DATE DUE

DEMCO 38-296

STRUGGLES
in the PROMISED LAND

STRUGGLES
in the PROMISED LAND

Toward a History of Black–Jewish Relations in the United States

Edited by

JACK SALZMAN & CORNEL WEST

New York // Oxford
OXFORD UNIVERSITY PRESS
1997

Oxford University Press

Oxford   New York
Athens   Auckland   Bangkok   Bogotá   Bombay
Buenos Aires   Calcutta   Cape Town   Dar es Salaam
Delhi   Florence   Hong Kong   Istanbul   Karachi
Kuala Lumpur   Madras   Madrid   Melbourne
Mexico City   Nairobi   Paris   Singapore
Taipei   Tokyo   Toronto

and associated companies in
Berlin   Ibadan

Library of Congress Cataloging-in-Publication Data
Struggles in the promised land :
toward a history of Black-Jewish relations in the United States/
edited by Jack Salzman and Cornel West.
p. cm.   Includes bibliographical references and index.
ISBN 0-19-508828-X.
1. Afro-Americans—Relations with Jews.
I. Salzman, Jack.   II. West, Cornel.
E185.61.S915   1997
305.896'073—dc21   96-45386

1 3 5 7 9 8 6 4 2
Printed in the United States of America
on acid-free paper

contents

STRUGGLES
in the PROMISED LAND

STRUGGLES IN THE PROMISED LAND

JACK SALZMAN

here was a time, not even so long ago, that "Grand Alliance" would have been a more appropriate title for a volume devoted to the relationship between African Americans and American Jews. Despite some cautionary voices, most scholars wrote of the relationship—and many still do—as one that worked well from the turn of the century through the middle of the civil rights movement. That presumed history has been told many times: Although African Americans arrived in the New World in 1620 and the first Jews settled in 1654, Blacks and Jews had little occasion to interact until the early part of the twentieth century. To be sure, there was the issue of Jewish involvement in the slave trade and of Jews as slave holders, but not until recently has such interaction been the cause of serious friction. Even the lynching of a Black and a Jew in Tennessee in 1868 and the invidious studies of scientific racists near the end of the nineteenth century did little to link the two groups.

For most people, the relationship started when American Blacks began to move North in large numbers and Eastern European Jews began to settle in the urban areas of the United States to escape pogroms in Europe. It was at that point, so the story went, that African Americans and American Jews began to forge a Grand Alliance for social justice. They were bound, some believed, by a heritage of slavery that marked the history of both peoples. And Zionism, the dream of some Jews for their own homeland, inspired for a while such influential Black Americans as Marcus Garvey and W. E. B. Du Bois.

The alliance was not always smooth, of course—accusations of Black anti-Semitism and Jewish racism are not new—but Blacks and Jews frequently found common cause in fighting for greater opportunities in such areas as education, housing, and employment. The lynching of Leo Frank in Atlanta in 1915 served as a painful reminder to many Jews of both their own vulnerability and their need to struggle against racism, just as Hitler's onslaught would make all too clear to many African Americans that the scourge of racism was not restricted to the

United States. So it was that some Blacks and Jews would find themselves working together to support labor unions, to make the world safe for democracy, and, finally, to bring to fruition in the civil rights movement the long unfulfilled dream of equality for all Americans.

That was, I must say, the understanding I brought with me when I was asked by The Jewish Museum in New York City to serve as a consultant to an exhibition it was planning on Black-Jewish relations. At the time, I was the director of the Center for American Culture Studies at Columbia University. In that capacity I had organized a number of public programs focusing on race relations in the United States, and had been asked by the American Jewish Committee to organize closed door sessions with members of the Jewish and African American communities. I was also about to undertake the editorship of a massive reference work, the *Encyclopedia of African American History and Culture*, which would take several years to complete. Since the proposed exhibition at The Jewish Museum fit well into the framework of what I already was doing, I was interested to see how the exhibition would address Black-Jewish relations. Like a number of other invited scholars I went to the museum for a three-hour meeting. A year later I was still working with members of the museum on the exhibition. In addition, I agreed to take responsibility for putting together the exhibition catalogue. (Not long after, I left Columbia and accepted a position at The Jewish Museum; but that's another story.) Both the exhibition, "Bridges and Boundaries: African Americans and American Jews," and the editing of the catalogue greatly altered my sense of the nature of the relationship between Jews and African Americans and ultimately led to the creation of this volume.[1]

Early discussions about the "Bridges and Boundaries" exhibition made certain assumptions: there had been a clear and definable history between American Jews and American Blacks; a once important alliance was in trouble; the bridges that once existed between African Americans and American Jews needed to be rebuilt, whatever the obstacles or boundaries. The question was how to present this history within the walls of a museum—or so it seemed. But as the weeks went by, it became all too clear that there was no readily definable history. By this I do not mean that we were caught in a relativist quandary as to which history to believe; I mean, more simply, that the history of the relationship between Blacks and Jews had not, and still has not, been written. There were, of course, several works—though fewer than one might have expected—that attempted to tell parts of the story.[2] There also were some books and essays that themselves were part of the untold history: Harold Cruse's *The Crisis of the Negro Intellectual*, James Baldwin's "I'm Antisemitic Because I'm Anti-White," Norman Podhoretz's "My Negro Problem—and Yours," among others.[3] The various parts, however, did not add up to a whole; neither the scholarly nor the anecdotal and personal provided an adequate historical narrative to explain the "peculiar entanglement."

And that entanglement was becoming more and more contested—and has continued to be so. Martin Bernal's *Black Athena* opened a heated debate about the center of Western civilization that fed into the teaching and writings of such Afro-centrists as Molefi Asante, Leonard Jeffries, and Tony Martin. Despite the scholarly debates that Bernal's writings engendered—his critics, such as Mary Lefkowitz and Emily Vermeule, were ferociously contemptuous of his conclusions[4]—it was less Afro-centricism that led to a further entanglement between Blacks and Jews than it was some contentions by Tony Martin and particularly by Leonard Jeffries. Although little known outside New York City, Jeffries became the center of considerable controversy in New York when he publicly proclaimed in 1991 that, among other matters, Jews had played a large part in the slave trade and that Jews controlled Hollywood and the media. Although Jeffries insisted that he was not anti-Semitic and that his contentions were historically indisputable, his comments, played up in the New York press, eventually resulted in his removal as head of the Department of Afro-American studies at City College (whose president he referred to as the "head Jew"). Despite the fact that Jeffries did not receive much support or sympathy from most African Americans, some Jews were disturbed by what they saw as the failure of prominent African American leaders to denounce Jeffries, while many Blacks and some Jews were distressed by what they saw as a violation of Jeffries' right to free speech. The language of race and racism, as always, became a contested arena.

But the critical attention given to Leonard Jeffries was minor compared to the furor aroused by Louis Farrakhan and his followers. Farrakhan first gained national visibility in 1978, when he began to rebuild the Nation of Islam three years after the death of Elijah Muhammad. It was not until 1991, however—the same year in which Leonard Jeffries delivered his widely excoriated talk in Albany, New York—that he really attracted the ire of the institutional Jewish community. In that year, the Nation of Islam published *The Secret Relationship Between Blacks and Jews: Volume One*, a work that purports to look at Jewish involvement in the slave trade and argues that Jews "carved for themselves a monumental culpability in slavery." Within two years the Anti-Defamation League published *Jew-Hatred as History*, an analysis of *The Secret Relationship* which made no attempt to argue that the work was anything but "a mendacious work of anti-Semitic propaganda." To many, *The Secret Relationship* was as virulently anti-Semitic as *The Protocols of the Learned Elders of Zion* (that the two books could be found together in the bookstalls of Nation of Islam street vendors in Harlem and other large urban settings only reinforced the comparison). Jewish institutional leaders began to urge Black leaders to renounce Farrakhan, a call that reached a crescendo in late 1993 when Khalid Abdul Muhammad, the Nation's national spokesman, delivered a speech at Kean College in New Jersey in which he referred to Jews as "blood suckers of the Black nation and the Black community" and Adolph Hitler as "wickedly great." When Farrakhan demoted Muhammad but failed to refute what his former national spokesman had said, Jewish fear and anger increased. If Black leaders did not renounce Farrakhan, it was clear proof that Blacks were anti-Semitic. The more Jewish institutional leaders asked African American leaders to renounce

Farrakhan, the more strident the refusal became. They might not have much regard for Farrakhan, but they were not going to be told what to do: charges of Black anti-Semitism were countered with cries of Jewish racism.

The discontent became most marked when in 1995 Farrakhan announced that he would organize a march of one million Black men on Washington, D.C. Jewish institutional organizations were undecided on the position they wanted to take. Although none were supportive of the idea, most preferred to remain silent about the march, lest they seem once again to be telling Black Americans what they should and should not do. The march itself elicited a spectrum of responses. The white press, including the Jewish press, emphasized the length and discursive nature of Farrakhan's speech, as well as the National Park Service's attendance estimate of 400,000, rather than one million, people. Many Black women object-ed to their exclusion from the march, while many African American gays and les-bians expressed their anger at the Nation's homophobic stance. Some African Americans, like Adolph Reed and Roger Wilkins, saw the march as the end result of the desperate state of poor African Americans and the refusal of white people to heed the need of many African Americans. "By ignoring moderate Black lead-ers," Wilkins commented on the day of the march (October 16), "they sowed the seeds for the emergence of Farrakhan as a more important figure."[5] As for the Jews, many seemed angered by the march: it was not possible, some felt, to sep-arate the spirit of the march and the good will that was evidenced on the part of the marchers from the anti-Semitic rhetoric of the march's organizer. To partici-pate in the event was to be in league with Farrakhan. So my colleague Cornel West was taken to task for sharing the platform with Farrakhan. West, who only months earlier had been the subject of an insidious attack in *The New Republic*, was chastised by Jews on both the Left and Right, including old friends like Michael Walzer and Michael Lerner.[6] Although West had spent his public life insisting that a dialogue of inclusion was imperative to human progress, dialogue with Farrakhan was deemed untenable. Jews were wary of Farrakhan's anti-Semitic rhetoric, and comparisons between Farrakhan and Adolph Hitler were not uncommon in many Jewish communities.

Farrakhan and the Nation of Islam were not the only source of uneasiness for Jews in 1995. When Michael Jackson's album *HIStory* was released in June of that year, there was an outcry over the song "They Don't Care About Us," which con-tained the lines "Jew me, sue me, everybody do me/ Kick me, kike me, don't you Black or white me." Jackson soon rerecorded the song, and the lines were changed. But there was no changing the verdict of the celebrated O.J. Simpson trial. When the jury found Simpson not guilty of the murder of Nicole Brown and Ron Goldman, the country truly seemed to become divided along racial lines. Jews (and other whites) for the most part reacted with stunned disbelief; many Blacks cheered the verdict, their distrust of the police validated by the jury's deci-sion. (The verdict, Greg Tate wrote in *The Village Voice*, may "represent the first time in history that a majority Black jury has wielded an apparatus of state power against the will of the nation's white citizenry.")[7] But for Jews, the Jackson and Simpson media events functioned as a prelude to Farrakhan and the march. Some people felt that more moderate voices should have organized the march. But all that seemed unrealistic. Neither Ben Chavis, Kwasi Mfumi, nor Jesse Jackson had the authority to attract so many African Americans to a rally. Whether whites liked it or not, only Farrakhan—whom West referred to as "white America's worst nightmare"—could pull it off, and he did.[8] So intense was the distrust of Farrakhan and the Nation of Islam, that there seemed no room for a discussion of the real issues surrounding Farrakhan: What was it about him that resonated so strongly with so many Black students? And if Farrakhan was to be feared and rejected as a rabid anti-Semite, who in the United States had a meaningfully realistic program that would alter the devastation of human lives taking place in parts of the Black community? These questions had no acceptable answers. The challenge of Farrakhan, then, as West put it in a discussion with Michael Lerner, "is the degree to which others will now provide alternative leadership to Farrakhan, by building on the King legacy and King's vision of the direction for the Black community."[9] But for all of West's hope that the fear and anxiety Farrakhan arouses in whites might result in a more pronounced progressive leadership, that hope shows almost no sign of becoming a reality. If anything, race does seem to be the issue that most defines and divides the United States as we make our way into the twenty-first century.

And as we make our way toward the millennium, there is little indication that the liberal coalition occasionally formed by Blacks and Jews has any real chance of being reestablished. It is too easy to contend, as some do, that the relationship has never been worse; among other things, that would suggest that there was a time when it really was strong. But to suggest so would be a mistake. What little can be said with certainty is simply this: the peculiar entanglements of Blacks and Jews have, at times, provided an important impetus for social justice in the United States and, at other times, have been the cause of great tension. Beyond this, matters become murkier. For a while, there was much talk about Black-Jewish dialogue, and groups in various parts of the country would meet to look for "common ground." But, increasingly, many African Americans seem to have lost interest in "dialoguing," in trying to understand what went wrong. Jobs, not talk, is necessarily their prime agenda. So, too, with alliances: with the change in demographics, both African Americans and American Jews are starting to seek new relations with Latinos and Asian-Americans. Simply put, common ground is in a state of dramatic flux.

Indeed, halfway through the last decade of the twentieth century there is little reason to think that there is much common ground between African Americans and American Jews. The argument that both Jews and Blacks have a shared heritage of enslavement makes little sense in the United States. Religious Blacks may have used the Old Testament as a source of inspiration for their own travails, but neither the story of Exodus nor the Jewish experience of voluntary immigration to the United States can be meaningfully compared to the way slavery has defined the lives of African Americans in this country. As former slave Charles Davenport commented, "De preachers would exhort us dat us was de chillen o' Israel in de wilderness an' de Lord done sent us to take dis land o' milk and honey. But how us gwine-a take land what's already been took?"[10] For many Jews (myself included), however, it is not the story told in Exodus but the Holocaust in Europe that serves to define their Jewishness. This has frequently led to an insistence on the singularity of that atrocity. The determination of the Nazis to systematically exterminate the Jewish people has made that event different from other atrocities. But not all people accept the uniqueness of the Holocaust; not all people believe the Holocaust should be singled out from other holocausts. For some African Americans—noted television host Tony Brown, for example— there have been numerous holocausts. To particularize one atrocity over others is to suggest that what happened to Jews was more horrific than the onslaught against American Indians or the ravages of the Middle Passage and slavery. For the Holocaust to be singled out by the creation of the United States Holocaust Memorial Museum on federal land was to make clear just how much financial and political power Jews had managed to attain.

All of this, of course, could only lead to the inevitable foolishness of comparative victimization: was Columbus's onslaught on American Indians worse than the Middle Passage, or was either as bad as Nazi Germany and the camps in Poland, to say nothing of the devastations in Biafra and Bosnia? For Jews, these arguments were compounded by the attacks of Holocaust deniers, a small group of pseudo-historians and right-wing fanatics who contended that the Holocaust never took place. What many non-Jews, Blacks and whites alike, were unable to appreciate fully was not only the extraordinary emotional tie Jews had to the memory of Auschwitz, Buchenwald, Bergen-Belsen, Treblinka, and the other camps of nightmare, but the fear and concern many Jews had that another pogrom was indeed possible—even in the United States. That fear, irrational though it may be, cannot be underestimated. It was at the core of the response to Jesse Jackson's "Hymietown" comment and the unwillingness to forget the remark, the sharp reaction in 1979 to Andrew Young's secret meeting with the U.N. representative of the Palestinian Liberation Organization, and the intensity of the response to Farrakhan: the sight of the Nation of Islam's "soldiers," combined with the rhetoric of a Khallid Muhammad and Farrakhan himself, resonates with all the symbolic power of a yellow Star of David and thousands of wearers of the Star rattling in cattle cars to their death. Memory, fear, and reality do not always go well together.

All this is prelude to the decision to put together this volume. There were also numerous personal considerations. Memory allows me to conjure up the remarkable Jackie Robinson running the bases at Ebbets Field in Brooklyn, and then being told that he, a Black man, was "an exception." Memory further recalls the "colored girl," the "schwarzer," who would occasionally come to do domestic work. (The importance of the relationship between domestic workers and their employers has yet to be adequately considered.) Memory, too, struggles with days in Brooklyn when I was a "Jew bastard" who somehow had killed Jesus; it tries to make sense of a scene in New Orleans in which a Black boy of about ten does a dance for three men who, instead of giving the boy money, ask that he dance some more, and the boy, with some exasperation, asks: "What are you, a Jew or something?" Where, one wonders, did he learn that, and what is to be done with such knowledge? And what is to be made of the haunting memory of a walk through a concentration camp, and the knowledge that grandparents, aunts, uncles, and cousins who did not leave Germany in early 1938 as I did, did not leave at all?

Memory of a somewhat faded past, of course, becomes entangled with more recent events: the murder of a rabbinical student in Brooklyn's Crown Heights and the killings in early 1996 in a Jewish-owned store in Harlem recall the worst of the tensions between African Americans and American Jews. Other moments equally convey a sense of bewilderment about the relationship between Blacks and Jews. Henry Louis Gates, Jr., publishes a piece in the *New York Times* on Black Anti-Semitism and is immediately revered by numerous Jews: money and invitations to speak on the subject flood his office at Harvard. But who will address the subject of Jewish racism? It is more difficult to document, more private in its manifestation, but no less corrosive. (Cynthia Ozick, wonderful wordsmith that she is, would have us believe that though there are Jewish racists, there is no such thing as Jewish racism. That's an important distinction, of course, but it really does beg the issue. It doesn't lessen the impact, for example, of Dick Gregory's contention that "Every Jew in America over 15 years old knows another Jew that doesn't like niggers.")[11] Equally disturbing: I am asked to convene a closed door session between some prominent Jews and African Americans to consider what might be done to improve the relationship between the two groups. Everything and anything is open to discussion, until someone wants to discuss Israel. Then, suddenly, there is no room for discussion. Israel and Farrakhan are breaking points of meeting after meeting. Soon, meetings seem superfluous.

Is another book on Black-Jewish relations superfluous too? Obviously, West and I think not. What I did find superfluous was a collection of essays that would expound on what should be done to make the relationship a strong one. I briefly discussed the idea of such a book with a prominent African American scholar, who wanted to see a volume by such personalities as Elie Wiesel and Wole Soyenka. "We all know the history," he said to me. "Let's put together a volume that will really get attention." But to what end, I wondered? What of significance do people like Wiesel and Soyenka have to say about Blacks and Jews at this point? That we must be more tolerant of one another—more accepting? That we must look for common ground? Maybe, finally, it is time that we stop talking about common ground and begin to confront, if we can, those differences that are as central to the way we define our lives as is the common ground we so desperately seek.

In any case, what brought West and me together was the conviction that we did not know all the history—that as we talked about the relationship between African Americans and American Jews we agreed that there was too much that was unknown, too many stories that were untold, too much that remained part of history's contested realm. We were less concerned with pondering, "What went wrong?"[12]—perhaps nothing did, after all—than discerning what had happened. The rhetoric of race was becoming more and more inflammatory, and the past was becoming anyone's story to tell. We wanted, at the very least, to undercut the rhetoric by trying to determine what might in fact have happened between Blacks and Jews during the slave trade, in Hollywood, and in the struggle for civil rights. As slippery as history may be, indeed because it is so elusive, we wanted to produce a volume that would provide the reader with a historical framework for a relationship that is most often defined by ideological passion.

II

Struggles in the Promised Land begins with two essays that precede the coming to America of either Blacks or Jews. In "The Curse of Ham: A Case of Rabbinic Racism," David M. Goldenberg offers a pointed refutation of the contention that ancient and medieval rabbinic literature reflect an invidious racism against Blacks. Goldenberg challenges the writings of such Black authors as St. Clair Drake and Tony Martin, as well as such white scholars as Thomas Gossett and Winthrop Jordan, whose lack of knowledge of rabbinic literature or ancient Jewish history has allowed them to erroneously argue that the source of anti-Black prejudice in Western civilization is to be found in rabbinic literature. William Jordan focuses his attention on "The Medieval Background" to show how both Blacks and Jews were demonized in the medieval world, how Jews and Blackness became represented as "allegorical evocations of the Devil and their moral inter-pretation as signs of evil." Although few Blacks in the Middle Ages had to endure the racist environment that was the lot of Jews, once the power and authority of Western European norms expanded around the globe, "people of color" began to feel the weight of a symbolic system that derided Blackness and Black people as much as it did Jews and Judaism.

The issue of Jewish involvement in both the slave trade and slavery itself is addressed by David Brion Davis and Jason Silverman. Both essays grow out of the unfortunate need to respond to the charges that "Jews" were heavily invested in and were major benefactors of slavery. That some people who were Jewish were involved in the slave trade and that more owned slaves in the South is not to be disputed. What is at issue is *why* that fact has become an issue. Relatively speaking, very few Jews engaged in the slave trade compared to people who were Protestant, Catholic, or Muslim; indeed, many more Africans took part than did Jews. But numbers aren't exactly the point. What is unsettling is the obvious: a Black man commits a crime and all Blacks are criminals; a Jew owns slaves and, suddenly, Jews control the slave trade—as, in the same conspiratorial vein, "they" control Hollywood and the media. The statement begs the obvious question: since Jews are hardly a homogeneous people, is there anything in Judaism that defined a Jew's relationship to slavery? The essays by Goldenberg, Davis, and Silverman all respond to that question. To speak of "The Jews," just as to speak of "The Blacks," always distorts, and almost always offends.

The significance of generalities is central to Hasia Diner's consideration of Black-Jewish relations between 1880 and 1935. When Black migration to northern cities from the South connected with Jewish immigration from Eastern Europe, Blacks and Jews began to exist for the other "as a kind of mythic mirror, by which they reflected and refracted on themselves and on their respective histories." Many Jews, Diner notes, considered the subjugation of African Americans "a stain of shame on the American flag"; many African Americans, at least institutional leaders, considered the efforts of Jews to succeed in the United States as a model for African Americans to emulate. But the actual interaction between Blacks and Jews was far more complex than the rhetoric of institutions. Jews may have hired Black domestics and sold goods in areas where other whites would not, but that did not mean that Blacks did not find the attitude of Jews paternalistic and demeaning. What Diner finally questions, however, is not the bad feeling that began to develop in urban areas, but what we actually know about the interaction between Blacks and Jews in large cities, as well as in small towns in the South. Were Jews as pervasive in the daily lives of African Americans as accounts would indicate, or were whites in general assumed to be Jewish? "The spottiness and ahistoricity of the popularly accepted generalizations," Diner notes, "render all statements about the past relationship particularly problematic."

Jonathan Kaufman continues the story begun by Diner, but his emphasis is substantially different. For Kaufman, cities initially were the scenes of cooperation between Jews and Blacks. After 1966, however, when Martin Luther King, Jr., decided to move the struggle for civil rights to the cities, they became more intense; at first a testing ground, cities became the battleground for Blacks and Jews as they moved from cooperation to confrontation. Two dramatic events that occurred in sections of Brooklyn, New York—the struggle for community control of schools in Ocean Hill–Brownsville in 1967 and the violence in Crown Heights in 1991—give shape to Kaufman's contention that the cities are where Jews attained their greatest success, while for African Americans cities represent both their greatest successes and their greatest failures.

The struggle for civil rights makes up the next part of *Struggles in the Promised Land*. If there is anything about the relationship between Blacks and Jews that has common consent, it is that the civil rights movement provided the occasion for a meaningful alliance. But even that assertion is now being scrutinized. At issue is not Jewish involvement in the civil rights movement—as distinct, perhaps, from the struggle for civil rights—but the extent and meaning of that involvement. Just how tangled even this part of the history has become can be witnessed by a quick reference to accounts by three writers: Jonathan Kaufman, Murray Friedman, and Jack Greenberg. In his essay for this volume, Kaufman confidently notes that young Jews from northern cities made up two-thirds to three-quarters of the white volunteers who took part in Freedom Summer in 1964 and that northern Jews contributed the large majority of funds to King and other civil rights organizations. In a similar vein, Murray Friedman undertook to write *What Went Wrong: The Creation & Collapse of the Black-Jewish Alliance* because, as a person who had spent more than thirty years in civil rights activities and never doubted that "the Black-Jewish alliance stood at the center of the great American experiment in democracy," he was deeply distressed that revisionist historians were trying to "obliterate the past and shape a future of acrimony and conflict."[13] But how we know the specifics of the past becomes all the more confusing when we turn to Jack Greenberg's *Crusaders in the Court*. There, Greenberg, who succeeded Thurgood Marshall as Director-Counsel of the NAACP Legal Defense and Educational Fund in 1961, writes that "while Jews have been among financial contributors to civil rights, this role has been exaggerated." Although Greenberg acknowledges that in proportion to the total population Jews have been overrepresented among the financial supporters of civil rights, it nevertheless would be unfair to claim that Jews were the financial mainstay of the civil rights movement.[14]

The essays in this volume by Nancy Weiss, Cheryl Greenberg, and Clayborne Carson do not resolve these conflicting accounts; it was beyond the charge of their pieces to do so. But their essays focus on other aspects of the struggle for civil rights that are just as complex. Both Weiss and Greenberg address, among other matters, the issue of Jewish self-interest in the movement for civil rights. Weiss concentrates on the contributions of Jews to the NAACP and the National Urban League in the early part of the twentieth century, and notes the significance of such Jewish figures as Felix Adler, Joel Spingarn, Louis Marshall, Henry Moskowitz, Lillian Wald, Julius Rosenwald, Jacob Schiff, and Stephen Wise. As anti-Semitism began to increase in the early part of the twentieth century, it clearly was in the interest of Jews to work with African Americans to fight against both religiously based and racially based prejudice. But such self-interest should not, must not, detract from the fact that although many non-Jews participated in the struggle for racial advancement, the contribution of Jews, as Weiss notes, "was unusual in its character and intensity...they helped importantly to shape and sustain the early twentieth century movement for civil rights."

Cheryl Greenberg, too, recognizes the importance of self-interest in the establishment of an alliance between Blacks and Jews. Indeed, it would be somewhat foolhardy to believe that political alliances grow out of anything but self-interest. At the same time, tensions and antagonisms begin to develop when self-interests are not allied. Thus, Greenburg shows how, at times, Jewish organizations decided not to become involved in causes of importance to African Americans because they felt it might lead to an increase in anti-Semitism. But despite this, from the rise of Nazi power in Germany through the end of the 1960s, Blacks and Jews did frequently work together to further the cause of social justice. By the end of the 1960s, however, the agendas of Blacks and Jews began to change rapidly, and there was a dramatic decline in the willingness of Jewish and Black institutions to cooperate with one another. That decline, of course, has become even more dramatic in the ensuing years.

The story of that decline is delineated by Clayborne Carson. The Black Power movement and the split over the struggle in the Middle East effectively ended the "Black-Jewish alliance." That term, "Black-Jewish alliance," has meaning, Carson argues, only as it applies to the involvement of Jewish professionals—Arthur Spingarn, Arnold Aronson, Kivie Kaplan, and Stanley Levison, for example—in civil rights organizations. With a shift in the civil rights movement from the South to the urban North, the voices of Stokely Carmichael and then Malcolm X suddenly began to compete with that of Martin Luther King, Jr. A coalition built on integration and nonviolence started to crumble: inner-city Blacks were unable to see how their lives had been made better by King and the Southern Christian Leadership Coalition (SLCC), and once-liberal Jews, fearful of the new Black agenda, began to turn toward the Right. (This shift by some Jews toward neo-conservatism should not have been unexpected, Carson contends, because the involvement by many Jews in the civil rights movement seems to have had little to do with their religious affiliation.) For Carson, the tensions that began to develop between Black and Jewish organizations with the introduction in 1966 of the Black Power slogan and the 1967 Arab-Israeli conflict has led almost inevitably to the rise of Louis Farrakhan and the further erosion of a belief in universalism.

Several important issues covered by Clayborne Carson also are addressed by Paul Buhle and Robin D.G. Kelley in their piece on the role of the Left in Black-Jewish relations. Our continued fear of the Communist Party's enduring presence in the United States has resulted in a failure to recognize adequately the importance of the Left in many areas of the history of this country, not the least of which was its central role in the relationship between Blacks and Jews. It is an enormously complex story, one that begins in the 1860s and covers, among other things, the North and South, the Scottsboro Boys, Hospital Workers Union, Local 1199, the Theatre Union, and Ocean Hill–Brownsville; it is a story that begins with great idealism, frequently reflects astonishing accomplishments, and ends with a sense of defeat and even betrayal. The importance of Jews in the struggle for social justice is not questioned. But, like Carson, Buhle and Kelley see the main thrust of Jewish concern as emanating almost entirely from secular left-leaning Jews. (The relationship between that political stance and Judaism still needs to be clearly defined.) Unlike Carson, however, Buhle and Kelley believe that the real break between progressive Blacks and Jews began before 1967. They mark the break with the Israeli occupation of the Suez Canal and the ambivalence that Old and New Left Jews had toward Zionism (at least until the 1967 war). For them, as for Carson, Ocean Hill–Brownsville irrevocably damaged the liberal alliance between Blacks and Jews. There, "Old Left Jewish radicals who had cultivated links with working-class Black and Latino communities were suddenly forced to choose between supporting a labor conflict and an important community issue affecting aggrieved populations of color." The struggle was ferocious, and almost thirty years later reconciliation still seems all but out of reach.

Ocean Hill–Brownsville is also of major concern to Earl Lewis, who writes about three phases in Black-Jewish educational relations. When the number of Jews living in the United States was small and contact limited, personal relations defined the nature of the educational relations between Blacks and Jews. To exemplify the nature of this relationship Lewis looks at a segment of Charleston's Jewish community, in particular the three sons born to Lydia Williams, a free woman of color, and a Jewish father who afforded them the educational opportunities that would allow them to rise to prominence. Their story is significant, Lewis argues, because it highlights the fact that from 1820 well into the beginning of the twentieth century the relationship between Blacks and Jews depended primarily on individual contacts rather than group relations. That began to change in the late nineteenth century when elites in both groups came of age and the relationship started to center on the formation of mutually beneficial institutions, such as the Tuskegee Institute and other sites of Black higher education. The final phase, for Lewis, is symbolized by the Ocean Hill–Brownsville controversy, which demonstrated what can happen when the histories of the two groups converge rather than merge. Despite some attempts to seek out common interests, difference and "otherness" came to dominate the discourse as Jews increasingly came to be seen as part of white America. In Ocean Hill–Brownsville, Lewis concludes, "what looked like reform from one side of the divide simply appeared as guardianship of the status quo from the other side." Although education, ideology, and politics always have been intermingled, Ocean Hill–Brownsville brought this delicate entanglement to the fore.

Far less delicate in the history of Black-Jewish relations is the presence of Hollywood. Like the contention that Jews were involved in a major way in the slave trade and slavery, so some people—Leonard Jeffries and Louis Farrakhan, for example—have insisted that "the Jews" control Hollywood. (This is also a favorite contention of several white groups, many of whom are white supremacists.) This control, the argument goes, not only demonstrates the enormous influence Jews have by their ability to define the content of this powerful industry; it also explains why so many movies contain racist stereotypes of Black Americans and why so few Black Americans have been "allowed" into the industry. Thomas Cripps, in his essay on African Americans and American Jews in Hollywood, presents an account that sharply undercuts the view of those who see Jews as engaged in cabalistic conspiracies. Blacks and Jews, Cripps believes, have long been "ambivalent allies," and with this as a focal point he looks at the way they affected one another in Hollywood, particularly during such times of crisis as the Great Depression and World War II. Certainly, many of Hollywood's most powerful figures were (and are) Jews, but their decisions, Cripps argues, had little to do with their Jewishness; they behaved, for better and worse, the way most white Americans did. It is clear that in matters of financial compensation and division of labor Blacks suffered. But, Cripps notes, many of the conservative trends that were detrimental to African Americans came from Southern whites and the influence of Catholicism. In times of national crisis, many Blacks and Jews, both within and outside the film industry, worked together to combat racism and fascism: If not all Jews in Hollywood were responsive to the social problems besieging the nation, many were; and if some Jews were indifferent (at best) to African Americans, many were not. To speak about a Jewish conspiracy in Hollywood, Cripps argues, is not only baseless but continues to add to the racial tension in the country.

The story of racial divide in the United States, of course, is as old as the country itself (for some, it is *the* story), and much of that story has of necessity focused on the South. But relatively little has been written about the relations between Blacks and Jews in the South. Certainly, the encounter between Blacks and Jews has been most telling in such cities as Chicago, Detroit, Washington, and, above all, New York. But as Deborah Dash Moore makes clear, although Blacks and Jews had a limited relationship in the South, that relationship has not been insignificant. To be sure, African Americans have always played a central role in the history of the South, while Jews were and continue to be marginal. There is virtually no aspect of Southern life that has not been affected by the presence of African Americans. Jews, on the other hand, had little impact on Southern life; and, in Eli Evans' phrase, there always has been a "loneliness of soul" at the core of every Jew who lives in the Bible Belt.[15] Put somewhat differently, African Americans helped define the very life of the South, while Jews usually chose to become part of it. A few common factors linked the two groups (among them the Ku Klux Klan, the lynching of Leo Frank, and the trials of the Scottsboro Boys); but for the most part, Jews who wanted to live in the South preferred to be white and Southern, and for the most part acted just like white Southerners. Consequently, the record of Southern Jewish activities during the civil rights movement, for example, is not distinguishable from that of other white Southerners. (And those Southern Jews who did take an active part in the civil rights movement, like the majority of Jewish activists, defined themselves by their politics, not by their religion.) At the same time, Jews often were disliked by African Americans simply because they were Jewish. As Richard Wright wrote in *Black Boy* (1945) about his early years in the South, "All of us Black people who lived in the neighborhood hated Jews, not because they exploited us but because we had been taught at home that Jews were 'Christ killers'."[16] Still, since the civil rights movement Blacks and Jews have found occasion to join in common cause, as they did in 1992 when they helped elect Douglas Wilder as the first Black governor of Virginia and that same year helped defeat David Duke in Louisiana. The paths of Jews and Blacks in the South still intersect only occasionally, but they do so more often than in the past and there is less ambivalence now than there once was.

Where Blacks and Jews do interact with some frequency—and have done so since the 1940s—is on issues of affirmative action and voting rights situations. And in these arenas, more, not less, ambivalence shapes the debates. Indeed, far more than Black anti-Semitism or Jewish racism, affirmative action is the focus of many of the current disagreements between Black and Jewish institutions. This difficult and potentially explosive subject for Blacks and Jews is explored in two essays: Jerome A. Chanes examines the evolution of a Jewish communal stance, and Theodore Shaw considers the importance of affirmative action, districting, and reapportionment for African Americans.

Chanes offers a telling overview of the complex attitude that Jewish communal organizations have had toward issues relating to affirmative action. To begin with, he makes clear that, although the basic ideology of Jews in America has been the notion that individual rights rather than group rights inform the workings of American society, only occasionally has the organized Jewish community spoken with unanimity on issues of civil rights. Not infrequently, self-interest has motivated Jewish involvement in civil rights issues. But, for all this, the organized Jewish community has been at the forefront of this struggle. At the same time, the organized Jewish community was strongly opposed to "anything that smacked of quotas," which historically "had compromised the ability of Jews to participate in the workings of society." Here, Chanes notes, was a major source of disagreement between Blacks and Jews: for Jews, quotas were a way of keeping people out; for African Americans, quotas were a way to let people in. Voting rights issues provide another source of contestation: like affirmative action, voting rights (reapportionment, redistricting) are dependent on the question of civil rights versus group rights. Although by the mid-1990s very few Jewish communities had been affected by voting-rights issues, reapportionment and redistricting have caused considerable tension between Jewish agencies and such Black civil rights groups as the NAACP Legal Defense and Education Fund, Inc. This tension was most dramatically brought to the attention of the general public when President Bill Clinton nominated Lani Guinier, a former staff member of the NAACP Legal Defense and Education Fund, Inc., to the post of assistant attorney general in the Department of Justice, where she would have run the Civil Rights Division. The first salvo against Guinier came from Chanes himself (in the English language Jewish *Forward*), and Guinier's failed nomination was frequently attributed to the opposition of the organized Jewish community, who in the words of an official at the NAACP Legal Defense Fund were raising "hell over a Black nominee who was trying to increase Black political representation."

Although Theodore Shaw was not that official, he has frequently represented the NAACP Legal Defense Fund in their struggle over voting rights issues. Shaw is not surprised that Jews have changed their stance on affirmative action or have taken the position that they have on voting rights issues. They have become part of the power elite in this country, and their actions are defined more by their whiteness than their religion. (Shaw, of course, does not ask what is perhaps best asked by a secular Jew like me: if Jews have become white, if they are no longer primarily defined by their Otherness, and have lost their impetus for social justice, what is the moral principle that distinguishes Jews from those around them? Assimilation, so desperately wanted, may come at too high a price.) For Jews, Shaw argues, the idea of "meritocracy" works. But for African Americans, race— no, skin color—still overshadows merit: to be Black in America is, in large part, to have merit redefined. Jews and Blacks come to affirmative action and voting rights issues from different experiences, from different places in America. The stakes for African Americans—in jobs, politics, and education—is much higher than it is for Jews. And recent court decisions, such as the Supreme Court's 1993 decision in *Shaw v. Reno* (which has led to "a widespread attack on political empowerment of African Americans and Latinos"), as well as the more conservative attitudes of American Jews, suggest that more difficult days are ahead for African America.

Perhaps not as contentious an issue as affirmative action, the position of African Americans toward Israel nevertheless is a dramatic flashpoint in Black-Jewish relations. Various aspects of this complex matter are explored by Waldo Martin and Gary Rubin. Martin puts into historical context the importance of Black Nationalism, and explores the ways in which the redefining of coalitions among Black radicals led to the unraveling of traditional intergroup coalition ties. As Israel aligned itself with the First World and revolutionary Black nationalists like Stokely Carmichael and Willie Ricks aligned themselves with the Third World, Martin notes, "the die was cast." The call for Black Power in 1966 was a defining moment in the history of the United States: the civil rights movement would never be the same, nor would the relationship between Blacks and Jews (or for that matter, the relationship between Blacks and other whites). Increasingly, tension arose between Jewish Power and Black Power. Black nationalists supported the revolution in Cuba and saw the war in Vietnam as an imperialist struggle against people of color. Israel, on the other hand, was seen as little more than a tool of American capitalism whose existence was predicated on the repression of Palestinians. There was little room or interest in the rhetoric of Black nationalists for the historical plight of Jews that made Israel so essential to a diasporic people. Just how influential the anti-Zionist stance of Black Nationalism has been outside the realm of Black activists remains somewhat unclear. What is more certain for Martin is that the moral authority emanating from the histories of both Blacks and Jews has been diminished "by the narrow and often stultifying demands of nationalism."

Gary Rubin takes a very different approach to African Americans and Israel than Waldo Martin. Rubin notes that several writers—Cynthia Ozick and Paul Berman, for example—have argued that the hostile attitude of African Americans toward Israel was a major factor in developing tensions between Blacks and Jews in the 1960s and that it remains a serious impediment to any coalition in the 1990s. The assertions of these writers, Rubin argues, is based on a simple syllogism: Criticism of Israel is wrong and hostile to Jews. Since important Black leaders have criticized Israel, important Black leaders are wrong and hostile to Jews. Rubin then sets out to question the presumptions underlying this syllogism. He reviews three decades of surveys of African American attitudes toward Jews, and concludes, among other matters, that African Americans as a whole show consistent support for Israel, even if that support is at a lower level than that of other groups. If anything, Israel-related issues seem to be of little interest to many African Americans. Certainly, the sharply critical statements by some African American leaders have "not penetrated to the general Black population." One might add to Rubin's conclusions the imperative of trying to distinguish between the attitudes of those voices that get heard and those that do not, and the difficulty of knowing how to make that distinction.

Struggles in the Promised Land concludes with personal and ruminative pieces by Patricia Williams, Letty Cottin Pogrebin, Michael Walzer, and Cornel West. Williams' piece ranges from Crown Heights to Art Spiegelman's *New Yorker* cover (February 14, 1993) of a Black woman and Hasidic man kissing to Phil Donahue's show devoted to American Jewish Princesses. Her intention is to show that "the irreducibility of the categories 'Black' and 'Jew' in racist and anti-Semitic imagination must be whittled away by persistently detailed descriptions of lived encounters among live neighbors." The hard work facing us, Williams writes, "is to come up with images that might suggest a model of hybridity that is fluid rather than static, a model of value that does not substitute a facile sociobiology for the actuality of culture."

Pogrebin also writes about a model of value, only hers is based on a Black-Jewish woman's dialogue group "that talked a blue streak for more than a decade and then went silent." There were several reasons why this group finally ran out of steam, but none more important than the fact that each side came in with different expectations. The Black women may have been ready to move from dialogue to action, Pogrebin writes, while for Jews "dialogue itself is the need—it's a short-term cure for Jewish insecurity." Despite the *sturm und drang*, Pogrebin says she would join another Black-Jewish dialogue group in a minute, for "it makes no sense for us to pull away from one another." Blacks and Jews comprise much of the moral conscience of the nation, Pogrebin writes, and if they were less competitive and more politically savvy they would link up and "make life uncomfortable for those who hate us."

Walzer's reflections, though of course framed differently than Pogrebin's, lead him to much the same place. Jewish involvement in the civil rights movement, like that in the labor movement or in the campaign against the Vietnam war, had more to do with the leftist politics of secular Jews than it did with their Jewishness. After spending a couple of years engaged in the civil rights movement, Walzer "drifted" out of his activism in the movement, and soon he and his friends were caught up in the opposition to America's involvement in Vietnam. Although he saw no Black-Jewish alliance in either struggle, he worries now about the role of Black Nationalism in arguing against integration. Separation, he believes, can only be destructive to African Americans. Blacks and Jews do not have to forge a formal alliance, Walzer argues; "coalition politics in a democracy is more rough and ready than that." But however rough and ready, the crucial steps toward an American left-liberalism must be taken if Blacks and Jews are to attain the egalitarian commitments that "orient and shape the everyday politics of both communities."

The tone of West's piece is quite different than Walzer's. Like Walzer, West provides us with a very personal piece about his involvement in the world of Black-Jewish relations. He begins by noting that although he grew up in a world without Jews, his worldview was shaped by the Jewish world. At the same time, he tells us, he took the retreat from affirmative action to be a sign of progressive or liberal failure of nerve and commitment. He also was never a Zionist; only a secular democratic state, he believes—with no special Jewish character—can secure Jewish survival. But much of what he reflects upon are the personal attacks upon him, and the implications of such attacks for a meaningful coalition of Blacks and Jews. Despite what he describes as the "sheer viciousness" of the attacks from the Jewish world on his work and life, he nevertheless persists in believing in the need to promote Black-Jewish coalitions. His investment in such alliances is, above all, a "moral endeavor that exemplifies ways in which the most hated group in European history and the most hated group in U.S. history can coalesce in the name of precious democratic ideals—ideals that serve as the sole countervailing force to hatred, fear, and greed." But a coalition between these two despised groups requires bonds of trust and cords of empathy. Without them, West writes, "Black-Jewish cooperation is but sounding brass and tinkling cymbal."

III

West's somewhat angry and disillusioned essay concludes *Struggles in the Promised Land.* Perhaps a more upbeat piece from a man whose public talks are always uplifting would have been more appropriate. But, somehow, I think not. The piece reflects his own growing concern, if not despair, about the possibilities for the dream that was America. We come from quite different backgrounds, West and I, he a Black Baptist from Oklahoma, I a white Jew from Brooklyn via Germany. We have lived quite different lives and struggled with different issues and demons. Our differences neither divide us nor bring us together. At the moment, I'm more troubled by Farrakhan than West, and I do not share his belief in the innocence of O.J. Simpson. I also am perhaps even more troubled than he about the conservative mood among many Jews and the banality of most progressive programs. He also is still more confident in the possibility for meaningful change in our political system than I, but then he also is more confident in his religious convictions than I. What has brought us together, as I said at the beginning of this introduction, is the conviction that knowing the past as well as we can, that, in this case, knowing what happened between Blacks and Jews, is not inconsequential. That conviction, in this case, grows out of a belief that to speak of the relationship between Blacks and Jews still resonates in a way that the relationship between no other two groups of people does. No doubt in the years to come we will speak more than we now do about Blacks and Latinos or Asians and Jews. But there is little reason to think, at least right now, that the forging of new alliances will have the same consequences for social justice in the United States as has the relationship between Blacks and Jews. For whatever the tensions that developed, however much alliances may have been determined by self-interest, no)matter how much one group may have felt betrayed by the other, the struggle for civil rights in this country has benefited enormously from the coming together of African Americans and American Jews. We are the poorer for what we have allowed to happen—what some have willed to happen—to the legacy of that struggle. We will continue to grow even poorer, I think, until we regain the conviction that without social justice and civil rights the United States has lost its purpose for being. This book, then, is meant to be both a corrective to the history of a relationship that has yet to be fully written and a reminder of the good that can come from even the most peculiar and difficult entanglements.

Notes

1. See *Bridges and Boundaries: African Americans and American Jews*, ed. Jack Salzman, with Adina Back and Gretchen Sullivan Sorin (New York, 1992).

2. See, for example, Hasia Diner, *In the Almost Promised Land: American Jews and Blacks 1915–1935* (Westport, CT, 1977); Nat Hentoff, ed., *Black Anti-Semitism and Jewish Racism* (New York, 1969); Jonathan Kaufman, *Broken Alliance: The Turbulent Times Between Blacks and Jews* (New York, 1988); Joseph R. Washington, ed., *Jews in Black Perspective: A Dialogue* (Rutherford, NJ, 1984); Robert G. Weisbord and Arthur Stein, *Bittersweet Encounter: The Afro-American and the American Jew* (Westport, CT, 1970).

3. Harold Cruse, *The Crisis of the Negro Intellectual* (New York, 1967). An excerpt from Cruse is reprinted in *Bridges and Boundaries*, as is the essay by Podhoretz. The pieces by Podhoretz and Baldwin are included in Paul Berman's collection, *Blacks and Jews: Alliances and Arguments* (New York, 1994).

4. The literature on Bernal's work, as well as Afro-centrism, continues to grow. Among other works, see Martin Bernal, *Black Athena: The Afroasiatic Roots of Classical Civilization.* 2 vols. (New Brunswick, NJ, 1987, 1991); Mary R. Lefkowitz, *Not Out of Africa: How Afrocentrism Became an Excuse to Teach Myth as History* (New York, 1996);

Mary R. Lefkowitz and Guy MacLean Rogers, eds., *Black Athena Revisited* (Chapel Hill, NC, 1996); Tony Martin, *The Jewish Onslaught: Despatches from the Wellesley Battlefront* (Dover, MA, 1993).

5. Quoted in *The New York Times*, October 17, 1995, p. A19.

6. For *The New Republic*'s attack on West, see Leon Wieseltier's "The Decline of the Black Intellectual" in the issue of March 6, 1995. The cover, stark black, with red and white print, contains the line, "Leon Wieseltier Rakes Over Cornel West."

7. Greg Tate, "Bigger's Got Back," *Village Voice*, October 17, 1995, pp. 27–28.

8. Cornel West, "Why I'm Marching on Washington," *The New York Times*, October 14, 1995, p. 19.

9. Michael Lerner and Cornel West, "After O.J. and the Farrakhan-led Million Man March: Is Healing Possible?" *Tikkun*, November/December 1995, p. 20.

10. See Norman Yetman, ed., *Voices of Slavery* (New York, 1970), p. 75.

11. The piece by Gates, "Black Demagogues and Pseudo-Scholars," appeared in *The New York Times*, July 20, 1992. For Ozick's contention that there is no Jewish racism, see her "Afterward" in Paul Berman's *Blacks and Jews*. Dick Gregory's comment is in *The New York Times*, September 7, 1969.

12. See Murray Friedman, *What Went Wrong? The Creation and Collapse of the Black-Jewish Alliance* (New York, 1995).

13. Friedman, p. 15.

14. Jack Greenberg, *Crusaders in the Courts: How a Dedicated Band of Lawyers Fought for the Civil Rights Revolution* (New York, 1994), pp. 50–53.

15. Eli N. Evans, *The Lonely Days Were Sundays: Reflections of a Jewish Southerner* (Jackson, MS, 1993), p. xxii.

16. Richard Wright, *Black Boy* (New York, 1945), p. 59.

one

THE CURSE OF HAM

A Case of Rabbinic Racism?

DAVID M. GOLDENBERG

n 1604 Fray Prudencio de Sandoval had this to say about the Jew and the Black:

> Who can deny that in the descendants of the Jews there persists and endures the evil inclination of their ancient ingratitude and lack of understanding, just as in the Negroes [there persists] the inseparable quality of their blackness.[1]

His linking of Jew and Black was not unusual. Indeed, the explicit and implicit comparison of these two peoples is found throughout western literature over many centuries. Leslie Fiedler may have been right when he said, "Surely the Negro cannot relish...this improbable and unwanted yoking any more than the Jew." Nevertheless, yoked they are, at least in the minds of the rest of the world. At various times and in various places, both peoples were said to be genetically diseased, physically and intellectually inferior, cursed by God, oversexed, more animal than human, ugly, smelly, and, of course, associated with the devil. From Jerome and Augustine, who saw biblical Ham as typologically the Jew while biologically the Black, to the 1930s American graffito "A nigger is a Jew turned inside out," these two peoples have been typecast as reflections of one another, and as substitutes for one another in society's categorization of the Other. Voltaire put it succinctly: "One regards the Jews the same way as one regards the Negroes, as a species of inferior humanity."[2]

This introductory backdrop highlights the Black-Jewish tension of our times. How ironic that these peoples, seen as mirror images of one another, have become modern-day antagonists. And, as we see again and again, the spring-taut tension of Black-Jewish relations has not left the academic world untouched.

Indeed, the most recent and pernicious attack against Judaism is now being mounted by several academics who base their assault on a purported scholarly reading of ancient and medieval rabbinic literature. Their claim: these texts reflect an invidious racism against Blacks, subsequently adopted by Christianity and Islam, which played itself out on the stage of history. In short, the source of anti-Black prejudice in Western civilization, it is alleged, is found in rabbinic literature.

However, an examination of the literature shows that the claim has nothing to stand on. Not one of the individuals who allege ancient rabbinic racism is an expert in rabbinic literature or in ancient Jewish history. In fact, an examination of the modern "scholarship" paints a sorry picture of the academy, for it shows how academics and others venture into cultural fields they do not understand, deal with concepts, languages, and literature they do not comprehend, and how they nevertheless readily devise theories, or repeat those of others, which are baseless and false.

The Claim: Judaism Is the Source of Anti-Black Racism

The proposition that ancient Jewish society invented anti-Black racism was first stated about thirty years ago and has been increasingly repeated in scholarly and nonscholarly works of all sorts. It should be noted at the outset that the authors of these claims do not fall into a single class. They are neither all Black nor are they all non-Jewish. The idea, in fact, seems to have originated—at least in its modern version—with the 1963 publications of three authors, one a Jew, two not, none of them Black. Thomas Gossett's *Race: The History of an Idea in America* claimed that two legends, which the author found in the *Jewish Encyclopedia* (1904), depict the origin of black skin as a curse of God, thus exhibiting "the most famous example of racism among Jews." Raphael Patai, an anthropologist, and Robert Graves, a novelist, published *Hebrew Myths: The Book of Genesis*, containing selections of rabbinic expositions on and about the Genesis myths. The authors wove together various strands of rabbinic traditions, inserting an editorial remark here and there, tendentiously creating (it is their own creation) a picture of Noah cursing his grandson Canaan and his descendants by endowing them with the following characteristics: black skin, negroid features, eternal slavery, hatred of their masters, and a love of theft, fornication, and lying.[3]

A few years later, in an article in the *Journal of African History*, Edith Sanders drew on these earlier works and implied a close link between modern racism and the rabbinic legends, which "endowed [the Negroes] with both certain physiognomical attributes and an undesirable character." Sanders' arguments are adopted in toto, although without attribution, by Joseph Harris who characterizes the rabbinic legends as embodying "a most decisive derogatory racial tradition."[4]

The American historian Winthrop Jordan took the charge one step further in his work *White over Black* (1968). Accepting the idea (Jordan read Gossett) that the rabbis saw the origin of black skin in a curse, Jordan claimed that the image of the lustful Negro in sixteenth- and seventeenth-century England also had its origin in rabbinic literature. From England, both ideas—blackness as curse and oversexed Negro—wound their way through the thoughts of European writers until they made their harmful appearance in the New World.[5]

Without Jordan's contribution, the theory of rabbinic racism might have died on the dusty shelves of university libraries. But *White over Black* was an otherwise important work—in fact, one of the most influential in Black historiography— and made a strong impact on the scholarship that followed. So much so, that the theory is now often repeated in scholarly works dealing with topics as diverse as British ideas about Africans' educability, the mythic world of the antebellum South, the French and Portuguese encounter with Africa, and color prejudice in English religion.[6] Rabbinic racism became an accepted fact in the canon of literature pertaining to Africans and race prejudice. Similarly, Jordan's sexual interpretation has influenced others who speak of a rabbinic "stereotype, defining Black people as unable to control their sexual impulses."[7]

The most recent full-scale discussion of "the highly pejorative images of Blacks in the Babylonian Talmud" is to be found in a work by the late Black anthropologist St. Clair Drake, *Black Folk Here and There*. The publication blurb for the book says it all: "St. Clair Drake brilliantly uncovers the genesis of cultural and phenotype denigration of dark-skinned peoples in the talmudic Judaic tradition...."This is reminiscent of the pronouncement of another academic, John Ralph Willis, who recently declared (drawing on the work of Sanders) that although the idea of blackness as curse "had its genesis in the Old Testament, its forcing bed was the Babylonian Talmud."[8]

Much of the accumulating wisdom of scholarship today seems to agree: rabbinic Judaism has "its own special mix of unflattering allusions to the color and character of dark-skinned Africans," it "associates darkness of hue with sin, slavery, and savagery," and it is where one finds a "growth of Jewish lore demeaning the Negro."[9] In its "depth of anti-Blackness," rabbinic Judaism "suggests how repugnant Blacks were to the chosen people," and how the Jews viewed Blacks "as the people devoid of ultimate worth and redeeming social human value."[10]

This attack on rabbinic Judaism has spread beyond the university campus. Black biblical interpreters, theologians, and religious leaders, drawing on Jordan, Graves-Patai, and others, repeat the accusation. Charles B. Copher writes of "the Babylonian Talmud, Midrashim, and legends [where] the reactions are wholly anti-Black," and Cain Hope Felder, whose work is generally balanced, refers to the "curse of Ham...which rabbis of the early Talmudic periods...used to denigrate Black people."[11] And now the Nation of Islam and Tony Martin, the controversial professor of Africana Studies at Wellesley College, have carried the attack to center stage of the public arena: "The Hamitic Myth (that is, the association of the African with the supposed curse of Noah), was invented by Jewish talmudic scholars....It provided the moral pretext upon which the entire [African slave] trade grew and flourished."[12]

Basing their arguments on translations, anthologies, and encyclopedia articles, these writers—drawing on one another, derivative and repetitive as they are, not one of them an expert in rabbinic literature—have created a modern American intellectual tradition. The tradition, however, disappears upon inspection. Academic tools are being manipulated, and ancient sources exploited, to serve purposes foreign to a real search for truth. And the sorriest aspect of this sordid drama is that most of those repeating the canards are innocent bystanders.

While the arguments of these authors are repeated from one book to the next, the tone undergoes sharp change. The objective language of Jordan and Gossett is gradually replaced by the voice of vehement attack in the works of some who follow them. There is clearly more at stake here than pure scholarship. It is, however, the argument and not the tone that is the subject of this essay.

The charge of ancient Jewish racism consists of three parts: (a) rabbinic statements project an anti-Black sentiment; (b) such sentiment is pervasive in rabbinic literature (Talmud and Midrash) and reflects a "talmudic view" of Blacks; and (c) this view is the source of racism in Western civilization. I shall deal with each of these claims in turn.

"Rabbinic Statements Project an Anti-Black Sentiment" The charge of "rabbinic racism" rests upon a total of five statements. Two of these occur in the earlier talmudic-midrashic corpus—the others are in later medieval sources—and view dark skin as a curse of God. The first (Talmud, *Sanhedrin* 108b) records the following folktale told by a third-century CE rabbi: God prohibited Noah and all the creatures in the ark from engaging in sex during the flood ("I have decided to destroy my world and you would create life!"). Three creatures transgressed—the dog, the raven, and Ham, son of Noah—and were punished. Ham's punishment was that he became black, a procreative (i.e., genetic) punishment for a procreative (i.e., sexual) sin.[13] The second story (Midrash, *Genesis Rabbah* 36.7), in an elaboration of the biblical narrative in Genesis 9 ("And Ham saw [Noah's] nakedness"), assumes that Ham castrated his father Noah. In retaliation Noah said to Ham: "You prevented me from doing that which is done in the dark [the sexual act], therefore may your progeny be black and ugly."[14]

First, it should be noted—it is often not—that these folktales are concerned with skin color, not race. Ham's progeny, the Bible tells us, comprised different ethnic groups: Egyptians, Libyans, Canaanites, Ethiopians. Still, the idea that dark skin is a punishment for a sinful act is disturbing to our twentieth-century Western ears.

But should we listen to a 1700-year-old Near Eastern text with twentieth-century Western ears? Historians train for years to learn to distance themselves culturally and chronologically from their own time and place, and to listen with the ears of their subjects.

When we do this we recognize immediately the literary form of the stories as an etiological myth. Early Jewish, Christian, and Islamic sources always assume that mankind derived from one original couple and that this couple had the same skin color as those investigating the question. Since a good part of humanity had a considerably darker complexion, these cultures were faced with the question of how relative lightness changed color. Their answer was divine extranatural intervention; in other words, an etiological myth. The stories thus account for the anomaly of dark skin in a lighter-skinned society. (Folk etymology may have also been involved, for the Hebrew "Ham" may have been understood—incorrectly— as deriving from *ḥum*, "dark," or "brown.")

Such tales explaining the origin of natural (or linguistic) phenomena are commonly found in Jewish literature, beginning with the Bible. The story of Adam and Eve in the Garden of Eden is an etiological myth meant to explain the snake's peculiar (legless) anatomy, woman's pain in childbirth, and man's toil in life. Linguistic etiologies based on the name of a person, place, or nation (folk etymologies), are similarly commonplace. An oft-cited example is the name "Moses" explained in the Bible as based on a Hebrew root meaning "to draw," "for I drew him out of the water" (Exodus 2:10).

The ancient Israelites did not invent the genre; etiological myths are common to all cultures, including African as well. A Cameroon folktale (later incorporated in the Uncle Remus stories) tells of the Mountain Spirit's two children who became dirty while playing. Their father sent them to the sea to wash. One jumped in and emerged clean again. The other was afraid of the water and only got the soles of his feet and the palms of his hands wet. When the father saw the children he turned to the dirty one and said: "Since you did not listen to me and did not wash, may you therefore become black and may your children and your children's children all become black. Only the soles of your feet and the palms of your hands will remain white."[15]

Etiological myths of course reflect views and attitudes of society, and there is no question that the two rabbinic stories imply an aesthetic preference for lighter skin color. There is no question that the authors considered their own skin color to be the norm and, therefore, the preferred. Such human conceit is, however, hardly peculiar to the Jews of antiquity. People everywhere find most desirable that which most closely resembles themselves. Social scientists call this human trait "somatic norm preference" and differentiate it from racism, a phenomenon determined by societal structures.[16]

It is this very distinction that historians have adopted to explain an apparent contradiction in classical antiquity. Greco-Roman society does not exhibit racist social structures and yet a number of the ancient writers express anti-Black sentiment. The answer: such sentiment just reflects a preference for the somatic norm and is really an ethnocentric expression of conformism to dominant aesthetic tastes.[17] Is there, however, more to the two rabbinic stories than a universal expression of somatic preference? After all, these tales see dark skin as a form of divine punishment. What does this say about underlying rabbinic attitudes?

The biblical story of the Tower of Babel will help us answer the question. One original couple, Adam and Eve, speaking one language (Hebrew of course, the preferred linguistic norm) cannot account for the world's multiplicity of languages. An etiological myth—this time in the Bible—was thus created as explanation. The divine punishment for mankind's sinful revolt against God was the introduction of the variety of human languages. As with human color, so with human speech variety is introduced into the world by means of etiology with divine punishment.

The role of divine punishment in these etiologies explains the existence of the nonnormal, that which was perceived as different. "Curses...served as explanation for enigmatic physiological or environmental peculiarities. The ancestor or prototype of those exhibiting such abnormalities was considered to have been cursed by God...or by some ancient hero."[18] There is no indication, however, in the many biblical and rabbinic etiological stories, that "nonnormal" aspects of the world—whether man's toil, woman's labor pains, non-Hebrew language, dark skin, or anything else—were viewed in a deprecatory light. They were seen and appreciated, rather, as manifestations of the world's variety. Here, for example, is the talmudic Rabbi Jonathan of Bet Guvrin on non-Hebrew languages: "There are four languages that beautifully serve particular functions. Greek for song, Latin for things military, Aramaic for elegy, and Hebrew for speech."[19] R. Jonathan's knowledge that Greek, Latin, and Aramaic may have had their remote mythic origin in divine punishment, did not impact upon his everyday, real-life perception of human languages, and did not prevent him from appreciating their beauty.

The African etiological myth from Cameroon is not very different in this respect. It too seeks to explain variations in nature—shading differences on the palm of the hand and the sole of the foot. In both the rabbinic and the African folktales, blackness is seen as divine "punishment" for disobedience. The Cameroon story says, "Since you did not listen to me and did not wash, may you therefore become black." The rabbinic story in effect says, "Since you did not listen to me and did not abstain from sex, may you therefore become black."[20]

Having examined the function and language of etiological myths in ancient society, we are now, only now, in a position to ask what do the rabbinic folktales tell us about the authors' view of dark skin? The answer: the rabbis had an aesthetic preference for their own skin color. There is no denying this, but such a universal ethnocentric attitude is far from the anti-Black perspective which is alleged. Reflecting neither animus nor racism, the ancient Jewish stories explain the variety of human color, while implicitly favoring the somatic norm of the writers.

How did the ancient Greeks and Romans account for variation in skin color? Their explanation sounds more "scientific" to our ears: people living in the southern regions are burned dark by the sun; those in the north are pale because of the lack of sun; those in the middle (Greece and Rome) are just right. It should not be supposed, however, that this environmental-climatic explanation for dark skin was based on egalitarian presuppositions. The climatic theory viewed darkness as a result of exposure to extreme heat on the normal, white, skin color ("roasted skin" as Lucretius, the Roman poet and philosopher, would say). Always behind this theory stood the assumption that the changed color was a kind of degeneration, and characteristic of inferiority (*decolor*, that is "discoloration," in the Latin texts).[21] Neither the Greeks and Romans nor the Jews saw darker skin as aesthetically pleasing. The one expressed this view by means of the environmental theory, the other by means of etiological myth with divine curse. The negative aesthetic sentiment is the same; the (culturally based) literary expression differs.[22]

In addition to the folktales just examined, those who allege rabbinic racism generally offer two further texts as proof for their claim. Here too, the claim is empty, for it is based on misunderstood readings of abridged and faulty translations. The first text is from the *Zohar*, a thirteenth-century kabbalistic work:

> **And Ham was the father of Canaan** (Genesis 9:18). [I.e.,] the refuse and dross of the gold, the stirring and rousing of the unclean spirit of the ancient serpent. It is for that reason that it is written the "father of Canaan," [namely, of Canaan] who brought curses into the world, of Canaan who was cursed, of Canaan who darkened the faces of mankind...."Ham, the father of Canaan," that is, [the father of] the world-darkener.[23]

Jordan (p. 18) sees in this passage a rabbinic curse of blackness, but in truth, the *Zohar* text has nothing whatsoever to do with Blacks or dark skin. This passage, rather, deals with the phenomenon of human mortality and refers to it as the "serpent's darkening the face of mankind" because of the role the biblical serpent played in introducing death into the world. A linguistic equivalency in the Bible ("Cursed be" said of both Canaan and the serpent in the Garden of Eden story) allowed the *Zohar*'s author to treat "Canaan" (Israel's ancient enemy) as a verbal substitute for the serpent and to say that "Canaan," that is, the serpent, was cursed and brought curses and death ("darkness") into the world.[24] This obvious meaning of "darkening the face of mankind" in our passage was commonly noted by both medieval and modern commentators alike.[25]

How did Jordan misunderstand the *Zohar*? Why would he see an allusion to the blackness of Ham when the *Zohar* speaks of "*Canaan*, the world-darkener"? Because, not knowing the original language, Jordan used a faulty English translation: "**And Ham was the father of Canaan** (Genesis 9:18). *Ham* represents the refuse and dross of the gold...."[26] The laconic Aramaic, however, does not have the word "Ham." It reads: "**And Ham was the father of Canaan** (Genesis 9:18). The refuse and dross of the gold...." with the implied subject of "the refuse and dross of the gold" being *Canaan*, not Ham, as can be seen by consulting the standard commentaries cited above. The English translation is, as any translation, an interpretation, and here the interpretation is incorrect.

Having convinced himself that the *Zohar* is speaking of Blacks, Jordan then compounded his misreading of the passage by seeing in it a reference to the Black's sexuality. Thus, rabbinic Judaism is responsible not only for derogation of black skin, but also for the stereotype of the oversexed Negro. "The depth and diffuse pervasiveness of these explosive associations [of blackness and sex] are dramatized in the mystic *Zohar*...where Ham, it was said, 'represents the refuse and dross of the gold, the stirring and rousing of the unclean spirit of the ancient serpent'" (p. 36). Apparently, the "ancient serpent" to Jordan's mind represents the Black penis!

In zoharic symbolism, our world, the domain of evil—represented by the primeval serpent—is described as the unclean world, likened to the dross that remains after gold has been refined (alluding to God's descending and gradually diminishing "light" in the process of creation). There is no penis in this passage, black or otherwise.[27]

It is not surprising that this mystical work of medieval Judaism, replete with complex and abstruse symbolism, would be misunderstood by one not familiar with the literature. Use of a translation does not improve comprehension. Nothing is helped in our case by the fact that part of the original Aramaic passage in the *Zohar* is not even included in the translation. Jordan naturally was unaware of this. Obviously, reading an abridged translation of an abstruse text loaded with symbolism and code words will produce an incorrect understanding. The *Zohar* passage says nothing about Blacks and nothing about sex.

The second text usually cited by those who wish to prove rabbinic "racism" derives from a work called *Tanḥuma*, a medieval collection of legends and rabbinic exegeses. Here is Graves and Patai's rendition (p. 121):

> Because you twisted your head around to see my nakedness, your grandchildren's hair shall be twisted into kinks, and their eyes red [sic]; again, because your lips jested at my misfortune, theirs shall swell; and because you neglected my nakedness, they shall go naked, and their male members shall be shamefully elongated. Men of this race are called Negroes.

It is not surprising that this rendition has provided much ammunition for the racist theorists. However, an exact translation of the original, devoid of stereotyped and preconceived notions, produces a significantly different reading:

> Ham's eyes turned red, since he looked at his father's nakedness; his lips became crooked, since he spoke with his mouth; the hair of his head and

beard became singed, since he turned his face around; and since he did not cover [his father's] nakedness, he went naked and his foreskin was extended. (*Noah*, section 13)

Is this an anti-Black statement? Does it speak of Blacks at all? What is it saying? The text is a difficult one which presents several problems (e.g., in the Bible it was precisely Ham who did *not* turn his head around), but let us focus only on "crooked lips" and "extended foreskin," literal translations of the original Hebrew *sefatayim ʿaqumot/ʿaqushot* and *nimshekhah ʿorlato*. What do these two terms mean? Elsewhere in rabbinic literature they bear the specific meanings of "movement of the lips" and "uncircumcised penis" (or, a penis on which an operation has been performed to rebuild a foreskin). Unfortunately, that does not make the passage any clearer. The text is admittedly an enigmatic one, whose precise meaning escapes philological investigation.

Nevertheless comparison with non-Jewish literature may provide some interpretive clues, for medieval Christian and Islamic sources commonly portray the black African with red eyes.[28] If the Jewish *Tanḥuma* text is describing the African, it would certainly not be unique in including red eyes in its description.

The same can be said for *Tanḥuma*'s "extended foreskin," which Graves and Patai assume to be a reference to penis size. If they are right, such a depiction of the African should be cause for no more surprise than the reference to red eyes. As early as Galen in the second century CE, we find a large penis said to be characteristic of Blacks. "The black with an oversize phallus was a traditional theme" in Greco-Roman art.[29]

But are Graves and Patai right? The fact is that, as stated, the Hebrew term in *Tanḥuma* has a quite specific meaning, and it has nothing to do with penis size. Similarly, the words translated by Graves and Patai as "swollen lips" cannot under any circumstances have that meaning.

We are back, then, to where we started: an enigmatic text. Some elements in the passage (red eyes, and singed/curly hair too) were commonly used—across cultures and times—to describe Blacks, while other elements (crooked lips, extended foreskin) remain unexplained.

It may be that *Tanḥuma* is not depicting any known people at all, but is rather engaging in imaginative fantasy. History has preserved a wide range of descriptions of distant and presumed wild and strange peoples, found from antiquity onward among pagan, Christian, Islamic, and Jewish writers. Beyond the limits of the known world, particularly in mysterious Africa, lived the fabulous races. "India and parts of Ethiopia especially teem with marvels," reported Pliny, who goes on to talk about the monstrous animals and humans existing in the extreme reaches of Africa.[30] During the Middle Ages, such accounts of the fabulous races of Africa were disseminated by means of John Mandeville's popular *Travels* (circa 1360).[31] Jean Devisse described the medieval Christian European view of Africa as "a land of geographic, physiological, and intellectual abnormality....Africa [was seen] as dangerous and the African as subhuman."[32] Some Christian works then combined the legends of monstrous races with biblical genealogy: the monstrous races are descendants of those (Adam, Ham, Cain) who had sinned.[33]

The medieval *Tanḥuma* text, containing legends and lore, may be representative of the same literary genre. If the sense of the passage as a whole is meant to depict the distant sub-Saharan African as strange, or even fantastic, it should not surprise us. Nor is it unusual that Jews, as others, combined such descriptions with biblical genealogy.

But is *Tanḥuma* in fact describing the black African? If so, where is the Black's most distinguishing characteristic—his skin color? This crucial point is probably what led Louis Ginzberg, author of the massive seven-volume *Legends of the Jews*, to conclude that the text does not in fact have Blacks in mind. (After all, in biblical/rabbinic thinking, Ham was also seen as the ancestor of the non-Black races of Egypt, Libya, and Canaan.) Ginzberg, perhaps the greatest scholar of rabbinic folklore, paraphrased *Tanḥuma* as referring only to the *non-Black* Canaanites: "The descendants of Ham, through Canaan therefore, have red eyes...."[34] All this does not faze Joseph Washington, who "proves" his argument of Jewish racism by assuming a rabbinic identification of Canaan as Black, an assumption that is absurd.[35] An accurate reading of the *Tanḥuma* passage, on the other hand, is made by A.A. Jackson, a Black Baptist minister, who recently concluded: "These Jewish traditions make no connection between Ham and blackness, no connection between the curse of Ham/Canaan and skin color."[36]

The *Tanḥuma* passage remains an enigma. It may refer to black Africans in descriptive language commonly used by different cultures. Or it may be portraying the distant and strange as fantastic. In either case, the passage would be in line with pagan, Christian, and Islamic views dating from well before *Tanḥuma*'s redaction (eighth–tenth centuries in the Islamic world) to well after it. On the other hand, it is possible that the passage does not refer to Blacks at all. Yet, in the face of such doubts, Graves and Patai are so certain that the text refers to Blacks, that they inject their own stereotypes into the translation and then top it off with the unwarranted gratuitous insertion "Men of this race are called Negroes." Thus was created, in 1963, a new rabbinic text. On such pillars was the house of "rabbinic racism" built.[37]

The three passages we have examined (excluding the *Zohar*), constitute the sum total of rabbinic texts purportedly expressing anti-Black attitudes. Some of the purveyors of "rabbinic racism" theories at this point may have realized the weakness of their position, for, scratching at the bottom of the barrel, they enlisted two medieval Jewish travelers as representatives of anti-Black rabbinic thinking. Eldad ha-Dani's (ninth century) reference to Africans' cannibalism and Benjamin of Tudela's (twelfth century) mention of Africans' animal-like behavior, nakedness, low intelligence, and promiscuity supposedly indicate a deep-rooted Jewish antipathy toward Blacks.

Leaving aside for the moment the question of how medieval travel diaries can be said to represent classical rabbinic thought, the descriptions found in Eldad and Benjamin are commonly and widely found in non-Jewish sources, whether ancient or medieval, and whether pagan, Christian, or Islamic.[38]

Given the universalism of the phenomenon that we are describing, it is somewhat disconcerting to find these two Jewish sources cited as unique instances of such views toward Blacks. Drake (2:27), for example, contrasts Eldad with reports of "Romans and Persians through the eleventh century," which however "do not speak of cannibalism among the people." Drake is here, as very often elsewhere on this topic, simply wrong.[39]

Indeed, such descriptions of black Africans are so common, that it is not Tudela who is exceptional but a fifteenth-century rabbi, Isaac Abrabanel. He responded with unconcealed anger to the comment of a tenth-century Karaite from Jerusalem, Yefet b. Ali, on the issue of Black sexuality. Yefet had interpreted a biblical verse (Amos 9:7) to refer to Black women "who are promiscuous and therefore no one knows who his father is." Abrabanel: "I don't know who told Yefet this practice of promiscuity among Black women, which he mentions. But in the country of my birth [Portugal] I have seen many of these people and their women are sexually loyal to their husbands unless they are prisoners and captive to their enemies. They are just like any other people."[40]

If we summarize the results of our investigation thus far, we find that the five Jewish texts reputed to show anti-Black racism actually present an entirely different picture. One text (*Zohar*) does not speak of Blacks at all; another (*Tanḥuma*) may not. Two others (Eldad and Benjamin) are late medieval compositions not part of the rabbinic canon, reflecting only the views of the individual authors, which are shared by—and much more prominent in—pagan, Christian, and Muslim writers. The remaining texts (Talmud and Midrash) show a preference for the somatic norm on the part of two authors of antiquity. Yet, despite these meagre findings, the racist theorists claim that anti-Black sentiment permeates rabbinic literature.

"Anti-Black Sentiment Is Pervasive in Rabbinic Literature and Reflects a 'Talmudic View' of Blacks" It is rather strange to consider such sentiment (assuming for the moment it existed) pervasive in rabbinic writings. The folktale of sex in the ark consists of 15 words in a total of some 2 1/2 million in the Talmud.

It is just as strange to hear that such views represent "the talmudic view" of Blacks. The rabbinic canon is not the work of a single author speaking with the voice of authoritative doctrine. Rather, this literature encompasses the thinking of over 1,500 individuals spanning five centuries and two countries covering almost 6,000 large-sized folio pages. Given the prodigious number of topics covered and variety of opinions expressed, it is ludicrous to speak of "the talmudic view of Blacks."

Furthermore, the rabbinic corpus is not only multitudinous; it is also multifarious. It includes discussions on all aspects of daily life, and on every area of human existence and thought: religion and superstition, medicine and astronomy, commerce and agriculture, magic, botany, zoology, biology, mathematics, history, customs, fables and folktales, among others. Some of this material expresses central tenets in Jewish life and thought; other material represents momentary opinions of individuals. Some statements reflect communal consensus; others the fancy or fantasy of one person. Much of this latter aggadic material was even termed "hocus pocus" *{sifre kosemim}* by one of the major personalities in the talmudic-rabbinic corpus, R. Zeira (third–fourth centuries CE).[41] Hai Gaon (d. 1038), the leading rabbinic personality of his age and head of the talmudic academy in Babylonia, spoke about the authority of aggadic (stories, folklore, etc.) dicta: "Aggadic statements are not halakhic (religio-legal) statements. Rather, they represent what anybody thinks up by way of exegesis....They are not decisive. Therefore we do not rely upon them as authoritative."[42]

The claim that two aggadic folktales, representing .0006 percent of the overall talmudic corpus and transmitted by two of 1500 personalities, represents "the talmudic view" sounds a little ridiculous. In 1680 Pere Richard Simon denounced Buxtorf the Elder and other Judaeophobic authors for "one of the commonest failings of Christian Hebraists, their tendency to regard fanciful Midrashim and other collections of rabbinic moral tales and obiter dicta as serious textual interpretation of the law."[43] Three hundred years ago the claim was anti-Christian; today it is anti-Black. The Talmud remains the seedbed of all evil in civilization.

"The Rabbinic View of Blacks Is the Source of Racism in Western Civilization" This claim rests upon the New World justification for Black slavery by appeal to a biblically ordained "Curse of Ham," the belief that Blacks, and Blacks alone, were cursed with eternal slavery. American pro-slavery writers of the antebellum period often supported their position by reference to this Curse, according to which:

> [Noah] was the first to plant a vineyard. He drank of the wine and became drunk, and he uncovered himself within his tent. Ham...saw his father's nakedness....When Noah woke up from his wine...he said: "Cursed be Canaan [Ham's son]; the lowest of slaves shall he be to his brothers." (Genesis 9:20–25)

Of course, the biblical account speaks only of slavery, not blackness. But those charging rabbinic racism do not wish to attack the Bible. Their target is the Talmud and Midrash. Their claim is that the Curse of Ham is a rabbinic invention.

But just as there is no Curse of Ham in biblical literature, so too there is no Curse of Ham—that is, a curse of slavery on Blacks—in the rabbinic texts. The biblical story is an etiology accounting for Canaanite slavery. The rabbinic stories, on the other hand, speak of blackness, not of slavery. They are, as we saw, etiologies accounting for the existence of dark-skinned people.

The Curse of Ham hinges on the assumed linkage of blackness and slavery. But such linkage is not found in the Bible or later Jewish literature. Neither of the two rabbinic folktales of the origin of darker-skinned people (sex in the ark; sex in the dark) occur in the context of Noah's curse of slavery.[44] Slavery and dark skin are two independent etiological myths. Nowhere in early Jewish literature—either rabbinic or, for that matter, nonrabbinic—is that distinction violated. Dark skin devolving on Ham comprises one set of traditions; slavery as Noah's curse on a non-Black Canaan comprises a second. The two traditions are never joined.

Never joined, that is, except in the minds of some moderns. Graves and Patai tried to weave together the various and distinct traditions in order to present a readable whole for a popular audience. In their treatment it is Canaan's progeny who are both enslaved and turned black. This popular but false treatment has perhaps caused more damage than any other, for it became the source for most of the "Judaism is racism" thinking. So, to take just two examples, Washington at the very outset of his book, refers to the "Jewish oral tradition" claiming that Blacks are "doubly damned," and Akbar Muhammad states that "Jewish theologians" are the source for the "dual act of God." The confusion between Canaan, who was enslaved, and Ham, who became black, begins unfortunately with the publication of Graves and Patai's book in 1963.[45]

Almost 900 years ago the rabbinic exegete Abraham ibn Ezra spoke out forcefully against a "doubly damned" Curse of Ham interpretation. He noted that, "there are those who say [he intends the Muslims] that the Blacks are slaves because of Noah's curse on Ham," and he refuted that claim by pointing to Nimrod, son of Kush [i.e., Black] the first post-deluvian king. Obviously, a king cannot be a slave. Ibn Ezra presses his point further when he comments on the biblical "Cursed be Canaan; he shall be a slave to his brothers": "i.e., to Kush, Mizraim, and Phut." Kush, the ancestor of the Blacks, is the master, not the slave. And if this is not yet abundantly clear, again he observes (to the verse "Ham is the father of Canaan"): "It says Canaan *and not Kush* because Canaan is the one who will be cursed." Similarly Naḥmanides, another medieval rabbinic scholar, stresses the same point.[46] Morever, in the rabbinic worldview, the association of slavery with Canaan, and not Ham, is implicit in the very linguistic classification used in the Talmud for the two categories of slaves: "Hebrew" and "Canaanite."

"Early rabbinic teachings distinguished the innocent black descendants of Kush from the accursed descendants of his brother Canaan."[47] The Curse of Ham is, indeed, an idea which spawned devastating consequences in history. It is not, however, an idea found in Judaism.

But it is found in those societies that institutionalized Black slavery. From the seventh century onward the concept appears as a recurring theme among Islamic writers who tightly link blackness and slavery. In some, blackness is added to the biblical story of the curse of slavery; in others, blackness and slavery occur together as curses in an extrabiblical framework; in still others, the biblical framework is there but those cursed with slavery come to the story already black. The common thread binding all these accounts together is the linkage of blackness and slavery.

A few examples from the Muslim authors will suffice. From Ibn Khaldūn (fourteenth century) quoting "genealogists" with whom he disagrees:

> Negroes are the children of Ham, the son of Noah, and...they were singled out to be black as the result of Noah's curse, which produced Ham's color and the slavery God inflicted upon his descendants.

And from Ṭabarī (ninth century) quoting others:

> [Noah] prayed that Ham's color would be changed and that his descendants would be slaves to the children of Shem and Japheth.

Or quoting the father of Ibn 'Aṭā' (647–732):

> Ham begat all those who are black and curly-haired....Noah prayed that the hair of Ham's descendants would not grow beyond their ears, and that wherever his descendants met the children of Shem, the latter would enslave them.[48]

The obvious meaning of "hair not growing beyond the ears" is made explicit in *The Book of the Zanj*:

> Ham was most beautiful in face and form, but God changed his color and that of his progeny because of the curse of Noah. [Noah] cursed Ham blackening his appearance and that of his progeny; and that they be made slaves to the sons of Shem and Japheth. This narrative is widely found in history books, as is recorded in the "Book of the Gold Ingot" (*Sabā'ik adh-dhahab*). When the prophet of God (Noah) partitioned the earth among his sons, Africa belonged to Ham. He begot sons who are the Negro, whose hair does not go below their ears, as we see them.[49]

The persistence of this linkage of slavery with blackness in the Islamic world is explained by Islam's long history of enslaving black Africans. (Even today in many Arabic dialects, the word for Black is 'abd, which actually means "slave.") Such linkage provided the justifying myth sustaining the social structure. In Jewish history, the Israelites conquered and enslaved the Canaanites and thus invented the attendant justifying myth: Noah's curse of the eponymous Canaan with eternal slavery. In Islamic history, it was not Canaan who was enslaved, but Black Africa. The biblical curse story was then reinterpreted to embrace both slavery and blackness—Islam's own etiological myth.[50] The same mythic justification was then adopted from Islam by other societies in which the Black became the slave. Christian Europe, after its discovery and enslavement of Black Africa, and antebellum America commonly relied upon the Curse of Ham to maintain the existing order.

One would expect those societies that enslaved the Black to justify, and thus support, their social structures with whatever means possible. The rabbinic etiology was one of several available means. In its original context, the etiology had an anthropogenic function (it explained the existence of dark skin in a relatively white world) in Near Eastern cultures of antiquity and late antiquity (it is also found in Samaritan and Christian writings of the fourth century),[51] but was later reused to serve a different purpose. When Blacks became identified with the slave class in the Islamic world and in the Christian world after the fifteenth century, the etiology was dusted off and reborn as the "Curse of Ham," thus providing justification for social structures that subjugated the Black. An ancient Near Eastern myth, taken out of context and given a new meaning, served well as one of many pegs upon which to hang a new commercially and socially driven racism.

It is ironic that ancient Jewish literature is ransacked to find racist sentiment, for, as we have seen, the best place to find such sentiment is in those societies that enslaved Blacks. Rabbinic Judaism, on the other hand, never had the temporal power to enslave anybody, certainly not Africa. This historical fact is reflected in the literature, for rabbinic sources contain not a hint of anti-Black racism in the comprehensive social structure detailed in the normative legal canon (*halakhah*).

Instead of attempting a truly historical investigation of racial prejudice in western civilization, the "new scholarship" has isolated three or four stories of ancient Jewish myth, extracting them from their intellectual environment, transporting them over a 1500-year period, untouched by historical and cultural developments, and has plunked them down in our own time as the finally revealed source of prejudice.

Assuming for the sake of argument, and contrary to the evidence, that Judaism's ancient folktales reflected anti-Black sentiment, we must then ask if and how these folktales were used to denigrate Blacks in Jewish history. We will not find any such use. But if the same question is asked of, first, Islamic, and then, Christian, societies, we will find that heavy usage indeed was made of the folktales. The stories served as raw material from which was fashioned the Curse of Ham, used to justify the social institution of Black slavery in those societies. That is why we first hear of the Curse in Islamic writings after the conquest of Africa in the seventh century, and in Christian writings after the European discovery of black Africa in the fifteenth century.

Scholars have long recognized the "inter-hermeneutic encounters" between Judaism, Christianity, and Islam. As these cultures encountered one another their traditions were reappropriated and recreated as they moved into the new historical environments.[52] The scholar of African oral traditions, David Henige, aptly compared this process to the principle of natural selection: "Those traditions that are best able to outlive changing circumstances are those that exist today...."

Surviving requires that they adapt to whatever changes they encounter."[53] In the
new Islamic and Christian worlds of Black slavery, the ancient Jewish etiology of
black skin was adapted to the new circumstances and became the Curse of Ham.

Rabbinic Views of Blacks

It should be abundantly clear by now that a historical assessment of rabbinic
thought requires a knowledge of the relevant languages, literatures, and discipli-
nary methodologies. Translations, anthologies, encyclopedia articles—the building blocks of the "rabbinic racism" theorists—will only result in a mass of incompetent misreadings and misunderstandings.[54]

A further impediment to an accurate evaluation of rabbinic views is an
approach which limits the evidence, an approach which often becomes what
David Brion Davis has described as "pounc[ing] upon quotations extracted arbi-
trarily from the Babylonian Talmud and other rabbinic sources."[55] If one is truly
interested in knowing what rabbinic Judaism thought about dark-skinned people, obviously all of the relevant literature must be examined for references direct
and indirect, in order to reconstruct a resulting attitude or attitudes.

When we undertake such an objective and thorough investigation, we find a
positive perception of Blacks running throughout the rabbinic corpus. The most
common reference to Blacks in the literature is that which treats biblical black
skin as a metaphor for that which is distinctive in a positive way. In an exposition on Moses' Ethiopian wife (Numbers 12:1), the rabbis say: "Just as the
Ethiopian is distinctive in his skin color, so was Zipporah distinctive in beauty
and good deeds." Several other biblical references to "Ethiopian" receive the same
metaphorical treatment. Saul, who according to rabbinic tradition is identified
with Kush of Psalms 7:1, was handsome ("distinctive in appearance"); the people
of Israel, whom God considers to be "like the Kushites" (Amos 9:7), were distinctive in fulfilling God's commandments, and so on.[56]

Not recognizing the metaphor as reflecting a positive view of black skin,
Drake, Copher, Brackman and others see rather rabbinic attempts "to explain
away the blackness of Moses' wife."[57] Apparently the snowballing effect of the
"new scholarship" finds anti-Black sentiment everywhere, as long as it's in a rabbinic text. However, any student of midrash will recognize in the exegesis a common, and innocuous, interpretive technique.

Metaphoric explanations of names and descriptions of biblical figures are
widespread in midrashic literature and are driven by two factors: the hermeneu-
tical desire to extrapolate as much as possible from the biblical text, and the literary characteristic of what one scholar has termed "retreat from anonymity."
Thus, the common attempt to identify the unknown (in our case, the Kushite)
with the known (in our case, Zipporah).[58]

An example is provided by the case of Iscah, daughter of Haran, brother of
Abraham (Genesis 11:29). Otherwise unknown, Iscah is identified with Sarah by

means of an "etymological" explanation of her name: "All gaze (*sakhin*) at her beauty, as it is written 'And the princes of Pharaoh saw her [i.e. Sarah] and praised her to Pharaoh" (Genesis 11:15).[59] "Iscah" is thus a description of the known Sarah. So too, in our case, "Kushit" is a description of the known Zipporah.

There are other rabbinic references to Blacks and black skin. Take for example the following passage in the eighth-century *Pirqe de-Rabbi Eliezer* (chapter 24), which tells of God "colorizing" the world, as it were.

> He blessed Noah and his sons—as it says: "And God blessed them," i.e. with their gifts, and he apportioned the entire earth to them as an inheritance. He blessed Shem and his sons [making them] black and beautiful and he gave them the habitable earth. He blessed Ham and his sons [making them] black as the raven and he gave them the sea coasts. He blessed Japheth and his sons [making] all of them white and he gave them the desert and fields. These are the portions he gave them as an inheritance.

The key word in this account is "blessed." According to this text God's endowing of various skin colors is part of his blessing to humanity. Obviously this text sees dark skin differently than the sex-in-the-ark (or, dark) folktales we saw above.

If there were a monolithic "rabbinic view" of dark skin as a curse, it would have been highly unlikely for *Pirqe*—based and dependent upon the earlier rabbinic views—to consider this color a blessing. And it would have been highly unlikely for this text to consider the color of Shem—and his descendants, the Jews—to be black. Naturally enough, it is a preferred shade of black to that of the Hamites, but it is considered by the author(s) to be black nonetheless.

Further insight to rabbinic views of Blacks might be gained from those texts treating other biblical references to a Kushi/Ethiopian. One does not find, for example, any attempt to "explain away" the father of the prophet Zephaniah, whose name is Kushi. On the contrary, rabbinic tradition has it that this "kushi" was a righteous man. Similarly, the Ethiopian Ebed-melech, who saved the prophet Jeremiah (Jeremiah 38:4–13) is considered to be one of the select few who did not die, but entered paradise alive. Other midrashic accounts cast him in the role of a king who converted to Judaism.[60] Clearly, a thorough investigation of the rabbinic corpus results in a very different picture from that which is alleged.

Rabbinic society was not an ideal world free of xenophobia. However, it was certainly not anti-Black. The various attitudes which emerge from rabbinic literature depict a society that barely thought about Blacks, qua Blacks, at all. The social structures of rabbinic society (as governed by, and embedded in, its legal literature) depict a world in which color was irrelevant.

This essay began by noting a perception of the Black as seen by the dominant society throughout history. It will end by noting a view of the Black as seen by the talmudic and midrashic rabbis. A little known, and never quoted (it is not found in translation), early midrashic commentary explains Isaiah's view of the messianic age. The prophet said: "[God] is coming to gather all nations" (Isaiah 66:18). The rabbinic paraphrase puts it this way:

Isaiah said: In the messianic period he who is light-skinned [*germani*] will take hold of the hand of him who is dark-skinned [*kushi*] and the dark-skinned will take hold of the hand of the light-skinned and arm in arm they will walk together.[61]

Notes

The publication of this essay is due in no small measure to three people. Prof. Bernard Lewis provided me inspiration and opportunity. My debt and gratitude to him is profound. Both Lewis and Prof. David Brion Davis read various drafts of the essay and offered valuable suggestions. My thanks are due to them as also to Prof. Benny Kraut for thoroughgoing stylistic improvements. To avoid confusion, in this essay I use "Black" in upper case to mean one whose descent is from sub-Saharan Africa.

1. As quoted in Y.H. Yerushalmi, *Assimilation and Racial Anti-Semitism: The Iberian and the German Models* (New York, 1982), p. 16.

2. "Negro and Jew: Encounter in America," *The Collected Essays of Leslie Fiedler* (New York, 1971) 1:460. Augustine, *Contra Faustum* 12.23, Corpus scriptorum ecclesiasticorum latinorum (Vienna, 1866–) 25:351. Jerome, *Dialogus contra Luceferianos* 22 (*Patrologiae cursus completus...series Latina*, ed. J.P. Migne [Paris, 1844–55] 23:185). Nathan Hurvitz, "Blacks and Jews in American Folklore," *Western Folklore* 33 (1974): 307. Voltaire in his *Essai sur les moeurs* as quoted by Poliakov, "Racism in Europe," *Caste and Race: Comparative Approaches*, ed. A. de Rueck and J. Knight (Boston, 1967), p. 224n.

3. Gossett (Dallas, 1963), p. 5; Graves-Patai, p. 121. Already in the 1940s, J.A. Rogers (*Sex and Race* [New York, 1940–44] 3:316–317, and later in *Nature Knows No Color-Line* [New York, 1952], pp. 9–10) noted that the idea of a curse of blackness on Ham "originates in the Talmud, Midrash, and other rabbinical writings." Rogers, however, was more interested in documenting this myth than he was in seeing in it the origin of racism in Western civilization. Somewhat earlier Raoul Allier, Dean of the Faculté libre de théologie protestante of Paris, condemned the rabbis: "Christian missionaries...must take the initiative to protest without delay the thesis [of blackness as curse], born in the ghetto, of the feverish and sadistic imagination of some rabbis" (*Une énigme troublante: la race nègre et la malédiction de Cham*. Les Cahiers Missionnaires no. 16 [Paris, 1930], pp. 16–19, 32), but Allier's work, in any case, seems to have been unknown to those who followed, at least in this country. (Allier was known to, and used by Albert Perbal, "La race nègre et la malédiction de Cham,"

Revue de l'Université d'Ottawa 10 [1940]: 156–177, and Martin Steins, *Das Bild des Schwarzen in der europäischen Kolonialliteratur 1870-1918* [Frankfurt a/M, 1972]).

4. Edith Sanders, "Hamitic Hypothesis," *Journal of African History* 10 (1969): 521–532. Harris, *Africans and Their History* (New York, 1972), pp. 14–15. Sanders and Graves-Patai are well critiqued by Ephraim Isaac, "Genesis, Judaism and the 'Sons of Ham,'" *Slavery and Abolition* 1 (1980): 3–17; reprinted in *Slaves and Slavery in Muslim Africa*, ed. John R. Willis (London, 1985) 1:75–91.

5. Winthrop Jordan, *White over Black: American Attitudes toward the Negro, 1550-1812* (Chapel Hill, NC, 1968), pp. 18, 35–37. Jordan's familiarity with Gossett's work is seen on p. 604 ("Essay on Sources").

6. Charles Lyons, *To Wash an Aethiop White: British Ideas about Black African Educability, 1530-1960* (New York, 1975); Thomas Peterson, *Ham and Japheth: The Mythic World of Whites in the Antebellum South* (Metuchen, NJ and London, 1978); William Cohen, *The French Encounter with Africans: White Responses to Blacks, 1530-1880* (Bloomington, IN, 1980); A.C. de C.M. Saunders, *A Social History of Black Slaves and Freedmen in Portugal, 1441-1555* (Cambridge, UK, 1982); Joseph R. Washington, *Anti-Blackness in English Religion, 1500-1800* (New York, 1984).

7. St. Claire Drake, *Black Folk Here and There*, volume 2 (Los Angeles, 1990), pp. 22–23. Joseph Washington (*Anti-Blackness in English Religion*, p. 10) makes a similar claim. On the impact of *White over Black*, see August Meier and Elliot Rudwick, *Black History and the Historical Profession, 1915-1980* (Urbana, 1986), p. 123. Jordan is even quoted, incorrectly, to prove that Ham's blackness begins with the Bible (H.L. Feingold, *Zion in America: The Jewish Experience from Colonial Times to the Present* [New York, 1974], p. 86).

8. St. Clair Drake, *Black Folk Here and There* 2:2, 17–30, 74 and 117; John Ralph Willis, ed., *Slaves and Slavery in Muslim Africa* 1:8.

9. Howard Brackman in his Ph.D. dissertation (UCLA, 1977), "The Ebb and Flow of Conflict: A History of Black-Jewish Relations Through 1900," pp. 6, 73, 79.

10. Joseph Washington, *Anti-Blackness in English Religion*, pp. 11 and 15.

11. Copher, "Blacks and Jews in Historical Interaction: The Biblical/African Experience," *The Journal of the Interdenominational Theological Center* 3 (1975): 16; reprinted in *African Presence in Early Asia* (New Brunswick, NJ; rev. ed., 1988), p. 185. A few years ago *The Washington Post* (September 14, 1991; p. B6) ran a story on Black biblicists and biblical interpretation. The writer reported that "some blacks believe the Bible was intentionally intepreted in this manner to perpetuate racist ideologies." This is immediately followed by a rehashing of the rabbinic racism claims by Charles Copher. Cain Hope Felder, *Troubling Biblical Waters: Race, Class, and Family* (New York, 1989), p. 38.

12. Tony Martin, *The Jewish Onslaught* (Dover, MA, 1993), p. 33. Martin relied on the Nation of Islam's racist publication *The Secret Relationship between Blacks and Jews* (Boston, 1991), p. 203: "It is also the [Jewish] misinterpretation of the Old Testament which offered the holy justification for oppression on purely racial grounds." The NOI continues to push this line in their other racist writings: "This 'curse' was the absolute basis for the Europeans' choice of dark-skinned Africans for chattel slavery....When the Jews invented it and promoted it to the world they sentenced the Black Race to a holocaust the likes of which no people have ever suffered" (*Philadelphia Blacks and Jews News*, Spring 1994 reprinted in R. Rockaway, *"The Jews Cannot Defeat Me": The Anti-Jewish Campaign of Louis Farrakhan and the Nation of Islam* [Tel Aviv, 1995], p. 42).

13. The idea that black skin came about due to a change in seminal composition had wide currency. See the church father Origen's *Commentary to Song of Songs* 2.2: "Among the whole of the Ethiopian race...there is a certain natural blackness because of seminal inheritance (*ex seminis carnalis successione nigredo*), that in those parts the sun burns with fiercer rays, and that having once been scorched, the bodies remain darkened in the transmission of the inborn defect (*infuscata corpora genuini vitii successione permaneant*). *Die griechischen christlichen Schriftsteller der ersten drei Jahrhunderte* (Leipzig, 1901–) 33:125. R.P. Lawson translates: "natural blackness inherited by all" and "bodies that have once been scorched and darkened, transmit a congenital stain to their posterity" for the bracketed words. *Ancient Christian Writers* (Westminster, MD, 1946–) 26: 107. Similarly, in a Persian version of Tabarī's *History* done by Abu 'Ali Mohammed Bal'amī (10th century), we find the same idea of altered genetic composition. Elaborating on the biblical story, Bal'amī says that Noah cursed Ham and said: "'May God change the semen of your loins.' After that all the people and fruit of the country of Ham became black." M. Hermann Zotenberg, ed. and trans. *Chronique de Abou-Djafar-Mo'hammed-ben-Djarir-ben-Yezid Tabarī traduite sur la version persane d'Abou-'Ali Mo'hammed Bel'ami* (Paris, 1867–1874) 1:115.

14. Precisely the same explanation for Aphrodite's (the love goddess) title as the "Black One" is given by Pausanius, the Greek geographer of the second century CE: people make love in the dark (*Description of Greece* 8.6.5). The *Sanhedrin* passage is paralleled in the Jerusalem Talmud, *Ta'anit* 1.6, 64d.

15. P. Simon Rosenhuber, *Märchen, Fabeln, Rätsel und Sprichwörter der Neger in Kamerun* (Limburg, 1926), pp. 56-57. The Uncle Remus tales incorporated African traditions: J.C. Harris, *Uncle Remus: His Songs and His Sayings* (1880), no. 33; in the Penguin edition (1982), ed. Robert Hemenway, on pp. 150–151. Cf. J.A. Rogers, pp. 60-61. Of course, there are African creation myths—the Uncle Remus story is one—that assume the original humans to have been black, some of whom then became white. A wide variety of black/white stories is found in the work of Veronika Görög-Karady who has collected 161 African accounts (myths, tales, songs, etc.), recorded since the beginning of the century, that represent the relationship between Africans and Europeans. A significant proportion of these are etiological origin myths that

explain the creation and/or the social stratification of the different races, and an additional group are African reformulations of mostly biblical origin myths. (*Noir et blancs: leur image dans la littérature orale africaine*, [Paris, 1976]. Studied further in: "Parental Preference and Racial Inequality: An Ideological Theme in African Oral Literature" in *Forms of Folklore in Africa: Narrative, Poetic, Gnomic, Dramatic*, ed. Bernth Lindfors [Austin, 1977], pp. 104–134; "Noirs et blancs: A propos de quelques mythes d'origine vili" in *Itinérances—in pays peul et ailleurs* [Paris, 1981] 2:79–95; and "Retelling Genesis: The Children of Eve and the Origin of Inequality" in *Genres, Forms, Meanings: Essays in African Oral Literature*, ed. V. Görög-Karady [Oxford, 1982], pp. 37–44.) An example of an African reformulation of a biblical story is that recorded by W.W. Reade from the inhabitants of Sierra Leone in 1864: Man was originally black; when God shouted at Cain for killing his brother, Cain turned white from fright; thus the origin of white people (*Savage Africa* [New York, 1864], p. 31 = *Noir et blancs*, no. 89, pp. 342–343; cf. J.A. Rogers, *Sex and Race* 1:11). A similar story, but with God confronting Adam who then turned white, was told by American ex-slaves (R.R. Earl, *Dark Symbols, Obscure Signs: God, Self, and Community in the Slave Mind* [Maryknoll, NY, 1993], pp. 47–48). Görög-Karady listed several "bathing" stories (nos. 37–48, pp. 292–298) although the Cameroon account is not one of them. Add also the following: An origins story told by an American ex-slave has the original humans, all black, living in a cave. Those who slept closest to the opening of the cave were turned white by the sun (R.R. Earl, *Dark Symbols*, pp. 49–50); a Yoruba creation story is recounted by R.E. Hood, "Creation Myths in Nigeria: A Theological Commentary," *The Journal of Religious Thought* 45 (1989): 71; an etiology of black and white people told by South Carolina Blacks speaking a Black-English dialect called Gullah in S.G. Stoney and G.M. Shelby, *Black Genesis: A Chronicle* (New York, 1930), pp. 161–171.

On the problem of filtering through the culture and language of the transcribers, see Ralph Austen, "Africans Speak, Colonialism Writes: The Transcription and Translation of Oral Literature before World War II," in the series *African Humanities* 8 (1990) of Boston University.

16. See the work of H. Hoetink, *The Two Variants in Caribbean Race Relations* (Oxford, 1967; originally published in Dutch in 1962). For some examples of this universal phenomenon, see the remarks of Sextus Empericus (ca. 200 CE) in his *Against the Ethicists* 43; Al-Hamadānī (ca. 900 CE) quoted in B. Lewis, *Race and Slavery in the Middle East* (New York, 1990), pp. 45–46; and Benjamin Franklin quoted in Jordan, *White over Black*, p. 143, cf. 102.

17. The somatic norm explanation is set out by Frank Snowden in *Before Color Prejudice: The Ancient View of Blacks* (Cambridge, MA, 1983), pp. 75–79, and *Blacks in Antiquity: Ethiopians in the Greco-Roman Experience* (Cambridge, MA, 1970), pp. 171–179, and especially by Lloyd Thompson in *Romans and Blacks* (Norman, OK, 1989), *passim*; see index, "somatic norm image."

18. S. Gevirtz, "Curse Motifs in the Old Testament and the Ancient Near East" (Ph.D. diss., University of Chicago, 1959), p. 258.

19. Jerusalem Talmud, *Megillah* 71b, bottom.

20. The function of punishment in these origin-myths is well documented by scholars of folklore. Here, for example, is Görög-Karady on the black/white etiologies of the Vili in the Congo: "The texts thus manifest a fundamental ethnocentrism....The Black constitutes the prototype of humanity from which all the 'races' have issued. What is more, [the Black] appears as the normal condition by which humanity is measured where all the other species of mankind—mixed breeds [*métis*] or whites—figure only as deviations or incomplete or unsatisfactory forms....The thematic nucleus of the majority of these Vili texts consists of a fault or misdeed imputed to the ancestor or one of the ancestors and to which the deviation of humanity issues directly." Or, "The racial differentiation flows directly from the nature of the crime....The transformation of skin color appears as the punishment for an evil action....All these texts affirm the culpability and justified mythic damnation of the white ancestor" (*Itinérances*, pp. 82–83, 88–89).

21. This was noted by William Cohen in regard to France's later adoption of the classical explanation. Cohen discusses the anthropological theory of polygenism which, as the climatic theory of antiquity, accounted for human racial variation. This too "established for blacks a separate destiny from whites—an innate inequality" (*French Encounter* [above, n. 6], p. 13). Indeed, polygenism was frequently cited as support for American slavery. Cohen's point was made also by Jean Devisse, but for the Islamic world. Commenting on Ibn Khaldūn's (14th century) rejection of the Curse theory of blackness in favor of the climatic theory, Devisse says: "This position is not ...so favorable as it may at first seem. True Ibn Khaldūn...did attribute the blackness of the Sūdān [Blacks] to the action of the sun....But this theory itself was turned against the Sūdān! A few lines further on, Ibn Khaldūn very seriously explains that, due to the very nature of climate, only the men of the 'temperate' zone can be characterized by *balance*. Thus we are brought back to the Mediterraneocentrism we have already talked about. Beyond the 'temperate' zone, whether to the north or to the south...climatic excesses engender dangerous excesses of character." Devisse is in *The Image of the Black in Western Art*, ed. Ladislas Bugner (Cambridge, MA, 1976), vol. 2.1, p. 221, n. 179. Lucretius is in *De rerum natura* 6.1109–1112.

22. In actuality the classical "scientific" explanation may have derived from the etiological myth of Phaeton who brought the sun chariot too close to the earth. "It was then, as men think, that the peoples of Aethiopia became black-skinned" (Ovid, *Metamorphoses* 2.235–236). Some discussion of the environmental theory in the Greco-Roman world will be found in Snowden, *Blacks in Antiquity*, pp. 170–179. See also K. Trüdinger, *Studien zur Geschichte der griechische-römischen Ethnographie* (Basel, 1918) and E. Honigmann, *Die sieben Klimata* (Heidelberg, 1929).

23. The text is found in ed. R. Margaliot, *Zohar, Tiqqune ha-Zohar, Zohar Hadash* (Jerusalem, 1940–53) 1:72b–73.

24. Cf. *Genesis Rabbah* 36.2 (ed. Theodor-Albeck, Jerusalem, 1965, p.336): "**And Ham was the father of Canaan,** [that is,] the father of the curse (*phth*)," which may stand behind the *Zohar* passage. For *phth* as "curse," see Saul Lieberman, *Hellenism in Jewish Palestine* (New York, 1950), pp. 12–13, n. 59, and idem, *Jewish Quarterly Review* 36 (1945–46): 346.

25. See, e.g., the following commentaries: Shim'on Labi (sixteenth century), *Sefer Ketem Paz* (Livorno, 1795), p. 207b; (Jerba, 1940), p. 179b; Moses Cordovero (sixteenth century), *'Or Yaqar* (Jerusalem, 1967) 4:91, s.v. *Kena'an de'ahshikh;* Judah Leib Ashlag (twentieth century), *Ha-Sulam* (Jerusalem, 1952) vol.3, "Noah," p.105, sec. 298.

"Darkening the face of mankind" is used elsewhere in the *Zohar* (2:149b) in explicating Genesis 1:2 ("darkness on the face of the deep") having nothing to do with Ham. The image is as obvious as it is common. See, for example, Hesiod, *Works and Days* 154–155: "Black death seized them and they left the bright light of the sun."

26. H. Sperling and M. Simon, *The Zohar* (London, 1934) 1:246–247.

27. Jordan's strange interpretation of the *Zohar* is followed (without attribution) by Joseph Washington, *Anti-Blackness in English Religion*, p. 12.

28. For Islamic sources, see, e.g., Jāhiz, *Kitāb al-Hayawān*, ed. Harun, 3:245, 5:35–36, translation in André Miquel, *La Géographie humaine du monde musulman jusqu'au milieu du 11ᵉ siècle*, 2nd ed. (Paris, 1973), 1:11; Mas'ūdī, *Kitāb al-tanbīh wa'l-ishrāf*, translated by B. Carra de Vaux as *Le livre de l'avertissement et de la revision* (Paris, 1896), pp. 38–40; Minoo Southgate, "The Negative Images of Blacks in Some Medieval Iranian Writings," *Iranian Studies* 17 (1984): 12; *Mukhtasar al-'ajā'ib*, trans. B. Carra de Vaux, *L'abrégé des merveilles* (Paris, 1898), ch. 6, pp. 99–100; ed. Paris, 1984, p. 105. Authorship is attributed to either Mas'ūdī or Ibrāhīm ibn Wasīf Shāh (d. before 1209). N. Levtzion and J.F.P. Hopkins, *Corpus of Early Arabic Sources for West African History* (Cambridge, 1981), pp. 37, 133, and 170. For Christian sources, see, e.g., the Old French *Les Narbonnais* quoted in W.W. Comfort, "The Literary Role of the Saracens in the French Epic," *Publications of the Modern Language Association* 55 (1940): 650–651, and Albertus Magnus in J.P. Tilmann, *An Appraisal of the Geographical Works of Albertus Magnus and His Contribution to Geographical Thought* (Ann Arbor, 1971), p. 101. In Christian writings the devil was commonly portrayed as an Ethiopian (i.e., a black African), and in such descriptions red (or, flaming, fiery, glowing) eyes was a typical feature. One example among many: *The Martyrdom of Bartholomew* (= *Pseudo-Abdias*, Book 8) in *The Ante-Nicene Fathers* 8:556. See Lloyd A. Thompson, *Romans and Blacks*, p. 113 and p. 213, n. 114; Jack Winkler, "Lollianos and the Desperadoes," *Journal of Hellenic Studies* 100 (1980): 155–181, p. 161. A full treatment of this subject, with more examples, will appear in my forthcoming book on the Curse of Ham.

29. Galen is preserved in quotation by the Arab historian Mas'ūdī, *Les praires d'or*, ed. Pellat (Paris, 1962), 1:69. The quotation is that of J. Desanges in *The Image of the*

Black in Western Art, ed. Ladislas Bugner, vol. 1/1, p. 312, n. 131; for another example, see ibid., pp. 221 (Snowden) and 278f. (J. Leclant). See also Jordan, *White over Black*, p. 159. On macrophallic Blacks in classical iconography, see Snowden, *Blacks in Antiquity*, pp. 23, 272–273. On the image of oversexed Blacks in Roman antiquity, see also J.P.V.D. Balsdon, *Romans and Aliens* (Chapel Hill, 1979), p. 218.

30. *Natural History* 7.2.21, 6.35.187.

31. *The Voiage and Travaile of Syr John Maundeville...* (reprint: London, 1932; Louvain, 1988) shows no reliance whatsoever upon rabbinic stories. It is therefore quite surprising to read that the "anti-Black influence of Jewish interpretation on that of Gentile Christian Europeans" can be detected in fourteenth-century England in the writings of Sir John Mandeville (Charles Copher, "Three Thousand Years of Biblical Interpretation with Reference to Black Peoples," *Journal of the Interdenominational Theological Center* 30 [1986]: 115–117; the article was reprinted in *African American Religious Studies: An Interdisciplinary Anthology*, ed. G. Wilmore [Durham, 1989]). A full catalogue of the fabulous-race descriptions can be found in J.B. Friedman, *The Monstrous Races in Medieval Art and Thought* (Cambridge, 1981).

32. In Ladislas Bugner, ed., *The Image of the Black in Western Art*, vol. 2/1, p. 52.

33. W.W. Comfort, "The Literary Role of the Saracens in the French Epic," *PMLA* 55 (1940): 651–654, and Ruth Mellinkoff, "Cain's Monstrous Progeny in *Beowulf*: Part II, Post-Diluvian Survival," *Anglo-Saxon England* 9 (1980): 192. The medieval works mentioned by these authors are the *Vienna Genesis* and the Irish *Lebor Na Huidre*. Similarly, the Old French *Chansons de geste* see Cain as the progenitor of the grotesque monster Saracens. See the chapter "Cain's Kin" in Friedman's *Monstrous Races* (pp. 87–107) for a discussion of the idea that the monstrous races derive from biblical figures who had sinned. Cf. also the Muslim al-Dīnawarī (9th century), who reports the tradition that the monsters of Africa are "descended from Noah who incurred the wrath of God so that he changed their form." (*Al-Akhbār al-Ṭiwāl* in N. Levtzion and J.F.P. Hopkins, *Corpus of Early Arabic Sources for West African History*, p. 23.)

34. *The Legends of the Jews* (Philadelphia, 1925) 1:169. Note also that the Canaanites did not practice circumcision (*Legends* 3:275), which may well have made them appear strange ("his foreskin was extended") to the Jew. Thomas Peterson (*Ham and Japheth: The Mythic World of Whites in the Antebellum South*, p. 44), quotes Ginzberg's paraphrase but replaces "through Canaan therefore" with ellipsis. By adding these words Ginzberg clearly understood the passage as not referring to Blacks, who are descended from Kush, not from Canaan. By removing this explanatory gloss, Peterson has Ginzberg say precisely what he took pains not to say.

35. *Anti-Blackness* (above, n. 6), p. 13. Washington must have confused Judaism with Islam. In Islam the association of Canaan with black Africa is common, and is found in two forms: either Canaan is a black African, or Kush is made the father or

the son of Canaan. The first form can be seen in *Mukhtaṣar al-ʿajāʾib*, trans. B. Carra de Vaux, *L'abrégé des merveilles* (Paris, 1898), pp. 99–101: "[Ham] had a son, after Canaan, Kush, who was black....Among the children of Canaan are the Nabīṭ, Nabīṭ signifies "black"....Among the children of Sūdān, son of Canaan, are...the Zanj." Other examples: *The Book of the Zanj* in E. Cerulli, *Somalia* 1 (Rome, 1957), p. 254, trans., p. 234, text; Ibn ʿAbd al-Ḥakam (9th century), *Futūḥ Miṣr*, ed. C.C. Torrey (New Haven, 1922), p. 8. The second form is found in Maqrīzī, *Ibn Faḍl Allah al-ʿOmarī: Masālik el Abṣār fi Mamālik el Amṣār*, ed. Gaudefroy-Demombynes (Paris, 1927), Appendix I, p. 85; Ibn Masʿūd apud Ṭabarī, trans. W. Brinner, p. 50; Dimashqī, *Nukhbat al-Dahr*, ed. C.M.J. Fraen and A.F. Mehren (St. Petersburg, 1866), p. 266; Ibn Saʿd, *Kitāb al-Ṭabaqāt al-Kabīr*, vol. 1/i, ed. E. Mittwoch (Leiden, 1905), p.19; Ṭabarī, trans. Brinner, pp. 105, 109, etc.; Masʿūdī, *Muruj (Praires)*, ed. Meynard 3:1–2, 240, *Les Praires d'or*, ed. Pellat 2:321, 418 n. 1.

Drake, like Washington, has confused Judaism with Islam when he claims that rabbinic literature "makes Kush the son of Canaan." Of course, no rabbinic reference is, or could be, cited, since such a genealogy contradicts the Bible. See also Washington, p. 6, where the same confusion is apparent: "Jewish explanations of the Genesis saga wherein Noah's son Ham (or variously his son or grandson Canaan) was black and the progenitor of black people."

36. *Examining the Record: An Exegetical and Homiletical Study of Blacks in the Bible* (New York, 1994), p. 10. A correct translation of the passage was recently published by Samuel A. Berman, in his English translation of the Genesis-Exodus portions of the work, *Midrash Tanhuma-Yelammedenu* (Hoboken, NJ, 1996), p. 67.

37. The degree of textual and interpretive uncertainty lying behind Graves and Patai's reconstruction brings to mind an evaluation of another of their theories. Commenting on their statement on matriarchal societies, T.O. Beidelman said that it "contains unbridled conjecture on the discredited theories of the reputed existence of early matriarchal societies" ("A Kagaru Version of the Sons of Noah: A Study in the Inculcation of the Idea of Racial Superiority," *Cahiers d'Etudes Africaines* 3.4, no. 12 [1963]: 479, n. 19).

38. For antiquity and late antiquity, see Homer, *Odyssey* 1.23; Diodorus 3.8.2; Jerome in *Patrologia Latina* 25:1091–1092; Agatharchides apud Diodorus 3.32–33; Strabo 17.2.1 (cf. 16.4.17); Herodotus 4.183; Diodorus 3.15.2; Origen, *De Principiis* 2.9.5; Juvenal 15.49f; Ptolemy, *Geographia* 4.8(9).3. For the medieval world, see Hayden White, "The Forms of Wildness: Archaeology of an Idea" in Dudley and Novak, ed., *The Wild Man Within*, p. 20; E. Miner, "The Wild Man Through the Looking Glass," ibid., p. 89; G.R. Crone, ed. and trans., *The Voyages of Cadamosto and Other Documents on Western Africa in the Second Half of the Fifteenth Century* (Cambridge, 1937), p. 54; Katherine George, "The Civilized West Looks at Primitive Africa: 1400-1800," *Isis* 49 (1958): 64, 66. Similarly, Muslim geographers commonly attribute nakedness, sexual permissiveness, cannibalism, and beastlike behavior to the

Blacks. See: Bernard Lewis, *Race and Slavery in the Middle East*, pp. 52–53 (and see pp. 47–48 and 122); André Miquel, *La géographie* 2:44, 144, 193, 198; Gerhard Rotter, *Die Stellung des Negers in der islamisch-arabischen Gessellschaft bis zum XVI Jahrhundert* (Ph.D. diss., Friedrich-Wilhelms Universität, Bonn, 1967), pp. 161 and 182; Minoo Southgate, "The Negative Images of Blacks in Some Medieval Iranian Writings," *Iranian Studies* 17 (1984): 4. The index to Levtzion and Hopkins's *Corpus of Early Arabic Sources for West African History* lists eight references under "Cannibal, -ism," to which eight more can be added (pp. 86, 200, 255, 274, 298 bis, 321, 406 n. 48), and twenty references under "Nudity" (add p. 354). Regarding "beastlike behavior" see *Corpus*, pp. 200, 205 bis, 206, 211, 214, 321–322, and Alfarabi in Ralph Lerner and Muhsin Mahdi, *Medieval Political Philosophy: A Sourcebook* (Glencoe IL, 1963), p. 42. Examples of reports on the Blacks' hypersexuality are found in Lewis, *Race and Slavery*, pp. 34, 45–46, 52, 60, 93–94, 97; idem., *Islam from the Prophet Muhammad to the Capture of Constantinople* (New York, 1974) 2:254–256; Miquel 2:44; Levtzion and Hopkins, *Corpus*, pp. 205 and 214; see also David Brion Davis, *Slavery and Human Progress* (New York, 1984), p. 44 (cf. Lewis, pp. 75–76). A full treatment of this subject, with more examples, will appear in my forthcoming book on the Curse of Ham.

39. Drake's entire section dealing with rabbinic sources (2:17–30) exhibits a large number of misreadings and misunderstandings and is studded with mistakes. The most serious error undergirds his major "discovery"—a supposed dichotomy between Palestinian Jews and the Babylonian Jewish diaspora. Drake finds anti-Black sentiment only in the latter, a development, he says, of the Jewish encounter with the Zanj, thousands of black slaves working the land of Mesopotamia. The cultural differences of the Zanj "may have incited fear, dislike, or even contempt among the Jewish exiles" (p. 29).

In setting out his claim Drake argues that: (a) a text found in Palestinian sources (Jerusalem Talmud, *Ta'anit* 1.6, 64d) is found only in Babylonian sources, (b) a Palestinian statement (R. Ḥiyya) is Babylonian, (c) *Genesis Rabbah*, a product of Israel, is a product of Babylonia, and (d) the presence of the Zanj in Mesopotamia, evidence for which begins in 689 CE, influenced the thinking of a Palestinian rabbi who lived 400 years earlier.

Thus, to prove his theory that "denigration of black slaves was quite consistent with Mesopotamian Jewish social stratification," Drake performs the following historical and geographic reconstruction: he puts Israel in Babylon and makes four centuries disappear. But Drake's historiography goes even further. Having invented a world, its characters, and their relationships, he attempts now to investigate its myths. The origin of the idea of black skin as curse, he claims, lies in its ideological justification of the Zanj enslavement. Discovering, however, that the evidence does not support his theory, for the talmudic folktale says nothing about enslavement, Drake calls this situation "curious."

Among historians it might be regarded as odd to posit a theory, note that it does not coincide with the facts, call it curious, and go on. As a nonhistorian trying to write history, Drake confronted two barriers: lack of knowledge of the source languages and cultures, and lack of knowledge of relevant historical methodologies. To overcome these impediments, Drake, an anthropologist by training, was forced to rely upon the mistranslations and misrepresentations noted above. It is indeed unfortunate that this eminent social scientist was so misled.

The date for the arrival of the Zanj follows François Renault, *La traite des noirs au Proche-Orient médiéval VIIe - XIVe siècles* (Paris, 1989), p. 25, and Alexandre Popovic, *La révolte des esclaves en Iraq au IIIe/IXe siècle* (Paris, 1976), p. 60.

40. *Commentary to the Bible*, to Amos 9:7, p. 109 in ed. Tel Aviv, 1960; in ed. Gregorio Ruiz, *Don Isaac Abrabanel y su comentario al libro de Amos* (Madrid, 1984), pp. 244–245.

41. Jerusalem Talmud, *Ma'aserot* 3.10, 51a.

42. B.M. Levin, *Osar ha-Geonim: Hagigah* (Jerusalem, 1931), p. 59.

43. Frank Manuel, *The Broken Staff* (Cambridge, MA, 1992), p. 136.

44. I am talking of internally cohesive narrative frameworks in which associations between elements are clear and necessary for the cohesion of the unit. I naturally exclude anthologies of traditions in which separate elements are strung together, such as in *Genesis Rabbah*. This is not to say that there are no relationships between discrete elements in such compositions, but that the relationships are of an external sort, not being inherently crucial to the narrative. The difference will become clear below when I discuss Islamic narratives of the Curse of Ham. On this issue, see Joseph Heinemann, *Aggadah and Its Development* [Hebrew] (Jerusalem, 1974), p. 181, who uses this distinction as a defining characteristic of the classical midrashic works as opposed to *Pirqe de-Rabbi Eliezer* or to the "rewritten Bible" genre. The former are "composed of hundreds of exegeses and explanations to various verses, such that each of them is independent and is not generally related to those that come before or after [in context]."

45. Washington, p. 1; Muhammad in Willis, ed., *Slaves and Slavery* (above, n. 4) 1:66–68. Jordan does recognize the distinction, as does Cain Hope Felder, who writes that "later Europeans adopted the so-called curse of Ham as a justification for slavery." (*Troubling Biblical Waters*, p. 38). Although it was not the Europeans, but the Muslims centuries before them, who combined blackness and servitude, Felder at least recognizes that the two were separate in rabbinic Judaism. J.A. Rogers' earlier work (*Nature Knows No Color-Line*, pp. 9–10) conflates and confuses the different rabbinic sources and thus adumbrates the later belief in a rabbinic dual curse.

An indication of the damage done by the Graves and Patai book is to be seen in the increasing reliance upon it by works such as Yosef ben-Jochannan's *Cultural Genocide in the Black and African Studies Curriculum* (New York, 1972), which quotes the work and repeatedly refers to it (p. 29 *et passim*).

46. Respective *Commentaries* to Genesis 9:25.

47. Davis, *Slavery and Human Progress*, p. 42. On this point, and the Curse of Ham generally, see B. Lewis, *Race and Slavery in the Middle East*, pp. 123–125, n. 9. Incredibly, Jan Nederveen Pieterse (*White on Black: Images of Africa and Blacks in Western Popular Culture* [New Haven, 1992], p. 44 and p. 237, n. 43) cites Davis here as a reference for his statement that "the association of the curse of Canaan with blackness arose...in medieval Talmudic texts," precisely the opposite of what Davis actually said.

48. Ibn Khaldūn, *Muqaddimah*, ed. E. Quatremère (Paris, 1858) 1:151; translation of F. Rosenthal, 2nd ed. (London, 1967) 1:169–170. Ṭabarī, *Tarikh*, ed. M.J. de Goeje, vol. 1 (Leiden, 1879), pp. 215, 223; translation of William M. Brinner, *The History of al-Ṭabarī*, vol. 2 (New York, 1987), pp. 14, 21. On Ibn Khaldūn's Muslim genealogists, see Walter J. Fischel, "Ibn Khaldūn: on the Bible, Judaism, and the Jews," *Ignace Goldziher Memorial Volume*, ed. S. Löwinger et al. (Jerusalem, 1958) 2:157.

49. My English follows the Italian translation of Enrico Cerulli, *Somalia* 1 (Rome, 1957), p. 254, text on p. 234. *The Kitāb al-Zunūj* is a late nineteenth-century redaction of earlier manuscripts. On the work, see Prins in the *Journal of East Africa Swahili Committee* 28 (1958): 26–40, and G.S.P. Freeman-Grenville, *The Swahili Coast, 2nd to 19th Centuries* (London, 1988), sec. II, pp. 8–9, originally published as *Uganda Museum Occasional Papers, No. 4: Discovering Africa's Past* (Kampala, 1959).

50. The identity of slave and Black in Islamic societies also explains the association of Canaan with black Africa (or with Kush) in Islamic sources; see n. 35. On this point, see Paul Kaplan, "*Ruler, Saint and Servant: Blacks in European Art to 1520*" (Ph.D. diss., Boston Univ., 1983), p. 172.

51. Samaritan: *Tibat Marqe*, ed. and trans. (into Hebrew) Z. Ben-Ḥayyim (Jerusalem, 1988), pp. 288–289, sec. 232a. Christian: Ephrem the Syrian quoted in a catena of patristic explanations and exegeses to the Pentateuch published by Paul de Lagarde, *Materialien zur Kritik und Geschichte des Pentateuchs* (Leipzig, 1867), part II, p. 86, and cited by M. Grünbaum, *Neue Beiträge zur semitischen Sagenkunde* (Lieden, 1893), p. 86.

52. See Steven Wasserstrom, "Jewish Pseudepigrapha in Muslim Literature: A Bibliographical and Methodological Sketch" in *Tracing the Threads: Studies in the Vitality of Jewish Pseudepigrapha*, ed. John C. Reeves (Atlanta, 1994), pp. 95, 99–100. The same phenomenon occurs as traditions move into new historical and ideological environments within the same culture. See Eli Yassif, "Traces of Folk Traditions of the Second Temple Period in Rabbinic Literature," *Journal of Jewish Studies* 39 (1988): 212–233.

53. *Oral Historiography* (London, 1982), p. 4.

54. Several have been pointed out during the course of this essay. A few more egregious errors may be noted.

Some authors assume that the idea of blackness as curse entered European thought from Jewish sources, by means of Christian interest in rabbinic exegesis. Jordan (p. 37) admits that "the measure of [such] influence...is problematical," but he accepts the proposition anyway. Washington (pp. 1, 10–11) is virulent in his denunciation: "The most maleficent traducement Israel's biblical tradition pressed upon England was the popular belief in anti-Blackness....The vitriolic and inflammatory castigation of Ham, whose 'dark' to 'black' and 'hot' associations were seared in the imagination of sixteenth-century Bible adherers, Englishmen inherited from Talmudic, Halakhahhistic [sic], and Midrashic literature....The depth of anti-Blackness communicated to Englishmen by the custodians of the Talmud and Pentateuch in their commentaries...." Thomas Peterson (pp. 43–44) attempts to trace the line of transmission further: the Ham myth entered America via a work by Bishop Thomas Newton, chaplain to King George II, published in London in 1759; Newton cites Augustin Calmet's *Dictionary of the Holy Bible*, published in Paris about thirty years earlier; Calmet's source was Jewish legends. It was these legends that "first suggested that blackness and slavery resulted from Noah's curse." Thus the source of the Curse of Ham in America is traced back to "rabbinical traditions." But here is what Calmet says:

> The author of Tharik-Thabari [i.e., *Ta'rīkh* written by Ṭabarī, the Islamic historian] says that Noah having cursed Ham and Canaan, the effect was that not only their posterity became subject to their brethren and was born, as we may say, in slavery, but likewise that the color of their skin suddenly became black; for they [i.e., the Arabic writers] maintain that all the blacks descend from Ham and Canaan.

(Quotation from *Calmet's Dictionary of the Holy Bible*, ed. C. Taylor [London, 1800], s.v. Ham, the edition used by Peterson. The work was first published in French in 1722–28. I am indebted to Dr. Peterson for placing at my disposal copies of Calmet which he had used.) It is surprising that, given the explicit reliance upon Ṭabarī (d. 923), Peterson would have considered "rabbinical traditions" as Calmet's source.

Another example is provided by the influential essay of William McKee Evans, "From the Land of Canaan to the Land of Guinea: The Strange Odyssey of the 'Sons of Ham'," *The American Historical Review* 85 (1980): 15–43. Evans attempts to study "the shifting ethnic identities of the 'sons of Ham'...from the Land of Canaan to the land of Guinea, [hoping to] learn something about the historical pressures that shaped modern white racial attitudes" (p. 16). Evans's entire thesis hangs on the assumption that "during the first Christian centuries most 'Canaanites' [i.e., non-Hebrew slaves] were in fact either Syrians or *Kushim* from black Africa" (p. 22). Thus the eternally enslaved Canaanites were interpreted to be Black Africans in Jewish sources, and this interpretation then moved on to Islam and Christianity. How does Evans know that most of the non-Hebrew slaves in Jewish Palestine in the first centuries were Syrians and Blacks? He cites two sources: S. Baron's *Social and Religious History of the Jews* and J. Klausner's chapter in *The World History of the Jewish People*. But Baron says nothing of the sort, and while Klausner does ("Negro slaves...were common"), he does so without citing any source. Undoubtedly he was relying on four rabbinic references to Black slaves, which only show that Black slaves existed in Israel at that time, perhaps even that most African Blacks in Israel were slaves. The references do not, however, provide evidence that most slaves were Black. On this point, see Samuel Krauss, *Talmudische Archäologie* (Leipzig, 1910) 2:85–86, "Unsere Quellen kennen besonders die Mohren als Sklaven," not die Sklaven als Mohren. There is no evidence that shows that most of the slaves were Black. As in Rome, so in the provinces, slaves undoubtedly came from a number of different areas.

As noted throughout this study, the various misreadings of the ancient and medieval sources are not even of the texts themselves, but of translations of the texts. Sometimes these misreadings bear laughable results. So, for example, the folktale referred to above, in which God prohibited those in the ark from engaging in sex, says that among those who transgressed were the dog and Ham, each committing the act with its own partner, a female dog and a female human respectively. A popular English translation (Soncino edition) of the rabbinic text puts it this way: "Ham and the dog copulated in the Ark." In Winthrop Jordan's work this became Ham "copulating with a dog" and from there to Charles Lyons' "Ham commits bestiality on the boat by copulating with a dog." Similarly, Joseph Washington (p. 10), Gene Rice ("The Curse that Never Was [Genesis 9:18-27]," *The Journal of Religious Thought* 29 [1972]: 25–26, n. 112), and apparently also William Evans (p. 26). The absurdity of this translation of the rabbinic text was recently noted by A.A. Jackson in his *Examining the Record*, p. 9.

55. David Brion Davis, *Slavery and Human Progress*, p. 337, n. 144.

56. *Sifre Numbers* 99 and parallels.

57. Drake 2:309; Copher, *Nile Vally Civilizations*, p. 173; Brackman 1:83–84. Brackman goes even further: "Not one rabbinic source accepted this interpretation [that 'Kushite' of Numbers means Black]," and "It is painfully obvious that their qualms over Numbers 12 were rooted in race prejudice" (1:79, 130). This is just an uninformed comment, for many rabbinic sources did interpret "Kushite" just that way. See: *Targum Pseudo-Jonathan* ad loc.; R. Meyuhas b. Elijah, *Commentary to Numbers*, ed. S. Freilich (Jerusalem, 1977), ad loc.; Samuel b. Meir (Rashbam), *Commentary to the Pentateuch*, ed. A.I. Bromberg, 2nd ed. (Jerusalem, 1969, based on ed. D. Rozen, Breslau, 1882), ad loc., p. 177; some of the Tosafot, *Da'at Zeqenim*, ad loc.; Ephraim b. Shimshon, *Commentary to the Pentateuch*, ed. J. Klugman (New York, 1992) 2:76; Hezekiah ben Manoah, *Hizzequni: Commentary to the Pentateuch*, ed. C.B. Chavel (Jerusalem, 1981); and anonymous commentators cited by Ibn Ezra, *Commentary on the Pentateuch*, ed. Asher Weiser (Jerusalem, 1977), ad loc. A variation, recorded by a medieval source as a tannaitic statement cited from *Sifre* (but not extant), states that Moses married the Ethiopian after Zipporah had died (quoted from a manuscript containing anonymous Ashkenazic Bible interpretations combined, and published, with those of Ephraim b. Shimshon, 2:86). Other rabbis claimed that Zipporah herself was

an Ethiopian, or, at least, a half-Ethiopian. Eliezer of Worms says that Jethro married an Ethiopian, from whom Zipporah was born (*Commentary to the Pentateuch*, ed. S. Kanivsky [New York, 1981], 3:43 to Numbers 12:1). The manuscript referred to above records the same tradition in the name of the talmudic sages (Ephraim b. Shimshon, *Commentary* 2:86.)

58. Isaac Heinemann, *Darkhe ha-'Aggadah*, 3rd ed. (Jerusalem, 1970), p. 28; see also, Eliezer Segal, "Sarah and Iscah: Method and Message in Midrashic Tradition," *Jewish Quarterly Review* 82 (1992): 417–429.

59. *Sifre Numbers* 99 (p. 98). For more examples see Heinemann loc. cit. and Segal, p. 419 n. 7.

60. Zephaniah: Talmud *Ta'anit* 15a. Ebed-melech: in many midrashic collections, anthologies, and medieval writings; see the references in Ginzberg, *Legends* 5:96 and 6:412, and in M. Higger, *Mesekhtot Ze'irot* (New York, 1929), pp. 74, 129–132.

61. Louis Ginzberg, *Ginze Schechter* (New York, 1928) 1:86.

two

THE MEDIEVAL BACKGROUND

WILLIAM CHESTER JORDAN

ost sophisticated Christian readers of religious texts in the European Middle Ages recognized four levels of interpretation. The first was literal and addressed the basic matters of physical reality. If the word "Jerusalem" appeared in scripture, its literal interpretation evoked the biblical or historical city in Israel. However, Jerusalem also connoted the Church allegorically, the believing soul morally, and the heavenly City of God mystically.[1] Similarly, the words "Jew" (Latin *Judeus* or any of its vernacular forms) and "Blackness" (*nigredo* with its vernacular synonyms) had various levels of meaning in the texts in which we find them. "Jew" literally denoted a person who professed the religion of Judaism either in biblical or contemporary times; "Blackness," the absence of light. Yet, allegorically the words "Jew" and "Blackness" conjured the Devil; morally they denoted evil; and mystically they evoked the Day of Judgment. Although this negative cast given to the two terms was not entirely unrelieved, derogatory and demeaning associations were those which predominated in the Middle Ages.

Jews and dark-skinned people in Europe, therefore, suffered under the same or similar symbolic and metaphorical impediments throughout the Middle Ages. The difference, of course, is that these symbols and metaphors, often refigured as stereotypes, had far more immediate and tragic consequences for the many Jews than for the few Blacks who lived in medieval Europe. Only in the long term, as a result of the colonization and enslavement of large numbers of dark-skinned people in the post-medieval period, would the consequences be comparable.

Medieval Images of the Jew

Before the eleventh century many Christian princes, like the Visigothic kings of Spain of the sixth and seventh centuries, and many clerics, such as Agobard, the ninth-century bishop of Lyons, himself an Iberian by birth, expressed and acted upon their strong negative feelings toward Jews.[2] On more than one occasion there were also "popular" attacks on Jewish communities in western Europe. Yet, despite instances of this sort, it is widely accepted by scholars that the intensity of anti-Jewish hatred and the number of violent attacks on Jews were far lower in the early Middle Ages than they were after 1096, the year of the massacres of Jews in the Rhineland during preparations for the First Crusade.[3] Moreover, the twelfth and thirteenth centuries, while frequently punctuated by exceptionally brutal anti-Jewish incidents, also witnessed the emergence of more consistently bad relations between Jews and Christians in ordinary daily life. This development did not take place everywhere according to the same timetable; it is generally agreed, for example, that northern Europe led the way in the worsening of relations. Nonetheless, the broad negative shift is discernible everywhere Jews lived in Latin Christendom by the end of the fourteenth century.[4]

Along with this shift went a degeneration in the "image" of the Jew. Polemics and similar sources aimed deliberately at humiliating or ridiculing Jews focused on their lack of "humaneness." According to many polemicists Jews were "felons" (anti-social); they were ritual murderers who martyred innocent children; and in persisting in their Judaism they wilfully joined their ancestors in bearing responsibility for the crucifixion of Jesus. Rowdy, drunken, perverse (as the stereotype went), they would always be anathema in a well-ordered, which was to say, Christian, society. At the same time their role—as usurers, bribers of rulers, and subverters of the faith of poor, uneducated Christians—was seen as jeopardizing Christian society.[5]

This rhetorical picture might be summarized by using the language of chivalry. Jews were said to lack *courtoisie*, *prud'homie*, and *débonnaireté*. Though hard to define, the first, usually translated "courtesy" or "courtliness," denoted civility and propriety; the second, almost untranslatable, represented the virtues of Christian knighthood which made a just society possible; the third, which the quasi-English "debonaire-ness" positively distorts, denoted the abundance of goodness required to transform a just society into a compassionate one. The Jews were found wanting on all counts.[6]

Slippage from this stereotypical picture into demonic and bestial metaphors and depictions, that is, into a denial of the essential humanity of Jews, was not unknown in the twelfth and thirteenth centuries, the classical period of high medieval civilization. The simian and other disagreeable images of usurers seen in manuscript paintings and in sculpture are a case in point, but there are many others.[7] Nonetheless, such slippage became increasingly common in the later Middle Ages, the Renaissance, and the Reformation. It was then, for example, that the *Judensau*, the representation of the Jew as a bloated sow nurturing Jews/piglets on excrement, became a common motif, especially in Germany.[8] At the same time the trio of the Jew, the Devil, and the Witch became irrevocably linked in the premodern imagination.[9]

Many reasons have been put forward to explain this worsening of the images and stereotypes of the Jew. The Crusades and the precarious situation of the crusader states (1095–1291) certainly sharpened perceptions of the Jew as enemy of the faith in tandem with hostility to Muslim enemies, and they also help explain the strongly negative stereotypes of the twelfth and thirteenth centuries. However, these factors alone could not produce the grotesquer images of the later Middle Ages and early modern period. In part the marginalization of Jewish business activity accentuated the transformation in perceptions. As crippling taxation and competition from Christian merchants forced Jews into ever less attractive occupations in the later thirteenth century, their activity—especially as moneylenders to the poorest, most vulnerable, and least creditworthy members of the Christian community—could be interpreted as a deliberate attempt to suck or bleed the poor dry. When the economy of Europe which enjoyed boom times for most of the twelfth and thirteenth centuries turned sour in the fourteenth century, and when long and recurring periods of famine and plague aggravated social struggles then and in the century following, Jews wherever they resided became a characteristic object of Christian fantasies: Were they in league with the Muslims?, with witches?, with Satan?[10]

Problems in the Church were another factor: first, the Babylonian Captivity with the papacy at Avignon rather than Rome (1305–1377), which appeared to some to signal the subservience of the papacy to the political interests of the French crown; then, the Great Schism (1378–1417), which divided Catholic from Catholic and produced two and then three claimants to the papal throne; finally, the Reformation—or the Protestant heresy, depending on viewpoint. And with all this revolutionary religious change went unceasing wars sometimes specifically aggravated by the religious conflicts. God seemed to be testing sinful humanity— with baneful repercussions for Jewish-Christian relations.

As a result, from the end of the thirteenth century through the sixteenth century there occurred numerous expulsions of Jews from various principalities and pogroms against Jews in those where they continued to live, itself a fact that in part led to ghettoization (ostensibly for the Jews' own protection and to make the task of missionizing among them more simple).[11] Where the threat of expulsion or the fears generated by pogroms prevailed and led to mass conversions, novel suspicions arose about the "New Christians" and their commitment to the Catholic faith. Jews' (or New Christians') alleged penchant for conspiracy took on an even brighter hue in the stereotype created by Christians.[12] And in any case, the Jews would never disappear. The strong eschatological belief that they would join Anti-Christ or that Anti-Christ would be a Jew completed the standard interpretation.[13]

In whatever way the worsening of the stereotypes over time may be explained, two factors need to be stressed in evaluating their importance. The mere existence of the stereotypes, however negative, did not inevitably or invariably produce physical violence or expulsion. Relations between Christians and Jews were occasionally cordial, and even if routine transactions and contacts were less easy going in the late Middle Ages than in some earlier periods, they were still frequent and often mutually beneficial.[14] Moreover, there was always a less unsavory view of biblical (Old Testament) Jews than of New Testament and contemporary Jews. Christian intellectuals read of the failings of the ancient Hebrews to live up to God's selection of them as His Chosen Ones, but they also had a consistently deep admiration of the patriarchs, prophets, and many of the kings of ancient Israel like David, Solomon, and Josiah. Something attracted Christian thinkers to the contemporary keepers of this heritage. Not that contemporary Jews were considered the *Verus Israel* or "True Israel" any longer, but they did have direct access to the Hebrew scriptures and associated Hebrew lore such as that found in the mystical writings of so-called cabalists. This "philo-Semitic" interest in contemporary Jews and their knowledge—linguistic and esoteric—was always a minor counterpoint to the grosser stereotypes that circulated among Christians, but it was genuine.[15]

If Christians expressed violent hatreds and mentally and literally painted distorted pictures of the Jews, a somewhat similar phenomenon is documented in polemical texts that reveal Jewish attitudes toward Christians and their religion. Many of these texts were of the highest order intellectually. Indeed, from the twelfth century on, a fully developed philosophical rebuttal to Christian theological positions was in place, largely in response to an increasingly strong tendency among Christian intellectuals to ridicule post-biblical Judaism and to try to win converts.[16]

There was a cruder reaction to Christian domination and attempts at humiliation as well. Among the oldest and most common charges was that Christianity was the religion of a people who worshiped wood or a wooden idol or a rotting corpse ("for they prostrate themselves," the medieval *Alenu*, the closing prayer of the daily liturgy among Jews, said, "before vanity and emptiness, and pray to a god who cannot save"). Yosef Yerushalmi has shown that there probably existed a set of prayers recited on Yom Kippur which, adapting material from the *Toledot Yesu* or Jewish counter-Gospel of Late Antiquity, slurred the founder of Christianity and his mother. By the fourteenth century the precise content of these prayers appears to have been known to Christian polemicists and inquisitors, probably through the medium of converts from Judaism. The prayers were said to "make...Christ an illegitimate son of a prostitute,...Mary a woman of voluptuousness and luxury, and they [the Jews] curse both of them together with the Roman faith and its adherents."[17]

It would not be difficult to assemble other such pieces of information. One thirteenth-century polemic routinely refers to Jesus' mother (Latin, Maria) by a nearly homonymic Aramaic word (Haria) which, properly translated, should be rendered in English as "Shit."[18] The great twelfth-century Jewish thinker, Joseph Kimhi, contrasted the proper deportment of Jewish girls with his stereotype of shameless gentile girls (that is to say, Christians) who, he alleged, stood around on every streetcorner courting disaster, as it were, and, by implication, opening themselves up to becoming latter-day women of "voluptuousness and luxury."[19]

Blackness

Although before the fifteenth century a few Black people lived in Europe, such as the trumpet and trombone playing slaves ordered to Lombardy by the Holy Roman Emperor Frederick II around 1240,[20] their number was never large or well distributed across the continent. Consequently, the kind of "marker" racism based on gross somatic differences and associated most forcefully with the modern United States and South Africa was rare.[21] In the Middle Ages ambivalence about dark-skinned peoples in particular arose largely from encounters with texts rather than from resentments arising out of personal interactions between people of different colors.[22] But the texts that employed Blackness as a negative symbolic marker for human beings were ubiquitous and penetrated a large number of genres. Only a sampling can be marshaled here, but that sample will demonstrate what was demonstrated above with regard to Jews and Judaism and for the same time period, namely, the range of negative interpretative readings—allegorical, moral, and mystical—to which medieval authors committed themselves.

Before doing so, however, it should be mentioned that as with any symbol there were more or less conflicting valences, depending on cultural context and tradition.[23] It was the Middle Ages, after all, that bequeathed the image of the Black magus, one of the three kings, who followed the star and worshiped Jesus as a child. The universalizing tenets of Christianity—its search for converts among all people—helped to fix this likeness in the European imagination. The now traditional Black king of the epiphany scene probably appeared for the first time in art in the mid-fourteenth century, but his roots go back to the "positive" depiction of Blacks serving the south Italian court of Emperor Frederick II in the early thirteenth century.[24] The Middle Ages also saw pictures of heroic Black saints, like Saint Gregory the Moor; word pictures of a fantastic parti-colored (half-Black/half-white) courtly knight of mixed parentage, Parzival's half-brother Feirefiz, a heathen who, once baptized, became a latter-day apostle; and the illustrated legend of Saints Cosmas and Damien (where the miraculous grafting of a Black man's leg onto a white man's stub is effected).[25] Indeed, one is tempted to say that this countervailing tendency (to impute positive or at least equivocal significance to Blackness and Black people as symbols) was richer and more powerful than anything European Christians achieved with regard to Judaism and Jews. Nonetheless, the weight of the evidence still points to a prevailing negative characterization of Blackness and Black people.

One example of this can come from the so-called hagiographic romances of the High Middle Ages. These vernacular stories, often based on ancient legends, were the updated versions of the lives of the saints, adapted for a new lay audience in the twelfth and later centuries. They were immensely popular, judging from surviving manuscripts. The Life of Saint Margaret of Antioch is one such story. It tells of the struggles between Margaret and various temptations, tempters, and enemies. In the version recently translated by Brigitte Cazelles, we can read of the episode in which Margaret is visited by "a dark man, / Who did not look like a Christian / But was blacker than an Egyptian" (ll. 310–12). Asked his name, he replies,

> "They call me Beelzebub,
> And rightly so.
> I am the king and lord of all the devils.
> I never cared for goodness,
> Loving only the worst of sins." (ll. 332–36)

Margaret will not be the loser in her encounter with the "dark man…blacker than an Egyptian," and in the course of their conversation and struggle where she overpowers him physically (with God's help), she will reveal him as loathsome, savage and bent, though unsuccessful, on her deflowering.

> "Ha!" she says, "mad and evil man,
> Despicable and foul creature,
> Beast full of iniquity,
> Threat to my virginity,
> Be careful not to harm me,
> If you ever want to get up!" (ll. 367–72)

In various versions of the story, the dark man thereupon vanishes or is banished to the underworld.[26]

The routine depiction of the Black man as devilish and full of vice ("loving only the worst of sins") responded to the allegorical and moral levels of interpretation and can also be seen in the visual arts. There in paintings of the crucifixion of Jesus, for example, one can see misshapen and hideous torturers. Like artists in all times the variety of ways to show the evil imputed to these tormentors was wide, but, as we might expect, an available and instantly understandable choice was depicting one or more of the crucifiers as swarthy or Black. The spongebearer, the oft distorted figure whom the Gospels record giving vinegar to Jesus on the cross, appears from time to time as a dark man with what scholars have called "negroid" features.[27]

The most learned discourses of the Middle Ages also contain material that emphasizes the allegedly unappealing or immoral characteristics of Black people. Take, for instance, the so-called *Quodlibets* or topics for university debate in the arts faculty of Paris in the thirteenth century. The question, "Are white men bold?" appears as one of these *Quodlibets*. No doubt intended for humorous (though learned) reflection among the professionally pacifist white *doctores* of the university, the orthodox and self-congratulatory answer was never in doubt. All one had to do was look up the matter in a good encyclopedia. A book by one of the most gifted encyclopedists of the High Middle Ages, the Dominican friar

Vincent of Beauvais, would have provided the answer. But to do so—and this was typical—the author had to summon up the counterimage of the Black man. In his discussion of complexions in the *Speculum naturale* of the mid-thirteenth century, Vincent contrasts the Ethiopian with the northern European. The Ethiopian, with his frizzy hair and black complexion, lacks spirit; the blond northman is brave and strapping. As Peter Biller remarks, Vincent was merely repeating statements that in various forms could be found in "well-known sources, Greek texts, the Latin encyclopaedic tradition, and Arabic authors" as well.[28]

Sometimes the implicit and explicit comparisons evoke, as we saw above in the story of Saint Margaret, the question of sexual mores, whether biologically conditioned or not. The manuscript from which Peter Biller cited the *Quodlibet* on the boldness of white men contains other topics meant, of course, to display learning and cleverness but also, it seems reasonable to believe, to titillate the celibate audience of learned white male clerics who would have followed the debates: "Whether a white woman has a greater appetite for men than a black woman." Or, again, "whether white women have greater appetites for intercourse than black women."[29]

At the outset of this essay it was pointed out that Jews and Blackness, besides their allegorical evocations of the Devil and their moral interpretation as signs of evil, were mystically identified with Judgment. In the final genre that I want to invoke here, sermons, the magniloquent homilies wherein preachers tried to construct vivid word pictures both to edify their audiences and congregations and to strike the fear of Doomsday into their hearts, just such evocations of Blackness occur. A particularly excellent example comes from the works of the great crusade preacher Eudes of Châteauroux, a papal legate and participant in discussions at the highest levels of the political system in medieval Europe. Eudes had earlier helped lead the assault on Jewish books that characterized the mid-thirteenth century, ordering the tracking down of as many copies of the Talmud as could be found in order to consign them to fire.[30]

Eudes's zeal burned not only against Judaism (or rather, in his view, the perversions of post-biblical Judaism) but against the venality of those in authority in the Church. In a stunning set of images preached in a sermon before a group of cardinals, he described what might befall cardinals (the *familiares* or associates of the pope) or even a pope himself who fell from virtue into vice. The passage is a fitting conclusion to this section on Blackness as a medieval trope.

As a sign of desolation and death [the preacher declaims] men clothe themselves in black. Demons are depicted in the colour black. The colour black is appropriated to the devil. Therefore when some great man has black garments—that is, *familiares* who are like the devil—it is a sign that he is dead. The pope, when he is dead, is clothed in black. For you know that the spirits of demons are named from sins: the spirit of fornication, the spirit of avarice, of cupidity, of pride,...The works of the supreme pontiff ought to shine above the works of others. But were they to be black, and were his face to be blackened—may God avert this—men might be right to be fearful about the imminence of judgement and condemnation. For the sun will be darkened and turned to blackness when judgement is imminent.[31]

Conclusion

The interpretative parallels between medieval Christians' conceptions of Jews and Judaism, on the one hand, and Black people and Blackness, on the other, were precise despite the fact that Jews did not have to remain Jews in the Middle Ages whereas Black people and their Blackness could never be sundered. We have seen that suspicion about the large numbers of converts to Christianity from Judaism in the very late Middle Ages and the early modern period laid the foundation for an equally invidious "biologicization" of anti-Jewish attitudes.[32] We might imagine a *Quodlibet* as to whether a Jew could "really" cease to be a Jew, and we could imagine, in turn, an even greater link between the interpretative discourse on Jews and Blacks as a result.

In fact, it is not necessary to imagine such convergence. Any number of texts—especially, pictorial—link Jews and Blacks in the Middle Ages. Although the color primarily associated with Jews by medieval Christians was yellow,[33] Jewish tormentors of Christ at the cross, as we have already noticed, do at times appear Black. Blacks appear in the crowd of scornful onlookers at the arrest in the Garden of Gethsemane and elsewhere as well. "How many generations of Christians," one scholar writes, "have been conditioned by looking at a grimacing black man torturing Christ or his saints."[34]

Moreover, the *Quodlibets* cited earlier in this essay are found in a manuscript that speculates on the biological nature of Jews. Christian debaters wondered "whether Jews suffered a flux" (widely attributed to them in popular culture) specifically because they were Jews. Medieval scholars were bothered by the fact that Jews and Christians had similar color ("because Christians and some Jews are of the same complexion"); it would have been easier to link a "humoral" distinction about the nature of bile and fluxes of bile to gross somatic difference. But northern European churchmen knew from experience that Jews were not black, no matter how much they permitted themselves occasionally to indulge symbolic (allegorical, moral, mystical) conflations of the two. Peter Biller, who has edited the entire *Quodlibet* and sets it into the wider context of medical and theological speculation on the relative importance of nature and nurture on the Jewish body, views these speculations as a kind of early intermediate stage to the full scale pseudoscientific racism of the modern period. In its own time it was never uncontested, however, because scholars—all of whom were churchmen—took the radically transforming potential of baptism so seriously.[35]

So, although similarities in the interpretation of the symbolic significance of Judaism and Jews and Blackness and Black people were strong and sometimes even precisely homologous, we must also remain aware of the important differences, at least with regard to the medieval economy of salvation and the still relatively weak authority of arguments about the immutable biological nature of Jews. We must also remain alert to a point made at the outset of this essay, namely, the differential impact of medieval ideas about Jews and Blacks, however negative they were, on social relations in the Middle Ages. Jews were living among people whose mental universe was profoundly shaped, if not absolutely conditioned, by the symbolic system described above. Few Blacks had to endure living in this environment. Only when the power and authority of western European norms expanded around the globe did "people of color" feel the weight of a symbolic system that derided Blackness and Black people as much, if in different ways, as it derided Judaism and its adherents. Sharing this burden as well as the burden of racist pseudoscience of the nineteenth and early twentieth centuries, Jews and people of color, one might hope, can actively share in the mission to overcome them.

Notes

1. The fourfold method of interpretation was common to Christian authors who wrote in many genres, even those as dry and apparently straightforward as chronicles; see *The Chronicle of Salimbene de Adam*, trans. Joseph Baird and others (Binghamton, New York, 1986), p. 680 (where the editors use the same Jerusalem example to highlight the method).

2. The focus of this essay is on western or Catholic Europe in the Middle Ages. Although there existed a strong current of anti-Judaism in the Byzantine East from Antiquity through the Middle Ages, it was on the whole less virulent than in the West. Its artistic expression was also different. Byzantine images of the Jew, according to one scholar, were "illustrative and not moralizing, descriptive and not accusatory"; Elisabeth Revel-Neher, *The Image of the Jew in Byzantine Art* (Oxford, 1992), p. 107.

3. This general, but not uncontested, view of the situation in western Europe is summed up in Gavin Langmuir, *History, Religion, and Antisemitism* (Berkeley, 1990), pp. 289–90.

4. Mark Cohen, *Under Crescent and Cross: The Jews in the Middle Ages* (Princeton, 1994), pp. 82–87, sums up the scholarship nicely.

5. For the comments in this paragraph I am drawing from an earlier work of my own, *The French Monarchy and the Jews from Philip Augustus to the Last Capetians* (Philadelphia, 1989), pp. 15–17, 27–29, 45–46, 68, 181, etc.

6. William Jordan, "Marian Devotion and the Talmud Trial of 1240," in *Religionsgespräche im Mittelalter*, ed. Bernard Lewis and Friedrich Niewöhner (Wiesbaden, 1992), pp. 71–75.

7. On images of avarice, see Lester Little, "Pride Goes before Avarice: Social Change and the Vices in Latin Christendom," *American Historical Review*, 76 (1971), 44; and Priscilla Baumann, "The Deadliest Sin: Warnings against Avarice and Usury on Romanesque Capitals in Auvergne," *Church History*, 59 (1990), 7–18. On demonic images, see Cohen, *Under Crescent and Cross*, pp. 171–72.

8. Isaiah Shachar, *The Judensau: A Medieval Anti-Jewish Motif and Its History* (London, 1974); Ruth Mellinkoff, *Outcasts: Signs of Otherness in Northern European Art of the Late Middle Ages*, 2 vols. (Berkeley, 1993), 1:93, 108.

9. Joshua Trachtenberg in his famous study, *The Devil and the Jews* (New Haven, 1944; reprinted 1983), pp. 207–16, while noting this conflation in the mental imagination, also remarked at the relatively small number of judicial accusations that it generated against Jews.

10. On the matters addressed in this and the following paragraph (and, of course, on the countervailing tendencies as well), there are some useful observations in John Edwards, *The Jews in Christian Europe 1400–1700* (London, 1988), pp. 11–65, and in Myriam Yardeni, *Anti-Jewish Mentalities in Early Modern Europe* (Lanham, Maryland, 1990), pp. 1–53.

11. For a convenient, if incomplete, list of expulsions, see Edwards, *Jews in Christian Europe*, pp. 10–12; on ghettoization, Kenneth Stow, *Alienated Minority: The Jews of Medieval Latin Europe* (Cambridge, MA, 1992), pp. 304–08.

12. On the large-scale conversions and some of the suspicions they engendered (especially in Spain, less so in Portugal), see Edwards, *Jews in Christian Europe*, pp. 29–35.

13. Richard Emmerson, *Antichrist in the Middle Ages: A Study of Medieval Apocalypticism, Art, and Literature* (Seattle, 1981), pp. 27, 46, 79–81, 90–91, 100–101, 127, 129, 134–35, 140, 144, 164–65, 170. Some Protestants recognized the eschatological role of Jews, their conversion at the Last Day to the religion of Christ, without accepting traditional interpretations of their relation to Anti-Christ: pp. 215, 217, 220.

14. For the most positive statement of this position for the fourteenth century, see Joseph Shatzmiller, *Shylock Reconsidered: Jews, Moneylending, and Medieval Society* (Berkeley, 1990).

15. On interest in Jewish learning in various periods (and the problematic results of such interest), see Beryl Smalley, *The Study of the Bible in the Middle Ages*, 3rd ed. (Oxford, 1983) with a summary of more recent work and interpretations in Jordan,

French Monarchy and the Jews, pp. 11–15. See also Edwards, *Jews in Christian Europe*, pp. 43–61.

16. Daniel Lasker, *Jewish Philosophical Polemics against Christianity in the Middle Ages* (New York, 1977).

17. The texts cited in this paragraph were translated and are discussed by Yosef Yerushalmi, "The Inquisition and the Jews of France in the Time of Bernard Gui," *Harvard Theological Review*, 63 (1970), 357–63.

18. David Berger, ed., *The Jewish-Christian Debate in the High Middle Ages: A Critical Edition of the Nizzahon Vetus* (Philadelphia, 1979), p. 215 (English), p. 150 (Hebrew). For propriety's sake Berger understandably does not use this word in his English translation.

19. The appropriate passages from Kimhi's work are translated into English in Robert Chazan, *Church, State and the Jew in the Middle Ages* (New York, 1980), p. 252.

20. David Abulafia, *Frederick II: A Medieval Emperor* (New York, 1992), p. 337.

21. Robert Bartlett, *The Making of Europe: Conquest, Colonization and Cultural Change, 950–1350* (Princeton, 1993), p. 197.

22. This section addresses medieval *Christians'* understandings of Blackness as a symbolic marker, since these had a powerful impact on later developments. Jewish views are discussed by David Goldenberg in another essay in this collection.

23. Michel Pastoureau, *Figures et couleurs: Études sur la symbolique et la sensibilité médiévales* (Paris, 1986), p. 40.

24. Paul Kaplan, "Black Africans in Hohenstaufen Iconography," *Gesta*, 26 (1987), 29–36.

25. *Lexikon der christlichen Ikonographie*, 8 vols., ed. Engelbert Kirschbaum and others (Rome and elsewhere, 1968–1976), 6, cc. 441–42 s.v. "Gregor der Mohr"; 7, cc. 343–52 s.v. "Kosmas und Damian." On the fascinating figure of Feirefiz, see Linda Parshall, *The Art of Narration in Wolfram's* Parzival *and Albrecht's* Jungerer Titurel (Cambridge, 1981), index s.v. "Feirefiz."

26. For a discussion of the Life and the quoted excerpts, see Brigitte Cazelles, *The Lady as Saint: A Collection of French Hagiographic Romances of the Thirteenth Century* (Philadelphia, 1991), pp. 216–37.

27. Ruth Mellinkoff, "Demonic Winged Headgear," *Viator*, 16 (1985), 374; William Jordan, "The Last Tormentor of Christ: An Image of the Jew in Ancient and Medieval Exegesis, Art, and Drama," *Jewish Quarterly Review*, 78 (1987), 36. (It must be stressed that the depictions are not usually based on real human beings known to the artist, but are extrapolations from textual descriptions or copies generated within a tradition which originates remotely in physical observation.)

28. Peter Biller, "Views of Jews from Paris around 1300: Christian or 'Scientific'," in *Christianity and Judaism*, ed. Diana Wood (Oxford, 1992), pp. 200–201. I wish to thank the author for bringing this article to my attention.

29. Biller, "Views of Jews from Paris," p. 200n.40; the content of neither of these *Quodlibets*, so far as I can determine, has been published in any modern edition.

30. Shlomo Simonsohn, *The Apostolic See and the Jews: History* (Toronto, 1991), pp. 302–06.

31. The original Latin and the English translation quoted may be found in Penny Cole, D. L. d'Avray, and J. Riley-Smith, "Application of Theology to Current Affairs: Memorial Sermons on the Dead of Mansurah and on Innocent IV," *Historical Research: Bulletin of the Institute of Historical Research*, 63 (1990), 243 and note.

32. It has been argued more than once that a biological essentialism has sometimes been embraced by a few Jewish thinkers who look upon converts to Judaism as less fully Jews than those born Jewish. The twelfth-century rabbi, Yehuda HaLevy, has been accused of taking this position. On occasion the position has been categorized as "racism" by scholars. Whether it deserves the name is hotly contested. The late Steven Schwarzchild took a very strong position in declaring it racism (though he was not absolutely wedded to the word; "ethnicism" would do). Schwarzchild also asserted that "One has to face up to it that he (Yehuda HaLevy) also speaks in what nowadays can only be called a racist way of Blacks, of women, etc." See Steven Schwarzchild, "Proselytism and Ethnicism in R. Yehuda HaLevy," in *Religionsgespräche im Mittelalter*, ed. Bernard Lewis and Friedrich Niewöhner (Wiesbaden, 1992), pp. 27–41. The conference at which the paper cited here was first read provoked equally strong opposition to the application of the modern category of racism to twelfth-century Jewish thought.

33. Pastoureau, *Figures et couleurs*, p. 41.

34. For the evidence of "Black Jews," see J. Vercoutter and others, *The Image of the Black in Western Art*, 4 vols. (New York, 1976), 2:i, 63, 80; ii, 73. The quotation is at 2:i, 80.

35. Biller, "Views of Jews from Paris," pp. 187–207. He edits the text at pp. 205-07; a translation appears on pp. 192–93. The quoted passage, "because Christians and Jews are of the same complexion," actually begins with the words "It is argued, that not," which is to say, the respondent challenges the contention that Jews by nature have fluxes, since some of them share an aspect of nature (color) with Christians. See also Gilbert Dahan, *Les Intellectuels chrétiens et les juifs* (Paris, 1990), pp. 528–30.

three

JEWS IN THE SLAVE TRADE

DAVID BRION DAVIS

To blame Jews for participating in the Atlantic slave trade is a bit like blaming Native Americans for contributing to the oil industry that now threatens the earth with atmospheric pollution and global warming. After eastern Indian tribes were expelled westward to Oklahoma, some members of the small Osage group profited from the immense reserves of oil discovered beneath their barren and seemingly unproductive land. In the early twentieth century, after tribal leaders distributed fabulous royalties to previously indigent Indians, oil riggers were soon outnumbered by swarms of white vultures including luxury car salesmen and fancy prostitutes. Money was so plentiful that, in addition to extravagant spending, Indian oil profits also led to the founding of the great Gilcrease Museum in Tulsa.

In somewhat similar fashion, a few of the Sephardi Jews and their descendants who were expelled from Spain and Portugal found refuge in Antwerp and then the Netherlands, where, thanks to geopolitical circumstances far beyond their control, the trade in sugar and slaves became as tempting an enterprise as modern oil. Like the oil and petrochemical industry, the slave system of Brazil and the Caribbean revolutionized the world economy, attracting investments from all quarters, creating thousands of new jobs, amassing capital, and benefiting consumers throughout the Western world, including West Africa, with a new array of cheap products. In addition, as Joseph C. Miller has written, this merchant capitalism had the effect in Africa of converting human beings "into cold metal...the Midas touch that rendered southern Atlantic slaving the Africans' 'way of death.'"[1] Yet just as the mass of North American Indians remained enclosed in reservations, far removed from the profits of drilling and refining oil, so the great mass of Europe's Jews were confined for centuries in separate, isolated communities well beyond the margins of the Atlantic slave system.

Although Jews and Native Americans have both suffered from centuries of persecution, caricature, and even mass killings, one profound difference qualifies any analogy. Even the radical environmentalists who see any participation in the oil industry as immoral or as verging on criminality would never dream of interpreting Indian oil profits as part of a larger Native American conspiracy. Yet partly because of their remarkable success in a variety of hostile environments, Jews have long been feared as the power behind otherwise inexplicable evils. For many centuries they were the only non-Christian minority in nations dedicated to the Christianization and thus the salvation of the world.[2]

Signifying an antithetical Other, individual Jews have been homogenized and reified as a "race"—a race responsible for crucifying the Savior, for resisting the dissemination of God's word, for manipulating kings and world markets, and for spreading the evils of both capitalism and communist revolution. Responsibility for the African slave trade (and even for creating and spreading AIDS) has recently been added to this long list of crimes. Such fantasies were long nourished by the achievements of a very small number of Jews who, barred from landholding, the army, and traditional crafts and professions, took advantage of their cosmopolitan knowledge and personal connections that favored access to markets, credit, and such highly desired commodities as diamonds, spices, wool, and sugar. Indeed, much of the historical evidence regarding Jewish involvement in the slave system is biased by deliberate Spanish efforts to encourage anti-Semitism in Holland and to blame Jewish refugees for fostering Dutch commercial expansion at the expense of Spain. Given this long history of conspiratorial fantasy and collective scapegoating, a selective search for Jewish slave traders becomes inherently anti-Semitic unless one keeps in view the larger context and the marginal place of Jews in the history of the overall system. It is easy enough to point to Jewish slave-trading firms in Amsterdam (the Belmontes), in Bordeaux (the Gradis and Méndez), and in Newport, Rhode Island (Aaron López and Jacob Rivera). But far from suggesting that Jews constituted a major force behind the exploitation of Africa, closer investigation shows that these merchants were the exception, far outnumbered by thousands of Catholics and Protestants who flocked to share in the great bonanza.

For four centuries the African slave trade was an integral and indispensable part of European expansion and settlement of the New World. Until the 1840s the flow of coerced African labor exceeded all the smaller streams of indentured white servants and voluntary white immigrants willing to endure the risks of life in the Western Hemisphere. The demand for labor was especially acute in the tropical and semitropical zones that produced the staples and thus the wealth most desired by Europeans. In the mid-eighteenth century the value of exports to Britain from the British West Indies was more than ten times that of exports from the colonies north of the Chesapeake—and thirty-one times greater if measured in terms of value per capita. The economy of the northern colonies depended in large measure on trade with Caribbean markets, which depended in turn on the continuing importation of African labor to replenish a population that was never allowed to sustain itself by natural increase.

Fortunately for the white planters, merchants, consumers, and other beneficiaries of this lethal system, West Africa offered a cheap and seemingly unlimited supply of slave labor. Long before the Portuguese African voyages of the fifteenth century, Arab merchants had perfected the trans-Saharan slave trade and had delivered hundreds of thousands of black slaves to regions extending from the Persian Gulf (via a seaborne trade from East Africa) to Sicily, Morocco, and Spain. Sharply divided by tribal disputes and rivalries, Africans never looked upon one another as a homogeneous "race"; accustomed to a variety of forms of servitude, many tribes or kingdoms developed highly sophisticated methods for recruiting captives and bartering slaves for coveted commodities which Arabs or the Portuguese could bring from distant lands. The political power and commercial networks of the Sokoto caliphate, the Asante, and the Yoruba states, to name only three examples, were wholly inconsistent with the popular picture of "primitive" people overawed and dominated by European military might.

Though first monopolized by the Portuguese, the Atlantic slave trade attracted ships from the Netherlands, France, Britain, Denmark, Spain, Sweden, and the English mainland colonies. Even the northern German ports sought to cash in on this lucrative traffic. How did Jews fit into this picture? To keep matters in perspective, one should keep in mind that in 1290 England expelled its entire Jewish population; only a scattering of migrants began to return in the later half of the seventeenth century. In France a series of expulsions and massacres in the fourteenth century virtually demolished the medieval Jewish communities. In Spain, beginning in the mid-fourteenth century, a much larger Jewish population was subjected to periodic massacres, forced conversion, mob attacks, and final expulsion in 1492. Many of the refugees fled to Muslim lands; the estimated 100,000 Jews who escaped into Portugal were compelled to accept Christianity. By the 1570s, which marked the beginning of Brazil's sugar boom based on African slave labor, Judaism as a religion had been virtually wiped out in England, France, the Germanies, Spain, Portugal, the Low Countries, and most of Italy; the great mass of Jewish survivors had emigrated to Poland, Lithuania, and Ottoman lands in the Balkans and Turkey. No professing Jews were allowed to contaminate the Spanish or Portuguese colonies of the New World. These sustained anti-Semitic crusades clearly reduced the opportunity Jews might have had for participating in the Atlantic slave system and certainly precluded any Jewish "initiation," "domination," or "control" of the slave trade. Yet the continuing persecution and exclusion, especially of the "New Christians" or Marranos, did lead to a desperate search for new commercial opportunities in the rebellious Spanish province of the Netherlands (the Dutch struggle for independence continued from 1568 to 1648).

One of the most convincing estimates of the total volume of the Atlantic slave trade, by Paul E. Lovejoy, comes to 11,698,000 slaves exported from Africa between 1450 and 1900.[3] For the first century most of the slaves were destined for the Iberian Peninsula, Madeira, São Tomé, and other sugar-producing islands off the African coast. In the next century these markets were replaced by Brazil and the Spanish colonies. Over half of the grand total, 6,133,000 slaves, were exported in the eighteenth century, and 28.5 percent in the nineteenth century. During the seventeenth century the Dutch took the lead over the Portuguese for perhaps as long as twenty-eight years, and the very small proportion of Jewish slave traders undoubtedly reached its peak. But the total Dutch share of the overall slave trade accounted for only 16 percent. During the crucial eighteenth century British ships transported nearly 42 percent of the slaves who left Africa; the Dutch share amounted to only 5.7 percent. In view of the absence of more conclusive data, and keeping in mind the fact that even Dutch slave trading was overwhelmingly in Protestant hands, these figures at least help to indicate the small parameters of any "Jewish contribution" to the total slave trade.

//

Jews and Jewish names are virtually absent from the texts and indexes of scholarly works on the Atlantic slave trade and from recent monographs on the French, Dutch, Portuguese, and British branches of the commerce. Clearly Jews were not prominent in the British Royal African Company or the Dutch West India Company (although in 1677 the WIC made an *asiento*[4] with Diego Nunes Belmonte which was never implemented). According to the eminent historian Seymour Drescher, who draws on the Dutch historians Pieter C. Emmer and Johanes Menne Postma, Jews played a very limited and subordinate role even at the height of the Dutch slave trade: "They did not serve on the *Heren X*, the directorate of the Dutch West India Company. Their investment share amounted to only 0.5 percent (or one two-hundredth) of the company's capital."[5] Few Jews appear among the merchants of Bristol, Liverpool, and London who purchased over 2.5 million Africans in the eighteenth century. Yet if we expand the issue beyond the slave trade itself, small numbers of Sephardi Jews and Marranos did play a crucial role in refining and marketing sugar and then in shifting transatlantic commerce, including the slave trade, from Portugal to northern Europe. We must always remember, however, that most Marranos or New Christians were Jews only in the Nazi racist sense of the concept. It was mainly persecution by the Inquisition that kept alive any sense of non-Christian identity for succeeding generations.

Throughout the Mediterranean, Jews had acquired expertise in refining and marketing sugar, which until the eighteenth century was a much-desired luxury only the wealthy could afford. Marranos and Italians were prominent in the international sugar trade of the fifteenth and sixteenth centuries. Some of them helped to establish sugar plantations in Madeira and São Tomé. Indeed, in 1493 when Portugal was flooded with Jewish refugees from Spain, the government forcibly baptized their children, large numbers of whom were separated from their parents and shipped off to São Tomé as colonists. Because Marranos were always suspected of harboring covert "Judaizing" tendencies, they were often eager to leave Portugal for safer locations, farther removed from the scrutiny of the Inquisition. The Marranos who moved to Brazil took with them the technical skills of artisans, foremen, and merchants, and played a leading part in developing the sugar export industry. Other Marranos, who sailed with Portuguese expeditions to the Kongo Kingdom and Angola, became expert at contracting for cargoes of slave labor. There can be no doubt that these New Christians played an important part in transforming Portugal into Europe's major supplier of slave-grown sugar. But as I have already indicated, the question then arises: To what extent were the Marranos Jews? This matter has been hotly debated, especially since a few of them were able to recover their religious heritage in Holland or in Dutch Brazil. Yet given the extent of intermarriage and loss of Jewish identity, most Marranos were "Jewish" only in their vulnerability to suspicion, persecution, and anti-Semitic fantasies of conspiracy.

Such fears were greatly stimulated by the leadership which Marranos and professing Jews took in marketing Portuguese East Indian spices and then sugar throughout northern Europe, especially after they became allied with the rebellious Dutch and heretical Protestants. The history of the Dutch Sephardi communities, including their fluctuating economic fortunes, depended in large measure on the Hollanders' relations with Spain, which from 1580 to 1640 controlled Portugal and its many colonies. Under pressure of Dutch attacks on the Flemish coast, many Marranos migrated around the turn of the seventeenth century from Antwerp, long the headquarters of sugar refining, to Amsterdam and Rotterdam. Although the Dutch barred professing Jews from many trades and occupations— it was apparently not until 1655 that two Jewish merchants received permission from the Amsterdam government to establish a sugar refinery—the Netherlands presented a climate of relative religious toleration that encouraged the founding of synagogues and the revival of a small Jewish religious community. The Twelve Years' Truce with Spain, from 1608 to 1621, helped the Dutch Sephardi merchants expand various branches of trade with the Iberian Peninsula, Brazil, and Africa. Their knowledge of Spanish and Portuguese, as well as the intricacies of international finance, gave them a particular advantage in procuring and marketing sugar.

Even though Jewish merchants suffered from the resumption of the war with Spain and from the expansion across Europe of the Thirty Years' War, they retained temporary control of sugar and its distribution, which should not be confused with control of the Dutch slave trade.[6] This involvement with sugar was largely the result of the Dutch conquest of northeastern Brazil in the early 1630s. By 1639 Jews constituted a substantial proportion of the white civilian population of Recife and owned about 6 percent of the sugar mills in Dutch Brazil. Jewish merchants bought a large share of the slaves transported by the Dutch West India Company and then retailed them to Portuguese planters on credit, arousing complaints of high prices and high interest rates. A few Amsterdam

Jews such as Diego Días Querido, originally a native of Portugal, challenged the WIC monopoly and chartered their own ships to transport slaves from Africa to Brazil or the Spanish Caribbean. But the Jewish presence in Brazil was short-lived. In the early 1650s, with the collapse of the Dutch occupation and the impending return of the Portuguese, Jews faced the choice of emigration or death. Most flocked back to Holland, bringing with them capital and new knowledge of sugar cultivation, sugar refining, and slave trading. The next quarter-century would mark the high point of Dutch Sephardi commercial success and involvement with the slave system.

Some of the emigrés from Brazil moved northwestward to the Caribbean, where they were soon joined by Jewish and Marrano entrepreneurs from Holland, some of whom had lived in Dutch Brazil. There were a number of reasons for the upsurge of interest in the Caribbean. By the 1650s the British island of Barbados had made a decisive conversion from tobacco to sugar, as African slaves and a new class of large planters replaced a population of white indentured servants. In 1662 Spain awarded an *asiento* to the Dutch West Indian Company, seeking a non-Portuguese source of African slaves for the Spanish Caribbean colonies. The main *asientista* was the Protestant banker Balthazar Coymans, and Jews had little to do with the WIC shipments of slaves from Africa. Still, in the 1670s Spain appointed Baron Manuel de Belmonte as its agent in Amsterdam to procure slaves. And it was in Curaçao, which Marranos had helped establish in 1651, that Jews found their main outlet for selling slaves and Dutch manufactured goods along the Spanish Main.

For a time Curaçao became the great *entrepôt* of the Caribbean, trading legally and illegally with Barbados and other rising British and French colonies as well as with the Spanish mainland. In the eighteenth century Jews made up about half the white population of Curaçao and seem to have been involved mainly in the transshipment of commodities other than slaves to the Spanish colonies. The mainland colonies never developed large plantation systems; their demand for slaves declined abruptly in the eighteenth century, since they could not begin to compete with colonies like Jamaica, St. Domingue, and Brazil, which imported their labor directly from Africa. The one colony where a significant number of Jews took up plantation agriculture was Suriname, or what later became Dutch Guiana. The religious freedom of the Dutch colonies allowed Jews to establish their own self-governing town, Joden Savanne (Jewish Savannah), in the interior jungle. There in the late seventeenth and early eighteenth centuries the Sephardim lived the life of sugar planters, extracting labor from African slaves in one of the most deadly and oppressive environments in the New World. During this period, however, Suriname never became a sugar-producing region on the scale of Jamaica and St. Domingue.

"The significant point," as I've written in another place,[7] "is not that a few Jewish slave dealers changed the course of history but that Jews found the threshold of liberation in a region dependent on black slavery." Before turning to the sobering and depressing part of this message, it should be stressed that even with regard to the Dutch Sephardi sugar trade, we are dealing with a few hundred families. And after the brief Dutch sugar boom had ended, Britain emerged as the world's greatest sugar importer and slave-trading nation. In Barbados, to be sure, there were fifty-four Jewish households in 1680. But these were not great slave traders or planters; they were mostly the managers of retail shops and money-lending firms who owned fewer slaves per household (three) than the non-Jewish residents of Bridgetown.

To keep matters in perspective, we should note that in the American South, in 1830, there were only 23 Jews among the 59,000 slaveholders owning twenty or more slaves and only four Jews among the 11,000 slaveholders owning fifty or more slaves. Even if each member of his Jewish slaveholding elite had owned 3,704—a ridiculous figure anywhere in the world—the total number would only equal the 100,000 slaves owned by black and colored planters in St. Domingue in 1789, on the eve of the Haitian Revolution. In actuality, the free people of color in the Caribbean greatly surpassed the much smaller number of Jews in slave ownership. Even in Charleston, South Carolina the percentage of free African Americans who owned slaves increased from one-half to three-quarters as one moved up the socioeconomic scale as indicated by the ownership of real estate.[8] While the thousands of black slave owners in the antebellum South included large numbers of freed people who had simply purchased family members or relatives, there were also colored planters, especially in Louisiana, who owned more than fifty or even one hundred slaves. The allure of profits and power transcended all distinctions of race, ethnicity, and religion.

No one should defend or apologize for the Jews who bought and sold slaves, or who forced slaves to cut cane on the estates of Joden Savanne. Yet Jews as a group were much less responsible for the crimes of the slave trade than were Catholics or Protestants—or Muslims, some of whom actually initiated the process of shipping black African slaves to distant markets—even if one adopts the absurd and dangerous though often seductive belief in collective guilt over centuries for members of religious, ethnic, or racial groups. In fact, by that criterion no group would be more culpable than the descendants of African ethnic groups who captured and enslaved other Africans in order to sell them to European traders in exchange for textiles, metal ware, guns, liquor, and other desired commodities. It is a disturbing thought, nonetheless, that many Sephardi Jews, including those who established the first synagogue in Curaçao and the first Jewish settlements in North America, found the path to their own liberation and affluence by participating in a system of commerce that subjected another people to contempt, dishonor, coerced labor, and degradation. It has even been said that the more enlightened rulers of eighteenth-century Europe were much swayed by the early achievements of enfranchised Jews in Dutch Brazil, the Caribbean, and North America. This is one aspect of the dismal truth that the New World— conceived as a land of limitless opportunity, breaking the crust of old restraints, traditions, and prejudices—was made possible only by the near extermination of indigenous populations and by the dehumanizing subjugation of the so-called African race.

Notes

* An earlier version of this essay appeared in *Culturefront: A Magazine of the Humanities*, Vol. 1, No. 2 (Fall 1992), 42–45. Thanks are given to the editor of that journal and the New York Council for the Humanities for permission to use the essay here. Some of the same material also appeared in an essay in *The New York Review of Books*, December 22, 1994, 14–16.

1. Joseph C. Miller, *The Way of Death* (Madison, WI, 1988).

2. For a fuller documented account of Jews and slavery, see my *Slavery and Human Progress* (New York, 1984), 82–101.

3. Paul E. Lovejoy, "The Volume of the Atlantic Slave Trade: A Synthesis," *Journal of African History*, Vol. 23 (1982), 473–500. But also see Joseph E. Inikori and Stanley L. Engerman, eds., *The Atlantic Slave Trade* (New York, 1992).

4. An *asiento* was a contract between an individual or company and the Spanish crown for the transport of Africans and their sale as slaves in the New World.

5. Seymour Drescher, "The Role of Jews in the Transatlantic Slave Trade," in *Immigrants and Minorities*, 12 (July 1993), 120.

6. As Seymour Drescher points out, wealthy Jews of Amsterdam and Hamburg did play "significant entrepreneurial or organizational roles" in the "minuscule Brandenburg, Swedish, and Courland slave trades," but these so-called Baltic trades "combined did not account for as much as 0.7 percent of Europe's transatlantic slave trade." Drescher notes one final irony: "the only major state in Europe whose people or rulers evinced no interest whatever in getting into the Afro-Caribbean system during the four centuries after Columbus's voyages was the kingdom of Poland, proportionally the most "Jewish" area of Europe until its final partition in the 1790s." Of course the irony is a new one, he adds, since "for five centuries, no one imagined European Jewry to be dominant in the transatlantic slave trade." Drescher, "The Role of Jews in the Transatlantic Slave Trade," 117, 122.

7. Davis, *Slavery and Human Progress*, 101.

8. Michael P. Johnson and James L. Roark, *Black Masters: A Free Family of Color in the Old South* (New York, 1984), 204.

four

"THE LAW OF THE LAND IS THE LAW"

Antebellum Jews, Slavery, and the Old South

JASON H. SILVERMAN

I f there was a Jewish Ashley Wilkes in the Old South surely it would have been Judah P. Benjamin. Master of the New Orleans plantation, *Bellechase*, and its some one hundred and forty slaves, Benjamin was in many ways an icon of the southern planter and gentleman. And, while no one would doubt that Benjamin was a true, *bona fide* antebellum southern slaveowner, his quiet attitude toward the "peculiar institution" perhaps reflects the deep and contradictory feelings shared by some of his fellow southern Jews seeking acceptance and assimilation. For, "though he entered the ranks of the planter class that ruled the [Old South]," wrote one of his biographers, "[Benjamin] never felt that slavery reflected the divine order of things. He was not taken in by distorted theories of the Bible; he never argued that Blacks were of a lower order; and he hated the cruelty of the overseers he heard about."[1]

An attorney and the first openly Jewish United States senator, Benjamin rose to become such a symbol of the antebellum South that he eventually occupied the three most significant cabinet positions in the Confederacy (attorney general, secretary of war, and secretary of state). And yet this undeniable symbol of what the Old South represented was vehemently critical of the most inhuman aspects of slavery and eloquently denounced its cruelties, though he stopped short of actually opposing the "peculiar institution" itself. Arguing a case early in his legal career, Benjamin articulated beliefs shared by many of his fellow southern slaveholding Jews. Albeit racist in tone, his argument nevertheless may be considered enlightened by the standards of his day and it bears quoting. "What is a slave?" Benjamin rhetorically asked the court.

He is a human being. He has feeling and passion and intellect. His heart,
like the heart of the white man, swells with love, burns with jealousy, aches

with sorrow, pines under restraint and discomfort, boils with revenge and ever cherishes the desire for liberty. His passions and feelings in some respects may not be as fervid and as delicate as those of the white, nor his intellect as acute; but passions and feelings he has, and in some respects, they are more violent and consequently more dangerous, from the very circumstances that his mind is comparatively weak and unenlightened. Considering the character of the slave, and the peculiar passions which, generated by nature, are strengthened and stimulated by his condition, he is prone to revolt in the near future of things and ever ready to conquer the liberty where a probable chance presents itself.[2]

Benjamin and his southern Jewish brethren, of course, were a small ethnic and religious minority in a land where the small slaveowning minority ruled. Indeed, out of a population of roughly 9 million in the South, there were around 20,000 Jews, constituting approximately 0.2 percent of the total southern white population. Of those, about 25 percent, or 5,000 Jews, owned slaves. If one accepts that almost 400,000 southerners owned slaves, then almost 5 percent of the white population owned slaves; and 1.25 percent of the slaveowners were Jews. But the owners of record were certainly not the only white southerners to be intimately involved with slavery, as a number of recent scholars have maintained. According to the census figures, a family in 1860 averaged five members. Thus, to obtain a more accurate picture of the number of southerners directly involved with slavery requires multiplying the number of titular owners by the average family size. The result, almost 2 million people, represents almost one-quarter of the white population (the same percentage as the southern Jews).[3]

Although perhaps not as successful as a Judah P. Benjamin, several thousand Jews of the Old South did own slaves and many others tangentially supported the institution. Theirs is certainly a story that bears telling within the historical context and perspective of the Old South.

"There is no American Jewish history," wrote the historian Lloyd Gartner, "that does not include assimilation." Defining assimilation not as the end to Jewish identity nor its diffusion but rather as a social process whereby a minority assumes the values and practices of the majority, Gartner very accurately describes the Jewish experience in the antebellum South. Not surprisingly, during their first century of existence in the South, from the mid-eighteenth century, Jews constituted an insignificant part of the population and the economy. Different in religion and ethnicity the Jews were a highly vulnerable minority within an increasingly clearly defined aristocratic region. Many southern Jews, particularly those in the urban areas of Charleston, Savannah, and New Orleans, actively sought entrance into the mythical southern aristocracy by erroneously claiming to be descendants of the noble Jews of Spain and Portugal, the Sephardim. This status, they hoped, would admit them into the planter class of southern gentlemen and thereby enable them to obtain complete social and economic acceptance from their Christian peers.[4]

With that end in mind, on a balmy spring day of March 19, 1841, at the consecration ceremonies of perhaps the most impressive synagogue in America at the time, Charleston's Beth Elohim, Gustavus Poznanski, the congregation's *hazan* or spiritual leader, emotionally expressed the southern Jewry's yearning to be a part of southern society. In what may have been the first major public expression of Jewish support for the southern ethos, Poznanski asserted: "This synagogue is our *temple*, this city our *Jerusalem*, this happy land our *Palestine*, and as our fathers defended with their lives *that* temple, *that* city, and *that* land, so will their sons defend *this* temple, *this* city, and *this* land." Delivered to an overflow audience of both Christians and Jews, Poznanski's remarks were addressed to a city where less than a decade before the Nullification movement had been born. To Poznanski and his southern Jewish brethren the message was not lost: the South demanded fealty from its people to the state before nation. To be accepted completely within southern society the Jews would have to either adapt or be ostracized, which was the fate of all who opposed slavery and the planter regime.[5]

The typical southern Jew tended to eschew rural areas. Most Jews, for a variety of reasons, felt safer in urban areas, where they could engage in each other's fellowship and find support within a visible Jewish community. If they desired to practice their religion actively, they could only do so in an urban area in which there were other Jews, not in sparsely populated rural areas. Furthermore, most immigrant Jews arrived in America virtually poverty-stricken, making it highly unlikely they would achieve aristocratic status in the xenophobic South. Thus, the average southern Jew was more likely to be a small trader eking out a marginal existence at an occupation which did not rank well on the social scale of the Old South. He considered himself fortunate to be able to pay his bills and perhaps eventually own a small shop, above which a few rooms provided a home to him and his family. In all likelihood, he lacked enough capital to purchase a slave even if he could determine a need for one. Yet, to survive in a potentially hostile environment he could not, or would not, ever become a vocal critic of the institution.

Some southern Jews, though, successfully climbed the socioeconomic ladder through careers as merchants or professionals. In general, these Jews of the South did indeed conform to the prevailing pattern of slave ownership, and some of them grew quite wealthy from the plantation economy. While there were instances of manumission among the Jews, in principle they were as staunchly supportive of the "peculiar institution" as were their non-Jewish counterparts. Wanting to participate as equals in the slave-based southern society, almost all Jewish residents acclimated themselves to southern values. True, their acceptance of slavery was hastened by the fear that opposing white southerners would unleash a firestorm of anti-Semitic prejudice; still, some southern Jews quickly assuaged any moral compunctions about slave owning. "The institution of slavery as it existed in the South was not so great a wrong as people believe," reflected Aaron Hirsch of Mississippi shortly after the Civil War. "The Negroes were brought here in a savage state," he mused, "they captured and ate each other in their African home. Here they were instructed to work, were civilized and got religion, and were perfectly happy."[6]

No pro-slavery southerner could have been more direct than Savannah Jewish leader Solomon Cohen when he wrote before the war that, "I believe that the institution of slavery [is] refining and civilizing to the whites—giving them an elevation of sentiment and ease of dignity of manners only attainable in societies under the restraining influence of a privileged class—and at the same time the only human institution that could elevate the Negro from barbarianism and develop the small amount of intellect with which he is endowed." For Jews like Cohen who could afford to purchase slaves and who believed they needed their labor, participation in the buying, trading, owning, and selling of slaves was expected. Like their Christian peers, some Jews, especially those living in southern urban areas, owned slaves as status symbols. In accepting southern society for what it was, these Jewish residents also conformed to the dominant pro-slavery ideology.[7]

For instance, no southern Jews were abolitionists; nor were many white southern Christians for that matter. No southern Jewish intellectual questioned the justice of slavery, although prominent Jews such as Judah P. Benjamin obviously felt queasy about owning slaves. In many ways, through their writings, men such as Texas newspaper editor Jacob De Cordova, South Carolina political essayist Isaac Harby, and Virginia journalist Samuel Mordecai contributed to the formation and dissemination of the pro-slavery doctrine. De Cordova emphatically wished "it distinctly understood that [my] feelings and education have always been pro-slavery." The prominent editor and political economist Jacob Cardozo minced no words: slavery was defensible on both economic and moral grounds. "Slavery brought not only great wealth to the South," he wrote, "but to the slaves a greater share of its enjoyment than in many regions where the relation between employer and employee was based on wages." As for the morality issue, Cardozo was nothing short of direct. "The reason the Almighty made the colored black," he asserted, "is to prove their inferiority." Nor did Cardozo mellow with the emancipation of the slaves after the Civil War. In his well read *Reminiscences of Charleston* Cardozo lamented the passing of the peculiar institution:

The owner of two hundred to five hundred slaves, with a princely income, has not only to submit to the most degraded employments, but he frequently cannot obtain them. In some instances, he has to drive a cart, or attend a retail grocery, while many have to obey the orders of an ignorant and coarse menial. There is something unnatural in this reverse of position—something revolting to my sense of propriety in this social degradation.

Although Cardozo was undeniably describing the social status of a minuscule number of southern Jews, nevertheless, no native white southerner could have expressed the myth and nobility of the Lost Cause any more passionately.[8]

And a very few Jews did indeed become prominent slaveowning planters in the Old South. Besides Judah P. Benjamin, Major Raphael J. Moses, who would become chief commissary officer of General Longstreet's Corps during the Civil War, owned a plantation with approximately fifty slaves near Columbus, Georgia. Charlestonian Nathan Nathans owned an impressive plantation on the Cooper River; other Jewish South Carolinians were Isaiah Moses who owned thirty-five slaves; Mordecai Cohen, who owned twenty-seven; and Isaac Lyons, Barnet Cohen, and Chapman Levy, all of whom maintained sizeable slave holdings. Various members of the Mordecai family owned plantations in Virginia and North Carolina. Moses Levy's plantation, *Parthenope*, was an impressive spread in Florida, a fitting image of anyone's romantic notion of the Old South. Joining Benjamin in Louisiana was J. Levy of Ascension Parish, who owned some forty slaves. Yet it must always be remembered that as successful as these Jewish planters were by southern standards, they represented a very tiny percentage of the 20,000 Jews who resided in the South before the Civil War and who could, or would, ever aspire to own a slave.[9]

For the successful urban Jews of the Old South, the situation was not unlike that of their rural counterparts. Prominent Jewish residents of Richmond, Virginia, for example, owned slaves as status symbols. The census of 1820 reveals that those few Jews who could afford slaves averaged three bondsmen per household. The most extensive slave holdings were by Jacob Mordecai, who also maintained a Henrico County farm. The Virginia Cardozos of neighboring Powhatan County also owned a farm that utilized slave labor. For most Richmond slaveowning Jews, however, slaves were used for domestic purposes or were hired out.[10]

The census returns of New Orleans indicate a similar pattern for the small number of affluent Jewish denizens of the Crescent City. In 1820 the six Jews who could be identified owned some twenty-three slaves. Ten years later although only twenty-two Jews could be identified (more than half of whom did not own slaves), ten of the group owned a total of seventy-five slaves. And in 1840 when sixty-two Jews were listed (a distinctly small number), they held a total of 348 slaves. These census returns, while underestimating the number of Jews in the area, are still a clear indicator that some Jews in New Orleans, like non-Jews, equated growing economic success and prosperity with slaveowning in the hopes of acquiring complete social acceptance.[11]

Even in Mobile, Alabama, which housed a much smaller, newer, and poorer Jewish population, some Jews purchased slaves in anticipation of becoming assimilated. The seventy-two identifiable Jews in the 1850 census owned a total of ninety slaves. For a few Jewish immigrants in Alabama, much like other fellow southerners, the road to success was paved by slave labor.[12]

On the whole, the Jews of Charleston, South Carolina, supported the institution of slavery. By 1830, 87 percent of the white households in Charleston had slaves; for the Jews the figure was 83 percent, perhaps the highest percentage in the urban South. By mid-century the Jews who could afford slaves averaged 5.5 slaves per household. And although many of the Jews of Charleston held bondsmen, their holdings appear to be quite small when compared to the white Christian slaveowners of the city.

Isaac Harby and Jacob Cardozo owned and edited two of Charleston's newspapers, the *Southern Patriot* and the *Evening News*, both of which condoned slavery. Harby penned a series of editorials under the pseudonym of Junius which attacked the abolitionists. South Carolina "can never consent to those newfangled doctrines," Harby wrote, "which, if carried to any extent might not only jeopardize the well-being of the Planting States, but...shake the married calm of the whole Union." And later he concluded that "our eyes [are now] opened to the character and sentiments of certain men [who seek to] *destroy the guarantee*, which secures the possession of slaves to their owners." Even more evidence of the support of Charleston's Jews for slavery can be seen in the speech by Judah Barrett Cohen to the first anniversary meeting of the South Carolina Historical Society, in which he exclaimed that "the state of South Carolina is bound to reverence those men to whom she owes her position to the present day. She owes much to Sir John Yeamans, who first introduced slaves,—that incalculable benefit to our soil and necessary to our climate."[13]

"It would seem realistic to conclude," surmised Bertram Wallace Korn, the dean of historians who study Jews and slavery, some thirty-four years ago, "that any Jew who could afford to own slaves and had a need for their services would do so." Indeed,

> Jewish owners of slaves were not exceptional figures. Slavery was an axiomatic foundation of the social pattern of the Old South. Jews wanted to acclimate themselves in every way to their environment; in both a social and psychological sense, they needed to be accepted as equals and fellow-citizens. It was therefore only a matter of financial circumstances and familial status whether they were to become slaveowners.[14]

For those Jews who owned slaves the records demonstrate that they were not significantly different from other masters in their treatment of bondsmen. Southern Jews were just as likely, or unlikely, to manumit their slaves and, if their last wills and testaments are any indication, Jews occasionally regarded their slaves as chattel, to be retained if possible, or to be sold if the situation warranted. The will of Emanuel Stern, for example, who died in New Orleans in 1828, instructed his executor to sell off his twelve-year-old slave Mathilda at auction. Mathilda brought $400, a profitable transaction since she was valued at $250 in the inventory. Yet, at the opposite end of the spectrum, was the unusual David Perayra Brandon of Charleston, who bequeathed in his will that his servant be left to his stepdaughter and her husband and implored that they "take him under their protection to treat him as well as they would do me and to give him Such portion of my Cloths as they think useful to him and never forsake him being the best friend I ever had." It is indeed hard to imagine many other white southerners remembering their servant as the "best friend I ever had." Perhaps more typical, though, for the Jews, as well as the non-Jews, was the will that simply bequeathed slaves to relatives or friends without specific instructions. Upon the death of their Jewish masters, slaves faced the prospect of being torn away from familiar surroundings and sold to less benevolent strangers—a potential fate, of course, for all slaves in the Old South.[15]

Incidents of cruel, sadistic, or violent Jewish slaveowners are rare, in part because such episodes generally occurred in the rural South where there were very few Jews. The most aberrant case on record is that of Joseph Cohen of Lynchburg, Virginia, who, in 1819, murdered his slave. Though court records for this case have not survived in their entirety, it is known that Cohen was indicted, tried, convicted, and sentenced for this crime in a fashion very much consistent with the law of the antebellum South. Conversely, urban Jews "appear to have been quite content to abide by the excessively cruel punishments meted out to Blacks who were caught by the law." And Jewish immigrants in the South were among the many who participated as public officials in the apprehension, prosecution, and incarceration of slaves. Jewish residents of Charleston, Richmond, Mobile, and New Orleans held such positions as constable, turnkey, sheriff, marshal, and detective.[16]

There were many Jewish merchants who participated in the selling of slaves as auctioneers, commission merchants, and brokers. "This was an avenue of commerce in which many Jews found their niche," wrote Bertram Korn, "because no stock of merchandise or investment of capital was required, at least at the beginning." However, contrary to popular myth, *none* of the major slave traders in the Old South were Jewish nor did they represent a large percentage of the traders in any particular community. In Richmond, Virginia, only three of seventy traders were Jewish; in Charleston, South Carolina, only four of forty-four; in Memphis, Tennessee, only one in twelve. In Kentucky and Mississippi, not a single Jewish name appears in the long list of slave traders. It is entirely possible that all of the Jewish slave traders in all of the southern urban areas bought and sold fewer slaves than did the one firm of Franklin and Armfield, the South's largest trader of slaves. In all likelihood, the largest Jewish slave trading firm in the antebellum South was the Davis family of Petersburg and Richmond, referred to by Harriet Beecher Stowe in her *A Key to Uncle Tom's Cabin* as "great slave traders" who buy their slaves at low prices, "trim, shave, wash them, [and] fatten them so that they may look sleek, and sell them to great profit."[17]

Much has been made of the fact that no Jewish southerner emerged as an outspoken critic of the slaveowning Old South.[18] This perhaps is subjecting a southern ethnic and religious minority to undue and unrealistic historical standards or criteria. For in truth, very few southerners of any race, religion, or creed stepped forward to challenge the planters' slavocracy. And when they did, such as in the case of Hinton Rowan Helper who attacked slavery in his controversial yet racist *The Impending Crisis of the South* (1857), they usually found themselves either figuratively or literally exiled. Still, such southern Jews as Judah P. Benjamin, David Levy Yulee of Florida, and Davis S. Kaufman of Texas are consistently heralded as prototypical pro-slavery advocates, an accurate if not somewhat parochial point.

Viewing the antebellum southern Jews as a historical monolith in regard to their attitude toward slaves and slavery runs the risk, of course, of being unfair, if not outright inaccurate. Rather than launch an ill-fated and very dangerous abolitionist assault from within the South, some southern Jews chose to fight a quiet and individual battle against the institution of slavery around them. For instance, Major Alfred Mordecai, brother to slaveowning planters, purchased only one slave in his life and then simply to manumit her. Unable to overtly oppose slavery in the South, Mordecai, in a melancholy tone, wrote that slavery was "the greatest misfortune and curse that could have befallen us." New Orleans merchant Judah Touro emancipated all of the slaves he purchased and then placed them within his employ to ensure their financial security. And North Carolinian Marx E. Lazarus wrote stinging critiques of slavery published in Moncure Conway's journal, *The Dial*. Thus, as Bertram Korn has perceptively noted, "Probably many Jews as well as non-Jews were caught in the dilemma of purchasing slaves just because they did not believe in slavery; since emancipation was virtually impossible all they could do was to become the most generous masters possible under the circumstances."[19]

The loudest Jewish voices against slavery were safely ensconced outside the South, where most of the more numerous and recent immigrants arrived in the 1830s and 1840s. Then, too, northern Jews, like their southern brethren, did not speak with one mind. Jewish critics of slavery ranged from the fierce Kansas editor Moritz Pinner and the Jews who marched with John Brown to Rabbi Morris Raphall of New York, who defended the biblical sanction of slavery and merely called for a humanization of slavery "from the Roman chattel model to the Hebraic humanistic model, that is from a system that callously treated the slave as an animated tool to one that looked compassionately upon the slave as a bonded human being endowed with protections against ill-treatment." More likely, most northern Jews were similar in attitude to such moderate abolitionists as Max Lilienthal, Isaac Wise, and Isaac Lesser. Articulate anti-slavery rabbis included David Einhorn of Baltimore and Sabato Morais of Philadelphia, who "contrary to the wishes of their nervous or opposing congregants, attacked slavery as a menace to the rights of Jews and all other minorities and preached support of the Union as the sole bastion of liberty."[20]

For the Jews who lived in the South, however, slavery was not a reprehensible "theory" to be opposed in speech, sermon, essay, or letter. Rather, it represented a very vivid reality of the existence of all southerners: an insidious institution which permeated virtually every aspect of the southern social fabric. Since Jews constituted only a tiny fragment of the southern population, even in the largest urban areas of New Orleans, Charleston, and Richmond their small numbers precluded any distinctively Jewish perspective to any social issue of the day save for anti-Semitism. It should not be surprising then, nor particularly significant, that most Jewish southerners would associate themselves with the majority planter mentality accepted by virtually all of their non-Jewish neighbors. For the more prominent and affluent southern Jews this was especially true, as they were quite likely to interact on a regular basis with the professional class of the Old South, from attorneys to physicians, from planters to merchants, all of whom either owned slaves or ideologically supported the institution of slavery.

Being Jewish did not play any significant role in the relationship between slaves and Jews, as religion and ethnicity did not for others in the Old South. Indeed, in all likelihood, if most southern Jews were asked about their attitudes toward slavery per se, they would have been very comfortable quoting the Talmud that "the law of the land is the law." But then again, so would the Christians. Despite the current controversies and accusations, perhaps the real issue was not whether one was Jewish in the antebellum South but rather whether one was white. Southern society, while very definitely assigning whites to rigidly defined classes and castes, nevertheless was a society built more fundamentally upon race, a reality which one could not, no matter how hard he or she might try, escape. For the Jews of the Old South, as well as their non-Jewish counterparts, a peaceful, if not profitable, life among the moonlight and magnolias meant regarding "slavery as part of the law which they were bound to uphold and follow," rather than scrutinizing the "failings of slavery in the light of the prophetic ethnic."

"Whatever prejudice there was in the South before the Civil War," wrote Bertram Korn, "aggravated every possible source of tension, [and] was directed largely against the alien Jew, the immigrant peddler, and petty store-keeper, the insecure newcomer, whose very survival was in the hands of his customers." This would, of course, apply to Jew and non-Jew alike. Failing to accept and adopt such strongly held popular beliefs as those which existed in the Old South would, in essence, be the death knell to anyone's hopes for success, regardless of their religion or ethnicity.[21]

This ubiquitous race consciousness in the South before the Civil War no doubt benefited Jewish residents and tended to mitigate their religious and ethnic background, unlike the social environment north of the Mason-Dixon Line. Whatever differences there existed among white southerners were subsumed in a society dedicated to maintaining the subordinate status of Blacks. In this fashion, the status of southern Jews, like that of other southern whites, was very much contingent upon the maintenance, if not expansion, of an institution that kept Blacks in bondage. "The Negroes," wrote one scholar, "acted as an escape valve in Southern society. The Jews gained in status and security from the very presence of this large mass of defenseless victims who were compelled to absorb all of the prejudices which might otherwise have been expressed more frequently in anti-Jewish sentiment."[22]

With such social and economic vested interests in slavery, it would be as unrealistic to expect antebellum southern Jews to eschew slavery as it would be to expect any southern white in the Old South to turn his back on the peculiar institution. Hence, when war came in 1861, the Jews of the Old South were as loyal to the Confederate cause as any other white southerner. Typical of this loyalty was the Shreveport, Louisiana, Jewish community, which resolved that "although we might be called Southern rebels; still, as law-abiding citizens, we solemnly pledge to stand by, protect, and honor the...Southern Confederacy with our lives, liberty, and all that is dear to us."

Whether newly arrived immigrant (and at least two-thirds of the southern Jews were) or native-born southerner, for the Jews, loyalty to the Confederacy was a matter of "personal gratitude and cultural affinity." Indeed, "nowhere else in the United States had Jews been offered the opportunity to participate so fully as equals in society....As a consequence, Jews had acclimated themselves to Southern values, had become imbued with Southern traditions, and therefore had become committed to the struggles and fortunes of the Confederacy." Devotion to their homeland, then, meant fighting for the perpetuation of slavery and the Old South. "Now, we of the South," wrote Solomon Cohen of Savannah in 1861, "seeing that public opinion, [and]...the North are against all that we hold valuable, [and] seeing that...our enemies have triumphed and that the government is about to pass into the hands of those who hate us and our institutions, feel that prudence and self-defense demand that we should protect ourselves, even while there is ruption of every tie that binds us to the union that we have loved so well." Had he been alive, John C. Calhoun could not have expressed the southern white sentiment any more eloquently.

And most southern Jews readily answered the call to fight for slavery, states' rights, and the Confederacy. University of Virginia student Gratz Cohen, who was to fall mortally wounded in battle, perhaps best expressed the mood of most southern Jews in one of the stanzas of a poem that he wrote imploring his fellow students to enlist:

> Go, for your soldier brothers need you by their side;
> Go, fight as we have fought and die as we have died;
> If need there be, a thousand deaths were better than disgrace;
> Better that every man should die than live a conquered race.[23]

On virtually every level of participation southern Jews served the Confederacy. Transforming their businesses into producers of war materials or enlisting in the Confederate army as *entire* families, elected or appointed as noncommissioned or commissioned officers, serving in the Confederate cabinet or state office, Jewish southerners established strong bonds of commonality with their Christian peers. "It was," as historian Louis Schmier has written, "usually sufficient to silence the loudest prejudiced voice, for such war experiences assured local non-Jewish residents that among them were men, Jews notwithstanding, who had defended and would continue to defend the South against the desecration of its soil and the deprivation of its liberty. In both a wartime and postwar South, struggling for an identity by glorifying its past and honoring its struggle, that was no small recommendation for accepting the Jews into their midst, for reassessing malicious stereotypes of Jews, and for preparing the way for those Jews who in the following decades were to immigrate to the South."[24]

The Jews of the Old South were neither the victors nor the vanquished. And, in fact, slavery played a more prominent role in the existence of antebellum southern Jewish life than the Jews themselves played in the emergence and maintenance of slavery. The historical rise and fall of American slavery would not have been affected at all were there no Jews living in the South; and, whatever minuscule part the Jews played in the historical drama would more than have been compensated for by other non-Jewish whites. That the Jews benefited, as did every other southern white, from the existence and labor of Black slaves is undeniable. But, southern Jews, like southerners in general, hovered between myth and reality. "They assumed a certain distance from the racial question," one scholar wrote, "but made every effort to see that religious and economic freedoms were not harmed by an overt distaste for the system…and a too visible reaction against the entire oppressive nature of Southern society. This was in keeping, after all, with the notion that Southern gentlemen—both Jew and Christian—were required to maintain a proper and correct attitude at all times. This was to be the proper response even if their make-believe could not hide the glaring inequalities around them." In the South, much of whose history has been shrouded in myth, the Jews were neither myth makers nor myth breakers. But one thing is for certain: in the building, maintaining, and enhancing of that myth, southern Jews were inconsequential at best and invisible at worst. They were, to borrow from Ralph Ellison, just barely inside "the groove of history."[25]

NOTES

I wish to express my deep appreciation to Thomas H. Appleton, Jr. and David Brion Davis for their invaluable comments on earlier drafts of this essay.

1. Eli N. Evans, *Judah P. Benjamin: The Jewish Confederate* (New York, 1988), p. 33. The subject of Jewish and other ethnic slaveowners will be covered in depth in my extended work, a study of immigration and ethnicity in Southern history, currently in preparation.

2. Evans, *Judah P. Benjamin*, pp. 38–39.

3. Much controversy surrounds the Nation of Islam's *The Secret Relationship Between Blacks and Jews*, vol. 1 (Boston, 1991), a document that largely distorts and takes out of context the demographical, historical, and historiographical data included in the works of many Jewish scholars. See all of the pertinent demographic data on the various and germane annual census rolls housed in the National Archives, Washington, D.C. See also William J. Cooper, Jr. and Thomas E. Terrill, *The American South: A History* (New York, 1990), pp. 204–7; and Howard David Brackman, "The Ebb and Flow of Conflict: A History of Black-Jewish Relations Through 1900" (Ph.D. dissertation, University of California, Los Angeles, 1977), pp. 223–390.

4. Lloyd P. Gartner, "Assimilation and American Jews," in Bela Vargo, ed., *Jewish Assimilation in Modern Times* (Boulder, 1981), pp. 171–75; Malcolm H. Stern, *First American Jewish Families* (Cincinnati, 1978), *passim*; and Abraham J. Peck, "That Other 'Peculiar Institution': Jews and Judaism in the Nineteenth Century South," *Modern Judaism* 7 (1987): 99–114.

5. James William Hagy, *This Happy Land: The Jews of Colonial and Antebellum Charleston* (Tuscaloosa, AL, 1993), pp. 245–46.

6. Jason H. Silverman, "Ashley Wilkes Revisited: The Immigrant as Slaveowner in the Old South," *Journal of Confederate History* 7 (1992): 123–35; Jacob Rader Marcus, *Memoirs of American Jews, 1775–1865* (3 vols., Philadelphia, 1955–56), 2:138. I am deeply indebted to the pioneering work of Bertram Wallace Korn, upon whose work I have relied for this essay as well as for my monograph. See his *Jews and Negro Slavery in the Old South, 1789–1865* (Elkins Park, Penn., 1961) and its reprinting in Leonard Dinnerstein and Mary Dale Palsson, eds., *Jews in the South* (Baton Rouge, 1973), pp. 89–134; see also Korn's *American Jewry and the Civil War* (Philadelphia, 1951). For more on Jews and slavery, see the special issue of the *American Jewish Archives* 13 (April 1961): 149–70; Nathan M. Kaganoff and Melvin Urofsky, eds., *Turn to the South: Essays on Southern Jewry* (Charlottesville, 1979); Samuel Proctor and Louis Schmier, eds., *Jews of the South: Selected Essays from the Southern Jewish Historical Society* (Macon, 1984); and Hugh H. Smythe and Martin S. Price, "The American Jew and Negro Slavery," *Midwest Journal* 7 (1955–1956): 315–19. Two recent volumes deserve mention for the valuable light they shed on topics very germane to this study. See Lawrence Mordekhai Thomas, *Vessels of Evil: American Slavery and the Holocaust* (Philadelphia, 1993); and Leonard Dinnerstein, *Anti-Semitism in America* (New York, 1994).

7. Korn, *Jews and Negro Slavery*, p. 61.

8. Ibid., p. 59; Jacob N. Cardozo, *Reminiscences of Charleston* (Charleston, 1866), p. 10.

9. Marcus, *Memoirs of American Jews*, 1:184; Korn, *Jews and Negro Slavery*, pp. 13–15.

10. Myron Berman, *Richmond's Jewry: Shabbat in Shockoe, 1769–1976* (Charlottesville, 1979), pp. 164–70.

11. Bertram Wallace Korn, *The Early Jews of New Orleans* (Waltham, MA, 1969), pp. 91–153; Elliott Ashkenazi, *The Business of Jews in Louisiana, 1840–1875* (Tuscaloosa, AL, 1988), *passim.* See also the *1820, 1830, and 1840 Mss. Census Returns for New Orleans and Vicinity*, National Archives, Washington, D.C.

12. *1850 Mss. Census Returns for Mobile*, National Archives, Washington, D.C. See also Bertram Wallace Korn, *The Jews of Mobile, Alabama, 1763–1841* (Cincinnati, 1970).

13. Hagy, *This Happy Land*, pp. 91–106.

14. Korn, *Jews and Negro Slavery*, p. 26.

15. Ibid., pp. 27, 28–29.

16. Helen Tunnicliff Catterall, *Judicial Cases Concerning American Slavery and the Negro* (4 vols., Washington, D.C., 1926–1936), 1: 131; Barnet A. Elzas, *The Jews of South Carolina* (Philadelphia, 1950), p. 142; Jacob Rader Marcus, *American Jewry: Documents of the Eighteenth Century* (Cincinnati, 1959), p. 63; Herbert T. Ezekiel and Gaston Lichtenstein, *The History of the Jews of Richmond from 1769–1917* (Richmond, 1917), pp. 77–78; Jack K. Williams, *Vogues in Villainy: Crime and Retribution in Ante-Bellum South Carolina* (Columbia, S.C., 1939), p. 73; Uriah Z. Engelman, *The Jews of Charleston* (Philadelphia, 1950); and Korn, *Jews and Negro Slavery*, p. 34.

17. Frederic Bancroft, *Slave Trading in the Old South* (Baltimore, 1931), pp. 97–98, 175–77, 251–52; Harriet Beecher Stowe, *A Key to Uncle Tom's Cabin* (Boston, 1853), p. 151; Korn, *Jews and Negro Slavery*, pp. 41, 45.

18. See *The Secret Relationship Between Blacks and Jews*, pp. 143–57. For more scholarly accounts, see Oscar R. Williams, Jr., "Historical Impressions of Black-Jewish Relations Prior to World War II," *Negro History Bulletin* 40 (1977): 728; and Jayme A. Sokolow, "Revolution and Reform: The Antebellum Jewish Abolitionists," *Melus* (1981–82): 27–28.

19. Stanley L. Falk, "Divided Loyalties in 1861," *Publications of the American Jewish Historical Society* 48 (March 1959): 149–50; Leon Huhner, *The Life of Judah Touro* (Philadelphia, 1946), p. 69; Korn, *Jews and Negro Slavery*, pp. 62–65.

20. Louis D. Schmier, "Jews," in Randall M. Miller and John David Smith, eds., *Dictionary of Afro-American Slavery* (Westport, CT, 1988), pp. 376–79.

21. Korn, *Jews and Negro Slavery*, pp. 66–67.

22. Robert G. Weisbord and Arthur Stein, *Bittersweet Encounter: The Afro-American and the American Jew* (Westport, CT, 1970), pp. 22–23.

23. The quotes in the preceding paragraphs are from Louis D. Schmier, "Jews," in Richard N. Current, ed., *Encyclopedia of the Confederacy*, 4 vols. (New York, 1993), 2: 845; see also Korn, *American Jewry and the Civil War, passim*; and the Civil War Centennial issue of *American Jewish Archives* 13 (April 1961) emphasizing Jews in the Confederacy.

24. Schmier, "Jews," p. 846.

25. Peck, "That Other 'Peculiar Institution,'" pp. 102–10.

five

BETWEEN WORDS AND DEEDS

Jews and Blacks in America, 1880–1935

HASIA R. DINER

On March 13, 1935, New York's widely circulating *Jewish Daily Forward* wistfully eulogized the Black actor Richard Harrison, star of the play "The Green Pastures," in which he had portrayed none other than "God, the Lawd." The play had been staged, according to the *Forward*, at a truly propitious moment.

> In this present moment of upheaval and unrest, of world catastrophe and world storm, there was no greater pleasure than to be carried away to that far more naive, sinless world, which the play presented...In this play...the souls of two nations are woven together...the soul of the Jew and the soul of the Negro.[1]

But given events of the same week, the *Forward's* poignant retrospective for Harrison might also have been read as a retrospective for a "far more naive" era in which Jews could truly believe that their souls and those of their Black neighbors had been "woven together."

Three days later, on March 16, a young boy named Lino Rivera helped himself to a pocket knife from the counter of Kress's Store on 125th Street in Harlem. An employee apprehended the youthful shoplifter and called for the police. Almost spontaneously, rumors spread like wildfire on the streets of what had only a decade earlier been described as the "Negro Mecca". Word had it that the teenager, after pilfering from a Jewish-owned store, had been killed in police custody. An angry crowd gathered outside. Within hours protesters, fired up by privation and a year-long politically intense "Don't Buy Where You Can't Work" campaign, appeared with signs and leaflets decrying the murder, which actually never took place. The protesters reiterated the message that had resounded for years on those same streets: despite the neighborhood's overwhelming Black population, its businesses, properties, institutions, and other economic resources firmly rested in the hands of whites, Jews.

The match hit the tinderbox. Mob violence spread through the streets of Harlem, with windows broken, stores looted, crowds surging, and violence spreading. By night's end, scores of people, mostly Black, bore the injuries of battle, and hundreds of stores, mostly Jewish-owned, lay vandalized and stripped.[2]

Only three days separated the obituary for Harrison in the Yiddish press from the angry Black rebellion on the streets of Harlem. How did these two happen at one and the same time? How could the Yiddish press cover the unfolding economic tension in Harlem and its overt anti-Semitic rhetoric while writing about the weaving together of the Jewish and Black souls? How could the rhetoric of Jewish and Black harmony persist at a time when Black orators in halls and street corners raged against the Jews as greedy, selfish exploiters? After all, what other group of white Americans identified themselves so passionately with Blacks and claimed to possess a linked consciousness with these most oppressed of Americans?

These contradictory phenomena underscored a long-standing discrepancy between the ways Blacks and Jews "saw" each other on a metaphoric level and the ways they "saw" each other in the flesh. First, each existed for the other as a kind of mythic mirror, in which they reflected and refracted on themselves and on their respective histories. Each functioned as a cultural metaphor for the other, using that vision of the other as a way of working out contemporary struggles and concerns for their respective futures. Jews wrote voluminously about the sufferings of Blacks in America, condemned racism, and chided their new land to live up to its avowed creed of democracy. Jews told each other that they bore a special mission in America: to bring it into line with its own rhetoric by aiding, supporting, and sympathizing with Black people as no other Americans would do.[3] Black educators, ministers, writers, and orators held up the noble image of the Jews. Jews, they maintained, had succeeded because *they* banded together, *they* lived cleanly, *they* saved their money, *they* used their intellect, and *they* never abandoned those left behind. In short, several generations of Black leaders told the masses of recently emancipated slaves and their immediate descendants struggling with poverty and oppression: Be like the Jews.[4]

At the individual level, Jews and Blacks interacted with each other at the backs of hundreds of peddlers' wagons, across the counters of rural and urban stores, and in union meetings in the needle trades industry. As merchant and customer, employer and employee, benefactor and beneficiary, Jews and Blacks lived in many of the same cities, sometimes sharing the same neighborhoods.[5]

How did the cultural overlay of the mythic encounter shape the literal one? How, conversely, did the unequal relationship of actual Jews and actual Blacks mold their rhetoric?

The years 1880–1935 marked momentous transitions in the lives of both groups: the massive Jewish transfer of population to the United States from Eastern Europe, and the beginnings of the Great Migration of rural, southern Blacks to the cities of the North. This period also marked the rise of Jim Crow, the constitutional sanction of segregation, the "normalization" of lynching, and race violence as facts of everyday life for America's Black population. For Jews, this half century saw the outbreak of pogroms in Russia at the beginning of the era and the triumph of Naziism on the other. Both peoples debated how best to organize and equip themselves in a larger, hostile world. In both communities, elites sought to shape the behavior of antiauthoritarian masses.

The leadership strata in both the Jewish and Black communities each used the image of the other as a device to frame contemporary concerns. In both cases elites offered ordinary people a complex image of the other in the context of more extensive communal discussions about their past as a group, the meaning of America, and prospects for survival. Shapers of opinion in the Jewish and Black communities each invented a whole range of images about the group's past, its present status, and hopes for the future. Intrinsic to those was the image of the "other."[6]

Blacks in the Eyes of Jews

For Jews, the image of Blacks—as victims of racism, as slaves and impoverished sharecroppers, as bearers of a noble history of struggle, and as the creators of a vibrant culture of music, theater, and art—figured prominently in the communal discourse about America.[7] From the highly Americanized, Reform-oriented world associated with, for example, *The American Israelite* and other English-language periodicals, through the Socialist-inspired Yiddish-language press, discussions of race, racism, and racial strivings conjoined the ways in which Jews thought of themselves with the ways in which they described Blacks. Jewish public opinion, whether in Yiddish or in English, acknowledged that the subjugation of African Americans amounted to a "stain of shame on the American flag" (an often repeated phrase in the Yiddish press) and that Black people "are so justified in protesting against bad treatment."

Jewish commentary on the status of Blacks in America transcended neutral reportage and even beyond passionate condemnations of racism. Rather, Jews publicly and specifically linked themselves and their history and fate with that of Blacks. Jews and Blacks, they declared, shared a field of understanding and a common political agenda. Employing the resonant words and graphic imagery of Jewish life—"pogrom," "ghetto," "auto-da-fé," "Cossacks," "black hundred," "blood libel"—Jews claimed to understand Blacks better than did other Americans.

Political and artistic discussions both focused on the ways in which Jews and Blacks understood each other. Novelist Meyer Levin said of the Black production, "Run, Little Chillun'!" "the play seemed a revelation out of traditions so deeply akin to our own Jewish traditions that at times it was difficult to keep from rushing onto the stage and joining in the singing, the ecstasy....'Run Little Chillun'!' is...a Chassidic play!"[8] A few years earlier a *Forward* review of Al Jolson's "The Jazz Singer," interpreted the performances of Jews in black face as a sign of intense cultural bonding:

> The son of a line of rabbis well knows how to sing the songs of the most cruelly wronged people in the world's history.[9]

These imaginary linkages complemented the prominent role played by individual Jewish women and men in various efforts aimed at improving the conditions of Black America. Extensive Jewish involvement in the civil rights movement made the words of the press seem very real. Indeed, W.E.B. Du Bois himself remarked in a 1923 interview with the *Forward* that "the Negro race looks to Jews for sympathy and understanding."[10]

Jewish women and men believed that the connections between the two peoples flowed from an organic similarity of circumstances as evidenced by the Hebrew Bible, they believed they bore an obligation to empathize and help, in keeping with the historic Jewish tradition. Furthermore, condemning racism and working for its eradication benefited Jews as well.

In an age of restrictive covenants against Jews in housing, quotas against them in elite universities, and discrimination in various sectors of employment, Jews had a common cause with a political movement that sought to remove invidious distinctions from public life. In an era when much of scientific thinking and popular culture considered Jews a "race" with a distinctive phenotype and innate mental and moral abilities, Jews shared with Blacks the goal of proving that race had no basis in biological fact and existed only as a sociological concept. "Sociological distinctions," as Melville Herskovitz wrote in his 1928 monograph, *The American Negro*, "are irrational and nonsensical. They exist because they *have* existed."[11]

Working against Black exclusion and oppression provided a stalking horse on a more abstract level for American Jewish writers, thinkers, and doers who fretted over the power of anti-Semitism in America and in Europe. Downplaying the extent of anti-Jewish action and sentiment in America, they held up the indisputably worse position of Blacks as an apt illustration of sinister forces which might, if unchecked, crush their aspirations for success in their latest diasporic home. Their acts on behalf of Black people defied centuries-old stereotypes of Jews as selfish, greedy, insular, and tribal. A 1924 news item in the *American Hebrew* fulfilled this function. The article boasted about a substantial investment by Julius Rosenwald in a black-owned insurance company which had teetered on the edge of bankruptcy. The firm's owner, Herman E. Perry, contending with a group of white bankers who threatened his business, turned to Rosenwald for help. Set against the backdrop of the ongoing controversy with Henry Ford over his publication of the anti-semitic "Protocols of the Elder's of Zion," *American*

Hebrew reported, "Here's an item for Ford's Folly. A group of Nordics in the South—white, 100 percent, American money lenders—were about to stop Herman E. Perry, Negro financier...when a JEW by the name of Julius Rosenwald stepped in.... [12]

Furthermore, the rhetoric which Jews used when inveighing against racism provided a way for Jewish leaders, concerned about the fate of Jewishness and Judaism in America, to justify the preservation of tradition, albeit in modified form. They believed that their efforts and concerns for American Blacks set Jews apart from other Americans, apart from, and indeed above, Christians. This championing of the cause of Blacks not only proved their credentials as Americans, conversant with the imagery of American ideals, but also provided them with a way of showing how useful Judaism could be in America. A 1942 cantata, "What is Torah?" written by Reconstructionists Judith Kaplan Eisenstein and Ira Eisenstein to mark the celebration of the late-spring holiday of Shavuoth, celebrating the giving of the Torah, aptly demonstrated the conjoining of the imagery of Jewish life and the Black predicament.

> Torah is the hope of the Negro people, plunged into poverty and despair....In all their tragic years upon this continent, the memory of Israel's struggle has kept their faith alive. [13]

Jews read and heard a message that something special existed between themselves and Blacks. Rabbis preached that unlike the Christians among whom they lived, Jews shared in the triumphs of Black Americans, triumphs which they in no small measure had helped to bring about. The Jewish cultural construction of Blacks operated along the lines of a morality tale whose narrative line demanded that Blacks be victims, albeit noble ones, who gratefully took the helping hands that Jews extended to them. Jews could stride across this historical stage as an *am kadosh*, a separate and holy people, different than the rest of America. Blacks, by virtue of their suffering, fell outside of the usual category of "goyim," occupying a unique locus in the Jewish understanding of the world.

Jews in the Eyes of Blacks

A popular joke made its way around Black America in the early twentieth century. It retold the Creation story, with a bite. The various races gathered around the feet of God, who had offered to grant each one some special gift to take to earth. The Anglo-Saxon, accordingly, asked for political power, while the Chinese character preferred to be left alone to achieve inner tranquility. A happy hunting ground constituted the American Indian's vision of the good life. The Black man wished for a million dollars. God lastly turned to the Jew. The Jew, it turns out, wanted only "the address of the Negro you gave the million dollars." [14]

This joke, collected by William Pickens, a field secretary for the NAACP, spoke volumes about the complicated ways in which Blacks in the late nineteenth and early twentieth centuries saw Jews. Encoded in it lay a vast range of images that Blacks projected about the "Jew" of these years: a combination of admiration, envy, and fear.

Jews assumed mythic proportion in the Black press and religious community. Talking about Jews became a way for Blacks to talk about themselves, to express their fears and aspirations, their anxieties and concerns. Jews did not, in short, simply constitute another group of whites. As a writer for the *Negro World* noted in 1924, "Who has housed and is still housing, the colored community...? Who forms the greater part of the faculties of the schools and colleges that educated the Negro? With whom do the Negroes enter into business communication? To whom can the Negro who wants to launch out on a business...go for a loan at any time? None else but the Jew."

No doubt the African American religious tradition can explain in part the broad uses of the Jews in Black rhetoric in this period. For a people suspended between slavery and freedom, the stories of Moses the liberator, the rigors of slavery, the yearning for freedom, and the glory of the Exodus offered powerful religious and political symbolism. While Black religious rhetoric associated Jews with the crucifixion of Jesus, it constantly promoted the heroic images of the suffering slaves transformed into the triumphant women and men who left Egypt.[15] The music and imaginative literature of Black Americans characterized Jews on some level as the living embodiment of the Exodus story. As Howard University professor Kelly Miller wrote in 1935 for the *Richmond Planet*, the stories of struggle and deliverance, of Noah, Daniel, Jonah, "are absorbed and relished [by the Negro] as if they were an indigenous part of Negro folklore."[16]

Jews were also represented in Black discourse as the heirs of centuries of oppression. Black writers and lecturers repeatedly emphasized that Jews had suffered harshly, and despite—or perhaps because of—that experience, had emerged successful. In 1876 the Reconstructionist governor of Mississippi, Pinckney B.S. Pinchback, exhorted an audience to ponder the fate of the Jews. "Like you," he reminded his listeners, a decade out of bondage, "they were once slaves and after they were emancipated they met with persecution." With hard work, he continued, they became "leaders of education and princes of the commercial world....What an example for you, my people, whose advantages are so great."[17] Booker Washington in 1912 echoed this sentiment, claiming that despite the "wear and tear of centuries of persecution," the Jews have risen "up to a position of power and preeminence."[18]

Jewish success, according to the range of Black commentary, grew out of Jewish business acumen. Commerce catapulted Jews out of oppression and into the upper realms of influence and achievement.[19] The *New York Age* went so far as to claim in 1906 that the Jews' "influence on Wall Street, through their European connections, is almost predominant."[20]

Black writers, educators, clergymen, and intellectuals offered a variety of speculative reasons to explain Jewish success in making money. Sociologist Kelly Miller suggested that the ability of the Jews to turn a profit might have some biological basis, whether "inborn or acquired." He concluded that Jewish economic prowess grew out of a combination of unique group characteristics and a willingness to sacrifice everything to make money: "the Jew seems to deem it his mission to cater to Christian needs and necessities. They violate their own Sabbath, gathering shekels, to supply Christians with their requirements for Sunday, Christmas, and Easter....When the Jews take a holiday, the Gentiles suffer for lack of their accustomed supply of creature comforts."[21]

Jews, the explanations further offered, banded together and helped out their less well-off brethren. Added to this, Jews worked hard, lived soberly, and invested, rather than squandered, their money. "You have never heard of Jews begging anybody for anything," commented one Atlanta writer in 1930, whereas the *Richmond Bee* claimed that "they have sense enough to invest their money productively....Success seems to attend their pathway."[22]

References to Jewish business acumen and personal success ran through the Black press, but positive statements mingled with defamatory ones. The same articles that praised Jewish achievement could easily include such statements as appeared in the *Globe* in 1883: "It is a peculiar race...parasitical and predatory...preying upon and devouring the substance of others rather than creating and devouring the substance of itself.[23]

If the explanation for the overwhelming Jewish fascination with the imagery of Black America grew out of a complex set of adjustments Jews made to their new American home, how can we then explain the ways in which Blacks manipulated the imagery of Jews? What underlying cultural dramas inspired African Americans to distinguish the Jews from other groups?

Jewish history and success, as Black commentators observed, did indeed provide a powerful metaphor and inspiration for African Americans. As they saw, Jews had achieved success after centuries of travail.

Communal Black rhetoric was also shaped by the connections that some African Americans had established with Jews in political, philanthropic, and civil rights endeavors in organizations like the NAACP and the Urban League, on the boards of Black schools, colleges, and social service agencies, and in outreach projects and unions.[24] Black newspapers documented the words and deeds of the Spingarn brothers, Stephen Wise, Jacob Schiff, Louis Marshall, rabbis Joseph Krauskopf, Rudolph Coffee, and many others. As a 1927 commentary in a New York newspaper, *The West Indian American,* reported, "A prominent Negro" had been asked, "Which group in America was fairest to the Black man?" "Emphatically," he had answered, "the Jews."[25]

The Black press asserted that Blacks *should* pin their political future on an alliance with Jews, who were both powerful and sympathetic to the struggle for equal rights. The *New York Age* in 1916 applauded the introduction of a civil rights bill to the state legislature by A.J. Levy. "The wise thing," counseled the editor, "for the Negro to do is to form as close an alliance with the Jews as is possible so that the latter in fighting for his own rights will in some degree fight for ours."[26]

Black writers, thinkers, and community activists put the Jews on a kind of mythic pedestal, at a moment when role models seemed especially necessary. Crime, marital desertion, prostitution, drunkenness, violence—a whole panoply of socially deviant behaviors—wracked Black America and threatened the community as a whole.[27] In both the pre-migration south and in the developing Black communities of the north, poverty and exclusion had bred a subculture of disreputability, certainly as measured by middle-class standards. An African American physician in Chicago, a key player in the local chapter of the Urban League, said it bluntly in 1904 in a public lecture, "Those of the race who are desirous of improving their general condition are prevented to a great extent by being compelled to live with those of their color who are shiftless, dissolute and immoral."[28]

Jews and their situation likewise could provide Blacks with a kind of meter of suffering, a gauge by which to assess how bad—or how good—they had it in America. By and large, the Black press saw the greater share of suffering as falling on the shoulders of their own people. Particularly in the realm of real, everyday politics, Black writers claimed that Jews had little to complain about, when measured against Blacks.

And comparisons between the fate of Black people in America and that of the Jews, particularly in Europe, presented an opportunity for African American commentators to once again note the tremendous power of Jews.

Whether writing about Jewish achievement, or ironically noting Jewish power to manipulate the press for their own ends, whether praising the Jews for their educational successes and their clean living, or chiding them for their willingness to do anything to turn a profit, Black imagings about Jews reflected Black concerns about their own status in America. Jews, especially to middle-class African Americans, thus served as hortatory and didactic devices in a community debate.

In sum, Jews and Blacks functioned as metaphors for each other. The invented "Jew" and the imaginary "Negro" fulfilled culturally thick, deeply complicated functions as the two groups of marginal outsiders contended with a white, gentile, host society. The communal rhetoric of one needed the mythic other.

Real Jews and Real Black People: The Encounter

However, mythic people did not move into neighborhoods and set up their homes near those already living there. Constructed characters did not sell clothing and flour, pins and needles to imaginary customers, taking cash or extending credit. Debates in union halls over strategies and goals took place among flesh and blood women and men. As Jews and Blacks met each other in these settings, they had to contend not only with the day-to-day tugs and pulls of relationships among strangers of unequal status, but also with the images that they carried with them. They had to square the actual people they met and saw with the figures who jumped out of the pages of magazines and the words of sermons. The actual meeting grounds between Blacks and Jews, as such, became complicated by the discourses already established in both communities.

Between 1880–1935, in both the south and north, in cities and in rural areas, Jews and Blacks interacted with each other to an extent that a century later we have yet truly to understand. The spottiness and ahistoricity of the popularly accepted generalizations—particularly in the context of a subject so explosive and culturally tense as this—render all statements about the past relationship particularly problematic.

Some historian should in fact follow up a lead provided by a 1928 African Amerian writer in Norfolk, Virginia. Remarking about the Jewish merchants around him, this observer wrote, that the Jew, "will run his store on the first floor, live on the second floor himself, and in some cases rent out a possible third floor to some family of Negroes. Six days out of seven he, his wife, and his children will see more of colored people than...even their fellow Jews."[29]

In the period of the late nineteenth and early twentieth centuries it seems that two kinds of Jewish-Black residential connections took place, neither of which has yet been studied. First, as described by the Norfolk writer, lone Jewish families lived in predominantly Black neighborhoods as store owners. Who were these Jews? Did they come to Black neighborhoods specifically seeking out the business of African Americans, who themselves established little in the way of small businesses? Or, did the Jewish families who served in Black neighborhoods represent the failures of their own community? What kinds of institutional connections did they have with their fellow Jews who had perhaps abandoned them as they fanned out to more comfortable homes?

Second, in many American cities, in the period from the late nineteenth century through the 1920s, Blacks and Jews did in fact reside near each other. Stray pieces of evidence, empirically or analytically undeveloped, indicate that Jews and Blacks occupied some of the same urban spaces throughout this era. A study of Atlanta Jews concluded that between 1896 and 1911, 19 percent of the city's Russian Jews lived on the edges of the heavily Black Decatur Street neighborhood.[30] In Detroit, as early as the 1870s, Jews and "the better classes of the colored people" moved into a predominantly German—presumably Christian—area of the near east side, making their homes side by side.[31] Black migrants began to flock to the predominantly Jewish Hastings Street section in the late 1910s and through the 1920s they occupied the neighborhood alongside Jews. Yet, by 1930, only a smattering of Jewish retail establishments remained.[32] In the 1920s an area in Cleveland, between East 55th and East 105th, with Euclid as its northern boundary and Woodland as its southern, served as the heart of Jewish Cleveland. Black families had made their homes in this neighborhood as early as the 1910s, and for a brief period in the 1920s the two groups lived together.[33] A 1942 study conducted at Howard University by Lunabelle Wedlock, focusing on the ways in which Black newspapers treated the rise of Naziism in Germany, uncovered Jewish-Black spatial propinquity additionally in Philadelphia, Pittsburgh, and Chicago.[34]

Obviously the most important, and explosive, locus for this transition played itself out in the upper reaches of New York City, in Harlem. Well-off American Jews, primarily upper-middle class merchants and white collar workers, began moving to Harlem in the 1870s. By 1900 it boasted an impressive panoply of dignified institutions of bourgeois Jewish life. But in 1905, the neighborhood began to change as less well-off Jews, Eastern European working class immigrants abandoning the lower East Side and other zones of first settlement, took advantage of a building boom in Harlem. As they moved in, the earlier Jewish denizens of the area began to move out for more spacious quarters. Since the humbler Jews far outnumbered the better-off ones, the size and density of the Jewish population grew in the 1910s and early 1920s.

As Jewish immigration from Europe came to a virtual standstill in 1924, and as other neighborhoods opened up for modest Jewish residence in the Bronx and Brooklyn, the Jewish movement into Harlem began to end. Jewish institutions, including synagogues, schools, community centers, kosher meat markets, and bakeries followed their patrons to other areas. The Jewish Welfare Board in 1924 attributed the sunset of Jewish Harlem to "restriction on immigration, desire to better oneself as economic status improves."

The first African Americans drifted northward to Harlem at the beginning of the century, just as the more economically marginal Jews had. Small in number at first, and relatively comfortable economically, Black families took up residence on the fringes of the neighborhood, and then over time moved closer and closer to 125th Street, the commercial center of the area. Like their Jewish counterparts, they began to create the infrastructures of communal life, in some cases buying up synagogues and converting them to churches. For a period from around 1905 through the mid-1920s, Blacks, increasingly humbler in class status, and poorer Jews lived together there. But, the Jews enjoyed the possibility of leaving Harlem when their economic situations improved. That is, those working class, lower East Side Jews who had streamed into Harlem in the first decade of the century began to move outward by the third, and by the fourth, had quite nearly completed their abandonment of the area. Black residents, on the other hand, had no such route outward. A combination of slow economic mobility, sometimes increased impoverishment, the influx of massive numbers of very poor migrants swept in by the Great Migration, and vicious discrimination in housing, locked Blacks in place. Thus the neighborhood became less and less Jewish as it became increasingly Black. The same Jewish Welfare Board assessment which linked Jewish outward mobility from Harlem to "making it" economically also recognized the realities of the racial situation, noting that Jews left also because of "the influx of negroes, Italians, and Spanish-speaking groups."[35]

How did Jews respond to changes in their neighborhoods? It appears that they moved out when they did not feel comfortable, although without closer research it is not possible to pinpoint the factors cited in the 1924 Jewish Welfare Board report. Would Jews have moved out of these neighborhoods anyhow even if the racial makeup of the neighborhood had not changed. Generally studies of Jewish residential patterns in the United States have historically shown that groups always moved in response to improved circumstances.[36] The exodus of Jewish institutions also played a role in this centrifugal phenomenon. Once synagogues and Hebrew schools moved out, members either had to found new institutions or follow their houses of worship and study. Consumers of kosher meat and other foods followed departing butchers and bakers, their only access to ritually acceptable food.[37]

By and large Jews did not respond violently to the increasing Black presence in their neighborhoods.[38] Contemporary observers and subsequent historians have shown that when Irish, Polish, and other whites of various backgrounds considered their neighborhoods "threatened" by Blacks seeking homes, they responded with physical force—"defending" their neighborhoods. Jews did not meet their Black neighbors with firebombs, guns, or clenched fists because their rapid rate of economic success allowed them to move. The "wandering Jews" had a centuries-long historic experience with picking up and settling themselves elsewhere, and perhaps Jews of the time felt they carried with them little in the way of a romantic commitment to a physical place. Thomas Kessner's important study comparing Jewish and Italian adjustment to New York City showed that Jews, despite greater economic mobility, had lower rates of home ownership and high rates of small business investment. Italians, on the other hand, viewed home ownership the highest of achievements at that point in their history in America. Jews may have had less stake in the maintenance of their turf.[39] Finally, Jews had close to no experience or taste for armed self-defense or preemptive aggression against others.

Nevertheless, the shifts in population from Jewish to Black did not take place without any controversy. Reports of friction between Jewish homeowners and the increasingly large pool of Black renters in Harlem showed up in the Black press as early as 1908. Meyer Jarmulowsky, a Jewish homeowner, indeed a major real estate developer, a member of the Property Owners' Improvement Association, and a key player in the immigrant eastern European Orthodox community, addressed a group, presumably Black, at Harlem's St. Philip's Church, on "The Housing Problem From the Owner's Point of View." The problem, as Jarmulowsky saw it, at least as described in the *New York Age*, amounted to a difference in one's economic perspective: the lessee and lessor had opposite interests in the development of the neighborhood. Jarmulowsky suggested then that a joint meeting be called to directly confront the problem. He clearly wanted to convince Blacks to cease any further forays into the neighborhood.[40] Evidence of Jewish participation in efforts to block further Black movement into Harlem in the 1920s actually showed up in the Jewish press, and both the Yiddish and English Jewish newspapers strongly condemned any Jewish participation in such organizations.[41]

While neighborhood life *may* have provided a setting for some encounters in the Jewish-Black encounter of the early twentieth century, in the world of work, no controversial issues divided them. Jews and Blacks did not compete against each other for jobs. They occupied such very different niches in the economy that they had no place to struggle and contest. The absence of direct competition partly explains the absence of physical violence in the meeting between Jews and Blacks, as distinct from the meeting between Blacks and Irish or Blacks and Poles on the docks of New York or the slaughter houses of Chicago. Jews, certainly when it came to making a living, had nothing to fear from Blacks; Blacks, on the other hand, never confronted a phalanx of resistant Jews, standing, literally or figuratively, armed at the factory gates.

The one part of the industrial world that Jews did dominate, the garment trades, at first attracted very few Black workers. And the point in time at which Blacks, primarily women, began to enter in serious numbers into these same factories coincided almost precisely with the Jewish movement outward.

The fact that employers did not pit Jews and Blacks against each other, threatening one with hiring the other as a way either to depress wages or to create a docile work force, lead to some fairly positive relationships that developed among Jews and Blacks in the garment trades. From the creation of the International Ladies' Garment Workers' Union in 1914 through the era of the Depression, the small, but growing, number of Blacks who worked in garment factories not only were welcomed into the union through special recruiting drives, but a few moved into positions of leadership on the local level. Its official publication *Justice* went out of its way to include photographs of African American members sitting in meetings, addressing their fellow workers, and relaxing at the union's resort, Unity House.[42]

Clearly, the Jewish-Black relationship that reverberated with the greatest emotional energy took place primarily in the realm of business. Jews sold to Blacks all over America, in communities of every size, selling merchandise of every type. But the specifics can only be sketchily pieced together. Statements in the Black press about "Jew stores," or observations by Black political activists about the stranglehold of Jewish stores on Black neighborhoods, need to be taken with caution.

Jewish business dealings in African American sections need to be historicized. Jewish business with non-Jewish customers hardly amounted to something new. Jews carried with them a centuries-old tradition of commerce and a legacy of being Europe's economic middlemen. Coming to America, opening small stores in black neighborhoods differed not at all from selling to Christians in Galicia, Bavaria, and elsewhere in Europe.[43]

Furthermore, in America, Jews sold to all sorts of non-Jews. The Jewish economy that came to dominate the Mississippi Delta or Chicago's "Black Belt" differed in fact very little from the Jewish economy either on the other side of the Atlantic or from that forming in vast stretches of white America.[44]

Additionally, Jews were not alone in selling to Blacks. In numerous American cities, in parts of the Mississippi Delta and other regions of the south, Chinese immigrants set up small stores to cater to Black customers.[45] Although by the early 1930s Harlem had become the flashpoint of tension and resentment by Blacks against Jewish merchants, many Italian, Greek, and Irish, as well as Chinese, shopkeepers, also sold goods to Blacks there.[46] Likewise, in the early decades of the twentieth century, Black immigrants from the West Indies also flocked to areas like Harlem and carved out a place for themselves in the realm of small business, and despite their shared racial heritage, they too were considered "foreign."

With all these caveats in mind, the fact remains that Jews did establish an intense and complicated business relationship with Black people across America.[47] They sold to various non-Jews, blacks among them. They engaged in commerce in many regions and neighborhoods, some where no Blacks dwelled, as well as in those where African Americans predominated. A Jewish economy in retailing developed as early as the 1840s in Oregon where few Blacks lived at that time. In some locales, Jewish shopkeepers set up businessess among their former, not so friendly, neighbors from Europe. In the western Pennsylvania coal fields and steel towns, Polish and other Slavic immigrants lived in areas served primarily by Jewish merchants; Poles on Chicago's West Side complained bitterly that they once again found themselves in thrall to Jewish grocers and purveyors of other goods. Slavic informants from the small towns of western Pennsylvania recalled growing up with the belief that "'Jews meant shopkeepers,'" and that Jews spent all their time coming up with ways to make money off the Slavic peoples. In Chicago in the early twentieth century, Polish community activists launched several "Swoj do Swojego" ("Patronize your own") campaigns. The Jewish economy of the Mississippi Delta or Chicago's "Black Belt" hardly differed from the Jewish economy forming elsewhere in America or that existed on the other side of the Atlantic.[48]

The commercial encounter became more pronounced in the aftermath of the Civil War and the end of slavery. Commentators as different as Black activist-intellectual W.E.B. Du Bois and the southern apologist historian E. Merton Coulter considered the entry of small numbers of Jewish merchants into the post-emancipation south as a notable event. Du Bois, in the 1903 edition of *Souls of Black Folk,* claimed that Reconstruction saw the transition of power "from the hands of Southern gentlemen...to those men who have come to take charge of the industrial exploitation of the New South...thrifty and avaricious Yankees, shrewd and unscrupulous Jews."[49] Coulter's history of Reconstruction placed the Jews directly in contact with Blacks. "The end of the war," he wrote, "saw an invasion of Jews to reap a harvest in trade; Sticking to their business and treating the freedman as an important businessman, not eschewing to call him 'Mister,' they secured a great amount of the Negro's trade."[50]

That "great amount" bears further analysis. Blacks flocked to Jewish-owned stores by choice, by compulsion, or by some kind of combination of the two, according to the Black press, imaginative literature, and the more general African American communal discourse. An informant to sociologist John Dollard, studying 1930s race relations for his classic *Caste and Class in a Southern Town*, said, "If there is a Jewish holiday, you cannot buy a pair of socks in this whole country." This same kind of rhetoric showed up in the pages of the Black press. The *Amsterdam News* remarked after Rosh Hashanah and Yom Kippur, 1925, "Harlem was the only community where literally all business was closed…and it was necessary for persons to walk from ten to fifteen blocks to find an open grocery store."[51]

Why did Black customers give so much business to Jewish shopkeepers? In some places they may have had no alternative. Only Jewish entrepreneurs may have opened a dry-goods or grocery store in proximity to an African American community. For Black consumers, shopping at a Jewish store represented their only way to secure daily necessities. Also, Jewish merchants advertised heavily in Black newspapers, making their goods known to readers of the *New York Age, Amsterdam News,* or *Pittsburgh Courier*, and in the process helped to keep these newspapers afloat.

Some contemporary commentators, however, claimed that Blacks preferred Jewish-owned stores over others. Certainly in the South, the respect that Jews showed to customers, regardless of race, made green the important color, rather than black or white. According to Dollard, "The Jews," as opposed to gentile southern whites, "let the Negro know that his dollar is as good as anyone else's." His sources, presumably Black people, "stressed that the Jews have treated Negroes with courtesy, or at least without discourtesy, in strictly business relations. They find some way of avoiding the "Mr." and "Mrs." question, such as by saying, "What can I do for you?"[52]

Testimony given to St. Clair Drake and Horace Cayton in Chicago demonstrated that this phenomenon did not stop at the Mason-Dixon line. Blacks in Bronzeville (Chicago) gravitated toward Jewish shops, which the authors estimated represented "three-fourths of the merchants" in the teeming Black metropolis. A consumer told Cayton and Drake quite bluntly, "You see, I can get credit from him and I can't from the A & P or a colored store. I like to trade at the A & P because you can pick up quite a bit of fresh vegetables and stuff, but I tried to get credit there and couldn't."[53]

But Black commentators and observers may have vastly exaggerated not only the power of the Jews, but the level of economic interaction. In 1942, one Harlem newspaper claimed that 95 percent of the area's merchants were Jews, a statement not borne out by any data collected at the time.[54] Commentators in the 1930s recognized that the issue between Jews and Blacks involved perception as much, or perhaps more, than reality. One observer noted, "The belief is widespread in the Negro that a large share of the exploiting landlords are Jewish." Roi Ottley and others, however, recognized that the "Jew" taken to be the landlord actually was the rent collector, employed by the landlord, usually a bank. Kenneth Clark, reconstructing the evolution of "Negro-Jewish" relations from the vantage point of 1946, remembered that "almost all landlords were thought to be Jews," implying that the Black people among whom he lived and grew up made the automatic assumption that "landlord" meant "Jew" regardless of truth.[55]

The rhetoric which not only sloppily labeled any store or apartment owned by a white person as "Jewish" also specifically linked Jews in Black neighborhoods to a range of practices demeaning to their Black clients. It accused *Jews* of selling shoddy goods at exorbitant prices. It condemned *Jews* for refusing to hire Black workers. It held up the *Jews* as cramming too many Black people into small, dirty apartments and then charging astronomical prices. Clearly such behaviors did occur. The Black press reported incidents of Jewish merchants assaulting Black customers, of Jewish real estate owners heedlessly not maintaining apartments. The Jewish press did so as well. The Yiddish press in particular reported on unscrupulous behavior by Jewish merchants against Black customers, and condemned such actions.[56]

The process by which Blacks linked all small business, and indeed almost all exploitive economic relationships, to Jews increased in the 1930s. As a new generation of Black people, urban dwellers, many born or raised in the north, experienced the ravages of the Depression, the imagery of Jews as unlike other white Americans transformed itself into an imagery of Jews as the "whitest" of Americans. Jews came to be defined as the worst exploiters. Roi Ottley noted that during the 1933 "Don't Buy Where You Can't Work" boycott of Harlem, "the Jew [was] bearing the brunt of the attack." Rhetoric from that campaign, and similar movements in Chicago and Pittsburgh, born of the economic dislocation and desperation of the Depression, directed itself at "white" merchants, always identified as "Jewish."[57]

But then in the decades of the late-nineteenth and early-twentieth centuries Jews and Blacks probably could not have a rational discourse about each other. Ultimately the "real" relationship between Jews and Blacks, the every day encounter between ordinary humans, never had a chance of being ordinary. Two peoples of such unequal economic and political stations met each other with a set of preconceived ideas about the other. The two communal rhetorical traditions basically stacked the deck against "normalcy." Jews operated on an ideological level in which Blacks functioned as the focus of their "mission," as the object of "proving" Jewish worth. By virtue of insisting that they had something special to offer their "stricken brothers," Jews could not, in the limited places where they met, interact with Black people as just like anyone else. African Americans on the other hand produced and consumed a vast body of communal mythology about the Jews as special, different, unlike all other white people. The gap between rhetoric and reality proved to be too great. Every day Jews and Blacks who looked into each others' eyes could never see each other as ordinary and real: each became at once larger and smaller than myth and than reality itself. Probably no two peoples in America emerged more disappointed from an encounter than did these two; probably no two peoples in American history spent more time reliving those encounters and reconstructing them to keep the myths alive.

Notes

1. *Jewish Daily Forward* (to be cited as *Forward*), March 13, 1935, p. 6.

2. Cheryl Lynn Greenberg, *"Or Does It Explode?": Black Harlem in The Great Depression* (New York, 1991).

3. Hasia R. Diner, *In the Almost Promised Land: American Jews and Blacks, 1915–1935* (Baltimore, 1995).

4. Arnold Shankman, *Ambivalent Friends: Afro-Americans View the Immigrant* (Westport, CT, 1982), pp. 111–48.

5. The actual history of Black-Jewish interaction has not yet been written. No historian has yet tackled such issues as Jewish business relations with Blacks or the ways in which Jews and Blacks inhabited and used the same neighborhoods. Jeffery Gurock, *When Harlem Was Jewish: 1870–1930* (New York, 1979) in a sketchy, undeveloped way points to the meeting of Jews and Blacks in Harlem. This work is mainly a study of Jews, and Blacks enter into the analysis here as minor players. On the other hand, social histories of Black communities may make reference to a Jewish presence, but again, such references are undeveloped. Cheryl Greenberg's, *"Or Does It Explode?"* analyzed the impact of the Depression on Black Harlem, a time of intense dispute between Black activists and Jewish merchants. While it contains numerous references to the lingering Jewish business presence in the neighborhood, it also does not treat the relationship in a thorough manner. The rhetoric is taken to be "true" in the sense that the author did not actually analyze how many Jewish merchants actually had stores in Harlem, how many employed anybody, how many employed Black workers, and the like. Steven Hertzberg's study, *Strangers in the Gate City: The Jews of Atlanta, 1845–1915* (Philadelphia: Jewish Publication Society of America, 1978) provides the most focused attention to the interaction of the two groups. Unfortunately, no scholar has picked up this kind of analysis for other cities, or for the country as a whole, in as detailed a manner. The interaction of Jews and Blacks in the garment unions has been covered in Diner, *In the Almost Promised Land*, pp. 199–235. This subject also deserves a closer investigation, particularly examining specific locals in specific cities, searching for the actual behaviors.

6. For some theoretical analysis of this kind of "construction" or "invention," see Eric Hobsbawm and Terence Ranger, *The Invention of Tradition* (Cambridge, 1983);

Benedict Anderson, *Imagined Communities: Reflections on the Origin and Spread of Nationalism* (London, 1983); Peter Berger and Thomas Luckmann, *Social Construction of Reality: A Treatise in the Sociology of Knowledge* (Garden City, NY, 1966).

7. All discussions about imagery fundamentally represent the perspective of the elite, however splintered that elite might be. The communal rhetoric appeared in newspapers, sermons, published literary works, and the like. By virtue of their appearance in these formats, such statements should not be confused with the range of opinions of "ordinary" people.

8. Diner, *Promised Land*, p. 113.

9. Diner, *Promised Land*, p. 69.

10. Diner, *Promised Land*, p. 151.

11. Melville Herskovitz, "What is Race?" *American Mercury* 2 (June 1924), 207–10.

12. Diner, *Promised Land*, pp. 190–91.

13. Ira Eisenstein and Judith Kaplan Eisenstein, "What is Torah?: A Cantata for Unison Chorus and Piano" (New York: Jewish Reconstructionist Foundation, 1942).

14. William Pickens, *American Aesop* (Boston, 1926), pp. 113–15.

15. Horace Mann Bond, "Negro Attitudes Toward Jews," *Jewish Social Studies* 27, 1 (January 1965), p. 4; E. Franklin Frazier, *The Negro Church in America* (New York, 1964), pp. 15–20; Richard Wright, *Black Boy* (New York, 1945), pp. 53–54.

16. Shankman, *Ambivalent Friends*, p. 115.

17. Shankman, *Ambivalent Friends*, pp. 116.

18. Booker T. Washington and Robert Park, *The Man Furthest Down* (Garden City, NY, 1912), p. 241.

19. Philip S. Foner, "Black-Jewish Relations in the Opening Years of the Twentieth Century," *Phylon* 36, 4 (Winter 1975), 361.

20. Steven Bloom, "Interactions Between Blacks and Jews in New York City, 1900–1930, as Reflected in the Black Press" (Ph.D. dissertation, New York University, 1973), p. 181.

21. Shankman, *Ambivalent Friends*, p. 122.

22. Shankman, *Ambivalent Friends*, pp. 126–28.

23. Seth Scheiner, *Negro Mecca: A History of the Negro in New York City, 1865–1920* (New York, 1965), p. 139.

24. Diner, *Promised Land*; Faith Rogow, *Gone To Another Meeting: The National Council of Jewish Women, 1893–1993* (Tuscaloosa, AL, 1993), p. 186, described how members of the Chicago chapter of the National Council of Jewish Women cooperated with Ida B. Wells after the 1919 race riots.

25. Quoted in Bloom, "Interactions Between Blacks and Jews," p. 229.

26. Bloom, "Interactions Between Blacks and Jews," p. 93.

27. See, for example, Roger Lane, *Roots of Violence in Black Philadelphia: 1860–1900* (Cambridge, MA, 1986).

28. James R. Grossman, *Land of Hope: Chicago, Black Southerners, and the Great Migration* (Chicago, 1989), p. 131. See also W.E.B. DuBois, *The Philadelphia Negro: A Social Study* (Philadelphia, 1899) pp. 78, 126, 127; and St. Clair Drake and Horace R. Cayton, *Black Metropolis: A Study of Negro Life in a Northern City* (New York, 1945), pp. 684, 710–15.

29. Quoted in Shankman, Arnold, "Friend or Foe?: Southern Blacks View the Jew, 1880–1935," in, *"Turn to the South": Essays on Southern Jewry*, ed. Nathan M. Kaganoff and Melvin I. Urofsky, eds. (Charlottesville, 1979), p. 122.

30. Hertzberg, *Strangers in the Gate City*, p. 115.

31. David Katzman, *Before the Ghetto: Black Detroit in the Nineteenth Century* (Urbana, IL, 1973), p. 73.

32. Sidney Bolkolsky, *Harmony and Dissonance: Voices of Jewish Identity in Detroit, 1914–1967* (Detroit, 1991), pp. 97, 100, 185.

33. Kenneth L. Kusmer, *A Ghetto Takes Shape: Black Cleveland, 1870–1920* (Urbana, IL, 1976), pp. 43, 171–72.

34. Lunabelle Wedlock, "The Reaction of Negro Publications," *The Reaction of Negro Publications and Organizations to German Anti-Semitism* (Washington, D.C., 1942) pp. 136–38, 156, 167–70.

35. Jeffrey S. Gurock, *When Harlem Was Jewish, 1870–1930*, (New York, 1979); Gilbert Osofsky, *Harlem: The Making of a Ghetto: Negro New York, 1890–1930* (New York, 1963), pp. 127–28.

36. Such a study not only needs to be done, but needs to be framed in a comparative context. Jewish geographic mobility out of neighborhoods that attracted African American newcomers needs to be juxtaposed with Jewish demographic patterns in places where whites of a range of ethnic backgrounds made up the new settlers to the area. Did Jews in places like Seattle, Minneapolis, Portland, Oregon or Portland, Maine, which had miniscule Black populations, stay put longer or did they too rapidly abandon neighborhoods of first and second settlement as they rose in economic status?

37. Additionally scholars need to look at the balance between Jewish home ownership versus renting as a factor in outward mobility. Who left neighborhoods first? Did Jewish homeowners sell when they moved or did they retain their property and rent them out?

38. The evidence for this assertion by necessity must be negative. The Black press, studied in Shankman, *Ambivalent Friends* and Bloom, "Interactions Between Blacks and Jews," makes *no* reference to Jewish use of physical violence as a way to keep Blacks out of neighborhoods they defined as "theirs."

39. Thomas Kessner, *The Golden Door: Italian and Jewish Immigrant Mobility in New York City, 1880–1915* (New York, 1977), pp. 132, 151.

40. Bloom, "Interactions Between Blacks and Jews," p. 167.

41. Gurock, *When Harlem Was Jewish*, p. 146.

42. Diner, *Promised Land*, pp. 199–235; the subject of Jewish-Black interaction in predominantly Jewish unions still needs a great deal more historical research.

43. This subject is also basically devoid of scholarship. We really do not know what kind of attitudes Jews developed in Europe toward their customers. Other than Jacob Katz, in his *Exclusivity and Tolerance: Studies in Jewish-Gentile Relations in Medieval and Modern Times* (New York, 1961), no historian of the Jewish experience has explored the attitudes and practices of Jewish merchants as they interacted with their non-Jewish clients. Such a study would go a long way toward contextualizing how Jewish business dealings with Blacks in America represented a new phenomenon or how much it merely continued a long-standing tradition.

44. For the origins and details of Jewish small business in America and its European roots, see, Hasia Diner, *A Time for Gathering: The Second Migration, 1880–1920* (Baltimore, 1992), pp. 60–73.

45. Shankman, *Ambivalent Friends*, pp. 18–21; Roi Ottley, *"New World A-Coming": Inside Black America* (New York, 1943), pp. 53–54; James W. Lowewen, *Mississippi Chinese: Between Black and White* (Cambridge, MA, 1971).

46. Ottley, *"New World,"* p. 118.

47. Black educator Horace Mann Bond stated it most succinctly as he remembered his Atlanta youth: "The Jew was the man who kept the pawnshop on Peter and Decatur Streets, where I sold papers on Saturday; he was the man who operated the clothing store where my father took his five boys to lay in a stock of clothes." (Horace Mann Bond, "The Negro Attitudes Toward Jews," *Jewish Social Studies* 27, 1 [January 1965], 4.) Kelly Miller made the same point. "The Jew," he boldly pronounced, "makes the most acceptable merchant among Negroes because he knows how to reduce race prejudice to a minimum" (*Survey* 52 [March 1, 1925], 711).

48. Steven Lowenstein, *The Jews of Oregon* (Portland: Jewish Historical Society of Oregon, 1987); William Toll, *The Making of an Ethnic Middle Class: Portland Jewry over Four Generations* (Albany, NY, 1982). See also Ewa Morawska, "A Replica of the 'Old Country' Relationship in the Ethnic Niche: East European Jews and Gentiles in Small-Town Western Pennsylvania, 1880'–1930'," *American Jewish History* 77, 1 (September, 1987), 27–86, particularly see, pp. 73, 75; Dominic A. Pacyga, *Polish Immigrants and Industrial Chicago: Workers on the South Side, 1880–1922* (Columbus, 1991), pp. 155, 224. And for the origins and details of Jewish small business in America and its European roots, see Hasia Diner, *A Time for Gathering: The Second Migration, 1880–1920* (Baltimore, 1992), pp. 60–73.

49. W.E.B. Du Bois, *The Souls of Black Folk* (Chicago, 1903), p. 169.

50. E. Merton Coulter, *The South During Reconstruction, 1865–1877* (Baton Rouge, LA, 1947), pp. 202–3.

51. Bloom, "Interactions Between Blacks and Jews," pp. 197–98.

52. John Dollard, *Caste and Class in a Southern Town* (New Haven, 1937), pp. 128–29.

53. Drake and Cayton, *Black Metropolis: A Study of Negro Life in a Northern City*, pp. 443–44.

54. Leonard Dinnerstein, *Antisemitism in America* (New York, 1994), p. 204.

55. Gurock, *When Harlem was Jewish*, p. 146; Kenneth B. Clark, "Candor About Negro-Jewish Relations," *Commentary* 1 (February 1946), 8.

56. Diner, *Promised Land*, pp. 72–73.

57. L.D. Reddick, "Anti-Semitism Among Negroes," *Negro Quarterly* 1, 2 (Summer 1942), 115.

SIX

BLACKS AND JEWS

The Struggle in the Cities

JONATHAN KAUFMAN

I n 1966, Martin Luther King, Jr. decided to move the Civil Rights struggle
north, to America's cities. He announced that he would begin a series of
demonstrations in Chicago. It would mark a new stage for the civil rights
movement, which up until then had fixated America with its battles and demonstrations in Montgomery and Birmingham, Alabama; Jackson, Mississippi;
Greensboro, North Carolina; and Albany, Georgia. It would also mark a new stage
in the relationship between Blacks and Jews. For decades Blacks and Jews had
been neighbors, economic and even political allies in the North. But after 1966,
their relationship would become more intense and more pointed. Cities were the
scene of the earliest cooperation between Blacks and Jews; they would soon
become the scenes of their most bitter conflicts. Through changes in neighborhoods and clashes over schools and jobs, the relationship between Blacks and Jews
would deteriorate until by the 1990s the two groups were barely on speaking
terms with each other. By that time, the conflict between Blacks and Jews was
nationalized, focusing on such issues as affirmative action and the anti-Semitic
remarks of Black leaders like Louis Farrakhan. But the scars and wounds left by
the battle of Blacks and Jews in America's cities still lingered. And as often as
some leaders in both communities urged Blacks and Jews to walk away from each
other, the two groups still remained tied to the cities, and each other, by what
King called an "inescapable web of mutuality." For twenty-five years America's
cities were the testing ground, and then the battleground, for Blacks and Jews as
they moved from cooperation to confrontation to competition and conflict.

II

Blacks and Jews had a long history of interaction and conflict in the cities even
before King brought the civil rights movement north to Chicago. The waves of

Jews who poured into America's cities from Poland, Russia, and Eastern Europe after 1880 were shaped by economics and ideology to be intrigued by the plight of the American Blacks they soon encountered. To be sure many Jews arriving in the United States felt an uneasiness about Blacks, whose lives and skin color were so different from their own. The racial slur *schwartze*—Yiddish for "Black"—did not originate in the South among rednecks, but in the Jewish tenements of New York's Lower East Side and in the working-class Jewish neighborhoods of Brooklyn and Chicago. Many Jews quickly assimilated racism and prejudice along with other American values.

But in the political universe of immigrant Jews, Blacks were not part of the problem. They were part of the solution. Jews in America before 1880 had cut a low political profile on the issues of slavery and social reform. During the Civil War there had been Jews, mostly in the South, who supported slavery and Jews, mostly in the North, who opposed it. But the new arrivals came imbued with the ideology of socialism and quickly hurled themselves into politics, union organizing, and public life.[1] In New York, Jewish immigrants formed the most militant labor unions. They marched with picket signs printed in Hebrew and Yiddish and forced passage of progressive labor laws. Jewish names dominated the labor movement. Even among those Jews who did not consider themselves socialist, the commitment to improving the lot of workers was strong: two Jews, Samuel Gompers and Leo Strasser, led the American Federation of Labor. The catechism of socialism impelled an alliance with Blacks: The brotherhood of the workers would overthrow the bosses and banish racism, anti-Semitism, war, and exploitation. Socialism in America also gave Jews an opportunity to help people less fortunate than themselves. There was something heady in the chance to help people whose sufferings dwarfed Jewish sufferings and who seemed happy to get the help. "You colored workers were exploited and mistreated in the shop worse than any other group," David Dubinsky, head of the Jewish-dominated International Ladies' Garment Workers' Union, told a rally of Harlem workers in 1934.[2]

When Leo Frank was lynched in Georgia in 1913, it seemed to cement in the minds of many Jews the idea that Blacks and Jews in America shared a community of interests. Who better than the Jews could understand Black suffering? Following the East St. Louis riot in 1917 in which thirty-nine Blacks were killed, the Yiddish *Forward*, the most influential paper among Jewish immigrants in New York, compared the riot to the Kishinev pogrom in Russia in 1903, when more than fifty Jews were killed: "Kishinev and St. Louis—the same soil, the same people. It is a distance of four and a half thousand miles between these two cities and yet they are so close and so similar to each other....Actually twin sisters, which could easily be mistaken for each other." Just before Memorial Day, 1927, the *Forward* asked indignantly: "Where is the spirit of freedom with which our America is always priding itself? And where is the holiness of the constitution which is so often mentioned? And Monday, the 30th of May, the American people decorated the graves of those who fell in the great battle to free the slaves in America and free America from the stain and shame of slavery. The slaves are today not free and on America, the stain of the shame of slavery is still evident."[3]

What socialists believed as faith, communists believed as ideology. Most Jews were not communists. But in the 1920s, 1930s, and 1940s, many communists were Jews. For those Jews who adopted or flirted with communism, a commitment to Blacks stood as the centerpiece of their beliefs. The communists were the first party to run a Black on the national ticket, nominating James W. Ford for Vice President in 1932, 1936, and 1940. When the men known as the Scottsboro boys were accused of raping two white women in Alabama, the lawyer that rushed to defend them was Samuel Liebowitz, a Jew from Brooklyn, who became a folk hero among southern Blacks. When the Communist Party turned its attention to organizing Harlem, a disproportionate number of organizers were Jewish.[4]

A Jew growing up in Brooklyn, in the Bronx, or on Chicago's South Side, a Jewish neighborhood, did not have to be socialist or communist to inhale the talk of socialism and equality that blew all around. It permeated life, creating a world view in which Blacks were objects of sympathy rather than hate, potential allies rather than foes, people who could be helped and who could make Jews feel good for having helped them. Many Jews prided themselves on employing Black maids when no one else would, on renting apartments to Blacks when no one else would, and on making sure their used clothing went to Blacks who were less fortunate and so obviously in need.

For their part, Blacks growing up in the north had a far more ambivalent view of Jews, shaped by economic contact that almost always put Blacks one step below Jews on the urban economic ladder. Whereas Jews often saw themselves reaching out to "help" Blacks by extending them credit at stores, giving them jobs as maids, passing on old clothes to their children, Blacks bristled at the patronizing attitude that seemed to lurk behind every act of generosity. They chafed at the vast economic disparity between Blacks and Jews.

Blacks in northern ghettos in the 1930s and 1940s often preferred working for Jews. They were more courteous and often more generous. But wages were still low and conditions often insulting. In an article for a Harlem newspaper in 1933, two Black women wrote of the "Bronx slave market" in which Black women worked as maids for white, usually Jewish, families. In 1935, when rioting broke out in Harlem, it was directed against Jewish merchants and stores. Roi Ottley, a Black author writing in 1943, charged that Jews had introduced the idea of installment buying into Black life, inducing Blacks to spend beyond their means, leading to a build up of resentment and anger. Jewish-owned pawnshops, Ottley said, required Blacks to leave a suit for a month for a two-dollar loan—and then charged an additional one-dollar storage fee. Jews drove a hard bargain.[5]

For many Blacks, Jews were different from white people. There was "Mr. Charlie," Black slang for whites, and there was "Mr. Goldberg," Black slang for Jews. At their worst, Jews were the conniving tricksters who took advantage of innocent Blacks beaten down by the oppression of white society. They were like the driver on the plantation, the hated middleman who did the white man's dirty work.

Or Jews were insincere. Under the guise of "helping" Blacks and being their "friend," Jews patronized Blacks and exploited them. Jews would leave neighborhoods as Blacks moved in. But they kept their businesses there: the apartment buildings they had bought, the stores they owned and ran. During the Depression, Black activists in Harlem launched a "Don't Buy Where You Can't Work" campaign. Black leaders approached Blumstein's, the largest store in Harlem, which was owned by a Jewish family. Ottley reported that Blumstein "remained adamant to requests or to persuasion to employ Negroes as clerical workers and salesgirls. As a sponsor of Negro charitable institutions, and as the employer of Negro elevator operators, porters, and maids, he explained that he had done his share for Negroes, and refuses to budge an inch in response to demand for more jobs."[6]

Such an attitude infuriated Blacks. It reeked of condescension. Encounters between Blacks and Jews always seemed to involve Jews reaching out and "helping" Blacks, "teaching" them, "guiding" them. Many Black intellectuals ended their flirtation with the Communist Party bitter not only at the communists but at Jews they felt had treated them condescendingly. "How can the average public school Negro be expected to understand the exigencies of the capitalist system as it applies to both Jew and Gentile in America...since both groups act strangely like Hitlerian Aryans...when it comes to colored folks?" asked Langston Hughes, bitter after a feud with Jewish communists.[7]

//

Despite these differences, Blacks and Jews in the 1940s formed two of the pillars of the Democratic Party in America's cities. When Blacks began to run for political office and initiate school desegregation battles in the early 1960s in cities like Boston, New York, and Chicago, they turned to Jews for help. Young Jews, most of them from northern cities, made up two-thirds to three-quarters of the white volunteers who went south to ride busses through Alabama or organize Freedom Summer in Mississippi in 1964. Northern Jews contributed two-thirds to three-quarters of the money raised by King and other civil rights groups.

And yet, despite these links, Blacks and Jews still did not really know each other very well. Black and Jewish interests were also beginning to change just as the cooperation between Blacks and Jews was reaching its peak in the mid-1960s. Jews had embarked on their long climb into the professions and were beginning to move into the establishment. They were becoming part of the white American elite. Jewish parents who had felt a common link with Blacks because they too were denied access to law school and medical schools and country clubs were now seeing their sons and daughters flood into these professional schools and break down social barriers. The demands of the civil rights movement were changing too. In 1963, from the steps of the Lincoln Memorial, King had issued his call for an America where everyone was judged on the "content of their character." By 1966, Stokely Carmichael was electrifying Black crowds with calls for "Black Power." The goals of the civil rights movement were shifting—from demands for political and legal equality to demands for economic equality, from demands for equal opportunity to demands for equal results. Although Blacks and Jews had known each other for decades in the cities, although they had sometimes clashed on an individual level, Black and Jewish interests had not come into direct conflict. In the south, Blacks and Jews united in part because they faced a common enemy: the racist white southerner. Now that the civil rights movement was coming north, all that was about to change.

II

The first sign that Blacks and Jews were destined to clash in America's cities came, ironically, at the same time the alliance between Blacks and Jews reached its symbolic high point in the south. In the summer of 1964, three civil rights workers, Michael Schwerner, Andrew Goodman, and James Chaney—two young Jews from New York and a Black from Mississippi—were kidnapped and murdered in Mississippi. The search for their bodies took months, and when their bodies were unearthed, found caked with the red clay dirt of the Mississippi Delta, their murders seemed to symbolize the cooperation between Blacks and Jews. But that summer of 1964 was also the first summer of major rioting in northern cities. While FBI agents combed the Mississippi woods for Schwerner, Chaney, and Goodman, riots erupted in New York and a handful of other cities, with Jewish-owned stores the targets of burning and looting. Federal studies after the riots were over indicated that Jews owned 30 percent of the stores in these ghetto neighborhoods.

Most Jews, transfixed like most Americans on the drama unfolding in the south, had thought most Blacks were like the integrationist Martin Luther King. They were ignorant of the growing anger in the northern ghettos as well as of the long history of Black nationalism in northern cities like New York where Marcus Garvey had been a powerful influence in the 1920s. They were wary and suspicious of the growing power of Malcolm X and the Nation of Islam. But it was now Malcolm X who symbolized and gave voice to the frustrations and despair of northern ghettos. When the first riots broke out in Harlem in 1964, Malcolm X was in Cairo, Egypt at a conference. Black teenagers roamed the streets shouting at police, "Malcolm! We want Malcolm! Wait until Malcolm comes."

A few months after the 1964 summer riots, Nathan Glazer, a Jewish sociologist, took to the pages of *Commentary* to argue that a sea change was occurring in the civil rights movement. "As the Negro masses have become more active and more militant in their own interests, their feelings have forced themselves to the surface; and Jewish leaders—of unions, of defense and civil rights organizations—

as well as businessmen, housewives, and homeowners, have been confronted for the first time with demands from Negro organizations that, they find, cannot serve as the basis of a common effort."[8] It took just a few years for Glazer to turn out to be prophetic.

//

The Ocean Hill–Brownsville school district in New York was the first place the conflict between Blacks and Jews erupted into open hostility.[9] Located in a blighted section of Brooklyn, Ocean Hill–Brownsville epitomized the failure of New York to educate its Black students. In 1966, standardized reading tests showed Black twelve-year-olds reading two years behind white twelve-year-olds. Only 8 percent of New York's teachers were Black. There were no Black high school principals, and only a handful of Black school administrators. Back in 1954, a few weeks after the Supreme Court outlawed school segregation, Kenneth Clark, the NAACP Legal Defense Fund's star witness, had charged that New York's schools were segregated, with all-Black schools having fewer experienced teachers and Black students crammed into older, poorly maintained buildings. Over the next ten years, city officials proposed plan after plan to integrate the schools. Conditions for Black students just got worse.

In the south, Blacks hobbled by poor schooling knew where the problem lay—with a segregated school system and white politicians and administrators who refused to give Black schools sufficient money, supplies, and books. In New York the problem was much the same, but the face of the enemy was Jewish. New York's public schools were both the historic avenue of success for the city's Jews as well as employer to a significant part of the Jewish middle class. Up through the 1940s, New York's school bureaucracy and classrooms had been run mostly by Irish teachers and supervisors. Following the Second World War, however, Jews graduating from the public city colleges had poured into the system, valuing its job security and good benefits. By 1967 approximately two-thirds of New York's teachers, supervisors, and principals were Jewish. In a city where over half the students were Black or Hispanic, the school teaching staffs and administrators were overwhelmingly white and Jewish. Many of these Jews were liberal, indeed many had supported civil rights. But in the battle of Blacks and Jews the two sides found themselves opposed.

The battle over Ocean Hill–Brownsville began when city officials, responding to Black demands for better education, decided in 1967 to "decentralize" the schools. The city Board of Education announced plans to establish community boards made up of local parents and residents. These boards presumably would give Black and Hispanic parents more influence over the education of their children. Ocean Hill–Brownsville was to be the first model.

From the very start, the seeds of conflict were evident in the different words the two sides used to describe the educational experiment. The largely Jewish teacher's union called it "decentralization"—reducing bureaucracy and giving more power to teachers as well as parents. Black parents called it "community control"—putting the real power in the hands of local parents and residents. To run the Ocean Hill–Brownsville school district, the new community school board chose Rhody McCoy, a Black New York school administrator angered by the traditional exam and seniority system that he believed kept Blacks like himself from rising in the New York school system. Unlike the Blacks who dominated television coverage of the civil rights movement in the early 1960s, McCoy had long given up on Martin Luther King and had become interested instead in the philosophy of Malcolm X, frequently travelling to Malcolm's house for long discussions. McCoy saw the Ocean Hill–Brownsville experiment as a chance to establish the first step in a Black-run and Black-controlled school system stretching from elementary school through college.

McCoy's opponent, the head of the New York Teacher's union, was Albert Shanker. Shanker, like most of his members, was Jewish. And, like many of his members, he was a liberal who had long been active in civil rights. In 1963, Shanker had led a delegation to the March on Washington.

From the start of the experiment, McCoy moved to assert the authority of the school board. The new board interviewed teachers, quizzing them on their responsiveness to the problems of Black children, especially poor Black children. Dissatisfied with the performance of ten teachers, the board dismissed them in the spring of 1968, saying they should all be transferred to other districts. At the time, neither McCoy nor anyone on the board took note that all the fired teachers were Jewish.

Shanker led the teacher's union out on strike. Within two days, the Board of Education agreed to guarantee that the ten teachers plus all remaining union teachers who wanted to go back would be reinstated in Ocean Hill–Brownsville. But the day the teachers returned to Ocean Hill–Brownsville, McCoy summoned them to a meeting in the auditorium of the district's largest school. Supporters of the community board lined the walls. McCoy told the teachers that they were not wanted here and would not get class assignments. Outside, pickets yelled taunts at the teachers. Inside the auditorium, people chanted and jeered. McCoy told the teachers to go home. They walked out in single file, through a gauntlet of angry Blacks.

Then New York snapped. For months, Shanker had been concerned by the persistent reports of anti-Semitism and intimidation in Ocean Hill–Brownsville. If McCoy could dismiss teachers at his whim, then no teacher's job could be safe, especially—judging by the tenor of things in Ocean Hill–Brownsville—in a school system that was more than 50 percent minority and the teachers overwhelmingly white and Jewish.

Shanker felt he had to protect his people. As the second strike began in mid-September 1968, Shanker received copies of leaflets that teachers said had been put in their mailboxes in the Ocean Hill–Brownsville schools. Shanker ordered

500,000 copies printed, to be distributed throughout the city. People should see, he said, what his teachers were up against.

One handout quoted an anonymous leaflet placed in teachers' mailboxes in Junior High School 271:

> If African American History and Culture is to be taught to our Black Children it Must be Done By African Americans who Identify With And Who Understand The Problem.

> It Is Impossible For The Middle East Murderers of Colored People to Possibly Bring To This Important Task The Insight, The Concern, The Exposing Of The Truth That is a *Must* If the Years Of Brainwashing And Self-Hatred That Has Been Taught To Our Black Children By Those Bloodsucking Exploiters and Murderers Is To Be OverCome. The Idea Behind This Program Is Beautiful, But When The Money Changers Heard About It, They Took Over, As Is Their Custom In The Black Community, If African American History And Culture Is Important To Our Children To Raise Their Esteem Of Themselves [sic], They Are The Only Persons Who Can Do The job Are African American Brothers And Sisters, And Not the So-Called Liberal Jewish Friend. We Know From His Tricky, Deceitful Maneuvers That He is Really Our Enemy and *He* is Responsible For The Serious Educational Retardation Of Our Black Children. We Call On All Concerned Black Teachers, Parents, And Friends to Write To The Board of Education, To the Mayor, To The State Commissioner of Education To Protest The Take Over Of This Crucial Program By People Who Are Unfit By Tradition And By Inclination To Do Even An Adequate Job.

Other union handouts reprinted inflammatory statements by activist Les Campbell and anti-Semitic slurs that had circulated around the fringes of the Ocean Hill–Brownsville dispute.

As a device to win the strike, Shanker's decision to print the handouts was a brilliant tactical move. Overnight it changed the debate from one over community control and decentralization—over which many in the city, including Jews, were divided—into a debate over anti-Semitism in the Black community. Are these the kind of things, Shanker asked, that you want said in your schools? Are these the kind of people you want running the schools and teaching children? Many Jews were already unhappy with the rising militancy and anti-white sentiment emanating from the more militant parts of the civil rights movement. Most Jews in New York still considered themselves liberals, but many, especially in working-class neighborhoods, were becoming scared. Crime had skyrocketed in the 1960s, rising faster than at any other time since the 1930s. Two years earlier, in 1966, New York Mayor John Lindsay had proposed establishing a civilian review board to consider complaints of police brutality. With the eruption of the slogan "Black Power," the forthcoming election quickly became a referendum on "law and order" and the fear of crime. Most liberal unions and reform groups, and the major Jewish organizations, backed the proposal. Conservatives and the police opposed it. When November came, the civilian review board was defeated. Polls showed that a majority of Jews had voted against it. The heaviest Jewish opposition was in Brooklyn and Queens, where working- and middle-class Jews lived. Tensions were roiling in ghettos, in civil rights organizations, and in Black and Jewish neighborhoods across the city. The rising Black militancy was demanding power, real power. To many Jews, middle-class liberals as well as working class conservatives, these demands for economic equality and the rumblings of anti-Semitism coming from Ocean Hill–Brownsville now seemed to threaten them directly.

Passions in New York reached a peak when Julius Lester, then a Black activist and public radio talk show host, invited a Black teacher from Ocean Hill–Brownsville onto his show to read a poem written by a Black student. The poem, the teacher said, was dedicated to Albert Shanker. It began: "Jew-boy with your yarmulke/Jew-boy I wish you were dead."

In fact, as McCoy and others claimed repeatedly throughout the strike, several of the union handouts were inaccurate, quoting statements out of context. None of the anti-Semitic leaflets represented official Ocean Hill–Brownsville policy. Lester repudiated the poem on his show, saying it showed where anger and bigotry could lead. For all the talk of Black Power and fear of anti-Semitism in Ocean Hill–Brownsville, 70 percent of the teachers the community board in Ocean Hill–Brownsville approved—before the strike and during the strike— were white. Half were Jewish. The important thing, McCoy emphasized over and over again, was not their background but the fact that the neighborhood parents had approved them.

In the end McCoy and the Ocean Hill–Brownsville school board lost. The striking teachers demanded that McCoy and the board be removed before they would return to work. After weeks of bitter confrontation, the New York Board of Education agreed. The Ocean Hill–Brownsville experiment was suspended. McCoy and the board were dismissed from their jobs.

The Ocean Hill–Brownsville school strike and the bitterness it created was part and preview of clashes that would recur between Blacks and Jews, especially over affirmative action. McCoy had demanded Black control over Black lives. Even more, he wanted control over white lives as well: the right to replace white principals with Black principals, the right to hire, and fire, white teachers as well as Black teachers. McCoy wanted to scuttle an examination system that Jewish teachers and supervisors had based their careers on—but which had prevented Blacks in any significant numbers from becoming schoolteachers. These issues, in the form of affirmative action and quotas, in challenges to civil service rules and fights with unions, in debates over seniority rules versus discrimination, would dominate the 1970s and 1980s. Jews, who had been at the cutting edge of Black demands for freedom in the 1950s and 1960s, were now at the cutting edge of the next phase of Black demands. Only this time it was they who were being cut.

The sound heard in New York in 1968 and 1969 was the sound of a coalition ripping itself apart.

The Ocean Hill–Brownsville clash was the most public sign in the late 1960s that the alliance between Blacks and Jews was coming to an end. But there was another change, little noticed at the time, which was to have as great an impact, especially in Jewish minds. This was the steady change of many city neighborhoods from Jewish to Black.

The enormous influx of Blacks into American cities pushed the existing ghettos past the bursting point. In Chicago, for example, Blacks were crammed into two areas: the gradually expanding "Black Belt" that began just south of the downtown Loop, detoured briefly around the University of Chicago, and ran several miles southward; and the newer West Side ghetto where in 1966 Martin Luther King took an apartment to symbolize his concern for the plight of poor people.

Reinforcing these bureaucratic and financial barriers to open housing was steady violence that echoed like a drum beat through Chicago's tight-knit ethnic neighborhoods whenever Blacks had the audacity to move in. In the summer of 1951, a mob of 2,000 whites in the white, working-class suburb of Cicero, bordering Chicago's western edge, stormed an apartment building that had a Black family living inside. In 1957, 6,000 whites attacked Black picnickers in Calumet Park on the Southeast Side. Through the late 1950s, vigilantes threatened and fire bombed a small group of Black families living in the Trumbull Park Homes, a public housing development that had become "accidentally" integrated when a light-skinned Black family moved in.[10]

Still, the burgeoning size of the Black population meant Blacks had to move somewhere. Hemmed in by violence and homeowners who refused to sell to them, they followed the path of least resistance. That path in Chicago—as in New York, Boston, and dozens of other cities—was to move into Jewish neighborhoods.

Unlike the Italians and Slavs of Chicago's Trumbull Park or the Irish-Americans of South Boston, Jews did not fire bomb houses or chase Blacks down the street when they moved into "their" previously all-white neighborhood. When Blacks moved into Jewish areas, the Jews simply moved out. Often this was made easier by the fact that the Jewish areas were relatively poor and the more successful immigrants wanted to move away anyway. But it was also true that, all things being equal, many Jews would have preferred not to have moved. Their ties to the old neighborhood remained strong. The other side of Black complaints about Jewish landlords and store owners was that the Jews had been in the neighborhood first and had been unwilling—or, as the area deteriorated, unable—to sell all their property.

The move of Blacks into Jewish neighborhoods was often hastened by the white power structure in cities that excluded or restricted the influence of Blacks and Jews. In Boston, banks and the city established a special loan program, known as "B-BURG" which granted low cost mortgages to Blacks—only if they bought in the Jewish neighborhood of Mattapan. Under pressure from King, Chicago's business leaders and Mayor Richard Daley agreed to set up a "summit conference" that would push open housing throughout Chicago. Invited to attend one of the meetings in 1967, Rabbi Robert Marx, head of the Jewish Council on Urban Affairs, a liberal Jewish civil rights group, found that the business leaders—most of whom were neither Black nor Jewish—had chosen five neighborhoods to start integration. Three of them were Jewish neighborhoods. The Jewish areas, one of the businessmen told Marx, would be "easier to integrate." Marx left the meeting convinced that Jewish neighborhoods were being sacrificed to protect other institutions, including the Catholic Church, which had a great deal of property and schools in Chicago's stubbornly white enclaves.[11]

The large-scale movement of Blacks into once-Jewish neighborhoods was a phenomenon repeated across the country, and accounted for the fact that so many Black churches in Brooklyn, Hartford, and Cleveland hung painted signs reading "Mt. Hope Baptist Church" or "Mt. Zion A.M.E. Church" over the entrances of former synagogues. Many Blacks felt that Jews, despite their liberal rhetoric, had abandoned their neighborhoods as soon as Blacks began to move in. Stores closed. Crime rose. City services deteriorated. For Jews too poor or too old to move out of these neighborhoods, the disruption caused by the crime and violence that accompanied the change from working-class and middle-class white neighborhood to poor Black neighborhood was profound. Indeed, by the end of the 1960s there seemed not to be a Jewish family in America who did not have a grandmother or elderly aunt or friend trapped in a once Jewish, now Black neighborhood, hemmed in by fear of violence and crime. Blacks in these neighborhoods suffered under the same fears, of course. But by the late 1960s, the writings of Jewish intellectuals distancing Jews from the civil rights movement were being matched by an inchoate fear and anger gripping the mass of rank-and-file Jews, an anger which perversely mirrored the widespread support the civil rights movement had enjoyed among Jews just ten years before. The change in city neighborhoods had driven yet another wedge between Blacks and Jews.

II

By the 1970s America's cities had come to represent the very different way the American dream had worked for Blacks and Jews. America's cities had worked for Jews. They had arrived as immigrants, gone to public schools and colleges, lived in city neighborhoods, and climbed up the economic ladder of success through civil service jobs and jobs in the private sector. But cities had not worked for many Blacks. Increasingly many Blacks remained trapped in ghettos, unable to break through to prosperity. The downtown office towers that had beckoned Jewish immigrants seemed to mock Blacks. And when Jewish neo-conservative intellectuals began to examine the state of Black America in the 1970s and 1980s, they seemed to scold them for not taking advantage of cities the way the Jews had. "People have begun to think that New York's problems are not the kind that can be solved by spending money," Martin Peretz, a leading Jewish neo-conservative wrote in an editorial in his magazine *New Republic* following the 1977 Harlem riot in New York. "No city has been more generous in terms of the amount of money or the variety of programs it has offered to help the poor. None paid its civil servants better. None was more generous with its education system; New York City even opened its university to all residents. Thousands of lives may have been made better by this generosity, but there is no evidence that the sum total of poverty and violence was reduced, and those are the curses of New York."[12]

Many Blacks felt deceived. Their dreams lay shattered in cities; Jews, like most whites, increasingly seemed unwilling to help. The new hostility of many Jews to Blacks seemed epitomized by Mayor Edward Koch in New York, whose reign as mayor polarized the city and embittered Blacks. Though a veteran of Civil Rights protests in the 1960s and a longtime liberal, Koch moved more to the right as mayor and repeatedly jabbed at Black politicians he believed were anti-Semitic and hostile to Jews—declaring in 1988 that Jews would be "crazy" to vote for the Rev. Jesse Jackson in his presidential bid.

Despite this anger and bitterness Blacks and Jews were still able to work together in one important area in the 1980s: Urban politics. Throughout the 1980s Jews in cities were the only whites that consistently voted for Black candidates running for local office. Many of the new generation of Black politicians, like William Gray in Philadelphia, relied on Jews for contributions and support. Whites typically shied away from backing a Black candidate for mayor. Jews did not. Their support ranged from the 32 percent who voted for Wilson Goode, the first Black mayor of Philadelphia, to the 75 percent of Jews who backed Tom Bradley, the longtime Black mayor of Los Angeles.

The support of Jews as "swing voters" was crucial in cities where Blacks made up more than 40 percent of the population but less than a majority. In Chicago in 1983, Harold Washington had won 18 percent of the white vote but 33 percent of the Jewish vote—even though he was running against a Jewish opponent. Those Jewish votes, along with overwhelming support from Blacks, helped give Washington victory. In 1987, Washington had increased his Jewish support, and his margin of victory.

The importance of the Jewish vote was magnified by the willingness of Jewish Democratic contributors and fundraisers to support local Black candidates across the country. Jews were crucial in electing David Dinkins the first Black mayor of New York in 1989. By the late 1980s the power of the Black-Jewish coalition behind Bradley in Los Angeles was so strong that it scared most other contenders out of the race.

II

But the cooperation in politics could not hide the tensions that still simmered between Blacks and Jews. In 1991, for the first time, tensions between Blacks and Jews broke out into open violence in Crown Heights, in Brooklyn.[13]

For years, Blacks and Hasidic Jews had lived in uneasy proximity in Crown Heights. Crown Heights had once been a Jewish neighborhood. Like many Jewish neighborhoods, it had changed complexion in the 1950s and 1960s. Blacks had moved in, crime had increased, city services had deteriorated. Many Jews had left. But a group of Hasidic Jews, known as the Lubavitchers, considered it the center of their religious community and were determined to stay. This was not a neighborhood where Blacks and Jews mingled. The Hasidic Jews in Crown Heights were an insular, self-sustaining community that shut out anyone who was not part of their sect—Black or white, Jewish or Christian or Moslem. These were not Jews who had once marched with Martin Luther King, Jr. They were conservative and ultra-orthodox. They voted Republican, were pro-life, and set up anti-crime patrols that targeted Black residents. They focused their political energy on Israel, their own internal conflicts, and getting better services from the city of New York. Blacks were at first mystified by the Hasidic Jews, distinctive in their black coats, black hats, and side curls. Later many came to resent them. The Hasidic Jews were wealthier and competed with Blacks for scarce housing. Many Blacks believed the Hasidic Jews got better police protection and better city services than they did.

On a hot August night, a car bringing home the leader of the Hasidic sect ran a red light and struck a 7-year-old Black boy, Gavin Cato. An angry crowd of Blacks gathered. What happened next is disputed. An ambulance from a Jewish ambulance service arrived. Police directed the ambulance to take away the Jewish driver of the car who was surrounded by angry Blacks and was in danger. A minute later, a city ambulance arrived and took Cato to the hospital, where he died. Crowds of Blacks, enraged that the driver of the car was not immediately arrested and that the Jewish driver had been taken away by ambulance before Cato, surged through the streets. Three hours later, a group of Black teenagers descended upon Yankel Rosenbaum, a 29-year-old Hasidic Jewish scholar visiting from Australia. "Kill the Jew!" they shouted, and stabbed Rosenbaum to death. The Black teenager arrested for killing Rosenbaum, Lemerick Nelson, Jr., was later acquitted.

Four days of attacks and rioting followed. Blacks attacked Jewish buildings and stores, breaking windows, looting stores, and setting fire to cars. They threw stones at Jewish and white passers by. David Dinkins, the Black mayor of New York, hesitated to deploy vast numbers of police to stop the rioting. He and the city's Black police chief hoped the rioting could be contained and tempers calmed by restraining the police. Dinkins went to Crown Heights to appeal for calm.

Dinkins had been elected as a peacemaker; he was a politician used to finessing differences between groups and harnessing them into a political coalition. In Crown Heights, that strategy proved disastrous. The attacks against Jews continued for four days; Dinkins himself was unaware of the chaos enveloping Crown Heights. It was only when he was booed and jeered by angry Black residents when he visited the neighborhood that Dinkins realized the depth of the problem. Dinkins finally flooded Crown Heights with police and brought the rioting to a halt. But the damage had been done. Dinkins was seen as indecisive and out of touch with a riot in his own city. Jews dubbed the rioting the first American pogrom. Many Blacks saw it as an explosion over injustice and long simmering tensions. They said the Hasidic Jews, with their all-Jewish schools, their all-Jewish houses, and their Jewish patrols had created an American apartheid. When the police arrested 163 people to end the rioting, the *Amsterdam News*, New York's largest Black newspaper headlined, "Many Blacks, No Jews arrested."

Because New York was home to most prominent Black as well as Jewish organizations, as well as the media center of the country, news and pictures of the Crown Heights riot spread rapidly across the country, inflaming tensions between Blacks and Jews far from the streets of Brooklyn. Together with the resurgence of Louis Farrakhan and his attacks on Jews two years later, Crown Heights represented the nadir of Black-Jewish relations.

//

By the 1990s, Jews, like most whites, had moved to the suburbs. Their concerns were increasingly dominated by national issues such as affirmative action and the growing debate over "diversity" as well as by internal debates over intermarriage and the future of the American Jewish community. For most Blacks, certainly for most poor Blacks, the debate over Black-Jewish relations was a distant speck on the horizon. Their concerns were far more immediate: jobs, poverty, school, crime, drug abuse, the collapse of inner-city Black neighborhoods. Back in the 1960s it used to be said that of the five people a Black kid in Harlem meets in the course of the day, the schoolteacher, the social worker, the store owner, the landlord, and the cop, four were Jewish and one—the cop—was Irish. To a child growing up in Harlem, whose view of the world extended only as far as his neighborhood, it could indeed seem as if Jews controlled the world. That was no longer true. Koreans, Palestinians, and Blacks have taken the place of Jews in the ghettos. The cooperation and conflicts that occurred from the 1930s to the 1960s from Blacks and Jews rubbing up against each other—as landlord and tenant, storekeeper and shopper, schoolteacher and parent—no longer existed.

And yet, more broadly, cities remained the primary arena of Black-Jewish contact. Much of Jewish power and influence is tied to the health and future of cities—whether it is the financial and media center of New York, where Jews make up a significant proportion of idea-shapers and decision-makers, or the entertainment capital of Los Angeles. For Blacks, cities represent both their greatest successes—the rise of urban Black politicians and a growing Black middle class—and their greatest failure—the imploding, alienated Black underclass. Three decades have passed since Martin Luther King moved into a ghetto apartment in Chicago and brought the civil rights movement to America's cities. Struggle as they may, Blacks and Jews still remain caught in what King called an "inescapable web of mutuality."

Notes

1. The role of Jews in early reform movements and their transformation into opponents of discrimination is discussed in an essay by Oscar Handlin in Nathan Glazer, Joseph L. Blau, Herman D. Stein, Oscar and Mary F. Handlin, *The Characteristics of American Jews* (New York, 1965).

2. Hasia Diner, *In the Almost Promised Land* (Westport, CT, 1977), pp. 217–20.

3. Ibid; pp. 36–81. Diner cites extensive quotes from the *Forward*, including those cited here.

4. Mark Naison, *Communists in Harlem During the Depression* (Urbana, IL, 1983), pp. 321–27.

5. Roi Ottley, *New World A-Coming* (Boston, 1943), pp. 124–26.

6. Ibid., pp. 114–15.

7. See Jonathan Kaufman, *Broken Alliance*, rev. ed. (New York, 1988), p. 39.

8. "Negroes and Jews: The New Challenge to Pluralism," reprinted in Nathan Glazer, *Ethnic Dilemmas: 1964–1982* (Cambridge, MA, 1983), pp. 29–43.

9. The history of the Ocean Hill–Brownsville conflict is recounted in Jonathan Kaufman, *Broken Alliance: The Turbulent Times Between Blacks and Jews in America* (New York, 1994), pp. 127–64.

10. The growth and development of Chicago's ghettos are described in Arnold Hirsch, *Making the Second Ghetto: Race and Housing in Chicago, 1940–1960* (New York, 1983).

11. Kaufman, *Broken Alliance*, pp. 187–88.

12. "The Mugging of New York," *The New Republic*, July 30, 1977.

13. The story of the Crown Heights riot is recounted in Kaufman, *Broken Alliance*, pp. 286–89.

seven

LONG-DISTANCE RUNNERS
OF THE CIVIL RIGHTS MOVEMENT

The Contribution of Jews to the NAACP
and the National Urban League
in the Early Twentieth Century

NANCY J. WEISS

L ooking back in 1973 on a lifetime of close association with Jews in the
National Association for the Advancement of Colored People, Roy Wilkins,
the NAACP's executive secretary, reflected on the role that Jews had played
in the struggle for civil rights. "They are very quick...to aid the downtrodden,"
he said, "they're very keen, intellectually, in seeing their own plight mirrored in
somebody else's treatment, they're very generous in their giving to these causes."
While Wilkins was not arguing that Jews, of all sympathetic whites, had been
uniquely helpful, his appreciation for their contributions was unambiguous: "They
have supplied sympathy, understanding, intellectual achievement and skills, comprehension over and above the regular comprehension of similar groups...and,
most of all, they have never forgotten...what a hard time they had."[1]

In 1994, in the keynote address at the National Urban League's annual convention, the new president of the organization, Hugh P. Price, sounded a similar
theme. "Many whites of good will have accompanied us on our long journey for
racial, social and economic justice," he declared. "None has matched the Jewish
community as long-distance runners in the civil rights movement."[2]

This chapter explores the contribution of Jews to the NAACP and the
National Urban League from their founding in the Progressive Era to the eve of
the Second World War. It tells the story of a small number of individuals who
took up the struggle for racial equality well before it would be joined by the principal organizations for Jewish advancement. Influenced by religion and social concern, acting out of a combination of altruism and self-interest, they committed

their prestige, energy, and resources to the cause of racial advancement in the earliest decades of the modern movement for civil rights.[3]

The chapter begins by sketching the obstacles that stood in the way of cooperation between Blacks and Jews and turns next to the influences that brought them together. It focuses especially on the critical roles that Jews played in the governance and financing of both the NAACP and the National Urban League—and, in the case of the NAACP, on their impact in shaping the organization's legal efforts, perhaps the most significant accomplishments of the Association's early years.

I

That even a small number of Jews should have chosen to take up the cause of Blacks in the early twentieth century was by no means predetermined. Such an alliance had to overcome differences in outlook and experience that expressed themselves in tension, even outright prejudice, between the two groups. As white Americans, Jews shared to some degree in the racial attitudes and practices that undergirded the rigid institutionalization of segregation and discrimination in the era of Jim Crow. Like other whites in the border states and the Deep South, Jews participated in state campaigns to proscribe the rights and liberties of Blacks. In Maryland, for example, two prominent members of the Baltimore Jewish community who figured importantly in the successful effort to bar Blacks from the polls argued for disfranchisement as a means of protecting white society from "depraved negroes": "The race issue is not a political one," one of them explained, "but in this state is one of self-preservation. The white race must prevail over barbarism, and this can best be achieved by reducing the Negro vote to the utmost minimum in Maryland." When Jews expressed racist views, they were widely quoted in the Black press. A leader of B'nai B'rith in Philadelphia, for example, underscored what he considered to be the absurdity of comparing "the advanced stage of intellectual and moral development of the Jews in general with the limited progress that the masses of Negroes in America have made." He took pains, as well, to refute the notion that there was any similarity between the pogroms that Jews were suffering in Russia and the contemporaneous anti-Black riots and lynchings in the United States. While the pogroms involved innocent people and the complicity of the authorities, that was not true of violent acts against Blacks; "with rare exceptions," those "originate[d] in crimes committed by individual Negroes" and were directed against the perpetrators, and they were usually "resisted by the officers of the law."[4]

As Blacks and Jews rubbed up against each other in the cities of the border states and the North, racial prejudice manifested itself in numerous ways. The two groups encountered one another with increasing frequency as tenants and landlords, employees and employers, customers and shopkeepers, or simply as neighbors—all of those relationships fraught with tension and frustration.

Jewish-owned stores in the ghetto might sell to, but not employ, Blacks; outside the ghetto, such stores might refuse to allow Blacks to try on clothing or sit at lunch counters, or decline to serve Blacks at all. Jews who employed Blacks generally hired them in menial capacities at low wages. Jewish landlords charged Black tenants high rents for overcrowded, poorly maintained facilities, and Jews led or joined in efforts to contain Blacks in ghetto neighborhoods. There were numerous incidents of Jewish disparagement or harassment of Blacks; "Nigger" and "Schwartze" became commonly used epithets.[5]

If Jews were prejudiced against Blacks, the reverse was also true. The tensions showed up in a none-too-subtle strain of Black anti-Semitism. Richard Wright recalled of his boyhood in Arkansas that everyone in his neighborhood "hated Jews, not because they exploited us, but because we had been taught at home and in Sunday school that Jews were 'Christ killers'....To hold an attitude of antagonism or distrust toward Jews was bred in us from childhood; it was not merely racial prejudice, it was a part of our cultural heritage." Horace Mann Bond remembered a youthful encounter with the son of the Jewish grocer in his neighborhood in Atlanta: "Nigger, Nigger, Nigger, Nigger," the boy taunted; "You Christ-killer!" Bond retorted. The boy burst into tears, leaving Bond surprised and dismayed to realize that he had so easily embraced "one of the 'bad' words that I had been taught never, never, never to use."[6]

Booker T. Washington, who had made the mistake in print of calling Jews a race distinct from whites, sprinkled his speeches with references to Jews as exploitative storekeepers and usurious creditors until a trusted white adviser counseled him that such expressions would surely not help his efforts to raise funds for Tuskegee Institute among whites in the North. W. E. B. Du Bois, who traveled across the Atlantic in the summer of 1895, found two of the Jews he met aboard ship congenial, but the rest distasteful: "There is in them all that slyness that lack of straight-forward openheartedness which goes straight against me."[7] The first edition of Du Bois's classic book, *The Souls of Black Folk* (1903), described Jews as "heir[s] of the slave-baron," "shrewd and unscrupulous," given to "deception and flattery," "cajoling and lying."[8]

Langston Hughes voiced some of the complexity of the urban encounter of Blacks and Jews in his book of poems, *Fine Clothes to the Jew*:

> When hard luck overtakes you
> Nothin' for you to do.
> When hard luck overtakes you
> Nothin' for you to do.
> Gather up yo' fine clothes
> An' sell 'em to de Jew.

James Baldwin, growing up in Harlem, captured the tensions more sharply: "I remember meeting no Negro...in my family or out of it, who would really ever trust a Jew, and few who did not, indeed, exhibit for them the blackest contempt."9

//

For all of the pressures and prejudices that pulled Blacks and Jews apart, other influences led them to find common cause. Blacks saw Jews as models whom they would do well to emulate; Jews saw Blacks as fellow victims whose protection and advancement had some bearing on their own.

It was widely believed that Jews set an important example for Blacks in triumphing over adversity. Leading Black newspapers frequently admonished their readers, "Let Us Learn From the Jews." "Where everything else had been denied him—political rights, social standing, even the privilege of owning real estate— the Jew yet conquered," the *A.M.E. Church Review* observed admiringly. "Two things he could and did get—money and education." "The Israelite gives us our finest object lesson in the possibilities growing out of thrift and economy," the *Colored American* echoed. "The Jew has learned that money is taken by the world as a measure of worth. Can we not learn the same?"10

The most important Black leaders of the day, too, came to portray the Jewish experience as a template for their race. They saw obvious similarities between the lot of Jews and the struggle of Blacks for human dignity and political and economic advancement. Jews had come to the United States largely to escape persecution; drawing strength from race pride and group solidarity, they had overcome poverty and prejudice to climb the ladder of success. Booker T. Washington held Jews up as a "very bright and striking example": "The history of [the Jew's] struggles and persecutions and how he has risen in spite of them should be carefully studied by my people....The Negro has much to learn from the Jew." James Weldon Johnson called Jews "the example which we should set before us for solving our own problem." W. E. B. Du Bois urged Blacks to "look at [Jews] with admiration and emulate them."11

As for the natural affinity between Blacks and Jews, both groups recognized that, to some degree, they shared common ground. The Black minister Reverdy C. Ransom made the point plainly in an address at the Free Synagogue in New York in 1911: "Since the Negro and the Jew know what it is to suffer on account of race prejudice they should be the first to unite and take the leadership of humanity in working to establish the brotherhood of man." The Black newspaper, the *New York Age*, characterized Blacks and Jews as outcasts of mankind, fighting for their rights against a common enemy. The Black Socialist paper, *The Messenger*, drew the parallel this way: "Despised and oppressed through centuries, the Jews know what oppression means and consequently they have always been tender and sympathetic toward the Negroes who have been their companions in drinking the bitter dregs of race prejudice." Kelly Miller, the dean of Howard University, called Blacks and Jews "partners in distress."12

Jewish spokesmen made the same point. Addressing a meeting of the NAACP at his synagogue in Philadelphia in 1913, Rabbi Joseph Krauskopf said: "There is no people who can feel as deeply the purpose which has moved you to organize this body as can the Jew. There is no people who can understand its motives as well as we can understand them; and there is no people who can sympathize as deeply with you as we can." Speaking at the annual meeting of the NAACP in Town Hall in New York in 1923, Rabbi Stephen S. Wise articulated a similar case: "I come to you tonight as a Jew and a Jewish teacher because I know as few men have had cause to know how injustice hurts, how it kills and how long continued oppression may degrade."[13] The shared experience of oppression bred a special kinship, and that kinship, in turn, nurtured Jewish commitment to the struggle for racial advancement.

Generalizing about a Jewish commitment, however, obscures the key point. The early civil rights movement attracted a particular subset of the American Jewish community: German (or, in a very few cases, Austrian) Jews, predominantly immigrants or children of immigrants; adherents of Reform Judaism (or, in some cases, of its secular offshoot, the Society for Ethical Culture); men and women of means—chiefly bankers, lawyers, merchants, and philanthropists (along with a smaller number of educators, social workers, and rabbis, the majority of them independently wealthy)—who were active participants in the reform causes of their day; and city-dwellers, concentrated chiefly in New York. Their interest in racial justice was rooted in the complex interplay of religious belief, social concern, and pragmatic self-interest. The principal motivation was altruistic, the product of the nexus of Reform Judaism and social justice progressivism. But there was also an element of self-interest, the outgrowth of a pragmatic assessment that helping to improve the situation of Blacks could redound to the benefit of Jews.[14]

From Reform Judaism came the impulse to take up the fight for social justice. Judaism had always had an important ethical component; there was a longstanding tradition of social justice in Jewish culture. The distinctively American brand of Reform that took root in the United States in the second half of the nineteenth century modernized the religiosity of the traditional faith and intensified its emphasis on ethical commitment.[15] Rabbi Emil G. Hirsch of Congregation Sinai, the leading Reform temple in Chicago, called social justice the flower that grows on the "well rooted and well ordered stock" of religion. Stephen S. Wise, the rabbi who founded the Free Synagogue in New York, accounted for his commitment "to seek out ways in which I could be of service to those who suffered injustice" by explaining: "For me the supreme declaration of our Hebrew Bible was and remains: 'Justice, Justice shalt thou pursue'—whether it be easy or hard, whether it be justice to white or black, Jew or Christian."[16]

A small group of Jews carried the ethical component of Reform Judaism to such an extreme that they made it the centerpiece of a substitute faith. Their leader was Felix Adler, the son of Samuel Adler, the rabbi of the most prestigious

American Reform congregation, Temple Emanu-El in New York. Expected to succeed his father in the pulpit, the younger Adler traveled to Germany following his graduation from Columbia University to pursue advanced studies in preparation for the rabbinate. But his exposure there to modern science, Kantian philosophy, Biblical criticism, and the history of religions shook the foundations of his Jewish faith. No longer persuaded of the validity of a distinctive Jewish theology, rejecting theism as the very foundation of religion, he began to preach a universalist, humanitarian commitment to applied social ethics—to reconceptualize religion in terms of social reform. In 1876, Adler founded the Society for Ethical Culture in New York.[17] The Ethical Culture movement was grounded in a "passionate belief in the...power of the moral law and the duty to apply it to society, especially to the problems of industrialization, urbanization, and the working poor." It took as its motto "Not the creed, but the deed"; it was "dedicated to the inherent worth of each individual, to personal and communal ethical growth, and to the application of an ethical perspective to every social context." It taught its followers, in Adler's words, to look at "the man at the bottom" as "an object not primarily of pity, but rather of respect."[18]

The emphasis of Reform Judaism and Ethical Culture on social justice intersected directly with the preoccupations of early twentieth century progressive reform. The social justice movements of the Progressive Era strove, among other things, to improve the living and working conditions of the exploited and disadvantaged in urban America. Racial reform was one of those efforts. As we shall see, for Jews and Jewish-born adherents of Ethical Culture, involvement in the work of the NAACP and the National Urban League fitted within a web of diverse commitments to social betterment.

It fitted also within a framework of plain self-interest. Carving out a sphere of their own in finance and commerce, German Jews had prospered in the United States in the nineteenth century. The more prominent they became, however, the more they began to confront acts of anti-Semitic discrimination. With the migration to the United States in the late nineteenth and early twentieth centuries of large numbers of Eastern European Jews, nascent patterns of discrimination intensified. Jews now encountered significant restrictions in a variety of spheres, from hotels and social clubs to employment, housing, and education. While the analogy was not exact, there were suggestive parallels in the increasingly pervasive discrimination against Blacks in the same period. Violence yielded yet another disturbing commonality. Pogroms in Russia in 1903 and 1906 bore unmistakable similarities to the race riots in Atlanta in 1906, or Springfield, Illinois, in 1908, or East St. Louis, Illinois, in 1917. ("Kishinev and St. Louis," the *Jewish Daily Forward* noted, "—the same soil, the same people.") The resurgent Ku Klux Klan made Jews and Blacks common targets of race-based hatred. Perhaps most frightening of all was the Leo Frank case of 1913, which brought the spectre of American anti-Semitism into full public view. Frank, the young Jewish manager of a pencil factory in Atlanta, was convicted on the basis of the false testimony of a Black janitor of the rape and murder of a young white girl in his employ. Efforts to appeal the conviction failed repeatedly. In 1915, following the commutation of the sentence to life imprisonment, Frank was lynched by an angry white mob.[19]

It did not require much of a stretch to make the connection between religiously based and racially based prejudice and discrimination, nor to see that securing the rights of one group would redound to the advantage of the other. The *New York Age* captured the point precisely when it called for a close alliance between Blacks and Jews in the hope that "the latter in fighting for his own rights will in some degree fight for ours also." The advantage of the alliance worked the other way as well: in fighting for the rights of Blacks, Jews could not help but contribute to ensuring their own.[20]

Those compatible interests help to explain the motivations of the Jews who devoted their energies to the work of the NAACP. For those who involved themselves in the National Urban League, the connections were of a different kind. The work of the Urban League focused primarily on finding jobs and providing social services for Blacks who were new to the cities. It offered travelers' aid at docks and railroad stations, temporary shelters for migrant women, and information about low-cost housing; it sponsored big brother and big sister programs, boys' and girls' clubs, and recreational programs for children and adults; it counseled families new to the city on the most elementary matters of behavior, dress, sanitation, health, and homemaking. These were the same kinds of services that German Jews were providing for Eastern European Jews through immigrant aid societies and settlement houses.[21]

Not only was the social service work of the Urban League familiar to the Jews who funded and worked for those agencies, but it was powered by the same objective. The Urban League worked to socialize Black migrants from the South in the ways of the city, to mold their behavior in its own middle-class image. The instruction began at the most rudimentary level: "Use the toothbrush, the hairbrush and comb, and soap and water freely"; "DON'T carry on loud conversations or use vulgar or obscene language in street cars, streets, or in public places"; "Get a job, get there on time, be regular, master it, dignify it."[22] The rudiments of a well-ordered urban life—proper housekeeping, cleanliness, deportment, punctuality, efficiency, good citizenship—were precisely what German Jews were trying to teach Eastern European Jewish immigrants. Both efforts involved socializing people new to the cities, people whose alien ways threatened to disrupt the established social and economic order. Both were vehicles through which German Jews could seek to impose some control on the rapidly changing urban environment.

II

The participation of Jews in the NAACP and the National Urban League came chiefly in the areas of governance and financial support; in the case of the NAACP, as has been noted previously, Jews also played a major role in shaping its legal program. Exploring in some detail the involvement of Jews with the two agencies in each of these areas will illustrate the scope and significance of their contribution.

From the outset, a small number of Jews took part in the various governing committees of the NAACP. In the wake of the Springfield race riot of 1908, Henry Moskowitz, a social worker at the Madison Street Settlement in New York who was associated with the Ethical Culture movement, was one of five drafters of the "Call" to a conference in 1909 "to discuss means for securing political and civil equality for the Negro." Among the sixty signers of the "Call," four can be positively identified as Jews: Moskowitz, Lillian Wald, the founder of the Henry Street Settlement in New York, and two rabbis known for their outspoken commitment to social justice, Stephen Wise and Emil Hirsch. The Committee of Forty, the executive committee of the National Negro Committee, included six members who can be positively identified as Jews: Moskowitz; Wald; Wise; Jacob W. Mack, a shirt manufacturer in New York; Edwin R. A. Seligman, a professor of political economy at Columbia University; and Joseph Silverman, the rabbi holding Samuel Adler's former pulpit at Temple Emanu-El. Among the forty-five members of the NAACP's first general committee, seven can be positively identified as Jews: Mack; Moskowitz; Seligman; Wald; Wise; Rita Wallach Morgenthau, a social worker at the Henry Street Settlement; and Jacob H. Schiff, the banker and philanthropist who had become a great supporter of Tuskegee Institute. Of the thirty men and women elected to the Association's first board of directors, four can be positively identified as Jews: Silverman, Wald, Walter E. Sachs, a banker at Goldman, Sachs and Company, and Joel E. Spingarn.[23]

The case for Jewish influence in the NAACP comes not from disproportionate numbers, but from the critical roles played by particular individuals in the organization's early decades.[24] Surely the most influential in the agency's formative years was Joel Elias Spingarn, who would become the chairman of the NAACP board. The son of a Viennese immigrant who prospered in the wholesale tobacco business in New York, Spingarn earned a Ph.D. in comparative literature at Columbia University in 1899. He joined the Columbia faculty that year and rose to the chairmanship of the Department of Comparative Languages and Literature, but he resigned abruptly in 1911 in protest over the University's dismissal of a prominent faculty member without due process. Thereafter, Spingarn fashioned a life that combined literary pursuits with active engagement in political and social reform. The author of several volumes of poetry and literary criticism, he was one of the founders of the publishing house of Harcourt, Brace. He bought a country estate in Dutchess County, New York, and immersed himself in reform politics as the publisher of a local paper, a proponent of women's suffrage, and an active participant in the affairs of the Progressive Party. In the words of Langston Hughes, he was "a scholar steeped in the humanities" who "had the interest of all human beings at heart."[25]

The NAACP, among all of Spingarn's involvements in the 1910s, captured his attention and claimed the largest share of his efforts. He first became interested in the Association in 1910 when he read a newspaper account of the plight of Steve Greene, an illiterate Black tenant farmer in Crittenden County, Arkansas, who had killed his former employer and landlord in self-defense and escaped to Chicago. Greene fell into the hands of the police, who deprived him of food and drink for four days while they questioned him about the shooting. He was identified as the assailant by the nephew of the man he had shot, who boasted that a mob was waiting to burn him back in Arkansas.

The NAACP was working to block Greene's extradition and to raise funds for his legal defense, and Spingarn sent a check for $100. Years later, he reflected on what it was that had struck him about that case as distinct from many others. A man could never adequately explain, he said, "by what strange current of emotion he is moved...why one injustice appeals to him more than another, but I know that at that moment I said, 'I don't care what happens, Steve Green[e] will never be extradited to Arkansas.'"[26]

At the invitation of Oswald Garrison Villard, the grandson of the abolitionist William Lloyd Garrison and the editor of the *New York Evening Post*, Spingarn agreed, at year's end, to join the NAACP executive committee. By January 1914, he had succeeded Villard as chairman of the board.

Almost from the moment Spingarn signed on, he made the NAACP virtually a full-time job. He took on an array of tasks—fundraising, publicity, coordination and support of branches—that would, by the 1920s, become the responsibility of a salaried professional staff. At his own expense, beginning in 1913, he traveled the country for three years on a "New Abolition" speaking tour, making stops in more than twenty cities to solicit funds, recruit members, and publicize the NAACP's program. In 1914, he endowed an annual award, the Spingarn Medal, to be given by the NAACP to a Black man or woman of unusual distinction and achievement. As well, Spingarn took a strong hand in shaping the Association's earliest campaigns against residential segregation ordinances, Jim Crow transportation statutes, civil service segregation, and lynching.

When Spingarn went into the Army in World War I, he temporarily relinquished the chairmanship to Mary White Ovington, a social worker among Blacks and immigrants in New York whose commitment to the NAACP bore the stamp of her abolitionist heritage. In 1919, Ovington formally assumed the chairmanship, whereupon Spingarn became treasurer of the Association. In 1931, Spingarn was elected to the NAACP presidency to succeed Moorfield Storey, a prominent Boston lawyer and past president of the American Bar Association; in 1932, he again assumed the NAACP chairmanship as well. Continuing to shape the Association's financial policy, he exercised a close watch over the activities of the salaried executives, particularly the NAACP secretary, Walter White. He was much involved, as well, in mediating between White and Du Bois, then editor of

The Crisis, who ultimately left the Association in a conflict over the management and financing of the magazine and, more broadly, the basic philosophy and program of the organization.[27]

Spingarn handed the chairmanship over to the Black physician Louis T. Wright when his term ended in 1935 but continued as president until his death in 1939 (he was succeeded by his brother, Arthur B. Spingarn). The following year, Du Bois dedicated his autobiography, *Dusk of Dawn*, to Joel Spingarn's memory. "Scholar and Knight" was the way Du Bois described him—"one of those vivid, enthusiastic but clear-thinking idealists which from age to age the Jewish race has given the world."[28]

//

The NAACP's legal activities became the major vehicle through which Jews shaped the programmatic work of the Association. Beginning in 1913, Arthur Spingarn and his law partner, Charles H. Studin, both members of the NAACP board, took up the organization's legal work, which they handled, on a volunteer basis, from their office in Manhattan. Roy Wilkins later described Arthur Spingarn as "the Association's entire 'legal department' for virtually a quarter of a century."[29]

As chairman of the legal committee, Spingarn was responsible for overseeing the cases that provided the NAACP's earliest victories in the courts: *Guinn v. United States* (1915), in which the Supreme Court declared Oklahoma's "grandfather clause" unconstitutional, and *Buchanan v. Warley* (1917), in which the Court struck down a municipal residential segregation ordinance in Louisville, Kentucky. In the 1920s, the centrality of the legal committee work put Spingarn in a position "to play a more crucial role" in the ongoing business of the NAACP "than any other Board member, white or Black." Spingarn frequently attended staff meetings, and he was a trusted adviser to the NAACP secretary, James Weldon Johnson, and the assistant secretary, Walter White. With the salaried executive staff assuming more responsibility for the operations of the Association than they had in the 1910s, Spingarn coordinated the legal program with White, who served as the liaison between the staff and the board on legal matters. Spingarn "advised which cases should be selected"; White, working closely with him, "screened requests for legal aid, handled negotiations with local lawyers, and carried out much of the [legal] committee's routine business."[30]

The lawyers who served on the legal committee from the 1910s through the 1930s included a number of prominent Jews in addition to Spingarn: Morris L. Ernst, Felix Frankfurter, Arthur Garfield Hays, Louis Marshall, and James Marshall. Members of the committee advised on strategy, participated in the framing of briefs, and argued cases in the federal courts. The heavy reliance on prominent white attorneys was partly a matter of strategy, since the Association obviously benefited from the experience and connections they brought to the table. But it was also a matter of necessity, since most Black lawyers, hampered by segregation and discrimination, lacked the training, influence, and standing that the Association badly needed.[31]

The most prominent of the NAACP lawyers in the 1920s was surely Louis Marshall. A New Yorker of German Jewish descent, Marshall was widely respected for his distinction as a constitutional lawyer: he had built a highly successful legal practice, centered especially in corporate law, but ranging broadly to include the defense of minority rights; it was said that over the course of his career, he appeared more frequently in the United States Supreme Court than anyone, save government attorneys. A founder and longtime president of the American Jewish Committee, chairman of the board of the Jewish Theological Seminary, and president of Temple Emanu-El in New York City, he was distinguished, as well, for his leadership in Jewish communal affairs.[32]

The NAACP had been trying for four years to interest Marshall in its work (he would provide a "tower of strength," they thought) before he agreed in November 1923 to join the legal committee and the board. He was concerned about the increasingly repressive atmosphere of the 1920s: with the upsurge of lynching and threats of racial violence, Jews as well as Blacks were especially at risk. As he wrote in accepting the NAACP's invitation, with "the Ku Klux Klan...sowing the seeds of discord throughout the country, it is the duty of those who believe in the maintenance of America's best traditions to unite in counteracting that evil influence."[33]

The particular event that piqued Marshall's interest in the NAACP was its Supreme Court victory in 1923 in the Arkansas peonage case, *Moore v. Dempsey*. The case involved a group of Black sharecroppers in Phillips County, Arkansas, who were trying to organize a union to better their economic situation. Stirred by rumors that the Black farmers were planning to massacre whites and seize their property, whites fired into an organizing meeting, killing a number of the participants. Blacks returned the fire, and at least one of the assailants was killed. As news of the confrontation spread, armed mobs of whites fanned out across the countryside, hunting down Blacks and killing them on sight. By the time the violence subsided, more than 200 Blacks and a small number of whites had lost their lives. Seventy-nine Blacks were indicted on charges of murder and insurrection. In a hasty trial, conducted in the presence of an armed mob, twelve of the defendants were sentenced to death, and the remainder to prison terms ranging from twenty years to life. Moorfield Storey, arguing the case before the Supreme Court, persuaded the justices that the "mob spirit" in the Arkansas courtroom had made it impossible for the defendants to get a fair trial. That was the argument that Marshall had used unsuccessfully in 1915 in seeking to persuade the Supreme Court to overturn Leo Frank's conviction. Storey told the Court that its stance in the Frank case had been a mistake. Now Justice Oliver Wendell Holmes, who had dissented from the Frank decision, wrote the majority opinion. The Court's reversal struck Marshall as "a great achievement in constitutional law." He sent the

NAACP a check for $100 as a "thank-offering" along with a fulsome letter of con-
gratulations to Walter White: "The stone that the builders rejected" had become
the cornerstone of an important new guarantee of individual rights, he wrote;
"due process of law now means, not merely a right to be heard before a court, but
that it must be before a court that is not paralyzed by mob domination."[34]

Over the next half dozen years, Marshall threw himself into the Association's
legal work with such intensity that Kelly Miller later characterized him as "the
Attorney General for the N.A.A.C.P." Marshall took the leading role in the organization's battle against disfranchisement and residential segregation. He plotted
strategy, drafted briefs, and—in *Corrigan v. Buckley* (1926), a case involving the
legality of restrictive covenants, and in *Nixon v. Herndon* (1927), the first of a series
of cases involving the constitutionality of white primaries in Texas—presented
oral arguments in the Supreme Court. When Marshall died unexpectedly in 1929,
he was deeply involved in developing the brief for the second Texas primary case,
Nixon v. Condon (1932). "What fretted him most" when he fell ill, a close associate later recorded, "was that he had some work to do at home; that there was an
important case to be argued involving questions affecting the rights of the
Negroes." Marshall's son, James, took over as lead counsel in *Nixon v. Condon*, and
subsequently joined both the NAACP legal committee and the board.[35]

For Louis Marshall, doing battle for the legal rights of Black Americans was
part and parcel of a broader commitment to ensuring the civil liberties and rights
of all minorities. He took up the cause of Socialists and pacifists, Jews and
Catholics, Indians and Japanese-Americans, aliens and immigrants. He was animated by what one colleague described as "his passion for justice, his hatred of
wrong": "His tongue and his pen were ready in his defense of Jew or Gentile alike,
of white man or Negro, when he was called to champion their cause." But he was
also impelled by the knowledge that the rights of other minorities needed to be
secure if the rights of Jews were to be guaranteed.[36] The experience of belonging
to an oppressed minority helped to explain his commitment to racial advancement. Addressing the annual meeting of the NAACP in 1926, Marshall made the
connection explicitly: "I belong to an ancient race which has had even longer
experience of oppression than you have....We were subjected to indignities in
comparison with which to sit in a 'Jim Crow' car is to occupy a palace." At the
time of Marshall's death, Alfred Segal, the president of B'nai B'rith, wrote that
being a Jew was "no narrow identity to him; it had to do with all the duties at
the common altar. To be a Jew was to be a servant of mankind: to champion the
Negro against discrimination." In a memorial tribute, Marshall's close associate,
Cyrus Adler, commented along the same lines: "It may be, because he was a Jew
and was aware of the oppression to which minorities are subject, that he took up
the cause of the Negro."[37]

Marshall's death came, by coincidence, within months of Moorfield Storey's.
Walter White observed of their passing: "It is going to be almost impossible to
replace these two men who were our greatest legal assets as well as immensely

helpful through the prestige which each had." Their particular contributions as volunteers would never be replicated, not only because of their singular personal qualities and professional distinction, but because of the increasing prominence in the Association's legal work of an elite group of Black lawyers, culminating in the appointment in 1935 of the first salaried special counsel, Charles H. Houston, the dean of the Howard University Law School. (At the decade's end, Houston would be succeeded as special counsel by his most famous student, Thurgood Marshall.) For two decades thereafter, however, the Black lawyers would pursue a strategy influenced in significant measure by the work of a Rumanian Jew. Nathan Margold, a Harvard-trained lawyer who was a protege of Felix Frankfurter, had been retained by the NAACP in 1930 to frame a long-range plan for civil rights litigation (the money for the project had come from the Garland Fund, known formally as the American Fund for Public Service). The Margold Report (1931) laid out a strategy for a direct attack on "the practice of segregation, *as now provided for and administered*"—that is, for a litigation campaign designed to demonstrate that segregation, as practiced, was "accompanied irremediably by discrimination," and was therefore unconstitutional. The distinguished Black lawyer William H. Hastie later called the Margold Report "the Bible of the NAACP legal drive."[38]

While the legal arena was the principal vehicle for Jewish involvement in the NAACP's program in its early decades, Jews made contributions, as well, to its many political activities. Joel Spingarn and Henry Moskowitz joined with Jane Addams in 1912 in an unsuccessful effort to insert a civil rights plank, drafted by W. E. B. Du Bois, in the Progressive Party platform. Jacob Schiff and Stephen Wise lobbied President Wilson to change his policies concerning segregation in the federal civil service. Joel Spingarn, Lillian Wald, Jacob Schiff, Stephen Wise, and others joined in the protest against D. W. Griffith's film, *The Birth of a Nation*, because of its inflammatory, racist portrayal of Blacks. In the 1920s and 1930s, many Jews lent their efforts to the NAACP's campaign for anti-lynching legislation. Jews played a significant role, as well, in the NAACP's publicity campaign, writing articles and pamphlets, delivering lectures, and generally using their connections to bring the NAACP's message to the white professional, civic, and social circles in which they moved. In addition, the NAACP's first salaried director of publicity was a Jewish reporter for the *New York Evening Post*, Herbert J. Seligmann, who handled the Association's dealings with the press from 1919 through 1932.[39]

II

Finally, Jews played a significant role in providing financial support for the NAACP's work. As Hasia Diner has pointed out, "Jews were natural potential contributors for two reasons": many Jews in the early twentieth century had substantial resources, and the long tradition of Jewish philanthropy disposed them to be generous. (Roy Wilkins remarked years later, "Jewish people...have a tradition of giving to things in which they believe or wish to support....It's part of their religion....It's a social response and responsibility....It really has been a revelation, the way they believe in giving.") The result was important financial support for the NAACP from some of the wealthiest Jews of the day: Jacob Schiff and his son-in-law, Felix Warburg, both bankers at Kuhn, Loeb & Company; Julius Rosenwald, the Chicago philanthropist who was president of Sears, Roebuck; Samuel Fels, the soap manufacturer; and Herbert H. Lehman, a partner in the New York banking house, Lehman Brothers, who had retired from the family firm to make his career in politics.[40]

The contributions came, in part, because the Jews who were the most actively involved in the work of the NAACP used their connections to persuade other Jews to give as well. Arthur Spingarn was one such emissary; Louis Marshall was another. Judge Julian Mack, a Zionist leader who was a member of the NAACP branch in Chicago, regularly sent Association literature to Julius Rosenwald. Herbert Lehman solicited contributions from friends whom he thought might be "interested in the work of the association." James Weldon Johnson and Walter White turned to Spingarn, Marshall, Lehman, and Marshall's son-in-law, Jacob Billikopf, the director of the Federation of Jewish Charities of Philadelphia, for advice on the best approach to potential Jewish donors. "Here is the new draft of the letter to go to wealthy Jews," White wrote to Spingarn. "Will you read it and telephone me your opinion." Eager to make the case for the NAACP to a new partner at Lehman Brothers, White asked Lehman to make the introduction. Seeking a share for the NAACP of the estate of a Jew who had bequeathed $100,000 for charitable causes, White turned to Billikopf and James Marshall for help. Marshall agreed to approach the executors, and Billikopf advised him on strategy: "Play up the names of Father, Julius Rosenwald, and various other Jewish benefactors. The personal element may play a part in the equation."[41]

With the NAACP in desperate financial straits in the depths of the Depression, Jews played a significant role in keeping the organization going. As a membership organization that depended heavily on income from its branches, the Association was particularly vulnerable to the economic crisis. The year 1930 brought "one of the most acute financial situations it [had] ever encountered." Jacob Billikopf made the connection to William Rosenwald, a philanthropist who was the youngest son of Julius Rosenwald, who agreed to make a gift of $1,000 a year for three years if four other individuals would do the same. Herbert Lehman, Samuel Fels, Felix and Frieda Schiff Warburg, and Harold Guinzberg, the publisher of Viking Press, met Rosenwald's challenge; the only non-Jew to respond was Edsel Ford of the automobile family. Smaller pledges were made by a number of individuals, several of them Jewish. All told, the Rosenwald offer resulted in $26,250 in pledges over the three years, nearly half of the contributions received by the Association in that period.[42]

In 1933, with the NAACP's finances again in a "most dolorous" state, it was

Lehman who offered the challenge grant: he would make a gift of $1,000 a year for three years, provided that the Association could secure four other gifts of the same size. ("Among my many interests none has been more compelling than that of civil rights," he later reflected.) Lehman renewed the offer in 1936. Among other sources, the NAACP obtained the matching gifts from William Rosenwald, Samuel Fels, and the New York Foundation, where Lehman was a longtime trustee. Lehman's generosity made such an important difference to the Association's financial solvency in the difficult years of the 1930s that Roy Wilkins was prompted to write, "In a very real sense you were one of the saviours of this movement."[43]

III

The essential contribution of Jews to the work of the NAACP found important parallels in the major role that Jews played, principally in governance and finance, in sustaining the National Urban League. Whereas the contribution of Jews to the governance of the NAACP came chiefly through the work of individual officers, in the case of the National Urban League it came through the significant overrepresentation of Jews among the members of the national board. In the 1910s, of the twenty-eight white Urban League board members whose religious affiliations are known, six were Jews or Jewish-born members of Ethical Culture Societies: Felix Adler, then a professor of social and political ethics at Columbia University; Abraham Lefkowitz, a teacher and labor organizer in New York (and the sole Eastern European Jew in the group); and four members of two of the leading New York German Jewish banking families—Ella Sachs Plotz and her brother Paul J. Sachs, and Edwin R. A. Seligman and his brother George. In the 1920s, the number of Jews on the board grew to ten out of the twenty-eight whites whose religious affiliations are known. Adler, Lefkowitz, Ella Sachs Plotz, Paul Sachs, and George Seligman continued to serve, and the new members included another Sachs sibling, Arthur; Julius Rosenwald's wife, Augusta Nusbaum Rosenwald, and their daughter, Adele Rosenwald Levy, both of Chicago; Dorothy Straus, a New York lawyer; and Lucy Goldschmidt Moses, a New York philanthropist. In the 1930s, of the twenty-six white board members whose religious affiliations can be identified, seven were Jews: Lefkowitz; Levy; Moses; Arthur Sachs; Straus; Alice Naumburg Proskauer, a New Yorker active in civic and philanthropic affairs; and Joseph N. Ulman, a judge on the Supreme Bench of Baltimore.[44]

These men and women's support for racial reform stemmed from religious commitment, social conscience, personal ties, and family connections. Adler and Seligman provide cases in point. Both were German Jews by birth (Seligman's father, Joseph, the founder of the international banking house, J. & W. Seligman & Company, was widely regarded as the leading Jewish financier in New York); both came to embrace Ethical Culture (Seligman served as president of the Society for Ethical Culture from 1908 to 1921). Both brought their energies, connections, and resources to many of the most important economic and social reform movements of their time. A pioneer in the establishment of free kindergartens, manual training schools, and public health nursing, Adler worked for the reform of tenement houses and the eradication of vice in New York City, and served for many years as chairman of the National Child Labor Committee. Seligman worked on behalf of tenement house reform, the settlement house movement, reform of municipal government, and conservation. In 1912, he drafted the New York State platform for the Progressive Party. As well, both men had a personal reason for associating themselves with the Urban League, since George Edmund Haynes, the Black sociologist who was the co-founder of the agency, had been their student at Columbia.[45]

A handful of German Jewish families made the National Urban League a family project. Edwin Seligman's interest in the Urban League was reinforced by two of his brothers, Isaac Newton Seligman and Alfred Lincoln Seligman, both bankers, who had been among the founders of the Committee for Improving the Industrial Condition of Negroes in New York (1906), an agency that anticipated much of the work of the National Urban League and eventually became part of its nucleus. To supplement his own commitment to the Urban League, Edwin Seligman enlisted still other members of his family to work on behalf of the fledgling agency: another brother, George Washington Seligman, a lawyer and Ethical Culturist with a strong interest in educational efforts on behalf of Blacks, served on the board for the better part of the 1910s and 1920s; following George's death, his wife, Alice Benedict Wadsworth Seligman, who had established her own credentials in promoting the social welfare of Blacks through her work for the Sojourner Truth House in Harlem, replaced him on the Urban League board.[46]

Another of the great German Jewish banking families, the Sachses, also made the Urban League a family concern. The first to take a seat on the board was Paul J. Sachs, the grandson of Marcus Goldman and the oldest son of Samuel Sachs, the founders of the family banking firm of Goldman, Sachs & Company. After a decade as a partner at Goldman, Sachs, Paul Sachs joined the faculty at Harvard University, where he taught fine arts for more than thirty years. Serving with him on the Urban League board was his sister, Ella, who was also a member of the board at Fisk University. When Paul Sachs stepped down from the Urban League board, his brother Arthur, who would shortly retire from Goldman, Sachs to devote full time to philanthropy, took his seat.

In accounting for her commitment to the National Urban League, Ella Sachs Plotz explained that her "interest in the colored race" had been "early aroused" by her grandfather, Marcus Goldman. "A great admirer of Booker T. Washington," Goldman had often told her stories about incidents in Washington's life. On a trip to Tuskegee Institute in 1915 at the invitation of Julius Rosenwald, Ella Sachs met Ruth Standish Baldwin, co-founder with George Haynes of the Urban League. "Ever since then," she said, "I have worked heart and soul for the colored people to help create a better understanding between the white and black races."[47]

It was Paul Sachs who brought the National Urban League to the attention of his close friend Rosenwald, a German Jew who was in the process of becoming the most important individual benefactor of Blacks in the United States.[48] Privately, Rosenwald used to tell his family that his interest in Blacks stemmed from his childhood in Springfield, Illinois, where he was deeply affected by the spirit of the great emancipator, Abraham Lincoln. Publicly, he explained it this way: "Whether it is because I belong to a people who have known centuries of persecution, or whether it is because naturally I am inclined to sympathize with the oppressed, I have always felt keenly for the colored race." His "sympathies," he said, had "remained more or less dormant" until he read a biography of William H. Baldwin, the late husband of Ruth Standish Baldwin, who had been president of the Long Island Rail Road, chairman of the board of Tuskegee, and a close friend and trusted adviser of Booker T. Washington. Rosenwald was particularly impressed by Baldwin's contention that one of the major challenges of the day was finding the means for Blacks and whites to live together "with decency and forbearance." As Rosenwald observed, "Nothing will so test the sincerity of our religion, our moral obligation, or even our common self respect, as will the exigencies of this, which is among the greatest of all our problems." Rosenwald was impressed, too, when he read Washington's autobiography, *Up from Slavery*. The two first met in 1911 and quickly struck up a warm friendship. The next year, Rosenwald joined the board at Tuskegee, where he continued to serve until his death.[49]

Thanks in significant measure to Washington's influence, Rosenwald made Black education and social welfare his major philanthropic commitment. Through the Julius Rosenwald Fund, over a thirty-year period, he spent more than $20 million to build rural schoolhouses, train teachers, improve Black colleges and universities, develop health services for Blacks, advance race relations, and provide fellowships to enable talented Black students and scholars to complete their schooling and advance their careers. His purpose in these benefactions, he said, was to promote "better American citizenship"; uplifting Blacks, he felt, would benefit whites as well.[50]

In the 1910s, Rosenwald's annual gifts of $2,000 made him the National Urban League's second largest contributor. (John D. Rockefeller, Jr., who gave an average gift of $3,000, was the largest. Together, their gifts sometimes accounted for as much as a third of the League's annual budget.)[51] Along with the personal benefactions came a direct link to the management of the League's affairs in the 1920s, as Rosenwald's wife, Augusta Nusbaum Rosenwald, was elected to the board in 1920; following her death in 1929, their daughter, Adele Rosenwald Levy, took her seat.

While there is no evidence that Rosenwald used those ties explicitly to influence the direction of the Urban League, the presence on the board of close family members surely provided a means for communicating his views to the leadership of the organization, and it gave him an intimate perspective on the League's operations. In the late 1920s, however, as the Julius Rosenwald Fund took over Rosenwald's philanthropic activities, direct efforts were made to change the way the Urban League operated. The Fund tried to force the League to merge with the NAACP and to oust Eugene Kinckle Jones as executive secretary. It is not clear whether the Fund ignored, or considered and then set aside, the differences in philosophy and method that made the two organizations distinctive. As the new president of the Fund, Edwin R. Embree, explained, from the Fund's perspective, the proposed merger made good sense in terms of efficiency and economy; by combining forces, the NAACP and the Urban League would avoid duplication of effort, enhance their influence, and—not incidentally—save money.

There was also another motive for the merger, and that was the dislike for Jones on the part of Alfred K. Stern, Rosenwald's son-in-law, his administrative assistant at the Fund, and a member of the board of the Chicago Urban League. Stern put the case bluntly to Rosenwald in 1929 when he said that he and Embree were of the view that Jones was "incompetent" to run the organization. Beyond that, Stern—who had a reputation for being opinionated and for insisting that others defer to his ideas—found Jones to be personally uncongenial, possibly because he was unwilling to bend to Stern's bidding. The proposed merger would provide an excuse for replacing Jones; in Stern's plan, Will W. Alexander, a white southern liberal who was directing the Commission on Interracial Cooperation, would have headed the new organization, and Jones would have been relegated to the role of an assistant to Alexander, in charge of programs for improving the economic conditions of Blacks. Short of that, if the two organizations continued to operate separately, Stern believed that substantial reorganization was in order at the League; at the very least, Jones ought to be forced to retire, and the Chicago League (where the board had ignored a number of Stern's directives about policy) reorganized as well, with a new board and a new executive secretary.

Stern made no secret of the fact that there was a pricetag on the continuation of Rosenwald funding for the Urban League. But the League was unable—or unwilling—to bear the costs of acceding to his wishes. Recognizing the stakes, the Chicago League tried to meet some of Stern's criticisms, but the effort failed to appease him (the expansion of the League's industrial relations activities, for example, undertaken expressly in order to assuage Stern's concerns about the effectiveness of the agency's program, backfired when the League appointed as the department's new director a man Stern considered to be wrong for the job). At the national level, Jones further fueled Stern's displeasure by not removing the Chicago executive secretary. And both the National Urban League and the NAACP stood firm against the pressures for merger of the two organizations.

Stern's interventions raised a spectre that would continue, in various forms, to concern Black Americans as the civil rights struggle unfolded: Did Jewish support for the movement necessarily come at the cost of ownership and control?

There is little indication that other Jews were exerting (or seeking to exert) the kind of heavy-handed influence that was Stern's stock in trade. In Stern's case, however, the insistence on linking funding and control had significant consequences for the Urban League; preserving the organization's independence and integrity carried real costs. The Rosenwald Fund reduced and eventually withdrew its support of the National Urban League during the 1930s. As well, Stern resigned from the board of the Chicago Urban League and persuaded Rosenwald to withdraw his support. Stern also campaigned, albeit with little success, to get other foundations and businesses to follow suit. The cumulative effect of these moves, coming on the eve of the depression, was to gravely threaten the Chicago affiliate's financial security.[52]

II

Other Jews, less intrusive than the Rosenwald Fund, played major roles in funding the National Urban League.[53] The League's rolls carried the names of the great German Jewish banking families of New York. Sachses, Schiffs, Seligmans, and Warburgs were steady donors from the time of the League's founding; in the 1920s, no fewer than ten Sachses and eight Seligmans made annual contributions, and Goldmans, Guggenheims, and Wertheims showed up as regular donors as well. Despite the great wealth of these families, some of their individual contributions were very small—$25, $50, $100, $250 a year. But Jewish donors held a disproportionate place among the handful of individuals who made the largest annual gifts. A thousand dollars was a major gift in the League's early decades—in a typical year in the 1920s, for example, there would be five or six individual donors who made gifts of that size, two or three of whom would be Jews. (In addition to Rosenwald, these donors included Samuel and Louise Goldman Sachs, who made substantial annual gifts after their daughter Ella's death in 1922, and Felix and Frieda Schiff Warburg, who became major donors beginning in 1927.) From time to time, too, Jews were the source of unusual, outsized benefactions.

It was the private foundations, however, that made the critical difference in the National Urban League's financial survival, and here, too, Jews played a major role. In the 1920s, the average annual income of the National Urban League was $55,100 (the range was roughly from $26,000 to $75,000). The Rockefellers provided the lion's share of the funding: throughout the decade, the Laura Spelman Rockefeller Memorial alone accounted for one-fifth to one-sixth of the League's annual income; for the period 1925–29, John D. Rockefeller, Jr., himself, together with the Memorial (or, beginning in 1929, its successor, the Spelman Fund of New York), accounted for more than one quarter. The National Urban League attracted only two other regular contributors of comparable size. One was the Carnegie Corporation of New York, which made annual grants of $8,000 for five years in the 1920s and in other years contributed upward of $2,500. The other was the Altman Foundation, established in 1913 by the German Jewish merchant and philanthropist Benjamin Altman, the owner of the New York department store, B. Altman & Company, to support charitable and educational institutions in New York. The Altman Foundation's annual contributions to the Urban League averaged $2,100 from 1920 through 1923 and $7,500 from 1924 through 1930.[54]

In the 1930s, the average annual income of the National Urban League was $66,325 (the approximate range was from $56,000 to $92,000). Again, the Rockefellers were the principal donors. From 1932 to 1939, the Spelman Fund, John D. Rockefeller, Jr., himself, and the Davison Fund, which he created in 1934 to handle his personal contributions, accounted for 20 to 30 percent of the League's annual income. At the same time, two Jewish foundations—the New York Foundation and the Friedsam Foundation—emerged as the League's other leading funders.

Established in 1909 as a result of a bequest from Louis A. Heinsheimer (its capital would be significantly augmented in the 1920s through additional bequests from Lionel J. Salomon and Alfred M. Heinsheimer), the New York Foundation was one of the oldest philanthropic foundations in the United States. "Intergroup relations" was one of the areas in which it concentrated its efforts; in making grants, it looked for organizations "endeavoring not to alleviate the distress of the Negro, but to remedy the causes of this distress," and it considered the Urban League to be "a leading force in the field." The Foundation had close ties to the League. Its longtime president was Felix Warburg, a banker at Kuhn, Loeb & Company and a major force in Jewish philanthropy (he was the founding chairman of the Federation for the Support of Jewish Philanthropies in New York, the first chairman of the Joint Distribution Committee, and a founder of the United Jewish Appeal). Warburg was a substantial contributor to Tuskegee Institute (Booker T. Washington described him as "a nobleman by instinct; a big, broad, liberal, refined, warm-hearted man") and had been a founding member of the Committee for Improving the Industrial Condition of Negroes in New York. A financial supporter of the Urban League from its earliest years, he had become, by the late 1920s, one of its principal individual donors. The New York Foundation's longest-serving trustees included three other members of Warburg's family—his father-in-law, Jacob Schiff, his brother, Paul Warburg, and his brother-in-law, Mortimer Schiff—all bankers at Kuhn, Loeb, and all regular contributors to the Urban League. (Felix's son, Frederick Warburg, also a supporter of the League, joined the board of the Foundation after his father's death in 1937.) The New York Foundation supported the Urban League from the time of its founding; it was one of the most important donors to the National Urban League in the 1910s and to the New York Urban League in the 1920s. For the years 1932–39, the Foundation's annual gifts to the National Urban League averaged $6,800.[55]

Beginning in 1935, the Friedsam Foundation also entered the lists as one of the National Urban League's most substantial donors. The Foundation had been

established in 1932 with capital from the estate of Michael Friedsam, a philanthropist, art collector, and civic leader who had succeeded Benjamin Altman as
president of B. Altman & Company as well as the Altman Foundation. The
Friedsam Foundation made gifts to the Urban League of $10,000 in 1935, 1936,
and 1937—identical to those of the Spelman Fund, and the largest gifts received
by the organization. (In the same period, the Carnegie Corporation was making
contributions of $5,000 a year.) From 1935 through 1939, the Friedsam and New
York Foundations together accounted for more than 20 percent of the Urban
League's total income.[56]

The connections between Jewish leadership and financial support and the
well-being of the National Urban League also played themselves out on the local
level as individual Jews became mainstays of efforts to establish and sustain Urban
League affiliates. In Newark, when William M. Ashby, executive secretary of the
fledgling Negro Welfare League of New Jersey, set out to establish a home for the
young Black women who were flocking to the city in the great migration from
the rural South, he turned to Caroline Bamberger Fuld, the sister of the department store executive Louis Bamberger, who made a personal contribution and
helped him raise the balance of the money. At the same time, the League counted on "quite a substantial donation" from her husband, Felix Fuld (a partner with
Bamberger in the Newark department store, L. Bamberger & Company), to support its annual operations.[57]

In Pittsburgh, the May family, German Jews who had built up a substantial
drug store empire in the early part of the century, played the critical role. Walter
May, one of the Pittsburgh Urban League's founders, served both as the agency's
first president (1918–20) and as its "principal 'angel.'" His younger brother,
Edwin, served the League for fifteen years, both as president (1924–26) and as
"perennial treasurer."[58]

In Baltimore, Joseph N. Ulman, the judge on the Supreme Bench of
Baltimore who was president of the Hebrew Benevolent Society, served as the
Urban League's second president (1928–36). In White Plains, Max Meyer, a Jew-
turned-Ethical Culturist, held the Urban League presidency from the agency's
founding in 1919 until his death in 1952. His successor, Richard Maass, who
would subsequently serve as president of the American Jewish Committee, later
reflected on the mutually beneficial relationship between the Urban League and
the White Plains Jewish community: "There were a large number of Jews on the
board of the Urban League," he said. "Our problem was more to get WASPs,
white non-Jews on."[59]

II

The record of Jewish involvement in the NAACP and the National Urban League
in the early years of the twentieth century led many Blacks to characterize Jews
as their particular allies. W. E. B. Du Bois made the case in an understated fash-

ion when he told the *Jewish Daily Forward* that "the Negro race looks to Jews for sympathy and understanding." Other commentators took a more categorical view: "They have stood by us and have aided us when all other groups in America have turned their backs on us," the Black newspaper, the *Chicago Defender*, asserted. Or, as the *Messenger* expressed it, "The Jewish people have been fairer and squarer in their treatment of Negroes than any other people in the world."[60]

Statements like the latter, of course, oversimplified the record of white participation in the struggle for racial advancement. Of course there were many non-Jews who played critical roles. But there is no doubt that the contribution of Jews was unusual in its character and intensity. As we have seen, Jews loomed large in the governance and financial support of both the NAACP and the National Urban League, and in the development of the NAACP's legal program. In so doing, they helped importantly to shape and sustain the early twentieth-century movement for Black civil rights.

NOTES

1. Roy Wilkins interview, Aug. 21, 1973, pp. 26–27, American Jewish Committee's Oral History Collection, Jewish Division, New York Public Library.

2. Quoted in *New York Times*, July 24, 1994, p. 18.

3. In taking this approach, this essay confirms the hypothesis posited in John Bracey and August Meier, "Towards a Research Agenda on Blacks and Jews in United States History," *Journal of American Ethnic History*, XII (Spring 1993), 65–66. The principal published accounts thus far are Hasia R. Diner, *In the Almost Promised Land: American Jews and Blacks, 1915–1935* (Westport, CT, 1977), and David Levering Lewis, "Parallels and Divergences: Assimilationist Strategies of Afro-American and Jewish Elites from 1910 to the Early 1930s," *Journal of American History*, LXXI (Dec. 1984), 543–64. For a particularly thoughtful brief summary, see Murray Friedman, "Civil Rights," in Jack Fischel and Sanford Pinsker, eds., *Jewish-American History and Culture: An Encyclopedia* (New York, 1992), pp. 87–91.

4. *Baltimore Sun*, Oct. 18, 22, 1903, and Solomon Cohen letter to *The Public*, Aug. 22, 1903, quoted in Philip S. Foner, "Black-Jewish Relations in the Opening Years of the Twentieth Century," *Phylon*, XXXVI (Winter 1975), 365 and 363–64, respectively.

5. See, among other sources, Robert G. Weisbord and Arthur Stein, *Bittersweet Encounter: The Afro-American and the American Jew* (Westport, CT, 1970), pp. 34–35, 43–44; Seth M. Scheiner, *Negro Mecca: A History of the Negro in New York City, 1865–1920* (New York, 1965), p. 133.

6. Richard Wright, *Black Boy: A Record of Childhood and Youth* (New York, 1945), pp. 53–54; Horace Mann Bond, "Negro Attitudes toward Jews," *Jewish Social Studies*, XXVII (Jan. 1965), 3–4.

7. Louis R. Harlan, "Booker T. Washington's Discovery of Jews," in J. Morgan Kousser and James M. McPherson, eds., *Region, Race, and Reconstruction: Essays in Honor of C. Vann Woodward* (New York, 1982), pp. 267–69; Du Bois quoted in Francis L. Broderick, *W. E. B. Du Bois: Negro Leader in a Time of Crisis* (Stanford, 1959), pp. 26–27, n.

8. Resisting at first the suggestion of some prominent Jews that such statements were offensive, Du Bois finally reconsidered and revised the passages at issue in the Jubilee Edition of the book. See Herbert Aptheker, "*The Souls of Black Folk*: A Comparison of the 1903 and 1952 Editions," *Negro History Bulletin*, XXXIV (Jan. 1971), 15–17.

9. Langston Hughes, "Hard Luck," *Fine Clothes to the Jew* (New York, 1929), p. 18; James Baldwin, "The Harlem Ghetto: Winter 1948," *Commentary*, V (Feb. 1948), 169.

10. *Christian Recorder*, Sept. 1, 1899, *Washington Bee*, Aug. 11, 1899, *New York Age*, Feb. 8, 1899; *A. M. E. Church Review*, IX (1892–1893), 8; *Colored American*, Apr. 22, 1899, all quoted in Foner, "Black-Jewish Relations," pp. 360–61. See also Scheiner, *Negro Mecca*, pp. 132–33.

11. Booker T. Washington, *The Future of the American Negro* (1899), and manuscript of an article, "Race Prejudice in Europe," Dec. 5, 1911, in Louis R. Harlan and Raymond W. Smock, eds., *The Booker T. Washington Papers*, vol. V (Urbana, 1976), p. 369, and vol. XI (Urbana, 1981), p. 397, respectively; James Weldon Johnson, "Prejudice Minus Discrimination," *New York Age*, Jan. 28, 1915 (on the same theme, see also Johnson's columns of Feb. 3, 1916, and Feb. 2, 1918); [W. E. B. Du Bois,] "Organization," *Crisis*, IX (Mar. 1915), 235, in Herbert Aptheker, ed., *Selections from THE CRISIS*, vol. I, *1911–25* (Millwood, NY, 1983), p. 91.

12. *New York Age*, Feb. 16, 1911 (Ransom), May 7, 1914; *Messenger*, I (Nov. 1917), 18; *New York Amsterdam News*, Apr. 16, 1930 (Miller), all quoted in Steven Bloom, "Interactions between Blacks and Jews in New York City, 1900–1930, as Reflected in the Black Press" (Ph.D. dissertation, New York University, 1973), pp. 75, 84, 230, and 229, respectively.

13. Krauskopf in *Crisis*, VI (June 1913), 86; *Chicago Defender*, Jan. 13, 1923, both quoted in Bloom, "Interactions between Blacks and Jews," pp. 230, 290. Wise spoke about the commonality between Blacks and Jews in his address to the NAACP's annual meeting in 1934: "You, too, have been wronged. You, too, have been deeply wounded....Even as we shall survive Hitlerism in Germany and in other lands so you will survive the trials and the injustices and the abysmal wrongs of which you are the victims." Rabbi Stephen S. Wise, "Parallel Between Hitlerism and the Persecution of Negroes in America," *Crisis*, XLI (May 1934), 128–29.

14. For a different interpretation—that German-Jewish and Afro-American elites, sharing "an ideology of extreme cultural assimilationism," chose in self-defense

against "threats to their hegemony" to engage in "overt and covert mutual assistance" to advance their interests—see Lewis, "Parallels and Divergences," pp. 543–44ff.

15. On Reform Judaism, see Nathan Glazer, *American Judaism* (2nd ed., Chicago, 1972), p. 48; Michael A. Meyer, *Response to Modernity: A History of the Reform Movement in Judaism* (New York, 1988), chs. 6, 7; Leonard Dinnerstein, *Antisemitism in America* (New York, 1994), pp. 208–209.

16. Leonard J. Mervis, "The Social Justice Movement and the American Reform Rabbi," *American Jewish Archives*, VII (June 1955), 202 (Hirsch quote); Stephen Wise, *Challenging Years: The Autobiography of Stephen Wise* (New York, 1949), p. 110.

17. Benny Kraut, *From Reform Judaism to Ethical Culture: The Religious Evolution of Felix Adler* (Cincinnati, 1979), chs. 1, 2; Howard B. Radest, *Toward Common Ground: The Story of the Ethical Societies in the United States* (New York, 1969), chs. 1, 2. While Jews dominated the early boards of the New York Society and comprised the large majority of Adler's audiences, a number of his principal associates in the leadership of the Ethical Culture movement were not Jewish. Kraut, *Reform Judaism*, pp. 110, 125–26, 185.

18. Benny Kraut, "Felix Adler," and "Ethical Culture," in Mircea Eliade, ed., *The Encyclopedia of Religion* (New York, 1987), I, 30 ("inherent worth"), and V, 171–72 ("passionate belief"; "Not the creed"); Felix Adler, *The Ethical Society: What It Means* (n.d., probably 1917 or 1918), Survey Associates Papers, Folder 340, Social Welfare History Archives Center, University of Minnesota ("man at the bottom").

19. John Higham, *Send These to Me: Jews and Other Immigrants in Urban America* (New York, 1975), pp. 138–73; Dinnerstein, *Antisemitism in America*, pp. 181–84; *Jewish Daily Forward*, July 1917, quoted in Diner, *In the Almost Promised Land*, p. 75.

20. *New York Age*, June 22, 1916, quoted in Bloom, "Interactions between Blacks and Jews," p. 78. Hasia Diner argues that civil rights provided a cover or an outlet for Jews who were at once anxious about American anti-Semitism and eager to secure their status; it enabled them to express indirectly the frustrations they felt with American society, and, at the same time, by showing how very American they had become, to "prove their worth to their Gentile neighbors." *In the Almost Promised Land*, esp. pp. xv–xvi, 237.

21. Among the immigrant aid societies, the Association for the Protection of Jewish Immigrants, the Hebrew Immigrant Aid Society, and the Baron de Hirsch Fund provided important models; among settlement houses, that was true especially of the Henry Street Settlement and the Educational Alliance. On the relationship of German and Eastern European Jews in New York, see Moses Rischin, *The Promised City: New York's Jews, 1870–1914* (Cambridge, MA, 1962), chs. 6, 10.

22. The first and third admonitions come from Urban League of the St. Louis Provident Association, *A New Day* (n.d.), Social Welfare History Archives Center,

University of Minnesota; the second comes from an untitled Detroit Urban League pamphlet, with heading "Helpful Hints" on the inside page, Detroit Urban League Papers, Box 18, Folder 12, Michigan Historical Collections of the University of Michigan.

23. Diner, *In the Almost Promised Land*, p. 122; Charles Flint Kellogg, *NAACP: A History of the National Association for the Advancement of Colored People*, vol. I: 1909–1920 (Baltimore, 1967), pp. 297–301, 305–306 ("Call" quoted on p. 297). The signers of the "Call" also included three non-Jews who played leading roles in the Ethical Culture movement: John Lovejoy Elliott, Anna Garlin Spencer, and William M. Salter. Radest, *Toward Common Ground*, p. 171.

24. Only four Jews have been positively identified among the members of the NAACP board in the 1920s, only five in the 1930s. The lists of board members are published in the annual reports of the organization.

25. B. Joyce Ross, *J. E. Spingarn and the Rise of the NAACP, 1911–1939* (New York, 1972), pp. 3–12; David Levering Lewis, *W. E. B. Du Bois: Biography of a Race, 1868–1919* (New York, 1993), ch. 17; Langston Hughes, *Fight for Freedom: The Story of the NAACP* (New York, 1962), p. 27.

26. Kellogg, *NAACP*, pp. 62–63; Spingarn quoted in Ross, *J. E. Spingarn*, p. 20.

27. Ross, *J. E. Spingarn, passim*; Kellogg, *NAACP, passim*.

28. W. E. B. Du Bois, *Dusk of Dawn: An Essay toward an Autobiography of a Race Concept* (New York, 1940; paperback ed., 1968), dedication and p. 255.

29. Mary White Ovington, *The Walls Came Tumbling Down* (New York, 1947), p. 109; Hughes, *Fight for Freedom*, p. 27; Roy Wilkins, "Jewish-Negro Relations: An Evaluation," *American Judaism*, XII (Spring 1963), 4.

30. Diner, *In the Almost Promised Land*, p. 129; Elliott Rudwick and August Meier, "The Rise of the Black Secretariat in the NAACP, 1909–35," in Meier and Rudwick, *Along the Color Line: Explorations in the Black Experience* (Urbana, 1976), pp. 113–14 (source of the quotes).

31. Diner, *In the Almost Promised Land*, p. 129; August Meier and Elliott Rudwick, "Attorneys Black and White: A Case Study of Race Relations within the NAACP," in Meier and Rudwick, *Along the Color Line*, p. 132.

32. Oscar Handlin, "Introduction," in Charles Reznikoff, ed., *Louis Marshall, Champion of Liberty: Selected Papers and Addresses* (Philadelphia, 1957), I, ix–xliii; *Dictionary of American Biography*, XII (New York, 1933), 326–28.

33. "Tower of strength" was Spingarn's phrase; see Meier and Rudwick, "Attorneys Black and White," p. 166, n. 55. The Marshall quote is from Louis Marshall to Moorfield Storey, Nov. 30, 1923, in Reznikoff, ed., *Louis Marshall, Champion of Liberty*, I, 426.

34. Walter White, *A Man Called White: The Autobiography of Walter White* (New York, 1948), pp. 47–53; Ovington, *The Walls Came Tumbling Down*, pp. 154–63; Kellogg, *NAACP*, pp. 242–45; Meier and Rudwick, "Attorneys Black and White," pp. 138–39; Louis Marshall to Walter White, Mar. 12, 1923, New York Foundation Archives, folder marked "NAACP— General, Prior to 1940," New York Foundation, New York City.

35. *New York Amsterdam News*, Apr. 16, 1930 (Miller), quoted in Bloom, "Interactions between Blacks and Jews," p. 284; Cyrus Adler, "Louis Marshall, A Biographical Sketch," in *Louis Marshall: A Biographical Sketch by Cyrus Adler and Memorial Addresses by Cyrus Adler, Irving Lehman, Horace Stern* (New York, 1931), p. 65. *Corrigan v. Buckley* involved "the validity of a restrictive covenant in an agreement between the owners of private property"; the Court "held that the inhibitions of the constitutional provisions invoked applied only to government action as distinguished from that of private individuals" (Reznikoff, ed., *Louis Marshall*, I, 465 n.). In 1948, in *Shelley v. Kraemer*, the Court embraced Marshall's argument that privately arranged restrictive covenants were not legally enforceable. (On Marshall's role in *Corrigan v. Buckley*, see his correspondence with James Weldon Johnson [Sept. 25, 1924], Moorfield Storey [Dec. 12, 1924, Sept. 24, 1925], and Senator William E. Borah [Apr. 19, 1926], in *ibid.*, pp. 459–65.) In *Nixon v. Herndon*, the Court accepted Marshall's argument that a state law barring Blacks from participating in Democratic Party primary elections in Texas violated the Fourteenth Amendment. (See Marshall's brief in *ibid.*, pp. 426–47.) In *Nixon v. Condon*, the Court invalidated a Texas law giving political parties the power to prescribe the qualifications of their members on the grounds that they were, in effect, acting as agents of the state. (On *Nixon v. Condon*, see Marshall's correspondence with William T. Andrews [Jan. 26, 1929] and Fred C. Knollenberg [Apr. 17, 1929], in *ibid.*, pp. 447–59, and James Marshall Oral History Memoir, Apr. 11, June 6, 1974, pp. 67, 151, American Jewish Committee's Oral History Collection, Jewish Division, New York Public Library.)

36. Irving Lehman memorial address, Nov. 10, 1929, in *Louis Marshall: A Biographical Sketch...and Memorial Addresses*, p. 93 (source of the quote); Morton Rosenstock, *Louis Marshall: Defender of Jewish Rights* (Detroit, 1965), pp. 28, 274; James Marshall Oral History Memoir, Apr. 11, 1974, pp. 69–70.

37. Marshall quoted in Diner, *In the Almost Promised Land*, pp. 151–52; Segal quoted in *ibid.*, p. 132; Adler, "Louis Marshall, A Biographical Sketch," pp. 20–21.

38. Meier and Rudwick, "Attorneys Black and White," p. 141 (White quote); Mark V. Tushnet, *The NAACP's Legal Strategy against Segregated Education, 1925–1950* (Chapel Hill, 1987), chs. 1–2 (Margold Report quoted on p. 28); Richard Kluger, *Simple Justice: The History of Brown v. Board of Education and Black America's Struggle for Equality* (New York, 1975), pp. 166–69, 232–33 (Hastie quote is on p. 169).

39. Diner, *In the Almost Promised Land*, pp. 133–42; Cyrus Adler, *Jacob H. Schiff:*

His Life and Letters (Garden City, NY, 1929), I, 315; Wise, *Challenging Years*, pp. 117, 172–73; Herbert H. Lehman to Walter White, Feb. 12, 1934, and White to Caroline Flexner, May 8, 1934, Herbert H. Lehman Papers, Special Files, Folder 931c, Rare Book and Manuscript Library, Columbia University; Mervis, "The Social Justice Movement and the American Reform Rabbi," pp. 194–95, 209.

40. Diner, *In the Almost Promised Land*, pp. 124–25; Roy Wilkins interview, June 4, 1957, p. 20, Herbert H. Lehman Oral History Project, Rare Book and Manuscript Library, Columbia University. See also the observation of Oswald Garrison Villard that Jews "responded more quickly, often more generously" in support of philanthropic causes: "I have never appealed to them for aid for the Negro, for the sick, the poor, the distressed, or for any philanthropy and been rebuffed." *Fighting Years: Memoirs of a Liberal Editor* (New York, 1939), p. 529.

41. Herbert H. Lehman to Walter White, Feb. 27 (Lehman quote), Mar. 17, 1939, Lehman Papers, Special Files, NAACP Folder (c. 30–38); White to Walter T. Brown, June 18, 1935; Lehman to John D. Hertz, June 21, 1935, both in *ibid.*, Folder 931c; Diner, *In the Almost Promised Land*, p. 126 (White and Billikopf quotes).

42. NAACP, *Twenty-First Annual Report, 1930*, pp. 55–56. The Association counted contributions separately from membership income. The sum of the contributions for the early 1930s was calculated from the relevant annual reports.

43. In the Lehman Papers, Special Files, see: Walter White to Caroline Flexner, Apr. 19, 1933 ("most dolorous"), Folder 931c; Herbert H. Lehman to Roy Wilkins, Jan. 2, 1959 ("more compelling"), and Wilkins to Lehman, May 29, 1962 ("saviours of the movement"), Folder 937. In the New York Foundation Archives, see: White to William F. Fuerst, Feb. 6, 1934; Application of the National Association for the Advancement of Colored People to the New York Foundation for Renewal of Grant of $1,000, May 14, 1936; Fuerst to White, May 18, 1933, Feb. 23, 1934, Apr. 18, 1935, May 21, 1936, Sept. 27, 1937, all in the NAACP folder; and White to Fuerst, Oct. 11, 1939, in the folder "NAACP—General, Prior to 1940." The New York Foundation had made more modest contributions to the NAACP in the years 1911–15 and again in 1920–23; see the annual financial statements, which are held at the Foundation's offices in New York City.

44. The rudiments of this analysis are laid out in Nancy J. Weiss, *The National Urban League, 1910–1940* (New York, 1974), pp. 52–54, 155. Even if all of the white Urban Leaguers whose religious affiliations have not been established (eight in the 1910s, eleven in the 1920s, twelve in the 1930s) were Christians, Jews would still have been significantly overrepresented: one sixth of white board members in the 1910s, one quarter in the 1920s, and almost one fifth in the 1930s.

45. On Adler, see *Dictionary of American Biography*, XXI (New York, 1944), 13–14, and Kraut, "Felix Adler," p. 29–30. On Seligman, see *Who's Who in America,*

VI (1910–11), 1712; *Dictionary of American Biography*, XXII (New York, 1958), 606–609.

46. *Who's Who in America*, VI (1910–11), 1712–13; *New York Times*, June 25, 1912, p. 1, June 28, 1912, p. 13; *National Cyclopaedia of American Biography*, XXX (New York, 1943), 264.

47. *Who Was Who in America*, IV (Chicago, 1968), 822; Arthur Sachs to Nancy J. Weiss, Sept. 28, Oct. 12, 1971; Ella Sachs Plotz quoted in "Who's Who in the Urban League Movement," *Urban League Bulletin* (May 1922), 8, Robert R. Moton Papers, National Urban League folder, Tuskegee Institute.

48. It was Sachs who took the lead in entreating Rosenwald to support the Urban League in its earliest years. See, for example, Paul J. Sachs to Julius Rosenwald, June 27, 1914, Julius Rosenwald Papers, Box 18, University of Chicago Library; Rosenwald to Sachs, June 30, 1914, *ibid.* (in which Rosenwald recalled "the verbal guarantee I made in your office in New York, 6/25/13, to pay 20%" of the League's annual budget for five years "when 100% of the budget has been guaranteed"); L. Hollingsworth Wood to George Edmund Haynes, George Edmund Haynes Papers, Erastus Milo Cravath Library, Fisk University; Sachs to Wood, May 22, 1915, L. Hollingsworth Wood Papers (at the time I used them, in the custody of Mrs. L. Hollingsworth Wood and Mr. and Mrs. James Wood, Mount Kisco, NY).

49. The story of the Lincoln influence comes from Rosenwald's grandson, Philip Stern, as recounted by Susan Willens, Aug. 20, 1994, Princeton, NJ. The published account comes from Pauline K. Angell, "Julius Rosenwald," *American Jewish Year Book*, XXXIV (Philadelphia, 1932), 160–61. Paul Sachs brought Baldwin's biography and Washington's autobiography to Rosenwald's attention. Peter M. Ascoli to Nancy Weiss Malkiel, Feb. 6, 1995.

50. Edwin R. Embree and Julia Waxman, *Investment in People: The Story of the Julius Rosenwald Fund* (New York, 1949), provides the most complete account of the Rosenwald philanthropies. The Rosenwald quote comes from an interview in the Chicago *Broad Ax*, Feb. 19, 1921.

51. In fiscal 1912, the League's annual budget was under $15,000; five years after, it had grown by roughly 60 percent. Rosenwald's annual contributions to the National Urban League are listed on an undated sheet marked "National Urban League," Rosenwald Papers, Box 75. In 1922, Rosenwald's gift was reduced to $1,500; for the remainder of the 1920s, it was usually $1,000. Rosenwald was the financial mainstay of the Chicago Urban League in its earliest years; see Arvarh E. Strickland, *History of the Chicago Urban League* (Urbana, 1966), pp. 32–34, 37–38, 74–78, 96–98.

52. A. Gilbert Belles, "The Julius Rosenwald Fund: Efforts in Race Relations, 1928–1948" (Ph.D. dissertation, Vanderbilt University, 1972), ch. 8; Raymond S.

Rubinow to Julius Rosenwald, Nov. 27, 1929, Rosenwald Papers, Box 75; Strickland, *History of the Chicago Urban League*, pp. 97–102, 105–106; Guichard Parris and Lester Brooks, *Blacks in the City: A History of the National Urban League* (Boston, 1971), pp. 202–203 ("incompetent").

53. The following account of Jewish financial support for the National Urban League is drawn, unless otherwise noted, from records of annual contributions to the League, which can be found in the following sources: for the 1910s, lists of contributors in the Wood Papers, the Haynes Papers, and the Rockefeller Family Archives, Record Group 2, Rockefeller Archive Center, Pocantico Hills, NY; for the period 1919–1931, the annual *Financial Statement and List of Contributors of the National Urban League*, printed pamphlets in the National Urban League Papers, Manuscript Division, Library of Congress; for the remainder of the 1930s, principally memoranda of meetings to discuss yearly requests for funding for the National Urban League in the Rockefeller Family Archives, as well as scattered correspondence in the Carnegie Corporation Archives, New York City.

54. On the Altman Foundation, see *Foundation Directory*, 3rd ed. (New York, 1967), p. 499. Another Jewish foundation, the Hofheimer Foundation, established in 1919 by Nathan Hofheimer "to improve the living conditions of unfortunate persons through research and publications and by the establishment of benevolent agencies" (*ibid.*, p. 594), occasionally provided smaller gifts—$1,500 in several years in the mid-1920s, $1,000 in several years in the mid-1930s.

55. New York Foundation, *Forty Year Report, 1909–1949* (New York, n.d.), pp. 5, 29, 50. Its contributions to the National and New York Urban Leagues are recorded in its annual financial statements. For the period 1935–39, the Foundation was also making substantial annual gifts (they averaged $2,000) to the New York Urban League. On Felix Warburg, see David Farrer, *The Warburgs: The Story of a Family* (New York, 1975), chs. 6, 9. The Booker T. Washington quote comes from a letter to Marcus M. Marks, May 24, 1904, in Harlan and Smock, eds., *The Booker T. Washington Papers*, vol. VII (Urbana, 1977), p. 512.

56. The Friedsam Foundation shared an office and a common set of officers with the Altman Foundation. It had a lifespan of twenty years. *American Foundations and Their Fields*, vol. IV (New York, 1939), pp. 39, 73; *New York Times*, Apr. 8, 1931, pp. 1, 16; telephone conversation with Karen L. Rosa, vice president and executive director, Altman Foundation, Dec. 12, 1994. A gift of $10,000 in the mid-1930s is equivalent to approximately $100,000 in mid-1990s purchasing power.

57. William M. Ashby, "Some Unimportant Incidents in the Life of an Unimportant Man Who is Eighty and Still Alive" (n.d.), pp. 92–93, 109, Free Public Library, Newark, NJ.

58. Arthur J. Edmunds, *Daybreakers: The Story of the Urban League of Pittsburgh, The First Sixty-Five Years* (Pittsburgh, 1983), pp. 44–45.

59. Baltimore Urban League, *Souvenir Program and Annual Report, Silver Anniversary Observance, February 12–22, 1950*, p. 5, courtesy of the Baltimore Urban League; Richard Maass interview, Dec. 10, 1980, Jan. 6, 1981, pp. 65, 68 (quote on p. 68), American Jewish Committee's Oral History Collection, Jewish Division, New York Public Library.

60. Du Bois quoted in Diner, *In the Almost Promised Land*, p. 71; *Chicago Defender*, Feb. 11, 1928, and *Messenger*, II (July 1919), 6, quoted in Bloom, "Interactions between Blacks and Jews," pp. 232 and 227, respectively.

eight

NEGOTIATING COALITION

Black and Jewish Civil Rights Agencies in the Twentieth Century

CHERYL GREENBERG

frican American and Jewish American communities have long sought to organize for their own advancement through a variety of institutions, from mass to elite, from nationalist to integrationist, from conservative to radical. During the middle-twentieth century agencies advocating liberalism, coalition building, and integration into the political, economic, and social mainstream have been the most prominent. Examining the relationships between these organizations in the Black and Jewish communities, therefore, offers a profitable approach to Black-Jewish relations during the period of the modern civil rights movement. Such a study avoids the dangers of generalizing from the actions of a few (the "but Goodman and Schwerner were Jewish" argument) and has the added advantage of allowing us to trace developments over time, as organizational decisions and tactics changed. Budgets and staff allocation reveal the priorities of these groups, and are thus invaluable in understanding the extent to which Black-Jewish collaboration went beyond rhetoric or good intentions. Furthermore, these agencies may in fact be the clearest representation of their communities that can be identified. Organizations that were economically supported by their community and claimed to speak for it constantly monitored their community's feelings because moving too far ahead or behind group sentiment spelled financial and political disaster. Tracing the positions and priorities of successful ethnic organizations not only reveals the level of commitment the organized community felt toward civil rights questions, but almost as reliably also uncovers broader community views.

Most prominent among the African American organizations in the early twentieth century were the National Association for the Advancement of Colored People (NAACP), National Urban League (NUL), and National Association of

Colored Women (NACW). Within two decades these were joined by the National Council of Negro Women (NCNW). Pressing them from the left were the National Negro Congress and A. Philip Randolph's Brotherhood of Sleeping Car Porters, along with several prominent African American Communists, while the Garvey movement and its Universal Negro Improvement Association embodied widespread nationalist sentiment that liberal organizations ignored at their peril. Local and religious organizations also competed for the allegiance of the community. Among Jews, the American Jewish Committee (AJC), American Jewish Congress (AJCongress), National Council of Jewish Women (NCJW), Anti-Defamation League of B'nai Brith (ADL), and later the Jewish Labor Committee (JLC) navigated a path within boundaries marked by Zionist nationalists, religious conservatives, and radical anti-religious, socialist, and communist groups. These Black and Jewish organizations, very different from one another but all dedicated to liberalism, pluralism, and integrationism, emerged as leaders in their communities by the 1940s, and were supported by a wider segment of their communities than groups of any other political position. It was these groups that made the deliberate choice to cooperate with agencies outside their own communities in order to further their goals. Although these cooperative networks became extensive, embracing a variety of ethnic, racial, religious, and political groups, for a variety of reasons the collaboration between organizations of Blacks and Jews moved ahead most swiftly and with most dramatic effect. Yet this relationship, often called an alliance because of the sustained and close nature of the contacts, was not without its tensions. These tensions were in many ways rooted in American society and culture, and they contributed to the dramatic decline in cooperation between the two communities by the late 1960s. Both the positive strengths of the Black-Jewish political relationship and its significant tensions are the subject of this chapter.

Although both Blacks and Jews had been in the United States from the earliest days of colonization, relations between them had never stood out in sharper distinction than with other groups. Religious parochialism and bigotry had strained relations between Jews and both white and Black Christians, while slavery and racism defined relations between all African Americans and whites of every religion. Thus Black-Jewish tensions existed only insofar as most Jews were white, and most African Americans were Christian. The low number of Jews living in the south, and the resulting infrequency of contact, also lessened the likelihood of a distinct relationship between them. Had Jews played a prominent part in either pro-slavery or anti-slavery activity, the case might have been different, but although individual Jews and local Jewish groups took positions on both sides of the debate and the Civil War, the organized Jewish community was too small (and often, too fearful of anti-Semitism) to be of much consequence.

All this changed with the Black migration north and the Eastern European Jewish migration to American urban centers. By the early twentieth century, a sizable northern and urban Black community, freer from constraints than their compatriots in the south, had begun the long struggle for the jobs, services, and opportunities so long denied them. They formed organizations to help in that struggle and to help acculturate the new migrants, and came increasingly in contact with immigrants, among them, Jews. Meanwhile anti-Semitism rose with the immigration of these Eastern European Jews: economic, educational, and social restrictions actually increased during this period. To cope with this threat, and to help the immigrants assimilate more quickly, the established Jewish community created its own defense organizations. The immigrants quickly responded by establishing groups of their own.

Although Black and Jewish civil rights organizations had similar agendas, they rarely worked together on a sustained basis in these early years, although individuals from the two communities certainly cooperated, and agencies did work together on specific occasions where the issues overlapped directly. For example, several prominent Jews joined the Call to found the NAACP. The ADL, formed after the persecution of Leo Frank, a Jew who was later lynched, involved itself in anti-lynching activities from the start. Nevertheless, there was virtually no sustained or structured contact or collaboration.

In part, the communities' mandates were different. Despite their shared concern with the consequences of bigotry, racism was far more virulent than anti-Semitism. Discrimination against Jews, while real and severe, was virtually never as physically dangerous, ubiquitous, or economically destructive as that routinely practiced against African Americans. Thus at the forefront for Black agencies were issues such as physical violence, exclusion from skilled and white-collar work, denial of political rights, and segregation. Jewish groups focused more on social discrimination, restrictions on employment and in higher education, and immigration quotas. In part, too, neither community enjoyed much wealth or power, and thus their organizations remained small and weak for several decades. It was barely possible to meet the most pressing needs of one's own community, much less to look beyond them and tackle broader and less immediate issues.

The two communities also enjoyed a different relationship with the dominant culture. Most Jews were white people, and although anti-Semitism was real, race was the deeper rift in American society. White ethnic groups have shifted from ethnic to white over time since most rewards and opportunities in America were apportioned not by ethnicity or religion but by race, and Jews were no exception to this pattern. Jews were no more eager to embrace the cause of a pariah people than any other white community. Further, most immigrant Jews had come from urban areas, and often had job skills unavailable to most Black rural agricultural workers. The combination of better skills and lesser discrimination brought most Jews more quickly out of the ranks of the poorest urbanites, and increased class differences between the two groups.

Nevertheless, a relationship did emerge between them. More Jews than virtually any other white immigrant group could be found among the left, and Jewish tradition had long stressed the obligation to help all the oppressed "because you were strangers in the land of Egypt." Slave Christianity relied far more on the Old Testament than traditional white Christianity had, and many Black Christians identified with the trials of the children of Israel because they viewed their own plight in similar terms. Both communities viewed themselves as victims of persecution, which helped foster a bond (often cultivated or promoted by their leadership) based on a sense of a shared oppression. Hasia Diner has documented a Jewish interest in and concern with the problems of African Americans from the earliest years of the twentieth century, and even nationalist Blacks like Marcus Garvey commented positively (on at least some occasions) on the example of community and commitment set by similarly persecuted Jews. Indeed, while anti-Semitism has always been present in the Black community, and Jews have held racist beliefs, every contemporary study has documented that Jews were less racist than other whites, and Blacks less anti-Semitic than other Christians.[1] Thus at least on the rhetorical level, a certain affinity between Blacks and Jews mitigated some of the violent tensions that marked relations between Blacks and many other white ethnic groups, or between Jews and some white Christians.

It also brought Blacks and Jews into closer proximity, which both improved relations and exacerbated tensions. Jews were less likely than their white Gentile neighbors to flee neighborhoods into which African Americans moved, and even after leaving, continued to maintain their stores and other services there. This expanded the possibilities for social interaction, but led as well to economic competition and Black complaints of Jewish exploitation. Many Jews entered social service fields and became social workers and teachers in Black areas, again the source of both mutual education and the resentments inherent in hierarchical power structures. Generally more leftist in their politics, and less tainted by American racist notions, Jewish-organized or dominated trade unions were more likely to recruit or accept African American members. Nevertheless, because of seniority, more Jews than Blacks could be found in these unions' leadership ranks, as Herbert Hill and others have documented.[2] Thus while Jews enjoyed the reputation of being less racist, they also entered more often into hierarchical economic relations with African Americans, sowing the seeds for resentment based on class.

Beyond rhetorical interest, or interest born of a sense of common suffering, however, most Blacks and Jews gave little thought to the plight of the other, reflected in the lack of contact or cooperation between their representative organizations. This began to change with the rise of German Fascism, and the impact of that political movement on the concerns of both communities. For Jews, of course, the dangers were obvious. Nazi ideology espoused anti-Semitism (and racism) and posed an immediate threat to the Jews of Germany and later of all Europe. Violence against Jews, economic, educational, and travel restrictions, and segregation followed in quick succession, with little sustained protest from other European nations or the U.S. Jewish organizations turned to the plight of their European coreligionists, and also began to pay close attention to the possible spread of Nazi or Fascist thought in the United States. To that end, they contacted every possible ally, including African American organizations, to help.

But African American agencies had their own reasons to become involved in the struggle against Fascism, beyond sympathy with the plight of another persecuted minority. Nazism revealed the vicious and dangerous implications of all forms of racism, and Black groups moved to exploit white America's expressed outrage against Nazi atrocities by drawing explicit parallels with race relations at home. While sincerely opposing anti-Jewish violence and Fascism generally, Black organizations quite overtly used the political situation to raise their own issues more dramatically in the public eye. After the U.S. State Department publicly invited 29 nations to provide havens for German refugees in March of 1938, Roy Wilkins of the NAACP urged Walter White "most strongly that the Association take note publicly in some fashion that will attract attention....I feel that this opening is a made-to-order one for us....The obvious thing to do is to dispatch a telegram to the State Department and the President, calling attention to the plight of the Negro in this country." That day, White cabled Secretary of State Cordell Hull.

AMERICAN NEGROES APPLAUD ACTION OF UNITED STATES GOVERN-
MENT...IN OFFERING HAVEN TO JEWISH POLITICAL REFUGEES...BUT WE
WOULD BE EVEN MORE ENTHUSIASTIC IF OUR GOVERNMENT COULD BE
EQUALLY INDIGNANT AT THE LYNCHING, BURNING ALIVE AND TOR-
TURE...OF AMERICAN CITIZENS BY AMERICAN MOBS...WHICH HAVE
SHAMED AMERICA...FOR A MUCH LONGER TIME THAN PERSECUTION
UNDER ADOLF HITLER.[3]

They used domestic issues similarly. When Walter White wrote President Roosevelt that he was "very much disturbed, as I know you are, at the spread of anti-Semitism in certain quarters in Washington," he explained that "My reason for writing you about this is that this ties in with an attempt by certain persons ...to tie in anti-Semitism with prejudice against Dr. Robert C. Weaver [U.S. Housing Authority]" to block appropriations for public housing serving African Americans. "Frankly, I don't know what the complete answer is to this tendency to express anti-Semitism and anti-Negro feeling with housing the victim except that I would urge that more Administrative support of housing instead of less would be the best answer."[4] For both Jews and Blacks, then, this earliest collaboration emerged primarily out of clear and explicit self-interest, albeit a self-interest that coincided with a broader moral stance.

Jews more than other whites recognized the danger of racism that Nazism raised. Even while spending most of their organized efforts on the immediate dangers of Nazism at home and abroad, Jewish organizations did begin to pay attention to the problems facing African Americans by the late 1930s. The NCJW added an anti-lynching plank to its platform in 1935, for example, and four years later the AJC joined the NAACP in meetings with Black and Jewish newspaper editors to explore tensions between the two communities, generally over employment and customer relations. The ADL lent strong support to the effort to integrate the armed forces, at least on a voluntary basis. Nevertheless, such cooperation was halting and at least some Jewish leaders were extremely reluctant to move toward closer ties with Black organizations. The AJC meetings, for example, came only after a great deal of pressure from Charles Houston and Walter White of the NAACP. Responding to complaints about allegedly anti-Semitic remarks made by a Chicago NAACP representative, Houston wrote to A. Ovrum Tapper, the ACLU's Chicago attorney,

> You can depend on my doing everything in my power to have my people see that anti-Semitism is Negro suicide.
> But I wish on your side you would try to show some of the wealthy Jews the fundamental identity between race persecution of minorities, regardless who. Walter White has been trying for some time to get an unpublicized conference of Jewish leaders and representative Negroes to discuss the whole question of Negro-Jewish relations, but he has been unable to get anywhere."

Jewish organizations focused on African Americans as much to scrutinize them for changes in the level of anti-Semitism as to challenge American racism. Jewish groups were far more reluctant to take on questions of Black civil rights directly, partly out of fear that their already tenuous position in America might be further jeopardized by any perceived alliance with an even more reviled group. As Philip Frankel of the ADL put it in 1943, "The difficulties facing the Jews, as a minority group, are sad enough without tying ourselves up with another minority group of less influence, and by so doing, probably taking on some of their troubles—a group whose difficulties, in my estimation, are even more deplorable than our own."[6]

Not only were Blacks similarly outcast in American political life, Black organizations occasionally embraced more confrontational tactics to further their goals. While Jews sought access to officials in power to convince them to intervene in the European conflict, and therefore took the most conciliatory and politic stance possible, Black groups recognized that their similarly conciliatory tactics during World War I had resulted in no benefits for them. Therefore when A. Philip Randolph proposed a mass March on Washington to insist on equitable opportunities for Black soldiers and workers during wartime, Black organizations signed on, while many Jewish groups read it as a sign of possibly subversive activity. Responding to a query about the possibility of working with Randolph, Paul Richman of the ADL warned Director Leonard Finder, "I wonder if you are aware that the Department of Justice is watching him closely for subversive activities in connection with his 'March on Washington' movement. He has been causing the

President…a great deal of anxiety with statements involving threat, bordering on sedition." Richard Gutstadt concurred. "The danger of our working with a man like Philip Randolph is that he is considered extremely left-wing….The violence of his recommendations…might conceivably affect our relations with some government bureaus because Randolph does not hesitate to whip the Negroes up to the adoption of methods calculated seriously to embarrass Washington."[7] Indeed, many Jewish organizations feared any aggressive tactics might slow the war effort. A 1942 ADL report warned of

> the dangers attendant on the current demands of the Negro leaders for an immediate solution of the social aspects of the Negro problems.
>
> …It is courting disaster for Jewish organizations and interests to be tied in intimately with Negro causes and leadership under present conditions. It is certain that the[se] demands of the Negro leadership will lead to violent resistance in the southern and border states, and that extreme bitterness will be engendered in both races. The disloyal attitudes of the Negro leadership and a large percentage of their followers might break into a national scandal at any moment. It is important that Jewish leadership…not allow sentimental considerations to prevent them from protecting the Jews of this country from an unnecessary and terrible stigma.[8]

Nevertheless, wartime brought ample opportunities for Blacks and Jews to continue collaborating on issues of mutual self-interest. One—ironically, given initial Jewish opposition—was the product of the threatened March on Washington: the signing of a Fair Employment Practices Act which prohibited discrimination in war industries on the basis of race or religion. Enforcing the Act, expanding it to all industries, and making it permanent brought Jewish and Black groups into frequent and productive contact. Although the dream of a permanent FEPC was never realized, the leaders of the Committee for a Permanent FEPC were an African American and a Jew, and both communities worked together to pass state and local Fair Employment laws.[9]

The race riots which spread throughout the country during the war years also brought Black and Jewish agencies together. In response to the violence or threat of violence, cities and states established "unity committees" and similar ad hoc structures to examine the state of race relations and ameliorate the worst of the problems. Jewish groups, concerned with racial violence, also saw the opportunity to promote a broader message of tolerance and anti-bigotry that would challenge anti-Semitism as it would racism, and participated along with African American and other groups in these unity committees all across the country. Some committees were pure window dressing, with only the power of rhetoric behind them, but others had quite a bit of power and made effective policy recommendations or legal changes.[10] In each instance, not only did Black and Jewish leaders have the opportunity to meet one another and work together, they also each educated themselves about the other community. They identified shared problems to be fought together, and came to appreciate a bit better each group's separate burdens. When mutual action proved effective, it encouraged further cooperation.

At the same time, because of wartime successes in organizing, general post-war prosperity, and broad repugnance toward fascism, these liberal, integrationist, pro-tolerance organizations grew in size and prestige, which in turn gave them more resources with which to pursue broader agendas. Thus the benefits of coop-eration and the means to cooperate more fully coincided in the post-war years and a Black and Jewish political partnership, often called an "alliance," was born. This alliance was never seamless, and full collaboration was never achieved—nor sought. Nevertheless, the number of programs and goals now shared by defense agencies in the two communities had multiplied, and the initial experience of cooperation had set the stage for continued and expanded collaboration.

These mutual efforts were still based in self-interest. What had changed was the broader definition in both communities of what self-interest entailed, and the recognition of the power of joint action. Nazi hatred of Jews and Gypsies had resulted in genocide, and the internment of west-coast Japanese in this country, including American citizens, demonstrated that Americans could not be relied upon to resist making similar racial generalizations (which of course lynching and Jim Crow had already shown). The backlash against such bigotry, and a recogni-tion of its potential perils, brought a new shift in social thinking to an embrace of pluralism. Ill-defined as it was in the public mind, pluralism called for the recognition of the contributions of racial, ethnic, and religious groups, and both a celebration of cultural differences and a deeper presumed unanimity of values and beliefs.[11] Often expressed as "tolerance" or "brotherhood," public commit-ment to pluralism was certainly more rhetorical than real, but it nevertheless brought the questions of anti-Semitism and racism to the fore, and cast them both in a new light. Now they were symptoms of the same broader evil, and the most effective way to oppose discrimination against one group was to couch it in argu-ments against all discrimination based on heritage. Every anti-racist tract and every piece of anti-discrimination legislation demanded toleration and equality for the holy trinity of "race, religion, and national origin." Thus for African American groups to cooperate in the struggle against anti-Semitism, for Jewish groups to support Black civil rights, or for both to fight bigotry against Asian or Mexican Americans (whose causes were increasingly joined in this period as well) was in fact to challenge restrictions on their own group.

The fight against restrictive housing covenants clearly demonstrates this iden-tity of interest. Both African Americans and Jewish Americans (as well as Asians and occasionally other white ethnics) were routinely barred from renting or buy-ing real estate in certain neighborhoods whose residents had signed a "restrictive covenant." Although the NAACP brought the cases to the Supreme Court *(Shelley v. Kraemer, Hodge v. Hurd,* and *Sipes v. McGhee)* that declared such covenants unenforceable, it came armed with advice and briefs from the ADL, AJC, Jewish War Veterans, AJCongress, and JLC, all of whom had fought restrictive housing covenants against Jews, and all of whom recognized the decision's direct benefit for their own constituency.[12] As Rabbi Berman of the AJCongress remarked, "I think the [AJ] Congress has made a great gain…in that we are helping the Jews…to understand that this is a common struggle and not something we are doing out of the graciousness of our hearts for Negroes."[13]

Similarly, lifting immigration and citizenship barriers was a joint effort for mutual benefit. Using a broad-brush opposition to discrimination enabled Jews to argue that existing laws unfairly excluded European Jewish refugees, Japanese to argue against Asian exclusion clauses, and African Americans to promote immigration from the Caribbean and Africa. The Leadership Conference on Civil Rights, Civil Liberties Clearing House, and other coalitions of progressive organizations within which Jewish and Black groups were well represented testified before Congressional committees on hundreds of bills protecting civil rights and civil liberties of all minorities, as did every major Black and Jewish organization. In fact, the chairman of the Leadership Conference, Walter White, was Black, and its secretary, Arnold Aronson, was Jewish. The AJCongress and NAACP jointly produced *Civil Rights in the United States: A Balance Sheet of Group Relations*, annual book-length assessments of civil rights advances and setbacks from 1948 to 1952, which focused primarily on racial and religious discrimination.[14]

Black and Jewish agencies cooperated on local and state issues as well. Again, broad anti-discrimination language ensured that both communities would benefit. Jewish groups, often joined by the local chapters of the NAACP, labored to convince employers to stop requesting applicants' race or religion on applications, and newspapers to stop accepting advertisements for jobs or resorts that mentioned racial or religious restrictions. They spearheaded the drive to end quotas and restrictions in New York colleges and professional schools, supported by Black groups that saw clear benefits for their own community. Black organizations obtained the aid of Jewish ones to open housing and employment opportunities, and to persuade newspapers to cease identifying Black criminals by race, and Catholic or Jewish ones by religion. All over the south both Black and Jewish groups fought for restrictions against the racist, anti-Semitic Ku Klux Klan, including anti-mask legislation, and monitored their activities.[15]

Violence also brought cooperation. In Peekskill a Paul Robeson concert provoked attacks against both Blacks and Jews by anti-Communist rioters, and the NAACP, NUL, ADL, AJC, NCJW and others joined in demands for investigation and action. Similarly, dynamite attacks in 1951 and '52 against Blacks and Jews in Miami and the desecration of synagogues and Black churches there, culminating in the bombing death of NAACP chapter president Henry Moore and his wife, brought both communities' organizations together in mutual defense. A housing riot on Peoria Street in Chicago protesting the arrival of Black tenants turned anti-Semitic as well because it was a Jewish family that had rented to them. The ADL, AJCongress, and the NAACP wrote investigative reports of this and similar disturbances, and collaborated on their responses.[16] Meier Steinbrink, President of the ADL, recognized the power of such cooperation in a 1949 fund-raising letter for the NAACP to be sent to potential Jewish donors.

> I want to cite three of the many achievements of the NAACP which make all Americans and particularly members of the Anti-Defamation League indebted to the NAACP.
>
> It was the NAACP which started the fight...against restrictive covenants which culminated in the Supreme Court victory in 1948. Our Anti-Defamation League filed a brief amicus curiae....
>
> And it was the NAACP which caused the United States Supreme Court to reverse its unfortunate decision in the Leo Frank case...in Moore vs. Dempsey....
>
> It was the Association which called the meeting on August 6, 1946 of 41 organizations of which the ADL was one out of which came the President's Committee on Civil Rights.[17]

Still, while this was mutual effort in the name of self-interest, most programs jointly undertaken in fact had a greater impact on one community or the other. Thus, for example, Jewish groups joined or spearheaded efforts to desegregate restaurants and beaches, from which they were rarely excluded, as well as country clubs and resorts which generally excluded both populations. African American organizations added their voices to efforts to resettle refugees, the bulk of whom were Jewish, and joined the battle against quotas in higher education which, though raised against both Blacks and Jews, affected Jews more since they constituted a larger proportion of the applicant pool. This represented a further development in the Black-Jewish political relationship; increasingly by the end of the 1940s, Black and Jewish groups joined in efforts primarily or exclusively benefiting the other. The definition of self-interest, which had expanded during wartime to include mutually overlapping concerns of discrimination, had expanded again. Taking their own words seriously, defense agencies argued that protecting the rights of one minority group protected the rights of all. As Isaac Toubin, Associate Director of the AJCongress, wrote in 1953:

> We must be concerned with safeguarding the democratic process as the best way to preserve our integrity and our identity as Jews. But democracy frequently ceases...at the boundaries of race, color and creed. It is not always the same race, color or creed that is subjected to abuse, but this abuse, no matter what its target, always poses the identical threat....The only really significant way to guarantee or protect or extend Jewish rights

is to round out democracy wherever it is imperfect....It involves fighting on dozens of fronts to establish and safeguard the rights of all groups in America wherever those rights are curtailed.[18]

African Americans spent a good amount of time and effort in support of Jewish causes such as immigration reform and, most important for Jewish organizations, support for the state of Israel. Walter White spent months convincing the Haitian and Liberian delegations to the UN to support the 1947 partition plan, to the delight of Jewish groups. "Please accept my personal thanks and those of the AJCongress for the magnificent job you did on the partition proposal," Will Maslow wrote to White. "It was indeed heartening to see how effectively you work. I am sure that Haiti's shift was the direct result of your efforts."[19]

Jewish organizations also spent much of their time furthering the cause of Black civil rights even when Jewish interests were not at stake. Sometimes new, temporary coalitions would form around particular issues, such as the Committee for Civil Rights in East Manhattan which sought to integrate restaurants near the new United Nations building. Other times, a national Jewish organization or its local affiliate would spearhead the campaign, in consultation with African American agencies. The AJCongress spent a decade in litigation against Stuyvesant Town in New York City which refused to accept Black tenants despite municipal aid and state and city anti-discrimination laws. For years the ADL fought the American Bowling Congress on the question of permitting the participation of Black bowlers. The major Jewish organizations filed supporting briefs in every significant civil rights case before the Supreme Court and most state courts, including *Brown v. Board of Education* and the Thompson restaurant case in Washington, D.C. brought by Mary Church Terrell and the Coordinating Committee for the Enforcement of D.C. Anti-Discrimination Laws.[20]

These examples of collaboration went far beyond direct or even indirect self-interest, as both communities moved toward a sense of the indissoluble nature of equality. Far more public on each other's issues than was any other ethnic, racial, or religious community as a whole, Black-Jewish cooperation brought tremendous power to the civil rights struggle.

Nevertheless, priorities certainly differed between the communities, and even between agencies within the same community, and not every cause of discrimination was taken up as avidly by one group as by another. Jews remained more fearful of direct confrontation, for example, and therefore almost unanimously opposed CORE's 1947 Journey of Reconciliation to integrate southern interstate transport. (The NAACP and NUL also kept their distance.) Most African American groups tempered their criticism of anti-Semitism with reminders of instances in which Jews exploited Blacks.[21]

Separate considerations often led to differences in approach as well. Faced with urgent needs and gross inequality, African American agencies focused on civil rights almost exclusively, and responded so slowly to requests for help on Jewish issues that the AJCongress, the most liberal and perhaps the staunchest Jewish advocate of Black civil rights, lamented in 1960:

> our organizational structure is completely committed to the elimination of all forms of prejudice....We adhere to this position even though corresponding Negro support of Jewish objectives...has not been extensive. Faced with problems far more severe than those of the Jewish community, Negro defense activities have been shaped far more by their own immediate and pressing problems than by general principles....If one views the situation in terms of striking a balance, there is a large Negro deficit.[22]

For their part, Jews, eager to be accepted among their white gentile neighbors, often hesitated to act in ways that might alienate them. Thus the AJC tempered its call to action against the Miami dynamiting spree with, "At the same time, there is a relationship of Jews to white Christians that needs to be maintained on friendly terms."[23] Deciding that its top priority, the promotion of tolerance as a broad virtue, could be disregarded in certain circumstances, the Institute for American Democracy, funded primarily by the ADL, produced two sets of "brotherhood" comics for children. In one, a scene of children included a Black boy. The other, for use in the south, depicted an entirely white crowd. As Walter White noted in a letter of protest, "It seems to me that if members of the ADL living in the south cannot stand up for the brotherhood of all human beings, including Negroes, there is little point spending money to print 'brotherhood' literature at all." In his reply, ADL's Ben Epstein admitted being

> as shocked as you were....The IAD, largely subsidized by the ADL, nevertheless operates somewhat independently and in this specific instance we are vigorously opposed to what was done....This does not at all detract from the fact that some materials will be more acceptable in the South than others.

ADL's Alex Miller noted that Black leaders expected that "Jews, as fellow objects of persecution, should be the first to rush to the aid of the Negroes." Unfortunately, he lamented, "This is...completely at variance with the behavior pattern of the Southern Jewish community which has clothed itself quite completely in the mores of the area."[24]

Great bitterness on both sides was reflected in the often strained relations between Black and Jewish leaders. Jews were, after all, white people, and on occasion responded to problems as whites rather than as Jews. This was particularly true when the issue was one of class, since race had a hand in helping Jews achieve middle-class status. When confronted with exploitative behavior by Jewish merchants, the ADL responded, "if it [discrimination] be common practice...then however regrettable the practice may be, it is hardly fair to pick only upon the Jew[s]." After all, another argued, if only Jews altered their policies, "it would affect their business." As the president of Morgan State University declared (referring to Baltimore), "I would say that...the Jews are white people with all the white people's psychology and prejudices when it comes to dealing with Negroes."[25]

While such differences of position could be found all over the country, they were most pronounced in the south, where Jews proclaimed their commitment to racial equality but also demanded that their representative organizations cease public efforts for integration. Rabbi Berman described white Jewish flight from Chicago neighborhoods in the late 1940s as Black families moved in, while a Brooklyn delegate to the 1956 AJCongress convention complained that "unfortunately, and it grieves me to say it, the Jews have failed to cooperate with us [AJCongress] on very basic issues of democracy."[26] Speaking of northern cities, the AJCongress warned in 1960 that

contact between Negroes and Jews occurs most frequently along a front peculiarly productive of friction [with Jews in positions of economic power in Black areas. There is also]...the clash between new Negro members of the middle class and their Jewish competitors....A [further] factor...is the practice of discrimination against Negroes by Jews....Genuine social acceptance [of Blacks] by Jews is at a minimum and generally we find the usual fear, panic and flight to the suburbs. In such situations Jews act, in the main, like other whites.

As Walter White warned Will Maslow, "We have got a lot to do within our own ranks, Will, and the time is quite short to do it."[27]

Other tensions ran still deeper. The differential success Jews enjoyed in achieving middle-class status left them more accepting of compromise, and less conscious of the limits of liberalism than many in the Black community. As the AJCongress presciently noted in 1960,

Negroes are re-evaluating their alliances....One of its results has been a mistrust of "liberals" in the struggle for civil rights. And we must recognize, for good or ill, that the Jews, more than any other group, are generally so identified....The willingness of Jewish and other groups to accept, on occasion, a partial victory (because of the danger that demanding too much will result in getting nothing) has caused resentment in Negro ranks. They often feel that this compromises their position and demonstrates a lack of understanding on our part.[28]

Furthermore, anti-Semitism had declined far more quickly than had racism, and what remained was primarily social and non-governmental. Racism, on the other hand, remained firmly rooted in the law and in economic practice. Thus Jewish groups concerned about continued bigotry did not look to the legal or court system for change, but rather spent increasing amounts of effort in public relations or propaganda work: encouraging materials that highlighted tolerance and diversity.[29] Although Jewish groups argued that these materials benefited African Americans as well, since the message was broadly construed, racism was in fact far less responsive to such techniques, and in any case the central problems of racism lay in the deep structures of society rather than solely in the minds of individuals. Institutional racism had to be tackled in very different ways. So long as these methods included court and legislative work, Jewish groups continued to support civil rights efforts, even though they had little impact on anti-Semitism. When tactics turned to more direct action, most Jewish groups balked. Street demonstrations and mass marches reminded many Jews of the demagogy and appeal to the mob of fascists like Hitler. Although Jews themselves had employed boycotts against German products during World War II, even boycotts now seemed dangerously anti-democratic.[30] The more radical of these civil rights efforts challenged the very notions of liberalism that had allowed Jews to achieve so much in America, and this also proved threatening.

Already suspicious of mass action, Jewish groups grew increasingly uneasy as the 1960s progressed, with SNCC's emerging criticism of the liberalism of Kennedy, the Democratic Party, and the establishment more generally; Martin Luther King, Jr.'s opposition to the Vietnam War and its implied criticism of the wisdom of the power structure; the general move toward nationalism in a Black community dispirited by white recalcitrance and liberal inaction; and a rising sense of anti-colonial sentiment that moved many Black groups to embrace the Palestinian cause. While Jewish youths were well represented in the ranks of activist civil rights organizations like SNCC, their parents in the AJC, ADL, or NCJW remained far more suspicious. When the civil rights movement moved north, into the neighborhoods of these liberal Jews, the question of integration took on a different tone. With concerns now couched in class rather than racial terms, Jews fled to suburbs almost as quickly as white Christians to avoid what they perceived as the deterioration of their schools and neighborhoods. They pointed to riots as evidence of civil rights agendas run amok.

Suddenly, it became clear, the most basic visions of the two communities conflicted. African Americans recognized that earlier trust in the courts, the legislature, or the goodwill of well-meaning whites was misplaced, or at best naive. Just laws could still be administered unjustly. One could not rely on white administrators and employers to suddenly see the error of their ways and accept Black people equally. Only concerted pressure compelled the changes wrought by the civil rights movement, and only continued pressure would move the process further. It was not enough to press white people into hiring Black workers: Black entrepreneurial activity and economic nationalism would provide an independent base from which to rise. Affirmative action, and numerical quotas to demonstrate its successful implementation, replaced attempts to convince employers or colleges to accept qualified candidates without regard to race, because that strategy had allowed racists to argue that only white candidates were qualified.

Jews, on the other hand, held tenaciously to the ideal of a race-blind society, and viewed nationalism and race-based solutions to the problem of inequality as a dangerous undermining of that ideal. Although economic nationalism had always played a part in Jewish life, Jews nonetheless saw their success as rooted in liberal notions of merit and fair play—exactly those categories under attack. Their pluralist vision had worked for them; despite the arguments of Black nationalists few Jews could see its underlying coercive assimilationism.

These fundamental disagreements came to a head in the first open break between Black and Jewish civil rights agencies, in the court cases over affirmative action. In *De Funis v. Odegaard* (1974) and *Regents of University of California v. Bakke* (1978), Jewish and Black groups lined up on opposite sides.[31] This conflict, shocking for its visibility and apparent suddenness, was actually the logical culmination of years of slow divergence of interest, vision, and priority. And much to the dismay of Jews on the left, these divisions grew rather than lessened over the next two decades. As more time passed, more Jews attained middle-class and even upper-class status, and anti-Semitism retreated into fewer strongholds more on the periphery of society, Jews as a group began moving rightward politically, and their organizations followed. Aided by the embrace of Israel by the right, and of Palestinians by the left, Jews in the 1980s continued to vote more liberally than their pocketbook interests might dictate, but less liberally than in the past. Jewish agencies turned their focus inward, toward support of Israel and Soviet Jews, and to challenge the growing rate of intermarriage which seemed to threaten Jewish continuity in the United States. Now living primarily in suburbs, Jews and their agencies paid less attention to the problems of poverty and urban life than before.

Meanwhile, the gap between Black and white incomes and life chances, which had begun to shrink in the 1960s, widened again. The backlash against civil rights resulted in a weakening of civil rights laws, greater educational segregation than ever, and a new racist rhetoric of "us" and "them" which cast African Americans outside the boundary of American society. Black organizations now faced very different problems than did their Jewish counterparts. A disgust with white society and liberalism's betrayals (embodied ironically by Jews since they represented such a large proportion of the liberals perceived as betraying them) and a growing interest in nationalism and internal unity have marked African American communities, both rich and poor, and have been reflected in the changing attitudes of Black defense organizations. At the same time, some nationalist rhetoric has been overtly anti-white and anti-Semitic, which has infuriated and pained Jews. Although most liberal Black leaders have repudiated such sentiments, they also insist on the importance of working with everyone in the Black community to tackle such intractable political and economic problems. It is hardly surprising, then, that as Jewish and Black interests and concerns diverged, their level of collaboration declined.

Nevertheless, cooperation did not cease. While Jewish groups moved rightward from where they had been, they remained on the liberal side of the political spectrum, particularly in regard to domestic policies and social issues. Thus large areas of overlapping interest remained. Black and Jewish groups worked together on aid to public education, anti-poverty, hunger and homelessness programs, abortion rights, and similar causes. Further, like Black organizations, Jewish groups continued to monitor all cases of bigotry and continued their tolerance work. The ADL, for example, long in the business of producing diversity programs, launched "A World of Difference" in 1985 to help schools, workplaces, and civic groups appreciate ethnic, racial, and religious diversity and work more effectively with those different from themselves. Like the NAACP, it also keeps watch on hate groups like skinheads, the Klan, and neo-Nazis. Collaboration on hate crimes brought passage of bias or hate-crime legislation in numerous states and cities across the country.

Compared to the earlier period, then, two things have changed. One is the makeup of the coalition on progressive issues. Once dominated by Jews and Blacks it is now far broader. Asian Americans, Latinos, gays and lesbians, a growing number of activist liberal church groups, some unions, and others perceiving themselves on the margins of society routinely join efforts to challenge inequality and poverty. Second, because of class and politics, organized Jewish interest in issues of central importance to this coalition is no longer as uniform or unambivalent. Thus while African American groups remain firmly within this coalition, Jewish agencies sometimes join and sometimes stand outside, and the Black-Jewish political relationship can no longer be characterized in any sense as an alliance.

Nevertheless, some sense of linkage remains, a remnant of earlier, productive collaboration and the shared sense of vulnerability and oppression that fostered that collaboration in the first place. That is why "Black-Jewish relations" still have far more resonance than do "Black-Italian relations" or "Jewish-Latino relations," and why the tensions and anger seem so bitter. On some level, both Blacks and Jews expect more from each other, and so feel betrayed by the apparently fundamental recent rifts. On the other hand, that sense of linkage suggests that the rift need not be permanent. If Jews and African Americans find a renewed mutuality of purpose, they already have a model for a productive relationship in their past collaboration, conducted despite overwhelming tensions and differences. And they may find that shared purpose. As our cities continue to deteriorate, their problems spill increasingly over into suburban areas. Expanding divisions between rich and poor threaten both productivity and security. If hatred and bigotry continue to express themselves not only in limited opportunities but in violence, one can only hope for a return to the recognition that the problems of one group are indeed the problems of us all.

Notes

1. Biblical injuctions: see, for example, Exodus 22:20 ("A stranger shall you not wrong; neither shall you oppress him, for you were strangers in the land of Egypt"), or Deuteronomy 10:19 ("Love you therefore the stranger for you were strangers in the land of Egypt"). Hasia Diner: *In the Almost Promised Land: American Jews and Blacks 1915–1935* (Wesport, CT, 1977). Garvey: Garvey modeled his struggle on Zionism and the Irish struggle for a free and independent Ireland. He even called his followers Zionists, according to E. David Cronon, *Black Moses: the Story of Marcus Garvey* (Madison, 1969), p. 199. References to Jews and Zionism (many of them negative) are scattered through his writing and his speeches. The best collections are Amy Jacques-Garvey, ed., *The Philosophy and Opinions of Marcus Garvey,* 2 vols (1923, 1925; repr. New York, 1968); Robert Hill et al., eds., *The Marcus Garvey and Universal Negro Improvement Association Papers*, 7 vols, (Berkeley, 1983–90). Also see Judith Stein, *The World of Marcus Garvey: Race and Class in Modern Society* (Baton Rouge, 1986). Opinion polls: see, for example, Eleanor Wolf, Vin Loving, Donald Marsh, "Negro-Jewish Relationships," Pamphlet, Wayne State Studies in Intergroup Conflicts in Detroit #1, 1944, p. 7, American Jewish Committee (AJC) Inactive Vertical File: "Negro Jewish Relations" (hereafter VF:NJR), AJC Library, New York, NY; Wolf, Loving, Marsh, "Some Aspects of Negro-Jewish Relationships in Detroit, Michigan," Part I, 1943 (funded by the Jewish Community Council and NAACP), Anti-Defamation League (ADL) microfilm: "Yellows 1944: Negro Race Problems" (hereafter Y 1944 nrp), ADL Library, New York, NY; L.D. Reddick, "Anti-Semitism Among Negroes," *Negro Quarterly* (Summer 1942): 113–17; James Robinson, "Some Apprehension, Much Hope," *ADL Bulletin* (December 1957): 4, 6; Harry Lyons, "Jewish-Negro Relationships in the Post War Period," pp. 4–5, 9–10, Report, ADL microfilm: Y 1944 nrp; Elmo Roper, "The Fortune Survey," *Fortune* (November 1942 and October 1947); H.L. Lurie, "Introductory Report on the Study Project of Negro-Jewish Relationships," 9 December 1943 in AJC Vertical File: "NJR: AJC 1938–1969" and in ADL microfilm: Y 1943 nrp: "Anti-Semitism among Negroes, in the opinion of the American Jewish Committee, has not been sufficiently extensive or menacing to receive a sustained and concentrated program," p. 1.

2. See, for example, Herbert Hill, "Black-Jewish Conflict in the Labor Context: Race, Jobs and Institutional Power," paper presented at the "Conference on Blacks and Jews: An Historical Perspective," Washington University, St. Louis, Mo., December 2–5, 1993.

3. Roy Wilkins to Walter White, Memorandum, 25 March 1938; White to Cordell Hull, Telegram, 25 March 1938; NAACP papers, box I C 208, Library of Congress Manuscript Division, Washington, D.C. When the *New York Times* printed only the first sentence of the telegram, "thus giving the impression that the Association endorsed the action of the State Department, without reservation, the National Office protested to the Times." Walter White, "Report of the Secretary to

the April Meeting of the Board," 7 April 1938, p. 3, NAACP I A 18. See also George Schuyler, "Abuses of Colored Citizens in U.S.," *World-Telegram*, 21 November 1938; NAACP Press Release, "NAACP Secretary Denounces Nazi Pogroms; Says All Must Unite to Protect Minority Rights Here and Save Democracy," and "Senator King, Sorry for Jews, Urged to Support Federal Anti-Lynch Bill," 18 November [1938?]; White to Chester Ames, 18 November 1938, all NAACP I C 208; Inter-Racial Committee of the District of Columbia, Resolution, 1938, NAACP I C 208 which ["recorded] its deep abhorrence" of the treatment of Jews under Nazi occupation, adding "At the same time, we cannot forbear to point out that in many particulars, the sufferings of this innocent minority...are strikingly like the sufferings of a similar minority in our own country."

4. Walter White to Franklin Roosevelt, 14 September 1940, NAACP II A 325.

5. Charles Houston to A. Ovrum Tapper, 5 December 1938. Also see Tapper to Houston, 2 December 1938; White to Houston, 5 and 7 December 1938, all NAACP I C 208. Several meetings were indeed held. NY meetings: White to William Hastie, 26 July 1939; White to [Thurgood] Marshall and [George] Murphy, Memorandum, 21 September 1939; White to Ted Poston, 15 September 1939; Hubert Delany to White, 20 September 1939; Lester Granger to White, 19 September 1939; White and Walter Mendelsohn to Marshall, 27 September 1939; George Murphy, Jr. to White, Memorandum, "For the Committee Studying Anti-Semitism in Harlem," 30 September 1939; White to [Roy] Wilkins, Marshall, Murphy, Memorandum, 9 October 1939; White to Marshall and to Elmer Carter, 4 December 1939; NAACP Press Release, "Yiddish Papers Tell Jews Their Problem is Same as Negro's," 8 December 1939, all NAACP I C 277; White, "Report of the Secretary to the October Meeting of the Board," 5 October 1939, p. 4, NAACP I A 18; AJC, "The Jewish Press and the Jewish-Negro Problem," Report, 6 November 1939, AJC VF: NJR; ADL, Untitled report of articles on Black-Jewish relations in the *Jewish Daily Forward*, October 1939, ADL microfilm, "Dittoes 1939: Negroes," ADL library; Arthur Alberts to Norton Belth, Memorandum re "Harlem: Negro grievances against Jews," 17 October 1939, AJC inactive VF. NCJW: NCJW and NCJW Juniors, National Committee on Legislation, "Social Betterment Through Legislation" [lists NCJW endorsements and dates, including anti-lynching position in 1935], NCJW papers, box 142, Library of Congress Manuscript Division.

6. Philip Frankel to Richard Gutstadt, 2 September 1943. His colleague, Louis Novins, made a similar assessment: "Although we have always been concerned about the Negro situation, we have never deemed it practicable to form a united front. It would be a dangerous policy...because we would not only have our own enemies, but would inherit the Negroes' enemies." Novins to Richard Beisler [?illegible] 2 June 1943, both ADL microfilm Y 1943 nrp.

7. Paul Richman to Leonard Finder, Memorandum re "Philip Randolph— Railway Porters' Brotherhood Union," 3 September 1942; Richard Gutstadt to

Finder, 14 September 1942. See also Finder to Richman, 4 September 1942; Stanley Jacobs [ADL] to Finder, 10 September 1942, "I could have told you that Philip Randolph is persona non grata with responsible officialdom in Washington, and his proposed March on Washington, which was stymied, would have had serious repercussions and proved most harmful to the war effort." Also Abe Rosenfeld to Finder, 22 July 1942 regarding Adam Clayton Powell, all ADL Y 1942 nrp.

8. Unidentified fragment of report or memorandum, ADL, n.d. [1942], ADL Y 1942 nrp.

9. Many of the papers of the Committee for a Permanent FEPC, the Leadership Conference for Civil Rights, and Civil Rights Mobilization can be found in NAACP files, especially boxes II A 351, 353, 186, some in NCJW Washington Bureau papers, box 18. Roy Wilkins followed A. Philip Randolph as chairman of the Committee; Arnold Aronson of NJCRAC served as secretary. See also, for example, Minutes of the NAACP Board of Directors, 11 October 1943, p. 5; 11 February 1946, pp. 3–4; 14 October 1946, pp. 2–3; 14 February 1949, p. 4, all NAACP I A 134–35; Arnold Aronson, NJCRAC (and National Council for a Permanent FEPC) to NJCRAC Committee on Employment Discrimination and Civil Rights, 17 January 1949; Isaiah Minkoff, "Report of the Executive Director to 6th Plenary Session, NJCRAC," April 1948, pp. 5–6; NJCRAC, Minutes of "informal dinner meeting" of "intergroup relations" agencies, 27 December 1951; all NAACP II A 386–87; ADL National Committee Meeting Minutes, ADL warehouse box 176, and "nrp" files in ADL micro 1945–1958; NCJW, Civil Rights Council materials and "Planks Recommended for Inclusion in 1948 National Party Platforms," 16 June 1948, NCJW box 73; "FEPC: Its Development and Trends," n.d.; "Legislative Highlights," May 1943, pp. 2–4, NCJW box 142; AJCong Commission on Law and Social Action (CLSA) papers, AJCong library, New York, NY.

10. See, for example, ADL, "City and State Inter-racial and Good Will Commissions," June 1944, pp. 2–5, ADL Y 1944 nrp; Charles Collier, Jr., Citywide Citizens' Committee on Harlem, to Leonard Finder, 2 September 1943, ADL Y 1943 nrp; AJCong, CLSA, "Report of Activities July–September, 1947," p. 2, NAACP II A 360.

11. Pluralism, first coined by Jewish sociologist Horace Kallen in 1924, has had a long and convoluted history, due in large measure to the fuzziness of the concept in the public mind. At first including only white ethnics in its description of the American cultural scene, separatist in its prognosis, and essentialist in its definitions ("Men may change their clothes, their politics, ...their philosophies to a greater or lesser extent; they cannot change their grandfathers," Kallen argued in a famous passage in *Culture and Democracy in the United States* [New York, 1924] p. 122), it later became more assimilationist in its tone, abandoned essentialism for cultural identities voluntarily chosen, and by the 1940s included non-white groups as well. Alain Locke, the Black philosopher, was the first to apply cultural pluralism to African Americans;

see, for example, Leonard Harris, ed., *The Philosophy of Alain Locke* (Philadelphia, 1989). Kallen himself later repented of his early essentialism. For an excellent history of the many meanings of pluralism see Philip Gleason, *Speaking of Diversity* (Baltimore, 1992).

12. See, for example, Meier Steinbrink, ADL, to Mr. ___ [sic], fundraising letter on behalf of the NAACP, 18 May 1949, NAACP II A 363; "'Covenants' Hit by Jewish Groups in Court Brief," *ADL Bulletin* 4 (December 1947): 1; AJCong, CLSA, "Monthly Report," July 1946, NAACP II A 360. *Shelley v. Kraemer* 334 U.S.1 (1948), *Sipes v. McGhee* 334 U.S.1 (1948), *Hurd v. Hodge* 334 U.S.24 (1948).

13. Rabbi Berman, AJCongress Executive Committee Meeting, Minutes, 11 December 1949, p. 107, AJCong papers, box "admin and exec cmttee mins 46–50."

14. Testimony can be found in the papers of the NCJW, NCNW, ADL, AJC, AJCong, NAACP, NUL, JLC, and similar organizations, as well as in the papers of each coalition. *The Balance Sheet* pamphlets were jointly published by the AJCong and NAACP.

15. There are many such examples, found throughout the records of these agencies, on both the local and national level, including a Black and Jewish effort to challenge degrading stereotypes in Hollywood, the production of tolerance literature for schools, churches and civic groups, meetings with local newspaper editors over coverage, editorial policy, or advertising guidelines, or challenging racial and religious quotas in private professional and graduate schools. To take just one, the AJCong challenged the Commercial Travelers Mutual Accident Association regarding their policy of restricting membership to "white male persons." H.E. Trevett, CTMAA to Mr. ___ [sic], 18 February 1942, NAACP II A 360. Anti-mask legislation prohibited the wearing of masks in public and was obviously directed at the Klan. Oftentimes Jewish organizations worked for Black civil rights in the south against the wishes of the local Jewish community; this was the source of a great deal of intra-community strife. For a fuller discussion of this topic see Cheryl Greenberg, "The Southern Jewish Community and the Struggle for Civil Rights," in Nancy Grant and V.P. Franklin, eds., "Blacks and Jews in American History." (forthcoming).

16. Peekskill: see, for example, ACLU, Americans for Democratic Action, AJCong, American Veterans Committee, Council Against Intolerance, NAACP, "Statement on Grand Jury Inquiry into Peekskill Riots," 22 September 1949, NAACP II A 467 (which contains a folder on the riot); NJCRAC, "Suggestions for the Guidance of Jewish Organizations In Connection with the Paul Robeson Concert Tour," 19 October 1949, ADL micro "Chicago reel 12"; AJC Domestic Affairs Committee, Minutes, 4 October 1949, p. 5, bound volume in AJC library; Gloster Current, NAACP, to NY Branches, 2 and 8 September 1949, NAACP II A 369; AJC VF "Riots, Peekskill New York." Miami and anti-Klan efforts: AJC Community files; ADL National Commission Meeting, 24–25 October 1952, p. 303, ADL warehouse

box 176; NUL Board of Trustees meetings, NUL papers, Library of Congress Manuscript Division; ADL "chisub: civil rights" reels; NAACP II A 362, 369; AJ Cong, CLSA, "Reports of Activities," in AJ Cong library; Alex Miller, ADL to Nelson Jackson, NUL, 21 February 1951, NUL SRO box A 124. Peoria St.: See, for example, AJCong Executive Committee minutes, 11 December 1949.

17. Steinbrink, from fundraising letter for ADL members, n.d. It appears Walter White actually wrote the letter, and Judge Steinbrink signed it. Cover memorandum, White to Mr. Wilkins and Mr. Moon, 18 May [?] 1949, NAACP II A 363. In *Moore v. Dempsey* 261 U.S. 86 (1923) the Supreme Court ruled that the Black defendants, denied adequate counsel and tried in a court whose atmosphere resembled a lynch mob, had been denied due process.

18. Isaac Toubin to Hyman Fliegel, *B'nai Zion Voice*, 13 July 1953, contained in Will Maslow to CRC Group Relations Agencies, Memorandum, 22 October 1953, NAACP II A 362.

19. Maslow to White, 1 December 1947, NAACP II A 360. Testimony, organizing, and programming efforts by Black groups on behalf of immigration reform and other issues can be found in NAACP, NCNW, and NUL files, and occasionally in AJCong CLSA, AJC, and ADL files as well.

20. D.C.: Isaac Franck, Jewish Community Council for Greater Washington to Arnold Forster et al., 28 May 1951; Frances Levenson and Sol Rabkin, Memorandum re "Washington D.C. Civil Rights Statutes," 13 June 1951, both ADL Y 1949-52 nrp. CCREM: its papers can be found in the Columbia University Rare Book and Manuscript Division, New York, NY. Also see NAACP II A 370. Brown: The AJCong, AJC, ADL, NCJW, JLC, Central Conference of American Rabbis, and several other Jewish groups filed amicus briefs, and the Julius Rosenwald Fund and AJC funded Kenneth Clark's famous doll study. See, for example, Shad Polier, "Law and Social Action," *Congress Weekly* 17 (27 November 1950): 3; Arnold Forster, Interview, 13 August 1991, New York, NY; John Slawson, AJC Oral History Memoirs, pp. 34–6, New York Public Library; Kenneth and Mamie Clark, "Detailed Statement of Plan of Work," for Julius Rosenwald Fund, n.d. [1940?], provided by Ben Keppel. Testimony regarding anti-discrimination, anti-segregation, and immigration bills can be found by year in the papers of the NCJW (especially the Washington, D.C. branch), JLC, NCNW, NUL, NUL Southern Regional Office, AJCong CLSA (including Stuyvesant Town litigation) and AJC NJR and Community files, and ADL nrp (ABC materials can be found in 1949–52) and "chisub civ rts" microfilm records and its "Civil Rights Committee Meetings" files. The NAACP papers contain not only its own testimony on numerous issues, but copies of Jewish groups' testimony, organized by subject, date, and agency. There are literally thousands of examples of Black and Jewish groups taking up issues of primary or exclusive importance to the other, including struggles against racist store owners or employers, aiding the settling of refugees in resentful neighborhoods, or protesting segregation.

21. CORE: Samuel Markle to William Sachs, 28 December 1946, ADL Y 1946 nrp. All these organizations changed their minds after the fact and praised CORE's effort. Black temporizing: for example, a 1944 NAACP resolution "urge[s] the Board of Directors of the NAACP to adopt a program of action...for the purpose of eliminating anti-Semitism among Negroes, and...discovering and eliminating anti-Negro prejudice and practices...which foster anti-Semitism among Negroes." Resolutions Adopted at the War-Time Conference, National Association for the Advancement of Colored People, Chicago, 12–16 July 1944, p. 12, NAACP II A 28. "The Urban League has stated publicly its opposition to any campaign that is in the nature of an attack against a whole race of people but at the same time has expressed its recognition of the fact that there might be certain unfair and over-reaching practices carried on by Jewish merchants...which give rise to criticism and indignation." Earl Dickerson to White, 5 July 1938, NAACP I C 208. See also Cheryl Greenberg, "Class Tensions and the Black-Jewish 'Alliance,'" OAH Annual Meeting, Atlanta, Georgia, April 1994.

22. Nathan Edelstein, "Jewish Relationship With the Emerging Negro Community in the North, "Address to NJCRAC, 23 June 1960, pp. 8–9, AJC VF NJR: AJCong. He concluded that the imbalance should not deter Jews from embracing the civil rights struggle. "Jews are dedicated to the cause of justice and equality because it is best for all Americans."

23. Particularly since local Jews owning property in Miami's Black areas "share the feelings of other southern whites." S. Andhil Fineberg to John Slawson, AJC, Memorandum re "The Situation in Miami," 21 January 1951, p. 3, AJC VF Community files.

24. White to Ben Epstein, 2 June 1949; Epstein to White, 9 June 1949, NAACP II A 363. See also White's eulogy at Stephen Wise's memorial service, 25 May 1949, pp. 11–13, NAACP II A 362. Miller: Alex Miller to Lou Novins, Memorandum re "Negro-Jewish Relations," 16 August 1945, ADL Y 1945 nrp.

25. ADL: Richard Gutstadt to Paul Richman, 19 [10?] August 1941; Berland to Leonard Finder, 12 September 1941, Memorandum re "Article by Roy Wilkins (NY Amst Star)," ADL Y 1941 nrp. Baltimore: quoted in Stanley Jacobs to ADL Staff, Regional offices, CRCs, "Negro Press—Memo #2," 17 April 1942, p. 5, ADL Y 1942 nrp.

26. Berman: Minutes, AJCong Executive Committee, 11 December 1949, pp. 105–6. Brooklyn (Stanley Henderson): AJCong National Convention, 1956, Panel: "Integration," 13 April 1956, p. 73, AJCong box "Nat'l Conventions 54–58."

27. Edelstein, pp. 4–5; White to Maslow, 10 December 1947, NAACP II A 360.

28. Edelstein, p. 6.

29. See, for example, Maslow, "The Advancement of Community Relations Ob-

jectives Through Law and Legislation," 25 October 1954, NAACP II A 386, and Edelstein.

30. See, for example, AEB [Abel Berland] to BG [?], Memorandum re "Meeting of the Civic Service Committee," 6 August 1947, ADL Y 1947 nrp (regarding a CORE-led boycott in Chicago). This fear of mass mobilizations was shared by many white liberals in the late 1940s and 1950s. See, for example, Walter Jackson, "From Moderation to Engagement: White Liberal Intellectuals and Civil Rights 1954–59," Southern Historical Association meeting, 7 November 1992; Steven Gillon, *Politics and Vision* (New York, 1987).

31. *De Funis v. Odegaard* 416 U.S. 312 (1974), *Regents of University of California v. Bakke* 438 U.S.265 (1978). Actually the Union of American Hebrew Congregations (the Reform movement) and the NCJW filed briefs on the side of the defendants, along with Black organizations.

nine

BLACK-JEWISH UNIVERSALISM
IN THE ERA OF IDENTITY POLITICS

CLAYBORNE CARSON

The victories of the modern civil rights movement during the period from 1954 to 1965 were made possible by political coalitions that brought together African Americans and Jewish Americans. Yet ironically the increasing militancy of that movement also led many blacks and Jews to question assimilationist assumptions that had guided previous racial reform efforts. As black Americans turned from NAACP-led litigation and lobbying efforts to the mass civil rights protests and community-wide mobilizations of the early 1960s, blacks and Jews began to argue publicly with one another and among themselves over fundamental issues involving group identity and advancement strategies. Debate over these issues was particularly intense in urban black communities, where class divisions among blacks and between blacks and non-blacks persisted despite civil rights gains. After the June 1966 Mississippi voting rights march introduced the Black Power slogan to the nation, established civil rights leaders faced increasingly forceful challenges from competitors who derided nonviolent tactics and questioned the racial loyalties of leaders committed to interracialism and the maintenance of black-Jewish ties. In an era of identity politics and cultural conflict, the universalistic values and cosmopolitan perspectives which had characterized the civil rights movement exerted less and less influence over national politics and over the attitudes of African Americans and Jews. On a deeper, more general level, tensions and controversies in contemporary black-Jewish relations have reflected the worldwide decline of transracial, transcultural, and transnational movements seeking to realize egalitarian and democratic ideals.

The Supreme Court's *Brown v. Board of Education* decision in 1954 and the civil rights advances that followed were the culmination of reformist and revolutionary political movements that for the first time enabled blacks and Jews to play important transformative roles in American politics. The modern civil rights movement continued previous efforts to move beyond the Founding Fathers' expectation that a citizenry comprised mainly of Anglo-Saxon Protestants would exercise political power. As the issue of Jewish citizenship tested the limits of democratic universalism in Europe after the French Revolution, so too did the question of extending political rights to former slaves serve as the ultimate test of egalitarian ideals expressed in the Declaration of Independence. Jewish Americans played less prominent roles than did African Americans in nineteenth-century anti-slavery and civil rights struggles, but members of both groups spearheaded twentieth-century civil rights efforts that resuscitated the Fourteenth and Fifteenth Amendments. After World War II, civil rights reform gained momentum as proponents portrayed the southern Jim Crow system as an embarrassing regional anachronism that was contrary to irrefutable social science findings, and vulnerable to a determined legal and intellectual assault on its underlying values. With only a few voices of dissent, African-American leaders united with Jewish leaders in support of racial integration, and few spokespersons for either group questioned whether assimilation was the most feasible strategy for the advancement of their groups. The gradual elimination of prejudices rooted in traditional racial and ethnic identities was seen as consistent with the trend toward the universalization of American democratic principles and of modern mass culture. As sociologist Talcott Parsons explained using his singular academic diction, "only in a highly urbanized, hence individualized and pluralized society does the opportunity emerge for a saliently different minority group to diffuse itself though the society"; or as another observer more bluntly observed: "Perpetuation of ethnic differences is altogether out of line with the logic of American reality."[1]

As the oldest and best-funded civil rights organization, the NAACP served as the primary national nexus for an interracial civil rights coalition that would achieve major legal and legislative breakthroughs during the 1950s and 1960s. No organization had more black members than the NAACP, and many Jewish leaders saw the group and its legal arm, the Legal Defense and Education Fund, Inc. (LDF), as their principal instruments for promoting civil rights reform. Having attracted substantial Jewish support since its founding in 1909, the NAACP had by the 1940s established cooperative relationships with the major national Jewish groups—including the American Jewish Committee, American Jewish Congress, Anti-Defamation League of B'nai B'rith, and Jewish Labor Committee. This black-Jewish institutional relationship was formalized in 1951 through the creation of the Leadership Conference on Civil Rights. Under the guidance of Roy Wilkins of the NAACP, Arnold Aronson of the National Jewish Community Relations Council, and A. Philip Randolph, head of the Brotherhood of Sleeping Car Porters, the Leadership Conference would play a crucial role in mobilizing political support for the major civil rights legislation of the late 1950s and 1960s. Moreover, this high-level black-Jewish institutional relationship provided a framework for the involvement of a substantial number of Jewish lawyers, academics, and propagandists in a multipronged assault against bigotry and racial discrimination.

The NAACP's almost unchallenged dominance of African–American politics at the national level during the 1950s resulted from the decline of serious alternatives to its conventional reform strategy based on litigation, lobbying, and appeals for white support. Although black urban residents faced discrimination and hostility as they competed with other ethnic and racial groups for housing and jobs, their festering resentments did not find a militant political voice until the 1960s. With the decline of black nationalism after Marcus Garvey's imprisonment in the 1920s and with the Cold War repression of black leftist activism, there was no significant organized opposition to the NAACP and its assimilationist orientation. Gunnar Myrdal's *An American Dilemma*, published in 1944, had set the tone for postwar civil rights efforts by insisting that African-American advancement would result from the transformation of white racial attitudes and the realization of traditional liberal ideals rather than from racial separatism or a radical transformation of American society. According to Myrdal, it was "to the advantage of American Negroes as individuals and as a group to become assimilated into American culture, to acquire the traits held in esteem by the dominant white Americans."[2] The unanimous *Brown* decision appeared to represent not only the limit of what white Americans were willing to concede to Blacks, but also an African-American consensus regarding political goals. The cultural and political diversity that would become apparent in African-American communities by the late 1960s was at the time of the *Brown* decision manifested mainly through street corner oratory and apolitical religious sects, such as the Nation of Islam. Malcolm X later recalled that when he became minister of the Nation of Islam's New York Temple No. 7 in June 1954, his group attracted little interest in Harlem: "You could have said 'Muslim' to a thousand, and maybe only one would have asked you 'What's that?'"[3]

The 1956 bus boycott in Montgomery, Alabama, marked the beginning of a period of massive and sustained protest movements that sped the pace of civil rights reform; yet it also gave hints of a major departure from preceding civil rights reform efforts. The spread of mass protests in the South provided a new setting for Jewish civil rights activism that was quite different from Jewish involvement in the NAACP's conventional reform efforts. On the one hand, high-level institutional ties between the major civil rights and the major Jewish organizations remained intact during the civil rights protest era. Indeed, this institutional relationship grew stronger during the 1960s as the NAACP took the lead in transforming diffuse protest activity into coherent reform agendas. Jewish professionals played major roles in the preparation of legal briefs and legislative proposals or in campaigns on behalf of tolerance and racial understanding. Jack Greenberg, who became involved with the LDF in 1948 and later became its director, recalled that a "substantial number" of LDF lawyers and five of the six white lawyers who signed the *Brown* brief were Jewish.[4] If the term "black-Jewish alliance" should be used at all to describe relations between the two groups, it applies most accurately to the involvement of Jewish professionals in civil rights organizations and to the lasting black-Jewish institutional ties that have persist-ed, despite the conflicts described below, from the 1940s to the present.

On the other hand, in the aftermath of the Montgomery bus boycott, the expanding southern black protest movement attracted Jewish activists who were different in many respects from the Jewish reformers who supported the NAACP and conventional civil rights efforts. The former were typically younger and more often a product of secular leftist backgrounds than were the latter. The Jewish activists who immersed themselves in the expanding southern civil rights strug-gle were also unlikely to be representatives of Jewish organizations or even to identify themselves as Jewish rather than white. They were participants in a volatile black-led social movement that produced a set of emergent radical values that challenged the NAACP's conventional reform strategy and its underlying assimilationist assumptions. Jewish activists did not forge a formal alliance with their Black counterparts; instead, for a time at least, they saw themselves as part of a radical community devoted to direct action protests and to organizing com-munity efforts. While Jewish support for the NAACP's conventional strategy remained strong, many Jewish civil rights activists joined their black counter-parts in an effort to probe the boundaries of conventional liberalism.

When Martin Luther King, Jr., rose to national prominence during the Montgomery bus boycott, he stood between these competing elements, support-ing both the NAACP's efforts to build a broad interracial coalition in support of civil rights reform and grassroots efforts to mobilize the black Americans as an independent force for change. King was a unique leader capable of stimulating racial militancy while also attracting considerable support from Jews who expect-ed that the upsurge of southern black protest activity would benefit the cause of civil rights reform. When King decided to build upon the success of the boycott by establishing the Southern Christian Leadership Conference (SCLC), he quick-ly attracted support from a number of Jews, including some who also supported the NAACP. Among his earliest Jewish associates in the civil rights movement was businessman and philanthropist Kivie Kaplan, a Reform Jewish leader, who became a major NAACP fundraiser after joining the organization in 1932, and who would succeed Arthur Spingarn as the NAACP's president in 1966. Kaplan became acquainted with King during the latter's years as a graduate student at Boston University, and after 1956 he supported King's emergence as a nationally known civil rights leader. Stanley Levison, a radical lawyer allied with the Communist Party, contacted King shortly after the end of the boycott and helped him expand his influence outside the South. Levison became King's closest white advisor, serving in New York as a liaison between the SCLC leader and both the Jewish left and the American Jewish Congress. When King was arrested in Atlanta shortly before the 1960 presidential election, a Jewish lawyer, Morris Abram, helped secure his release after arranging for Democratic candidate John F. Kennedy to intervene in the case. King also maintained close relations with Rabbi Jacob Rothshild of Atlanta.

By the early 1960s King had become the best-known civil rights leader, and his firm commitment to nonviolence and interracial coalitions enabled him to allay the concerns that some Jews were beginning to have regarding black militancy. He was a frequent guest speaker at northern synagogues and at meetings of Jewish organizations. Of all the major civil rights leaders, King was also the most effective fundraiser. Lacking the NAACP's membership base, he was nevertheless able to build a strong base of financial support for the SCLC that relied heavily on Christian and Jewish religious institutions and on religiously motivated individuals.[5] For King the effort to establish black-Jewish ties was part of a broader effort to attract ecumenical support for the civil rights movement. A particularly important event in King's outreach efforts was his participation in the 1963 National Conference on Religion and Race in Chicago. At the conference he formed enduring ties with Rabbi Abraham Joshua Heschel, a professor at the Jewish Theological Seminary. Heschel delivered a major address at the conference calling for Jews to see the civil rights movement as an expression of Jewish values.[6] Heschel's decision to join King in the 1965 Selma to Montgomery voting rights march made him a highly visible symbol of Jewish support for the civil rights movement.[7]

While some Jews saw King as a reassuring presence in the civil rights protest movement, other Jews identified themselves with groups such as the Student Nonviolent Coordinating Committee (SNCC) and the Congress of Racial Equality (CORE), which challenged King's dominance of the southern struggle. Although SNCC was not nearly as successful as was King in garnering Jewish financial support, it attracted a core of Jewish activists who found more opportunities for sustained involvement in SNCC than in the clergy-dominated SCLC. In addition, the SNCC-dominated Mississippi Summer project of 1964 provided an unprecedented opening for intensive civil rights participation by Jewish activists. The extent and significance of this participation is a matter of dispute, however, for there is no hard evidence regarding the religious orientations of the civil rights activists who became immersed in the southern struggle. Jonathan Kaufman, for example, failed to identify the "historians" who estimated, based on a review of "the records," that "more than half the white Freedom Riders who went South were Jewish, as were two-thirds of the white students and organizers who flooded Mississippi to help register black voters in the summer of 1964." In fact the available scholarly studies of participants in the Freedom Summer found that only a fifth of those applying for the project indicated any type of religious affiliation and that most religiously affiliated applicants were Protestant Christians.[8] In addition, although there is no doubt that Jewish civil rights activism in the southern struggle was disproportionately large, such activism was most often rooted in leftist political backgrounds rather than in religious beliefs. To be sure, leftist backgrounds were more common among Jews than among white Christians, but they were also more common among secular Jews than among observant Jews. Although religious Jews such as Heschel were notably present at major civil rights mobilizations—such as the March on Washington and the Selma to Montgomery march—a quite different group of Jews were involved in the sustained direct action protests and voter registration projects of SNCC and CORE. The latter group rarely saw themselves as acting on behalf of the Jewish community and rejected the conventional litigation and lobbying strategies of the NAACP and its Jewish allies.[9] Despite the lack of evidence that militant activism in the southern struggle was motivated by Judaism, Murray Friedman of the American Jewish Committee nevertheless has contended that "the Jewish kids who went south were acting out, albeit unconsciously, a Jewish tradition. It is as if these boys were wearing their yarmulkes without knowing it."[10] Friedman and others have insisted that even secular Jewish activists were influenced by "the egalitarian strains within Judaism"; as one account put it: "While these Jews did not get involved because they were Jewish, there was something very Jewish about their getting involved."[11] This argument may have validity in explaining the fact that Jews as a group were more likely than other white Americans to support the civil rights goals, but it is hardly sufficient to explain why the least religious Jews were the ones most likely to be drawn toward the radical egalitarianism of SNCC and CORE. Although Michael Schwerner and Andrew Goodman, two of the civil rights workers who were murdered as a result of their involvement in the voting rights campaign, have often been cited as examples of Jewish commitment to the civil rights movement, these two martyrs were actually illustrative of the secular roots of Jewish activism. Lenora E. Berson has categorized Schwerner with college-educated "middle-class suburban Jews, who believed not in God but in the infinite perfectibility of man."[12] Neither Schwerner nor Goodman received religious funerals, and Goodman's mother later insisted "that it had never occurred to her that her son had gone south as a Jew."[13]

In short, the motivations and political orientations of Jewish activists cannot be readily summarized. Jewish activists in SNCC and many of those in CORE moved toward forms of radicalism that often alienated them from their own communities and placed them in opposition to the Jewish supporters of conventional civil rights reform efforts. There was also a measure of self-interest in Jewish participation in a movement that enabled them to affect political change in ways that did not engender anti-Jewish sentiments and that resulted in legislation prohibiting religious as well as racial discrimination.[14] Certainly by the mid-1960s there was a visible and growing gulf between the perspectives of Jews whose attitudes toward the civil rights movement were motivated by a sense of group interest, and those driven by egalitarian idealism. Although black-Jewish conflict was hardly visible before 1966, internal tensions were evident among both African Americans and Jewish Americans regarding the future direction of civil rights reform. The small number of idealistic Jewish activists who had become part of the black protest movement were far outnumbered by Jews who remained at a distance from political ferment occurring within black communities. Before themselves becoming a target of black militancy, Jewish civil rights activists of the period from 1963 to 1966 found themselves on both sides of the crucial tactical and ideological debates occurring within the black struggle. Jewish civil rights lawyers, for example, were divided along ideological lines. Jack Greenberg, who replaced Thurgood Marshall as head of the NAACP's Legal Defense Fund, argued strenuously during 1964 against SNCC's decision to accept legal assistance from the leftist National Lawyers Guild, a group with a large representation of Jewish lawyers, including Arthur Kinoy, Victor Rabinowitz, and William Kunstler. Later in the same year, Joe Rauh, who tried to arrange a compromise with the Lyndon Johnson administration over the seating of the Mississippi Freedom Democratic Party at the 1964 Democratic Convention, faced opposition from black SNCC workers and their Jewish allies. Despite the fact that SNCC was able to retain significant Jewish participation and Jewish financial backing until the late 1960s, its increasing militancy gradually narrowed its base, although Jewish New Left radicals continued to support the group's Black Power advocacy.

The increasing militancy of the civil rights movement exposed tensions that existed between African Americans and Jews regarding the usefulness of interracial political strategies and ultimately brought to the surface doubts about the assimilationist values that pervaded liberal racial reform efforts. Even as the civil rights movement achieved major legislative victories during the mid-1960s, there were indications that the liberal-left coalition was beginning to fracture as some observers began to raise questions about the direction of racial reform. Norman Podhoretz's oft-reprinted essay, "My Negro Problem—and Ours," published in July 1963, expressed the feelings of many Jews who saw themselves as civil rights supporters, but who were becoming increasingly disturbed by black militancy. Podhoretz's memories of a childhood encounter in his native Brooklyn with hostile urban black youths became a metaphor for the change in the relationship of Jews to blacks from benefactor and sympathizer to competitor and fellow victim. When Podhoretz was waylaid by members of an all-black relay team that had been disqualified in his team's favor, racial antagonism surfaced:

> My panic is now unmanageable. (How many times had I been surrounded like this and asked in soft tones, "Len' me a nickel, boy." How many times had I been called a liar for pleading poverty and pushed around, or searched, or beaten up, unless there happened to be someone in the marauding gang like Carl who liked me across that enormous divide of hatred and who would therefore say, "Aaah, c'mon, le's git someone else, *this* boy ain't got no money on 'im.") I scream at them through tears of rage and self-contempt, "Keep your F———n' filthy lousy black hand offa me! I swear I'll get the cops." This is all they need to hear, and the five of them set upon me. They bang me around, mostly in the stomach and on the arms and shoulders, and when several adults loitering near the candy store down the block notice what is going on and begin to shout, they run off and away.[15]

While Podhoretz expressed the personal fears of increasing numbers of Jews, Nathan Glazer's essay on black-Jewish relations, published in the December 1964 issue of *Commentary*, revealed a broader ambivalence about the relationship between Jewish group interests and those of African Americans. Glazer's essay appeared soon after the civil rights movement achieved one of its major victories in the passage of the Civil Rights Act of 1964; yet it also reflected growing northern white resistance to the shift in the focus of civil rights activism from the southern Jim Crow system to northern de facto segregation and employment discrimination. Glazer recognized that the black-Jewish alliance on behalf of civil rights reform was one of leaders rather than communities. Many urban blacks, Glazer noted, viewed a Jew "not as a co-worker or friend or ally, but, in a word, as an exploiter," while many Jews resisted "such demands as preferential union membership and...the primacy of integration over all other educational objectives." Glazer saw the interests of the two groups as diverging. While Jews continued to support the removal of racial barriers, he argued, they did not agree with civil rights leaders who insisted that "color-blind politics" were insufficient to bring about rapid advancement for the black masses. Glazer not only dissented from the policies that would later take the form of affirmative action programs, but he also attacked what he saw as "a radical challenge" by black leaders to the desire of Jews to maintain areas of "Jewish exclusiveness." He claimed that the civil rights movement was heading in a direction that would alienate most Jews and that would increasingly cause them to view their interests as similar to their "less liberal neighbors" who shared a common "interest in maintaining an area restricted to their own kind; an interest in managing the friendship and educational experience of their children; an interest in passing on advantages in money and skills to them."[16]

While Glazer's essay suggests that some Jews were beginning to question the direction of the civil rights movement, a much fiercer debate, reflecting the growing influence of Malcolm X, was beginning in African-American communities. At the time of his assassination in 1965 Malcolm X had only a small following, but his decision to leave Elijah Muhammad's Nation of Islam and to forge ties with civil rights militants signaled a convergence of black nationalism and the emergent ideas of the southern black struggle. Although Malcolm's Organization of Afro-American Unity attracted little black support during his lifetime, his posthumously published autobiography and speeches made his ideas a central element in the black consciousness movement of the late 1960s. His cogent criticisms of King and other mainstream civil rights leaders coincided with the insurgent challenges from within the civil rights movement. Thus, soon after the 1963 March on Washington, Malcolm scored points with disaffected urban blacks by charging that white supporters of the major civil rights leaders had placed them in charge of the march in order to stifle "the Black revolution" that resulted when "local leaders began to stir up [Black] people at the grass-roots level." "The same white element that put Kennedy into power—labor, the Catholics, the Jews, and liberal Protestants...joined the march on Washington," he insisted at a Northern

Negro Grass Roots Leadership Conference in Detroit. "They didn't integrate it, they infiltrated it. And as they took it over, it lost its militancy."[17] As mass militancy became more common among northern urban blacks, Malcolm's rhetorical militancy provided a means to express the frustration felt by urban blacks who saw few changes in their lives as a result of the civil rights movement. Malcolm set the tone for subsequent debates within black communities by questioning the militancy and racial loyalty of mainstream black leaders.

While Malcolm had often denounced interracialism and occasionally directed specific criticisms toward Jewish merchants in black communities, the deterioration of black-Jewish ties occurred for the most part after his death as his ideas were adapted by black militants who had participated in the civil rights struggle. James Baldwin's essays, published in 1963 as *The Fire Next Time*, reflected the changing sentiments of blacks who did not see themselves as black nationalists yet nonetheless regarded interracialism and assimilationism with increasing skepticism. In some respects, Baldwin's essays belied Glazer's suggestion that the new black militancy was headed toward assimilation. "White Americans find it as difficult as white people elsewhere do to divest themselves of the notion that they are in possession of some intrinsic values that black people need, or want," Baldwin complained. Although he continued to reject black nationalism, Baldwin reflected the view of many black activists who had become disillusioned with interracial liberalism:

> How can one respect, let alone adopt, the values of a people who do not, on any level whatever, live the way they say they do, or the way they say they should? I cannot accept the proposition that the four-hundred-year travail of the American Negro should result merely in his attainment of the present level of the American civilization....The only thing white people have that black people need, or should want, is power—and no one holds power forever.[18]

Jewish participation in the civil rights struggle became an issue as black militancy shifted its focus from a frontal attack on the southern Jim Crow system to a more diffuse effort to deal with the tangible and intangible consequences of racial oppression. By 1966 all the major civil rights organizations had begun to move from their previous focus on the South toward a broader assault on those issues that had not been addressed through civil rights legislation. King's Chicago Campaign illustrated the difficulty of utilizing civil rights protest tactics in a northern urban context. Although some Jews remained civil rights supporters even as the movement came north, Glazer's article foreshadowed the increasing discomfort many Jews felt as the civil rights movement became the Black Power movement. Broad-based Jewish support for the civil rights movement was based on the belief that it pursued ideals that were perceived to be consistent—or at least not in conflict—with the interest of Jews. Harold Cruse's influential polemic

Crisis of the Negro Intellectual, published in 1967, reflected this widespread questioning of the universalist assumptions that had sustained black-Jewish involvement in leftist causes. As one observer commented regarding the changing climate of black-Jewish relations during the late 1960s: "The urban confrontation between Jews and Negroes will result in a further alienation of Jews and in increased hostility between Jews and Negroes. The stores that will be boycotted, the tenements to be hit by rent strikes, the collection agents to be driven out are mostly Jewish, as are the remaining white politicians; for the only whites left in the ghetto, besides the police, are Jews."[19]

Given this socioeconomic context, it was hardly surprising that black discontent was expressed through anti-Jewish sentiments. Indeed, anti-Jewish invective had long been an aspect of black nationalism, especially in New York, where resentment of Jewish economic power had been a significant factor in the popularity of Malcolm X. The vehement Jewish reaction against black anti-Semitism, moreover, did not result as much from awareness of its existence as from its potential political potency. The novel aspect of the anti-Jewish rhetoric of the period after 1966 was that it came not from isolated orators but from former civil rights activists, who now saw themselves as competing for Malcolm X's constituency.

Perhaps the most poignant example of this transformation of black civil rights militancy to Black Power militancy involved Stokely Carmichael, who first used the Black Power slogan during the June 1966 Mississippi march that was held soon after his election as SNCC's chairman. Even as Carmichael began to include references to "honkies" in his speeches during the summer and fall of 1966, Jewish support for SNCC remained largely unaffected. Indeed, at the time when Carmichael first came to national prominence as the best-known Black Power proponent, there were few other black activists with deeper ties to the white Jewish left. He was one of a number of black militants who had been drawn to civil rights activism as a result of his involvement in the New York-centered radical community dominated by African Americans and Jews. While at the Bronx School of Science, Carmichael's closest friends were Jewish leftists, and his activism began when he joined his Jewish friends in a protest against an anti-Semitic statement made by a United Nations official. His acquaintance with Gene Dennis, the son of a Communist Party leader, led to his initial contacts with black radicals who were party members or sympathizers. During the first half of the 1960s, as Carmichael rose to prominence in SNCC, he continued to work closely with Jewish activists even as he was drawn toward black nationalist ideas. As the chairman of SNCC during 1966–1967 and as the best-known proponent of Black Power, Carmichael was a central figure both in the black-Jewish left and in the black-Jewish conflicts of the period after 1966. Like Harold Cruse, his increasingly anti-Jewish sentiment was rooted in a long personal history of interactions with Jewish leftists. The turning point in his attitudes came after his election to head of SNCC, when he attempted to leave behind his identity as a civil rights activist with interracial, leftist ties and began to establish his reputation as a black nationalist and Pan Africanist seeking to expand SNCC's influence in the urban North. In northern cities, Carmichael, like other veterans of the southern struggle, confronted Jews not as dedicated comrades but as an urban economic and political elite to be challenged. The transformation of his views was gradual, reflecting his difficulty in balancing his past ties with his overriding desire to mobilize African Americans. He stood uneasily between a black-Jewish radical political culture that now provided a negative referent for his evolving views and an urban black nationalist tradition that had largely eschewed civil rights activism.

As he spread the Black Power message during 1966 and early 1967, he initially depicted Jews as a group to be emulated rather than one to be resented. He often presented the statement of Rabbi Hillel as his favorite quotation: "If I am not for myself, who will be? If I am only for myself alone, who am I? If not now, when? If not you, who?" Speaking of the 1965 racial rebellion in Los Angeles he compared the powerlessness of blacks to the power held by white ethnic groups: "If that were a Jewish community, if that were an Irish community, if that were an Italian community, [Police Chief William Parker] would be done."[20] Similarly, in a widely published Black Power statement titled "Power and Racism," he compared his own socialization with that of a Jewish child: "White Tarzan used to beat up the black natives. I would sit there yelling, 'Kill the savages, kill 'em!' It was as if a Jewish boy watched Nazis taking Jews off to concentration camps and cheered them on. Today I want the chief to beat the hell out of Tarzan and send him back to Europe."[21] On other occasions he would remark: "To ask the Negroes to get in the Democratic Party is like asking Jews to join the Nazi Party." Carmichael consistently rejected the notion that he was a racist or an anti-Semite. When a Jewish civil rights supporter asked whether there was "an inconsistency in not fighting anti-semitism in SNCC but in asking Cohen and other Jews for support," he responded, "As for your question about anti-semitism, it is difficult to 'fight' something unless it exists. Nothing in our policies or programs suggests anti-semitism. SNCC is very aware of the support it has received, both 'physical' and financial, from American Jews and appreciates it."[22]

Despite such disclaimers, however, Carmichael and other former civil rights activists were determined to present themselves as free to express festering black resentments regardless of the feelings of white or Jewish supporters. Carmichael's former ties to Jews were a liability in his effort to compete with black separatists inside and outside SNCC who were less encumbered with an interracial past. Malcolm X had demonstrated the effectiveness of "Blacker than thou" oratory, and Carmichael became aware of his vulnerability during the infighting within SNCC over the issue of white participation. Although perceived outside SNCC as an anti-white firebrand, Carmichael was seen by black separatists inside the organization as unwilling to expel the white activists who remained in the group. The separatists were willing to use disruptive tactics and to direct personal attacks against Carmichael, James Forman, and other veteran SNCC leaders in order to

force them to end the group's ties to whites. As one of the separatists commented: "My loyalty is to the black people and not to SNCC necessarily. It's to SNCC
only in proportion as I determine its loyalty to black people."[23] The issue of white
participation in SNCC was resolved only after a fractious staff meeting in
December 1966, at which the separatists refused to allow discussion of other
issues until whites were expelled from the organization. The expulsion was finally
accomplished by a one-vote margin. After weathering this vicious internecine
battle among black militants, Carmichael moved from the class orientation he
had brought into SNCC toward a race-first perspective that rejected Marxism and
insisted that African Americans must be provided with "an African ideology
which speaks to our blackness—nothing else. It's not a question of right or left,
it's a question of black."[24]

By the time of the 1967 Arab-Israeli war, Carmichael's pro-Palestinian sentiments did not in themselves set him apart from the majority of black political
activists, but his determination to take an uncompromising public stand on the
issue was driven by a combination of personal convictions and internal racial politics. His enthusiastic support for the Palestinian cause was a visible indication of
his willingness to break with Jewish former allies and to consolidate his position
at the center of an increasingly contentious group of Black Power ideologues.
SNCC's position on the Middle East conflict was itself an expression of the group's
willingness to make a public break with its interracial past. Rather than carefully deliberating the issue and the consequences of taking a public stand on the
issue, a few SNCC members quickly prepared an article that seemed designed to
provoke Jewish former supporters. Published in the group's Newsletter, the article compiled thirty-two "documented facts," contending, among other things,
that during the initial Arab-Israeli war "Zionists conquered the Arab homes and
land through terror, force, and massacres." By itself, the Newsletter article would
have provoked controversy, but accompanying photographs and drawings by
SNCC artist Kofi Bailey heightened its emotional impact. The caption on one of
the photographs, which portray Zionists shooting Arab victims who were lined
up against a wall, noted "This is the Gaza Strip, Palestine, not Dachau, Germany."
When program Director Ralph Featherstone explained to reporters in Atlanta
that the article did not indicate that SNCC was anti-Semitic, he further inflamed
the emotions of Jews by criticizing Jewish store owners in American black ghettoes. Reacting to the article, the executive director of the American Jewish
Congress labeled it "shocking and vicious anti-Semitism."[25] Rabbi Harold
Saperstein, who had continued to support SNCC despite the controversy over
Black Power, was among those who withdrew support from the group, explaining that SNCC leaders' willingness "to become a mouthpiece for malicious Arab
propaganda undermines my confidence in their judgment."[26]

The criticisms of Israel expressed by Carmichael and other SNCC members
could not alter the course of Middle Eastern politics, but they did serve a purpose
as part of an effort by former civil rights workers to abandon past ties to Jewish

liberals and thereby claim roles as leaders of the black urban insurgency. Carmichael's subsequent willingness to assume increasingly extreme positions against interracial alliances was in part spurred by his struggle to remain the leading ideologue of the Black Power movement. By the summer of 1967 he had been replaced as SNCC's chair by H. Rap Brown, but Carmichael continued to attract attention during his tour of Third World countries, which included a speech in Havana, calling for urban guerrilla warfare in the United States, and a stop at a Palestinian camp. After returning to the United States and assuming the role of Prime Minister of the Black Panther Party, he continued to give the Arab-Israeli conflict a central place in his rhetoric. At a 1968 rally on behalf of imprisoned Black Panther leader Huey Newton, Carmichael insisted, "We can be for no one but the Arabs because Israel belonged to them, to the Arabs, in 1917. The British gave it to a group of Zionists who went to Israel, ran the Palestinian Arabs out with terrorist groups and organized the state and did not get anywhere until Hitler came along and they swelled the state in 1948. That country belongs to the Palestinians. Not only that. They are moving to take over Egypt. Egypt is our motherland—it's in Africa. Egypt belongs to us since 4,000 years ago and we sit here supporting the Zionists." Speaking in 1969 at a convention for Arab students in America, Carmichael admitted that he had once "been for the Jews" but had reformed.[27]

Although Carmichael exemplified the utilization of anti-Jewish rhetoric as an aspect of black leadership competition, he did not succeed in maintaining his leading position among black militants. His race-first emphasis placed him at odds with other Black Panther leaders, who were almost alone among Black Power advocates in their Marxian orientation. In 1969 Carmichael resigned his post in the party and left the United States to begin promoting Pan Africanism from his new base in Guinea. He subsequently revised his position on racial ideology to incorporate concepts of African socialism, but he remained adamant in his opposition to interracial political strategies in general and black-Jewish ties in particular. During his return visits to the United States his public statements at times seemed intended to offend Jews. For example, when he was asked in 1970 by television interviewer David Frost to name the white man he considered a "hero," Carmichael responded by citing Hitler as perhaps "the great[est] white man." On another occasion he remarked: "The vicious, illegal, immoral and unjust state of Israel is occupying our territory Egypt.…If Egypt is in trouble we too must be animated with such a love and a desire to serve our people and to serve justice and the cause of humanity that we too must be picking up guns and going to fight in Egypt against Zionism."[28] In a 1972 letter to a white woman who had previously supported his civil rights activities, Carmichael privately speculated on the reasons Jews "have always aroused the hatred of so many people." Recounting the history of Jewish expulsions from England and European nations, he concluded: "There must be a reason!…Their control today of europe and america is the same as it always has been. We know for example that the causes of W.W. II were planted in the treaties of W.W. I. We are told that at that time the decisions were made by what was then the big four, britain, france, italy and u.s.a. The secretaries of the leaders of these four countries except italy were Jews."[29] In another letter written a few weeks later, Carmichael condemned "the Jews" who used Hitler's atrocities to justify the creation of the state of Israel. "As soon as you say something about the Jews they throw Hitler in your face. You are made to feel guilty, yet when Black people talk about slavery they are the first to say they cannot feel guilty for what their ancestors have done!"[30]

Carmichael's pro-Palestinian stance did not in itself set him apart from other black militant leaders, but his decision to give that issue a central place in his speeches suggests the degree to which, for him and other black leaders, the Arab-Israeli conflict and the issue of Black-Jewish political ties assumed symbolic significance in African-American militant leadership competition. Carmichael's controversial statements on Israel provided a model for the use of rhetorical racism and anti-Semitism by black militants to build support among discontented blacks by focusing attention on the reluctance of more moderate black leaders to speak forthrightly on behalf of "Black" interests. As African-American political rhetoric became increasingly focused on issues of identity and racial conscious-ness, King and other leaders of the major civil rights organizations found them-selves on the defensive as many blacks turned their attention from issues such as discrimination and employment opportunity toward a focus on questions involv-ing racial identity and loyalty. In the aftermath of the 1967 Arab-Israeli war, black leaders were divided less over differences regarding poverty programs and civil rights legislation than over their stands on issues of symbolic importance. As would then be the case in future black-Jewish controversies, Carmichael and other Black Power proponents used opposition to Israel to demonstrate publicly their independence from Jewish control and to undermine the position of leaders who maintained their pro-Jewish positions. The pattern that would be repeated many times thereafter was established in 1967. After SNCC's statement in a newsletter, which normally reached only a few of the group's supporters, gained national notoriety, Jewish leaders called upon established black leaders to issue public con-demnations of the statement. Because King was personally committed to the maintenance of black-Jewish ties, he did not require such prompting, but his responses to anti-Jewish statements by blacks nevertheless became part of a pub-lic ritual that had less to do with Middle Eastern politics than with the ideolog-ical foment occurring within African-American and Jewish communities.[31] After SNCC's anti-Israeli statement appeared, King not only joined with other estab-lished black leaders in condemning its anti-Semitic overtones but also argued that anti-Zionism was "inherently antisemitic, and ever will be so."[32] King's respons-es, and that of other established black leaders, to anti-Israeli and anti-Jewish rhetoric were undoubtedly sincerely motivated, but they further undermined the black support of leaders who resisted the new politics of racial consciousness. King's Poor People's Campaign was a clear expression of his radical critique of

American society, but his reputation as a militant nevertheless suffered during the last year of his life among the angry black urban residents he hoped to mobilize for his nonviolent campaign. Although Carmichael and other proponents of Black Power saw themselves as more responsive to the needs of the black poor than the older civil rights leaders, their emphasis on racial unity often led them to place less emphasis on economic issues than King did. After the initial radicalism of the Black Power militancy encountered severe repression, the black consciousness movement turned inward toward an emphasis on defining racial identity and resolving the issue of who should lead the black community, instead of continuing to challenge white authority.

Because control of the black institutions was a fundamental aspect of the Black Power movement, it was hardly surprising that the Ocean Hill–Brownsville school dispute of 1968 reopened the wounds left by the black-Jewish contention over the 1967 Middle East war. That New York became the setting for this and many subsequent black-Jewish disputes was also not surprising, for it was there that the group interests of African Americans and Jews were most likely to collide. Moreover, the manner in which the efforts of blacks to control public schools in their communities quickly degenerated into ugly charges and countercharges of racism and anti-Semitism was also to be expected given the readiness of individuals on both sides to redefine the complex issue of school decentralization into simplistic group interest terms. Finally, the dispute was made more intense by the fact that Jews who had supported or even continued to support the civil rights movement—teachers' union president Albert Shanker had marched with King in Selma—found themselves in opposition to black civil rights veterans such as former SNCC activist Julius Lester who inflamed emotions when he read a student's anti-Semitic poem on a radio program he hosted.[33] One result of the dispute was the appearance of the Rabbi Meier Kahane's Jewish Defense League as a militant voice for Jewish group interest and a challenge to established Jewish leaders that was in some respects comparable to black separatist extremism.

Another response to the rise of black militancy came from Jewish neoconservatives, who made their own claim for ideological dominance in Jewish communities. Nathan Glazer's 1969 article in *Commentary* set the stage for the Jewish neoconservative movement by attacking not only black militants but also their Jewish radical defenders. As in black communities, Glazer's piece revealed how black-Jewish political ties were becoming a matter of contention among Jews. Glazer called upon "the chief Jewish defense agencies" to act on behalf of their constituencies and ridiculed Jewish radicals who gave support to black militancy: "All they can do is give the blacks guns, and allow themselves to become the first victims."[34] Within a few years, the outlines of the neoconservative position against black militancy had been presented in the pages of *Commentary* and other magazines by figures such as Glazer, Podhoretz, Irving Kristol, Midge Decter, and Milton Himmelfarb. Jewish neoconservatives agreed with their black militant opponents that many of the goals of the black struggles of the 1970s were departures from the traditional goals of the civil rights movement, but it was also the case that a profound political reorientation was occurring among Jews. As Jonathan Kaufman noted, the 1967 war "forced a reexamination not only of American Jewish attitudes toward Israel but of American Jewish attitudes toward themselves."[35] For both African Americans and Jews, the 1967 Arab-Israeli war signaled a shift from the universalistic values that had once prevailed in the civil rights movement toward an emphasis on political action based on more narrowly conceived group identities and interests. Kaufman observed that the black consciousness movement of the 1960s stimulated the Jewish consciousness revival of the 1970s.[36] Black Power advocates and supporters of Israel were on different sides of the Middle East conflict, but they agreed their own group must exercise a measure of exclusive political control on matters involving vital group interests.

This sense of Jewish exclusivity on the issue of Israel was threatened in the major manifestation of black-Jewish tensions during the late 1970s: the Andrew Young affair. In 1979 Young lost his position as ambassador to the United States and as the highest-ranking black member of Jimmy Carter's administration when he met secretly with the UN representative of the Palestinian Liberation Organization. Although Jewish leaders sought to avoid actions that would suggest that they had engineered Young's resignation, many African Americans saw it as a clear indication of the power that could be exercised by Jews against a black leader who took an even-handed stand on the Middle East conflict. The controversy reinforced the pervasive feeling among blacks that many of their leaders could not, or would not, speak out on the issues that divided blacks and Jews.

Given this background, the climate was established for the emergence of Nation of Islam leader Louis Farrakhan as a major spokesman for disenchanted and distrustful blacks. Although Farrakhan had been a Muslim leader since the late 1950s, he came to prominence only in 1984 when he injected himself into the black-Jewish controversy surrounding Jesse Jackson's presidential campaign. Jackson's campaign was initially damaged in February 1984 when he admitted to using the terms "Hymie" and "Hymietown" in a private conversation about New York Jews. He apologized for the remarks, which were revealed by a black *Washington Post* reporter, Milton Coleman, and insisted that he had not made the statements in a "spirit of meanness," but Farrakhan's spirited defense of Jackson brought even more criticisms from Jews. During the spring, Farrakhan further exacerbated Jackson's relations with Jews (and not coincidentally attracted enormous attention to himself) when he used the phrase "gutter religion" in reference to Jews whose actions he opposed. Although, at the time, most press reports focused on Jackson's partially successful effort to distance himself from Farrakhan, a by-product of the controversy was that Farrakhan took a major step toward becoming the principal national voice for black discontent. Having harmed Jackson's presidential aspirations in 1984, he was able to capitalize on his notoriety with such effectiveness that by 1995 he, rather than Jackson, would become the lead speaker and organizer for the Million Man March.

By the time of Farrakhan's emergence as a major African-American leader, the black-Jewish civil rights alliance had come to represent only one facet of a complex spectrum of African-American political alternatives. Leaders such as Farrakhan who did not believe in interracialism and rejected the idea of black-Jewish political ties had refined the technique of using occasional anti-Semitic comments as a means of stimulating anti-Jewish feelings among blacks, of garnering publicity, and of publicly demonstrating their willingness to express controversial views regardless of the feelings of non-blacks. Far more than Jackson and other black leaders who retained a vision of interracialism and black-Jewish cooperation, Farrakhan and those who followed his model benefited from a political climate that emphasized racial identity and loyalty and that reflected a worldwide trend away from universalistic political values.

In retrospect, the radical insurgencies of 1968 can be seen as the culmination of two centuries of reformist and revolutionary activity rooted in the Enlightenment and eighteenth-century democratic movements. The subsequent crises in black-Jewish relations reflected a generalized decline in popular support for socialism and other forms of radicalism that transcended racial, ethnic, and religious boundaries. Activists who had once joined in coalitions in pursuit of universalistic ideals have felt increasingly isolated within their own groups and have been unable to resist the apparent worldwide trend toward greater economic inequality and increasing conflict among racial, ethnic, and religious groups. Politics rooted in segregated enclaves and based on narrowly conceived notions of racial and cultural identity have challenged and in some places supplanted universalistic egalitarianism. The deep passions of ancient "tribal" and racial identities has, in the United States and elsewhere, undermined popular support for multicultural and multiracial democracy. Even African Americans and Jewish Americans—two groups that have historically supported twentieth-century democratizing movements in the United States—have at the end of the century become more noticeably divided among themselves about their nation's multiracial, multicultural democratic experiment.

Notes

1. Talcott Parsons, "Why 'Freedom Now,' Not Yesterday?" in Parsons and Kenneth B. Clark, *The Negro America* (Boston, 1966), p. xxiv; Will Hersberg, *Protestant, Catholic, and Jew* (New York, 1955), p. 23.

2. Myrdal, *An American Dilemma* (New York, 1964), pp. 928–29.

3. Malcolm X, with Alex Haley, *Autobiography of Malcolm X* (New York, 1965), p. 217. See, more generally, C. Eric Lincoln, *The Black Muslims in America* (Boston, 1961), and E. U. Essien-Udom, *Black Nationalism: The Search for Identity in America* (Chicago, 1962).

4. Jack Greenberg, *Crusaders in the Courts: How a Dedicated Band of Lawyers Fought for the Civil Rights Revolution* (New York, 1994), p. 50.

5. Although there have been many published estimates of the proportion of civil rights movement funding donated by Jews, hard evidence on this issue is not available. Jack Greenberg has dismissed the notion that donations from Jews were the principal source of movement funding and speculates that the "myth of dominant Jewish financial support for civil rights probably comes from the 1960s when Jewish celebrities gave to SNCC...and CORE and Martin Luther King, Jr. But they scarcely gave in similar amounts to mainstream organizations like LDF, the NAACP, and the Urban League"—Greenberg, *Crusaders in the Courts,* p. 51.

6. See the conference address of Heschel, as well as those of Rabbi Morris Adler and Dr. Julius Mark, in Mathew Ahmann, ed., *Race, Challenge to Religion* (Chicago, 1963).

7. Given the large proportion of secular Jews among Jewish civil rights activists, Murray Friedman overstates the case when he writes that Heschel "stirred not only the Jewish religious community but Jews young and old into direct action, galvanizing the whole spectrum of activists from fund-raisers to lawyers." See Friedman, with the assistance of Peter Binzen, *What Went Wrong? The Creation and Collapse of the Black-Jewish Alliance* (New York, 1985), p. 191.

8. See Doug McAdam, *Freedom Summer* (New York, 1988), pp. 48–50, 62–63. The other major study of the northern volunteers similarly provides no support for the notion that Jewish participation was dominant; see Mary Aickin Rothschild, *A Case of Black and White: Northern Volunteers and the Southern Freedom Summer, 1964–1965* (Westport, CT, 1982).

9. See Clayborne Carson, "Blacks and Jews in the Civil Rights Movement: The Case of SNCC," in Jack Salzman, ed., *Bridges and Boundaries: African Americans and American Jews* (New York, 1992), pp. 36–49.

10. Lenore E. Berson, *The Negroes and the Jews* (New York, 1971), pp. 123–24.

11. Friedman, *What Went Wrong?*, pp. 189–90; Jonathan Kaufman, *Broken Alliance: The Turbulent Times Between Blacks and Jews in America* (New York, 1988), p. 99.

12. Berson, *Negroes and the Jews*, pp. 121, 123. Berson quotes NAACP leader Aaron Henry's disappointment over the failure of Jews to support the civil rights movement: "We thought that naturally we would have the Jews on our side, because the enemies of the Jews were usually found in the same group that opposed us. But we don't have the Jews supporting us" (p. 121).

13. Friedman, *What Went Wrong?*, p. 189.

14. Although Jonathan Kaufman emphasized Jewish idealism, he conceded:

"Jews benefitted enormously from the terrain shaped by the civil rights movement. Jews were the first to use anti-discrimination laws to gain access to restricted apartment buildings in large cities. The growing tide of tolerance left by the civil rights movement opened opportunities for Jews as well as for blacks in law firms, corporations, and universities"—*Broken Alliance*, p. 101.

15. Norman Podhoretz, "My Negro Problem—and Ours," reprinted in Paul Berman, ed., *Blacks and Jews: Alliance and Arguments* (New York, 1994), pp. 81–82.

16. Glazer, "Negroes & Jews: The New Challenge to Pluralism," *Commentary*, December 1964, pp. 29–64. Sociologist Talcott Parsons reiterated Glazer's argument when he suggested in an article written in 1965 that "the Jewish community itself has been concerned about how far 'assimilation' should be allowed to progress"—"Full Citizenship for the Negro American? A Sociological Problem," in Parsons and Kenneth B. Clark, *The Negro America* (Boston, 1966), p. 726.

17. George Breitman, ed., *Malcolm X Speaks: Selected Speeches and Statements* (New York, 1965), pp. 13, 16.

18. Baldwin, *The Fire Next Time* (New York, 1963), pp. 108, 110.

19. Berson, *Negroes and the Jews*, p. 145.

20. Quoted on the television program, "Face the Nation," June 19, 1966.

21. "Power and Racism," in *Stokely Speaks* (New York, 1971), p. 26.

22. Stokely Carmichael to Mrs. Lorna Smith, November 8, 1966, the Stokely Carmichael-Lorna Smith Collection, Stanford University.

23. Clayborne Carson, *In Struggle: SNCC and the Black Awakening of the 1960s* (Cambridge, MA, 1981), p. 238.

24. Quoted in Carson, *In Struggle*, p. 282.

25. Carson, *In Struggle*, pp. 267–68.

26. Harold Saperstein to H. Rap Brown, quoted in Carson, "Blacks and Jews: The Case of SNCC," in Salzman, *Bridges and Boundaries*, p. 44.

27. Earl Raab, "The Black Revolution and the Jewish Question," *Commentary*, January 1969, p. 30.

28. Tambuza and Masa, "Interview with Stokely Carmichael," KPFK Radio recording, Los Angeles, California, February 1975.

29. Carmichael to Lorna Smith, 23 July 1972, Carmichael-Smith Collection, Stanford University, quoted in Becky Marcus, "Stokely Carmichael/Kwame Toure: The Reconstruction of Identity," Senior Honors Thesis, May 1992, Stanford University.

30. Carmichael to Smith, 9 August 1972, in Marcus thesis.

31. King's first statement against black anti-Semitism, entitled "My Jewish Brother," was issued February 26, 1966, shortly after a CORE activist in New York remarked to an audience that included a number of Jews, "Hitler made a mistake when he didn't kill enough of you." King's statement appeared in many newspapers.

32. "When people criticize Zionism, they mean Jews—this is God's own truth" (see "Letter to an Anti-Zionist Friend," *Saturday Review*, August 1967, p. 76). King provided a more well developed statement of his position and that of the SCLC in a September 28, 1967, letter to Rabbi Jacob M. Rothschild: "The Middle East problem embodies the related questions of security and development. Israel's right to exist as a state in security is incontestable. At the same time the great powers have the obligation to recognize that the Arab world is in a state of imposed poverty and backwardness that must threaten peace and harmony. Until a concerted and democratic program of assistance is affected, tensions cannot be relieved. Neither Israel nor its neighbors can live in peace without an underlying basis of economic and social development."

33. Among the many accounts of the Ocean Hill–Brownsville controversy are the following: Berson, *Negroes and the Jews*, chapter 14; Robert G. Weisbord and Arthur Stein, *Bittersweet Encounter: The Afro-American and the American Jew* (New York, 1970), chapter 8.

34. Glazer, "Blacks, Jews & the Intellectuals," *Commentary*, April 1969, p. 39.

35. Kaufman, *Broken Alliance*, p. 202. Kaufman reported Rabbi Heschel's observation: "I had not known how deeply Jewish I was" (p. 202).

36. Kaufman reported: "Following the end of World War II, there were only two full-time professors of Jewish history and thought at American universities; by 1985, 300 American colleges and universities were offering courses in Judaic studies and twenty-seven offered graduate programs. By the 1980s, polls found, American Jews in their twenties were more likely to attend a Seder than those in their sixties"— *Broken Alliance*, p. 213.

ten

ALLIES OF A DIFFERENT SORT

Jews and Blacks in the American Left

PAUL BUHLE AND ROBIN D. G. KELLEY

D iscussions of Jewish Americans and African Americans occasionally venture into the fringes of American liberalism, where Leftists dream of workers' revolution even when working for reform. Such discussions recall the golden age of a radical Black-Jewish alliance conditioned by a vanished socialist tradition. Like all memories, however, this one is very selective, revealing as much about the degree of mythmaking and self-deception in such recollections as the deep scars left by the collapse of the alliance. In this discourse, Black Nationalism usually figures as the culprit-deserter, with the vanquished hopes of the Great Society the tragic backdrop. On the other hand, Black nationalist intellectuals, most conspicuously Harold Cruse, recollect a history of Jewish paternalism suffocating native Black radicalism, of nationalist-minded Jews pushing for their own cultural autonomy at the expense of their darker comrades.[1]

As is often the case, the truth may lie somewhere in between these two opposing narratives. But the twisted tale of Black-Jewish relations on the Left is far too complicated to be constructed as the middle-ground of extremes. Neither version has a long view of the contradictions experienced by the two sides of the Black-Jewish dyad; instead the scope of inquiry is limited to the forty years after 1915. The fuller story, usually disguised within the history of labor, socialism, communism, and various branches of popular entertainment, has hardly begun to be told. Based upon archival research, oral histories, and relatively unexamined non-English language sources, a fresh narrative begins to emerge in outline. Irreducibly complex, it is a story of idealism, sometimes astonishing accomplishment, defeat and repression, egotism and wounded pride, even betrayal. By offering a condensed version of it, the authors of this essay seek to suggest new ways of thinking about the American Left at large as well as those Jewish and African American radicals who played such a vital role in it.

Beginnings

The particular legacy of the Left within labor and vice versa has had a decisive institutional impact upon interaction between Jews and African Americans, particularly during the twentieth century. Tracing this legacy returns the story to the birth of an organized Left in which socialist-oriented Jews and Blacks, each relatively few in number, came to represent forces far larger than themselves.

The International Workingmen's Association (or "First International," as it would later be called) brought Marxism and a modern Left onto American shores during the later 1860s, through a telling confluence of two distinct traditions. The first, usually considered the most important in the alliance, comprised the mostly German-American bloc of immigrant workers and intellectuals. As heirs to generations of political mobilization and cultural-educational association in the Old World, even before the Civil War Germans had created a culture of radical artisans whose eagerness to fight against Southern secession and slavery emboldened the radical wing of the young Republican Party and actually decimated the German-American radical ranks.[2]

They had nevertheless blazed the trail for the younger German-Americans of the 1870s–90s, who established a rich associational life, with newspapers, craft unions, and fraternal associations. All left-of-center, such institutions were largely restricted to their own linguistic and neighborhood culture, establishing an important pattern in the various ethnic sections of the American Left for generations, one with a crucial impact upon Black and Jewish interactions. Finding a place for their socialist values within a seemingly capitalist culture, ethnic radicals unintentionally walled themselves off from other communities, including African Americans. At its best, however, their evolving notion of group survival within a future socialism also evoked a conscious multiculturalism large enough to accommodate African Americans' special presence even before the immigrant radicals gained a sense of Blacks' central role in American history and culture.[3]

Yankee reformers, rooted in the abolitionist and perfectionist movements of the 1840s–60s, constituted the other wing of the International. Their political associations often had bolder commitments to universality (such as support for women's rights) than those of the immigrant socialists, but little comparable lasting power. Like the anti-racist or anti-imperialist movements of later generations on the Left, they represented sentiment more than fixed constituency and urgently needed allies successfully rooted in ethnic life. Like the German-Americans, they did possess one cause appealing to the scattering of Jewish middle class and the young Jewish immigrants first finding their way to labor and radical movements during the 1880s: the militant advocacy of Free Thought, a vision of life emancipated from conservative evangelical Protestant or Catholic hierarchy, or Jewish rabbinate.[4]

A fratricidal conflict between these two groups and the sudden collapse of the First International in 1871–72 eclipsed the influence of the "American" reformers, although the successor Socialist Labor Party (founded in 1878) recruited a handful of veteran Black reformers and a milieu of Yankees, especially women, during a rare moment of Left electoral upsurge. One of those Black reformers was the indefatigable orator and organizer Peter H. Clark of Cincinnati, Ohio. A leader in the National Colored Labor Union and hero during the Great Railroad Strike of 1877 in St. Louis, Clark shared the Socialist Labor Party ticket with Solomon Ruthenberg in their bid for Congressional seats in 1879. That an African American and a Jew were among the Party's first Congressional candidates had enormous symbolic importance, reflecting the unique ethnic make-up of the early SLP. To be sure, during 1878–80, for the last time in recorded history, the handful of African Americans may have equaled the similarly small number of Jews in socialist ranks. However, the SLP never really considered racism or anti-Semitism "working-class" issues. As later party leader Daniel DeLeon (himself of Sephardic background, a native of the Dutch Caribbean island of Curacao) succinctly put it, "there was no such thing as a race or 'Negro' question...there was only a social, a labor question, and no racial or religious question so far as the Socialist and labor movements were concerned."[5] In any case, the small and faction-ridden SLP was soon dwarfed by a new presence in the annals of working-class radicalism: the Knights of Labor. The meteoric rise of the Knights of Labor to more than a half-million members briefly created a unique inclusive association (except for proscribed Asian laborers) where large numbers of Black and white workers belonged to the same broad social movement under left-wing influence, albeit with limited Jewish presence. This configuration, too, fell away quickly, leaving behind a socialist and labor movement increasingly Jewish, with scarcely any African American presence.[6]

The consolidation of the American Federation of Labor over the body of the defeated Knights influenced labor, and the re-emerging Left, in melancholy ways. As elaborated by cigarmakers' Dutch-born Jewish leader Samuel Gompers, the AFL leadership viewed African Americans (also women and Asians) mainly as potential obstacles to labor's organizational consolidation. Not "skill" (since branches of many trades, including cigarmaking itself, had few more real skills than the "unskilled" trades) but ethnicity and gender served generally to demarcate which groups the AFL sought to represent and which it sought to marginalize or exclude entirely from the industrial workplace.[7]

Socialists within the AFL often resisted this drift toward particularism, but those rising to leadership levels from the 1880s to the 1910s, as a rule, did so with little vigor. An institutional conservatism around Gompers himself led the official labor movement toward a pragmatic acceptance of a capitalism which provided proper benefits for the uppermost sector (or "Aristocrats") of the working classes and accorded select others a minimum of representation. By the turn of the century, the United States had the largest difference among the industrial nations between the wages of the most fortunate workers and those of the least fortunate.

The bulk of impoverished Jewish workers, along with Italians, Slavs, and other immigrants considered unskilled, shared in many ways the bottom-most situation of African American laborers: starvation wages, brutish labor, and public execration as less-than-human "Hebes," "Hunkies," and "Dagos." Ethnic revolutionaries, scorning the ethnocentricity of the AFL leaders, led in effect a struggle *within* the working class between those who sought the broadest definitions of class and the most anti-capitalist of solutions, against those with a more collaborative approach to employers. Gompers himself set the tone in many respects for Jewish Socialist (and other) AFL leaders, including those who objected to his growing disdain for socialism. While they rejected the AFL's opposition to new immigration (i.e., of hard-pressed European Jewry) and usually continued to support the Socialist party at election-times, Jewish labor leaders increasingly sought amicable relations with employers and they mistrusted as impractical and disruptive the radical universalism of the Industrial Workers of the World and later that of the Communists. At least until proven wrong, these same Jewish labor leaders considered women workers and other Jewish workers in the lowest paid lines to be unsuited for organizing. They thereby left a gap for ardent Jewish radicals to embrace a larger vision of working class unity and anti-capitalist offensive. Here, for two generations, militant Jewish anti-racism found a political milieu.

The mass migration of Eastern European Jews to the United States, during the 1890s and again after 1905, significantly coincided with historic moments of lynching campaigns, Black Populist political insurgence, and deepening racism in American society at large. Concentrated in a handful of industrialized northern cities and limited largely to immigrant ghettos and sweatshops, proletarian Jews had limited actual contact with Blacks. Instead, images of African Americans were brought to Jewish ghettoes through the Yiddish press. Papers such as the socialist-oriented *Jewish Daily Forward*, *Morgn Journal*, and the *Tageblatt* carried a range of articles about African Americans, from essays that chronicled Black achievement to the sensational stories about Black rapists and criminals which were commonplace in the white Gentile press. For the most part, the Yiddish newspapers represented Black people as victims of racist oppression, focusing on the history of American slavery and racial violence. Jewish working-class identification with Black suffering is partly a product of the culture of *Yiddishkayt* ("Yiddishness"). Dwellers in a friendless and dangerous Diaspora, seekers of redemption (interpreted, almost until the foundation of Israel, more as the promise of world socialism than of a Jewish State), they felt a kinship with others viewed as similarly dispossessed and disinherited. Intellectual autodidacts to a surprising degree, they created socialist institutions far out of proportion with their numbers, and by the 1890s had already begun to mull the status of Blacks and Jews in a dominant culture both racist and anti-Semitic.[8]

Given the parallels between pogroms Russian Jews experienced prior to fleeing to the United States and the lynching of Southern African Americans, stories of lynching remained a dominant theme in Yiddish articles about Black life. Often, they made their socialist point by scoring the indifference of Jewish institutional leaders, eager for assimilation at any cost. Thus Baruch Vladeck, a leading Socialist figure among the post-1905 immigrants, described a race-riot that he personally witnessed in 1910 in Norfolk, Virginia (and precipitated by Black prizefighter Jack Johnson's victory over Jim Jeffries, the "Great White Hope") as akin to a Russian anti-Semitic pogrom. He was outraged by the refusal of Norfolk's Jews to take a stand in defense of the local Black community.[9]

Unfortunately, Vladeck's comrades within the Socialist Party, founded in 1901 after the disintegration of the SLP, had no consistent anti-racist policy. Here and there individual socialists led a rare interracial labor struggle (as beloved left humorist Oscar Ameringer did in New Orleans), publicized the horrors of lynching, published anti-racist books for children, and (especially among Christian Socialists) made special efforts to recruit African Americans or to work with Chicanos in the Southwest. In practice, the socialist movement acted on a localistic basis, often conceding ground to popular racist impulses and their codification in AFL practices. Milwaukee leader Victor Berger thus brazenly described African Americans as rapists. When questioned by its International Bureau about the Party's position on lynching, party leaders responded that

> nothing less than the abolition of the capitalist system and the substitution of the Socialist system can provide conditions under which the hunger maniacs, kleptomaniacs, sexual maniacs and all other offensive and *now-lynchable* human degenerates will cease to be begotten or produced.[10]

It was not surprising, then, that the Socialist Party failed to attract a Black following until the volatile war years. In the few places outside New York where African American socialists existed in numbers, mostly Louisiana, Oklahoma, and Texas, they generally met in segregated locals. Many Southern socialists courageously denounced Ku Klux Klan activities and dreamed of an interracial movement of the poor, but others boasted of maintaining a "white man's party." Torn by the factional divisions of the 1890s, Jews remained at first only minor players in this movement.[11]

A thin trickle of African American socialist intellectuals, most of them Christian socialists, pointed toward the need for a closer understanding of Black and Jewish experiences. These men of the cloth, perhaps more than their white comrades, recognized the unique forms of oppression African Americans and Jews faced in the Western world. Socialism, they believed, was the means to overcome ethnic difference and to remove racial and religious barriers standing in the way of true freedom. "While in [a Socialist meeting]," wrote Black Socialist Reverend George W. Slater, "a prominent Jewish merchant came to me—a gentile and Christian minister—and said: 'Comrade, isn't this great? Isn't it soul inspiring? Don't you find a bond of true brotherhood here?' And I said, emphatically, 'Yes.'"[12] Though reaching few readers, this effort at dialogue was crucial, for the speeches and writings of Black Christian Socialists like Slater, the Reverend

George Washington Woodbey, Reverend James T. Holly, and Reverend R.C. Ransom tried to dispel anti-Semitic myths and looked to the Old Testament and to Jewish law for a Biblical basis for socialism. In the shadow of the Dreyfus affair in France and on the eve of Leo Frank's lynching in Atlanta, these incredibly articulate and well-versed Christian ministers argued that many progressive principles must be sought in Jewish history and tradition—a tradition in which Reverend Woodbey, in particular, places Karl Marx. In a popular pamphlet titled *The Bible and Socialism* (1904), Woodbey wrote:

> It will be remembered that Marx, the greatest philosopher of modern times, belonged to that same wonderful Hebrew race that gave to the world Moses, the Lawgiver, the Kings and prophets, and Christ the Son of the Highest, with his apostles, who, together, gave us the Bible that, we claim, teaches Socialism. Doubtless Marx, like other young Hebrews, was made acquainted with the economic teachings of Moses, and all the rest of the Old Testament sages and prophets, whatever we find him believing after life.
>
> If we are able to show that the Bible opposes both rent, interest and profits, and the exploiting of the poor, then it stands just where the Socialists do.[13]

The Reverend goes on to make a persuasive case that the Book of Genesis in its original conception forbade the private ownership of land and once that law was broken it opened the floodgates to other violations—namely the charging of rent and interest. "This violation of law," he added, "lays at the foundation of the class struggle over the products which the capitalist is able to take from the worker, because of his private ownership of the earth." As slaves, Jews learned what it was like when their labor was exploited to enrich another. Woodbey reminded his readers that "the Jews had just been relieved from a condition in which others had been profiting at the expense of their labor in Egypt, so one of the first things in the law given them at Mount Sinai was a statute forbidding usury or interest." What is most remarkable about his text is his careful denunciation of the common tendency to equate (from Matthew 25:14–19) the "money lenders" with Jews. "It does not necessarily follow...that Christ had in view a Jew, when he used the parable. This money lender, who took his journey into a far country, was like the same class today who journey at others' expense."[14]

Unsteadily, lacking any official party encouragement, the dialogue continued. A few socialist intellectuals including Anna Strunsky Walling took part in the founding of the Niagara movement (predecessor of the NAACP) in 1905, indirectly assisting the rise of future Black leader W.E.B. Du Bois. But a minor Jewish intellectual figure, best known for his Yiddish writings about the need for a public system of social security, contributed the first of the important critiques of the Socialist Party's own position. I.M. Rubinow (using the pseudonym I.M.

Robbins) chose the *International Socialist Review*, the most militantly left-wing major socialist organ, to publish an unprecedented series of fifteen articles analyzing the situation and criticizing the socialists for failing to take an active role in support of basic civil and economic rights for African Americans. His conclusion was unambiguous:

> The Socialist Party must take a definite attitude on the Negro problem, and must not be afraid to proclaim. And this attitude must include something a good deal more tangible than the promise of "full products of one's labor in the cooperative commonwealth." It must include, if it is to be logical and honest, *a clear, unmistakable demand for the entire abolition of all legal restriction of the rights of the Negro....* The attitude of the Socialist movement must not only be passively correct and decent, but actively aggressive.[15]

Rubinow's powerful critique gained adherents among the tiny sector of Black socialists and among the party's left-wing, which had begun to demand solidarity with Asian-American, Mexican-American, and other nonwhite workers. For the most part, however, socialists stubbornly insisted that the "race question" had to be subordinate to the class struggle.[16]

The outbreak of mass strikes by unskilled and usually new immigrant workers, beginning in 1909, stimulated a wider vision of working-class radicalism and challenged both the Socialist Party and Samuel Gompers' increasingly conservative AFL. The Industrial Workers of the World (IWW), founded in 1905, ardently sought to organize the lowly worker of every kind and location, into a movement which bypassed political bodies by creating the infrastructure of a new, egalitarian society within the shell of the old one. Despite the attraction the Wobblies held for African Americans and the foreign-born, the IWW had little luck organizing African Americans, and when they succeeded their efforts were concentrated in Southern agriculture, primarily the lumber and sugar cane industries.[17] Jewish labor leaders for their part ferociously resisted IWW entreaties, instead entering established AFL unions or founding independent bodies like the Amalgamated Clothing Workers. The only significant example of Black-Jewish solidarity within the IWW took place on Philadelphia's waterfront during and after World War I. In this case, the IWW-affiliated Marine Transport Workers Union was a predominantly Black union led by one of the most talented African American labor leaders of the twentieth century, Benjamin Fletcher. Although 5,000 members of the 8,700 member union were Black, it is significant that the bulk of Fletcher's white support came from Jewish and Polish workers. Nevertheless, by 1923 Fletcher's experience with racist white workers overwhelmed his enthusiasm for "One Big Union." "Organized labor," he wrote, "for the most part be it radical or conservative, thinks and acts, in the terms of the White Race."[18]

Fletcher wasn't completely off the mark, even in regard to his beloved IWW.

The Wobblies never paid special attention to the specific situation of African Americans and they sought, too simply, to rise above the racism and ethnocentricity of the working class and its capitalist masters. To solve the class question, they argued, was to solve the race question. They also failed to recognize that the most downtrodden European immigrants had opportunities, over generations if not in their own lives, to become "white"—opportunities neither African Americans, Asians, and in some cases, Latinos did not enjoy. Anti-Semitism certainly didn't die, but assimilated Jews, Italians, and Slavs had a much better chance than assimilated Negroes.

Ironically, outside of the South and Midwest, the IWW had much more success attracting Jewish and Black intellectuals. The Wobbly vision of "socialism with its working clothes on" (as leader William D. Haywood put it), in no small part encouraged a working class bohemianism that embraced Black culture as part of a hopeful mix in the emerging society. The bohemian climate of Greenwich Village after 1910, the appearance of the "New Intellectuals" rebelling from narrow national traditions, a new art and even the rise of social science (despite its many contemporary racist uses) opened up American culture to the "Negro Question" just as younger Jewish radicals began to seek political and cultural reorientation. Thus the *New Review*, largely composed of Jewish intellectuals, enshrined W.E.B. Du Bois in its prestigious editorial committee, publishing his appeals for a serious socialist approach toward the Black community. The radical *Masses* magazine and its successor, *The Liberator*, exalted a small handful of Black radical writers including Claude McKay, who joined its editorial staff.[19] A. Philip Randolph's and Chandler Owen's socialistic race magazine, *The Messenger*, might properly be considered a Black *Masses*, so attuned was it to the "style" of the New Negro and to the cultural prospects at hand. It attracted Harlem's leading Black radicals, including Socialist Hubert Harrison (known as the "father of Harlem radicalism") and future Black Communists Richard B. Moore, Otto Huiswoud, Cyril Briggs, and Lovett Fort-Whiteman. More than any other Black publication, *The Messenger* enthusiastically supported the IWW, describing it as "the only labor organization in the United States which draws no race or color line."[20]

Both Randolph and Owens joined the Socialist Party, becoming the leading Black Left activists in New York City. They played a key role in the election campaign for Morris Hillquit, a Jewish Socialist who ran for mayor of New York in 1917. Although Hillquit lost, he nonetheless attracted 25 percent of the Harlem vote—a significant accomplishment due in no small part to the efforts of Randolph and Owens. They also developed close relations with predominantly Jewish trade unions such as the International Ladies' Garment Workers' Union, the Amalgamated Clothing Workers, and the International Furriers, all of whom provided critical financial support for *The Messenger*. In a letter to the socialist New York *Call* published in 1920, Randolph and Owen not only expressed their solidarity with Jewish workers but argued that they represented the strongest supporters of the Black working class in America. Jews, they argued, not only had a deeper understanding of class struggle than most of their fellow workers, but "they, too, have been the historic victims of persecution, injustice and wrong. They have a history that is replete with unspeakable outrages in well-nigh every alleged civilized country....Hence, the Jews have a deep and abiding feeling of love and human sympathy for the downtrodden and oppressed of all races. Their ears are not deaf to the bitter cries that come up from 15,000,000 of their Black brothers, who, since the systematic trade in them passed with the Civil War, have become, in the alleged land of the free and home of the brave, the mid-sills of the industrial world and the flotsam and jetsam of society."[21]

The world war brought government suppression of the IWW and of the Socialist press at a moment when Black migration northward might have brought a major radical coalescence with interracial movements toward a labor party and even toward a general strike (both of which took place at local levels). The disastrous split in the Socialist Party following Lenin's call for a Third International cut short the burgeoning of a socialist movement around A. Philip Randolph, whose campaign for State Comptroller under the Socialist ticket garnered an unprecedented 202,361 votes statewide, only 1,000 less than Eugene Debs polled in New York, the Socialists presidential candidate that year. The overwhelming support shown by Harlem's electorate, almost certainly buoyed by Jewish Harlemites, symbolized what could have been.[22]

The Communist Era

The rise of Black Nationalism seems meanwhile to have bypassed the white Left almost entirely, joined only at its early decline or demise by the urgent search for alliances. Of Marcus Garvey's key lieutenants, Hubert Harrison and W.A. Domingo were Socialist Party members. Cyril V. Briggs, a friend of Domingo's and an early admirer of Garvey's Universal Negro Improvement Association (UNIA), founded the African Blood Brotherhood (ABB), a secret, underground organization of radical Black nationalists led largely by West Indian immigrants. As the editor of the ABB's official organ, *The Crusader*, Briggs urged support for Socialist candidates, attacked Woodrow Wilson for not applying the concept of self-determination to Africa, and during the "Red Summer" of 1919, demanded "government of the Negro, by the Negro and for the Negro." Eventually, the ABB fell victim to its own internal logic as an advocate of class struggle: by the early 1920s it faded into a merger with the young Workers (Communist) Party.[23]

While the ABB embraced the wider left-wing world, Garvey moved to the right, firing Domingo from the editorship of the *Negro World* and expelling ABB and Workers Party members from the UNIA in 1921. His rhetoric became much more narrowly racial; he even expressed distrust of light-skinned Blacks and sought a secret agreement with the Ku Klux Klan. Yet, like earlier generations of Black nationalists, Garvey drew his vision of liberation from Jewish history and began calling his own back-to-Africa movement "Black Zionism"—a term the Communists used derisively in their 1925 Party platform.[24] Despite the

Communists' staunch opposition to "Zionism" of any kind—whether it be Jewish or Black—comrades such as Cyril V. Briggs, ex-UNIA activist "Queen Mother" Audley Moore, and others entering the Communist milieu would frequently measure the acceptance of Black Nationalism against that of Jewish nationalism, asserting even in moments of conflict that it was the Black-Jewish nexus which mattered most.

Virtually compelled by Moscow to accept the "Negro Question" as vital to an American revolution, American Communists had begun to work on the problem from another direction, through their practical activity. Because of their large immigrant membership, Communists rebuilt constituencies through appealing to class issues within ethnic groups. The "National Question," although complex and different in each case, uniformly saw nationalities as part of a world revolutionary force placed anomolously within the bulwark of world capitalism. The struggle against imperialism which Lenin highlighted abroad (and which played such a great role in appealing to groups which had seen their cultures crushed by empire) had a clear domestic application: capitalist America itself as a domestic empire whose especially oppressed groups (Blacks) had every need of solidarity with the proletariat at large and the communists in particular. By the Sixth World Congress of the Communist International in 1928, this formulation took on its most extreme form: African Americans residing in majority Black counties in the South, the Comintern argued, have the right to self-determination. Black peasants and proletarians not only have the right to rule their own territory but to secede from capitalist America if necessary.[25]

This view of race in America was revolutionary enough, as revolutionary as that held by Abolitionists generations earlier. At another level of political discourse, rank-and-file Jewish Communists faced the rigors and the promise of the "Negro Question" in daily life. If most of the other major ethnic blocs of Communist loyalists were insulated by geography (such as Finnish Americans in the Midwest Mesabi Range), industry, language, or personal choice, often reluctantly accepting aggressively anti-racist positions to assist Blacks as a strategy for uniting the working class, the case was different among several key groups of Jews. During the early 1930s, wherever the Party sought to organize large concentrations of African Americans, Jews were almost always the "shock troops." In Harlem, Jewish Communists fought evictions of Black residents, organized the jobless, and were often at the forefront of anti-racist campaigns. Cultural, historical, and above all personal experiences certainly help account for their prominent role in Black struggles. But for a variety of reasons including their own young age and the class and political conflicts within a badly divided Jewish community, they rarely emphasized their own identity as Jews. As historian Mark Naison points out, "Although many were products of the self-contained Jewish radical subculture, the bulk of the Jews who volunteered for work in Harlem were American born, English speaking, and enmeshed in a Communist version of an assimilationist dream."[26] Indeed, although the Communist Party would later adopt the language of a "Black-Jewish alliance," during the early 1930s their activity fell entirely within the slogan of "Black and white unite and fight." Thus, when the Communist Party declared war on the bourgeois reformist organizations such as the NAACP, followers on both sides rarely saw the conflict as one Black-Jewish alliance versus another. Perhaps for that very reason, more recent commentators have been unable to see beyond the romantic memory of a single grand alliance.

In the South, on the other hand, even the most assimilated Jewish Communists could hardly escape their identity, since anti-Communism and anti-Semitism went hand-in-hand. The Jewish community in the South was tiny compared to that in the northeast, and still fewer émigrés from the 1905 Russian Revolution made their way South. Prosperity—and sometimes survival—in Dixie meant not only assimilating to cultural norms but accepting white supremacy as a way of life. [27] The tense peace created between Southern Jews and "New South" WASP fathers began to unravel when Northern Communists—most of whom were Jews—crossed the Mason-Dixon line around 1929 to colonize the South. Radicals like Fred Beal, Vera Weisbord, William Dunne, James S. Allen (Sol Aurebach), Nat Ross, Blaine Owen (Boris Israel), and many, many others, risked their lives repeatedly for the sake of class and racial justice. A handful, like Harry Simms (born Harry Hirsch), one of the early leaders of the overwhelmingly Black Share Croppers Union, lost their lives.[28] The few Jewish Communists who were either native to the region or spent most of their lives in the South not only suffered the physical brutality of anti-labor and anti-radical repression, but experienced social ostracism from their own communities. The most prominent Southern Jewish radical was Birmingham-born Joseph Gelders, who not only endured a near-fatal beating because of his politics but lost many of his friends and acquaintances in Alabama's Jewish community. On the other hand, his family found acceptance and warmth in the interracial family of Southern Communists, most of whom were African Americans. Gelders' daughter Marge, who also followed him into the Communist Party, remembered the "close, comradely working relations between blacks and whites....We were hemmed in and hung up by the segregation system, but we did have social relations on an individual level, and they were very close."[29]

The event that generated the most interest among Blacks and Jews was the Communists campaign to defend nine young Black men falsely accused of raping two white women not far from Scottsboro, Alabama. The infamous Scottsboro case was not only portrayed in the mainstream Southern press as an example of foreign Communist meddling in local affairs, but because the Communist-led International Labor Defense hired two Jews, Samuel Leibowitz and Joseph Brodsky, as the principal attorneys in the case, Southern attacks on the ILD took on brazenly anti-Semitic overtones. The Southern Jewish community was hit especially hard. For example, Rabbi Benjamin Goldstein of Montgomery, Alabama's Temple Beth Or synagogue was forced to leave the state because of his support for the ILD. Faced with boycotts and Klan threats, Jewish merchants and other leading members of his congregation not only asked Goldstein to resign but issued a statement to the press repudiating any outside interference in Southern affairs and pledging their unequivocal support for segregation.[30]

Just as Scottsboro moved progressive Jews to action, the rise of fascism and the horrors of the Holocaust compelled radical African Americans to speak out against anti-Semitism. Several articles appeared in Black publications comparing the plight of Jews in Germany with that of Negroes in America. A handful of Black Communists and sympathizers joined Jewish Leftists on the battlefields of Spain, where they met fascist troops face-to-face. By defending the Spanish Republic, these volunteers were also avenging those Jews perishing in German concentration camps as well as those Ethiopians whose precious land Mussolini invaded in 1935.[31] Despite pockets of Black anti-Semitism during the 1930s among a few isolated Black nationalist groups, the struggle against fascism strengthened the Black-Jewish bond within Communist circles. Threats to European Jewry's very existence, combined with domestic anti-Semitism articulated by the Black Shirts, the American Nazi Party, and demagogues like radio priest Father Coughlin, brought about a renewed interest in Jewish identity within the Communist Party. Pamphlets and articles produced during the Popular Front highlighted Jewish contributions to labor and civil rights struggles. Black Communist leader James Ford himself wrote an influential pamphlet titled *Anti-Semitism and the Struggle for Democracy* in which he emphasized the role of Jews in the Black freedom struggle. During World War II, especially, leading Black spokesmen such as Paul Robeson, Adam Clayton Powell, Jr., and Communist leader Benjamin Davis, Jr., praised Jews for their support of African Americans.[32]

Meanwhile, Jewish intellectuals, of middle class or lower class origins and occupations, not only served as the majority of journalists and functionaries (and a disproportionate number of union leaders), but also played a crucial role in the wider culture of the Left. Here, from the dedicated Left newspaper or magazine editor (who urgently sought out Black writers and stories about the African American community), to the like-minded idealistic poet, cartoonist, dramaturge, and songwriter, the anti-racist alliance had its idealistic core. Movement poet Aaron Kramer thus began publishing at age 12 with a paean to the Scottsboro defendants, and Jewish left-wing summer camps typically rushed to include Black children and their parents. Non-communist radicals, from Norman Thomas's Socialist Party to the smaller Marxist groups, could claim a handful of such idealists, a few of them with far-reaching influence. But very few were Jewish.[33]

Communist and near-Communist intellectuals offered publications and theatrical or musical productions to a public audience disproportionately situated in greater New York City and vastly disproportionately Jewish. "Assimilated" Jewish communists who disdained any special or nationalist allegiance of their own often demonstrated their political commitment with their interest in

"Black" questions, which for them epitomized the colonized state of world politics and culture. Yiddish-speaking communists, the most stolidly working class (and often recently immigrated) section of American Jewry, developed a unique interest in what they took to be the folkishness that they, fellow sufferers of capitalism, could share. Both these sections of Jews, it is fair to say, felt the sting of anti-Semitism, and believed that only world revolution offered a solution to either group. Paradoxically, as the rise of fascism pushed early revolution off the map and the Popular Front took hold, the institutional cover of the New Deal allowed a far wider participation in public affairs and a popular culture which at times urged a drastic shift in race relations.

Themes explored for relatively small and politically committed working class audiences in the early 1930s gained tens of thousands of watchers and listeners (albeit with moderated political rhetoric) in Federal Theater productions a few years later. At the Left end of the theatrical spectrum, rising Jewish playwrights such as George Sklar staged provocative interracial dramas, notably Sklar's highly acclaimed *Stevedore* (co-written with Paul Peters). In film, Bernard Vorhaus co-wrote *Way Down South* (1939) with Langston Hughes and Clarence Muse, and a decade later Ben Maddows wrote the script for the anti-racist classic *Intruder in the Dust*. Significantly, these powerful productions were among the nation's earliest productions which did not feature African American actors in minstrel-show archetypes.[34] At another end, nightclub impresario Max Gordon opened the famed Village Vanguard in 1935 with a mixture of progressive-minded Black singers and left-wing Jewish stand-up comedy such as Leadbelly, Josh White, and Jack Gilford. Many of these same performers also worked at Cafe Society, Barney Josephson's after hours club well-known for breaking down racial barriers, paying employees union wages, lampooning the bourgeoisie, raising money for Popular Front causes, and being on J. Edgar Hoover's hit list. (Barney's brother Leon, incidentally, was a leading member of the Communist Party.)[35]

The Federal Theater folded as Congressional investigating committees accused it of being a Communist front and the New Deal wound to a close. But much of the talent that had gathered there reappeared in a handful of interracial films and theatrical productions during the 1940s–50s, once scattered "Negro" parts became an accepted element of Broadway and Hollywood. The musical side, from nightclubs to concerts to children's summer camps, had been fixed in the wild, left-wing, Jewish enthusiasm for the 1938 Carnegie Hall concert, "From Spirituals to Swing." Progressive Jewish impresarios at all levels made Black performers *de rigeur*, the more so if occasional songs could be sung in Yiddish as well (as by Paul Robeson, the all-time headline performer).

After Pearl Harbor

In a larger sense, the impress of Popular Front culture remained the most basic outline of an imagined interracial American society. When leading Yiddish pedagogue Itche Goldberg proclaimed in 1942 that the "melting pot has a scorched bottom," he argued for a multicultural, even multilingual, future which only a cooperative society could bring.[36] Black Communists, heavily situated among the Harlem intelligentsia and artistic crowd, could share this vision because they presumed that whites (i.e., Jews and some others) would patronize Black culture while elaborating their own. The Cold War devastated this working model of interracial unity without, however, destroying it entirely. Jewish artists had already seen the limits of public presentation in their Hollywood efforts. *Body and Soul* (1947), written and directed by two Jewish Communists, Abraham Polonsky and Robert Rossen, starred John Garfield and Canada Lee in an extraordinarily ambitious boxing film showing the destruction of an interracial friendship as a metaphor for capitalism's effect on human beings. It was one of the last credited productions by Polonsky for more than twenty years, and one of the last for Garfield and Lee (both personally destroyed by the effects of Blacklist).[37]

In the literary world, a group of anti-Stalinist Jewish intellectuals who emerged after the war as a dominant force on the high cultural landscape occasionally took up issues of race, and sometimes engaged in dialogue with Black writers like Ralph Ellison, Richard Wright, and James Baldwin. Too often, especially in *Commentary* and the *Partisan Review*, they used such issues mainly to slap at Black opponents of the Cold War, and to remind Black intellectuals of their good fortune as Americans. By contrast, Communists fallen on political hard times seized upon real Black-Jewish intellectual and artistic collaboration as one of their few remaining attractive features. The editorial board of *Masses and Mainstream*, for instance, was made up almost entirely of Jewish and Black artists and intellectuals, including W.E.B. Du Bois, Paul Robeson, Charles White, Theodore Ward, Lloyd Brown, Samuel Sillen, Herbert Aptheker, Howard Fast, Hugo Gellert, and Sidney Finklestein. At the height of the Cold War, Jewish Communist critics were celebrating Black literary achievements, highlighting a new generation of Black visual artists, and attacking Hollywood's portrayal of African Americans in popular film. *Masses and Mainstream* also became a vehicle for Black scholars writing on history and politics in the United States, Africa, and the Caribbean. Likewise, the Communist Party-influenced magazine *Jewish Life* devoted its entire February 1953 issue to African American history, reprinting the writings of Frederick Douglass as well as more contemporary essays by Black Communists.[38]

Even as the last moment of radical hope in a generation ebbed, remarkable occurrences suggested lost possibilities. The doomed Henry Wallace campaign of 1948 inspired without doubt the most interracial social network ever seen on the Left, and perhaps in American society at large. Bebop pioneer Dizzy Gillespie's appearance on the cover of *Life* magazine, surrounded by white teenagers, captured (or perhaps distorted) the surge of common generational sensibilities later recalled by many veteran radicals. Gillespie was not oblivious to the interracial culture of the pre-war Left, having known "a bunch of musicians more socially minded, who were closely connected to the Communist Party." And one of his greatest heroes was none other than Paul Robeson, whom Gillespie described as a "forerunner of Martin Luther King": "I'll always remember Paul Robeson as a politically committed artist. A few enlightened musicians recognized the importance of Paul Robeson, amongst them Teddy Wilson, Frankie Newton, and Pete Seeger—all of them very outspoken politically." At another level, Yiddish choral appearances with Paul Robeson reminded audiences of a deep folkish basis for sentiment.[39]

All this came to a shocking conclusion, as McCarthyism began and a series of calamities associated with suburbanization, inner city decay, drug epidemics, and gang violence literally swept several generations of interracial (and anti-racist, Jewish community) activists off the streets. The collapsing Communist Party added to its own troubles, alienating Jews by defending Stalin's depredations while attracting little African American admiration by the "trials" and expulsions of aged Jewish activists charged with taking vacations in racially segregated Florida. Furthermore, as the Jewish role in the Communist Party became more public and more pronounced, so did Black nationalist sentiment. During the 1950s, a growing number of Black Communists quit the Party, charging that it was "dominated" by Jews whose interest in African Americans was less than genuine. Although organizations like the Civil Rights Congress successfully rallied the faithful to protest new waves of Southern lynchings and arrests, by and large, a legally hamstrung Left spent its time defending itself and living through the large-scale disillusionment of its members, Black and Jewish alike.[40]

The Jewish Left retained a surprising vitality on Black-Jewish issues not because of Party leadership but because of the experience and dedication of mostly former Communists. On the political front, former Communists played key roles from the top of the Civil Rights movement to the local grass-roots organizer. Dr. Martin Luther King, Jr.'s top advisor, for example, was ex-Communist Stanley Levison. Southern African American leaders were often trained in left-wing organizations or schools, and Jews and Blacks in Northern metropolitan centers jointly protested segregated public facilities and racial discrimination in housing policy. On selected campuses in the 1950s, the Labor Youth League, overwhelmingly Jewish, often led such fights and, especially after the revelations about Stalin, turned their full attention toward civil rights support groups for the Southern movement.[41]

The Left arguably had still more success on the cultural front. There, for instance, eager Jewish audiences had been created for Harry Belafonte (who first made some of his appearances at Popular Front functions in the later 1940s, and became a standard figure in Jewish summer entertainment), Lorraine Hansberry (whose play, *Raisin in the Sun*, might be considered a final Popular Front aesthetic triumph, and which served as the model for the 1970s television series, *Good Times*), and notable progressives Ossie Davis and Ruby Dee. One might also include the late Arnold Perl, the credited co-author of the screenplay that became the basis for Spike Lee's film *Malcolm X*. The "folksong" movement, which generally featured Yankees like Woody Guthrie and Pete Seeger along with African American performers, was heavily Jewish in its audience and, somewhat more cryptically, in its "white" artists.[42] In these ways, the mostly Jewish Left and its showcased Black participants set the pace for cultural developments in the 1960s.

The Cold War and the economic recovery of the later 1940s also reconfigured the social democratic sector of the Jewish Left in key, albeit contradictory, ways. The shift of many thousands of Jews from the industrial working class to the regions of lower middle-class professionals (prototypically teachers and social workers) inevitably emphasized a degree of meritocratic personal advance along with whatever benefits unionization and politically based expansion of government agencies could bring. Even in the most caring professions, individuals found themselves enmeshed in a system whose "objectivity" promoted a subtle favoritism. So long as capitalism seemed to have failed, even meritocracy had sharp limits. With an expanding economy and a seemingly endless future of materialism (including suburbanization and generational upward-mobility) stretching ahead, "socialism" lost its tenacious hold upon a generation of Jewish voters for Franklin Roosevelt and American Labor Party (later, Liberal Party) candidates.

A certain fair-mindedness remained, and among aging social democrats or Labor (and socialist) Zionists as well as parts of a younger generation influenced by them, so did the desire for a Black-Jewish alliance that might transform American liberalism at large. In the twenty years after the outbreak of Cold War, resolutely anti-communist Jewish socialists formed committees for the racial integration of neighborhoods and unions, marched in local parades, and worked for liberal candidates such as Hubert Humphrey who argued for an inclusive society. Such unity had its limits, however. The "Red" unions, expunged and uprooted by the CIO, represented by and large the advanced wing of interracial unionism. Like the National Negro Labor Congress, effectively suppressed by mainstream union hostility and government investigation, such unions had been supported by Jews in the Popular Front orbit, while their demise was welcomed by Jewish anti-communists. The liberal entities encompassing anti-communist Left intellectuals, such as the Anti-Defamation League and American Jewish Committee with its *Commentary* magazine, had even worse records of cooperation with the FBI against Jewish and Black communists, of belittling Black radicals, and welcoming a blacklist which "accurately" pinpointed communist sympathizers for expulsion from positions of influence, from film industry to the labor movement. As Black civil rights attorney Conrad Lynn observed, the Jewish intellectuals with a background in socialism remained friendly to the idea of Black advancement but their real priorities lay elsewhere, with their own careers and with the stabilization of a liberal capitalist society whose institutions they accepted with fewer and fewer fundamental criticisms.[43]

The historically social democratic "Jewish unions," steadily less Jewish save in their bureaucracy, thus marched forward with increasingly nonwhite memberships. In a few cases, the mix of old Left Jewish labor leaders and dynamic Black militants inspired by Civil Rights and Black Power movements created some of labor's few bright spots during the 1960s and 1970s. The best-known example was the New York-based Hospital Workers Union, Local 1199. Initially made up of primarily Jewish male pharmacists, clerks, soda men, and Black porters and retail hospital workers in Harlem, 1199 was founded in the 1930s by Jewish Communists active in the CPUSA Trade Union Unity League. Its composition changed dramatically by the late fifties when a left-wing breakaway group within the union began organizing Black and Latino hospital service workers and waged a partially successful strike in 1959. Although it eventually abandoned its ties to the Communist Party, leaders like Leon Davis and Elliot Godoff (both Old Left Russian émigrés) as well as Moe Foner (brother of noted radical historians Jack and Philip—the latter emerging as one of the leading scholars on the history of labor and African Americans) ensured that 1199 would not take the complacent, apolitical road of most AFL-CIO unions. Like Cesar Chavez's United Farm Workers Union, 1199 retained a left-wing political culture, struggled against racial and gender inequality at the workplace and beyond, opposed the Vietnam War, actively supported the Civil Rights movement, aided the legal defense of the Black Panther Party, protested Israeli occupation of the West Bank, and pledged solidarity with democratic movements in Central America and South Africa. The union celebrated its multicultural make-up by sponsoring annual events such as "Salute to Freedom" (replacing its "Negro History Week" celebration), "Salute to Israel," and "Latin American Fiesta Night."[44]

Local (later District) 1199 remained a shining light of Black-Jewish-Latino solidarity and a remarkable example of progressive unionism until the early 1980s. A leadership secession crisis created by the retirement of president Leon Davis—the dominant force in the local for half a century, rising racial tensions within the union, economic recession, and cutbacks in the healthcare profession all contributed to a massive split in the once vital union. Unlike most other so-called Jewish unions, 1199's African American leadership turned out to be the more conservative force, resorting at times to red-baiting Black and Jewish activists aligned with Davis. On the other hand, aging giants of the traditionally Jewish garment trades, above all David Dubinsky of the ILGWU, had already established themselves as partners with international intelligence operations against the rebellious Third World nationalisms. Apart from visceral hatred of Communists and all who wavered in anti-Communism as an indispensable primary political issue, Jewish labor leaders increasingly viewed Israel as the beloved child of a West whose treatment of Palestinians and Arab populations was probably not harsh enough. Thus the idea that Arabs and African Americans alike were ungrateful, hopelessly backward troublemakers began to make its way into the respectable corridors of Jewish discourse in the 1950s.[45]

Mainstream Jewish leaders who might be properly regarded as the successors to the garment union dynasty did not at first place their institutional energy against the Civil Rights movement. Hoping to broaden the alliance with historic Black organizations and often in awe of Martin Luther King, Jr., middle-aged Jewish liberals with New Dealish and socialist or (often secretly) communist memories looked to idealistic young people to take up the fallen banners of social justice. Sometimes, especially at the local level of campus Hillel Foundations, they sponsored coalitions, primed advanced thought, and urged the awakening to conscience of a new Jewish generation. They were entirely committed, however, to the Johnson administration's vision of the Great Society as reform from the commanding heights of the post-New Deal coalition: they could not imagine the future arriving in any other way. As this impulse failed, and feeling themselves robbed of a liberal victory, key social democratic players turned their vitriol toward the student anti-war movement, and braced their ranks to support the Vietnam War. Especially after State Department support of the Six Day War in the Middle East refreshed their national loyalties and the hawkish AFL-CIO leadership made clear that it regarded lock-step patriotism as the price for bureaucratic cooperation, the mainstream Jewish institutions subtly shifted rightward and leaders quietly began to withdraw their support from Martin Luther King, Jr., who announced his opposition to the war and described America as the "most violent nation in the world." These events, less dramatic than the announcement of Black Power in several civil rights organizations, helped set the lines of fracture to come.

Black Nationalism, Zionism, and the Left

Nineteen sixty-seven is often viewed as marking the end of the grand alliance. It was the year Stokely Carmichael and other Black leaders in the Student Nonviolent Coordinating Committee (SNCC) adopted "Black Power" as their slogan and asked white members to devote their energies to fighting racism in white communities. The new directive created tension in the ranks since the majority of "whites" in SNCC at the time were young Jews who did not see the white community as their own and thus felt as if they had been exiled from the organization they helped to build. The second important development was SNCC's open solidarity with Third World liberation movements, including the Palestinians. The Black nationalist critique of Israel, in particular, and Zionism, in general, took on anti-Semitic overtones and ultimately eroded many ties remaining among young Jewish and Black radicals. Rapidly, the historic Civil Rights alliance crumbled: Jewish liberals felt betrayed and angry that African Americans had not been grateful for their support, and many Black nationalists began to see Jewish conspiracies at every turn.

Undoubtedly, the emergence of a particular brand of Black nationalism in the mid-1960s and Israel's policies toward the Middle East and apartheid in South Africa deeply damaged Black-Jewish relations within progressive circles. But as we have tried to suggest all along, the story is far more complicated. First, Israel had become a sore spot for African Americans in the Old Left a decade before the Six Day War. The Israeli occupation of the Suez Canal in 1956 sparked a contentious debate between Black Communist leaders like Benjamin Davis, Jr. and Edward Strong, who supported Egypt, and their Jewish comrades who stood behind Israel and even adopted the slogan "Arms for Israel." For their position, both Davis and Strong were accused of anti-Semitism, which hurt the former since his election to the New York City Council had depended heavily on Jewish votes. Davis not only accused Jewish liberals of pressuring Black newspaper editors to defend Israel's position, but he insisted that African Americans were right to support Egyptian President Gamal Abdel Nasser. In a letter to the *Daily Worker*, another Black Communist called on progressives to "ask themselves, why is it that Israel is today so completely isolated from the Bandung powers, the colonial peoples, Negro Americans and the Socialist bloc."[46]

Second, Old and New Left Jews of various kinds were ambivalent, if not outright hostile, toward Zionism. Before the Holocaust, Jewish Communists and socialists (excepting Labor Zionists) regarded Zionism as a bourgeois ideology. During the creation of Israel, some Communists had enlisted as fighters and the Left quite properly credited the Soviet Union with crucial early U.N. support for the Jewish state. The aftermath of near-genocide and the continuing revelations of Stalin's anti-Semitism inevitably compelled many left-wing Jews to rethink their positions on Israel without, however, placing it at the center of their worldview. Even the social democrats, set upon assimilation and a New Dealish revival, tended to treat Zionism as a competing ideology—until the 1967 war.[47]

During the later 1960s, then, the Jewish-Black relationship turned volatile for complex reasons often transcending the immediate issues. As Old Left Jews softened their criticisms of Israel, many New Left Jews echoed the anti-Zionist attacks waged by their Black militant allies and demanded self-determination for Palestinians. Others simply argued that Israel was an imperialist state and therefore should not be supported by any progressive Marxist movement. On the other hand, Black nationalism and its support for Third World liberation movements (including that of the Palestinians) prompted some New Left Jews to argue that support of ethnic nationalisms should extend to Israel. Thus, like the Old Left, the New Left was somewhat divided on the question. Jewish student journals like *The Jewish Radical* and *The Other Side* ran articles debating the Left's stance toward Israel, urging readers to embrace their own cultural particularism if they intended to advocate it among African Americans.[48]

Finally, although left-leaning Black nationalists were fairly uniform in their opposition to Israel, they did not deserve the blanket condemnation of being anti-Semitic any more than avid Zionists and other zealous supporters of Israel were uniformly anti-Black. Some were, no doubt, but many sought to divide anti-Zionism from anti-Semitism, warning that anti-Semitic expressions weakened the Black nationalist movement.[49] Here, still another irony might be located. As a stream of former young Zionists from the 1950s–60s, including Noam

Chomsky, became stalwart figures of the Left, a handful of Black nationalist leaders such as Stokely Carmichael began their political careers under the guidance of Old Left Jews. Perhaps the most important voice in support of Black Power and against Zionism, Carmichael cut his political teeth in high school through his relationship with Jewish Communists, notably Gene Dennis, Jr., the son of the New York Party leader. Through Dennis, he met Black Communists like Benjamin Davis, who clearly shaped his own socialist politics—indeed, long after the collapse of SNCC he continued to advocate socialism with the founding of his All African People's Revolutionary Party. (To compound the paradox: whereas Carmichael lived in a predominantly white neighborhood in the Bronx and attended the highly competitive magnet school, Bronx High School of Science, his classmate Gene Dennis lived in Harlem.) Eventually, Carmichael became involved in Left youth organizations, including the Young People's Socialist League. According to historian Clayborne Carson, Carmichael's first demonstration was in behalf of Israel. "Someone at the U.N. had said something anti-Semitic," he told Carson in a 1963 interview, "I can't exactly remember who, but [the Young People's Socialist League] drew up a big picket-line at the U.N."[50]

The crowning incident that brought the issues of Black Power and the Black-Jewish alliance to a head was the bitter 1968 New York City teacher's strike that pitted largely Jewish schoolteachers and their Old Left allies against Black and Puerto Rican communities in the Ocean Hill–Brownsville section of Brooklyn. The inability of New York City to integrate its schools led residents of poor Latino and African American communities to push for community control, which Mayor John Lindsay and the Board of Education granted to Ocean Hill–Brownsville residents. The newly formed governing board immediately got into trouble, however, when it attempted to reassign 19 white teachers. Albert Shanker and the UFT protested, waging three strikes in the fall of 1968 which ultimately led to the termination of the community control program and some limited compromise that gave schools with lower overall reading scores some flexibility over teacher hiring. The UFT was especially angry that community control would erode their ability to protect teachers' jobs—their primary responsibility as a teachers' union. Moreover, liberal Jewish educators (some of whom had longtime associations with the Left) felt betrayed by the community control board, particularly since UFT-affiliated teachers were responsible for developing a progressive, pluralistic curriculum that celebrated African American history and honored Civil Rights leaders such as Dr. Martin Luther King, Jr. On the other hand, community activists and Black teachers affiliated with the African American Teachers Association (ATA) regarded established white educators and their programs as paternalistic and out of touch with the social and material realities inner city children had to face. They rejected the prevailing view of poor Black and Puerto Rican kids as educationally disadvantaged or impaired and believed that teachers of their own race were needed to help build self-esteem and create a healthier environment for effective learning.[51]

The fight between Black and Puerto Rican community activists and the predominantly Jewish UFT irrevocably damaged the liberal Black-Jewish alliance. Old Left Jewish radicals who had cultivated links with working-class Black and Latino communities were suddenly forced to choose between supporting a labor conflict and an important community issue affecting aggrieved populations of color. Both sides fought for things progressive activists supported. But both sides fought tenaciously, consequently eliminating the possibility of reconciliation any time soon.

Whither the Alliance?

After the Ocean Hill–Brownsville conflict, the polarizations of the next quarter century had been firmly established. In a perverse twist of history and fate, the most influential Jewish Marxist of the mainstream, former Trotskyist leader Max Shachtman, used the Socialist Party/Social Democratic Federation (SP/SDF) as a launching pad for a major generational and political maneuver. Speech-writer for George Meany's attacks on the anti-war movement, Max Shachtman provided ideological (and often tactical) guidance to UFT leader Albert Shanker during the Jewish confrontations with African American activists.

Shachtman's ceaseless maneuvering pointed the way for a minor SP/SDF leader, Abraham Foxman, to move into the increasingly conservative leadership of the Anti-Defamation League (ADL). Still others from Shachtman's SP/SDF would become lead staffers in Jeane Kirkpatrick's United Nations office, in the neo-conservative Freedom House, and in their favorite agency, the National Endowment for Democracy. Linking their support of Israel to their broad cooperation with the Central Intelligence Agency during the "dirty wars" against insurgents in Central America (and for the Contra war against Nicaragua) and in the Front Line states in Southern Africa, they inevitably widened the breech between sections of Jewish officialdom and the Left, including the Congressional Black Caucus and Jewish progressives. By the early 1990s, this had reached the near-fratricidal level of ADL infiltration and disinformation against heavily Jewish environmental and Central America support groups.[52]

Three-quarters of a century earlier, in 1899, the *Jewish Daily Forward*, organ of expression for a bureaucratic Jewish socialism, had blessed the U.S. invasion of Cuba and the Philippines as bringing civilization to the savages.[53] In the new reading of American empire and world events, only the military strength and resolve of the world's greatest capitalist power could protect the Jewish State and, indeed, all civilization from the threatened depredations of fanatical Arabs.[54] Thus several aging Social Democrats and a handful of extremely well-placed protégés leaned heavily on the neoconservative side of international affairs, while the ADL was the most unsparing of Jesse Jackson's attackers within the Jewish community. At the end of the Cold War, manqué socialist rage sputtered mainly now toward questions of race and culture, in the pages of *Commentary* and the heavily

endowed think tanks. At what sometimes seemed the final round-up a of a tradition, those once fixed upon the visions of socialism turned their harsh gaze toward
the Popular Frontish elements of film and television and upon the neo-Popular
Front currents of academic multiculturalism as the hydra-headed foe.

And they were not entirely wrong, in their terms, to do so. Jewish memory
repeatedly pulled upon forbidden zones of socialist and even communist idealism, a past which they could bring back as their own exceptional democratic legacy. With the history of labor diminished, that past became more and more heavily colored, so to speak, with the dream of multicultural democracy. Jewish
Communists had not invented, but rather popularized and at times vulgarized,
the transracial notion of solidarity based upon their own identity as outsiders,
nonvictors in white domination of the world by the West. As young Jewish record
producers and journalists programmed and charted the hip-hop scene, leading
Jewish entertainers recuperated moments of the past Jewish Left in which Jews
found themselves victims, executioners, and above all bystanders to the unending
injustice of rich over poor and race over race.[55]

Meanwhile, the AFL-CIO's Executive Council, unified on the hopelessness of
labor organization at home and the hopes for guiding business unionism in the
post-communist world, marked the rendezvous of another kind of Jewish socialism in the domination of global North over South, suburb over inner-city, White
over Black. Of course, Jews outside of the Executive Council, from rank-and-file
unionists to middle-level leadership, have been among the most progressive voices pushing for trade union democracy and reform. More recently, Shanker and the
established leadership backed Lane Kirkland's heir apparent Tom Donohue,
despite protestations from the rank-and-file.[56] As many labor progressives celebrate John Sweeney's, Richard Trumka's, and Linda Chavez-Thompson's victory
over the old guard in 1995, it remains to be seen whether the new AFL-CIO will
become a site for the reconstruction of a radical Black-Jewish alliance. And with
Black Nationalism on the rise again and Jewish neoconservatives leading the fight
to dismantle affirmative action and the welfare state, the prospect of an alliance
anywhere seems dim.

But it would be far too early for any such conclusion. Unlike the enraged and
fearful white (and especially male) gentiles who pulled the electoral levers for
Republicans in 1994, Jews voted heavily against the broad swing rightward.[57] It
is more than possible that, with the dramatic rise of the Right, an exhausted
Black Nationalism and Jewish nationalism might find common roots or at least
the basis for a renewed modus vivendi.[58] Whether such a project takes flight
depends upon a vision of regeneration, with reborn urban cultures, an ability and
willingness to clean the wreckage left by an exploitative system, and hope for a
world beyond the ecological devastation at hand.

Notes

1. Robert Weisbord and Arthur Stein, *Bittersweet Encounter: The Afro-American and the American Jew* (Westport, CT, 1970); Harold Cruse, *The Crisis of the Negro Intellectual* (New York, 1967).

2. See, e.g., Bruce Carlan Levine, "Free Soil, Free Labor and Freimaenner: German Chicago in the Civil War Era," in Hartmut Keil and John B. Jentz, eds., *German Workers in Industrial Chicago, 1850–1910: A Comparative Perspective* (DeKalb, IL, 1983), 163–82. Like other accounts of antebellum German radicalism, this falls short by failing to note the small but significant Jewish presence among the movement's intellectuals.

3. See Christine Hess, "German Radicals in Industrial America: The Lehr and Wehr-Verein in Gilded Age Chicago," in ibid., 206–23; Paul Buhle, *Marxism in the United States* (London, 1990, 2nd edition), chapter 1; and the various essays in Hartmut Keil and John Jentz, eds., *German Workers Culture in Chicago* (Washington, D.C., 1990).

4. See Timothy Messer-Kruse, "The Yankee International: Marxism and the American Reform Tradition, 1831–1876" (Ph.D. diss., University of Wisconsin, 1994).

5. Oakley C. Johnson, "Marxism and the Negro Freedom Struggle (1876–1917)," *Journal of Human Relations* 13, no. 1 (1965), 25–27.

6. Adolf Douai, a German '48er of note and briefly the editor of an antebellum Abolitionist newspaper in Texas, was the most important veteran newspaper editor in the German-American socialist movement of the 1870s–80s, and the leading figure of a milieu of German-language, disproportionately Jewish (but very assimilated) intellectuals. As Philip S. Foner noted, Douai now and then made a special point of urging the organization of Black workers. Foner, *History of Labor in the U.S.*, vol. 1 (New York, 1947), 503. Ordinarily, Black workers were little discussed in the socialist papers of the day. See also Johnson, "Marxism and the Negro Freedom Struggle," 21–24; Philip S. Foner, *American Socialism and Black Americans* (Westport, CT, 1977); James R. Green, *Grass-Roots Socialism: Radical Movements in the Southwest, 1895–1943* (Baton Rouge, 1978).

7. Samuel Gompers said that as far as he could help it, "the caucasians are not going to let their standard of living be destroyed by negroes, Chinamen, Japs or any other." *American Federationist* (September 1905), 636, also quoted in Philip Foner and Ronald Lewis, eds., *The Black Worker: A Documentary History from Colonial Times to the Present*, vol. 5 (Philadelphia, 1980), 124. For more on the AFL's policies regarding race, see Sterling D. Spero and Abram L. Harris, *The Black Worker: The Negro and the Labor Movement* (New York, 1931), 53–104; Foner, *American Socialism and Black*

Americans, 102, 133, 262, 307–309, 342; Foner, *Organized Labor and the Black Worker* (New York, 1982); Marc Karson and Ronald Radosh, "The American Federation of Labor and the Negro Worker, 1894–1949," in Julius Jacobson, ed., *The Negro and the American Labor Movement* (Garden City, NJ, 1968); Bernard Mandel, "Samuel Gompers and the Negro Worker, 1886–1914," *Journal of Negro History* 40 (January 1955), 34–60.

8. See Paul Buhle, "The Jewish Left in the United States," in Paul Buhle and Dan Georgakas, eds., *The Immigrant Left in the United States* (Albany, NY, 1996), 77–118.

9. Hasia R. Diner, *In the Almost Promised Land: American Jews and Blacks, 1915–1935* (Westport, CT, 1977), 36–38; Robert Weisbord and Arthur Stein, *Bittersweet Encounter,* 32–33; Franklin Jonas, "The Early Life and Career of B. Charney Vladeck: A Study in Political Acculturation" (Ph.D. diss., New York University, 1970), chapter 2; Arthur Liebman, *Jews and the Left* (New York, 1979), 54–55. Of course, a few leading conservative Jews were not only indifferent to the plight of Black lynch victims but advocated lynching and vehemently rejected the analogy with pogroms. Tensions between Blacks and Jews came to a head after President Roosevelt sent a petition to the Russian Tsar in June, 1903, denouncing the massacre of Jews at Kishineff. African American leaders not only protested the fact that the petition included the names of Senators from Mississippi who had publicly justified lynching as a necessity to "maintain law and order," but they were taken aback when B'nai Brith leader Solomon Cohen criticized the Black press for comparing the plight of Jews and Blacks. Cohen argued that it was absurd "to contrast the advanced stage of intellectual and moral development of the Jews in general with the limited progress that masses of Negroes in America have made," and that lynching was justified since they generally are responses to "crimes committed by individual Negroes." Philip S. Foner, "Black-Jewish Relations in the Opening Years of the Twentieth Century," *Phylon* 36, no. 4 (Winter 1975), 362–363.

10. Quoted in Johnson, "Marxism and the Negro Freedom Struggle," 31.

11. Liebman, *Jews and the Left,* 45–47; on African Americans and the Socialist Party in the South and Southwest, see Green, *Grass-Roots Socialism;* Grady McWhiney, "Louisiana Socialists in the Early Twentieth Century: A Study of Rustic Radicalism." *Journal of Southern History* 20, no. 3 (1954), 315–36; E. F. Andrews, "Socialism and the Negro." *International Socialist Review* 5, no. 7 (January 1905), 524–26.

12. Philip Foner, ed., *Black Socialist Preacher* (San Francisco, 1983), 319, from the *Chicago Daily Socialist,* November 9, 1908.

13. Foner, ed., *Black Socialist Preacher,* 92–93.

14. Ibid., 103–4, 127.

15. Johnson, "Marxism and the Negro Freedom Struggle," 32–33.

16. See Robert Allen, *Reluctant Reformers: Racism and Social Reform Movements in the United States* (Washington, D.C., 1983), 212–15; Foner, *American Socialism and Black Americans*; Johnson, "Marxism and the Negro Freedom Struggle," 28–34; Lawrence Moore, "Flawed Fraternity: American Socialist Response and the Negro, 1901–1920," *Journal of Negro History* 33, no. 1 (1969), 1–14; Mark Naison, "Marxism and Black Radicalism in America: Notes on a Long (and Continuing) Journey," *Radical America*," 5, no. 3 (1971), 4–10; David A. Shannon, *The Socialist Party of America* (New York, 1955), 49–52; Sally M. Miller, "The Socialist Party and the Negro, 1901–1920," *Journal of Negro History*, 56 (July 1971), 229. Based on English language sources only, this and other accounts of the same subject remain incomplete. But Miller accurately reflects the approach as emphasizing class almost to the exclusion of race. Nationality groups came to recognize their own special plight almost inadvertently, until World War I compelled their attention, split the ranks of nearly all immigrant groups politically, and prompted the rise of the communist groupings which eventually sought to factor race into a complex approach.

17. On Blacks and the IWW, Selig Perlman and Philip Taft, *History of Labor in the United States* (New York, 1935), 247; Bernard A. Cook, "Covington Hall and Radical Rural Unionization in Louisiana," *Louisiana History* 18, no. 2 (1977), 230, 235; Melvyn Dubofsky, *We Shall Be All: A History of the IWW* (Chicago, 1969), 8–9, 210, 213–16; James F. Fickle, "Race, Class, and Radicalism: The Wobblies in the Southern Lumber Industry, 1900–1916," in Joseph Conlin, ed., *At the Point of Production: The Local Hist-ory of the IWW* (Westport, CT, 1981), 98–109; Merl E. Reed, "Lumberjacks and Longshoremen: The IWW in Louisiana," *Labor History* 13, no. 1 (Winter 1972), 44–58; James R. Green, "The Brotherhood of Timber Workers, 1910–1913: A Radical Response to Industrial Capitalism in the Southern U.S.A.," *Past and Present*, 60 (August 1973), 161–200; Philip Foner, "The IWW and the Black Worker," *Journal of Negro History* 55 (January 1970), 45–64; and portions of Spero and Harris, *The Black Worker*, esp. 329–335.

18. Foner, "The IWW and the Black Worker," 51; Herbert R. Northrup, *Organized Labor and the Negro* (New York, 1944), 144; Myland R. Brown, "The IWW and the Negro Worker" (Ed.D., Ball State University, 1968), 67; Spero and Harris, *The Black Worker*, 333–36: Irwin Marcus, "Benjamin Fletcher: Black Labor Leader," *Negro History Bulletin* 35 (October 1972), 131–40; Benjamin Fletcher, "Philadelphia Waterfront Unionism," *The Messenger* (June 1923), 740–41; quote from Benjamin Fletcher, "The Negro and Organized Labor," *The Messenger* 5, no. 7 (July 1923), 760.

19. Even *Modern Dance*, a specialized *Masses* with a disproportionately Jewish readership, praised the jazz dance as the sentiment of the new generation, rooted in African American culture. For an analysis of the significance of a young radical's zest for jazz dancing see Paul Buhle, *A Dreamer's Paradise Lost: Louis C. Fraina/Lewis Corey, 1892–1953* (Atlantic Highlands, NJ, 1995), chapter 2.

20. Quote from "Why Negroes Should Join the IWW," *The Messenger* 2, no. 7 (July 1919), 8; see also, Jervis Anderson, *A. Philip Randolph: A Biographical Portrait* (New York, 1972), 76–96; Theodore Kornweibel, Jr., *No Crystal Stair: Black Life and the Messenger, 1917–1928* (Westport, CT, 1975).

21. Anderson, *A. Philip Randolph*, 92–95; Foner, *American Socialism and Black Americans*; Philip S. Foner, ed., "'Colored and Jewish Workers'—A Document by A. Philip Randolph and Chandler Owen," *Jewish Currents* 21, no. 2 (February 1967), 4–7.

22. Research has not fully revealed the Jewish role in either Harlem or Chicago, but in the former case, Finns and Jews were the two most important ethnic radicals in the voting population; and in the second, Jewish communist organizers were a vital element even when the Jewish workforce was small.

23. "Program of the African Blood Brotherhood," *Communist Review* (London), April 1922, pp. 449–54; Mark Solomon, "Red and Black: Negroes and Communism, 1929–1932" (Ph.D. diss., Harvard University, 1972), 80–83; For more on the ABB, see Harry Haywood, *Black Bolshevik: Autobiography of An Afro-American Communist* (Chicago, 1978), 122–30; Mark Naison, *Communists in Harlem During the Depression* (Urbana, 1983), 3, 5–8, 17–18; Theodore Vincent, *Black Power and the Garvey Movement* (Berkeley, 1971), 74–85 and passim; Theodore Draper, *American Communism and Soviet Russia* (New York, 1960), 322–32; Foner, *Organized Labor and the Black Worker*, 148–49; Cedric J. Robinson, *Black Marxism: The Making of the Black Radical Tradition* (London, 1983), 296–301; David Samuels, "Five Afro-Caribbean Voices in American Culture, 1917–1929: Hubert H. Harrison, Wilfred A. Domingo, Richard B. Moore, Cyril Briggs and Claude McKay" (Ph.D. diss., University of Iowa, 1977); Theman Taylor, "Cyril Briggs and the African Blood Brotherhood: Effects of Communism on Black Nationalism, 1919–1935" (Ph.D. diss., University of California, Santa Barbara, 1981).

24. Workers (Communist) Party of America, *Fourth National Convention of the Workers (Communist) Party of America* (Chicago, 1925), 121 and 122; Robert Hill, ed., *The Marcus Garvey and Universal Negro Improvement Association Papers,* vol. 3 (Berkeley and Los Angeles, 1984), 675–81; James Jackson [Lovett Fort-Whiteman], "The Negro in America," *Communist International* (February 1925), 52; Robert Minor, "After Garvey—What?" *Workers Monthly* 5 (June 1926), 362–65.

25. The history of Comintern policy toward Blacks has been thoroughly documented by several scholars and participants, though there are sharp disagreements among them. For just a sampling of the primary and secondary literature, see Draper, *American Communism and Soviet Russia,* 320–350 passim; Roger E. Kanet, "The Comintern and the 'Negro Question': Communist Policy in the United States and Africa, 1921–1941," *Survey* 19, no. 4 (Autumn 1973), 87–122; Haywood, *Black Bolshevik*, 225; Robin D. G. Kelley, "'Afric's Sons with Banner Red': African

American Communists and the Politics of Culture, 1919–1934," in Sidney J. Lemelle and Robin D. G. Kelley, eds., *Imagining Home: Class, Culture, and Nationalism in the African Diaspora* (London, 1994), 35–54; Earl Ofari Hutchinson, *Blacks and Reds: Race and Class Conflict, 1919–1990* (East Lansing, 1995), 43–56; John W. VanZanten, "Communist Theory and the American Negro Question." *Review of Politics* 29 (1967), 435–56; Solomon, "Red and Black," 108–55; Margaret Jackson, "Evolution of the Communist Party's Position on the American Negro Question" (master's thesis, Howard University, 1938); Frank A. Scott, "An Inquiry into the Communist Program for the National Self-Determination of Negroes in the Black Belt" (master's thesis, Howard University, 1951); Wilson Record, "The Development of the Communist Position on the Negro Question in the United States," *Phylon* 19, no. 3 (1958), 306–26. The critical primary documents include Billings [Otto Huiswoud], "Report on the Negro Question," *International Press Correspondence* 3, no. 2 (1923), 14–16; "Theses on the Negro Question" is available in *Bulletin of the IV Congress of the Communist International* no. 27 (December 7, 1922), 8–10; "Sixth World Congress of the Communist International (Full Report)," *International Press Correspondence* 8, no. 74 (October 25, 1928), 1345–47; James S. Allen, *The Negro Question in the United States* (New York, 1936); Communist Party USA, *The Communist Position on the Negro Question* (New York, 1930).

26. Naison, *Communists in Harlem*, 321–22. Indeed, the Harlem CP's political manual, distributed around 1939 or 1940, identifies Negroes, Puerto Ricans, Italians, and West Indians as separate ethnic groups but makes no mention of Jews. In many respects they are rendered invisible. Harlem Division of the Communist Party, *A Political Manual for Harlem* (Mimeograph, ca. 1939) in Robin D. G. Kelley's possession.

27. See for instance, Mark Elovitz, *A Century of Jewish Life in Dixie: The Birmingham Experience* (University, AL, 1974), esp. 54, 101; Cowett, *Birmingham's Rabbi: Morris Newfield and Alabama, 1895–1940*, (University, AL, 1986), 137–38.

28. William F. Dunne, *Gastonia: Citadel of the Class Struggle in the New South* (New York, 1929); Fred Beal, *Proletarian Journey* (New York, 1937), 27–135; Vera Buch Weisbord, *A Radical Life* (Bloomington, IN, 1977); Robin D. G. Kelley, *Hammer and Hoe: Alabama Communists During the Great Depression* (Chapel Hill, NC, 1990), 7, 27–29. Simms was gunned down during a coal miner's strike in Kentucky in 1932.

29. Kelley, *Hammer and Hoe*, 128–31, 178–88, 207 (quote). On the beating of Joe Gelders, see Robert P. Ingalls, "Antiradical Violence in Birmingham during the 1930s," *Journal of Southern History* 47 (November 1981), 525–68.

30. Kelley, *Hammer and Hoe*, 87–88; Cowett, *Birmingham's Rabbi*, 148–49; Weisbord and Stein, *Bittersweet Encounter*, 33. The Yiddish press paid special attention to the Scottsboro case. According to Hasia Diner, "Of all the events in the history of race relations from 1915 to 1935, no single episode received as much attention from

the Yiddish press as did the Scottsboro case." From summer of 1931 to spring 1935, a total of 104 articles appeared in the *Forward* and *Morgn Journal-Tageblatt*. Diner, *In the Almost Promised Land*, 42. On the Scottsboro case generally, see Dan T. Carter, *Scottsboro: A Tragedy in the American South*, 1969; 2nd ed. (Baton Rouge, 1984); James Goodman, *Stories of Scottsboro: The Rape Case that Shocked 1930s America and Revived the Struggle for Equality* (New York, 1994).

31. David H. Pierce, "Fascism and the Negro," *Crisis* 42, no. 4 (April 1935), 107, 114; Rabbi Stephen S. Wise, "Parallel Between Hitlerism and the Persecution of Negroes in America," *Crisis* 41, no. 5 (May 1934), 127–29; Norman Thomas, "Can America Go Fascist?" *Crisis* 41, no. 1 (January 1934), 10–11; Harold Preece, "Fascism and the Negro," *Crisis* 41, no. 12 (December 1934), 355, 366; see also Lunabelle Wedlock, *The Reaction of Negro Publications and Organizations to German Anti-Semitism* (Washington, D. C., 1942). On African Americans and Jews in the Spanish Civil War, see Danny Duncan Collum and Victor Berch, eds., *African Americans and the Spanish Civil War: "This Ain't Ethiopia, But It'll Do"* (New York, 1992); Arthur Landis, *The Abraham Lincoln Brigade* (New York, 1967); Alvah Bessie, *Men in Battle: The Story of Americans in Spain* (New York, 1939); Edwin Rolfe, *The Lincoln Battalion: The Story of the Americans Who Fought in Spain in the International Brigades* (New York, 1974, orig. 1939); Robert Rosenstone, *Crusade of the Left: The Lincoln Battalion in the Spanish Civil War* (New York, 1969); James Yates, *Mississippi to Madrid: Memoir of a Black American in the Abraham Lincoln Brigade* (Seattle, 1989); John Coverdale, *Italian Intervention in the Spanish Civil War* (Princeton, 1975); Robert H. Whealey, *Hitler and Spain: the Nazi Role in the Spanish Civil War, 1936–1939* (Lexington, 1989).

32. Naison, *Communists in Harlem*, 324–25; Benjamin J. Davis, Jr., *Communist Councilman from Harlem* (New York, 1969), 106–7; Martin Bauml Duberman, *Paul Robeson* (New York, 1989). In 1954, Robeson gave a speech in which he compared the Cold War attack on the Left to Nazism. Paul Robeson, "Bonds of Brotherhood," *Jewish Life* 9 (Nov. 1954), 13–14.

33. This is not to deny that non-communist groups which were substantially Jewish in make-up sometimes provided a supportive milieu for individual Black activists and intellectuals. Ella Josephine Baker, for instance, received a Marxist education around the forums of the Communist (Opposition) Party and its publications during the 1930s. The heavily Jewish Trotskyist milieu greeted the appearance of Trinidadian Pan Africanist C.L.R. James with enthusiasm in 1938 and swiftly made him a political leader alongside E.R. McKinney. A small handful of Black Socialists enjoyed political support and even patronage, spending their careers in the vicinity of the needletrades' unions. But rarely was any explicit link of Jewishness and Blackness made in these quarters; more usually both sides of the dyad were denied in the name of a color-blind "internationalism."

34. See Jay Williams, *Stage Left* (New York, 1974), 114–17. In the next few years *Stevedore* was performed by Black companies in the Federal Theater. Originally produced by the Theatre Union (one of whose central figures, Albert Maltz, would become a member of the "Hollywood Ten" blacklistees), the play dealt with a Black dock worker falsely charged with raping a white woman because he was organizing a stevedore's union and because he was forcefully antiracist. In the climactic scene, white workers rush to join a Black neighborhood group in defending him against a racist mob. On at least one occasion, Bill "Bojangles" Robinson rushed up from the audience to join the action! The Theater Union was among the first to pay Black actors scale, and to seat African Americans in any audience seat. *Stevedore* played 22 weeks, and met with approving reviews. Four years earlier, a production of *Green Pastures* had won raves and a Pulitzer Prize by reviving the Uncle Remus view of Black life in the old South, notably paying its Black cast subscale and playing in segregated theaters.

35. Unfortunately but predictably, Gordon's memoir, *Live At the Village Vanguard* (New York, 1980), carefully understates the Left's role as performers and patrons, noting only as musicians those noted communists and leftists, like Woody Guthrie and Josh White, who took a part in the early days. On the Cafe Society, see John Hammond, with Irving Townsend, *John Hammond on Record* (New York, 1977), 206–10.

36. Buhle, *Marxism in the U.S.A.*, 289.

37. See the description of this film in Robert Sklar, *City Boys* (Princeton, 1992), 183–89. Abraham Polonsky, returning from the Blacklist, sought to make a series of films starring Harry Belafonte on civil rights-related themes. Only one, *Odds Against Tomorrow* (1959), was completed, but because it lost money he could not see his plan through to completion. Others blacklisted, notably Martin Ritt (*Sounder*), made supportive anti-racist films during the 1960s–70s. None had the bite of *Body and Soul*.

The degree of cooperation achieved between left-wing Blacks and Jews does not, of course, resolve the many ambiguities of the relationship. Harold Cruse argued forcefully that the Communist Party had given a latitude to Jewish nationalism, including an autonomous Jewish press, never allowed to Blacks, and that the Popular Front aesthetic (as in the case of Lorraine Hansberry) had been carefully crafted to meet white audience approval. Harold Cruse, *The Crisis of the Negro Intellectual* (New York, 1967), 267–301. Cruse missed the decisive point not in ideology so much as in political and cultural support: even the Yiddish newspaper *Morgn Freiheit* had vastly more readers than the Harlem edition of the *Daily Worker*, and at some points (the early 1920s and later 1950s) more readers than the *Worker* itself. Black left-wing theater and *Freedomways* magazine survived, however, in no small part because of Jewish support.

38. See for example, Samuel Sillen, "Charles W. Chestnut: A Pioneer Negro Novelist," *Masses and Mainstream* 6, no. 2 (February 1953), 8–14; Sidney Finkelstein, "Charles White's Humanist Art," *Masses and Mainstream* 6, no. 2 (February 1953), 43–46; V.J. Jerome wrote small pamphlet, *The Negro in Hollywood Films* (New York, 1951) published by *Masses and Mainstream*. On the New York intellectuals, see Alan Wald, *The New York Intellectuals* (Chapel Hill, NC, 1987); Judy Kutulas, *The Long War: The Intellectual People's Front and Anti-Stalinism, 1930–1940* (Durham, NC, 1995), 209–33.

39. See Dizzy Gillespie, with Al Fraser, *To Be, or Not...to Bop* (New York, 1979), 287; Kenneth L. Kann, *Comrades and Chicken Ranchers* (Ithaca, NY, 1993). Despite the admiration beboppers like Gillespie and Charlie Parker felt for Robeson, the leading Communist cultural critics had little admiration for bebop. They generally characterized the music as "mindless" improvisation with pretensions of high culture, comparing it unfavorably to Negro spirituals and early swing jazz. See Abner W. Berry, "The Future of Negro Music," *Masses and Mainstream* 6, no. 2 (February 1953), 15–22; Sidney Finklestein, *Jazz: A People's Music* (New York, 1948).

40. Naison, *Communists in Harlem*, 326; Leibman, *Jews and the Left*, 507–14; Cruse, *Crisis of the Negro Intellectual*, 164–70; Melech Epstein, *The Jew and Communism, 1919–1941* (New York, 1959); Gerald Horne, *Communist Front?: The Civil Rights Congress, 1946–1956* (Rutherford, NJ, 1988). Cruse argues, with some insight, that the stylized cultural policies of the Harlem Communists (as reflected in Paul Robeson's *Freedom* tabloid of the early 1950s) restrained creative approaches of Black intellectuals. But as Cruse makes too much of the Jewish intellectuals' role among Black communists, he fails to capture the complexity and the variety of artistic approaches among Black radicals, demanding (for instance) that *Raisin in the Sun* be more than a "family" drama when the road to commercial success lay in that direction as it would for many non-Black productions fitted to commercial styles. Moreover, the folk and jazz stylings of musicians around the Left, the canvas-work, poetry, and fiction cannot be confined to "realism" or "naturalism," whatever the preferences of *Daily Worker* reviewers may have been. The same is true for the Yiddish sector which saw a last efflorescence in the 1950s.

41. Maurice Isserman, *If I Had a Hammer: The Death of the Old Left and the Birth of the New Left* (New York, 1987), 33, 143, 186–88.

42. Half-Jewish Joan Baez, the early Bob Dylan, and a multitude of others should be included. On the folksong movements, see Robbie Lieberman, *"My Song is My Weapon": People's Songs, American Communism, and the Politics of Culture, 1930–1950,* (Urbana, IL, 1989).

43. Conrad Lynn, *There Is a Fountain* (Brooklyn, 1993 edition), 108. Indeed, even A. Philip Randolph's formation of the Negro American Labor Council could create

tensions for liberal Jewish labor leaders who believed Randolph's criticisms of the AFL-CIO's treatment of race were divisive. Founded in 1959 and patterned, ironically, after the Jewish Labor Committee and the American Jewish Committee's National Labor Service, NALC found itself in a contentious relationship with Jewish trade unionists and Civil Rights supporters. Given the divisiveness that comes with the rise of Black Power, it is quite ironic that Randolph—a strong critic of anti-Semitism and defender of Israel—is portrayed as a Negro militant contributing to the downfall of the Black-Jewish alliance. See Tom Brooks, "Negro Militants, Jewish Liberals, and the Unions," *Commentary* 32, no. 3 (September 1961), 209–16.

44. Leon Fink and Brian Greenberg, *Upheaval in the Quite Zone: A History of Hospital Workers' Union, Local 1199* (Urbana, IL, 1989), 181–208.

45. Fink and Greenberg, *Upheaval in the Quiet Zone*, 209–43; Paul Buhle, "Pages from Labor History," *New Politics* 5, no. 3 (Summer 1995), 55–64.

46. Gerald Horne, *Black Liberation/Red Scare: Ben Davis and the Communist Party* (London and Toronto, 1994), 283–84. Black Party leader Abner Berry actually opposed Davis and Strong's view. Berry argued that African Americans were neutral on the matter, supporting Israel and sympathizing with Egypt. *Daily Worker*, February 26, 1957, April 2, 1957.

47. Arthur Liebman, "The Ties That Bind: The Jewish Support for the Left in the United States," *American Jewish Historical Quarterly* 66, no. 2 (December 1976), 317–20; Morris U. Schappes, *The Jewish Question and the Left—Old and New: A Challenge to the New Left* (New York: Jewish Currents Reprint no. 7, 1970). During the late 1960s and early 70s, the CPUSA continued to criticize Israel's war against Palestinians and their involvement in Africa—a position in line with the Israeli Communist Party. See Tawfik Zayyad, "Israel's Setbacks in Africa," *Political Affairs* 52, no. 7 (July 1973), 55–65.

48. Balfour Brickner, "Jewish Youth, Israel and the Third World," *Reconstructionist* 36, no. 3 (March 27, 1970), 7–13; Robert G. Weisbord and Arthur Stein, "Black Nationalism and the Arab-Israeli Conflict," *Patterns of Prejudice* 3 (November–December 1969), 1–9; Liebman, *Jews and the Left,* 564–68.

49. See, for example, Eddie Ellis, "Semitism in the Black Ghetto," *Liberator* 6, no. 1 (Jan. 1966), 6–7, no. 2 (February 1966), 14–15; and no. 4 (April 1966), 14–16, a fairly vicious attack on Jews that also attempts to critique anti-Semitism. Several Black critics, including James Baldwin, found the piece offensive nonetheless and wrote responses to it in the pages of *Freedomways*. See *Freedomways*, 7 no. 1 (Winter 1967), 75–78.

50. Clayborne Carson, Jr., "Blacks and Jews in the Civil Rights Movement," in Joseph R. Washington, Jr., ed., *Jews in Black Perspectives* (Rutherford, NJ, 1984), 118.

51. Jerald E. Podair, "'White' Values, 'Black' Values: The Ocean Hill–Brownsville Controversy and New York City Culture, 1965–1975," *Radical History Review* 59 (Spring 1994), 36–59; see also, Jonathan Kaufman, *Broken Alliance* (New York, 1988); Martin Mayer, *The Teachers Strike, New York, 1968* (New York, 1969); Maurice Berube and Marilyn Gittell, eds., *Confrontation at Ocean Hill–Brownsville* (New York, 1969).

52. Robert I. Friedman, "The Enemy from Within: How the Anti-Defamation League Turned the Notion of Human Rights on its Head, Spying on Progressives and Funneling Information to Law Enforcement," *Village Voice*, May 11, 1993.

53. Matthew J. Jacobs, "Special Sorrows: Irish-, Polish- and Jewish-Americans, Nationalism and the Diaspora Immigrant" (Ph.D. diss., Brown University, 1992).

54. See Beth Sims, *Workers of the World Undermined* (Boston, 1992), 38–40, on the AFL-CIO role.

55. When Jewish neoconservative Allan Bloom exalted Plato so as to curse Black music as degenerate, he acutely identified (to the applause of many formerly socialist Jewish readers) both the continuing claims upon Western values and the curious hatred of mass culture which Jews and Blacks had done so much to create. Bloom had of course never been on the Left, but he found his most important sponsor (and author of the book's Forward) in manqué Marxist Saul Bellow, who, like neoconservative wizard Irving Kristol (father of William Kristol, Dan Quayle's aide-de-camp and sharpshooter on Jewish questions) was a Trotskyist of earlier days. See Allan Bloom, *The Closing of the American Mind* (New York, 1987). During the early 1990s, Bellow tended to withdraw from provocative (and outrageously racist) statements made earlier in support of the book; yet he remained a weathervane in the Jewish left-turned-right. Prominent SDUSA intellectuals, anxiously searching for an issue after the Cold War, inevitably found it in the presumably baneful effects of multiculturalism in the American university. *The Partisan Review*, a favorite vehicle for the inevitable denunciations perhaps even more than *Commentary* or the *New Leader*, thus ended its own long journey from extreme Left to extreme Right of an overwhelmingly Jewish constituency.

56. Robert I. Friedman, "The Enemy from Within"; on the AFL-CIO and Central Intelligence Agency, see Daniel Cantor and Juliet Schor, *Tunnel Vision: Labor, the World Economy and Central America* (Boston, 1987).

57. Even here, the imprint of the Popular Front remains. In the historically social democratic *Dissent* magazine and elsewhere, blame for the collapse of the alliance is generally placed upon African Americans, with the rightward drift of Jewish institutions and the role of Jewish-owned big business from Wall Street to corporations to Congress generally slighted if not entirely ignored. Among those left journals outside

Popular Front traditions but unreservedly supportive of African Americans (and critical of Jewish establishment activities), *New Politics* is perhaps the finest example. Its secular Jewish leaning has never been disputed.

58. This hope finds some expression in Michael Lerner and Cornel West, *Jews and Blacks: Let the Healing Begin* (New York, 1995).

eleven

THE NEED TO REMEMBER

Three Phases in Black and Jewish Educational Relations

EARL LEWIS

He comes to collect the rent, so you know him in that role. He runs the grocery store and he give you credit, so you know him in that role. He runs the drug store and he bandages your wounds, and you know him in that role...You don't really know him from anybody else, but...you deal with it one way or another.

When I was growing up it was a time, after all, of the Second World War. My best friends in high school were Jewish. It was a very, very important moment in my life because it was a time when I realized in a way...my friends...were not so far from the fiery furnace after all.

Noted author James Baldwin used his childhood memories of Jewish friends, merchants, and acquaintances to frame a discussion of Blacks and Jews in American society. Baldwin had often seen the need to lean on those memories; he did so again in a 1984 lecture to students at the University of Massachusetts-Amherst, where he taught prior to his death.[1] At the time, he had no way of knowing that his words would stir a controversy about academic freedom, education, race, and Black-Jewish relations that pitted one iconoclastic scholar against his colleagues, and interestingly exposed a twist in the intricacies of a fluid historical relationship.[2] That day, Baldwin called on memory—both his own and that of all African Americans. He asked them to recall the ways in which Blacks and Jews, each with a history of deep oppression, found themselves sharing social, cultural, and political space in the ghettos, ethnic enclaves, towns, and cities of America. His call to memory worked because whether it was raised in Harlem, Philadelphia, Detroit, Norfolk, or Atlanta, Black Americans had accessible memories of Jews as neighbors, friends, and merchants.

What we remember and why we remember certain aspects of the relationship and not others is key for understanding the peculiar entanglement of Blacks and Jews. What does it mean, after all, that successive generations of African American parents mark the Jewish merchant by race, ethnicity, and religion? Is it merely a function of clarifying a middleman's role in what at times looked and looks like a colonial economy? As important, why are the 1950s and 1960s offered as a "golden age" in intergroup relations? Is this somewhat romantic portrait an exaggeration or distortion? Or is the perceptible level of enmity in the post-1970 period exaggerated, the result of using events in New York to paint a national portrait? In fact, would a thorough probing of the overlapping worlds of Blacks and Jews look different if we examined individuals rather than institutions?

Baldwin understood that although the history of Black-Jewish relations is as old as the nation, the pace and depths of that relationship changed in form and character after the 1890s. Without saying so, he assumed markers such as "He comes to collect the rent" would provide sufficient historical context. Implied, therefore, is a generous, and perhaps misguided, belief that his students had full command of history. How many actually did is unknowable of course. It is clear, however, that context was important to memory in this case.

Indeed, through the Civil War, Jews accounted for less than 1 percent of the American population, especially in the South where more than 90 percent of all Blacks lived. After the war an expanding industrial economy fueled the need for workers. In response, millions arrived from Europe, including millions of Eastern European Jews. The Jewish newcomers differed from more assimilated German Jews who had preceded them in both material wealth and background. Moreover, second in volume only to Italian immigrants, who had the largest return migration of any immigrant group, Eastern European Jews settled in America with intentions of staying. The overwhelming majority settled in urban centers in the North and Midwest.[3]

During the same period, the demand for labor, oppressive racial conditions, and changes in the agricultural economy of the rural South produced a dramatic relocation of African Americans. Between 1900 and 1920 more than 1.5 million Blacks left the rural South; about three times that number would leave between 1940 and 1970.[4] As a result, millions of Jewish immigrants entered American cities just as millions of African Americans left the rural countryside. In these spaces the groups forged a relationship—one of love, friendship, and recrimination, or one that was personal, then institutional, and at times oppositional.

Thus Baldwin's retreat to memory poses interesting challenges for writing the history of African American and Jewish involvement in education. To begin, the details complicate the conventional narrative of encounter and alliance. In the shadows of slavery, an initial relationship was forged. During the antebellum period that relationship highlighted ties between parents and children—countering the tendency to view Blacks and Jews as distinct and separate populations. With massive immigration and migration individual relations surrendered to broader group alliances. Beginning in the 1900s and crystallizing by the 1920s, elites from both communities formed fragile yet lasting ties. The fragility of those enduring connections became all the more obvious in the late 1960s, as younger members of both communities distanced themselves from the old elites and campaigned for group and community privileges. This last phase also coincided with a noticeable shift in the importance of identity politics, a turn of events that obscured the nature of a historical relationship.[5]

Framing the Personal

Most Americans born in the first half of the nineteenth century had limited educational opportunities. Few states educated their residents for free. By and large, chances of receiving a quality education improved if one were male, white, and well-to-do. The country actually had a long tradition of training wealthy young white males for the clergy or providing the sons of plantation owners with their own tutors. This practice of educating an elite or leadership class continued through the early nineteenth century, stymieing the demand for universal free public education until well after the Civil War.[6]

Although notable exceptions emerged in northern cities such as Philadelphia and a few southern locales, most whites, irrespective of region, cringed at the thought of formally educating Blacks. In the South, many felt such efforts were wasted; others feared that education would make African Americans unsuitable slaves. More important, levels of unease percolated and hardened into outright opposition after several well-publicized slave revolts were planned and executed by literate leaders—that is, Gabriel Prosser, Denmark Vesey, and Nat Turner. Thereafter, from 1800 through 1865, opposition to the education of Blacks increased. By the 1840s and 1850s, most southern states officially prohibited formal instruction. Even in the North and Midwest, whites prohibited or objected to publicly supported educational opportunities for Blacks. When Blacks and their allies pushed for inclusion, as they did in Boston, prejudice lingered long after the laws had changed.[7]

The move toward prohibition must be understood as part of a historical process. In the space created by revolutionary ideology and the Revolutionary War, a notable number of Blacks secured their freedom, accumulated property, and for a time built independent institutions, including schools. Independent African schools, for example, appeared in several places between 1789 and 1810, only to come under increasingly hostile scrutiny by the second decade of the nineteenth century.[8]

Neither the increased examination nor the generally unfriendly atmosphere deterred African Americans altogether. Some, like noted abolitionist and orator

Frederick Douglass, tricked white kids into teaching them how to read and write after white adults ended the practice. At times, emboldened Blacks and committed whites simply ignored legal prohibitions until forced to cease their activities. Prominent examples of breaches in protocol captivated white Richmonders in 1811 and Norfolkians in 1853. In the end, both communities punished those among them who dared teach Blacks.[9]

Even in the North educational opportunities for Blacks were mostly separate and unequal. African Americans recognized this. Delegates to the 1832 National Negro Convention maintained, "If we ever expect to see the influence of prejudice decrease and ourselves respected, it must be by the blessings of an enlightened education."[10] There were a few notable exceptions of course, particularly in Philadelphia. There prominent citizens championed schooling for free Blacks as early as the 1790s and built the Institute for Colored Youth in the 1840s, which trained a generation of African American leaders. Elsewhere white northerners flatly refused to educate Blacks or insisted that at the very least they attend separate schools.[11]

Certainly opposition to educational opportunities stemmed in large measure from the overt threats to the institution of slavery. But education also threatened to expose the intricacies of a mythic relationship. When colonial assemblies legislated against intraracial sex for all but white men, they at once wrote the racial politics of sex into the nation's history. Although successive generations of African Americans wore the imprint of such unions on their visages, they remained distant until African Americans, in writing themselves into being through autobiographies, acknowledged such relations. When Frederick Douglass furtively mentioned his father in his autobiography, he indicted that father as a co-conspirator in his own bondage.[12] Education and literacy, especially from the pen of one as eloquent as Douglass, underscored the institution of slavery's ability to distort all relationships, including those between fathers and sons.

Jews, meanwhile, constituted a numerically insignificant proportion of the slave-owning population and a small percentage of the nation's pre-Civil War white population (roughly 15,000 in 1840). Significant demographic changes came after the war, and with these changes came attendant alterations in educational opportunities. Through the period when their numbers remained small, few states introduced legislation to limit the education of Jews. For the most part their racial and class positions mattered more than their religion or ethnicity. Still, the majority of Americans Jews lived in communities chiefly dependent upon other co-religionists.[13]

Given the relatively small population of Jews, and their only marginal presence in the South, the majority of them had little interaction with the majority of Blacks. Consequently, one can talk about a Black and Jewish educational history for the nineteenth century, but one is hard pressed to talk about a Black and Jewish educational relationship. The exception sprang from intimate relationships between Black women and white Jewish men.

One Significant Example

During the quarter of a century after the American Revolutionary War, the largest Jewish community in the nation resided in Charleston, South Carolina. It was the slave South, and the Jewish families who settled there assumed a white privilege and, for the most part, the perspective of the region. In fact, by 1850 well over half of those for whom records remained listed their place of birth as South Carolina. It was a community settled first by Sephardic Jews (from southern Europe) and thereafter by Ashkenazic Jews (from central Europe). In a social milieu that afforded them economic integration and an ease of social interaction, they came to resemble their Gentile neighbors in one important respect: roughly 87 percent of non-Jewish whites owned slaves by 1830 as compared to 83 percent of Jewish households.[14]

Yet Charleston's was not entirely a conventional community. The Reform tradition in Judaism had its birth in the city among those who came of age in the 1820s. Counted among the leaders was Isaac Nunes Cardozo, the younger brother of Jacob Nunes Cardozo, a noted journalist and economics writer, and the son of David Cardozo, a local rabbi or teacher. Isaac Cardozo served as Vice President of the Reform Society for a number of years, and delivered a key speech on the importance of reform. Some sources describe the younger Cardozo as a prominent businessman and expert on economics; others make no mention of his occupation; still others insisted he worked as a weigher in the Charleston Customs House for almost a quarter of a century. Whatever his employment status, Isaac found comfort in the bosom of a community at ease with itself.[15]

Next to religion, education anchored Jewish life in Charleston. That Isaac might value learning is not at all surprising given his father's occupation, his brother's stature, and the Charleston community's embrace of education. Generally, education was reserved for elites, and academies serviced the select few, who through accident of birth entered this privileged world. Charleston's Jews were not oblivious to such privilege, but their academies seemed to service a broader cross section of co-religionists. In this regard, education became part of a more progressive force in the community, occasioning the training of boys and girls, separately, and together.[16]

Sometimes the training that the young and old received occurred outside the sanctioned space of the classroom. Most noted were the interracial affairs of the heart that led writers such as de Tocqueville to comment on the significance of race in the America he encountered. In his treatise on American democracy he observed, "Among the Americans of the South, Nature sometimes, reclaiming her rights, does for a moment establish equality between white and Black."[17] The historical record is dotted with the names of men and women who entered such relationships. Moreover, some of these affairs assumed the quality of a marriage— long, respectful, and emotionally and materially satisfying. Savannah resident Moses Nunes, for example, took the unusual steps of preserving for prosperity the sincerity of his love for "Mulatta Rose" and their children. His will legalized their freedom and left them land, thirteen slaves, and other assets. It also established the avenue for his son James to ease into the white world, marry a white woman, and assume the privileges of race and station.[18]

More typically we understand the antebellum period as a time of absolute male prerogative. For Black women, male prerogative often gave way to male power and sexual abuse. In slave narratives, court proceedings, and oral interviews women recounted the horrors of rape and abuse. The law did little to protect their virtue and Black members of slave societies were often defenseless to prevent such crimes. Slavery registered most Black women as property; as property, they had no rights in person other than their own will to fight back and resist.[19]

Into the world of interracial relationships entered Isaac and Jacob Nunes Cardozo, the father (or fathers) of Henry, Francis, and Thomas Cardozo, important figures in reconstruction politics and affairs. Scholars disagree over which of the brothers entered the world of interracial love and fatherhood—perhaps both did. Early works claimed it was Jacob whereas more recent works follow the claims of family members that Isaac fathered this branch of the Cardozo family. Neither man married, although by the standards of the day they were quite desirable mates. Jacob became the more noted, serving as editor and owner of both the *Southern Patriot* (1821–45) and the *Charleston Evening News* (1845–47). He officially supported slavery even while denying this option for himself; he published two books on political economy and actively opposed the split of the Union. Isaac, meanwhile, lived a more circumscribed life. Aside from his activities on behalf of reforming Judaism, he seemingly shied away from the public stage.[20]

Insofar as reconciling the patrimony of Jacob or Isaac is beyond the scope of this essay, we surrender to contemporary scholarship: Isaac rather than Jacob fathered the three Cardozo sons.[21] More troubling, the historical record remains virtually silent on the particulars of his love. All we know is that Isaac met and fell in love with a mixed African and Native American free woman, frequently identified as Lydia Williams. Cross-racial relationships existed in antebellum South Carolina, and especially antebellum Charleston. Such relationships crossed the divide of class, religion, and nationality and include some of the most prominent names in America, among them Grimké. In 1860, census enumerators even counted seventy-one South Carolina households consisting of free people of color and whites.[22]

In this regard little separated Jews and Gentiles: men of both groups transgressed the boundaries of race and entered long-term relationships with Black women. Aside from the general descriptions of her status and parentage, none of the standard biographies provides further detail about Isaac Cardozo's paramour. Like many Black women, her deeds and actions were shrouded by the important accomplishments of the men in her life—first her partner and later her sons. Isaac gained prominence as a religious reformer. Her biracial sons, Henry, Francis, and Thomas, acquired considerable stature and distinction after the Civil War. Henry, several years older than his presumptive brothers, served in the postwar South Carolina legislature, representing Kershaw County from 1870–1874. After that he pastored at Wesley A. M. E. Church in Columbia and edited a denominational paper. Francis played critical roles in reconstruction politics in South Carolina, serving as both secretary of state and state treasurer. Thomas entered the political fray in North Carolina and later Mississippi, where he became superintendent of schools from 1874–1876.

The younger Cardozos achieved their prominence in large part because of the role education played in their lives. Little is known about what their father or mother said about their sons' education; nonetheless, Francis and Thomas both attended private schools in Charleston for free Blacks of color. Here we might conclude that the father, who remained involved in the lives of his partner and sons until his death in 1855, paid those bills.

It is equally possible that the sons paid their own way. Once he reached twelve, Francis entered an apprenticeship, wherein he learned to become a carpenter. Upon Isaac's death, Thomas was also apprenticed; the seventeen-year-old worked for a rice-threshing manufacturer for two years before moving to New York with his mother and resuming his education. Francis, we know, used his skills to set aside funds for a European education. After five years as an apprentice and four as a journeyman, Francis had saved $1,000. With these funds he studied first at the University of Glasgow, and then in London and Edinburgh, where he received three years of theological training. He returned to the United States as one of the best educated men of his generation.[23]

Whether his father assisted him in any way before he reached adulthood is not clear. Francis was eighteen when his father died, and did not leave for Scotland for another three years. More significant, Francis embraced Christianity as an adult and not Judaism (had he been given the choice). He trained at Presbyterian seminaries abroad and pastored at a Congregationalist church upon his return. At the end of the war, Francis and Thomas worked for the American Missionary Association (AMA) as teachers and educators. In fact, both would alternate between the bruising theater of reconstruction politics and the equally challenging world of educating freedpeople. In helping to found Avery Institute, a normal school, Francis would write that training Black teachers to train Black students "is the object for which I left all of the superior advantages and privileges of the North...."[24]

The Cardozo story is significant because it highlights the still unfocused educational relationship between Blacks and Jews. From the 1820s well into the first decades of the twentieth century, the relationship turned on individual contacts rather than group relations. With the number of Jews remaining a fraction of 1 percent nationally—and in the South—possible contacts were rare except in enclaves such as Charleston. Isaac aided his sons because they were his progeny; he knew them and, we are to assume, loved them. They aided the cause of a larger Black world because dominant ideology and life experiences defined them as

Black. Nothing suggests that Isaac set out to aid the multitudes of enslaved Blacks; few who came of age in antebellum America would have thought such actions reasonable. This changed as the country made the awkward transition from slavery to emancipation to segregation. The venture into the politics of philanthropy made it possible.

The Politics of Philanthropy

Freedpeople had many aspirations after the Civil War, including the right to exercise the franchise, to sell their labor, and to reconnect with loved ones. However, few desires struck contemporaries as powerfully and dramatically as the quest for an education. Across the South, African Americans overwhelmed missionaries sent South by the American Missionary Association (AMA) and other agencies. Long denied proper training, after difficult starts, Blacks made progress. Charlotte Forten, member of one of Philadelphia's leading families of color and a teacher-missionary, gushed in 1862 from the liberated Sea Islands of South Carolina, "It is a great happiness to teach them. I wish some of those persons at the North who say the race is…inferior, could see…these children, so long oppressed and deprived of every privilege, learn and understand." Freedpeople equated education with equality and power. They soon inundated Freedmen's Bureau institutions, exchanged their immediate need for child labor for the long-term benefit of educated youngsters, and even tolerated the twin offerings of the gospel and the primer. In 1870 alone, more than 247,000 Black students enrolled in Bureau schools.[25]

In the anxious years of reconstruction, Blacks and non-Jewish whites sowed a relationship that had profound implications for Blacks and Jews a generation later. Given the starting point, primary and secondary school education remained a concern for much of the nineteenth century. But beginning in the 1860s, some acknowledged the importance of training a generation of college educated freedpeople. Building on ties birthed in abolitionism, white caretakers, dependent on largesse, built the first phase of Black colleges in the late 1860s. Bearing the names of white benefactors—Howard, Fisk, or Biddle—or attesting to their locations—Hampton or Atlanta—these new schools marked the birth of philanthropic interest in Black education.[26]

Some scholars have questioned the motives of those whites who oversaw Black institutions and the philanthropists who gave of their wealth, time, and counsel. Without question, men such as Samuel Armstrong, who founded and directed highly influential Hampton Institute in its formative years, fancied Blacks other than their equals. They viewed themselves as missionaries sent by God to do good among the less fortunate—yes, even the inferior. It did not matter that they knew, or knew of, Blacks of accomplishment. Whites as much as Blacks fell under the sway of a racial vision of America. Armstrong, for instance, counseled Blacks to accept their lot by training for their place as loyal, cheap, southern labor.[27]

The extension of the Armstrong perspective evolved in tandem with the dramatic growth and alteration of the nation's economy. Between the Civil War and 1900, America's corporate culture changed profoundly. A new class of professional managers took over the day-to-day operations of many companies, beginning with railroads. Concomitantly, business sectors standardized operations and pricing. Spurred by an extraordinary savings rate that increased from a significant 10–12 percent in the 1850s to a staggering 18–20 percent between 1865 and 1914, capital was available to inventors, entrepreneurs, and corporations. This investment capital provided the revenues needed to fuel an industrial revolution. As important, America's corporate leaders embarked on a campaign of consolidation. This practice drove out competition and generated huge profits and personal fortunes for those who survived. Some would call the new capitalists "Robber Barons"; others called them friends and donors.[28]

Booker T. Washington, Hampton graduate and perhaps the most important African American leader to emerge after the Civil War, preferred the later label. Washington took the Hampton model of disciplined industrial training to Tuskegee, Alabama, where he created an educational institution and political fiefdom of unequaled endowment. At Tuskegee Institute Washington also developed a style of cultivating new capitalists into benefactors. He did so by exploiting the politics of racial belief.

Washington biographer Louis Harlan called him an astute politician. Like many politicians, Washington cultivated relationships, sometimes compromising principle for results. Thus he appeared quite at ease with William H. Baldwin's pronouncement that Blacks were the real alternative to the threat of unionized labor. Baldwin, a railroad executive and soon to be philanthropist, joined the Tuskegee board of trustees in 1894. A lifelong opponent of classical higher education for Blacks, the northern-born and educated Baldwin argued that industrial education trained Blacks for their roles as the backbone of the southern economy. In an 1899 address he maintained, "properly directed he...will willingly fill the more menial positions, and do the heavy work, at less wages, than the American white man or any foreign race which has yet come to our shores." So sure was Baldwin of Washington and industrial education that he enlisted scores of others in funding industrial education for Blacks.[29]

The sure-footedness of Washington and his advisors meant much to southern Blacks, even as the limits of their visions soon prompted a lively debate over the hazards of a singular approach to the education of the Black masses. This debate did not stop Robert G. Ogden, Andrew Carnegie, John D. Rockefeller, George Foster Peabody, and others from raising and donating millions for the education of Black southerners. Rockefeller, for example, gave $53 million to the General Education Board between 1902 and 1909, primarily for training Black teachers.[30]

Hundreds of miles to the north a new wave of European Jews, who fled the pogroms in Eastern Europe, began to establish themselves. They came by the millions and they stayed. The majority settled in New York, New Jersey,

Pennsylvania, and New England, with only a sprinkling venturing south of the Mason-Dixon line. Generally speaking, these newcomers suffered the travails of immigrants seeking to establish themselves in a new land.[31]

Although many years passed before the newly settled Jews amassed fortunes of any note, several of their more established co-religionists were quite wealthy by the turn of the century. Overwhelmingly of German Jewish background, many of these elites were self-consciously assimilationists. They made their money in real estate, banking, department stores, and business. More important, they totally accepted their faith's belief in the importance of giving. From the 1840s through the 1880s, when German Jewish immigration peaked, those who could built schools such as Hebrew Union College (1875), social welfare institutions, and charities.

As this group became more assimilated into a larger America, exogamous issues also attracted their attention. Of course the oldtimers did not totally ignore the newcomers from Russia, Poland, and other parts of Eastern Europe. Settlement houses were created and funded, committees were established to ease the transition, and advice on becoming Americans was readily dispensed. Still, barred from the directorships and trusteeships of leading Gentile-controlled organizations, they searched for other outlets for their money and opinions. At the same time, through the establishment of a number of national organizations, including the American Jewish Committee, these Jewish leaders became better known to one another. Many hoped to thwart the palpable rise of anti-Semitism by providing a larger public service.[32]

Meantime, Booker T. Washington, who voiced some of the same prejudices toward Jews as other Americans, began to court the favor of Julius Rosenwald, among others. William Baldwin died in 1905, and Washington, ever the astute observer, had noticed that the wealth was shifting from the old abolitionist families of New England to the industrial tycoons of New York and Chicago. In an urge to attract their favor, he wrote Baldwin in 1904 of his intention of inviting Paul M. Warburg "or some Hebrew of his standing" to join the school's governing board. Warburg served for five years, during which time he introduced Washington to members of his banking firm as well as others, including the immensely wealthy Jacob Schiff.[33]

It was Julius Rosenwald, president of Sears, Roebuck, and Company, who cemented ties between Jews and the educational needs of Blacks. Several months after reading Washington's autobiography *Up From Slavery*, and two years after Warburg's 1909 departure, he joined the Institute's board of trustees. During his tenure Rosenwald transported friends by private trains to see the fine work of the Wizard—Washington's fetching appellation. Rosenwald donated overstocked or slightly irregular clothes and shoes, which Washington sold to students for a modest sum; he gave faculty and staff bonuses; and he enlisted help from the nation's wealthy, many of whom were Jewish, in Washington's projects. After Washington's death in 1915, Rosenwald made the first of two major contributions. With funds mostly from his own accounts, he spent nearly $4 million constructing rural schools across the South.

Rosenwald's second effort marked a break with the past. Increasingly the clear preference for industrial education eviscerated. Campus protests roiled Black colleges in the 1920s, with students protesting stifling moral codes and limited, at times outdated, curricula. In the wake of such complaints the Rosenwald Fund (1928–48) supported individuals and institutions of higher learning such as Dillard, Fisk, and Atlanta University. In fact, a number of leading Black intellectuals of the Jim Crow era called themselves Rosenwald Fund alumni. The list included educators such as Horace Mann Bond, Charles S. Johnson, E. Franklin Frazier, and Kenneth Clark, writers such as Langston Hughes and Arna Bontemps, and painters and artists such as Jacob Lawrence.[34]

Thus the second phase of this educational relationship emanated from the birth of an institutional infrastructure predicated on Black advancement. Key to this effort was a shared commitment to civil rights by Black and Jewish elites. After all, many of the same men who used parts of their fortunes to provide educational opportunities also supported civil rights organizations. The chief beneficiaries were the National Association for the Advancement of Colored People (NAACP) and the National Urban League (NUL). Both organizations began as a partnership between Blacks and whites—a white group that was disproportionately Jewish. The partnership is partially explained by the vulnerability both populations felt in a post-World War I America where each became ready scapegoats.

On this point, one scholar has argued that it was a partnership of mutual need. Elite Blacks needed the material assistance that Jewish friends could provide. In turn, elite Jews hoped Black advancement would, in the words of NAACP activist Louis Marshall, "incidentally benefit Jews" by demonstrating how far even a non-white group might ascend, unhampered by prejudice and discrimination.[35] Like most alliances, other, less comforting, sources of conflict were shunted aside. Black leaders at the national level played down the intense economic competition implicit in James Baldwin's reference to the Jewish merchant. Questions of Jewish racism and Black anti-Semitism became part of a nicely choreographed dance to remind both communities of the importance of civil rights. Ironically, perhaps, the success of the pre-World War II generation fueled the intense animosities that erupted in the 1960s and 1970s, a conflict that in New York at the least overshadowed the moments of solidarity so critical to memories of the civil rights era in both communities.

Moving Toward Parallels of Cooperation and Confrontation

For Blacks and Jews, World War II proved an irreversible turning point. The horrors of Naziism revealed in stark clarity the dangers of allowing racism to become a consuming ideology. As a result millions of Jews accepted as an article of faith the noble promise "Never again." Mindful of German atrocities, scores of Blacks nonetheless aligned themselves with the conservative Black sage George Schuyler, who professed that the Black man's battle was with the "Hitlers at home." Yet on a metaphoric—when not on an actual—level, members of both communities understood the importance of fighting Naziism abroad and racism at home. In that sense, the events of World War II solidified the connections between anti-Semitism and racism.

Against the broad backdrop of this neatly scripted narrative, millions of Blacks and Jews lived more complicated existences. If events before World War II—such as the lynching of Leo Frank—graphically reminded the nation of Jews' tenuous claims to whiteness, that changed after the war. By the 1950s a consensus emerged: all with European ancestry were white. Although more research is in order, perceptions of whiteness structured relations between individual Jews and individual Blacks, often sabotaging the promise of group cooperation.

To the young Norman Podhoretz, for example, intense recollections of childhood whippings by neighborhood Blacks complicated perceptions of Blacks as aggrieved Americans. In his Brooklyn world they had power, wealth, and influence; he and his group were the subordinates. By his own account he feared, envied, and hated Blacks. Podhoretz knew that his schoolmates were attacking his whiteness as much as his Jewishness, but in the immediacy of the pain that did not matter. And even in the reflective quiet of time, the process of becoming "white," of having assimilated into the amalgam of American life, rubbed out other images of cooperation and interracial alliances. Even after he moved to the safe quarters of the Upper West side, he feared, envied, and hated what he thought he knew.[36]

Yet Blacks and Jews had worked together on a number of fronts between the 1920s and the early 1950s. Even if some may have overstated the depths of such cooperation, especially in leftist circles, sustained examples of intergroup alliance existed. Jews and Blacks continued their efforts on behalf of civil rights. In cities such as Detroit, Blacks and Jews united in progressive causes during the 1930s and 1940s. After the war, the Detroit Civil Rights Federation sponsored several forums on race relations, one specifically on anti-Semitism and another on racism. This two-pronged approach attracted the attention and criticisms of some, even as it highlighted the conditions for common ground. Such associations extended into the workplace. A coalition of Blacks and Jews actively pursued minority rights within the United Auto Workers after World War II, through Local 600.[37]

We tragically misunderstand the human condition, if we assume brotherhood and cooperation were the extent of the interaction. Each individual has many identities, with some at times more central than others. This made it possible for some to endorse broad alliances and others to criticize them, with each acting in the best interests of their communities. In Detroit and Harlem, for example, the 1930s, 1940s, and 1950s were punctuated by periods of intense antipathy and hostility. Some branded the Rev. Charles Hill of Detroit communist, dangerous, and anti-Black for his support of crossracial cooperation. As early as the 1930s, economic competition in Harlem pitted Black residents and activists against Jewish residents, merchants, and landlords. In support of economic boycotts directed at non-Blacks, some African Americans introduced the poker-hot language of bigotry. In the exchanges Jews became "the exploiters of the colored people," and "Harlem's worst enemies."[38]

Nor were these insecurities solely the preoccupation of job-insecure northern Blacks. Black militancy had an unsettling effect on southern Jews. Many voiced their discomfort with northern Jews who embraced civil rights for Blacks. After all, non-Jewish white racists easily attributed the fight for Black civil rights to a Jewish conspiracy (suggesting that even as late as 1960 some Gentiles viewed Jews as other than "white.") American Nazi figure George Lincoln Rockwell published a pamphlet that called desegregation a grand plot by Jews to take over the nation by creating a mongrel race. Following the Supreme Court decision in the *Brown* case and during the height of the school-closing crisis in late 1950s Virginia, the level of anti-Jewish sentiment increased. Letters circulated through the Hampton Roads section of Virginia with the directive "The time has obviously come for white Americans to take action if this Jew-inspired program for compulsory mongrelization is to be defeated." Nor were racist comments or the responses engendered limited to Virginia. A Jewish resident of Macon, Georgia fretted, "When a rabbi from New Haven...takes part in a demonstration, you have no idea the position Jewry in our state is placed." More hysterically, one Jewish leader from Alabama charged northern counterparts, "You're like Hitler. You stir up anti-Semitism against us."[39]

When Jewish students added their names to the growing list of civil rights martyrs, episodes of fear and recrimination exposed real rifts among the socially conservative and the socially liberal. These encounters highlight the dangers of painting this complicated history of interaction with too broad a stroke. Throughout the tumult of the 1950s and 1960s, socially conscious Jewish Americans lent their suasion to the cause of civil rights, risked their lives to desegregate America, provided funds and moral support to Martin Luther King and other activists, and taught Blacks in schools and colleges. Even the more conservative maintained relations with Black customers and tenants, counseled Black Americans on the virtues of going slow, agonized when Black youth embraced Israel's enemies, and openly feared the consequences of a Black ascendancy.[40] Still, in the interstices of an old relationship the personal and the institutional prevailed—they marked Black-Jewish interaction.

Community Confrontation

Until the 1960s, however, Blacks and Jews had never confronted one another as real competitors for civic control. Sure, intergroup conflict surfaced from time to time, most notably during race riots. Yet, even during the riots in Harlem (1935 and 1943) and in Detroit (1943), Blacks targeted property rather than individuals. Few publicly assailed Jews because of their religion. Until the late 1960s, most Americans could accept that religion and race were parts, but not the entire measure, of the individual. But as the nation made the transition from civil rights to Black Power, it also shifted from a politics of identity to identity politics. The latter, unlike the former, assumed that race, gender, sexual orientation, or religious affiliation were the most important measures of a person; that in the end, each individual was one thing rather than a complex interaction of many, often competing, parts.

Moreover, while southern Blacks argued for the attainment of basic civil rights, northern Blacks stepped up their demands for community control. As activists in Chicago would demonstrate, one of their first demands centered on control of local schools. Although the Chicago example had more to do with destablizing the absolute hold that Mayor Richard Daley had over city affairs, it served as a real primer for launching broader confrontations. In Chicago, Blacks worked to unseat the school superintendent and to shift the balance of power to community groups professedly interested in the educational aspirations of Black children.[41]

A similar emphasis took shape in New York City. When it was projected to become an overwhelmingly Black and Puerto Rican school district by 1970, Black parents and civil rights activists demanded more control over local school districts. Black parents first raised the issue in the spring of 1966; upset over terms under which Intermediate School 201 would open, they threatened, and then led, a school boycott. By the fall, increasing demands for more community control pitted parents against teachers, their union (United Federation of Teachers), and UFT President Albert Shanker. More than a localized effort, the quest for community control thrust residents and local governments into the vortex of a national movement. By February 1967, with emotions still raw, the city school board agreed to a pilot. Several experimental districts were to be set up across the city. The state followed in April with instructions for the Mayor to produce a decentralization plan by December. Sensing a general shift, New York Mayor John Lindsay sought assistance from Ford Foundation head McGeorge Bundy. A former official in the Kennedy administration, Bundy proposed a plan to cede considerable power to a series of community-based school boards.[42]

The basic outline of the first months of what became known as the Ocean Hill–Brownsville controversy not only strips the encounter of its high drama but fails to explain why this affair became viewed as a confrontation between Jews and Blacks. Although members of both communities publicly disagreed over affirmative action in higher education and other issues, the 1960s are conventionally viewed as a crowning moment of intergroup cooperation. Nonetheless, the tremors of change were everywhere. In Boston, the lending habits of banks and mortgage companies sowed the ground for conflict. Believing the Jewish community more liberal and politically less potent, financial institutions created a narrow swath of real estate to answer Black demands for decent housing—it so happened the property cut through the primarily Jewish communities of Dorchester, Roxbury, and Mattapan. Soon Black militants confronted Jewish merchants and civic leaders and clashed over housing integration, Black entitlement, Jewish culpability, and a list of factors real and imagined. Caught in the crossfire were long-time residents of Dorchester and Roxbury, stunned by the rapid transition of a community from white and Jewish to Black and somewhat isolated.[43]

Proclaiming, as did delegates at the 1972 Gary Convention, that "our cities are…dying grounds. [And] the schools are unable—or unwilling—to educate our children for the real world of our struggles," residents of the Ocean Hill–Brownsville section of Brooklyn demanded action, too. Blacks had lived in Brooklyn since the founding of the nation; in 1790 they accounted for 1 in 3 residents, a share they would not reclaim until the late twentieth century. The school conflict was born of the twentieth century, however. In 1940 Blacks accounted for just 4.0 percent of the population. A declining overall population and a sixfold increase in the Black population pushed African Americans to 25.2 percent of the New York City total by 1970. As of 1968, Brooklyn held the largest proportion of Blacks in the five boroughs of New York City (39 percent).[44]

Significantly, the majority of Blacks lived among other Blacks. This close proximity and sense of shared grievances stitched together a racial tapestry made from the commingling of West Indian, southern, and northern Black threads. From the fragments of this quilted world formed a racialized community that acknowledged differences even as it coalesced around themes of common complaint. Little bound that community as much as the goal of community empowerment.[45] Black, disproportionately poor, and symbolically disfranchised, many members believed community control was the answer to a complex of befuddling problems. It was not so simple of course, but in the late 1960s few knew this.

Elsewhere in the city, questions of race and desegregation had already shaped the perceptions of some Jews. In 1963, 87 percent of those attending PS 149 were white, whereas almost 100 percent of those attending nearby PS 92 were Black and Puerto Rican. To correct this racial imbalance, officials proposed grade-level consolidation. First and second graders would attend PS 92; third through sixth graders would go to PS 149.

This was not just a story about race, however. Reflecting a curious postwar bifurcation in the city's schools, the overwhelming majority of whites were also Jewish, including three quarters of those attending PS 149. A good number were new to the area. They had moved from the Bronx and Brooklyn for better opportunities, better schools, and to avoid the sizable influx of Blacks and Puerto Ricans. When pressed many acknowledged that they worried less about their children attending schools with Blacks than about their neighborhoods becoming majority Black. Some apprehension had to do with the bug-a-boo of depreciated real estate value. But faced with the possibility of sustained contact, Jews, just as Blacks, worried about empowerment and control.[46]

This pattern of concern erupted and intensified in Ocean Hill–Brownsville during 1967 and 1968. Various commentators have argued over the details of the controversy for more than a quarter of a century.[47] Here is not the place to rehearse those debates; rather, it is the place to highlight the importance of postwar migration and the attendant rise of segregated communities. For the third phase in Black-Jewish educational relations emerged from the spatial configurations of 1960s urban America, which dramatized differences.

In part, the third phase grew out of different migration histories. Jewish migration to New York and Brooklyn had long ended by the time the second wave of Black migrants reached the city. Many Black migrants arrived between 1940 and 1960, just as the children and grandchildren of former Jewish immigrants secured their places in classrooms and in school administration. Formerly excluded from higher education as a result of language barriers, family needs, and bigotry, New York's Jewish population now claimed a somewhat fragile hold on the ladder to mobility.

Thus when the conflict erupted, many white teachers acted in their own interests. They chafed at the prospects of community-based groups summarily firing teachers without due process—which happened in the early months of the controversy. They also feared for job and economic security. One teacher wrote,

> The public school teachers in this city are in the main a "lower-middle-class" group of people; that is, they reflect the values, thinking, goals, and life-style of a group of people whose parents were working class. They are people who did not have "things" and now want "things."

Wanting things and protecting gains became watchwords in the battle between community control and union protection.[48]

By 1967 teacher interest and union prerogative symbolized Jewish control to a number of Blacks. At the time, 90 percent of the teachers in New York City were white; more than half of the students were Black or Puerto Rican. The majority of the teachers were Jewish and they belonged to the UFT.[49] To these teachers, the union represented their best protector. Many harbored memories of an earlier time, when the school system systematically excluded them. They fought for an examination board, collective bargaining, seniority rules, a contract, and guarantees of due process—that is, the professional treatment of school teachers.

Yet what looked like reform from one side of the divide simply appeared as guardianship of the status quo from the other side. Much as with James Baldwin, individual experiences became the architecture of group perspectives. It was no longer the teacher who happened to be Jewish, it was the "Jewish teacher." Even when parents and teachers agreed about the need to redo or reform individual schools, their places in the matrix of social relations produced suspicion, contempt, and often anger. Both groups, for example, readily agreed that the principal of JHS 178 had lost control. Students ran the halls and some teachers had abandoned their classrooms. Yet parents were frustrated by reform-minded teachers reluctant to ignore eligibility lists, seniority, and collective bargaining agreements. Teachers viewed these hard won gains as sacrosanct; parents viewed the rules and the teachers as obstacles.

The poker-style gamesmanship of both sides continued though 1968, with each confrontation followed by a raising of the ante. After a threatened strike by Ocean Hill parents, teachers waged a 14-day strike over wages, disciplining unruly students, and policy-making. Some parents (and some teachers) saw the strike as further disregard for the well-being of the children. Parents soon picketed teachers. Tensions exploded again in May 1968, when a community board and its superintendent, Rhody McCoy, transfered 13 teachers, 5 assistant principals, and 1 principal without securing other employment for them—as promised. With UFT support, 350 teachers walked off the job. The state legislature settled the immediate issue—though not the question of community control—in April 1969 when it divided the city into more than 30 districts.[50]

The residue of interethnic suspicion lasted well after the controversy ended, one suspects. Certainly some Blacks demonstrated their susceptibility to the racist virus of anti-Semitism, and as the Botein Report on racial and religious prejudice concluded, "Over and over again we found evidence of...vicious anti-Black attitudes on the parts of some white people." Still, Jews and Blacks mobilized to fight such prejudices. Teachers of both races praised intergroup cooperation, criticized union leadership for seemingly fanning the flames of discord, and highlighted the continued involvement of white and Jewish teachers in Ocean Hill–Brownsville. Meanwhile, more conservative UFT members rejected radicalism and those members who supported community control, undermining the view that this was simply a battle between a Black community and white, overwhelmingly Jewish, teachers.[51]

Placed in historical context, therefore, the Ocean Hill–Brownsville controversy symbolized what happened when two group histories converged more than merged. When the Jewish community was small and contact limited, educational relations turned on personal relationships. When elites in both groups came of age, as they did in the late nineteenth and early twentieth centuries, the relationship revolved around the formation of mutually beneficial institutions. By the third phase, however, personal relationships and institutional arrangements had not disappeared altogether, but now a wider cross section of both communities knew each other. Some found the terms for common ground, pursuing civil rights and equal opportunity. Others encountered the "other" and recoiled. For those Blacks and Jews, ancient prejudices found new meanings as they struggled to maintain or secure their place in American life.

That James Baldwin had Jewish friends and that his Jewish friends had a Black friend is both the promise and the challenge. Each generation or two has defined the terms of an educational relationship. At times that relationship adopted the character of an alliance, and at times it assumed the qualities of a confrontation. History shows that individual Blacks and Jews have formed lasting, deeply personal relationships that defy simple categorization. After all, there are and have been hundreds of Americans who are both Black and Jewish. But given that 99 percent of all Blacks marry other Blacks, such possibilities remain rare. Instead, history shows the conditions for intergroup cooperation and the terms for cooperation to give way to conflict.

Fortunately, historical actors are multipositional; as such race, religion, ethnicity, class, and gender are part of the constellation of identities that make us who we are. Thus it was possible for Baldwin to have close Jewish friends, and to worry about the encroachment of Naziism, even as he held stereotypical views of the Jewish merchant or landlord. The challenge, therefore, is freeing ourselves to imagine the full range of human attitudes—both historically and currently. Once freed, we might combine the promise and the challenge required to understand the peculiar entanglement of Blacks and Jews.

Notes

1. Epigraph is from James Baldwin, Lecture, February 28, 1984, University of Massachusetts-Amherst, reprinted in *The Black Scholar* (November/December 1988): 3.

2. The *Black Scholar* spotlighted the conflict between Julius Lester, Black and Jewish, and his former colleagues in the Department of Afro-American Studies at the University of Massachusetts in the same issue it reprinted Baldwin's lecture. *Black Scholar* (November/December 1988): 16–43.

3. Only about 1 in 20 Jewish immigrants returned to Europe. Sucheng Chan, "European and Asian Immigration Into the United States Comparative Perspective, 1829s to 1920s," in Virginia Yans-McLaughlin, ed., *Immigration Reconsidered* (New York, 1990), pp. 37–69; return rates, p. 39.

4. Earl Lewis, "Expectations, Economic Opportunities, and Life in the Industrial Age: Black Migration to Norfolk, Virginia, 1910–1945," in Joe W. Trotter, Jr., ed., *The Great Migration in Historical Perspective* (Bloomington: Indiana University Press, 1991), pp. 22–23. Reynolds Farley and Walter Allen, *The Color Line and the Quality of Life in America* (New York, 1989), p. 113.

5. I don't mean to suggest that personal and institutional contact disappeared as the relationship matured. Rather, at different times certain patterns moved to the fore.

6. Lawrence Cremin, *American Education: The National Experience, 1783–1876* (New York, 1981); and *American Education: The Metropolitan Experience, 1876–1980* (New York, 1988), especially chapters 1–3.

7. Ira Berlin, *Slaves Without Masters* (New York, 1974), pp. 76–78, 303–306; Leon Litwack, *North of Slavery* (Chicago, 1961), pp. 113–52; and Robert L. McCaul, *The Black Struggle for Public Schooling in Nineteenth-Century Illinois* (Carbondale, IL, 1987).

8. Berlin, *Slaves Without Masters*, pp. 76–78.

9. On Douglass, see Frederick Douglass, *Narrative of the Life of Frederick Douglass* (New York, 1973; 1845), pp. 35–41, and William S. McFeely, *Frederick Douglass* (New York, 1991), pp. 29–32. When Christopher McPherson advertised his school, he was arrested and shipped to an insane asylum. On Richmond, see Berlin, *Slaves Without Masters*, pp. 76–77. Norfolk resident Margaret Douglass created a stir when she admitted teaching free Black children in the basements of some of the city's leading white churches. See Tommy Lee Bogger, "The Slave and Free Black Community In Norfolk, Virginia, 1775–1865," (Ph.D. diss., University of Virginia, 1976), pp. 217–221.

10. Litwack, *North of Slavery*, p. 132.

11. Interestingly, by the 1890s Italians and Jews made up a majority of the students at the Institute. Even in Philadelphia five bloody race riots in two decades curtailed the meaning of freedom and opportunity. For a history of education, racial conflict, and Black aspirations see, Vincent P. Franklin, *The Education of Black Philadelphia* (Philadelphia, 1979), pp. 3–15; Gary Nash, *Forging Freedom* (Cambridge, MA, 1988), pp. 203–10; and Roger Lane, *William Dorsey's Philadelphia & Ours* (New York, 1991), especially chapter 5.

12. Douglass began his first autobiography with the indicting words: "My father was a white man. He was admitted to be such by all I ever heard speak of my parentage" (p. 1). Douglass would rewrite his life story on two other occasions, even distancing himself from this claim, but the charge forever exposed whites as co-conspirators in the story of race in America.

13. As a result, in 1870 Detroit, nearly 82 percent of Jews worked as peddlers or traders. Such businesses favored those with limited capital and reliable networks of similarly situated workers crisscrossing the nation. In time, many of these peddlers parlayed savings into the purchase of small businesses—in some cases still larger businesses. Leonard Dinnerstein and Mary Dale Palsson, eds., *Jews in the South* (Baton Rouge, LA, 1973); Abraham Karp, *Haven and Home: A History of Jews in America* (New York, 1985); Shelly Tenebaum, "The Jews," in Mary Kupiec Cayton, Elliott J. Gorn, and Peter W. Williams, *Encyclopedia of American Social History* (New York, 1993), pp. 770–75.

14. James William Hagy, *This Happy Land: The Jews of Colonial and Antebellum Charleston* (Tuscaloosa, AL, 1993), pp. 1, 12–27, and 91.

15. For a sample of the conflicting biographical profiles, see Eric Foner, *Freedom's Lawmakers* (New York, 1993), pp. 39–40; Bertram Wallace Korn, "Jews and Negro Slavery in the Old South, 1789–1865," in Dinnerstein and Palsson, eds., *Jews in the South,* pp. 117–19; Joel Williamson, *After Slavery* (Chapel Hill, NC, 1965), p. 210. Hagy, *This Happy Land*, pp. 100, 152–54.

16. Hagy, *This Happy Land*, pp. 174–76.

17. George Lawrence, trans., and J.P. Mayer, ed., Alexis De Tocqueville, *Democracy in America* (New York, 1988), pp. 343–44.

18. Hagy, *This Happy Land*, p. 100; Korn, "Jews and Negro Slavery in the Old South," pp. 116–17. Similar accounts of interracial love are documented across the South. See, for example, Thomas E. Buckley, "Unfixing Race: Class, Power, and Identity in an Interracial Family," *Virginia Magazine of History and Biography* 102 (July 1994): 349–380, or Adele Logan Alexander, *Ambiguous Lives* (Fayetteville, AR, 1991), pp. 63–90.

19. Deborah Gray White, *Arn't I a Woman?: Female Slaves in the Plantation South* (New York, 1985); A. Leon Higginbotham, "Race, Sex, Education, and Missouri Jurisprudence: Shelley v. Kraemer in Historical Perspective," *Washington University Law Quarterly* 67 (1989): 684–685; and Melton A. McLaurin, *Celia, A Slave* (Athens, GA, 1991).

20. Again, for a sample of the conflicting biographical profiles, see Foner, *Freedom's Lawmakers*, pp. 39–40; Korn, "Jews and Negro Slavery in the Old South, 1789–1865," pp. 117–19; Williamson, *After Slavery*, pp. 210. Foner identified the father as Isaac, but offered a description that more closely fits Jacob. Korn acknowledged the controversy over patrimony but decided to identify Isaac as the father since that is what Francis's descendants prefer. Williamson believed Jacob was the father. Hagy, meanwhile, found no definite evidence and concluded that either brother could have been the father. Hagy, *This Happy Land*, pp. 100, 152–54, 213–14.

21. There is not only a question of patrimony but also of filial connection. All sources list Francis and Thomas as brothers; their relationship to Henry goes unacknowledged in all but one instance. Henry (1830–1886), who was several years older than Francis (1837–1903) and Thomas (1838–1881), is called their brother by Korn. Even contemporary sources identify Lydia Williams as his mother—i.e., Foner, *Freedom's Lawmakers*, p.40. By Charleston standards the Cardozo's were a small group, and Isaac and Jacob the only unattached men of marriage age around 1830. It is highly probable therefore that the three were possibly brothers and at least first cousins. For further details see Francis L. Cardozo Family Papers, Library of Congress.

22. Michael P. Johnson and James L. Roark, *Black Masters* (New York, 1984), p.

53; Dickson D. Bruce, Jr., *Archibald Grimké* (Baton Rouge, LA, 1993), pp. 2–17; Bernard E. Powers, Jr., *Black Charlestonians* (Fayetteville, AR, 1994), p. 154.

23. There is no mention of Henry's educational background. Foner, *Freedom's Lawmakers*, pp. 39–40; Korn, "Jews and Negro Slavery in the Old South," pp. 117–19; Williamson, *After Slavery*, pp. 210; Hagy, *This Happy Land*, p. 100; and Thomas Holt, *Black Over White* (Urbana, IL, 1977), pp. 36, 54, 64–65, 122–33, and 230.

24. We don't know why Francis, Thomas, and presumably Henry favored Christianity to Judaism. Hagy noted, for example, that antebellum Charleston synagogues generally restricted membership to whites only. Yet, Billy Simmons attended Beth Elohim as a Black, a slave, and a Jew. It is conceivable that Isaac did not want the larger community to scrutinize his socially compromised relationship and decided against raising his sons in his faith. Also, by the 1830s Christian denominations had made allowances for the inclusion of Blacks and Charleston had several churches for people of color. Hagy, *This Happy Land*, pp. 101–102. Foner, *Freedom's Lawmakers*, p. 39.

25. Dorothy Sterling, ed., *We Are Your Sisters* (New York, 1984), p. 280; Leon Litwack, *Been In the Storm So Long* (New York, 1979), pp. 472–94; John Hope Franklin and Alfred A. Moss, Jr., *From Slavery to Freedom*, 6th ed. (New York, 1988), p. 210.

26. See James D. Anderson, *The Education of Blacks in the South, 1860–1935* (Chapel Hill, NC, 1988), especially chapters 1 and 2.

27. Anderson, *The Education of Blacks in the South,* pp. 33–50. Anderson more directly equates postwar educational efforts with new forms of servitude in his dissertation, "Education For Servitude: The Social Purposes of Schooling in the Black South, 1870–1930" (Ph.D. diss., University of Illinois at Urbana-Champaign, 1973), pp. 1–5. Donald Spivey, *Schooling for the New Slavery* (Westport, CT, 1978).

28. Alfred Chandler, *The Visible Hand: The Managerial Revolution in American Business* (Cambridge, MA, 1977), pp. 122–87; Walter Lafeber, *The American Search for Opportunity, 1865–1913* (Cambridge, MA, 1993), p. 22.

29. Louis Harlan, *Booker T. Washington: The Making of a Black Leader, 1856–1901* (New York, 1972), pp. 215–16; and *Booker T. Washington: The Wizard of Tuskegee, 1901–1915* (New York, 1983), pp. 128–42; Anderson, *The Education of Blacks in the South*, pp. 80–102, quote p. 82.

30. W.E.B. Du Bois, *The Souls of Black Folk* (1903) in *Three Negro Classics* (New York, 1965), pp. 240–52; Raymond B. Fosdick, *Adventure in Giving* (New York, 1962), pp. vii–25; Franklin and Moss, *From Slavery to Freedom*, p. 241. For an overview of philanthropic activities, see J. M. Stephen Peeps, "Northern Philanthropy and the

Emergence of Black Higher Education: Do-Gooders, Compromisers, or Co-Conspirators," *Journal of Negro Education* 50 (1981): 251–69.

31. Leonard Dinnerstein, Roger L. Nichols, and David Reimers, *Natives and Strangers* (New York, 1990), pp. 136–37; Hamilton Holt, ed., *The Life Stories of Undistinguished Americans As Told by Themselves* (London, 1990), pp. 21–28; Susan Glenn, *Daughters of the Shtetl: Life and Labor in the Immigrant Generation* (Ithaca, NY, 1990).

32. David Levering Lewis, "Parallels and Divergences: Assimilationist Strategies of Afro-American and Jewish Elites from 1910 to the Early 1930s," *The Journal of American History* 71 (December 1984): 543–64.

33. Louis Harlan, "Booker T. Washington's Discovery of Jews," in J. Morgan Kousser and James M. McPherson, *Region, Race, and Reconstruction* (New York, 1982), pp. 267–79; on Warburg, p. 272. Harlan, *Booker T. Washington: The Wizard of Tuskegee*, pp. 140–42.

34. Harlan, "Booker T. Washington's Discovery of Jews," pp. 272–75; Lewis, "Parallels and Divergences," pp. 555–56.

35. Lewis, "Parallels and Divergences," pp. 559–63; David Levering Lewis, *W.E.B. Du Bois: Biography of a Race* (New York, 1993), pp. 386–407, 486–90.

36. Sense of African American horror at the atrocities in Nazi-occupied territory in Europe was relayed by Walter White to Stephen Wise in 1943; a facsimile of the letter is reproduced in Jack Salzman, ed., *Bridges and Boundaries: African Americans and American Jews* (New York, 1992), p. 213. Whiteness is reflected in increasing patterns of cross-ethnic marriages. According to recent findings, such marriages are now the rule rather than the exception. By the mid-1980s as many as 1 in 3 Jews married non-Jews: see Richard Alba, *Ethnic Identity: The Transformation of White America* (New Haven, 1990), pp. 12–15. Discussions of Black perceptions of Jews as whites are offered by Letty Cottin Pogrebin ("Blacks and Jews: Different Kinds of Survival") and Barbara Smith ("Between a Rock and a Hard Place: Relationships Between Black and Jewish Women") in Salzman, ed., *Bridges and Boundaries*, pp. 132–40. The personal pain of becoming white through rough encounters with Blacks is discussed in Norman Podhoretz, "My Negro Problem—And Ours," in *Bridges and Boundaries*, pp. 108–17.

37. Marshall Field Stevenson, Jr., "Points of Departure, Acts of Resolve: Black-Jewish Relations In Detroit, 1937–1962" (Ph.D. diss., University of Michigan, 1988), chapters 3–4.

38. Interestingly, for all of the writing on Black-Jewish relations, much remains speculative since there is still a great deal to know. What was life like for the Jewish scholars, sent by conscience or opportunity, who taught at predominantly Black col-

leges in the postwar South? How do we understand the relationship between Blacks and Jews, when Blacks were in positions of authority? How do we effectively address the taboos of interracial sex? These questions may seem beyond the purview of an article on education, but these and other questions had a tremendous effect on the third phase of the Black-Jewish educational relationship. On the need for more research on Black-Jewish relations, see John Bracey and August Meier, "Towards a Research Agenda on Blacks and Jews in United States History," *Journal of American Ethnic History* 12 (Spring 1993): 60–67. On Hill and a Left-Jewish alliance, see Angela Denise Dillard, "From the Reverend Charles Hill to the Reverend Albert Cleage, Jr.: Change and Continuity in the Patterns of Civil Rights Mobilization in Detroit, 1935–1968" (Ph.D. diss., University of Michigan, 1995), chapters 3–4. Stevenson, "Points of Departure," pp. 137–55. Cheryl Lynn Greenberg, *Or Does it Explode? Black Harlem In the Great Depression* (New York, 1991), pp. 122–28.

39. Competition and conflict between Black and Jewish southerners was not new. During the 1920s Black residents of Norfolk, Virginia complained bitterly of anti-Black sentiment—Earl Lewis, *In Their Own Interests* (Berkeley, 1991), pp. 79–80. Moreover, anti-Jewish sentiment increased noticeably as the civil rights struggle went on, explaining a feeling of unease. Murray Friedman, "One Episode in Southern Jewry's Response to Desegregation: An Historical Memoir," *American Jewish Archives* 33 (November 1981): 170–83, and "Virginia Jewry in the School Crisis: Anti-Semitism and Desegregation," *Commentary* 19 (January 1959): 17–22; and Leonard Dinnerstein, "Southern Jewry and the Desegregation Crisis, 1954–1970," *American Jewish Historical Quarterly* 62 (1972–73): 231–41, quote, p. 235.

40. Clayborne Carson, "Blacks and Jews in the Civil Rights Movement: The Case of SNCC," and Taylor Branch, "Blacks and Jews: The Uncivil War," in Salzman, ed., *Bridges and Boundaries*, pp. 36–49 and 50–69, respectively.

41. Hints of the shift to identity politics are mentioned in William L. Van Deburg, *New Day In Babylon: The Black Power Movement and American Culture, 1965–1975* (Chicago, 1992), pp. 1–61. A full elaboration of the transition from a politics of identity to identity politics is discussed in Earl Lewis, "Race, the State, and Social Construction," in Stanley I. Kutler, ed., *Encyclopedia of the United States in the Twentieth Century* (New York, 1995); James R. Ralph, Jr., *Northern Protest: Martin Luther King, Jr., Chicago, and the Civil Rights Movement* (Cambridge, MA, 1993), pp. 7–28.

42. A chronology of events is offered in Barbara Carter, *Pickets, Parents, and Power: The Story Behind the New York Teachers's Strike* (New York, 1971), Chronology.

43. Hillel Levine and Lawrence Harmon, *The Death of an American Jewish Community* (New York, 1992); and Ronald P. Formisano, *Boston Against Busing* (Chapel Hill, NC, 1991), pp. 13–14.

44. As quoted in Van Deburg, *New Day In Babylon*, p. 113. David M. Ment, "Education and the Black Community in Nineteenth-Century Brooklyn," in *Educating an Urban People*, ed. Diana Ravitch and Ronald K. Goodman (New York, 1981), p. 27. Harold X. Connolly, *A Ghetto Grows in Brooklyn* (New York, 1977), pp. 129–36, 141–42. Throughout much of America, postwar suburbanization was designed to exclude rather than include Blacks. Their greater concentration in inner cities reflected housing and lending practices—Kenneth Jackson, *Crabgrass Frontiers* (New York, 1985), pp. 241–42.

45. Connolly, *A Ghetto Grows in Brooklyn*, pp. 135–41, 212–22. Van Deburg, *New Day In Babylon*, pp. 112–29.

46. Kurt Lang and Gladys Land, "Resistance of School Desegregation: A Case Study of Backlash Among Jews," *Sociological Inquiry* 35 (Winter 1965): 94–106.

47. A list of works on the controversy includes Maurice Berube and Marilyn Gittell, eds., *Confrontation at Ocean Hill–Brownsville: The New York School Strikes of 1968* (New York, 1969); Thomas R. Brooks, "Tragedy at Ocean Hill," *Dissent* 16 (January–February 1969): 28–40; Carter, *Pickets, Parents, and Power*; Mario Fantini, Marilyn Gittell, and Richard Magate, *Community Control and Urban School* (New York, 1970); Martin Mayer, *The Teachers Strike: New York, 1968* (New York, 1969), chapter 12; Marjorie Murphy, *Blackboard Unions* (Ithaca, 1990), pp. 233–46; Diane Ravitch, *The Great School Wars: New York City, 1805–1973* (New York, 1974); and David Rogers, *110 Livington Street Revisited: Decentralization in Action* (New York, 1983).

48. On the early history of Jewish involvement in New York City education, see Selma Berrol, "The Open City: Jews, Jobs, and Schools in New York City, 1880–1915," in Ravitch and Goodman, eds., *Educating an Urban People*, pp. 101–15, and Sherry Gorelick, *City College and the Jewish Poor* (New Brunswick, NJ, 1981). Quote from Berube and Gittell, eds., *Confrontation at Ocean Hill–Brownsville*, pp. 209–10.

49. In fact, of the 541 teachers in the Ocean Hill–Brownsville demonstration project, an advertisement listed 70 percent as white; of that percentage, 50 percent as Jewish. Reprinted in Berube and Gittell, eds., *Confrontation at Ocean Hill–Brownsville*, pp. 170–73. Student figures noted in Connolly, *A Ghetto Grows in Brooklyn*, pp. 220–21.

50. *New York Times*, 5 January, 8 March, 18 August, 5, 7, 10, 13, 21, 30 September, and 26, 30 October 1968. Berube and Gittell, eds., *Confrontation at Ocean Hill–Brownsville*, pp. 104–75; Carter, *Pickets, Parents, and Power*, pp. 7–42, 107–29; Murphy, *Blackboard Unions*, pp. 233–46.

51. Curiously, the patently anti-Semitic flyer attributed to Blacks identified a community group that did not exist. Certainly members of the Black community were capable of producing such statements. Nonetheless, in light of the scope of

CONINTELPRO activities by the FBI and other law enforcement groups, one might also suspect agent provocateurs. Berube and Gittell, eds., *Confrontation at Ocean Hill–Brownsville*, pp. 170–76; Murphy, *Blackboard Unions*, pp. 240–45.

twelve

AFRICAN AMERICANS AND JEWS IN HOLLYWOOD

Antagonistic Allies

THOMAS CRIPPS

F ew ethnic groups in America have enjoyed such a close association in the popular mind as have African Americans and Jews. And yet their shared affinities have often been clouded by ambiguities. From the earliest days of the alliance—such as in the heavily Jewish founding of the NAACP in 1909 or in the origins of Black-oriented Jewish foundations such as the Rosenwald Fund—lack of mutual trust has often blurred the shared goals of their common cause: the struggle to end racial and ethnic discrimination. Among Blacks in particular the alliance has been strained by a lingering sense that however philanthropic Jews had been, they also possessed the power to push buttons that allowed them to dictate the terms of the alliance. In such cases, stereotypes regain their ability to define diverse groups as one dimensional demons—Jewish conspirators or moneygrubbers as against Black wastrels and criminals.

I propose to take up this theme of the ambivalent allies as it applies to African Americans and Jews in Hollywood, particularly with respect to their intergroup relations during times of social crisis such as the Great Depression and World War II.

In the history of moviemaking, the Black and Jewish alliance often suffered schisms that fractured its sense of common cause. But the central issue here is one of perception by African Americans of their shifting place in American life rather than a matter of actual Jewish social behavior. Indeed, Jews behaved politically like the generality of Americans, save for a generalized Jewish leftward slant that Michael Lerner, editor of the Jewish journal, *Tikkun*, spoke of thus: "Jews earn like Episcopalians but vote like Puerto Ricans."[2]

Nonetheless, when it came to moviemaking most observers saw that Jews enjoyed a special seat of power that clearly reinforced the notion of a Jewish cabal that pulled the wires behind almost every scene. As early as 1918, for example, Julius Rosenwald, the first Jewish president of the mailorder firm of Sears Roebuck, enjoyed both a reputation as a "friend of the Negro" and as a man willing to place demands upon those to whom he donated money. "I really feel ashamed to have so much money," he once said of a career during which he gave away $63 million to causes that included Blacks. "I belong to a race that has suffered," he told a colored YMCA that he had underwritten. But he also snappishly told white patrons of the YMCA that "I won't give a cent unless you will include in it the building of a Colored Men's YMCA," and then admonished a Black audience to take a hand on their own behalf. "You are going to run it," he said, "what a chance for you to make good!"[3]

The Hollywood version of this sort of having one's way helped shape a mold from which the moguls in all their arrogance were cast. Harry Cohn of Columbia was the bossy "White Fang" who *gave* ulcers to others rather than acquired them; journalists spoke of the moguls' "fiefdoms"; and actors routinely described their bosses as "a bunch of Jewish gangsters." As Frank Whitbeck, a publicist at Metro, recalled his first encounter with Jewish power he had only just muttered something about "a fat Jewish s.o.b." when a friend warned him that in Hollywood "there is no such thing as a *Jewish* sonofabitch!"[4]

But it was their power, not their Jewishness, that rankled the less powerful. Rosenwald's charity, for example, had its limits. When a coalition of Black and white allies joined to make *The Birth of a Race* (1918) as an antidote to the calculated racism of D. W. Griffith's epic of post-Civil War Reconstruction, *The Birth of a Nation* (1915), Rosenwald had offered his encouragement. But he quickly removed to a distance when one of the group let drop a hint that the philanthropist had agreed to guarantee the project against all losses.[5] It was this sense that a Jewish foot always rested on the braking pedal that stirred resentment among the beholden.

Across this gulf that divided rich from poor, stereotypes readily defined the respective groups to each other. Jews seemed to acquire money by means of some cabalistic formula—"never buy retail," or other incantation—while Blacks seemed fecklessly improvident; Jews saved, while Blacks sought immediate gratification. In mutually hard times, Jews and Blacks embraced the legend that both were victims of the same sort of oppression and thus were meant for each other as allies; in prosperous times when, however, Black fortunes lagged, Blacks found the legend wanting. Harold Cruse, for example, carped at "the myth that the Negroes' best friend is the Jew," and demanded that the African American "seriously reassess his relationship with American Jews." Thus when the Black director, Spike Lee, addressed a conference on the place of African Americans in movies, he drew upon a history of Black group-suspicions when he told his audience that he asked Warner Bros. to drop "gracefully" the celebrated director, Norman Jewison, from directing its often delayed bio-pic of Malcolm X.[6]

Stereotypes aside, the legend of a fruitful symbiosis of Jewish and Black political ambitions served Blacks well. But in their actual histories in America, the two groups only superficially shared a common heritage, whatever surface similarities drew them together. Blacks had been the victims of a Southern rural culture rooted first in slavery and then in its residual forms such as peonage, sharecropping, and political proscription. Jews, on the other hand, had come to this country in full flight from the pogroms of Czarist Russia and Wilhelmine Germany, but in possession of their own urban culture that embraced both skills and ideologies that anticipated eventual success in cities: trade unionism, socialism, cultural cohesion in the form of rabbinical devotion to scholarship, and crafts such as tailoring, all of which provided a cultural seasoning against the rigors of immigrant life. Thus Blacks fled to Northern cities as refugees while Jews fled to them as to familiar havens.

Therefore, Jews came to American cities with an edge—an inventory of skills and experiences that enabled them to enter raffish, marginal businesses apart from the staid enterprises that excluded them. Popular culture provided one of these accessible avenues. Particularly vaudeville, the popular, cheap traveling shows "creat[ed] a community of city dweller, by establishing norms of taste and behavior," as Albert McLean wrote in *American Vaudeville*.[7]

As a result of the drift of a Jewish entrepreneurial elite toward the marginal ventures of popular theatre, Jews stood poised to enter the business of moviemaking through the doorway provided by exhibiting and distributing movies rather than making them. Lacking not only these prospects but also the pool of urban skills with which to succeed at them, Blacks soon came to accept the division of labor that followed: Jewish management, exhibition, distribution, and booking, as against Black performing. Thus, whatever the merits of, say, "race movies" made by Jews for Black audiences, African Americans stood at a distance from the industry. Typically, Robert Levy's Reol firm made race movies, sometimes from original Black material such as the work of Paul Laurence Dunbar, distributed their work through Alfred Sack's bookers, and showed the films in theatres such as Frank Schiffman's *Apollo* in Harlem. Meanwhile even such an independently minded Black filmmaker as Oscar Micheaux (who often filmed his own novels) borrowed from white "angels" such as Schiffman or contracted out their lab work to Guffante and other labs willing to accept negatives as collateral against unpaid bills.

The drift of the times took a similar course in the production of the mainstream narrative movies that eventually grew into "classical" Hollywood fare. Movies at first had been produced by an old-stock, Anglo-Saxon and Irish elite that had included enterprising inventors such as Thomas Edison and W. K. L. Dickson, pioneering moviemakers such as the English J. Stuart Blackton and Albert E. Smith, and Thomas Ince. At their worst, they simply dealt in old stereotypes inherited from minstrelsy, melodrama, and vaudeville, while at their best they sometimes portrayed ethnic characters in a sweetly sentimental light. Such was the case in D. W. Griffith's *His Trust Fulfilled* (1910), in which a former slave's character is measured only by his fealty to his former mistress, and in his *The Romance of a Jewess* (1908), in which a "mixed" marriage is seen as morally advanced over the grumpy particularism of Jewish and Irish parents.

Gradually, beginning at the onset of the Great War, as Jews began to penetrate the oligopoly of old-stock patentholders (who had formed a patents "trust"), the Black image on the screen changed only in various marginal ways. Early on, Jews and Blacks alike had been hazed with unseemly ardor in the two-reel movies that were popular on the eve of Hollywood's birth. In *The Fights of Nations* (1907), for example, Blacks in "Sunny Africa, Eighth Avenue" fought with razors and danced preternaturally well, while the Jews vied with each other in fevered bouts of verbal duelling that broke off only when a gentile—an Irish cop, for example—drew the Jews together in cunning conspiracy.[8] As to moviemaking itself, William Selig's *A Night in the Jungle* (1915), like almost any jungle yarn of its day, placed its Blacks on the edge of the action with scant investment in the outcome of the plot. And, like Sam Lubin's *How Rastus Got His Pork Chops* (1910), many movies drew upon the hoariest of Southern racial lore, none of which could be traced back to Jewish cultural sources.

But with the onset of World War I, many liberal Jews stood against Griffith's *The Birth of a Nation* (1915) either by joining Rabbi Stephen Wise and the NAACP in the raucous demonstrations in the office of the Mayor of New York, or by joining with Rosenwald in backing some sort of cinematic challenge to Griffith such as *The Birth of a Race*.

Seemingly mere randomness rather than Jewishness set the racial agendas of moviemakers. In this connection the career of William Selig is instructive. Early on, like many figures in show business, he had managed "a genuine fast Black show" that played the Southern theatrical circuits. Later, he carried the experience into moviemaking in the form of such two-reelers as *Interrupted Crap Game* in which "darkies" break off from their gambling in order to pursue a plump chicken. Yet, paradoxically, Selig's Polyscope firm joined Rosenwald in the quest to make *The Birth of a Race*, a project also taken up in first-draft form by the German Jewish financier, Jacob Schiff, and one of the first studios to move westward to Hollywood, Carl Laemmle's IMP firm, which eventually formed the core of a real estate venture and movie company called Universal Pictures.[9] Clearly, as in all situational politics, the setting and the stakes, rather than ethnicity, set the agenda and the ideology.[10]

If the Jewish presence in this pre-Hollywood era seemed ambivalent, it must be seen that African Americans were shrewd enough to respond to both its aspects. On the one hand, Jews seemed magisterial in their knowledge of business practice; on the other, Blacks feared Jewish entrepreneurs would swamp struggling Black infant industries. "I have always been leery of the man with the thing [film cans] under his arm [as shoestring Black bookers were obliged to do]," wrote the Black critic, Tony Langston, to George P. Johnson, a cofounder of the Black Lincoln Motion Picture Company. "I learned this along with the Jews, and you know they are the last word in smartness when this game is concerned." Yet Johnson's perception of the entry of Jews into race moviemaking scared him as much as it tutored him. "The Jews are making ready for an attack upon the Negro field in the Movies," he warned the Black publisher, Robert L. Vann, only months after the Great War had ended.[11]

Meanwhile, the war had set in motion forces that transformed moviemaking in ways that defined a classical Hollywood style, opened up the entire war-weary world to the resulting products, and brought into national consciousness the image of the omnipotent Jewish mogul. Much worse news for the few Black moviemaking firms was a nationwide influenza epidemic that wiped out marginal companies while it left stronger survivors in position to form the oligopoly that became the Hollywood system of script-to-screen dominance of the marketplace. Moreover, the survivors enjoyed unaccustomed access to funds as a result of their new hegemony, with the result that the Jewish Wall Street brokers Kuhn and Loeb, Goldman and Sachs, and others, as well as the San Francisco immigrant banker, A. P. Giannini, routinely lent capital.

Still other factors joined with fiscal matters to diminish Black access to the process of moviemaking. Almost every one of the emerging "majors" took on as advisors on regional and racial matters nativeborn white Southerners—Steve Lynch and Y. Frank Freeman at Paramount, Lamar Trotti and Nunnally Johnson at Fox, Francis Harmon in the Motion Picture Association of America (MPAA) itself, among others. This meant that whenever Black material sailed "over the transom" into producers' hands it went immediately to some white man such as King Vidor whose *Hallelujah!* (1929) derived from "his own observations...on the everyday life of the Negro," or to Marc Connelly who directed his own *Green Pastures* (1935) which he had drawn from his reading of Roark Bradford's book of Southern Black fables, *Old Man Adam and His Chillun.*[12]

Reinforcing these conservative trends was the Production Code Administration of the MPAA, eventually a creature of Catholicism rather than of Jews in that its "don'ts and be carefuls" that segregated Black characters from white in order to assuage white fears of miscegenation were drafted by the Jesuit, Fr. Daniel Lord of the St. Louis Province; the Catholic layman and tradepaper publisher, Martin Quigley; and Joseph Breen who succeeded to the office of "czar" of the MPAA following the retirement of its first ruler, the Presbyterian Republican, Will Hays.[13] Together with the Hollywood Blacks who played the only roles that emerged from this politically conservative system, the MPAA provided the most structured ideological control over the Black image on the screen—without the intrusion of a single Jewish hand.

To take only one instance of this system in process, we could do no better than to turn to the old Fox lot in 1929 (before it became "the goy studio" in 1935 as a result of a merger with Darryl F. Zanuck's 20th Century studio). Winfield Sheehan, a veteran manager of the studio founded by William Fox and led by Joseph Schenck, drove onto the lot where he brushed against Clarence Muse, a veteran of Black theatre and race movies who had been lingering at the gate hoping for a gig. The studio, in fact, had been looking for a capable Black actor to star in *Hearts in Dixie*, a pet project that Sheehan had promoted with the result that it had grown from a sentimental two-reeler into a feature-length celebration of Dixie. In it Muse became Nappus, an exceptionally wise man whose ponderously resonant voice dominated his scenes. Moreover, the movie, along with Metro's *Hallelujah!* created a brief vogue for all-Black material and may have served as teaser to the movie version of Marc Connelly's Pulitzer-prize musical drama, *Green Pastures* (1935).

Thereafter, Muse not only became famous as Nappus but also redefined at least one sort of social role for Blacks in Hollywood. Clearly, despite an unctuous manner that made young Black activists wince, Muse advanced the cause of Blacks in Hollywood. His quiet dignity, his advice to young Black performers, his reputed study of the law, his solid training on the stage, his complex mix of Black cultural nationalism and assimilationism, and his resistance to wartime NAACP activism that seemed to run counter to Muse's hope of "build[ing] ourselves into" Hollywood all conspired to give Muse an authority among Blacks precisely because in Sheehan he possessed a "friend at court" on the white movie lots.[14] Later, he acquired yet another friend at court, the young Frank Capra, for whom he appeared in *Dirigible*, *Broadway Bill*, and other movies.

Why should Sheehan's Jewish bosses have taken counsel from Muse? Perhaps because they were as assimilationist as Muse seemed. A look at the movies on the screens at the onset of the Great Crash reveals a rage for a comic assimilationism that almost every studio played to: *Kosher Kitty Kelly*, *Clancy's Kosher Wedding*, the *Cohens and the Kellys* series, and others of the decade that saw Anne Nichols's play, *Abie's Irish Rose* run on Broadway for years. The apogee of the era came in the form of *The Jazz Singer* (1927), Samson Raphaelson's own assimilationist account of a cantor's son who becomes a jazz singer. Far from a fluke of faddishness, the ideology of universalism extended into almost every immigrant-themed movie thereafter, often embracing African Americans in the resulting lovefeast as in the 1946 remake of *Abie's Irish Rose* (following its success as an ongoing radio series) when at the wedding that forms the climax of the movie the Black servant intones her own "Mazeltov." Even in their own lives, the moguls reflected their immigrants' wish to belong by voting Republican, modulating, even muting, their Jewishness, and marrying *goyishe* women. To find in these drives the source of Jewish conspiracy is as absurd as to find a Jewish predominance in another field, that of furriers, a plot against foxes and ermines.[15]

But what of African Americans? Did they take Jewish Hollywood as conspiracy or merely as a ruling class with whom they could deal? Certainly both in the trades and in the Black press the relationship between the two groups of outsiders was celebrated as sanguine. As early as 1922, Jewish-edited *Variety* praised *Love is an Awful Thing* for its "Bert Williams touches...that are most welcome" while complaining of "needless" quivering Negro servants. Whenever some odd racist tract appeared, *Variety* predicted: "There is no chance for this picture to get a nick-el anywhere...the Sunday night audience laughed it practically out of the the-atre." Or the Jewish editors reported on trends such as the "clumsy housemaids [who] seem to have gone out of style." Meanwhile, the Black press played both nag and cheerleader. Every review seemed to weigh movies against Hollywood's history. The *Amsterdam News*, for example, praised Cecil B. DeMille's proposed *Porgy* which "will portray the human everyday life of the American colored man" only months after the *Afro-American* complained of a "lack of pictures with Negro characters teaching Negro ideals." "Never before has the Southern Negro had the good fortune to be selected to take part in a clean cut motion picture" such as *Uncle Tom's Cabin*, said another review.[16]

More than any other movie, *The Jazz Singer* enjoyed a special place at the inter-section of African American and Jewish cultures. In its way, Raphaelson and Paul Sloane's movie brought Blacks and Jews together on the screen in an urban set-ting that seemed to follow from the bold Black movies of 1927 through 1929: *Uncle Tom's Cabin* (1927) with the restoration of its abolitionist core; *Hearts in Dixie* (1929), with its tragic treatment of Black Southern rural life; *Hallelujah!* (1929), King Vidor's and Wanda Tuchock's contrasting of Black pastoral life with that of the poor Black city; and *Show Boat* (1929) with its racial moral worn on its sleeve in the form of the bittersweet miscegenation subplot and Oscar Hammerstein and Jerome Kern's powerfully defining ballad, "Old Man River."

The title role of *The Jazz Singer* seemed to feed not only a general white need to cultivate a parody of Black musical and performing style, but also a specifically Jewish response to their immigration to America. Much as Eric Lott has argued of Blackface minstrelsy—that the "theft" of African American performance cul-ture by having white people parody it while masked by burnt cork helped give identity to the white working class by portraying what white men were *not*—so too Michael Rogin has carried the argument onto the movie screen. To him, it seemed that as "Blackface made white Americans out of Irish immigrants," so movies did for the Jews of the twentieth century who "occupied an insecure posi-tion between whites and people of color."[17]

But meaning need not stop here. Both Blacks and Jews, if they in fact did not draw inferences similar to those made by Lott and Rogin, nonetheless appreciat-ed the link between their two ethnic cultures. While it is true that the Black *Pittsburgh Courier* in 1923 reported that Jolson "seriously doubted his ability to register [Blackface] as well upon the screen as upon the stage," the doubt focused on lame and stale racial comedy in a failed script, *His Darker Self*, that both D. W. Griffith and Jolson abandoned, rather than in Jolson's performance. Later, follow-ing the success of *The Jazz Singer* in 1930, the *Amsterdam News* claimed of Jolson's rendering of Blackness: "every colored performer is proud of him."[18]

Certainly Jewish producers shared some sort of appreciation of Black culture and its place in their lives. In a year's time spanning 1929 and 1930, for exam-ple, Jewish producers of short films integrated Black musical performance into the new medium of soundfilm in a rich cycle of Black musical performance so prolific that *Variety* gave it a headline—"Colored People in Many Short Talkers." Murray Roth's *Yamacraw* (1930) was typical in its stylized, sentimental treatment of the Black squalor of the "New South" that drives a young Black man (Jimmy Mordecai) northward to an urban life that tested his character in other ways—the ways of the street and the saloon. As it often did, Jewish *Variety* praised these shorts, finding *Yamacraw* "a jazz symphony of Negro life that is arresting in movement as well as dramatic in idea."[19]

Moreover, as though the onset of the Great Depression had thrust them together in common cause against still more burdensome economic forces, Blacks and Jews in Hollywood seemed to march in step. Perhaps they followed a course that various social critics have noticed. That is, from their inventory of cultural options they selected mutually satisfying tactics arising from a loose alliance of like-minded "conscience-liberals." As disparate observers as the Italian Marxist, Antonio Gramsci, through the liberal capitalist critics, John Kenneth Galbraith and James K. Feibleman, have found that times of crisis provide moments in which the oppressed and their allies may rebargain the terms of their social status.[20]

Certainly this alliance seemed emergent during the Great Depression. Not only did the decade begin with the cycle of Black performance shorts, including Duke Ellington's *Black and Tan Fantasy* (1929) with its wry treatment of a down-and-out composer and the dancer who hoofed so that he might live to compose, but it carried onward to 1935 when Ellington's *Symphony in Black* (1935) boldly evoked African American history in four movements: the "middle passage," oppressive toil, religious epiphany, and the urbane jazz age.

Moreover, Blacks participated. Briefly, until his early death, the Black writer Wallace Thurman enjoyed a contract with a Hollywood studio. In 1933, John Krimsky, one of the producers of the film of Eugene O'Neill's *The Emperor Jones*, insisted on diluting the playwright's primitivism by asking James Weldon Johnson of the NAACP and his brother, Rosamond, to contribute a prologue. In it, Jones (Paul Robeson), the Pullman porter whose *hubris* led him to a Caribbean crown (and a tragic death), is given a pastoral Black past rather than a tomtom beating in his breast as the psychologically plausible motive for his rise and fall.[21]

Such gestures earned Black attention, contending with Black concerns such as that of the Black movie pioneer, Bill Foster, who fairly shouted at James Weldon Johnson that "If the Negro wants Big Pictures of Negro life today they [sic] will have to produce them himself [or risk others']…controlling the Equipment [and] then the door will be closed." Muse, on the other hand, thought "Hollywood's not prejudiced; they'll buy anything that's successful," to which Johnson added a corollary that whites so far had handled Black material adequately because of a *Black* "reluctance…to see what they consider lower phases of Negro life." Indeed, after the Black congressman, Oscar DePriest, saw *Hallelujah!* he insisted that African America stood "on the threshold of civic and cultural emancipation." And by the middle of the Depression, the Negrophile writer, Carl Van Vechten, summed up, among other news items, the arrival of Bill Robinson and Paul Robeson in Hollywood, and the release of unsentimental movies such as *Slave Ship*, by predicting to Johnson "I think this is likely to be a NEGRO WINTER."[22]

By the end of the decade, the sort of gestures that evoked such fulsome praise had become calculated and firmly linked to an endemic anti-fascism that had been rising in the wake of the assumption to power of Mussolini, Hitler, Franco, and Tojo in totalitarian states. Indeed, in the transformation of the regional novel, *Gone with the Wind* into a national movie epic, David O. Selznick specifically linked the need for a modernized portrayal of Blacks to the international war against fascism. "In our picture I think we have to be awfully careful that the Negroes come out on the right side of the ledger," rather than, as he told his writer, risk their movie becoming "an advertisement for intolerant societies in these fascist-ridden times." Later, many Black activists, in spite of themselves, joined the house organ of the NAACP in finding in *Gone with the Wind* "no reason for Negroes to feel indignant." Later still, when Sol Lesser attempted a sort of B-movie version of the regionalisms of *Gone with the Wind* in his *Way Down South*, he, like Selznick, wished for fairly drawn Black imagery. But unlike Selznick, he went right to the source by engaging Clarence Muse and the poet, Langston Hughes, to write as Black a movie as they could. Never mind that draft-by-draft the movie compromised and embraced many Hollywood conventions; it had begun as a product of a Jewish-Black alliance. "Messrs. Muse and Hughes are to be given the utmost liberty in developing the Second Draft Screenplay," he wrote to his production unit, "so that it will contain every element of their conception of the story."[23]

Clearly, the mood of "conscience-liberalism" established by the onset of World War II placed African Americans in an enhanced bargaining position in Hollywood. Indeed, Sime Silverman's *Variety* gave such politics a banner headline: "Better Breaks for Negroes in H'wood." And Jews saw the changes—particularly those that seemed results of lobbying by Walter White of the NAACP—as especially sanguine. One of White's Jewish correspondents saw in the casting of a Black doctor in a Metro B-movie, *Dr. Kildaire's New Assistant*, an event "as stirring and as promising as any of the principles set forth in the Atlantic Charter [the pact that had defined the earliest of Allied war aims]." Routinely thereafter, critics celebrated war movies such as *Sahara* (1943) as "an outstanding contribution toward the objective stated by Mr. White."[24]

Such movies came from a cadre of Jewish "moguls" who even in prewar days had formed a Hollywood Anti-Nazi League to stand against Hitler's anti-Semitism even before the government did. They almost relished the role of propaganda warriors. In one instance of a polyethnic movie about a lost platoon, *Bataan* (1943), the cast featured obligatory soldiers that included the Jewish Sergeant Feinberg and a Black Corporal, Wesley Epps, a preacher and an artful demolition man. But when White learned during production that the Black role had been written out, he wired the MGM producer, Howard Dietz, and successfully pressed to have the role restored. Thus both the movie and its making symbolized the compelling wartime powers of the ethnic alliance. By war's end, the ethnic angle had begun to embrace Jews still more widely as in the case of Dore Schary's *Till the End of Time* (1946), in which a wounded veteran spits in the eye of a recruiter for a racist veterans' group, a gesture he offers in memory of "Maxie Klein," a dead buddy left on the beach on Guadalcanal.[25]

For their part, African Americans zealously took up White's agenda and made it their own. William G. Nunn, the publisher of the *Pittsburgh Courier*, for example, called for a "Double V" for victory simultaneously over foreign (and anti-Semitic) fascism and domestic racism. Such activism signaled the formation of a broadly based coalition that embraced Black publicists, White's lobbying in Hollywood, a link to the 20th Century-Fox boardroom through its chairman, the defeated presidential candidate, Wendell Willkie, who served as special counsel to the NAACP, and the Jewish studio chiefs themselves. As the screenwriter, Sidney Buchman, put it: "Hollywood as a whole has recently been made aware of the Negro's true position in America and our responsibility toward the subject." And speaking of his own contribution, the script for *Talk of the Town* (1942), in which he had written a Black role of substance, his motive was the "fundamental thing in this war we are fighting."[26]

Outside of Hollywood, in the circles of documentary and propaganda filmmakers the story was the same. At every turn, Jews pressed both studios and their government for opportunities to portray on film Black images that reflected the liberalizing propaganda aims of the Western Alliance. The "race movie" distributor, Ted Toddy, proposed to the War Department a saga of the Black 99th Pursuit Squadron with Paul Robeson as its star; Alfred Sack picked up *Marching On*, an espionage yarn directed by Spencer Williams, director of the evocative *The Blood of Jesus* (1940); the historian, Saul Padover, proposed to his wartime boss in Agriculture a film that would extend racial propaganda into peacetime by means of a documentary portraying the African American as "an average human being"; Gene Weltfish transformed *Race: Science and Politics*, a book by the anthropologist, Ruth Benedict, into an anti-racism comicbook and thence into the UPA movie, *The Brotherhood of Man*; and both Paramount and Warner, among other majors, pressed on with short theatrical movies on racism long after the impending end of the war rendered them both militarily obsolescent and profitless.[27]

The resulting agenda that had been set both by NAACP lobbying in Hollywood and by each new movie that pressed against former constraints on Black movie portrayals led to a Black and Jewish frame of mind that prodded the studios against inertia or backsliding. Upon the completion of the Pentagon's own *The Negro Soldier*, the studio bosses concurred in Harry Cohn's hyperbolic praise of it as "the greatest War Department movie ever made," while Edwin R. Embree, director of the Black-oriented Rosenwald Fund, urged "many of us...to enlist in the cause…to help spread the news to commercial theatres." Roy Wilkins of the NAACP extended the sentiment into the postwar era when he predicted that the Pentagon's considerably bolder sequel, *Teamwork*, "would do much to promote racial unity *now and for the future.*"[28]

So taken were these Black and Jewish activists with the prospects for a postwar liberalized national conscience that they sought to head off the release of *We've Come a Long, Long Way*, a rival to *The Negro Soldier*, that had been compiled by an independently active team of the "race movie" maker Jack Goldberg and the Black evangelist, Elder Solomon Lightfoot Michaux. At stake was their fear that a prolonged rivalry between *The Negro Soldier* and the privately made Goldberg/Michaux movie would create an unseemly "Jewish vs. Negro situation" that might undo the bicultural alliance war had helped revive.[29]

Of course, in any alliance the principals should have expected to compromise goals and even to dilute some of their ethnicity in the interest of promoting their common cause. The historian Kenneth M. Stampp spoke for the age in which unity against foreign enemies obliged propagandists to emphasize ethnic "tolerance" and even "brotherhood" when he asserted that "… innately Negroes *are*, after all, only white men with Black skins."[30] Unavoidably, the war became a touchstone of these sentiments borne by every liberal conscience. As a Jewish soldier says in the war movie, *The Pride of the Marines* (1946): "Don't tell me we can't make it work in peace like we did in war." One such movie, *The House I Live In* (1946), an Oscar-winning two-reeler written by the eventually politically blacklisted writer, Albert Maltz, directed by Mervyn LeRoy, underwritten by Dore Schary's RKO studio, and starring Frank Sinatra, featured a theme that sang of "all races and religions…that's America to me."[31]

The alliance even withstood postwar conservative countermeasures, particularly in the form of the congressional Un-American Activities Committee that masked its assault behind a campaign to root out "communists" in Hollywood. Under such pressure it seemed to Jews and Blacks alike that wartime ideals had to be kept alive in the form of both polemics and movies. And yet Jews, as usual, despite a leftward leaning, could be found on both sides of the issue. Mayer remained a Republican stalwart; Roy Cohn served as counsel to Senator McCarthy's investigators; and Dore Schary, the otherwise doctrinaire liberal, both composed and signed the "Waldorf agreement," a deceptively phrased response to proscription of political expression that ended by agreeing to fire communists because their scripts would be unsalable to good Americans.

Nonetheless, Hollywood Jews also stood in their accustomed place on the left as well. Samuel Goldwyn, for example, wrote a piece for the Urban League's *Opportunity*, entitled "How I Became Interested in Social Justice" (by reading of Allied war aims in The Atlantic Charter!). Norman Granz, already famous for his "Jazz at the Philharmonic" concerts, produced the Oscar-winning short, *Jammin' the Blues*, that seemed so authentically Black that the columnist, Walter Winchell, thought it had been shot from a hidden camera. Abraham Polonsky, eventually blacklisted for his politics, wrote *Body and Soul* (1947), in which he used the boxing ring as a trope for unrestrained capitalism by centering on "a Black man [Canada Lee]...to defy the conventions around us," a sequence the *New York Times* reviewer praised as "one of the finer things of the film." John Garfield (Julius Garfinkle), the actor, successfully pressed for a remake of Ernest Hemingway's *To Have and Have Not* (1944), this time including an elided Black role. The result was *The Breaking Point* (1951) in which Juano Hernandez restored the role of the Black deckhand for which the critic, Seymour Peck, offered an "especially grateful" review. By then every major studio, including the "goy" studio, 20th Century-Fox, had produced its own "message movie" that harked back to the racial ideals of wartime propaganda and worked them into various peacetime angles—among them Schary's *Intruder in the Dust* for Mayer's studio, Zanuck's *Pinky* and Joseph Mankiewicz's *No Way Out* for Fox, and Stanley Kramer's *Home of the Brave* for Columbia.[32]

Here it must be said that Hollywood Jews were not playing the role of a sort of ideological Lady Bountiful spreading goodness to the benighted. Rather, African Americans, driven partly by the example of Walter White during the war, took an uncommonly direct hand in their collective fate. Critics such as Bob Ellis in the Black *California Eagle*, embracing the universalist ideology of the day, urged their readers to see the message movies because they seemed to assert that "Negroes are like everyone else," or, like George Norford in *Opportunity*, marked each new success as "another step for Hollywood." Within the ranks of moviemakers themselves Blacks tried to affect films at their source. Walter White's daughter, for example, worked closely with Philip Dunne, the cowriter of *Pinky*, while Henry Lee Moon of the NAACP read Ben Maddow's script for *Intruder in the Dust* and pronounced it "the kind of film we can endorse" and told White to "give Hollywood the 'Go' sign." And at the point of release, Dore Schary exhorted Metro's salesmen: "don't be afraid of" controversial movies of advocacy.[33]

Thereafter, through the era of the civil rights movement Black fortunes in Hollywood were linked directly to a cadre of Jewish leftists. Their work, at first, took two parallel courses: the one taken by Harry Belafonte as a picaresque Black hero as in Max Youngstein and Abraham Polonsky's *Odds Against Tomorrow* (1959), the other taken by Sidney Poitier in a series of squarer, more circumspect roles as doctor, African national, Anglican priest, angry rebel who sees the light, shrewd cop—always in the good hands of the Jewish keepers of his image: Lew Schreiber, Martin Baum, Sydney Pollack, Aaron Rosenberg, David Susskind, Pandro S. Berman, Stanley Kramer, and Joel Glickman.

And yet, if Jews invested in such movies for the dual purposes of serving a progressive cause and turning a profit, they also ran into the self-imposed barrier of their own universalism—a barrier inherited from their own assimilationist lives as well as from the ethnically phrased nationalism of the war years. Such sentiments allowed scant room for the expression of the racial nationalism that African

Americans often turned to when their collective lot improved enough to seem to threaten their identity as a people. In moments like these they sometimes embraced the African Zionism of Marcus Garvey or the vibrant raffishness of the urban streetscape that always seemed most impervious to assimilation into the centers of American life—much in the way that the journalist, Murray Kempton, had formulated: "in bad times men cherish the elegant and in good ones they exalt the raffish."[34]

Almost predictably, Black urban youth rebelled against Poitier's increasingly stuffy image and turned to, as *Variety* called them, "blaxploitation movies." Here again, the trend toward making movies that focused upon or pleased African Americans derived not so much from Jewishness as from the generality of Americans who wished to get on with some reform that would confront endemic racism, which was not abating even in the face of evermore deeply moving television demonstrations of Black fortitude and Southern white intransigence. Indeed, by the decade of the 1960s, with the civil rights movement at its most accessible on daily television news broadcasts, one producer spoke of the medium as "the chosen instrument of the civil rights movement."[35]

The ensuing Civil Rights Acts that marked the era gave moviemen a means of diversifying the racial makeup of both their crews and their movies—all in a painless form defined by law rather than by the actions of a few bold pioneers. A mandated Office of Economic Opportunity obliged studios to keep records of hiring practices and their results. Soon, all of the studio guilds created apprenticeships and jobs for minorities, particularly in television programs that by then constituted a greater portion of output than did movies. The agency files soon swelled, either with apologies for this or that show that had not met its racial goals because "the nature of the programming did not call for negro talent," or with boasts, as Sheldon Leonard of Bill Cosby's series, *I Spy*, reported, that a "majority of the actors in this series will be from minority groups." The NAACP through its Labor Secretary, Herbert Hill, pressed the guilds for greater voluntary efforts by threatening them with challenges to their legitimacy before the National Labor Relations Board. A committee of studio bosses led by Joel Freeman, Schary, Morrie Weiner, Joseph Schenck, and Maurice Benjamin met and heard proposals directed at "cementing the bonds of friendship" across racial lines.[36] Finally, as work rules and membership roles changed under these pressures, the development of "Cinemobiles" by the firm of Fouad Said gave moviemakers a capacity to move whole units of crews out of Hollywood itself and into locations where relaxed work rules (and lower wages) opened up still more opportunities for African American journeymen.[37]

The resulting blaxploitation movies—that is, movies made with a view to their consumption by a narrowly defined Black audience—came to the nation's screens in a dizzying variety that defies any generalization that a specifically Jewish consciousness had imposed on them a conspiratorial uniformity that "messed with" young Black minds. If anything, Blacks of the time felt they had taken a hand in shaping Hollywood's future. The genre of "action" movies, wrote the Black journalist, Walter Burrell, in the Black pop-magazine, *Soul*, "has more profoundly, financially and sociologically altered the motion picture medium than anything since the...turn of the century."[38]

Unquestionably, Hollywood remained in mainly Jewish hands both through the studio bosses and many of their bankers. But Federal law, conscience-liberalism of moviemakers and their audiences, Black pressure not only from national Black activists and polemicists but from the local Hollywood/Beverly Hills branch of the NAACP, and increasingly bold Blacks on the sets—Gordon Parks, Ivan Dixon, and others—broke the monopoly of creativity that had kept Black roles in a narrow compass.

The result was an emerging image of Blacks as angry, urbane rebels who joined other images of a white "counterculture" that had also broken with Hollywood convention. Black audiences suddenly stood revealed. They filled the cavernously empty downtown picture palaces, almost certainly saved Mayer's old MGM lot from closure, and filled the trade papers with fables of success. A "complete metamorphosis," said *Variety* of the transformation of midtown Buffalo; a "cultural revolution," wrote the Black journalist, Chuck Stone; and only an occasional Black voice complained of the "warping" of Black minds by focusing on urban violence. Some of them merely aimed for a detective mode "like it was with Bogart," only Black; others actively sought Black writers; veteran Hollywood writers learned to write from a hip angle about "a woman with much girl in her and a man with no boy in him"; they quickly learned to insert an "elder" in place of a "witchdoctor"; and in order to reach the targeted market "fustest," they reminded each other to "hire a Black man or woman" and to buy space in the house organ of the Congress on Racial Equality (CORE).[39]

Of course it could not last. But more than any social phenomenon since World War II, the cycle had responded to a rising tide of popular Black nationalism, and introduced Black moviemakers into a formerly white monopoly (during the ensuing years the Black members of the Directors Guild of America rose from less than a dozen to more than six hundred, many of them women).[40] Rather than a Jewish cabal behind the walls of the movielots, it was many other forces which conspired to apply a brake to the trend: for in order to make a profit, a movie needed a share of the world market, which included Black investors such as the sorority, Delta Sigma Theta, occasional crossover audiences that would bring in white money, eventual television sales, bankable stars, and plausible motives other than revenge and guerrilla warfare. Often, the "quick-and-dirty" footage, the inexperienced crews, the scatological language, the gratuitous sex and violence, the transitory and often professionally limited actors, and the often apolitical mode of blaxploitation movies precluded the creation of a genre that pleased Blacks while reaching the necessarily broader marketplace.

As in earlier times, when shared goals seemed so elusive as to be unattainable and yet already attained goals seemed to threaten the roots of ethnicity itself,

African Americans and Jews withdrew into their respective ghettoes of the mind where culture identities might be cultivated in a sealed-off nutrient broth. The entry of Blacks and Jews into a cultural mainstream—in this case Hollywood—threatened to end in a featureless homogeneity. As the Black bourgeoisie blanched at the prospect of separation both from "the brother on the block" and from "Mother Africa," so Jews feared the loss of Jewishness as the incidence of inter-marriage across lines of faith increased. But the two groups remained linked by forces of history and circumstance that the rise and fall of cycles of moviemaking and of ethnic antipathies could not diminish.

Notes

1. In more elaborate form, this notion was taken up by Glazer in a morning seminar on the occasion of the inaugural of President Rudenstein in Harvard University in the fall of 1991.

2. Lerner interviewed by James Bock, *Sun* (Baltimore), Feb. 17, 1994.

3. Nina Mjagkij, "A Peculiar Alliance: Julius Rosenwald, the YMCA, and African Americans, 1910–1933," *American Jewish Archives*, 14 (Fall/Winter 1992), 598.

4. Melvyn Douglas, himself Jewish, quoted in *Sun* (Baltimore), Aug. 9, 1981; Whitbeck quoted in Beth Day, *This Was Hollywood: An Affectionate History of Filmland's Golden Years* (London, 1960), 45.

5. Thomas Cripps, *Slow Fade to Black: The Negro in American Film, 1900–1940* (New York, 1977), Chap. 3.

6. Cruse quoted in an anonymous "book notice" in *American Jewish Archives*, 14 (Fall/Winter 1992), 657; Spike Lee quoted in *New York Times*, March 28, 1994, as he appeared at a conference on Blacks in film at the New York University Tisch School of the Arts.

7. Albert F. McLean, Jr., *American Vaudeville as Ritual* (Lexington, 1965), 7–8.

8. *The Fights of Nations* (1907), print in Library of Congress.

9. Laemmle's removal to Southern California was itself a step toward Jewish hegemony in moviemaking in that it was meant to break the hold of the "motion picture patents trust," a creature of the old-stock moviemen of the East Coast.

10. See Selig's catalogue, *Special List of Films Made Expressly for Selig* (Chicago, 1900), 8–9; review of *How Rastus Got His Pork Chops* cited in footnote 30, Chap. 1, Cripps, *Slow Fade to Black*; Selig's "fast Black show" cited in Terry Ramsaye, *A Million and One Nights* (New York, 1926), 303.

11. Tony Langston to George P. Johnson, Nov. 24, 1916, in George P. Johnson Collection, Special Collections Library, UCLA; Johnson to Robert L. Vann, *Pittsburgh Courier* publisher, March 27, 1920, ibid.

12. *Variety*, Aug. 22, 1928, 7, on Vidor; on Connelly, see Thomas Cripps, "Introduction" to Marc Connelly, *The Green Pastures* (Madison, WI, 1979), passim.

13. See Leonard J. Leff and Jerrold L. Simmons, *The Dame in the Kimono: Hollywood, Censorship, & the Production Code from the 1920s to the 1960s* (New York, 1990), 3–54, for a brief institutional history.

14. Cripps, *Slow Fade to Black*, 108; and interviews with Muse.

15. Neal Gabler, *An Empire of Their Own: How the Jews Invented Hollywood* (New York, 1988), Chaps. 6, 7.

16. Cripps, *Slow Fade to Black*, 139, on *Love is an Awful Thing*; *Variety*, April 22, 1925, 44, on *The Toll of Justice*; April 27, 1927, 20, on "housemaids"; *Amsterdam News*, April 2, 1936, on *Porgy*; *Afro-American*, Aug. 29, 1925; and *Amsterdam News*, Sept. 15, 1926.

17. See Eric Lott, *Love and Theft: Blackface Minstrelsy and the American Working Class* (New York, 1993), 4, for his goal: "I am after some sense of how precariously nineteenth-century white working people lived their whiteness." Michael Rogin, "Making America Home: Racial Masquerade and Ethnic Assimilation in the Transition to Talking Pictures," *Journal of American History*, 79, 3 (Dec. 1992), 1052, quoted. See also his "Blackface, White Noise: The Jewish Jazz Singer Finds His Voice," *Critical Inquiry*, 18, 3 (Spring 1992), 417–53.

18. *Pittsburgh Courier*, Dec. 29, 1923 and *Amsterdam News*, July 9, 1930.

19. *Variety*, May 8, 1929, 23.

20. On Antonio Gramsci, see Stuart Hall, "Gramsci's Relevance for the Study of Race and Ethnicity," *Journal of Communication Inquiry*, 10 (Summer 1986), 5–27; on Galbraith's notion of "countervailing powers" as a force for change, see his *American Capitalism: The Concept of Countervailing Power* (Boston, 1972), passim; and on Feibleman's idea that crises such as wars draw antagonists together in common cause, see his *The Theory of Culture* (New York, 1946, 1968), 7, 43, 96; and on my own notion of "conscience-liberalism," see my *Making Movies Black: The Hollywood Message Movie from World War II to the Civil Rights Era* (New York, 1993), x–xi.

21. Interview between John Krimsky and the author, New Brunswick, NJ, spring 1976.

22. Foster to Johnson, n.d.; Johnson to Mary Ruta, May 7, 1932; Van Vechten to Johnson, Sept. 27, 1935, all in James Weldon Johnson collection, Beineke Library, Yale University, all cited in Cripps, *Slow Fade to Black*.

23. Selznick to Sidney Howard, Jan. 6, 1937, in Rudy Behlmer, ed., *Memoir from David O. Selznick* (New York, 1972), 151; *Crisis*, 48 (Jan. 1940), 17; Sol Lesser quoted from Cripps, *Making Movies Black*, 22.

24. Lola Kovner to Walter White, Nov. 28, 1942 in NAACP Records, Library of Congress.

25. Cripps, *Making Movies Black*, 72–77, 89–92.

26. Cripps, *Making Movies Black*, 104–105; Sidney Buchman to Booker Brown, in *Courier*, Oct. 31, 1942 and Sept. 19, 1942; "Rogue's Regiment," *Ebony*, Sept. 1948, 31–33, cited in Cripps, *Making Movies Black*, 65, 67.

27. Cripps, *Making Movies Black*, 163, 167; Padover quoted, 157.

28. Cohn quoted in Truman Gibson to Anatole Litvak, April 14, 1944; Edwin R. Embree to Philleo Nash, June 29, 1944; Roy Wilkins to Gen. A. D. Surles, Aug. 22, 1945, all cited in Cripps, *Making Movies Black*, Chap. 4.

29. Walter White to Thurgood Marshall, May 4, 1944, cited in Cripps, *Making Movies Black*, Chap. 3.

30. Kenneth M. Stampp, *The Peculiar Institution: Slavery in the Ante-Bellum South* (New York, 1956, 1964), vii. Such a sentiment speaks not so much to Stampp's own enduring convictions but to the ideology of an age in which racial caste dominated and thus ideals of universalism colored the rhetoric of conscience-liberals.

31. *The House I Live In* quoted in Cripps, *Making Movies Black*, 200. As political rhetoric, Jews often eschewed special pleading for themselves, preferring, for example, to condemn Nazism for its treatment of "all civilian populations" rather than a "particular tragedy visited upon Jews." See Lowell Mellett to American Jewish Council, Feb. 1945, in *Making Movies Black*, 217.

32. *Opportunity*, Summer 1948, 100–101; interview between Polonsky and the author, July 1977; Garfield and Canada Lee, "Our Part in Body and Soul," *Opportunity*, Winter 1948, 20–21; on Peck, see Cripps, *Making Movies Black*, 258, and on "message movies," Chap. 8.

33. *California Eagle*, Aug. 18, 1949; George Norford, "The Future in Films," *Opportunity*, Summer 1948, 108–109; Moon to White, Dec. 28, 1948, in NAACP Records; and on message movies, Cripps, *Making Movies Black*, Chap. 8.

34. Kempton quoted in Liz Smith's column, *Sun* (Baltimore), May 5, 1982.

35. Quoted in Cripps, "The Noble Black Savage: A Problem in the Politics of Television Art," *Journal of Popular Culture*, 8 (Spring 1975), 690.

36. Cosby reported in *Los Angeles Sentinel*, Oct. 1, 1969; Committee for Use of Negro Roles, minutes, April 19, 1962, Screen Actors Guild records, Hollywood, CA. See also Ronald Jacobs to Charles Boren, MPAA records.

37. On Cinemobile, interview between Jon Triesault and the author, June 1977; and on MPAA efforts to introduce Blacks into television drama: Phil Benjamin to Roy Metzler, May 12, 1965; Ralph Winters to Tony Frederick, May 21, 1965; Ed Perlstein to Charles Boren, April 27, 1965, in MPAA records.

38. Walter Burrell, "Black Films," *Soul*, Dec. 18, 1972, 2–3.

39. *Newsweek*, Dec. 7, 1970, 62–74, on "counterculture"; *Variety*, Aug. 4, 1965, 22, quoted; *Philadelphia Daily News*, June 1, 1972, on Stone; *Newsweek*, Aug. 8, 1972, 88, on "warping"; on scripts, see Sterling Silliphant draft of *Shaft*; Silliphant to Daniel Melnick, MGM, Nov. 27, 1972, Silliphant mss, UCLA; Roger Lewis to Mort Segal, MGM, Sept. 3, 1971, MGM Legal File.

40. Directors Guild of America, *Directory of Members* [1991] (Los Angeles, 1991), 481–92.

thirteen

SEPARATE PATHS

Blacks and Jews in the Twentieth-Century South

DEBORAH DASH MOORE

One third of the population of the South is of the Negro race. No enterprise seeking the material, civil, or moral welfare of this section can disregard this element of our population and reach the highest success." With these words Booker T. Washington began his Atlanta Exposition Address in 1895, a speech that catapulted him from a position as an innovative educator and builder of the Tuskegee Institute to the forefront of African American leadership. By the beginning of the twentieth century, Washington was widely acclaimed as America's preeminent Black man, with more influence than any of his peers. His views on questions of race and relations of whites and Blacks gained him access to the White House as well as to the homes of wealthy white men.[1] As for immigrants, Washington did not see them as integral to the South. "To those of the white race who look to the incoming of those of foreign birth and strange tongue and habits for the prosperity of the South," he observed in the same address, "were I permitted I would repeat what I say to my own race, 'Cast down your bucket where you are.' Cast it down among the eight millions of Negroes whose habits you know...." Washington concluded the paragraph with a metaphor that would become as famous as his call to cast down your bucket: "In all things purely social," he assured his listeners, "we can be as separate as the fingers, yet one as the hand in all things essential to mutual progress."[2]

Less than a decade passed before Washington's "Atlanta Compromise," as it came to be known, was challenged by a young scholar teaching sociology at Atlanta University. W. E. B. Du Bois observed "among educated and thoughtful colored men in all parts of the land a feeling of deep regret, sorrow, and apprehension at the wide currency and ascendancy which some of Mr. Washington's theories have gained." Du Bois singled out three things that "Mr. Washington distinctly asks that Black people give up, at least for the present....First, political power, Second, insistence on civil rights, Third, higher education of Negro youth...." Du Bois took issue with all three. He insisted that he was not alone in his criticism but that other African Americans agreed with him:

> that the way for a people to gain their reasonable rights is not by voluntarily throwing them away and insisting that they do not want them, that the way for a people to gain respect is not by continually belittling and ridiculing themselves, that on the contrary, Negroes must insist continually, in season and out of season, that voting is necessary to modern manhood, that color discrimination is barbarism, and that Black boys need education as well as white boys.[3]

Southern whites took little notice of Du Bois's collection of essays, published as *The Souls of Black Folk*,[4] yet it signaled the beginning of a significant debate among African Americans over both the goals of Black endeavor in the South and the best means to achieve them. A similar debate was long in progress among Europe's Jews, who argued among themselves over what, in fact, constituted a genuine emancipation, how to obtain it, and how they should cope with virulent antisemitism. Their argument ultimately was cut short by war, mass migration, the extermination of six million Jews, and asylum in the new State of Israel for the survivors.

Neither the Washington-Du Bois debate nor the arguments raging in Europe engaged the small minority of American Jews who settled in the South in the early decades of the twentieth century. Undoubtedly some were aware of the rising number of lynchings of Black men in the South; the decade from 1896 to 1905 saw over 700 lynchings in the South, a number that declined to just under 500 in the next ten years.[5] Lynchings were popular among southern white folk: they were often advertised in advance and special trains were occasionally added to bring crowds to the selected spot. In 1937 Karl Friedman's Cincinnati relatives came down "out of civilization" to visit his family in Birmingham, where they had settled two decades earlier. Friedman recalled that "my father invited his sisters and brothers who came for the Bar Mitzvah to view a Saturday night lynching in downtown Birmingham." Their response, he remembered, varied. "Some were willing. Some were appalled. All believed it was going to happen."[6] Some Jews may have recognized in the new laws of segregation, legal discrimination, and voting exclusion a systematic effort to establish a social, legal, and political system that subordinated Blacks to whites in all areas of life. But many Jews, especially those who were recent immigrants and "of strange tongue and habits," as Washington noted, merely accepted the southern way of life as they found it and sought to adjust their behavior to fit in as aspiring white Americans. Unlike the millions of Blacks living in the South whose "material, civil, and moral welfare" was integral to the section's economic, social, political, and cultural development, Jews made up a fraction of a percent of the total population and attracted attention only for their religious divergence from the region's dominant Protestantism.

The history of Jews and Blacks in the South reveals enormous contrasts and few similarities. Differences include demographic and settlement patterns, occupational distribution, forms of culture, religion, and community life, even politics and the prejudice and discrimination endured by each group. Visible Jewish presence in the South is considered so atypical that when large numbers of Jews (that is, over 100,000) actually did settle in a southern city, as they did in Miami and Miami Beach after World War II, the entire area of South Florida was soon dismissed as no longer southern and jokingly referred to as a suburb of New York City. Jews have been and remain marginal to the South. Their marginality is intrinsic to their existence as southern Jews.[7] African Americans have been and remain central to the South. It is impossible to imagine southern culture, politics, religion, economy, or in short, any aspect of southern life, without African Americans. "Race determined the neighborhoods in which people lived, the movies they could attend, the churches in which they worshiped, and the cemeteries in which they would be buried."[8] Not only did the burden of slavery and a history of segregation and "state-sponsored racial oppression and authoritarianism"[9] shape the South in the twentieth century, but so did the moral and religious vision of its Black minority. In the popular mind as well as in reality, the South would not be the South without Black Americans. Jews, by contrast, offer an interesting footnote to understanding the region, an opportunity to examine the possibilities and cost of religious and ethnic diversity in a society sharply divided along color lines.

The eight million African Americans living in the South at the turn of the century increased to ten million by mid-century, but fifty years of migration to northern and midwestern cities reduced their percentage of the total population from one-third to one-fifth. In many rural, Black belt counties in South Carolina, Georgia, Alabama, Mississippi, and northern Louisiana, African Americans remained a majority in the second half of the twentieth century, though over a million left the South in both the 1940s and 1950s.[10] Indeed, a steady and accelerating stream of southerners left the region: one out of 10 in the 1920s, one out of seven in the 1930s, and one out of five in the 1940s. From the region with over 90 percent of all Black Americans at the beginning of the century, the South became home to little more than one-half eighty years later.[11] After World War II, these patterns gradually changed, but not until the 1960s did more people move into the South than out of it. In the early 1970s the South became part of the Sunbelt, a region of booming population and economic opportunity that attracted Americans, including Black Americans, from a declining rustbelt.[12] For the first time, beginning in the mid-seventies, "the number of Blacks moving into the South exceeded the number departing for other regions of the country."[13] As southern cities grew due in part to federal largesse and the rise of the "gunbelt,"[14] and as southern agriculture became mechanized and cotton acreage was reduced (both of which discriminated against African Americans since they were denied jobs running the machinery and refused benefits under federal agricultural programs), the heavy preponderance of Blacks in rural areas shifted. The migration from field to factory boosted Black population in cities. By 1950 more Blacks than whites lived in cities in Georgia and by 1960 less than a quarter of all African Americans lived in the rural South.[15] African Americans particularly found the largest southern cities attractive and by 1980 Atlanta, Birmingham, New Orleans, and Richmond had Black majorities.[16] In the closing decades of the century, Blacks moved to the suburbs as well, leaving only a dwindling minority on farms.

Most of the several hundred thousand Jews in the South before mid-century lived in its cities and towns, distinguishing themselves not only from their fellow southerners, Black and white, but from their fellow Jews, who typically preferred metropolises like New York and Chicago. Even in some of the bigger New and Old South cities like Birmingham, Memphis, Charleston, New Orleans, Atlanta, and Richmond there were merely a few thousand Jews. Larger numbers did not move down until after World War II, which introduced a generation of Jewish GIs to the South. Jews settled in selected cities, drawn in substantial numbers first to Miami and neighboring Florida cities, and then to Atlanta and suburban Alexandria, Virginia. These three metropolitan areas hardly offer a characteristic view of the South, yet they account for the majority of southern Jews in the closing decades of the twentieth century.[17] When people think of the southern Jewish experience, they often conjure up the exceptional experience of small town Jews, of settlements ranging from several hundred to several dozen, where Jews lived close to the southern way of life yet nonetheless apart from it. In his collection of essays, *The Lonely Days Were Sundays*, native Southerner Eli Evans explains that the "phrase was epigrammatic of the emotional terrain of the immigrant generation of Jews who arrived in the small towns of the South in the eighteenth and nineteenth centuries. And that loneliness of soul is at the core of every Jew who lives in the Bible Belt," although urban experience characterizes Jews in the twentieth-century South.[18]

Irrespective of where they settled (except, of course, for Miami), Jews usually worked in middleman minority occupations not considered typically southern: as peddlers, shopkeepers, merchants, manufacturers, and occasionally professionals (doctors, dentists, druggists).[19] Main street was their domain. Initially Jews lived behind or above their stores; as they prospered they moved to white residential sections of town. In the early years of the century, unmarried Jewish women worked in their parents' store or as teachers or office workers. Later, most Jewish women took care of the household and, when they could afford to hire household workers, devoted some of their time to volunteer work. In the last decades of the century, inspired by the feminist movement, Jewish women have sought careers, which they often combined with marriage and motherhood.

By contrast, African Americans worked at a wide range of occupations from sharecropper and farmer, to day laborer and industrial worker, to a handful of middle and upper class positions, including storekeepers, teachers, entrepreneurs, and professionals serving a segregated society. What Sarah Hughes wrote of Virginia was true for the rest of the South: "Segregation permeated the economy during the first seventy years of the century. There were Black restaurants, hotels, grocery stores, barbershops, blacksmiths, cleaners, gas stations, and resorts."[20] In a society driven by caste, Black entrepreneurs occasionally found a precarious niche. Unlike Jews, many of whom were self-employed, Blacks largely worked for others, usually whites, restricted by custom and prejudice to the least desirable jobs in each sector of the economy. "Even trained college graduates took jobs as porters and baggage handlers. And we couldn't do a whole lot about it," reflected Warren Cochrane about work in Atlanta.[21] Despite economic oppression and subordination that forced women as well as men to work outside the home, African Americans in the South sustained stable families during the first half of the century. Married and unmarried women worked alongside their men in the fields and farms as well as in service occupations in cities and small towns. A few became teachers, midwives, and nurses. Middle-class standing was reflected less through women withdrawing from paid labor than through home ownership, education, and standards of public and private rectitude.

Separation forced by segregation characterized community life. Probably the single most important communal institution was the Black church. Virtually all African Americans, seeking individual salvation and collective spirituality, joined a church, which was usually either Baptist or Methodist. The church not only offered Sunday services and schooling, but it also sponsored social welfare, and civic and cultural activities. In her study of Indianola, Mississippi, during the Depression, Hortense Powdermaker observed: "No week passed without my attendance at some Negro social function—a chitterling supper in a church basement, an entertainment to raise funds, a meeting of the Ladies' Missionary society in a member's home. During some weeks there were two or three socials."[22] Ministers led the Black community, articulated collective aspirations, and served as ambassadors to white society. The church expressed African Americans' hopes and sacralized aspects of their culture. "The church services were powerful, with an almost ritualized intensity," recalled an African American of his Mississippi childhood. "Always, our prayers were for fair play, justice for all people, and freedom from fear. We echoed President Roosevelt's sentiments, and added our own."[23] Music, especially, gave voice to both sacred and secular dimensions of life. Black churches made music integral to their worship services, thus contributing to a dynamic relationship between the everyday world of work and sorrows and the sacred realm of prayer and ecstasy.

Synagogues assumed far less centrality in the Jewish community, though far greater percentages of Jews joined them in the South than in the North. Reform Judaism dominated Jewish religious expression during the first half of the century. In the largest cities where some Jewish religious diversity existed, Reform congregations attracted the more wealthy and established Jews. In Greensboro, North Carolina, after World War II "approximately half the members of the Reform Temple were raised outside the South, compared with nine out of ten in the Conservative Temple. The upper class of Southern origins, as elsewhere in the South, was concentrated in the former. They, as in the South generally, were the ones who belonged to the most esteemed country club, were members of law firms and other enterprises with Gentiles, and circulated socially with the local Gentile elite."[24] In smaller towns, Jews considered themselves fortunate if they could support a single congregation and a Reform rabbi. Like their Black peers, Reform rabbis accepted the responsibility of representing their community to the white Christian world. "Handsome and robust, something of a scholar, an eloquent speaker, and a sophisticated but enthusiastic participant in civic affairs," Rabbi Edward N. Calisch of Richmond's Beth Ahavath Temple personified the southern Reform rabbi of the first half of the century. "He exchanged pulpits with Protestant clergymen; he delivered patriotic speeches during both World Wars; he lunched with President Taft at the White House and with Lord Reading at the vice-regal palace in India; he was treasurer of the English Speaking Union, president of the Richmond Peace Council, and president of the Richmond alumni chapter of Phi Beta Kappa; in 1939 the *Richmond Times-Dispatch* put his name on its Roll of Honor as one of the ten outstanding men of Virginia."[25]

Usually accepted as white, and not summarily excluded from participation in civic affairs as were African Americans, Jews tried to maintain communal institutions focused upon internal Jewish needs, such as community centers, B'nai B'rith lodges, social welfare organizations, as well as women's clubs and Zionist groups, while supporting white community endeavors not connected with the church, such as cultural activities, better business and chamber of commerce groups, and philanthropic endeavors. Their success in this dual enterprise depended upon politics; during the heyday of the Ku Klux Klan after its reestablishment in 1915 in Georgia, Jews generally found themselves unwelcome in both political and civic endeavors. This chilly environment warmed substantially during World War II, and southern Jews faced the dawning of the postwar civil rights era feeling integrated into the white community. Observers in the 1960s discovered even among relatively small Jewish populations that two communities often coexisted, divided sharply by their "degree of Southernness." These divisions extended to country club and college fraternity memberships, as well as to ideology, specifically support for Zionism. Opposition to Zionism, and by extension Jewish nationalism and ethnicity, coincided with a high degree of "Southernness." Irrespective of ideology, however, southern Jews uncovered no antisemitism among their neighbors, although many feared that it might be "stirred up" by political change.[26] Outsiders visiting their fellow Jews rarely understood such sentiments, those heartfelt expressions by southern Jews of their sense of belonging to a white community whose heritage they saw as their own. Coming down to Mississippi to help with legal defense of those involved in the voter registration drive, Marvin Braiterman, a lawyer, decided to attend services at a local synagogue to escape the tensions of the week. "We know right from wrong, and the difference between our God and the segregationist God they talk about down here," his Jewish hosts told him. "But their God runs Mississippi, not ours. We have to work quietly, secretly. We have to play ball. Anti-Semitism is always right around the corner." Braiterman suggested that "your silence either makes things get worse, or things get worse in spite of it. You might as well open your mouths and do something about what you think." His hosts responded, "No. No. What you're talking about is suicide." Yet all Braiterman could suggest in response was that Jews leave Mississippi.[27]

Profound discrimination, prejudice, and the entire oppressive weight of a segregated society left Black southerners with no illusions regarding the parameters of their community. As in all other aspects of life, race defined communal endeavor. African Americans created in the South as comprehensive a community as they could afford, including education and cultural activities, social welfare assistance and health projects, and modest civic associations. They did this in an environment of fear of reprisals should their actions somehow threaten a precarious status quo and provide an excuse for white violence. Even where they did not organize, their segregated social patterns contributed to shaping collective cultural expressions. In larger cities where a Black middle class gained a secure foothold, class distinctions divided the African American community. In his classic study *Black Bourgeoisie*, E. Franklin Frazier ridiculed the pretensions of these strivers and condemned their efforts to imitate white society, advocating instead a rejection of its biased pretensions and recognition of the rich cultural creativity of the Black working classes. Frazier scorned the internalization of white values and fear of economic reprisals and violence that led middle-class African Americans to avoid protesting an unjust white society.[28]

Although African Americans were forbidden to mix in white society, Black culture repeatedly crossed the divide. In some areas, such as music and dance, white southerners were aware of the borrowing and cultural exchange; in other areas, such as literature and architecture, the process of exchange and cultural transformation was often obscured. Both self-consciously and unconsciously, Black southerners influenced the culture of the region: its folkways and diet, its literature and art, its music and dance. Through their impact on the South, African Americans influenced many aspects of American popular culture and produced what has often been considered most characteristically American. By contrast, southern Jews failed to produce the kinds of cultural contributions typical of their Western European coreligionists despite familiarity with minority status through a long diaspora history. Like German Jews, southern Jews were less than one percent of the population; unlike German Jews, their intellectual and artistic achievements have been modest. Most southern Jews appeared to have assimilated regional mores rather than interacting with them and responding creatively to the challenges of shaping a new culture. "They did not affect the South so much as they imbibed its values and became part of it," historian Melvin Urofsky concluded.[29] Perhaps the desire for a better life inherent in migration drew Jews eager to accommodate. When Ronald Bern's grandfather bought the railroad ticket that took him south to Anderson, South Carolina, he had no particular destination in mind other than one that was quiet and warm.[30] Seeking economic opportunity, southern Jews were largely unwilling to stand aloof from southern culture. Jewish religious observances borrowed little of the enthusiasm and spirituality of the evangelical Protestantism of Black and white southerners, but rather took southern Episcopalian sobriety and decorum as a model.

Given these disparate and contrasting Black and Jewish worlds that coexisted in the South, it is not surprising that politics rarely brought them together. Prior to 1915, Jews participated in electoral politics and occasionally won election to municipal or state office. The nadir of Jewish involvement in southern politics came during the heyday of the Ku Klux Klan, which attacked Jews and Catholics as well as Blacks.[31] African Americans, on the other hand, suffered their most bitter political defeats in the years prior to World War I, the era that generated the acrimonious debate between Washington and Du Bois. Those years saw the largest numbers of lynchings, a flourish of mob violence designed to terrorize Blacks, deny them their civil rights, and prevent them from voting. Segregation and systematic discrimination were entrenched. Black soldiers returned from World War I convinced that they needed to continue the fight for democracy and freedom at home. Chalmers Archer discovered "no change in the way we lived," when he arrived back in southern Mississippi. "The day I came home, my mother was in the field helping my brother Nick. It was then that I decided that she should no longer do any type of field work," he recalled. "I was a war hero from France, and that's the only way I could let out my frustrations. That was the one change in our lives that I could make."[32] During the interwar years, African Americans pressed for anti-lynching laws on both state and federal levels, brought cases to court challenging the refusal of registrars to let Blacks register to vote, fought against unequal school conditions and pay for teachers, and worked with New Deal liberals to eliminate the poll tax. Although they achieved few substantive changes, "expectations rose; Black powerlessness decreased; white hostility diminished. Together, these gave the proponents of civil rights hope."[33]

World War II changed southern Jewish attitudes toward politics, but not enough to bring them into convergence with African Americans' increasing demands for equal civil rights and for an end to desegregation. Jews migrating to the South after the war carried their politics in their suitcases, but since 80 percent of these northern newcomers went down to Miami, they exerted little influence on the emerging civil rights movement.[34] A handful of young rabbis joined forces with Christian clergy across the color line, but most feared to speak out lest they lose their positions. Many Black ministers also were cautious, yet they were ready to provide leadership when African Americans challenged segregation. Martin Luther King, Jr. responded to a request for leadership of the

Montgomery bus boycott though he did not initiate the protest. His moral vision and philosophy of Christian love and nonviolence, however, soon inspired and shaped the civil rights movement. Following the 1954 Supreme Court decision in *Brown vs. Board of Education*, which overturned the separate but equal doctrine upholding legal segregation, the movement to desegregate southern institutions expanded. The Court's decision put civil rights on the nation's political agenda. Southern Jews found themselves caught between the demands of racist white Southerners, who organized White Citizens Councils beginning in 1954, and the expectations of liberal northern Jews whose Jewish defense organizations actively supported equal rights. Imagining themselves between a rock and a hard place, most southern Jews were immobilized. Even a series of synagogue bombings by white antisemites in five southern cities in 1957–1958 failed to resolve their dilemma.[35]

The shift from protest to politics—especially the voter registration drives organized by SNCC in 1964 that drew large numbers of northern Jewish students to the South—exacerbated southern Jewish discomfort. The rabbi of Meridian, Mississippi, urged Michael Schwerner to leave, fearing that white anger at Schwerner might turn against local Jews. "He argued that Schwerner was already labeled 'that goddamned bearded atheist communist Jew,' and that consequently he was not helping Negroes but hurting Jews," Lenora Berson reported. "Progress will come with time and from within; it will not be made by outside agitation," the rabbi concluded.[36] Birmingham rabbis joined Christian clergy in urging King to be patient in his demands for change, criticizing his nonviolent philosophy for provoking white violence. Writing from his jail cell in 1963, King observed that "Lamentably, it is an historical fact that privileged groups seldom give up their privileges voluntarily." As for waiting, King remarked bitterly that "'Wait' has almost always meant 'Never'":

> Perhaps it is easy for those who have never felt the stinging darts of segregation to say, "Wait." But when you have seen vicious mobs lynch your mothers and fathers at will and drown your sisters and brothers at whim; when you have seen hate-filled policemen curse, kick, and even kill your black brothers and sisters; when you see the vast majority of your twenty million Negro brothers smothering in an airtight cage of poverty in the midst of an affluent society;...when you are humiliated day in and day out by nagging signs reading "white" and "colored"; when your first name becomes "nigger," your middle name becomes "boy"...and your wife and mother are never given the respected title "Mrs."; when you are forever fighting a degenerating sense of "nobodiness"—then you will understand why we find it difficult to wait.[37]

Although few Jews championed the policy of "massive resistance" advocated by white southern segregationists, only after the rise of Black Power did more Jews recognize the possibility of supporting the demands of moderate Black leaders by joining forces with white Christians to denounce violence and espouse gradual change.

Once large numbers of African Americans acquired the vote and entered southern politics, Jews discovered ways to build coalitions to sustain liberal change. The 1969 election of Sam Massell, Jr., Atlanta's first Jewish mayor, drew substantial Black support and helped topple the city's white power structure. Jews subsequently reciprocated in 1973 by voting for Maynard Jackson, Atlanta's first African American mayor.[38] Especially in such cities as Atlanta, New Orleans, and Richmond, Jews were willing to vote for Black politicians who championed pragmatic politics that encouraged economic growth and racial accommodation.[39] In the 1970s and 1980s, despite the resort to gerrymandering district boundaries to minimize Black political power, African Americans scored substantial gains, not only in local elections but even in statewide contests. Virginia elected Douglas Wilder as its first African American governor in 1992; since Blacks made up only 20 percent of the state's population, Wilder won with the support of many whites, including Jews. Political cooperation with African Americans was possible in the post-civil rights era because Jews could cooperate with African Americans as whites, not as Jews. Sufficient diversity and flexibility existed among southern whites so that Jews did not fear rousing either white or Black antisemitism. Jews could help create and sustain a political atmosphere not dominated by appeals to race prejudice and massive white resistance to civil rights. Jews have also joined with African Americans to defeat outspoken bigots like David Duke when he ran for governor of Louisiana in 1992.

Such political cooperation, with its potential implications of cordial relations between leading African Americans and southern Jews, represents a significant departure from earlier patterns of conflict and avoidance. Because their histories present divergent paths of widely different significance for the southern experience, rarely did either Blacks or Jews serve as a reference point for the other. More often Jews and Blacks in the South saw each other triangulated in relation to northern Jews. Those urban, ethnic, and often politically radical Jews read various meanings into southern Black suffering, protest, and resistance. Southern Jews were aware of how their northern coreligionists interpreted and judged southern mores, though they usually rejected both interpretation and judgment. When Baruch Charney Vladeck, a Jewish socialist and later member of the New York City Council, witnessed an anti-Negro riot in Norfolk, Virginia, in July 1910, he was shocked. Comparing it to a Russian pogrom, or anti-Jewish violence sanctioned by the state, he urged his fellow Jews to intervene on behalf of the African Americans. "He was told that he did not comprehend the situation. Blacks were 'nothing but animals.'"[40]

Some Black leaders distinguished Jews as a white minority group, usually through reference to northern Jews or Jewish suffering in Europe, but Jews figured significantly as a distinctive white minority neither in the consciousness nor in the lives of most southern Blacks. Most African Americans saw Jews through the lens of Protestant Christianity. "All of us Black people who lived in the neighborhood hated Jews, not because they exploited us but because we had been taught at home and in Sunday school that Jews were 'Christ killers,'" the novelist Richard Wright wrote about his youth in Arkansas and Tennessee. "To hold an attitude of antagonism or distrust toward Jews was bred in us from childhood; it was not merely racial prejudice, it was part of our cultural heritage."41 African Americans generally shared the norms of southern Christian society's biased attitudes toward Jews; southern Jews usually followed southern racist conventions in their attitudes and behavior toward Blacks.42 Even when living and working among African Americans, Jews did not participate in the life of the surrounding Black community on either a formal or informal basis.

Occasional moments of conflict did erupt between Blacks and Jews, vividly indicating their contrasting positions in southern society. The most traumatic moment for Jews came from events that unfolded in 1913. On Confederate Memorial Day a teenage white worker, Mary Phagan, stopped by an Atlanta pencil factory to pick up her pay envelope from the manager, Leo Frank, on her way to celebrate the holiday. She never made it to the parade. Early the next day, the night watchman found her body in the basement. Her brutal murder led to the arrest, trial, and conviction of Frank, the northern educated Jewish superintendent who was an active member of Atlanta's Jewish community. Despite lack of evidence and Frank's obvious innocence, the case aroused enormous passions and unleashed such vitriolic antisemitism in Georgia and throughout the South, that when the governor commuted his death sentence, Frank was taken out of prison, brought back to Mary Phagan's home town of Marietta, and lynched. Frank's lynching in 1915, the only lynching of a Jew in America, stimulated the establishment of the second Ku Klux Klan. White Southerners vilified Frank as a Yankee, a Jew, a capitalist, a sexual pervert—in short, someone seeking to destroy the South and its way of life. Jews saw the Frank case as a horrible example of antisemitism, analogous not only to the recent Mendel Beiliss ritual murder trial in Russia but to the famous Dreyfus Affair in France. It was impossible to ignore the vociferous antisemitism. "There were mobs outside of the courthouse. It was hot, it was the summertime. And the mobs outside were hollering, 'Kill the Jew!' and 'Lynch the Jew!'..." Clarence Feibelman recalled. "I'd be on the streetcar and sometimes I'd get off and walk past there, and it was just harrowing to hear those people. It made your blood run cold."43 The crowd even threatened to lynch the jury if it failed to convict.

Southern Jews, especially those in Atlanta, convinced of Frank's innocence (the conviction was overturned many years later), made common cause with the white Christian business elite in their efforts to obtain clemency for Frank and used racial stereotypes to defend Frank and to blame the Black factory sweeper, Jim Conley, upon whose testimony Frank was convicted. African Americans responded with virtually the same unanimity that gripped Jews: the former rallied around

Conley as the latter did around Frank. "For several decades the Frank case hung like a threatening cloud over the Jewish community, confirmation that economic success was no protection against bigotry," concluded Steven Hertzberg, historian of Atlanta Jews. It stimulated a momentary unity among native-born and immigrant Atlanta Jews and gave southern Jews a bitter taste of the experience of seeing one of their own lynched. "Two years later in the spring of 1917, Irving Engel and a group of U.S. Army officer candidates entered a Marietta drug store where 'they were still selling photographs…of Leo Frank in his nightshirt hanging by the neck from a tree with his feet crossed at the ankles.'"[44] The lynching of Leo Frank intimidated Jews, especially native-born Jews who had assumed that their white skin gave them immunity from persecution in the South.[45]

The antisemitic environment surrounding the case reached African Americans as well. The Black scholar, Horace Mann Bond, remembered an incident shortly after moving to Atlanta in 1916 that captured the antagonism even between children.

> I was walking along a street near my house, and had to pass a small grocery store located in our neighborhood. There was a small boy—perhaps six years old—looking through the picket fence that surrounded the store. As I passed he began to chant: "Nigger, Nigger, Nigger, Nigger." You may not believe it, but this was the first time I could remember anyone calling me a "Nigger." And my response still surprises me; I retorted to the boy, "You Christ-killer!" And the little boy burst into tears, and I have felt badly about it ever since.

In retrospect, Bond concluded that "'the word I used hung immanent in the Atlanta air'" during a time "when the Leo Frank lynching was front-page news and back-fence gossip." "Somehow," Bond recalled, the epithet "had entered my mind, and remained like a knife, waiting only for opportunity for release."[46] The Leo Frank case provided that moment by pitting the testimony of an African American against the testimony of a Jew and led to conflict between the two groups. It also demonstrated Jewish vulnerability to antisemitism in league with a reactionary populism that usually targeted Blacks. Though less often manipulated as anti-Black racism, antisemitism remained a potentially powerful force to mobilize whites against big business and working class radicalism.

Similar political forces appeared almost two decades later when nine African American teenagers were pulled from a freight train in Paint Rock, Alabama, and falsely accused of rape by two white women also riding the train. The trials of the nine "Scottsboro boys," as they came to be known, attracted nationwide attention largely due to publicity efforts by the Communist Party and the NAACP that focused on the "legal lynching" taking place in Alabama. In the case of Scottsboro, however, African Americans made common cause with northern Jews, suggesting that working class radicalism could overcome racism, antisemitism, and sexual conservatism. The prominence of Jewish lawyers, Joseph Brodsky and especially Samuel Leibowitz who served as defense attorney for several trials, implicated southern Jews in the case. Furthermore, the prosecutor's explicitly antisemitic charge to the jury—"Show them, show them that Alabama justice cannot be bought and sold with Jew money from New York"[47]—with its echoes of accusations hurled at Leo Frank, forced southern Jews to confront several difficult choices: they could support the African American defendants and join not only their northern coreligionists but also a small number of concerned white Christians willing to speak out against popular sentiment; or they could remain silent in the hope that their neighbors would not confuse them with their northern coreligionists, especially Jewish communists; or they could join the majority white Christian community that condemned the Black defendants and championed their conviction for the heinous crime of raping a white woman. Rabbi Benjamin Goldstein of Montgomery's Temple Beth Or chose the first alternative. Beginning in 1931 he told his congregation "and all who would listen" that he thought the Scottsboro boys were innocent. Two years later, he presided at a meeting in the Black Congregational Church in Birmingham to form a coalition of local support, even though he recognized that all of the white speakers risked losing their jobs. He was right. Two months later the temple board gave him an ultimatum: "Sever all connection with the Scottsboro Case or resign. He agreed to resign."[48] Most other southern Jews appeared to have chosen to keep a low profile. However, they were aware that they risked attack as communists if they did not actively villify the Scottsboro Boys.

The charge of being communists acquired even greater salience in the postwar era of anti-communist investigations and hysteria. White southerners leveled the charge against African Americans seeking to end desegregation and against civil rights organizations like the NAACP, forcing the latter to make public its membership lists and then attacking individuals for having joined as members. In some states, like Alabama, the campaign against the NAACP succeeded, forcing Black activists to create alternative organizations. However, relatively few African Americans in the South were attracted to communism or to socialism. Neither tradition nor structure existed upon which these ideologies could be built. Many more found in Christian radicalism a vision that inspired them to act and also resonated with some white Christians. Others preferred the nationalist dimensions of separatism, albeit not its accommodationist aspects, and recognized with Washington the need for African Americans to run their own organizations and build up their own independent communal life. Thus the debate over ends and means that divided African Americans in the South at the turn of the century returned with the civil rights era. This time southern Jews paid more attention, listening for those Black voices with which they agreed as well as those they opposed. The end of colonialism in Africa inspired many African Americans, much as the establishment of the State of Israel—and especially Israel's military victory in 1967—inspired many southern Jews. Yet few found the parallels sufficient to lead to cooperation. Despite efforts to exclude communists from participation in civil rights organizations, left wing radicals often were the whites most willing to champion an egalitarian society and to oppose racism. Those Jews most drawn to the southern struggle to create an egalitarian society usually were alienated from their religion. They were eager to erase ethnic, religious, and racial differences among Americans. In making common cause with African Americans, most Jewish activists in the South discarded their Jewish identity, seeing it as largely irrelevant to their struggle for social justice. Thus these marginal Jews rarely served as a bridge between southern Jews and southern Blacks.

Economic, political, and social changes altered the character of both the Jewish and African American experience in the post-civil rights South. Racial tensions diminished after 1975. Segregation ended in its legal and state-supported forms. Black political power materialized. Population grew due to migration from other states. Urbanization and a booming economy created a growing pie of opportunity. Certainly, it is easier to be an African American or Jew in the South at the end of the century than it was at the beginning. Opportunities once closed to Blacks due to their skin color and to Jews due to their religion are now available. Both Jews and Blacks can appreciate some of the region's virtues. Remigration rates of educated northern Blacks to the South indicate the powerful draw of a strong economy and a pleasant way of life, not marred by state-sponsored oppression. "I'm moving South for the same reasons my father came here from Mississippi," Taylor Wilson, a Black electrician from Chicago explained. "He was looking for a better way of life."[49] Often college-educated, the new Black migrants achieve higher incomes than native-born residents and are virtually at a par with southern whites in similar occupations.[50] Jews, too, have settled in the region in such numbers that the South now exceeds the Midwest in its percentage of American Jewish population.[51] Among the thousands of Jewish newcomers to Atlanta in the 1980s, few probably had ever heard of Leo Frank, and some settled in Marietta, now a suburb of Atlanta, unaware of its bitter history. Local grocery stores now stock Passover supplies in the spring instead of photographs of Frank's lynching.[52] Some Jews have even discovered the South to be their new promised land and are putting down roots, giving up the wandering spirit for a blessed sense of security.[53] Others carry a bit of soil of the homeland with them when they are forced to live up north, symbolic of the southern ways they cherish and hope to impart to their children.[54]

Continuities with the old days also remain. Inequalities between Blacks and whites endure, perpetuated by social and economic patterns as resistant to change as the old segregated society. "Ownership of property, land, and private businesses remains a central part of the American Dream of success, a dream that has eluded millions of Blacks," Robert Bullard observed.[55] Segregation itself, no longer legal but still present in fact, continues to nurture two separate societies divided by race. The Black church is still one of the most powerful institutions within the community and ministers are influential leaders, despite modest inroads made by Islam. African Americans retain an independent communal structure and a diverse and variegated community that includes many types of organizations ranging from modest rural cooperatives to well-established colleges and universities. However, these now coexist with Black participation in civic endeavors, especially in the larger cities, so that the Black community divides some of its energies between its own internal world and white society, as the Jewish community had done earlier in the century.

Southern Jews are still more likely to join a congregation than northern Jews and they often retain a deep identification with romanticized white southern history and society. Although assimilation, intermarriage, and conversion have affected more of them than northern Jews, most southern Jews will admit or assert that they never personally experienced antisemitism. Reflecting on his youth in Newport News, Virginia, growing up during the civil rights era in "a home where the Sabbaths and holidays were marked with festive meals and observances, and where the State of Israel was placed at the very center of our consciousness," David Ellenson described the South he experienced as "far removed from that of the Ku Klux Klan and the nightmares and fears Northern Jews have of the South. Indeed, I do not recall encountering even one overt incident of antisemitism." He loved history and the heritage of Virginia: "George Washington, Thomas Jefferson, Robert E. Lee and Stonewall Jackson—all of them were figures actively present in my life...." Yet there was another side to his experience:

> For me, as a Jewish boy in the South, the lonely days were not confined to Sundays. I was in the South and I partook of and was informed by its heritage and manners—but as a Jew I was not of it. As I look back upon my childhood and think of my many Jewish friends from that time, I am amazed how many of them do not seem to have experienced it as I did. For them, Virginia is home. For me, it is also a place of intimacy. More profoundly, it is a place of alienation. Part of me felt I never really belonged.[56]

Despite many changes, there lingers a sense of marginality to Jewish experience in the South. Jews live in a world they did not make.

African Americans are helping to change the South in the late twentieth century in ways that both Washington and Du Bois would have welcomed. Although it is rare to encounter among African Americans the kind of romantic attachment to white southern myths that exists among Jews, many southern Blacks recognize the South as their home even with its bitter history of racism. Despite identification with very different southern traditions, Blacks and Jews have drawn closer together in recent years through shared visions of a future that might preserve the best attributes of southern society—its "lack of pretension, honesty in relations to others, loyalty to one's family and friends, and self-confidence in one's worth and one's values."[57] The separate paths remain separate, but they converge more often than in the past and there is less ambivalence on such occasions.

Notes

I am grateful to Mark Wagner for his diligent research assistance.

1. August Meier and Francis Broderick, "Introduction," *Negro Protest Thought in the Twentieth Century*, ed. Francis L. Broderick and August Meier, American Heritage Series (Indianapolis, 1965), xix–xxi.

2. Booker T. Washington, "Atlanta Exposition Address" in *Negro Protest Thought in the Twentieth Century*, ed. Francis L. Broderick and August Meier, American Heritage Series (Indianapolis, 1965), 4–5.

3. W. E. Burghardt Du Bois, *The Souls of Black Folk* (1903, repr.; Greenwich, CT, 1961), 48, 51.

4. Georgia's *Atlanta Constitution* criticized it as "the thought of a negro of northern education who has lived among his brethren of the South, yet who cannot fully feel the meaning of some things which these brethren know by instinct—and which the southern-bred white knows by a similar instinct—certain things which are by both accepted as facts." Quoted in Saunders Redding, "Introduction," in *The Souls of Black Folk,* x.

5. George A. Davis and O. Fred Donaldson, ed., *Blacks in the United States: A Geographic Perspective* (Boston, 1975), 65.

6. Quoted in Mark H. Elovitz, *A Century of Jewish Life in Dixie: The Birmingham Experience* (University, AL, 1974), 85–86.

7. Deborah Dash Moore, *To the Golden Cities: Pursuing the American Jewish Dream in Miami and L.A.* (New York, 1994), 32; Stephen J. Whitfield, "Blood and Sand: The Jewish Community of South Florida," *American Jewish History*, 82 (1994), 73–96.

8. Sarah S. Hughes, "The Twentieth Century," "Don't Grieve After Me," in *The Black Experience in Virginia 1916–1986*, ed. Philip Morgan (Hampton, VA: Hampton Institute, 1986), 66.

9. William Cohen, *Black Mobility and the Southern White Quest for Racial Control 1861–1915* (Baton Rouge, LA, 1991), 298.

10. Davis and Donaldson, *Blacks in the United States*, 30–37.

11. Robert D. Bullard, "The Lure of the New South," in *In Search of the New South: The Black Urban Experience in the 1970s and 1980s*, ed. Robert D. Bullard (Tuscaloosa, AL, 1989), 7.

12. David R. Goldfield, *The Promised Land: The South since 1945* (Arlington Heights, IL, 1987), 23–24, 40, 133.

13. Bullard, "The Lure of the New South," 5.

14. "Over the half-century since World War II,...defense contracting has produced a new economic map of the United States," that resembles a gunbelt. "The soutwestern states, Texas, and the Great Plains make up the holster; Florida represents the handcuffs ready to be slipped on the wrists of the villains; New England is the bullet clip." Ann Markusen, Peter Hall, Scott Campbell and Sabina Deitrick, *The Rise of the Gunbelt: The Military Remapping of Industrial America* (New York, 1991), 3–4.

15. Goldfield, *The Promised Land*, 40, 133; Davis and Donaldson, *Blacks in the United States*, 54–61.

16. Bullard, "The Lure of the New South," 7.

17. Ira M. Sheskin, "The Migration of Jews to Sunbelt Cities," paper presented at Sunbelt Conference, Miami, 1986, 1, Table 12; "Metropolitan Atlanta Jewish Population Study: Summary of Major Findings" (February 1985), 2–3.

18. Eli Evans, *The Lonely Days Were Sundays* (Jackson, MS, 1993), xxii.

19. For a brief description of the socioeconomic structure of the Jewish community in Miami, see Moore, *To the Golden Cities*, 64–67.

20. Hughes, "The Twentieth Century," 75.

21. Clifford M. Kuhn, Harlon E. Joye, and E. Bernard West, *Living Atlanta: An Oral History of the City, 1914–1948* (Athens, GA, 1990), 10.

22. Hortense Powdermaker, *After Freedom: A Cultural Study in the Deep South* (1939, repr.; Boston: Atheneum, 1968), xix.

23. Chalmers Archer, Jr., *Growing Up Black in Rural Mississippi: Memories of a Family, Heritage of a Place* (New York, 1992), 65.

24. Alfred O. Hero, Jr. "Southern Jews," in *Jews in the South*, ed. Leonard Dinnerstein and Mary Dale Palsson (Baton Rouge, LA, 1973), 231.

25. David and Adele Bernstein, "Slow Revolution in Richmond, Va.: A New Pattern in the Making," in *Jews in the South*, ed. Dinnerstein and Palsson, 254.

26. Theodore Lowi, "Southern Jews: The Two Communities," in *A Coat of Many Colors: Jewish Subcommunities in the United States*, ed. Abraham D. Lavender (Westport, CT, 1977), 100–107, quote on 100.

27. Marvin Braiterman, "Mississippi Marranos," in *Jews in the South*, ed. Dinnerstein and Palsson, 355, 357. For a recent example of such attitudes, see Marshall Goldberg and Jeremy Mindich, "Letter from Mississippi," *Forward*, 2 (December 1994), 1, 5.

28. E. Franklin Frazier, *Black Bourgeoisie* (New York, 1957), 195–238.

29. Melvin I. Urofsky, "Preface," in *"Turn to the South": Essays on Southern Jewry*, ed. Nathan M. Kaganoff and Melvin I. Urofsky (Charlottesville, VA, 1979), xii.

30. Ronald L. Bern, "Utilizing the Southern Jewish Experience in Literature," in *"Turn to the South": Essays on Southern Jewry*, ed. Kaganoff and Urofsky, 155.

31. Raymond Arsenault, "Charles Jacobson of Arkansas: A Jewish Politician in the Land of the Razorbacks, 1891–1915," in *"Turn to the South": Essays on Southern Jewry*, ed. Kaganoff and Urofsky, 56, 70.

32. Archer, *Growing Up Black in Rural Mississippi*, 26.

33. Harvard Sitkoff, *A New Deal for Blacks: The Emergence of Civil Rights as a National Issue*, volume 1: The Depression Decade (New York, 1978), 133–36, 249–63, 269–95, quote on 330–31.

34. Sit-ins sponsored by CORE in Miami in 1959 in which Jews participated to desegregate lunch counters in downtown department stores neither set a precedent for the Greensboro student sit-ins that stimulated hundreds of such actions in the spring of 1960 nor inspired the students to adopt the tactic. Jews actually appeared on both sides of the Miami struggle: as CORE activists and as the owner and managers of the department store. Moore, *To the Golden Cities*, 171–72. On their lack of influence, see Goldfield, *The Promised Land*, 95.

35. The bombs occurred in Miami, Nashville, Jacksonville, Birmingham, and Atlanta. Robert G. Weisbord and Arthur Stein, *Bittersweet Encounter: The Afro-American and the American Jew* (Westport, CT, 1970), 137. Another set of synagogue bombings took place in 1967 in Atlanta, Charlotte, and Gastonia, North Carolina, and Gadsden, Alabama; a bomb also exploded at the house of Rabbi Perry Nussbaum of Jackson, Mississippi. Nussbaum supported integration. Leonard Dinnerstein, *Antisemitism in America* (New York, 1994), 190.

36. Lenora E. Berson, *The Negroes and the Jews* (New York, 1971), 121.

37. Martin Luther King, Jr., "Letter from a Birmingham Jail," quoted in Goldfield, *The Promised Land*, 107.

38. Steven Hertzberg, *Strangers Within the Gate City: The Jews of Atlanta, 1845–1915* (Philadelphia: Jewish Publication Society, 1978), 217, 221.

39. Ronald H. Bayor, "Race, Ethnicity and Political Change in the Urban Sunbelt South," in *Shades of the Sunbelt: Essays on Ethnicity, Race, and the Urban South*, ed. Randall M. Miller and George E. Pozzetta (New York, 1988), 129–32; Beverly Hendrix Wright, "New Orleans: A City That Care Forgot," in *In Search of the New South*, ed. Bullard, 67–73.

40. Robert G. Weisbord and Arthur Stein, *Bittersweet Encounter*, 32.

41. Quoted in Dinnerstein, *Antisemitism in America*, 198.

42. Powdermaker inquired "into possible differences in attitudes between the Christian and Jewish people in the vicinity. Neither observation nor the results of the questionnaire [administered to the sisterhood of an area synagogue] gave evidence that there was any difference." *After Freedom*, xx.

43. Kuhn, Joye and West, *Living Atlanta*, 12.

44. Quoted in Elovitz, *A Century of Jewish Life in Dixie*, 84.

45. The Leo Frank case has attracted a lot of scholarly attention because "in it the central conflicts of early twentieth-century southern history erupted," as Nancy MacLean has argued. See her essay, "The Leo Frank Case Reconsidered: Gender and Sexual Politics in the Making of Reactionary Populism," *Journal of American History* (December 1991), 917–48, quote on 918. I have quoted from Steven Hertzberg, *Strangers Within the Gate City* 202–15, quotes on 205, 215. See also Leonard Dinnerstein, *The Leo Frank Case* (New York, 1968).

46. Quoted in Weisbord and Stein, *Bittersweet Encounter,* 72.

47. Quoted in Dan T. Carter, *Scottsboro: A Tragedy of the American South* (New York, 1969), 235.

48. Carter, *Scottsboro*, 254–59, quotes on 258–59; see also James Goodman, *Stories of Scottsboro* (New York, 1994).

49. Quoted in Goldfield, *The Promised Land*, 216.

50. Bullard, "The Lure of the New South," 6.

51. Barry A. Kosmin, Sidney Goldstein, Joseph Waksberg, Nava Lerer, Ariella Keysar, Jeffrey Scheckner, *Highlights of the CJF 1990 National Jewish Population Survey* (New York: Council of Jewish Federations, 1991), 21–26.

52. Hertzberg, *Strangers Within the Gate City*, 222.

53. Goldfield, *The Promised Land*, xi.

54. Evans, *The Lonely Days Were Sundays*, 332–33.

55. Robert D. Bullard, "Conclusion: Problems and Prospects," in *In Search of the New South*, p. 164.

56. David Ellenson, "A Separate Life," paper forthcoming in *Jewish Spiritual Journeys*, ed. Lawarence Hoffman and Arnold Jacob Wolf (New York, 1996), 2–3, 5.

57. Abraham D. Lavender, "Shalom Y'All: Accent on Southern Jewry," *Contemporary Jewry*, 3:2 (Spring/Summer), 41.

fourteen

AFFIRMATIVE ACTION

Jewish Ideals, Jewish Interests

JEROME A. CHANES

The recounting of history, like a Hindu god, takes many forms.[1] Nowhere is this more true than in the narrative of the Jewish encounter with affirmative action, and its implications for Black-Jewish relations. Since the early 1970s, few issues have been more salient on the Jewish community's domestic public-affairs agenda. Clearly—almost tautologically, inasmuch as race-based affirmative action deals with race—the Jewish stance on affirmative action has had profound implications for the relationship between Blacks and Jews.

Contrary to conventional wisdom, Black-Jewish relations over the past decade have had very little to do with anti-Semitism in the African American community, and almost everything to do with public-affairs issues, especially affirmative action. The affirmative-action controversy stemmed from the long-standing Black-Jewish coalition, and subsequently led to fault lines in the coalition.[2] With all the *Sturm und Drang* surrounding this issue, some observers of intergroup relations believe that the fallout from affirmative action has had a great impact as well on Jewish intra-communal relations. Still, the bitter divisions between Blacks and Jews over affirmative action were more striking and helped shape the relationship for twenty-five years.

//

A word about terminology: There is no easy answer to the question, What is "affirmative action"? Indeed, in large measure the ambiguity over the term's definition itself has resulted in a sizable zone of ambiguity with respect to stances on the issue. "Affirmative action" lacks precise legal definition; in some ways the best approach is to paraphrase former U.S. Supreme Court Justice Potter Stewart's comment about obscenity: "I can't define it, but I know it when I see it."

The term's very lack of concreteness, at least in popular usage, has given rise to the numerous intergroup semantic and policy struggles that have accompanied the history of these programs, and that gave heat to the battle. Affirmative action covers a wide array of concepts: acting as a "gateway" for members of minority groups to become part of a pool from which they can enter a workplace or educational institution; the elimination of discriminatory practices; employing "goals and timetables" to set and measure progress; using quotas. One "official," workmanlike definition has it "broadly encompassing any measure, beyond simple termination of discriminatory practice, adopted to correct or compensate for past or present discrimination or to prevent discrimination from recurring in the future."[3]

The elusive term "goals and timetables" that often accompanies affirmative-action plans has meant "quotas" to some, and legitimate, benign, targets to others. In its strictest sense, the phrase refers to targets set for employing minorities and women, along with time frames for achieving these goals. Under the original Executive Order on Affirmative Action 11246, employers were encouraged to make good-faith efforts, but there were no legal penalties if they were unable to meet the goals. Executive Order 11246 provided for "goals and timetables," but prohibited quotas.

Affirmative action was a product not of the 1960s, when it became a national issue, but of an awareness from the early 1940s that eliminating employment discrimination would not be sufficient to overcome the effects of decades of opportunities denied to minority-group members, especially Blacks. The obstacles that had accrued over the period of slavery and over a century of segregation—at best, second-class citizenship—by the middle of the twentieth century inhered in American society. Special polices and programs were required to surmount these obstacles.

The question of using numerical formulae in the struggle for economic justice was raised as early as the 1920s. The federal government adopted a numerical racial hiring policy as part of the Public Works Administration (PWA), created in 1933 by Title VII of the New Deal National Industrial Recovery Act.[4]

Thirty years later, the Civil Rights Act of 1964 legislated "color-blind" equal employment opportunity via both voluntary compliance and judicial enforcement (through litigation) of the right of individuals not to be discriminated against because of race. But the Civil Rights Act, simply declaring in effect "racial neutrality," could not do the job. Racial (and gender) discrimination had become too deeply entrenched.

In 1961, President John F. Kennedy issued Executive Order 10925, which outlawed discrimination by federal contractors and mandated: "The contractor shall take affirmative action to ensure that applicants are employed...without regard to their race, color, creed, or national origin." The Kennedy order is note-worthy in that it defined affirmative action as an employer's obligation.

By the mid-1960s it became increasingly clear that Executive Order 10925 had had little impact with respect to the hiring record of government contractors. In September 1965, one year after the passage of the Civil Rights Act, President Lyndon B. Johnson issued *his* affirmative action order, Executive Order 11246, which added to the requirements of Order 10925 several compliance require-ments, including goals and timetables, and enforcement authorities.[5] Executive Order 11246 is generally considered to mark the beginning of what we now know as "affirmative action."

Unfortunately—and here lay the crucial flaw—these two civil-rights direc-tives mandated and legitimized affirmative action—but failed to define it. Definitions ultimately came from the federal courts.

A Note on the Jewish Community and the Civil Rights Movement: First Stirrings

To understand the stances of the organized Jewish community on affirmative action, it is useful first to explore the whys and wherefores of this community's involvement in the civil-rights movement. This involvement is an exemplar of how the organized Jewish community makes an issue a priority on its agenda.

Contrary to conventional wisdom, the beginnings of the Jewish involvement in civil rights—specifically, in fair employment practices legislation—came not in the 1950s but a decade earlier, after President Franklin D. Roosevelt issued Executive Order 8802 in 1941.[6] To avert a march on Washington threatened by union leader and civil-rights activist A. Philip Randolph—who saw the expanding industrial base as a vehicle to alleviate discrimination against Black employment—FDR issued Executive Order 8802, which outlawed discrimina-tion in defense industries (later expanded to include all federal contractors) and which created the Fair Employment Practices Committee (FEPC) to oversee enforcement. Plagued with serious employment discrimination in their own community, Jewish leaders saw their own opportunity, and in turn created the "Coordinating Committee of Jewish Organizations Concerned with Discrimination in the War Industries," which was incorporated in 1944 into the newly formed National Community Relations Advisory Council (NCRAC).[7] Toward the end of the War, as conservatives threatened to abolish the FEPC—the one agency that "gave teeth" to Executive Order 8802—Jewish groups became involved with the National Council for a Permanent FEPC, started by Randolph in 1943. This coalition marked the beginning of the "civil-rights movement."

Jewish groups hardly expressed unanimous support in the 1940s for making common cause with Blacks. At an early NCRAC Plenary Session, in a forum on "Relations with Negroes," a vigorous debate took place on the wisdom of coali-tion-building with Blacks. Rabbi Stephen S. Wise, an American Jewish Congress and NAACP leader, made the case for continued involvement based on Jewish self-interest. The Wise rationale, a rearticulation of the original reasons for Jewish involvement in the civil-rights struggle, is key to understanding Jewish involvement in, or opposition to, aspects of affirmative action.

But it was the growing Jewish community-relations council movement that saw the Black communities as natural allies. During the 1940s, the community-relations councils (CRCs) were spearheads of the technique of coalition, and CRCs established local human-relations councils and committees as vehicles for Black-Jewish relations and pioneered the technique of coalition-building.

Affirmative Action and the Organized Jewish Community: Three Cases that Set the Stage

From the beginning, affirmative action posed a broad and profound dilemma for the Jewish community. The community's core ideology was the quintessentially American notion that individual rights, rather than group rights, inform the workings of the society. This ideology defined American associationalism, exceptionalism, and voluntarism. Individual rights, protected by the Bill of Rights, primarily the First Amendment and most centrally the separation of church and state, was the prime guarantor of the Jewish polity's ability to participate in the public-affairs arena.

Further—and this is the crux of the strategic underpinnings of the civil-rights movement—the focus was not on the discrimination practiced by the individual bigot, but on results that could be achieved in terms of societal remedies.[8] In the years following World War II, the "authoritarian-personality" theory—theories of frustration-aggression, anxiety-aggression, projection and scapegoating—illumined the landscape of bigotry. This approach particularly fit the image of Hitlerism as consummate personal diabolism and pathology.

However valid this *causative* perspective may have been, it provided no strong *remedial* seat. Moreover, in other areas, the "good-will" approach to the world, focusing on individual attitudes, was being replaced by what might be characterized as *societal* therapy. The civil-rights movement generally bypassed individual attitudes—who cares, really?—and addressed the social, legal, and, more recently, political structure out of which bigoted attitudes grow. Social structure—"de-institutionalizing" discrimination—rather than psychopathology was the analytic fulcrum for the civil rights movement. The civil-rights leadership recognized that social systems create values and conflicts in which people are trapped, and so emphasized group power, rather than individual good will. This approach led naturally to the next step: race-based affirmative-action programs.

Yet Jews had a horror of anything that smacked of quotas; they could point to numerous instances in Jewish history, including the not-too-distant American past, when quotas had compromised Jews' ability to participate in the workings of society. To many Jews, federal agencies' affirmative-action efforts threatened individual rights, particularly the merit system, and by extension Jewish security.

For Jews, education was a powerful symbol. Higher education especially had become their primary vehicle for "making it" in American society. Jews vividly remembered ceilings placed on Jewish admissions by a number of universities during the first half of the twentieth century.

II

It is useful to trace along a time line how the Jewish organizational consensus position on affirmative action developed, and to explore the fault lines among national Jewish groups on the issue. The policy statements of the National Jewish Community Relations Advisory Council (NJCRAC)[9] can serve as general bellwethers of where the Jewish community stood on the issue. NJCRAC noted the opposition of the organized Jewish community to quotas as early as 1969.[10] The NJCRAC *Joint Program Plan* (*JPP*), an annual compendium and analysis of the Jewish public-affairs agenda, noted in its 1969–70 statement its opposition to quotas. Based firmly on individual rights, it also provided a tactical rationale for minorities to oppose quotas: "Racial or religious or ethnic quotas are regarded... as inconsistent with the concept of equality of opportunity, which should be based on *individual qualification* alone. In the long run, quotas must prove injurious even to those who benefit from them at any given time" (emphasis added).[11]

In 1971, the first major national debate among Jewish agencies over affirmative action took place at the NJCRAC Plenum. Argument centered on the quota issue. For Jews, remembering the *numerus clausus* policies in universities, a quota was a ceiling: a "no more than" idea, a way of keeping people *out*. For Blacks, a quota was a floor: "no less than," to let people *in*. This distinction was a key to the debates that followed.[12]

The issue came to a head at the 1972 NJCRAC Plenum. NJCRAC's position, reflecting the Jewish community's consensus view, was adopted following an intense debate,[13] and was published in a *Joint Program Plan* section entitled "Affirmative Action, Preferential Treatment, and Quotas." NJCRAC categorically asserted, "We oppose all quotas." But this seemingly unequivocal stance might have been more categorical had it not been followed immediately by "But we do not oppose—indeed, we endorse—setting specific target goals and time tables, not determined by population percentages, for rectifying the imbalances resulting from past discrimination; so long as such goals and time tables are used to evaluate good faith efforts and not as rigid requirements."[14] This nuanced distinction reverberated in subsequent debates among and within Jewish groups.

The delicately shaded 1972 position was as close to a definitive position on affirmative action as the Jewish community could get, and it "fuzzed over" divisions between some national agencies, and between some national Jewish groups and the local CRCs. Indeed, the communities played a major role in the debate at the 1972 Plenum in advancing the position ultimately adopted, despite opposition from three national bodies.[15]

NJCRAC's 1972 position on affirmative action was repeated more-or-less yearly, with some variations in language, throughout the decade. The organizations generally supported affirmative-action plans that were not explicitly racial, such as those considering economic or social disadvantage;[16] or those designed to weed out practices that served in fact to weed out minorities.[17] There was, throughout, the suggestion that the organized Jewish community was a bit uncomfortable about opposing a program that was so important to the Black community. In 1973 NJCRAC took pains to point out that there was no proof that race-conscious programs targeted Jews (that year's *JPP* somewhat paradoxically warned against devising affirmative-action plans that would impose special burdens on Jews).

NJCRAC's subsequent statements on affirmative action varied slightly, reflecting both situations addressed that year and, more importantly, growing disagreement among NJCRAC's constituent agencies. NJCRAC's positions careened from recognition of the limited use of racial criteria,[18] to absolute opposition to all such programs. "Goals and timetables" were considered permissible, not as much because of what they *would* do, but because several agencies perceived them as not being rigidly enforced, and hence less of a danger of degenerating into quotas.[19]

NJCRAC made an effort during the 1970s to bite the bullet with respect to how affirmative action would implicate Black-Jewish relations, but most formulations skirted the core issue of opposition to quotas. In response to the complaint that opposition to quotas was dividing the Jewish and Black communities, NJCRAC repeatedly urged initiatives that would enhance social and economic programs to aid Blacks, such as public employment, thus obviating the need for race-conscious affirmative-action programs to ensure minority access. This solution was consistent with NJCRAC's long-established approach to social justice, namely increasing government responsibility.

A forum on "Affirmative Action, Preferential Treatment, and Quotas" at the 1973 NJCRAC Plenum, a commentary to the 1972 NJCRAC position, reaffirmed the growing consensus that quotas should be rejected, but that blanket opposition to specific court-ordered remedies was unwise public policy.

In June 1975, NJCRAC issued a comprehensive statement that attempted to bridge gaps and articulate its consensus on affirmative action.[20] The NJCRAC "Position on Affirmative Action" affirmed support of programs that would bring members of minority groups to the "gateways," while reiterating Jewish communal opposition to quotas. One canny analyst noted that NJCRAC's position was

evidently motivated by the understanding that the battle over race-conscious affirmative action was a battle over economically-valuable benefits. Later, however, [the program] was more than a claim for valuable benefit....[S]uch programs acknowledged that minority groups were an integral part of society, that no aspect of society was complete without their presence, and that, unless encouraged to do so, minorities and women would not seek employment or attendance at institutions where they would be alone. The failure to grasp these broader applications was a serious shortcoming [in the NJCRAC position].[21]

In fact the position masked several areas of disagreement, some clear, some murky. The Anti-Defamation League (ADL), an early critic of many forms of affirmative action,[22] viewed affirmative action as a gateway, and opposed goals and timetables as being tantamount to quotas, and, in fact, objected to all departures from "merit" selection.[23] The American Jewish Committee (AJC) also opposed quotas, but supported "flexible" goals and timetables.[24] The American Jewish Congress (AJCongress) went through a tortuous debate that resulted in opposing quotas but supporting the use of goals and timetables if ordered by a court or administrative agency following a proof or finding of discrimination.[25] Among the religious bodies, the Union of Orthodox Jewish Congregations of America, representing the mainstream "centrist" traditionally observant religious community, opposed anything that suggested "group privileges," including goals and timetables.[26] The Union of American Hebrew Congregations (Reform) expressed a blanket support of goals and timetables. The National Council of Jewish Women did not address specifically the question of goals and timetables, but asserted a blanket support of affirmative action and a blanket opposition to "quota systems in the public and private sector."[27] Women's American ORT, a membership organization, appeared to be the only agency to support quotas, and not merely goals and timetables, noting [we] "support quotas under very narrowly-defined circumstances, approving the use of court-ordered quotas in cases of proven, prior discrimination."[28]

II

There were a number of affirmative-action situations—sometimes crystallized in federal-court activity—that engaged the Jewish community's attention, with implications for intergroup relations. Contrary to conventional wisdom,[29] Jewish groups, including the three influential "defense" agencies—the American Jewish Congress, the American Jewish Committee, and the Anti-Defamation League—and Jewish community-relations councils around the United States, diverged in their stances on affirmative action, notwithstanding the fact that they joined on single briefs in a number of cases. A quick review of the early landmark United States Supreme Court cases in this area demonstrates where Jewish groups were—and were not.

One event highlighted Jewish sensitivities to affirmative action in academia, and presaged involvement in Supreme Court activity that followed. From 1972 to 1975 six national Jewish organizations[30] engaged the Department of Health, Education, and Welfare (HEW) over proposed revision of HEW guidelines on hiring practices of colleges and universities which received federal grants. While they reached agreement in principle with HEW, it was widely believed that HEW policies and pressures had actually fostered reverse discrimination in several instances because universities feared the loss of government funds as a penalty for noncompliance. In any event, the Jewish organizational stance on the HEW matter angered Black spokesmen, and increased tensions between the two communities. Typical was the assertion by Carlton B. Goodlett, a prominent Black journalist: "If Jews are not prepared to accept a quota system as a means of quantitatively evaluating the eradication of racism in America, when then?"[31] This statement prefigured a generation of African American reaction to Jewish stances on affirmative action.

II

During the 1970s and 1980s, Supreme Court decisions expanded the rubric of acceptable affirmative-action practices. First the 1978 *Bakke* ruling said that race could be taken into account; the 1979 *Weber* case permitted the voluntary adoption by private employers of race-conscious programs; the 1980 *Fullilove* case permitted the "setting aside" by Congress of a percentage of federal funds in a public-works program for minority contractors.

The first Supreme Court test of race-conscious affirmative action was *DeFunis v. Odegaard* (1974), in which DeFunis, a white, Jewish applicant, challenged the University of Washington Law School's refusal to admit him, while the school accepted less qualified minorities under a special affirmative-action program. While the school denied having a quota, it did acknowledge that its goal was to achieve a reasonable representation of minorities in the university. The ADL, AJCongress, and AJC—the three "defense" agencies—all filed *amicus* briefs in the case in favor of DeFunis. The case did not reach a decision in the Supreme Court, because DeFunis, under a special order, was a student in the law school and was within weeks of graduation, and the case was therefore moot.

The firestorm over *DeFunis* had barely died down when an almost identical case was decided by the Supreme Court: *Bakke v. Regents, University of California*. *Bakke* is worth exploring in some detail for here *was* the first affirmative-action case decided by the High Court; and because *Bakke* had ramifications for Black-Jewish relations.

Deluged by *amicus* briefs in *Bakke*, most of which supported the constitutionality of the minority-admissions program, the Supreme Court split three ways. Four justices said the admissions program was legal; four said it was not. Justice Lewis Powell held that reserving a number of seats for minorities was racial discrimination, subject to the same strict judicial scrutiny as any other form of discrimination.

Predictably, Jewish organizations were split. The American Jewish Committee and the American Jewish Congress, with several white ethnic groups, filed a single friend-of-the-court brief, urging that race should not be a factor, but also that universities should take into account the hardships of an applicant. The ADL brief was along the same lines. While the National Council of Jewish Women and the Union of American Hebrew Congregations clearly sympathized with the program, significant numbers of their own constituents were unhappy about their agencies' participation in the case (as they had done in *DeFunis*), and they sat out *Bakke*.

The Jewish community generally hailed the *Bakke* decision as a victory because it outlawed rigid racial quotas. NJCRAC, however, noted that its constituent agencies had in fact been divided over the application of the anti-quota principle to *Bakke*.

The Black community had mixed feelings about *Bakke*, which did recognize the validity of some forms of race-conscious programs: Justice Powell did say that race could be a factor in admissions, which was considered a victory. Yet there was no escaping from the fact that *Bakke* recognized, for the first time, the validity of some "reverse-discrimination" claims, a precedent that concerned Blacks.

Significant Black-Jewish tension grew out of *Bakke* largely from the fact that Jewish groups had actually gone into the case.[32] The African American press excoriated Bayard Rustin and other Black leaders for marching in lockstep with friends from the national Jewish community-relations agencies in their opposition to affirmative action. The Leadership Conference on Civil Rights (LCCR), a coalition begun in 1950 by Black and Jewish leaders, ducked any number of affirmative-action cases—including *Bakke*. Operating as a consensus coalition, the LCCR realized that without Jewish support a consensus was impossible. This exacerbated Black-Jewish tensions on the organizational level as well.[33]

In the aftermath of *Bakke*, the Equal Employment Opportunity Commission (EEOC) recommended guidelines for handling reverse discrimination cases. The draft guidelines provided that if an employer made a "reasonable assessment" and found that affirmative action was an "appropriate" remedy, the commission would not take action against the company on the basis of reverse discrimination. Jewish defense organizations expressed deep concern that those guidelines gave the employers the impression that the guidelines mandated a proportional-representation system in hiring, and that they would have to institute a race-conscious employment plan, even in the absence of evidence of discriminatory practice.

One other landmark affirmative-action case illustrated both Jewish and intergroup sensitivities toward this issue. *DeFunis* and *Bakke* both involved admission to institutions of higher learning, presenting the quota issue to which Jews were very sensitive; there were few American Jews who did not have a *numerus clausus* tale to tell.[34] *United Steelworkers v. Weber* (1979), however, involved a blue-collar reverse-discrimination situation. Brian Weber, a white employee, was rejected by a training program that had been established as part of an affirmative-action program by a company with few skilled Black craftspersons, subject to "goals and timetables," and facing the loss of government contracts. When Weber alleged discrimination under the Civil Rights Act of 1964, the voluntary plan was upheld by the Supreme Court.

Jewish groups mostly sat out *Weber*, offering different views as to why they did so. The ADL, which did file pro-Weber and lost, suggested that the decision was narrow in that it did not require replacing white employees with Blacks. ADL maintained that a "blue-collar" principle had as much merit as a "white-collar" principle. AJC and AJCongress did not file briefs, for several reasons: Jews did not have as clear a stake in a steel mill as they had in a university; Weber's employer may have in fact discriminated against minorities, so the plan was justified; in *Weber* the Blacks were just as qualified as the whites, whereas in *Bakke* the Blacks admitted were less qualified than the whites admitted; finally, and most probably, the failure to support *Weber* was at least partly intended to improve Black-Jewish relations.

After the *Weber* decision, Jewish organizations called for meetings with Black groups to make an effort to devise mutually acceptable affirmative-action plans. These emollient calls came to naught. In 1980, immediately following *Weber*, NJCRAC noted that "affirmative action remains a subject of sharp dispute, notably between Blacks and Jews."[35]

Sharp dispute also characterized Jewish internal discourse. The divisions between Jewish groups over affirmative action occasionally resulted in explosive rhetoric that was aired in public. In June 1986, Rabbi David Saperstein, director of the Religious Action Center of Reform Judaism and a premier—if controversial—tactician in the Black-Jewish civil-rights coalition, suggested at an NAACP convention that, in the ADL's opposition to preferential treatment, the ADL might be out of step with the Jewish community. ADL national director Nathan Perlmutter reacted viscerally. "Kissing backsides isn't the way to strengthen relationships," snapped Perlmutter. He continued, "Every poll taken on [affirmative action] reveals that the majority of Americans, including Jews, oppose racial quotas."[36] Perlmutter missed Saperstein's point, as Saperstein missed his. Clearly, *intra*group relations were as sensitive on this issue as were intergroup relations.

Affirmative Action and the Organized Jewish Community: The 1980s and 1990s

After *Bakke* and *Weber*, working-class whites, and many Jews, feared that their rights and opportunities were being curtailed. For Blacks, there was considerable uncertainty about affirmative-action programs. In *Fullilove v. Klutznick* (1980), the

Supreme Court approved a congressionally mandated public-works program that required a 10-percent "set-aside" for federal expenditures with minority business interests.

Again, given a situation that involved the strong likelihood of actual discrimination, during a period in which there were substantial tensions between Blacks and Jews, and in a context in which it was not likely that many Jews would be affected, Jewish groups took a pass on this case. Only the ADL filed a brief in *Fullilove* arguing that the set-aside was counter to the principles of "color-blindness."

Following *Fullilove*, NJCRAC in 1981 introduced a small but important revision in its 1975 position, which had said that gender discrimination was different from racial discrimination. Its 1981 position equated the two groups. Additionally, three agencies—AJCongress, the Union of American Hebrew Congregations, and Women's American ORT—argued that the position ought to support the use of quotas in narrowly defined instances, as a remedy for proven past discrimination. They failed to carry the day after intense debate.[37]

This change points out a number of dynamics at work in the early 1980s. First, and most important, there had been a change in the legal landscape: the Supreme Court had affirmed the constitutionality of affirmative action. Although much political and social opposition to affirmative-action plans still existed, the *Zeitgeist* was different from that of the late 1970s.

Second, opposition to quotas increasingly was disruptive to Black-Jewish relations. As one observer put it, "The desire to maintain those relations, fueled in very large part by a nostalgia for the heady days of the civil-rights movement, led to a desire to play down the divisive issue of affirmative action."[38] Many Blacks were unhappy and impatient with Jewish obsessions about reverse discrimination and quotas. Observed NAACP leader Benjamin Hooks: "The term 'quota,' which traditionally meant the *exclusion* of Jews, was now being used by many Jews to warn against the attempts to *include* Blacks in aspects of our society and economy from which we were previously excluded."[39]

Two cases in the 1980s—*Firefighters Local Union #1784 v. Stotts* (1984) and *Wygant v. Jackson Board of Education* (1986)—restricted affirmative action, both testing seniority rights. Affirmative action bounced back in two later cases, *Local 28, Sheet Metal Workers v. EEOC* (1986) and *U.S. v. Paradise* (1987). Both tested a court-ordered quota for admitting Blacks—to the union and to a public job, respectively—where there were judicial findings of prior discrimination. Here, the Court allowed the quotas.

A major to-do was made of the fact that, at long last, four major Jewish groups (AJC, AJCongress, and the rabbinic and congregational bodies of Reform Judaism, the Union of American Hebrew Congregations and the Central Conference of American Rabbis)—joined with Blacks (the NAACP Legal Defense and Education Fund, Inc.) in an "Inc. Fund" brief in support of quotas in those circumstances.

//

During much of the 1980s the affirmative action issue lacked salience for the organized Jewish community for several reasons: first, some of the "Black-power" fire had gone out of Black-Jewish disputes by the middle of the decade, and affirmative action was less of a sore spot than it had been earlier. Second, the Jewish community was more secure than it had been in the 1970s.

Third, and perhaps most significantly, Jewish groups had many new issues, each demanding attention, on their collective table. A burgeoning Christian "religious right," a new generation of church-state situations, ripples and rumbles in the Soviet-Jewry issue—all nudged affirmative action to the corner of Jewish organizational consciousness.

The most recent Jewish organizational involvement in affirmative-action situations concerned not the Supreme Court, but the protracted struggle over passage of the Civil Rights Act of 1991. The embattled bill, which finally achieved passage in the 102nd Congress, after a two-year struggle, had become a flash-point in the relationship between President George Bush and Blacks, and within the Jewish community as well. The Civil Rights Act was Congress's first successful effort to reverse the effects of the conservative Rehnquist Supreme Court, which had itself reversed the tide of previous Court decisions that generally were favorable to affirmative action. Six cases handed down during the 1988–89 term (and four other rulings since 1985) had restricted the reach of federal laws involving gender, racial, religious, and ethnic discrimination in hiring, promotion, and termination. Passage of the legislation, which would make it easier for a plaintiff to prove the discriminatory effect of employment practices and require employers to defend the legitimacy of such practices—and not the other way around, as the High Court decisions would have it—had been frustrated since first introduced in 1989, during the 101st Congress.

The debate over support of the bill exposed numerous fault lines within the Jewish community. At the end of the day most Jewish groups, excepting two organizations representing the Orthodox Jewish community, Agudath Israel of America and the Union of Orthodox Jewish Congregations of America, supported the measure. AJC summed up the support expressed by twelve Jewish groups and by NJCRAC—in effect virtually the entire universe of Jewish community relations: "The Civil Rights Act is about fairness and opportunity...[it] has nothing to do with quotas."

//

Recently, several Jewish agencies have reexamined their stances on affirmative action. For example, in 1987 the ADL modified its affirmative-action policy:

[c]ourt-ordered preferential relief, *including quotas* [emphasis added], may be appropriate under the following limited conditions:

1. There is a long-standing history of systematic and egregious discrimination; and
2. The workforce is substantially segregated (i.e., token representatives at most, and not merely underrepresented in relation to the population, pool, or workforce) by race, gender, or ethnicity; and
3. Appropriate remedies such as programs of training, education, and vigorous recruitment...have been unsuccessful; and
4. Implementation of preferential relief is explicitly limited to a defined duration, at which time its continuation must be re-evaluated in light of then-existing conditions.[40]

Thus, if a history of "egregious discrimination" and nothing more than a token minority-group presence existed in an industry or workplace, race could be considered as the determining factor. Absent these narrow circumstances, the ADL was opposed to goals and timetables, which it believed were quotas.

Significantly the ADL, following what the Supreme Court had already mandated, went *further* than goals and timetables. But at its November 1995 annual meeting, ADL's National Commission rejected by a solid vote a policy that would have lowered the threshold of race for the ADL as an affirmative-action trigger for remedies such as preferential treatment. The proposed policy in essence said that race should be *a* factor (again, not the predominant one) in hiring, even without "egregious discrimination" or "token presence." The split in the voting was largely generational, with younger leaders more inclined to consider race as a factor.

AJCongress, in recent years a "hard-liner" on cognate affirmative-action issues, such as redistricting, in 1994 and 1995 studied the threshold at which goals and timetables should kick in. Ultimately, while still opposing quotas, AJCongress supported court-ordered goals and timetables given a finding of discrimination.

For the third time since 1975, NJCRAC engaged in another go-around on affirmative action in 1994, and following much discussion left its policy unchanged. The 1995–96 *Joint Program Plan*, in a message to "hard-liners" in the Jewish community, said,

Although misuse of affirmative action has been acknowledged in some cases, and anecdotal evidence of reverse discrimination has been provided, there is at present little hard statistical evidence of widespread abuse. According to a 1992 Urban Institute study, reverse discrimination is rare. On the other hand, research is available which documents continued workplace discrimination against Blacks, other minorities, and women.[41]

//

The world at the close of 1995 had turned over many times since 1965. In 1995, ideologically fueled abuses in some programs spurred demands by members of a Republican-controlled Congress and other political leaders to demand an end to all affirmative-action programs.[42] In July 1995, President Bill Clinton defended government affirmative-action initiatives and called for a review of current programs to guard against abuses, improve effectiveness, and guarantee fairness. In *Adarand v. Pena* (1995), the latest Supreme Court ruling to come down the pike, the Court—itself hardly immune to the *Zeitgeist* of the 1990s—established strict scrutiny for all federal programs.[43] Most Jewish groups, whatever their views on goals and timetables, reaffirmed support for these programs.[44]

A few local Jewish communities were beset with problems of their own as affirmative action was under siege in their states or localities. A number of legislative initiatives were introduced on the state level that sought to eliminate race-based preference programs. In California, where affirmative action was under severe attack in the mid-1990s, the California Civil Rights Initiative (CCRI), proposed as a ballot initiative for the 1996 elections, asked voters to amend the state constitution to make it illegal to grant preference on the basis of sex, color, ethnicity, or national origin—in effect, to eliminate all state-mandated race-conscious programs in every sphere of life. CCRI spawned comparable efforts in a number of states. Marching against the tide of public sentiment, local Jewish communities mobilized in 1995 against these initiatives.

A Coda for the Nineties: The Voting Rights Dilemma

The issue of districting and reapportionment stemming from the provisions of the Voting Rights Act of 1965 and the 1982 amendments thereto has presented a new set of dilemmas for Jews, even though very few Jewish communities have been affected by reapportionment. The political hot potato of the 1990s, redistricting is an issue that has been long on rhetoric and very short on understanding, differing in some key respects from the affirmative-action question, at whose heart is the quota issue. Central to voting rights in the 1980s and 1990s is the question of group empowerment.[45] But this factor is precisely what links the two matters: at the heart of each is the bottom-line question of individual rights *versus* group rights. The most dramatic manifestations of this fundamental question have in recent years been found in voting-rights situations.

The Voting Rights Act of 1965 had one and only one aim: to remedy Black disenfranchisement in the South.[46] In that it provided ballots for southern Blacks, the legislation worked, and worked remarkably well. Yet when it allegedly enhanced minority-group political power—which, in fact, it did not—the legislation was viewed by many as flawed.

The two operative provisions of the Voting Rights Act, which together became the focus of a generation of controversy, are on their faces simple. Section 2 prohibits in elections any device that discriminates; Section 5, the "preclearance" provision, which requires the Justice Department's approval for any new voting (or other) procedure, aims to guard against renewed disenfranchisement—"retrogression," in the words of the Supreme Court—so as to prevent the use of the back door to let in disenfranchisement once the front door was locked. "Preclearance" protected Blacks against obvious disenfranchisement devices, while also being useful in preventing more subtle "diluting" practices.

Three key events set the stage for controversy: the 1980 U.S. Supreme Court decision in *City of Mobile v. Bolden*; the 1982 congressional debate over and passage of amendments to the 1965 act; and the 1986 Supreme Court decision in *Thornburg v. Gingles*.

In interpreting Section 2 of the Voting Rights Act, *Mobile v. Bolden* contradicted prior court decisions and ruled that in order to violate the act, a discriminatory *intent*, and not merely a discriminatory *result*, had to be demonstrated. The Court in essence said that as long as voting methods in a given district had not been designed to keep Blacks from holding office, Blacks and whites are still considered on an equal political footing.

Predictably, Blacks (and the civil-rights movement generally) were exceedingly unhappy with *Bolden*; they wanted an "effect," and not an "intent," test. When, in 1982, the act was before Congress for its third renewal, there was an extended debate, which resulted in the "Dole Compromise." Crafted by Senator Robert Dole (R-KS), the amendments included an "effect" test: Congress outlawed electoral practices that *result* in denial of equal political opportunity based on race. Also included was explicit language that no one, including members of a "protected" group,[47] has a right to proportional representation. In other words, the fact that minority-group members may not be elected in numbers proportionate to their population does not constitute a violation of Section 2.

As is clear from the amendment's legislative history, its aim was to enable minority voters to shape electoral districts so as to minimize racism's impact in communities where racism was yet a factor.

Here's where the trouble began.

The third, and most difficult to understand, development was the Supreme Court's decision in *Thornburg v. Gingles* (1986), which dealt with multi-member districts (similar in concept to "at-large" districts). One issue here was the question of proportional representation, explicitly outlawed in the amended Section 2. Another was the question of minority-group representation in multi-member districts. It was this question that the Court analyzed in *Gingles*. The Court reasoned that minorities, in a democracy, will lose elections. Tautologically, that is what a minority is. But the Congress in effect had decreed, "Yes, but not for certain minorities." If a minority group is never able to elect its members in a multi-member district, a single-member district must be created, in which the "minority" (now perhaps a majority) will win. In order to create such a "majority-minority" district, said the Court, three criteria, which make racially polarized voting the real test of vote dilution, must be met: first, there are sufficient numbers of the minority group, and the group is geographically compact enough, to elect someone from a single-member district (in other words, to be able to create a "majority-minority" district); second, the minority community must be "politically cohesive," that is, it must express common electoral or political aspirations; and third, a pattern of racial polarization must be demonstrated—majority-community block voting that has usually led to the defeat of minority-supported candidates.

Race was the deciding factor in *Gingles*, and thereafter race became the central feature of most districting and reapportionment situations.[48] The *Gingles* interpretation of the 1982 amendments, which in essence gave sanction to legislatures and courts to redistrict, or to create entirely new legislative districts, for the purpose of increasing the possibility of electing minority-group members, had consequences for other groups. Yet groups not "protected" under federal statute were effectively deprived of representation as a consequence.

Where were Jewish groups in all of this? The organized Jewish community, across the board, supported the 1965 Voting Rights Act, but its attitudes toward the 1982 amendments did not signify an orgasmic frenzy. Some agencies supported the amendments; some sat them out, and were silent. One agency, the American Jewish Congress, opposed them, predicting possible negative consequences for the Jewish community, even though few Jews had to date been affected by reapportionment under the Voting Rights Act (the Chasidim of Williamsburgh in *UJO v. Carey* were a noteworthy exception).[49]

In fact, one of the first post-*Gingles* cases to reach the Supreme Court did involve a Jewish community, that of Dade County, Florida, including Miami and Miami Beach. *Johnson v. DeGrandy* (originally *Wetherell v. DeGrandy*) tested the validity of a redistricting plan for state legislative seats. The plan was developed in June 1992 by a federal district court in Florida, which found a plan previously crafted by the state legislature to be insufficient in its response to Section 2 of the Voting Rights Act. (Section 2 is violated if members of a "protected" class "have less opportunity than other members of the electorate to participate in the political process and to elect representatives of their choice.")[50]

As plaintiff, the Florida House of Representatives maintained that the district court's plan went beyond the requirements of the Voting Rights Act, and violated the act's spirit by effectively disenfranchising other populations. For the Jewish community, the issue in *DeGrandy* was that the court's proposed remedy would create Hispanic districts at the expense of other, including Jewish, communities—in effect, giving to a community that already has plenty by taking away from another that had less.[51]

In a 7-2 decision handed down in 1994, the Supreme Court rejected the district court's judgment and interpretation, and in effect rejected a "maximization" standard as contrary to the original purposes of the Voting Rights Act. Yet the

Court accepted that proportionality should continue to be an important factor in assessing Section 2 claims.

As for Jewish groups' involvement, AJCongress, joined by the Greater Miami Jewish Federation (the local umbrella for Jewish social and community services), filed an *amicus curiae* brief in support of the legislature's plan. The ADL, while not supporting any party in the case, asserted that courts are not required to maximize the number of "majority-minority" districts when evaluating the reapportionment plan under the Voting Rights Act. Most other Jewish groups, reflecting their ambiguous stances on redistricting, stayed out of *DeGrandy*.

Other significant cases decided during the 1990s have had little direct fallout for Jews. One of the most significant cases since *Gingles* tested a bizarrely shaped district in North Carolina. The Supreme Court in *Shaw v. Reno* (1993) ruled that North Carolina state officials, in their efforts to justify a serpentine district to boost Black or Hispanic representation, might have violated the rights of white voters. To Jewish organizations, concerned about reverse discrimination as well as Black-Jewish relations, *Shaw v. Reno* went beyond the districting issue. The decision appeared to be consistent with the ruling in *Richmond v. Croson* (1989) that racial preferences, such as minority "set-asides," are unconstitutional because they violate the Constitution's equal-protection guarantees, unless there is distinct evidence that they are needed to correct a specific past discrimination and not a generalized societal discrimination. Although no Jewish organization entered *Shaw* as a friend of the court, "many of them welcomed the decision."[52]

If analysts thought that the Supreme Court could not make things murkier, in fact the High Court did just that in *Miller v. Johnson* (1995). In a 5–4 decision that confused Jewish and Black groups alike, the Court articulated a new test for using race in drawing legislative districts, saying that a district, even one not bizarrely shaped, could be found constitutionally suspect if race was the "predominant factor" in drawing the district lines. Jewish and civil-rights agencies immediately asked, What is the threshold at which race becomes the "predominant factor"?[53]

II

To date, very few Jewish communities have been affected by voting-rights situations.[54] But as new reapportionment schemes involving members of Congress are tested in the courts, this is likely to change. Nonetheless, the issue of districting and reapportionment has been viewed as a source of tension between Jewish agencies and Black civil-rights groups such as the NAACP Legal Defense and Education Fund, Inc. Jewish organizations have had to make the case that even if they may in some instances, based on local circumstances, argue against civil-rights groups in voting-rights cases, their motive is not opposition to minority-group political empowerment.

The dilemma for the organized Jewish community was articulated in a series of NJCRAC analyses of voting rights in the 1993–94, 1994–95, and 1995–96 *Joint Program Plans*. In 1994 the NJCRAC acknowledged

> discomfort with remedies that appear weighted in the direction of assur-
> ing electoral success for groups, while at the same time recognizing the
> need to deal with a history of racially-polarized voting that has meant that
> Blacks rarely win elections in non-"majority-minority" districts. In addi-
> tion, it is necessary [for Jewish communal groups] to consider the very real
> potential of strained relations with other groups who view such remedies
> as central to their efforts of political empowerment.[55]

In 1995 NJCRAC reminded the Jewish community of the political implications that inhered in voting-rights situations:

> Because districting is a "zero-sum" exercise, any vehicle that enhances rep-
> resentation of one group necessarily comes at the expense of other groups,
> including possibly a Jewish community. [The Jewish community] needs to
> examine the implications of the voting rights debate for coalitional rela-
> tionships....The organized Jewish community will need to articulate to its
> coalition partners in minority communities that the Jewish community's
> approach to voting rights is highly nuanced....The fact that a Jewish com-
> munity agency may participate or intervene in a specific case, or may deter-
> mine that race-based districting is inappropriate, is not done out of hostil-
> ity to minority interests, but out of principled differences as to how best
> achieve a "color-blind" society.[56]

By 1995 no Jewish agency—including AJCongress, which in 1982 opposed
the amendments—was willing to say that race could *never* be a factor in districting, making the stances of the Jewish groups entirely congruent to their postures
on affirmative action.

What the voting-rights issue brought home to the Jewish community was the
fact that their world was no longer irenic. The traditional guarantors of constitutional protections—the federal courts—could no longer be relied upon. The
courts were mandated by the Voting Rights Act to protect the "protected"
minorities, of which the Jewish community was not one. Whatever protection to
be afforded the Jewish (and other communities) would need to come from state
legislatures. Thus the Jewish communal traditional approach to law and social
action was turned on its head in the early districting cases. The rationale for entering as *amici* voting rights cases was along these lines.

//

A development in the voting-rights controversy—a side-show, really, but
nonetheless revealing in terms of Jewish communal response on matters related to

group rights—was President Clinton's April 1993 nomination of Lani Guinier to be Assistant Attorney General in the Department of Justice. Guinier, a professor at the University of Pennsylvania School of Law and for eight years a staff member of the NAACP Legal Defense and Education Fund, Inc., was tapped for a particularly sensitive position. Her work would largely involve enforcing the provisions of the Voting Rights Act. Based on her scholarly papers, Guinier appeared to advocate interpreting the Voting Rights Act so that it could require electoral results to be in direct proportion to the number of Blacks and other minorities in the population—in a nutshell, proportional representation, the hot button for the Jewish community. There was, however, a strong and legitimate disagreement over the interpretation of Guinier's writings, with Guinier herself saying that her writings did not advocate simple proportional representation, but offered a more nuanced theory.

The opening bell in the Guinier controversy was an April 1993 article in the Jewish weekly the *Forward*, in which this author noted that the Jewish community always had been committed to individual rather than group rights and cautioned, "The Jewish community has serious questions about a plan that suggests that any group is entitled to representation in numbers equal to the proportion of those numbers in the population." I added that there were serious ramifications for intergroup relations under such schemes.[57]

Some Jewish groups went even further in expressing reservations and even disapproval of the nominee. AJCongress, distinguishing between its stance on goals and timetables and stark proportional representation, characterized Guinier's views as "wrong, inconsistent with both statutory and constitutional provisions ...and simply bad public policy."[58] "The civil-rights agenda will not be helped by Professor Guinier's distortion of the Voting Rights Act," said the Union of Orthodox Jewish Congregations of America, "which would subordinate the broader consensus of wider coalitions to the ability of specially empowered interest groups to manipulate the political process."[59] The ADL likewise declined to support Guinier, citing the nominee's refusal to respond to a NJCRAC invitation on behalf of Jewish groups to meet with her to discuss her views on the Voting Rights Act. "Short of Professor Guinier's rejection or significant modification of her prior views, we would oppose her nomination."[60] AJC, AJCongress, and the ADL abstained from endorsing Guinier in a May 11 Leadership Conference on Civil Rights vote.

On 3 June 1993 President Clinton, after reading Guinier's writings and claiming to disagree with some of her views, withdrew his controversial nomination. Guinier herself insisted that she never said what people claimed she had. The issue appeared to be less Lani Guinier's position on voting rights issues, and more the Clinton Administration's refusal to permit the nominee to present her views publicly (or to meet with Jewish groups). The fact was that her writings on voting rights *were* complex, and ought not have been pigeonholed; nor was it accurate to characterize her as the "quota queen."[61]

Jewish groups, having spent weeks trying to define their positions on the

Guinier issue, heaved a collective sigh of relief. But allegations that the organized Jewish community had "sunk" the nomination soon surfaced, with many Blacks—not understanding, or caring about, the finer points of the Voting Rights Act—believing that the Jewish community was, in the words of an NAACP Legal Defense Fund official, "[r]aising hell over a Black nominee who was trying to increase Black political representation."

//

This quote is a good place to end. Perceptions continue to mask realities as both communities continue their efforts at negotiating race-based affirmative action. The careful distinctions crafted by the Supreme Court and Congress over two decades are being eroded by the radical political impulses of the 1990s. As America becomes an increasingly multi-ethnic and multi-religious society— 2300 religions and sects, at last count—our communal organizations need to make common cause to ensure equitable approaches toward the ending of barriers to discrimination, so that all people may make their fullest contribution to society.

APPENDIX

*National Jewish Community Relations Advisory Council
Position on Affirmative Action*

(adopted June 1975) as amended January 1981

We recognize that past discrimination and other deprivations leave their mark on future generations; that, in the words of the late President Lyndon B. Johnson, "Until we overcome unequal history, we cannot overcome unequal opportunity."

Members of racial, religious, ethnic and other groups have all too often been the victims of such unequal history in our country. American Indians are the victims of the most severe discrimination. By far the largest of the groups are the blacks, whose history in America began in slavery and has been marred—in law as well as in practice—by denial, deprivation and segregation solely because of race. Many Spanish-speaking persons, including Puerto Ricans, Mexican-Americans and other Hispanics, also are grossly discriminated against, as members of a group.

Sex discrimination, too, has long been practiced in our society, depriving women of equality of opportunity.

A just society has an obligation to seek to overcome the evils of past discrimination and other deprivations—inferior education, lack of training, inadequate preparation—by affording special help to its victims, so as to hasten their productive participation in society.

If it fails to do so, our society will harbor inequality for generations, with attendant increases in inter-group hostility. The security of Jews as a group will not be immune from those consequences.

We reaffirm our support of affirmative actions, by both government and the private sector, that provide:

(a) Compensatory education, training, retraining, apprenticeship, job counseling and placement, financial assistance and other forms of help for the deprived and disadvantaged, to enable them as speedily as possible to realize their potential capabilities for participation in the main stream of American life. The sole criterion of eligibility for such special services must be individual need: the services must not be limited or offered preferentially on the basis of race, color, national origin, religion, or sex.

(b) Intensive recruitment of qualified and qualifiable individuals, utilizing not only traditional referral sources, but all those public and private resources that reach members of disadvantaged groups.

(c) An ongoing review of established job and admissions requirements, including examinations and other selection methods, to make certain that they are performance-related and free of bias.

Among the relevant qualifications for certain posts in certain circumstances, a special ability to deal with a particular race or religion or ethnic group or sex may be one. However, we reject the proposition that race, color, or ethnicity is a qualification or disqualification for any post.

Merit and Qualification: We believe that individual merit is the touchstone of equality of opportunity. At the same time, we recognize that individual merit is not susceptible of precise mathematical definition and that test scores, however unbiased, are not the only relevant criteria for determining merit and qualifications. Also relevant in determining merit and qualifications are such factors as poverty, cultural deprivation, inadequate schooling, discrimination, or other deprivation in the individual's experience, as well as such personal characteristics as motivation, determination, perseverance, and resourcefulness; and we believe that all such factors should be taken into account.

Quotas: Experience has shown that implementation of affirmative action programs has resulted in practices that are inconsistent with the principle of nondiscrimination and the goal of equal opportunity such programs are designed to achieve. We oppose such practices, foremost among which is the use of quotas and proportional representation in hiring, upgrading, and admission of members of minority groups.*

We regard quotas as inconsistent with principles of equality; and as harmful in the long run to all, including those groups, some individual members of which may benefit from specific quotas under specific circumstances at specific times.

The government is responsible for vigorously enforcing affirmative action programs. It is equally responsible for preventing abuses in such programs. Measures to help meet these responsiblilities must be built into all affirmative action programs. We urge that steps be taken to assure that field personnel are familiar with this policy and comply with its provisions. Grievance procedures should be set up to provide speedy and effective adjudication of all complaints.

We recognize the need for numerical data and statistical procedures to measure and help assure the effectiveness of affirmative action programs. However, such data and procedures must not be used to conceal the application in fact of quotas or other discriminatory practices. Such information must be gathered and compiled without infringing upon the principles of privacy and nondiscrimination.

Periodic enumerations of work forces or student bodies, based on observation or other techniques, may properly be used to evaluate affirmative action policies, provided that (1) questions concerning race, color, ethnicity, place of birth, or religion do not appear on application forms, (2) individuals are at no time required to identify themselves by any of the above, and (3) no records of any individual's race, religion, or ethnic origin are maintained by an employer or educational institution.

*The NJCRAC Plenary Session has not taken any position, or ever voted, on the question of court orders directing the use of quotas for specified time periods in cases in which this is deemed by the court the only available remedy for systematic, sustained discrimination. A motion at the 1981 Plenary Session that such limited use of quotas not be opposed was tabled to a time certain, viz., the 1982 NJCRAC Plenary Session.

Notes

1. The author gratefully acknowledges the counsel of Arnold Aronson, formerly of the staff of the National Jewish Community Relations Advisory Council (NJCRAC); Marc D. Stern, whose insights and suggestions were of inestimable value in preparing this chapter; Albert D. Chernin, who suggested numerous points worthy of exploration; Martin J. Raffel; Dr. Leonard Cole; and David Szonyi for his editorial suggestions.

2. On Black anti-Semitism and Black-Jewish relations, see Jerome A. Chanes, *Antisemitism in America Today: Outspoken Experts Explode the Myths* (New York, 1995), chapters by Gary E. Rubin, Jonathan Rieder, and Jerome A. Chanes. *Cf.* in this regard Gary E. Rubin, "Rising Black-Jewish Tensions in the USA," *Analysis* 5 (November 1993):1–6.

3. *Report of the Citizen's Commission on Civil Rights* (June 1984).

4. For details on the PWA "minimum percentage clause," and for a useful capsule summary of early affirmative-action programs, see Robert J. Weiss, "Affirmative Action: A Brief History," *The Journal of Intergroup Relations* 15, 2 (Summer 1987): 40–53.

5. Noteworthy as one of the benchmarks in the history of affirmative action is Lyndon Johnson's 1961 speech at Howard University, in which he laid out a conceptual framework for affirmative action.

6. The "civil-rights" struggles of the 1930s surrounded the question of whether it was legitimate for government to force employers to abide by fair employment practice rules.

7. Later renamed the National Jewish Community Relations Advisory Council (NJCRAC).

8. The American Jewish Congress in the 1940s pioneered in the Jewish community the use of law and social action as vehicles for achieving societal aims. But the use of these techniques was not without controversy within the Jewish community; indeed, there were many voices who, citing the realities of a Jewish community that was not very well organized and that felt vulnerable, were opposed to the use of these techniques, which were viewed as confrontational.

9. NJCRAC, an umbrella body comprising thirteen national Jewish organizations (including the three Jewish "defense agencies" and the congregational bodies of the three American Jewish religious movements), and 117 community relations councils around the United States, develops consensus positions around issues on the public-affairs agenda, and serves as the national planning and coordinating body for Jewish public affairs. NJCRAC serves as the instrument for community relations for some 200 Jewish communities. To the extent that there is a Jewish "position" on

public-policy matters, that position is articulated in NJCRAC's annual *Joint Program Plan*.

10. As early as 1963, however, the American Jewish Committee had developed a "Statement on Quotas and Race Relations." (See note 19.)

11. 1969–70 *JPP*, p. 14.

12. The analysis was developed by Albert D. Chernin of the Philadelphia JCRC, and further explored by Benjamin Epstein of the Anti-Defamation League and Bert Gold of the American Jewish Committee, at the session on affirmative action at the 1971 NJCRAC Plenum Session.

13. The intensity of the debate was reflected in the fact that a roll-call vote was necessary to tally the votes of the delegates.

14. 1972–73 *JPP*, p. 23.

15. The Anti-Defamation League, the Jewish Labor Committee, and the Union of Orthodox Jewish Congregations of America were not in agreement with the recommended position on goals and timetables, and therefore dissented in the *Joint Program Plan*. (These agencies did not record a dissent at the Plenum.) The National Council of Jewish Women—flip-flopping through the years on affirmative action—did not formally dissent from the position, but during the debate joined those national agencies in opposing the position.

16. 1973–74 *JPP*, p. 35.

17. 1974–76 *JPP*, pp. 27–29.

18. "Among the relevant qualifications for certain posts in certain circumstances...a particular race or religious or ethnic group may be one," from 1973–74 *JPP*, p. 28. See as well 1970–71 *JPP*.

19. On this issue there was dissent by a number of NJCRAC agencies. See 1973–74 *JPP*, pp. 27–28.

20. See Appendix.

21. Marc D. Stern, "Affirmative Action, the Law, and the Jews," in *Survey of Jewish Affairs* 1990 (London: Institute of Jewish Affairs, 1990), 147–48.

22. See, for example, Larry M. Lavinsky, "Preferential Treatment: A Legal View," *ADL Bulletin* (January 1973): 1–2, 6–8.

23. ADL policy statements, October 1969 and January 1972.

24. American Jewish Committee, "Statement on Affirmative Action," 1977. AJC was the first of the agencies to take a stab at developing a cohesive approach to affirmative action. In November 1963, the AJC Executive Board issued a "Statement

on Quotas and Race Relations" that firmly came down on the side of individual, rather than group, rights. The early AJC statement called for an expansion of a number of federal education, employment, and housing programs in order to render "special assistance to special categories of people upon whom society has enforced special burdens."

25. American Jewish Congress, Resolution, 1974; interview with Marc D. Stern, 20 November 1995.

26. 1976 position statement.

27. NCJW 1985–87 National Resolutions.

28. Letter from Sandra Isenstein, national president, to *New York Jewish Week*, 14 April 1995.

29. Wisdom expressed in popular treatments such as Jonathan Kaufman's *Broken Alliance: The Turbulent Times Between Blacks and Jews in America* (New York, 1988), 217, 222–24, and *passim*, in which Kaufman lumps together the "defense" agencies as if they were marching in lockstep with respect to their positions.

30. Agudath Israel of America, American Jewish Committee, American Jewish Congress, Anti-Defamation League, Jewish Labor Committee, and Jewish War Veterans.

31. *Amsterdam News* (New York), 29 September 1973.

32. More than in *DeFunis*, in which no decision was rendered.

33. Interview with Arnold Aronson, 8 November 1995.

34. Again, the key distinction with respect to quotas needs to be drawn: the Jewish view of quotas as a means of keeping people out as against the "affirmative-action" view of letting people in.

35. NJCRAC 1980–81 *JPP*, p. 47.

36. Anti-Defamation League press release, 26 June 1985.

37. NJCRAC 1982–83 *JPP*, p. 36.

38. Marc D. Stern, "Affirmative Action, the Law, and the Jews," 156.

39. NAACP Statement, 22 August 1983.

40. ADL "Resolution on Affirmative Action: Court Ordered Preferential Relief," October 1987.

41. P. 34.

42. The Federal Equal Opportunity Act introduced in the 104th Congress (1995), sponsored by Senator Robert Dole (R-KS) and Representative Charles Canady

(R-FL), would eliminate all federal preference programs based on race, gender, and ethnicity.

43. *Adarand* held that federal affirmative-action programs must be "narrowly tailored" to address specific examples of discrimination. This landmark decision calls into question the validity of set-aside programs that are not predicated upon specific evidence of discrimination.

44. NJCRAC Consultation on Affirmative Action, April 1995.

45. A useful brief summary of the voting rights issue is Samuel Rabinove, *The Voting Rights Dilemma: The Legacy of Discrimination*, AJC Legal Papers (New York: The American Jewish Committee, 1994). For a more extended treatment, which unfortunately provides a narrative only to 1984, see Abigail M. Thernstrom, *Whose Votes Count? Affirmative Action and Minority Voting Rights* (Cambridge, MA, 1987).

46. The Voting Rights Act is based on Section 2 of the Fifteenth Amendment, empowering Congress to enforce the provisions of the amendment. The main provisions of the Voting Rights Act are:

1. Literacy tests and other devices found to be discriminatory as qualifications for voting in any federal, state, or local election, where the right to vote had been denied by race, were suspended.
2. Provided for federal examiners to conduct registration and observe voting in states and/or counties covered by the act (seven states plus two dozen discrete counties).
3. The U.S. Attorney General was directed to initiate suits to determine the constitutionality of poll taxes.
4. Civil and criminal protection was extended to qualified voters seeking to vote, as well as to those who urge or help others to vote.
5. When a state or political subdivision covered by the act seeks to change its voting qualifications or procedures from those in effect on 1 November 1964, it must obtain approval from the U.S. Attorney General or initiate a federal court suit.

47. That is, groups whose "members have less opportunity than other members of the electorate to participate in the political process and to elect representatives of their choice." Voting Rights Act of 1965, Title I, Section 2(b).

48. Even prior to the 1982 amendments, the Supreme Court in *United Jewish Organizations of Williamsburgh (UJO) v. Carey* had upheld the use of racial quotas to assure that non-whites had majorities in certain legislative districts. The Supreme Court said that whites in New York State had more-than-sufficient representation, suggesting, in effect, that the whites of (for example) Kingston were akin in their political, social, and economic needs to the Chasidic Jewish whites of Williamsburgh.

49. Although the American Jewish Congress developed its position on what it viewed as intrinsic flaws in the amendments, Jewish communal interests were not far afield in the minds of AJCongress leadership. (Interview with Marc D. Stern, 11 May 1993.)

50. From Voting Rights Act of 1965, as amended through 1982, Title I, Section 2.

51. The plan proposed by the Florida House of Representatives and rejected by the federal district court made an effort not only to comply with the twin Voting Rights Act mandates of "One person, one vote," and the requirement that minority groups have effective political voice, but also to give voice and representation to other groups in the area, including the Jewish community. The plan was unacceptable to the court, which viewed its mandate as *maximizing* the minority-group political voice.

52. NJCRAC 1994–95 *JPP*, p. 44.

53. The Supreme Court announced that it would review in its 1995–96 term districting cases from Texas and North Carolina, signaling that it might be ready, at long last, to address the tough questions surrounding "predominant factor" and to dispel some of the murkiness in which interpretations of the 1982 amendments are immersed. As of this writing (November 1995), *Bush v. Vera* and *Shaw v. Hunt* had not been decided.

54. One Jewish member of Congress, nine-term Democratic Representative Stephen J. Solarz of New York, was personally a victim of interpretation of the Voting Rights Act by the New York State Legislature when it redrew the 12th Congressional District based on 1990 census data. The district had been originally heavily Jewish, but now it was newly shaped as a Hispanic district, snaking through Manhattan, Brooklyn, and Queens, lurching from neighborhood to neighborhood to take in a Hispanic block or two. In a September 1992 primary Solarz lost to a Puerto-Rican challenger, one of five Democratic rivals, all Hispanic.

55. NJCRAC 1994–95 *JPP*, p. 44.

56. NJCRAC 1995–96 *JPP*, p. 45.

57. *Forward*, 7 April 1993.

58. American Jewish Congress press release, 26 May 1993.

59. UOJCA press release, 2 June 1993.

60. ADL press release, 26 May 1993.

61. Thus Clint Bolick, writing in the *Wall Street Journal*.

fifteen

AFFIRMATIVE ACTION

African American and Jewish Perspectives

THEODORE M. SHAW

In the annals of the struggle for racial justice in the United States, the alliance between African Americans and Jews has been particularly noteworthy. The Jewish community has contributed to the Civil Rights movement beyond its proportions, and some Jewish individuals have played extraordinary roles.[1] Additionally, Jewish organizations have been central players in the civil rights movement. In fact, it is not too much to say that the alliance between African Americans and Jews is one of the great stories of the struggle for civil rights in the United States, indeed, "the movement."[2] Yet in recent years that alliance has been tested; some claim that it has fallen apart.[3]

The relationship between African Americans and Jews does not lend itself to sweeping analyses. While tensions have arisen over the issues of affirmative action and redistricting, even on these issues the Jewish community has not been of one mind. This article examines the controversies surrounding the redistricting battles that have followed the Supreme Court's ruling in *Shaw v. Reno*, especially as they have played out between some organizations (primarily the A.D.L.) and individuals within the Jewish community and those in the black community who have been attempting to preserve the political gains achieved pursuant to the Voting Rights Act. To the extent that there has been opposition to redistricting that produces "majority-minority" districts, it occurs within the context of some disagreement within and between the black and Jewish communities and their representative organization."While it would be unfair to call Jews the financial mainstay of the civil rights movement, as some have said, in proportion to the population they have been overrepresented among the financial supporters of civil rights."

In a sense, Jewish opposition is not particularly remarkable. Support for affirmative action and minority political empowerment is on the decline; the charge made by the Supreme Court in 1883 in *The Civil Rights Cases*, that African Americans were seeking a privileged status as "a special favorite of the laws," is once again in vogue, and a period eerily reminiscent of the post-Reconstruction era has been ushered in, with racial recidivism in the courts and in the social order. In the mind's eye of many African Americans, 1996 looks very much like 1896.[4] In a series of rulings beginning in 1993, the Supreme Court has allowed white voters, in southern states with long histories of racial discrimination and continued exclusion of minorities from full participation in the political process, to attack congressional districts drawn pursuant to the Voting Rights Act. The Court has also made it more difficult to maintain federal minority contracting affirmative action programs; federal affirmative action is now subject to strict scrutiny,[5] the most exacting standard of judicial review, which has been applied to local and state affirmative action programs since 1989.[6] Purporting to follow the themes voiced by the Supreme Court in the voting rights and minority contracting cases, the U.S. Court of Appeals for the Fifth Circuit has declared race based affirmative action in university admissions to be unconstitutional. In 1978, in *Board of Regents of the University of California v. Bakke*, the Supreme Court ruled that while quotas are unconstitutional, race can be one factor among others considered by admissions offices in pursuit of intellectual diversity, as long as educational institutions considered all applicants for all positions regardless of race. *Bakke* has provided the formulation on which colleges, universities, and graduate and professional schools throughout the nation have admitted minority students even though their test scores or GPA's may be lower than some white students who are admitted. In *Hopwood v. State of Texas* (1996), the Fifth Circuit has said that *Bakke* is no longer good law, if it ever was, and that race can *never* be taken into consideration in admissions without a specific finding of racial discrimination. The Supreme Court declined to review *Hopwood*.[7]

The stakes for African Americans are extremely high. Employment opportunities, political representation, economic development and educational opportunities are all at risk. If the current era represents "the second Redemption", i.e., an end to expanding opportunities brought about by the Civil Rights Movement, more difficult days are ahead for African Americans. Who will be their allies? Some Jewish organizations and individuals in academia, the media and politics are outspoken opponents of affirmative action. In the new millennium America the black-Jewish alliance of the halcyon days of the Civil Rights Movement may be a thing of the past; African Americans, historically the most despised group in America, may be isolated in their struggle for racial and economic justice.

Yet, why should the black-Jewish relationship be the subject of special attention? What is it about Jews that deserves sorting them out from other white people with respect to their relationship with blacks?

The issue of black-Jewish relationships is hopelessly shrouded in confusion, misunderstanding and ahistoricism. The simplistic view is that African Americans and Jews share common interests because of their respective histories as oppressed peoples. The Old Testament story of Moses leading his people out of bondage in Egypt has always had deep resonance for black people in America. When the slaves sang "Go down Moses, way down in Egypt land, tell Old Pharaoh let my people go," their song was a prayer for liberation. blacks and Jews share common enemies: the Ku Klux Klan and other white supremacist organizations target blacks and Jews in the same breath. If the old maxim "The enemy of my enemy is my friend" survives, surely blacks and Jews must be allies.

On a purely principled basis, blacks and Jews do share a common interest. Justice *is* indivisible. It is not possible to claim with any integrity that one is opposed to racism as a matter of principle without being opposed to anti-semitism, or vice versa. They are two heads on the same monster. But we do not live in a world of pure principle. There is racism in the Jewish community; there is anti-semitism in the black community. Many black Americans see Jews as a super-empowered and wealthy minority who are, at the end of the day, still white and therefore part of the class of race-privileged Americans. Still others have bought into the ugly ideology of anti-semitism and the stereotypes that serve that ideology. Many black Americans, peering up from the bottom, cannot comprehend the insecurities that plague Jews regardless of how privileged and powerful they may have become. They lose sight of the fact that privilege and power did not protect European Jews in the 1920s, 1930s and 1940s, or that not all Jews are privileged and powerful. Perhaps there is even the belief that anti-semitism within the black community cannot really threaten Jews given the relative powerlessness of the black community.

Jews, on the other hand, *are* white.[8] Their relationship with African Americans has been very complex, but for the most part it has not been one of equals. Jews were among the storeowners, landlords and employers in communities in which they interacted with African Americans.[9] Their involvement in the early Civil Rights Movement and in civil rights organizations working on behalf of African Americans was not limited to the role of supporters; often they were among the leaders. There were no comparable roles for African Americans in the affairs of the Jewish community.

In part this unevenness is a manifestation of the different experiences of African Americans and Jews in the United States. Whatever the experience of Jews with anti-semitic discrimination, they have nonetheless attained success in education, politics, and business to a degree disproportionate to their numbers.[10] The issue of Jewish empowerment is dangerous ground for those outside of the Jewish community. It is also a point of some uneasiness within the Jewish community. Still, there is no denying that Jews have attained positions of power previously denied to them. J. J. Goldberg, for example, notes that in 1995 there were nine Jews in the U.S. Senate and twenty-four Jews in the House of Representatives. In addition, according to Martin Lipset and Earl Raab, during the last three decades Jews have made up twenty-six percent of reporters, editors, and executives at major print and broadcast media, fifty-nine percent of the writers, producers, and directors on the fifty top grossing motion pictures, forty percent of the partners in leading law firms in New York and Washington, sixteen of the top forty on the Forbes 400 and twenty-three percent of the total list, seven and a half percent of senior executives of the nation's largest businesses, and thirteen percent of executives under 40.[11] Without begrudging one iota of these extraordinary accomplishments, and with a keen sensitivity to the way in which anti-semites and hatemongers may distort and manipulate the significance of these statistics, it is nonetheless true that the relative empowerment positions of the black and Jewish communities, and how that power is achieved, may inform the substantive disputes between the two communities around affirmative action and redistricting in a way that sheds light on a fundamental change in that relationship.

For Jews the idea of "meritocracy" works. And for Jews, the possibility of consistently winning political support of non-Jews has meant that they have attained significant representation in Congress and in other legislative bodies. For Jews in the political process, coalition building is not just a possibility, it is the name of the game. For African Americans, particularly in the South, the stubborn persistence of racial polarization in the political process has meant that, with rare exceptions, black candidates could not win political elections in majority white electoral districts. Race remains the great American divide, and it simply affects African Americans in a way which is not duplicated for any other group.[12]

For African Americans, the notion of "meritocracy" is not sacrosanct, for experience has shown them that regardless of merit, race has been an impediment to opportunity. Moreover, structural inequality along racial fault lines exist from the moment of birth, so that supposedly objective measures of merit and ability ultimately reflect something other than who is truly deserving of opportunity. Usually they reflect the benefits of privilege, in a self reifying process of unnatural selection that becomes enshrined as "merit."

Thus Jews and African Americans come to the issue of affirmative action from different experiences. Yet Jews' status as another minority group that has experienced American discrimination means that the opposition of some Jews to affirmative action has special resonance. Jews have been prominent among the leading voices of American liberalism, and "liberals" have been important voices on the issues of race. The Jewish experience with American discrimination informs their views on affirmative action, particularly in the critical effort to define it. The struggle over definition is, of course, half the battle. In the "linguistic reductionism" that dominates current political discourse, its opponents assert that affirmative action means "quotas." In the battle for public opinion they know that if they can sell this "affirmative action equals quotas" argument, they win.

The concept of quotas understandably elicits strong negative reaction from some Jews. In the early part of this century, discrimination against Jews was open and notorious. Many of the nation's most prestigious colleges and universities led the way in imposing ceiling quotas on Jewish enrollment and employment. Quotas were exclusionary and odious; they were maintained for the purpose of excluding Jews who were otherwise qualified from educational and employment opportunities. Quotas and other forms of discrimination against Jews were part of an American caste system in which anti-semitism was a significant part. Consequently, the abolition of quotas was an important element of the remedy for discrimination against Jews. In the Jewish anti-discrimination paradigm, quotas are anathema. With the elimination of ceiling quotas, Jews experienced increased educational, occupational, and economic success.

If J. J. Goldberg is correct in contending that Jews are now well-represented among America's power elite and that, while anti-semitism persists, it is more episodic than structural, then Jewish opposition to affirmative action is unremarkable. It is not worthy of special attention because it reflects a waning of the importance of Jewish identity to the affirmative action struggle in which Jewishness is incidental to white-ness. The focus on Jewish opposition to affirmative action is therefore misplaced. When Jewish individuals and institutions oppose affirmative action, their opposition must be viewed within the context of their position as beneficiaries of white privilege and as part of the mainstream, if not the power elite. The Jewish experience with discrimination may bring little of special value to the discussion of race-based affirmative action, although some Jews and Jewish institutions do claim to have special voice as opponents of affirmative action. The Anti-Defamation League's involvement in the Congressional redistricting cases following *Shaw v. Reno* is but one example.[13]

In Georgia no African American was elected to Congress in the Twentieth Century until Andy Young in 1974. In 1992 Cynthia McKinney was elected from Georgia's Eleventh Congressional District. White voters then challenged the state's congressional districting plan in *Miller v. Johnson*, and the Anti-Defamation League (ADL) filed an amicus brief in support of the plaintiffs. Racially polarized voting, i.e. the persistent refusal on the part of white voters to vote for black candidates, regardless of qualifications, precluded the election of black representatives in Georgia as it did elsewhere in the South and in the Nation. Under the Voting Rights Act of 1965 and its 1982 amendments, the Supreme Court has held that where a racial minority group is sufficiently large in number, is geographically compact enough, is politically cohesive enough, and has experienced racially polarized voting against its candidates of choice, districts must be drawn to allow them a fair chance to participate meaningfully in the electoral process. In practice this has meant that where these four preconditions, which the Supreme Court set forth in *Thornburg v. Gingles*, are met, legislatures have been required to draw "majority-minority" districts.[14]

In the Supreme Court's 1993 decision in *Shaw v. Reno*, the Court ruled that white voters in North Carolina could sue under the equal protection clause of the Fourteenth Amendment, even if they cannot make the traditionally requisite showing of vote dilution. Writing for the Court, Justice O'Connor referred to

North Carolina's Eleventh Congressional District, which elected African American Mel Watt, as "bizarre", and stated:

> A reapportionment plan that includes in one district individuals who belong to the same race, but who are otherwise widely separated by geographical and political boundaries, and who may have little in common with one another but the color of their skin, bears an uncomfortable resemblance to political apartheid.

In Justice O'Connor's view, the creation of majority black congressional districts such as the one at issue in *Shaw* frustrated "the multiracial, multireligious communities that our Constitution seeks to weld together as one."[15] The 5–4 majority in *Shaw* also opined that creating majority-minority districts reinforces the perception that members of the same racial group, regardless of their age, education, economic status, or community in which they live—think alike, share the same political interests, and will prefer the same candidates at the polls and that "[w]hen a district obviously is created solely to effectuate the perceived common interests of one racial group, elected officials are more likely to believe that their primary obligation is to represent only members of that group, rather than their constituency as a whole." Although the injuries traditionally alleged before federal court jurisdiction was exercised in voting rights cases were not present in *Shaw*, Justice O'Connor explained that under the new "analytically distinct" cause of action the Court was recognizing, the challenged reapportionment legislation "reinforces racial stereotypes and threatens to undermine our system of representative democracy by signaling to elected officials that they represent a particular racial group rather than their constituency as a whole." Thus, "[r]acial gerrymandering, even for remedial purposes, may balkanize us into competing racial factions; it threatens to carry us further from the goal of a political system in which race no longer matters—a goal that the Fourteenth and Fifteenth Amendments embody, and to which the nation continues to aspire."[16]

The Supreme Court's *Shaw* opinion has opened the floodgates to litigation by white plaintiffs who have launched a widespread attack on political empowerment of African Americans and Latinos that was accomplished pursuant to the Voting Rights Act. The ill-founded assumptions lurking in the *Shaw* opinion are well imbedded in social and political discourse, and trial court judges have openly expressed hostility to the Voting Rights Act and its political progeny. The ironies and fallacies are obvious. In the name of protecting African Americans from being stereotyped, the federal courts are striking down districts that provide them with opportunities to elect candidates from their communities.[17] *Shaw* was remanded to the three-judge trial court after the Supreme Court determined that white voters could challenge districts that are so "bizarre" in appearance that they can be interpreted as attempts to "segregate" voters among congressional districts. After a trial the court ruled that while the challenged districts did look "bizarre," there was a compelling state interest supporting the district and it was therefore constitutional.[18] The Supreme Court, however, in its second ruling on the *Shaw* case, invalidated North Carolina's redistricting plan "because the State's reapportionment scheme is not narrowly tailored to serve a compelling state interest.[19]

Meanwhile, congressional redistricting cases from other states proceeded. In 1995, the Supreme Court heard oral argument in *United States v. Hays* and *Miller v. Johnson*. In the former case the Supreme Court avoided a ruling simply on the merits of the case, by determining that the plaintiffs did not have standing to sue because they did not live in Louisiana's challenged District 4, represented by Cleo Fields (only the second African American congressman from Louisiana since Reconstruction). The Court's standing decision did not have any lasting significant impact on the *Hays* litigation. On remand the lawyers representing the plaintiffs simply intervened another group of white voters and the three-judge federal court moved quickly to afford them the same relief as they had earlier provided to the original plaintiffs.[20] In *Miller* the Supreme Court went beyond its *Shaw* decision that white plaintiffs could challenge majority-minority districts that had a "bizarre" appearance. The Court now ruled that bizarreness was simply one indication that a district may be unconstitutional; where race was the predominant factor in the creation of a district, even if it did not look bizarre, white voters could also maintain a constitutional challenge.[21] In all significant respects, the Supreme Court's *Miller* opinion adopted the ADL position.

After remand in *Miller* the three-judge federal court allowed additional white plaintiffs to intervene to challenge Georgia's second congressional district represented by Sanford Bishop, an African American. Georgia conceded the unconstitutionality of the second district, thus leaving the fifth, represented by Civil Rights Movement veteran John Lewis, as the only district in the State with an African American representative. Drunk with the wine of success, the white plaintiffs in Georgia attempted to expand their attack on black political empowerment by attacking twenty state legislative districts that were majority black. Although the federal court did not allow them to challenge the state redistricting plan in the federal redistricting lawsuit, lawyers for the white opponents of majority-minority districts filed a separate lawsuit that led to the invalidation of six state legislative districts.

Three Congressional districts in Texas, two in Georgia, one in Louisiana, and one in Florida have been declared unconstitutional. Challenges in the states of Virginia, New York, and Illinois are pending. Two congressional districts in North Carolina, while upheld by the federal trial courts, are at risk on appeal to the U.S. Supreme Court. In addition to Georgia, challenges to state legislative redistricting schemes have been brought in Florida, South Carolina, and Texas. In North Carolina, white voters have filed *Shaw* and *Miller* type claims aimed at decreasing black representation on the Durham County School Board. In Arkansas, white voters attempted to undo a court-ordered redistricting plan that resolved long-standing litigation concerning judicial elections. In sum, since the Supreme Court decided *Shaw v. Reno* in 1993, white voters have attacked electoral plans which have afforded minority political opportunities on the congressional, state, and local levels. Each success encourages more challenges. Unless the federal courts signal a halt, or at least some limitations on the assault on majority-minority districts, political opportunities for African Americans, especially in southern jurisdictions, will be significantly curtailed. This is the context in which the ADL's brief in *Miller v. Johnson* must be considered.

The backdrop against which the ADL's decision to support white plaintiffs in *Miller v. Johnson* must be viewed extends beyond the merits of the Georgia case. Tensions between African Americans and Jews were evident in *United Jewish Organizations of Williamsburgh (U.J.O.) v. Carey*, which the Supreme Court decided in 1977. *U.J.O.* involved a challenge to a New York State legislative redistricting scheme which split a Hasidic Jewish community in the Williamsburgh section of Brooklyn that had previously formed a majority of the voters in a state senate district. Prior to the adoption of the new plan, Hasidic Jews were concentrated in an assembly district that was 39 percent white and in a Senate district that was 63 percent white. The Justice Department exercised authority under Section 5 of the Voting Rights Act and rejected New York's 1972 redistricting plan because the legislature failed to demonstrate that the redistricting had neither the purpose nor effect of abridging the right to vote for reasons of race or color. The Hasidic plaintiffs argued that the challenged plan diluted the value of their franchise in order to achieve a racial quota, and that they were assigned to electoral districts solely on the basis of race.[22]

The Supreme Court ruled, contrary to the arguments of the *U.J.O.* plaintiffs, that neither the Fourteenth nor the Fifteenth Amendment prohibited consideration of race by legislatures seeking to comply with the Voting Rights Act. Moreover, the plaintiffs could not successfully claim that they suffered a constitutional injury because white voters continued to hold more than a proportionate share of the state legislative seats. The Court rejected the plaintiffs' quota arguments and further ruled that the legislature could constitutionally employ numerical objectives in attempting to assure that groups protected under the Voting Rights Act are afforded a fair opportunity to choose their political representatives.

The Court's decision in *U.J.O.* reflected nuances and tensions between African American and Jews that reveal fundamental differences in how each group negotiates its status as a minority. The *U.J.O.* plaintiffs eschewed any attempt to seek special recognition within the political process even as they complained that the challenged legislative districting plan "diluted the value of their franchise." Since the plan left white voters over-represented, the dilution claim could not have been based on their status as white voters; it must have been a reference to their status as Jewish voters. Thus, in spite of their disclaimer that they were not seeking "permanent recognition as a community in legislative reapportionment," and even as they argued that race should not be considered in the districting process, the *U.J.O.* plaintiffs advanced a claim aimed at protecting their political interest as Jews.[23]

The legal ambiguities in the *U.J.O.* plaintiffs' claims mirror an apparent inconsistency in the manner in which Jews opposed to majority-minority electoral districts (or for that matter, affirmative action in employment or education) argue that color blindness empties African Americans' race and its attendant historical experiences of any content worthy of special recognition or treatment even as their Jewish-ness is a point of religious, cultural and historical identity and provides the lens through which they see the world.[24] Jews' historical experience, culminating in the Holocaust, as an of oppressed, often hated minority is in part the *raison d'etre* for the Nation-State of Israel. While pre-Holocaust Zionists asserted a biblical and historical claim to Palestine, Israel also exists as the result of a brutal genocidal experience which Jews have pledged never to allow to happen again. Thus, like African Americans, Jews' common interests are founded, at least in part, on their status as an oppressed minority group.[25] When some Jews argue that majority-minority districts for African Americans constitute unfair discrimination against white (or Jewish) Americans and that African Americans have no common interests that demand protection in view of historical and continuing racial discrimination in the political process and elsewhere in American life, their opposition reflects an approach to individual/group identity issues that is very different from that applied to matters of concern to the Jewish community. The ADL engaged in precisely this contradiction when it filed its amicus brief in *Miller*.[26]

The ADL's amicus curiae brief in *Miller* stated that it "submits this brief to advance its conviction that redistricting substantially motivated by racial considerations impairs the liberties secured by the Equal Protection Clause of the Fourteenth Amendment to the United States Constitution." In the ADL's view, "such state action offends core equal protection principles, is inimical to democratic values, and undermines the fundamental importance of the franchise to our society and democratic system of government."[27] The ADL's position in *Miller* was vindicated by a 5–4 vote of the Court. It is, however, like the Supreme Court's analysis, flawed in that it ignores the entire context in which majority-minority districts are drawn pursuant to the Voting Rights Act, and in that it views the interests and participation of African Americans voters in a bizarre fashion. Like the Court, the ADL simply ignores the overwhelming power of racial bloc voting by white voters. In jurisdiction after jurisdiction in state after state throughout the South, African American candidates had never been elected to Congress or to state and local offices before the advent of the Voting Rights Act. Louisiana is not atypical. In Louisiana, since Reconstruction, no black candidate has been elected to Congress from a majority white district; no black candidate has been elected to the state legislature from a majority white district. No black person has been elected to statewide office. And in 1991, if left to the majority (55 percent) of white voters, David Duke would have been elected Governor of Louisiana.[28]

Racially polarized voting[29] similar to that which has dominated and continues to dominate Louisiana politics is not the exception in the South; it is the rule. Nor is racially polarized voting strictly a Southern phenomenon. Only two of the forty African American members of the 104th Congress were elected from majority white districts; in the Twentieth Century only two African Americans have served in the U.S. Senate. Are African Americans who seek the creation of a few majority-minority districts, as long as racially polarized voting continues to guarantee that no one from their community will be elected to Congress or to other legislatures, advancing a "constitutionally indefensible" position, in the words of the Washington Legal Foundation? Why does the creation of majority-minority districts presume "that only a member of a certain race can or will effectually represent his or her constituents?" Do majority white districts, in which racial bloc voting by white voters negates any opportunity for black candidates to win elected office, rest on the same presumption—"that only a member of a certain race can or will effectively represent his or her constituents?" The vast majority of candidates for whom black voters cast ballots are white, as are the vast majority of elected officials who represent black voters. Moreover, there is a long history of majority black jurisdictions electing white representatives.[30]

In the absence of majority black districts, Congress and other legislative bodies on the state and local level would be virtually all white. If African Americans feel that there should be some electoral districts in America where they have a majority because to quote Golda Meir, "as a minority, we have quite a history," is that, in the Washington Legal Foundation's words, "inimical to democratic values," and is it really true that it "undermines the fundamental importance of the franchise to our society and to our democratic system of government?" Are "bizarre" looking majority black districts and districts where race was consciously considered to assure that minorities could elect their representatives of choice more a threat to democracy than a racially segregated Congress? Is drawing majority-minority districts to counter white bloc voting really "doing violence to fundamental constitutional precepts," as the ADL argues?[31] The race problem in American politics is not rooted in the insistence on the part of black voters that they have electoral districts where they are guaranteed that black candidates will automatically win; what they seek is districts where they will have an *opportunity* to win. The problem is the persistence of racism on the part of white voters that, left unchecked, continues to marginalize black voters and deny them the opportunity for full participation in the democratic electoral process.

//

There is a contradiction, even a hypocrisy, concerning the legal, social, and political discourse about race today. Anyone reading the Supreme Court's opinion in *Shaw v. Reno*, where it in effect accuses the proponents of majority-minority congressional districts of advocating "political apartheid" and racial balkanization, frustrating "the multiracial, and multireligious communities that our

Constitution seeks to weld together as one," would think that the Constitution has been interpreted to affirmatively promote racial desegregation. The plaintiffs in each of the challenges to majority-minority districts have never taken a single action to promote housing or school desegregation; most of the other critics of majority-minority districts have never done so either. As a nation, we have virtually given up on school desegregation, and "socially engineered" housing segregation dominates demographic patterns across the country.[32] Although white Americans flee schools and neighborhoods populated by black people, they are deeply offended when African Americans voluntarily embrace racial segregation. While majority-minority electoral districts cannot fairly be described as "segregation" (in spite of the Supreme Court's insistence otherwise), it is nonetheless ironic, at best, that when black people seek to empower themselves within the segregated communities that white Americans have created, they are accused of promoting racial "balkanization" and "political apartheid."

Just as unfair is the argument that majority-minority districts are hurting Democrats by concomitantly causing adjacent congressional districts to become more white, and thus more conservative.[33] Whatever the merits of that charge may be, why must black people be the ballast for the Democratic Party? Why do the critics not ask why white voters, left to their own devices, elect representatives with conservative agendas that these same critics apparently believe are undesirable? Why is the focal point of their ire not the white voters? No other community is asked to forego any meaningful opportunity to elect candidates from its midst; why expect black voters to do so? And as for the argument that majority black districts ultimately frustrate the interests of black communities (an argument that at least admits that such interests exists) because their elected representatives simply become a minority within a minority party, in many southern jurisdictions the election of white Democrats has not guaranteed that those interests will be protected.

As for African Americans and Jews, for the most part majority-minority districts do not present constant conflicts, since they have primarily been attacked in the South.[34] Nonetheless, redistricting has been a flashpoint of tensions for the two communities. Early in his Administration's tenure, President Bill Clinton nominated University of Pennsylvania law professor and former NAACP Legal Defense Fund voting rights lawyer Lani Guinier to be Assistant Attorney General of the Civil Rights Division of the U.S. Department of Justice. Conservative lawyer Clint Bolick was granted a platform by the *Wall Street Journal's* editorial staff to engage in an unprincipled attack on Professor Guinier that distorted her writings and her career into the label "Quota Queen." Guinier had written some law review articles suggesting a way out of the quandary of geographic districting that relied heavily on racial residential segregation. Her articles suggested consideration of alternative schemes such as cumulative voting, which has been adapted in some American jurisdictions and is commonplace in other democracies. In addition to the advantage of breaking the link between residential segregation, cumulative voting schemes challenge the proposition that the best form of democracy is one in which winners and losers are determined by who gets 51 percent or more and who gets 49 percent or less of the vote. Whatever the merits of such proposal, Guinier's articles were squarely within the parameters of the kinds of intellectual inquires undertaken by law school professors and, moreover, were aimed at decreasing racial polarization.

Unfortunately, Bolick's distortions were given currency, and some individuals within the Jewish community furthered the misinterpretation of her writings. Jerome Chanes, of the National Jewish Community Relations Advisory Council (NJCRAC), claims credit for sounding "the opening bell in an article in the Jewish weekly, *Forward*, against Professor Guinier's nomination, purportedly because she was advancing the goal of 'proportionate representation.'" The American Jewish Congress and the Union of Orthodox Jewish Congregations of America took public positions opposing Guinier's nomination consistent with, if not based on, the Bolick-Chanes distortions of the meaning of her writings.[35]

//

So we have come full circle. Once again at the turn of a new century, the Supreme Court has capped an era of racial retrenchment with a series of decisions limiting the scope of civil rights protection for African Americans. Once again the nation seems to be receding from the high water mark of black political representation and participation. Once again the issue of race (this time exacerbated by the class line) looms large before us. Once again African Americans are being chastised for seeking protection as "the special favorite of the laws."

Who will stand with African Americans in their efforts to achieve the full measure of American life? If Jews pursue the goal of a "color blind" society in which there can be no recognition of common interests among African Americans on the theory that such recognition will stereotype them, even while Jews and other ethnic groups pursue their common interests within the pluralistic American polity, the alliance that ushered in the modern Rights Era will not be repeated. Perhaps the passage of Jews from a status where Jewish-ness set them apart from the mainstream and led them to challenge exclusion based on religion and race to a status where white-ness places them among those whose interest is in maintaining the *status quo* has made the old coalition obsolete.

But perhaps African Americans and Jews can rediscover some common ground in some principled place. Perhaps we can all find some common ground there.

Notes

1. A chronicle of those contributions is beyond the scope of this article and, in any event, is well known by those with even a passing interest on the subject of black-Jewish relationships. Of particular note are the stories of philanthropist Julius

Rosenwald, N.A.A.C. P. Board members Rabbi Stephen Wise and Joel and Arthur Spingarn, N.A.A.C.P. legal strategist Nathan Margold, the American Jewish Congress' Will Maslow, N.A.A.C.P. Legal Defense Fund lawyer and Director-Counsel Jack Greenberg, Stanley Levison, a close friend and advisor to Dr. Martin Luther King, Jr., Arnold Aronson of the Leadership Conference on Civil Rights, and civil rights workers Andrew Goodman and Michael Schwerner, who lost their lives in Philadelphia, Mississippi during Freedom Summer, 1964. It has been estimated that almost half of the young white civil rights volunteers who travelled to the South during the Civil Rights Movement were Jewish.

2. In *Jewish Power, Inside the American Jewish Establishment* (New York, 1996), J. J. Goldberg argues that "[a] formal alliance of Jewish and black organizations orchestrated the post-Second World War civil rights campaign that led to equal-rights laws in dozens of states, and finally to the Federal Civil Rights and Voting Rights acts of the mid 1960s." (p. 24).

3. See Jonathan Kaufman, *Broken Alliance: The Turbulent Times Between Blacks and Jews in America* (New York, 1988).

4. In 1896 the Supreme Court decided *Plessy v. Ferguson*, which finally closed the book on the Reconstruction era and ushered in the "separate but equal" regime that was not overturned until *Brown v. Board of Education* in 1954.

5. *Adarand Construction Company v. Peña* (1995).

6. *City of Richmond, v. J. A. Croson Co.* (1989).

7. Ironically, because discrimination on the basis of gender is subject to intermediate scrutiny, and race is subject to strict scrutiny, the effect of the Fifth Circuit's ruling is that it is more difficult to pursue affirmative action on behalf of African Americans, the class of people for whom the Fourteenth Amendment was originally enacted, than it is on behalf of white women.

8. Of course, there are nonwhite Jews and even black Jews. They are relatively few in number, however, and for the purpose of this analysis are not germane.

9. A personal note: As a young boy in Harlem of the late 1950s and early 1960s, I can remember many Jewish owned stores and shops, especially along 125th Street. The relationship between Jewish store owners and the black community was multifaceted: storeowner-patron, employer-employee, outsider-insider, sometimes friendly and sometimes antagonistic.

Later in the Bronx, I lived in a public housing project a few miles from Parkchester, then a huge all-white, heavily Jewish, highly desirable housing complex owned by Metropolitan Life Insurance Company. Through the early sixties, black people were not allowed to live in Parkchester. My paternal grandmother, who did domestic work, was employed by a Jewish family in Parkchester, and by several other Jewish families throughout New York City. Her relationships with her various employers typified the range of black-white (and in this case, Jewish) relationships at the places where the races touched. In some instances, my grandmother's employers were distant, condescending and even exploitative. In others, she was embraced as a part (to the extent an employee can be) of the family. Like many black women who were domestic workers, my grandmother not only cooked, cleaned, washed, ironed and scrubbed, she also provided a great deal of care for the children of those families, whose clothes would eventually be handed down to my siblings and to me (for which we were eternally grateful). Whatever these relationships were (and they were many things), they were not the relationships of equals.

10. This success is exaggerated by those who harbor anti-semitic views, who claim that Jews control Congress, the media, Hollywood, higher education, the Federal Reserve System, and other power centers. Similar claims punctuated the political rhetoric of pre-World War II Germany and were the basis for anti-semitic fervor.

11. See Goldberg, pp. 46 and 280. For Lipset and Raab, see *Jews and the New American Scene* (Cambridge, MA, 1995), pp. 25–28.

12. This is not to say that African Americans occupy any place of primacy as victims of discrimination. To assert that one experience is unique does not mean that it is more important than another. Those who play the game of comparative victimization status engage in a senseless and foolish exercise. It is not possible to compare any experience with the Holocaust, just as it is impossible to honestly assert that any experience was more destructive to a people or to a nation than American slavery. Moreover, whatever power one may seek in victimization status is illusory. Discrimination and oppression do not breed real power; but they do require remediation.

13. It is no more true to say that all Jews are opposed to affirmative action then it is to say that all African Americans support it. The Jewish community is split on affirmative action issues, with many of its important voices in support. However, many other prominent Jews and some leading Jewish organizations have opposed affirmative action measures, and there is a common perception of a significant rift between African Americans and Jews over the issue.

14. The term "majority-minority" is not always an accurate representation of the composition of these districts. For example, at the time *Vera v. Richards* was filed, Texas' Thirtieth Congressional District in Dallas, represented by Congresswoman Eddie Bernice Johnson, was a forty-seven percent black voting age population district. White voters successfully challenged its constitutionality in *Vera v. Richards,* in which the Supreme Court during its 1995–96 term, ruled that it and two other majority-minority districts (Houston's 18th and 29th) were illegally drawn.

Even where majority black districts are less than 50% white often they are among the most racially integrated districts in the nation. North Carolina's 11th, for example, was 53 percent black; Cynthia McKinney's district, declared unconstitutional in Georgia, was 63 percent black.

15. One wonders to what constitutional command Justice O'Connor's opinion referred. While her opinion quoted Justice Douglas' dissent in *Wright v. Rockefeller,* the Supreme Court has never held that the Constitution encompassed an affirmative right to an integrated society. The Fourteenth Amendment's equal protection clause, and for that matter all other constitutional and statutory provisions addressing racial discrimination, are prohibitions against discrimination, not commands to weld together "multiracial, multireligious communities."

Lawyers for minority plaintiffs in school and housing desegregation cases have faced high and often insurmountable barriers when they seek to weld together multiracial communities. See, for example, *Milliken v. Bradley* (1974) and *Missouri v. Jenkins* (1995).

16. See 125 L.E2d 511 at 529; 125L.E2d of 530, 532; 125 L.E2d at 535.

17. The Supreme Court and lower federal courts have credited the arguments by white plaintiffs in the *Shaw* line of cases that majority-minority electoral districts stereotype African Americans by assuming they all think alike. It is somewhat anomalous that white plaintiffs who have no demonstrated history of concern about the well-being of African Americans (as evidenced by their own depositions taken in these cases) should presume to have the standing to determine that this "stereotype," which does not inevitably follow as a consequence of majority-minority districts, is more harmful than the submersion of black voters' political influence in white racial bloc voting. Even more troubling is the Supreme Court's embrace of these dubious concerns.

18. Under Supreme Court jurisprudence, governmental actions that infringe upon "fundamental rights" (such as speech, privacy or the exercise of religion) or that involve "suspect classifications" (e.g. race, ethnicity or national origin) are subject to "strict scrutiny." They can survive only if they are necessary to meet a "compelling state interest," usually to remedy past discrimination, and even then the remedy must be "narrowly tailored" to minimize its effect on others. See *Kovematsu v. United States* (1944).

19. *Shaw v. Hunt* (1996).

20. Although the Supreme Court ruled that the original plaintiffs did not have standing, it was the wrong standing decision. The correct standing decision would have applied the pre-existing case law and determined that plaintiffs could not demonstrate a concrete injury that justified the exercise of a federal court's jurisdiction. Justices White and Stevens in *Shaw* and Justice Stevens in the Georgia case, *Miller v. Johnson,* dissented on the ground that plaintiffs had not demonstrated that they were injured and thus lacked standing. One amicus brief, submitted by the Washington Legal Foundation, argued the remarkable proposition that white plaintiffs suffered an injury "regardless whether the 'threat' to representative democracy comes to pass or whether elected officials catch the 'signal' that they have been sent regarding who (sic) they are supposed to be representing." In other words, according

to this conservative legal organization supporting white plaintiffs, no matter how solicitous a black elected official from a majority black district may be of the concerns of his or her white constituents, no matter how well he or she may represent the interests of *all* constituents, white voters suffer an injury.

21. In the "analytically distinct" cause of action recognized in *Shaw*, bizarreness was central to the conclusion that the challenged district was drawn to segregate voters between districts. Now the Court announced a standard that expanded opportunities to attack majority-minority districts beyond those extreme cases where the shape of a district was alleged to be so tortured as to suggest that it could only be understood as an attempt to "segregate" voters along racial lines. The Court's *Miller* decision put it on a collision course with the Voting Rights Act. If it means what it appears to mean, any time an electoral district is drawn to comply with the Voting Rights Act it can be said that race was the predominant factor in its creation. Were it not for racial considerations, i.e., the *remedial* goals of the Voting Rights Act, the challenged district would not have been created. After *Miller*, all electoral districts drawn pursuant to the Voting Rights Act are theoretically, if not actually, vulnerable.

22. The latter claim presaged the claims of plaintiffs in the *Shaw v. Reno* cases. Significantly, it did not allege that they were discriminated against as Jews; rather the claim that they were discriminated against on grounds of race must have gone to their status as white voters. Indeed, the plaintiffs specifically disavowed any effort to seek permanent recognition as a community in legislative reapportionment.

23. No doubt, their status as white voters was still relevant to their arguments; since Jews were not a protected group under the Voting Rights Act their claim was constitutional as opposed to statutory. Since the Constitution requires proof of discriminatory intent, the *U.J.O.* plaintiffs would have had to prove that the legislature intentionally discriminated against them as Jews when it drew the redistricting plan, a claim that they were unlikely to be able to support.

24. One might argue that Judaism, as a religion, is not comparable to race. Judaism is, as are all religions, a system of beliefs shared by the faithful. To be a Jew is to share religious, cultural, and historical experiences that have substantive meaning that people willingly embrace. Whatever the different forms of Judaism may be, Jews are not heard arguing that there is no common Jewish interest or community.

One might further argue that race is a social (and therefore an artificial) construct that is not built on a system of common beliefs and experiences willingly shared by African Americans. To the extent that black Americans do share a common experience, the argument would continue, it is one that treated them as members of a group discriminated against solely on the basis of their skin color and not as individuals. The antidote would be color blind treatment of individuals and a movement away from group identity based on race.

This argument fails, however. While race and religion are different, the fact that race may be a social construct does not render its "ties that bind" any less powerful.

There is a culture that is shared by African Americans that they willingly embrace, quite apart from the pathologies that are traceable to slavery, American apartheid, and the historical attempts to destroy black culture. Thus, Jews who deny the legitimacy of black communal interests act inconsistently with their pursuit of Jewish communal interests.

25. This fact is reflected in the concern on the part of many Jewish organizations and their leaders that the prospect of peace in the Middle East will weaken Jewish identity and solidarity in the United States. In *Jewish Power*, J. J. Goldberg asks: in a world where embattled Israel is signing peace treaties, where oppressed Jewish communities from Moscow to Damascus are stepping into the light of freedom, what battles remain? Without threats, what will rally Jews to the flag?" (p. 19).

26. A full page advertisement placed by the U.J.A.–Federation of New York in the May 10, 1996 *New York Times* (A29) promoting a March for Israel's Future includes a Golda Meir quote that is easily adaptable for African Americans in the context of American, and especially Southern, electoral politics: "There should be some place on earth where we have a Jewish majority...as a minority, we have quite a history."

While undoubtedly many will argue that the comparison fails, African Americans can argue that for them, in view of past and *continuing* racial discrimination and polarization in the political arena, their ability to have a few congressional districts drawn to allow them to have the *opportunity* to elect representatives from their communities in jurisdictions where racism has made that impossible is as important to them as is the protection of the State of Israel as a nation where all Jews are guaranteed a haven from anti-Semitism and the threat of oppression. Thus, members of the Congressional Black Caucus, which has been a staunch supporter of Israel and of American Jews on issues related to Israel, might have understandably felt betrayed when the ADL filed a brief in support of the plaintiffs in *Miller v. Johnson*.

27. Brief Amicus Curiae of Anti-Defamation League in Support of Appellees. The ADL went on to recognize that "the goal of increasing specific minority group participation in the political process is commendable" but stated that it "equally insists that racial classification in redistricting—the premise of maximization and proportionality—is constitutionally indefensible, and in the end, will defeat the laudable motives of the appellants." The ADL's statement of interest concluded that "[t]he presumption that *only* a member of a certain race can or will effectually represent his or her constituents of the same race is antithetical to the goal of a society—and a Constitution blind to racial classifications." Of course, the argument that majority-minority districts rest upon the presumption identified by the ADL in its statement of interest is mistaken. Most elected officials who represent African Americans and for whom African Americans vote are white.

28. See Peter Applebaum, "Duke May Seem to be Wallace of 91" *New York Times*, Nov. 25, 1991, p. 14.

29. In the two day trial in *Hays v. Louisiana* on October 30–31, 1995, in which those attempting to defend the 55 percent black district under attack were limited to four hours including cross examination of plaintiffs' witnesses, and to one expert witness (despite numerous complex technical issues), one of the plaintiffs testified that he joined the litigation because of his concern over racial tensions created as a result of the challenged district, and that prior to the Louisiana legislature's adoption of the challenged plan, there were no such tensions in Louisiana politics.

30. Most recently, in November of 1995, Gary, Indiana, with a 90 percent black population, elected a white mayor, Scott King, over three black opposition candidates. See Richard Berke "Election Games," *New York Times,* Nov. 9, 1995, p. 1.

31. ADL Brief at 20.

32. See Douglas Massy and Nancy A. Denton, *American Apartheid* (Cambridge, MA, 1993).

33. Some "liberals" even blame the Republican Revolution of 1994, at least to the extent that the Democrats lost the U.S. House of Representatives, on majority-minority districts. While they may have had some marginal effect on the elections, the numbers do not work out. See Report by the NAACP Legal Defense Fund on the effect of Section 2 of the Voting Rights Act on the 1994 Congressional elections (on file at the NAACP Legal Defense Fund).

34. *Johnson v. DeGrandy*, which involved redistricting in the Miami area, pitted Jewish and Hispanic interests against one another, according to Jerome Chanes. Chanes also cites Stephen J. Solarz, who served nine times in Congress as a Democrat from Brooklyn, as a "victim of interpretation of the Voting Rights Act by the New York Legislature when it redrew the 12th Congressional District based on 1990 census data." Solarz opted to run in the new twelfth and was defeated by Nydia Valasquez, a Latina. The twelfth has now been challenged in a *Shaw* type case.

35. See Jerome Chanes' essay in this volume, especially pp. 313–14. Chanes considers the Guinier debate to be a "side show really, but nonetheless revealing in terms of Jewish communal responses on matters related to group rights." Cryptically and perhaps patronizingly, Chanes concludes that "allegations that the organized Jewish Community had 'sank' the nomination soon surfaced, with many Blacks—not understanding, or caring about, the finer points of the Voting Rights Act—taking the view that the Jewish Community was, in the words of an NAACP Legal Defense Fund official, [r]aising hell over a Black nominee who was trying to increase Black political presentation."

Whatever the view of the unidentified LDF official Chanes quotes, his rendition of the Guinier nomination demonstrates that the finer points of Lani Guinier's writings apparently escaped him.

the uncertainty of Black Americans toward Africa.

Both, however, also illustrate a vital historical fact. Like their white counterparts, Black Americans—notably during the modern civil rights and Black Power period—have exhibited rich, varied, and often contradictory attitudes toward Africa, Africans, and African peoples throughout the African diaspora. Indeed, the African connection has represented a central, defining issue in the development of Black American group consciousness. In turn, this evolving consciousness has been instrumental in the creation of a vital African American history and culture.

In a similar vein, the related attitudes of Black Americans toward the Third World and its peoples during the same period have been likewise rich, varied, and often contradictory. What Carmichael's plea illuminated as well was a growing identification between Blacks in this country and Third World peoples generally. The interrelated rise of the Black Power movement and Black consciousness deepened and expanded this sense of identification and solidarity. Increasingly during the 1960s, as a growing number of Black Americans saw themselves as an oppressed nation and people, they came likewise to see themselves as a part of the Third World and its peoples.

This essay examines the evolving relationships between the growth of Black nationalism, increasing Black American identification with Africa and the Third World, and the impact of these developments on the relationships between Blacks and Jews. It concentrates on the era of the modern Black liberation struggle, roughly 1954 to 1972. It argues that the dynamic growth of Black nationalism, especially during the movement's Black Power phase, must be understood within an international context that illuminates the intimate relationship between domestic developments and international developments. In particular, the escalating identification of Black Americans with Africa and the Third World directly influenced the escalating conflict between Blacks and Jews. This tension has to be understood, in other words, within the context of this crucial interplay between the domestic and the international.

The growth of a concern among Black Americans for Africa and the peoples of the African diaspora, as well as a concern for the Third World and its peoples, must be seen within the broad evolution of a Black American group consciousness. Most fundamentally, that consciousness has been predicated upon the necessity for group solidarity and struggle as the basis for survival and advancement in a hostile white American environment. This guiding sense of peoplehood—of racial awareness and pride—has been a recurrent and defining feature of the Black experience in America.

342 //

Blacks' fundamental Americanness over their Africanness. Indeed, the challenge of Carmichael's clarion call was to bring around the likes of Anne Moody's mother to his side: away from America and toward Africa.

The enduring challenge for Pan-Africanism remains negative and racist views of Africa in the American mind. These invidious views have strongly influenced the relationship of Black Americans to Africa. Consequently, the very persistence of positive and insightful characterizations of Africa, especially among Black Americans, has been a powerful counterpoint to a hegemonic anti-African offensive. In addition to exposing the range and complexity of Black American attitudes toward Africa, the above episodes—and the attitudes they represent—speak to an even deeper historical dilemma: the imperative of self-definition, its meanings, its consequences. Why, how, and with what results have African Americans seen themselves as a unique group, a "race," a nation? Or, what has been the historical trajectory of this Black "nation within a nation"?

During the Civil Rights–Black Power years, the ongoing quest for a viable self-defined collective Black identity became increasingly nationalist in character. Fighting for greater group autonomy and empowerment, Black nationalists of the Black Power years increasingly fostered a separatist politics. A fierce racialism took hold, colliding head-on with the intergroup coalition politics which had animated the interracialist civil rights years.

A most revealing example of this unraveling was the accelerating rift between Jews and Blacks. As Israel aligned itself with the First World, and revolutionary Black nationalism aligned itself with the Third World, the die was cast. From the perspective of revolutionary Black nationalism, the choice was plain. It was Black over white; national self-determination over neocolonialism; internationalism over imperialism; the Third World over the First World; identification with Palestinian self-determination over Israel.

A close look at various historical paths of Black nationalism demonstrates that its emergence in the late 1960s and early 1970s was a defining moment for Black nationalism as a historical tradition. This audacious series of efforts to rethink and to realize an authentic Black nation eventually collapsed under the weight of overwhelming obstacles, notably internal conflicts and outside opposition. More important, however, it was a critical component of the various Black voices which sought to come together to speak as one on behalf of an increasingly self-conscious Black American identification with Africa and the Third World.

Radical Blacks, especially nationalists, thus internationalized their understanding of worldwide liberation struggles principally within a Pan-African/Third World framework. Consequently, the exposure of Israeli ties to South Africa in concert with growing sympathy for the nationalist struggle of Palestinians loomed large in an increasingly critical radical Black interrogation of both Israel and Jewish American support for Israel. To understand this escalating critique from the point of view of Black nationalists, the conflict between competing nationalisms, Zionism and Ethiopianism (of the American variety), must be recognized and taken seriously.

I

In colonial British North America and subsequently the United States, a collective sensibility among Africans emerged. Before 1700, the bulk of this Black population consisted of African slaves, many from other New World slave societies. During the course of the eighteenth century, more and more slaves came directly from West and Central Africa. Both Old and New World provenance inspired uncommon efforts to reconstitute a rudimentary sense of community among Black slaves from a wide variety of African ethnic groups, or peoples. This incipient communal ethos included the New World offspring of African slaves: Creoles.

As historian Sterling Stuckey has perceptively argued, Black slaves in the Americas pioneered the development of an African consciousness.[3] This Pan-African sensibility powerfully shaped their identity as a New World people. New World African consciousness is diasporic and, therefore, clearly related to Old World African consciousness. It is also fundamentally different. These determining differences cannot be conflated or ignored. The most crucial difference is historical context: while African Americans are both Americans and Africans, over time they become more American than African. Herein lies the rub for Black nationalism and Pan-Africanism.

Building upon cultural commonalities from their African roots, New World Africans constructed mixed New World cultures which drew as well from their exposure to European and indigenous cultures. Out of these fundamentally African yet increasingly creole histories emerged the collective sensibilities which distinguished the development of New World African Americans.

Being both African and American as well as, prior to 1865, both slave and free complicated the collective sensibilities of Blacks in the United States. More narrowly defined collective identities rooted in differences such as a particular West/Central African ethnic group or a particular West/Central African religion eventually gave way to an increasingly more inclusive sense of group identity. Enduring the common oppression of slavery and anti-Black racism, on one hand, and building upon a common need to alleviate that oppression, on the other, inevitably encouraged the budding Pan-African American consciousness.

The Black American nation's collective sensibility also drew upon the communalism and group-centered forms of identity common among the African forebears of Africans in America. The social emphasis of their self-definition thus reinforced the tendency toward a sense of nationhood, as did the sense of shared religious tradition.[4]

Neither Black nationalism, nor the Black nation, should be confused with a nation-state. In light of their recognition of a union at once psychic and moral,

African Americans are preeminently a nation, with a collective sensibility sustained by a distinctive heritage. Regard the powerful twin need for self-definition and self-determination, sociologist E. U. Essien-Udom has argued that "If we understand nationalism broadly as the effort of a people to assert their identity and dignity as human beings, then...the share of Afro-Americans in the articulation of the 'African Personality' looms larger than is generally acknowledged." The crucial issue, Essien-Udom contended, is "the self-assertion of a people:... their unswerving assertion and defense of the dignity of the African Peoples not only in America but also those in Africa."[5]

That Africans and their descendents have lived within a white-dominated territory and nation-state has complicated the history of Black nationalism. Not surprisingly, therefore, territorial separatism has been an important element of Black nationalism since its earliest expressions. Early on innumerable New World Africans sought to create their own worlds apart from European American domination, such as maroon or runaway slave societies. A far more widespread and influential separatist thrust resulted in the development of relatively autonomous institutions. The most important of these was the Black church, especially the antebellum development of independent Black denominations. Within Black church or religious history as well as the larger early Black experience, special mention must be made of what religion historian Albert Raboteau has aptly termed the "invisible institution" of the slave church. In stark opposition to the proslavery religion of the slaveholders, slave religion provided a vital sanctuary for renewal and self-validation and vigorously promoted a collective Black identity and liberation struggle.[6]

Scattered evidence of proto-Black nationalist sentiment and institutions can thus be found before 1800. As a formal doctrine and movement, however, Black nationalism proper emerges alongside the nationalism of the new American nation in the late 1700s and early 1800s. This formative period illumines two interrelated aspects of the Black nationalist tradition with particular meaning for its resurgence in the 1960s and early 1970s. First and foremost, the dialectic between African American nationalism and American nationalism represents the ambivalence of African Americans toward both Africa and America. The second aspect—Black nationalism as a historically complex phenomenon—has followed directly from the deep-seated African American ambivalence toward both halves of itself. A critical examination of selected elements in the history of Black nationalism lays bare a complicated and multifaceted trajectory.

Black Americans, fundamentally hybrid like Americans generally, have created a liminal nation poised precariously between the American nation and increasingly distant memories of African nations. Consistent with this line of thinking, an influential number of 1960s activists concluded that African Americans, like other oppressed peoples of color, represented an internal colony of the United States. Black nationalists saw themselves engaged in a version of anti-colonial struggles worldwide.[7]

In spite of the creole origins of the United States, America's principal white architects, like Benjamin Franklin and Thomas Jefferson, invented dominant visions of the nation as a white nation; American nationalism has thus been envisioned as *white* American nationalism. Since the founding of the United States, Black Americans, especially integrationists and assimilationists like Frederick Douglass, have rejected such racialized and, for them, self-effacing characterizations of the American nation and American nationalism. From their perspective, both the American nation and American nationalism are intrinsically hybrid and inclusive. For them, the Black liberation struggle was principally an uphill battle to have the Black nation accepted within the family of nations which constitutes the larger American nation.[8]

In the first half of the nineteenth century, the reform of a racist white American nation and nationalism struck moderate Black nationalists like the Reverend Lewis Woodson, as well as militant Black nationalists like David Walker, as important but ultimately secondary. Most important for these Black nationalists and their successors has been Black self-articulation and Black-led efforts toward group-based "autonomy, unity, and identity."[9] Black nationalism, then, has been primarily about extending strengthened boundaries of community outward as a way to realize a viable Black nation.

In the late 1960s, these boundaries expanded exponentially to include a revitalized connection to Africans throughout the world, especially those engaged in national liberation struggles on the African continent. In addition, this African American nation bound itself with an increasingly powerful coalition of non-white nations throwing off the shackles of colonialism, neocolonialism, and imperialism: the Third World. An accelerating tendency toward interpreting the world in racialistic and Manichean terms greatly intensified with the emergence in 1966 of Black Power as the liberation struggle's principal rallying cry.

II

On the evening of June 16, 1966, SNCC's Stokely Carmichael was the last speaker at a Greenwood, Mississippi rally. This proved to be a pivotal stop along the march of various civil rights leaders who had rushed to continue from Memphis to Jackson the ill-fated trek of James Meredith, who earlier had been shot by a sniper. That evening Carmichael issued a resounding call for "Black Power." The effect on the audience was stunning. His SNCC colleague Willie Ricks joined Carmichael and asked the audience: "What do you want?" The reply was immediate and thunderous: "Black Power!"[10] This electrifying call-and-response eventually died down, but it proved to be a defining moment. The civil rights movement would never be the same.

The subsequent white-dominated and mass-mediated furor over Black Power was extraordinary, largely for its concerted and often racist opposition. The wildly conflicting interpretations of its meanings among Blacks and whites reflected both the term's fundamental ambiguity and, even more importantly, the profound challenge it posed to white supremacy. Black Power was nothing if not open to multiple and shifting interpretations. It was seen as everything from the most conservative Black capitalism to the most radical Black demands for territorial and financial reparations. Not surprisingly, the Black Power phase of the Black freedom struggle alienated innumerable white supporters, among them many Jewish supporters. The left, liberal, labor, and interracial coalition so vital to the functioning of the national civil rights agenda began to unravel in the context of the awesome white backlash to the Black Power movement.[11]

For sure, the excesses of Black Power contributed significantly to the perception among whites of Black Power as anti-white and racist. Excesses aside, however, Black Power was essentially a demand for Black nationalist renewal. As with Ghanaian nationalism, Irish nationalism, or Zionism, African American nationalism is principally about the creation and institutionalization of a group-based identity and politics. Even among radical Black separatists, the angle of vision is American as well as Black. As a result, the alluring call for a revitalized Black nationalism operated for Blacks in ways comparable to nationalist appeals rooted in racial/ethnic ties among other American racial/ethnic groups, such as Jewish Americans and Italian Americans.

The critical distinction between African American nationalism and other ethnic/racial-based nationalisms within and outside the United States has been the African American's lack of direct, emotive ties to a specific homeland because of the disruptive impact of slavery. Consequently, the establishment of direct Black ties to African provenance—even the literal invention of such ties—is all the more powerful. Ultimately, therefore, while historically important in its own right, Black nationalism has served most effectively to negotiate the relationship of African Americans to the United States.

Most fundamentally, then, for African Americans Black Power called upon Blacks to adopt more thoroughly and adeptly the traditional American pluralist approach to advancement, even if that advancement required countenancing varying degrees of Black separatism. Indeed separatism has been historically driven by enduring patterns of anti-Black discrimination among whites as much as the enduring Black quest for self-determination and group autonomy. A minority of radical Black separatist voices and organizations urged Blacks to reject the American way in favor of African and often socialist-inspired alternatives. The Nation of Islam under the Honorable Elijah Muhammed and Malcolm X, his most influential spokesman, preached an intriguing amalgam of a separate Black capitalist economy, a very conservative moral ethos, a Black supremacist cosmology, and a politics of withdrawal and nonengagement with the American system.[12]

The clarion call of Ricks and Carmichael for Black Power reverberated widely and deeply among Blacks. It graphically captured a shifting mood—from hope and optimism to rage and despair—among many Blacks. This was especially the case among untold numbers of Blacks in northern and western cities for whom the southern-based movement had not meant material advances. This stirring call also signaled a growing Black militancy, notably a growing Black receptivity toward more radical expressions of Black racial politics. Transformed by the proliferation of Black urban rebellions and escalating Black assertiveness, the civil rights movement in fact became the Black Power movement. A critical ingredient of this reenvisioned social movement was the efflorescence of radical varieties of Black nationalism.

Much of the sixties revitalization of Black nationalism revealed continuities with the history of Black nationalism and the ongoing Black liberation struggle. The renewed emphasis on race as the primary basis of identity, pride, unity, and advancement among African Americans clearly harked back to nineteenth- and earlier twentieth-century articulations of this premise, like the 1920s mass movement spawned by Marcus Garvey's Universal Negro Improvement Association. Indeed, as with Garveyism, racialism (or ethnic chauvinism) has often transgressed dualities like conservative and radical, integrationist and separatist, resistor and accommodationist, American and African. This powerful transgressive impact has extended to boundaries among African Americans themselves, like gender, class, skin color, and sexuality. In turn, the impact of searching beyond these same boundaries has led to powerful transgressions of the very boundary of race itself. As a result, while the concern for the best interests of "the race" has been historically omnipresent, its expressions have been exceedingly various and complicated.

Significant often overweening obstacles, including internal differences, have seriously compromised the extremely difficult (if not impossible) work of identifying and then realizing the best interests of "the race." Clearly, competing visions and agendas—such as those between separatists and integrationists—have sapped crucial energies and resources. Just as important, however, this vigorous Black debate has also yielded insights and advances. As in the case of the civil rights movement, philosophical and strategic disagreements among various individual leaders and groups often led to breakthroughs, notably in local-based struggles like sit-ins, desegregation struggles, and voter registration campaigns. This was especially evident in the spirit of compromise and tolerance undergirding the commitment to operational unity so vital to the plethora of local- and national-based organizations and leaders constituting the national movement. This powerful overriding commitment to group unity thus enabled the more moderate Southern Christian Leadership Conference to work closely with the increasingly aggressive Student Nonviolent Coordinating Committee. Even in times of intense disgreement, and even when the efforts were ill fated, these intraracial struggles to achieve unity revealed a strong nationalist current.

Between 1945 and 1965, the nationalist ethos of the Black civil rights insurgency was held in check by the government-led repression of alleged radicals and subversives. Communist-baiting combined with racist opposition to the Black

freedom struggle to undermine principaled Black leftist politics. This could perhaps best be seen in the government's sordid campaign to blacklist both Paul
Robeson and W.E.B. Du Bois. Neither leader nor the internationalist, Pan-
Africanist, communist/socialist visions they represented ever recovered.[13] An
important component of late sixties and early seventies Black radicalism was the
effort among various Black intellectual-activists like Angela Davis and organizations like the early Black Panther Party to revive the tradition of Marxist-inspired
analysis of the Black freedom struggle.

The fevered Cold War mentality likewise impeded serious Black support for
the Cuban Revolution, especially after the revolution's alignment with
Communism and Soviet Russia. Early Black support for the Cuban Revolution
grew out of sympathy for the Cuban people's freedom insurgency as well as that
movement's highly praised efforts to alleviate anti-Black racism and discrimination.[14]

For many Black nationalists, the Cuban example was at once instructive and
inspirational, in keeping with a Black nationalist vision which increasingly
aligned itself with the progressive struggles of peoples of color throughout the
Third World (including Vietnam). Therefore, during the sixties, the Cuban victory at the Bay of Pigs, and Cuban support for nationalist efforts in the Third
World were not lost on Black nationalists. Not surprisingly, therefore, Black
activists like Robert Williams and Assata Shakur sought refuge in Cuba to escape
official persecution for their insurgent political activities in the United States.[15]

Growing Black opposition to the war in Vietnam derived in part from the
developing Third World consciousness of the period. Although most African
Americans, like most Americans generally, continued to support the war, by the
late sixties Black opposition was intensifying. King's open opposition to the war
after 1966 coupled with that of SNCC and the Black Panther Party revealed
something of the range of that antiwar sentiment. King's opposition revealed the
depth of his commitment to nonviolence as well as his compulsion to exercise the
national moral leadership he personified. It also reflected his growing need and
willingness to support publicly the national antiwar movement. While King distanced himself from the increasingly nationalist politics of groups like SNCC, he
shared with them an awareness that the escalating political and financial costs of
the war were undermining support for the Black freedom struggle itself. Those
costs extended to lagging support for critical national initiatives like President
Lyndon Johnson's War on Poverty.

In addition, it was becoming clearer that Black soldiers were a disproportionate number of the war's combat troops and fatalities. Radical Black nationalists in
particular severely criticized this aspect of the Vietnam War as evidence of its
racist nature. On a different yet related level, the conflict was seen as a racist
American intrusion into the internal affairs of the Vietnamese nation. Consistent
with this line of argument, radical Black critics charged the government with pitting one nation of color—African Americans—against another—the Vietnamese.

Likewise, the dilemma of fighting for a country which failed to recognize some of its soldiers as full-fledged citizens received extensive airing among the war's Black opponents. As a popular line put it: "No Vietnamese ever called me a nigger." This antiwar posture invigorated the increasing tendency among Black nationalists to see the struggles of the Vietnamese and African Americans as comparable. Black nationalist opposition to the war also spoke forcefully to the need for the Third World to unite against the First, for peoples of color to unite against the white West, and for progressive nations to unite for nationalist self-determination and against colonialism, imperialism, and racism.

III

Most Blacks, especially those in the working and middle classes, found comfort in the Black pronouncements of Third Worldism, even though they neither formally analyzed nor embraced it. It remained primarily an ideological construct, a rhetorical device, promoted for a variety of ends by numerous Black activists, including internationalists and nationalists. Of course, these were often the same people. In the aftermath of his pilgrimmage to Mecca, his assassination, and the publication of his gripping autobiography, Malcolm X became the most influential African American voice urging his people to envision their own nationalist struggle as inextricably wedded to those of peoples of color. In tandem with the impact of Frantz Fanon's forceful arguments for the psychological and political necessity of Third Worldism as central to progressive nationalism among nations of color, those of Malcolm X proved especially compelling.[16]

For nationalist Blacks, particularly those with a Third World commitment, Pan-Africanism represented a compelling ideology precisely because it linked the histories and destinies of Africans worldwide: on the continent and throughout the diaspora. The lure of Pan-Africanism often proved irresistible for a variety of reasons. For one, Pan-Africanism spoke directly to a powerful need among many Black nationalists to identify with the mythic homeland: the "motherland" and the "fatherland." For another, it gave them specific independent African nations—like Ghana under Kwame Nkrumah—as models and projections for their nationalist hopes and dreams. Furthermore, as with Third Worldism, Pan-Africanism encouraged African Americans to see themselves as part of an increasingly mighty majority—peoples of color worldwide—rather than simply an oppressed minority nation of color within a white-dominated United States. In addition, a venerable heritage encompassing the likes of Edward W. Blyden in the nineteenth century and W.E.B. Du Bois in the twentieth, along with the series of twentieth-century international Pan-African congresses, gave the idea historical cogency.

Even more than in the case of Black Power, however, the calls for commitment to Pan-Africanism and Third Worldism often proved more rhetorical than real. In spite of the heightened awareness among Blacks about Third Worldism and Pan-

Africanism, the purported meanings and consequences of these ideologies for the actual day-to-day realities of Blacks—especially their liberation struggle—remained typically vague or nonexistent. In fact, the metaphysical, romantic, and abstract qualities of these ideologies ultimately rendered them too unrelated to mass Black consciousness and mass Black struggle.[17] While Third World coalitions and Pan-African groups in the United States grew in number, they often had limited influence and brief lives. Barriers to efforts to link the struggles of Third World peoples within the United States (Native Americans, Chicanos/Puerto Rican Americans, Asian Americans, as well as Blacks) often proved overwhelming. Not surprisingly, therefore, direct links between the domestic Black freedom struggle and those of people of color outside the United States often proved even harder to forge and to sustain.

At each level of struggle and analysis, from the local to the national to the international—Pan-African and Third World—the obstacles loomed larger. Just trying to maintain balance within and across embattled movements given to ideological exaggerations, political extremes, and militant posturing was an immense challenge. In addition to external pressures and opposition, the problem of internal contradictions and resistance also stymied attempts at coalition among nations of color both within and outside the United States. Advocates of Pan-Africanism and Third Worldism like Carmichael often obscured and downplayed these extremely difficult and important issues. Indeed nowhere were the prospects and perils of Third Worldism and Pan-Africanism more apparent than in the late sixties leadership and thought of Carmichael.

Among the many who aspired to fill the activist-intellectual vacuum created by the assassinations of King and Malcolm X, few could match his commitment to the cause, his eloquent bravado, and his ideological audacity. Much of what he said and did in this period significantly advanced the African American liberation struggle, notably his efforts to heighten African Americans' awareness of the deep-seated mutual dependency between Blackness—their sense of racial identity and consciousness—and Africanness. Along with a host of nationalist intellectuals and artists like Amiri Baraka, Carmichael helped Blacks to negotiate not only their complicated relationship to Africa, but their equally if not more complicated relationship to the Third World as well.

The ultimate problem proved to be the narrow and chauvinistic extremes of nationalism. In a multiethnic/multiracial society like the United States, Black advancement has historically necessitated alliances and coalitions with progressive non-Blacks in addition to the race-based identity, unity, and power intrinsic to Black Power, even Black nationalism. As previously argued, in light of America's inherent diversity, American nationalism has to be seen as a composite of its constituent nationalisms. Consequently, the fundamental problem was neither Black Power nor Black nationalism per se, but the unmitigated failure of Americans as a people to face up to the enduring and intertwined challenges of structural inequalities rooted in differences like race, class, gender, and sexuality.

A revealing example of this failure of vision and politics was the unraveling of elements within the Black-Jewish alliance so prominent within movements for minority advancement and intergroup understanding and cooperation in the twentieth century, like the NAACP. An especially revealing episode in this unraveling was the intense debate engendered by growing Black radical support for Palestinian nationalism and the Arab world. Carmichael in many ways personified this shift. Most important, he explained his shift from support for Israel and Zionism to support for Palestine and Arabs as part of his evolving Third World and Pan-African consciousness. "Just as the Vietnamese are fighting for humanity, just as the Arab is fighting for humanity, just as our forces in Africa are fighting for humanity, just as Latin Americans are fighting for humanity," he argued in a 1968 speech, "the Black man is fighting for humanity." He concluded that "We stand with the Third World."[18]

Israel, on the other hand, was another matter. The state of Israel, he maintained, had been created out of the forced removal of Palestinians from their homeland. Rejecting what he termed the "effective, offensive propaganda" of Zionism, he derisively spoke of "the so-called State of Israel" as "an unjust and certainly an immoral state." He argued that racism—most obviously the ruthless oppression of Palestinians—and imperialism were basic to Israel and Zionism. Likewise, in this and similar kinds of arguments, Israel was seen as part of the First World, and even more damning, as an agent of United States aggresssion abroad. "The United States is the greatest de-humanizer in the world, and Israel is nothing but a finger of the United States," Carmichael proclaimed.[19]

While tensions between Blacks and Jews clearly intensified in the late sixties, Black nationalism and Black Power are only a partial explanation. Equally if not more important was the resurgence of Zionism and Jewish consciousness in general. These developments intensified dramatically in the wake of the the Arab-Israeli Wars of 1967 and 1973. The perennial question of "Is it good for the Jews?" rubbed up against against the increasingly insistent question "Is it good for the Blacks?" The pivotal issue, as Howard Meyer suggested at the time, was the growing conflict between Jewish Power and Black Power, between Jewish nationalism (including Zionism) and African American nationalism.[20] This conflict has been historically persistent, if uneven and, in many instances, surmountable. Given the constraints of the American system, whether one sees the operative paradigm as group-based pluralism or ethnic/racial nationalism, heightened group-based particularity ascended in the late sixties and early seventies. Viewed within this context, the increasingly intractable tensions between Blacks and Jews as allies become more understandable.

The growing literature on Black-Jewish relations in the late sixties makes it clear that within both communities "the other" community was increasingly feared and thus increasingly demonized. Beneath the surface of the growing anti-Semitic rantings of various Black nationalists, like Amiri Baraka, lurked fear and loathing of "Jewish Power," real and symbolic. In the past, direct Black-Jewish confrontations centered largely on "landlord-tenant and merchant-customer" relations. Conflicts, often within Black neighborhoods, between Black tenants and customers on one hand, and Jewish landlords and merchants on the other, exacerbated Black concerns about community control and economic empowerment. In this context, Jews were seen as an integral element of the white power structure. These realities and perceptions undergirded James Baldwin's revealing 1967 critique of both Black anti-Semitism and anti-Black Jewish racism: "Negroes Are Anti-Semitic Because They're Anti-White." Militant Black nationalism in particular increasingly clashed with Jewish influence, in contexts ranging from the intellectual domain of Black Studies to the institutional domain of Black community control of schools.[21]

Similarly, innumerable Jews viewed the growth of Black militancy and Black nationalism, especially its anti-Semitic elements, as deeply troubling. These developments compelled many moderate to radical Jews to rethink their support for the Black freedom struggle. Many interrogated intensely individual and collective Jewish complicity in continuing patterns of anti-Black racism. Many found the prospect of Black Power fearful and threatening. The hyperbolic rhetoric, inflamed passions, militant actions, and turbulent politics of the period—nonracial and racial—fed these anxieties. Julius Lester's Black Power manifesto, *Look Out Whitey! Black Power's Gon' Get Your MaMa!* was meant to intensify rather than assuage white/Jewish fears.[22]

For many, the evocative symbol of the raised Black fist in solidarity with Black Power signified a frontal challenge to Jewish security as well as Jewish Power. Countless Jews—like many whites—equated Black Power with the Black urban insurrections sweeping the nation's cities in the late sixties. In many instances, these riots took a high toll on Jewish businesses and property in Black areas. In far too many minds, the images and reality of Black militancy conjured up stereotypes of Black anti-white (and anti-Jewish) retribution, Black violence, and Black criminality. Many no longer felt welcome or comfortable in intergroup efforts, including residential areas. Some influential figures, like Norman Podhoretz, discovered neoconservatism. For innumerable Jews—and Blacks—engaged in interracial projects, the estrangement was palpable and deep.[23]

But, as historian Clayborne Carson has perceptively noted, the history of Black-Jewish relations reflects tensions growing out of the separate and distinctive histories of both groups. "Jews and African Americans," he wrote, "have followed different strategies of group advancement and remain divided over the extent to which their own interests coincide with those of the other group." Notwithstanding parallels in the histories of both groups—including "slavery, collective oppression, and minority status in prodominantly white, Christian societies"—these histories are distinctive. This fundamental distinctiveness has fed the nationalism of both groups.[24] In the late sixties, growing attention to particularity among Blacks and Jews underscored their different yet at times overlapping and related historical experiences.

The far greater political and economic power of Jews in the United States compared to that of Blacks helps to explain the pointed emphasis among Black radicals on an argument for a greater Black moral power. Arguing from the point of view of the historical uniqueness of the oppression of American Blacks, these Black radicals articulated a common and enduring belief shared by innumerable Blacks and their staunchest allies for centuries. Thus, for example, for Stokely Carmichael, the horrors of anti-Semitism and six million Jewish deaths in the Holocaust and its consequences are tragic, undeniable, and unspeakable. Clearly, Jews, too, speak from a lofty moral perch. For Carmichael, however, that perch had been sullied by the politics of the establishment of Israel, the displacement and repression of Arabs, and growing evidence of Israeli ties to reactionary regimes like South Africa. Zionism, in his eyes, had tarnished Jewish moral capital.[25]

Even before the Black Power imperatives of Carmichael and his cohorts, a Black nationalist belief in a superior Black morality undergirded the nineteenth-century Black freedom struggle invigorated by the likes of activists like David Walker and Sojourner Truth. In our own century, this nationalist belief animated the civil rights movement inspired by Rosa Parks, led by King, criticized by Malcolm X, and personified by the likes of the towering Mississippi activist and ex-sharecropper Fannie Lou Hamer. That not all of these individuals or even most Blacks who identified with the movement also saw themselves as Black nationalists is beside the point. Instead, Black nationalism has historically shared with the wide-ranging, broad-based, and enduring Black freedom struggle a powerful sense of Blacks as "a nation within a nation." This special nation had been endowed with a God-given mission: "to redeem the soul of America." This extraordinary belief has profoundly shaped African American consciousness and history.[26]

That this vision has been reinforced by the strong identification of many Blacks with the Old Testament travails and triumphs of "God's Chosen People," the Jews, is important. As a result, the African American liberation struggle has often reinvented and represented itself as the modern and New World equivalent of the traditional and Old World Jewish quest for peoplehood. The historic patterns of conflict and cooperation between American Blacks and Jews have clearly had very real economic (or material) as well as political and social origins and consequences. Intimately interwoven with those patterns, however, has been the intense symbolic ties between the historical sense of divine mission among both Jews and Blacks. Deeply implicated in the nationalism of both groups, this sense of a special and higher spiritual calling has colored the separate histories of both groups in addition to the history of Black-Jewish interaction. Regrettably, the moral authority emanating from histories responding to that calling has been diminished among both groups by the narrow and often stultifying demands of nationalism.

Notes

1. "A New World to Build," 9 December 1968, A&T State University, Greensboro, NC, in Stokely Carmichael, *Stokely Speaks* (New York, 1971), 152–53.

2. Anne Moody, *Coming of Age in Mississippi* (New York, 1968), 170, 171.

3. Sterling Stuckey, *Slave Culture: Nationalist Theory and the Foundations of Black America* (New York, 1987), ix.

4. Stuckey, *Slave Culture*, 3–97.

5. John Hutchinson and Anthony D. Smith, eds., *Nationalism* (Oxford, 1994), 4, 5; Walker Conner, "A Nation is a Nation, is a State, is an Ethnic Group, is a...," *Ethnic and Racial Studies* 1:4 (October 1978), 383; E.U. Essien-Udom, "The Relation-ship of Afro-Americans to African Nationalism," *Freedomways* 2:4 (Fall 1962), 393, 396.

6. Albert Raboteau, *Slave Religion* (New York, 1978).

7. Robert L. Allen, *Black Awakening in Capitalist America: An Analytic History* (New York, 1969); John H. Bracey, Jr., in Bracey, August Meier, and Elliott Rudwick, eds., *Black Nationalism in America* (Indianapolis, 1970), lxi–lx.

8. Bracey, Meier, and Rudwick, eds., *Black Nationalism*; Leonard I. Sweet, *Black Images of America, 1784–1870* (New York, 1976); Wilson Moses, *The Golden Age of Black Nationalism 1850–1925* (New York, 1978); Stuckey, *Slave Culture*; Harold Cruse, *The Crisis of the Negro Intellectual* (New York, 1967); Waldo E. Martin, Jr., *The Mind of Frederick Douglass* (Chapel Hill, 1985); Nell Irvin Painter, "Martin R. Delany: Elitism and Black Nationalism," in Leon Litwack and August Meier, eds., *Black Leaders of the Nineteenth Century* (Urbana, 1988), 149–71. Douglass, a conservative Black nationalist at best, worked with both white and Black America to realize a more inclusive American nation and nationalism, as did self-avowed Black nationalists more squarely within the tradition than Douglass, like Delany. Indeed, Black nationalists of all stripes have understood that the indispensable work of enhancing these intergroup bonds has been vital to the creation of a Black nation, within or outside the United States.

9. Hutchinson and Smith, *Nationalism*, 4, 5.

10. Clayborne Carson, *In Struggle: SNCC and the Black Awakening of the 1960s* (Cambridge, MA, 1981), 209–10.

11. William L. Van DeBurg, *New Day in Babylon: The Black Power Movement and American Culture, 1965–1975* (Chicago, 1992), 11–28; Carson, *In Struggle*, 215–28.

12. E.U. Essien-Udom, *Black Nationalism: A Search for an Identity in America* (Chicago, 1962).

13. Martin Bauml Duberman, *Paul Robeson* (New York, 1988); Gerald Horne,

Black and Red: W.E.B. Du Bois and the Afro-American Response to the Cold War, 1944–1963 (Albany, 1986).

14. Van Gosse, *Where the Boys Are: Cuba, Cold War America and the Making of a New Left* (New York, 1993), 120–23, 131–32, 147–54, 219–20.

15. Additional support for the Cuban Revolution as a beacon for oppressed peoples came from Angela Davis, Eldridge Cleaver, and Stokely Carmichael. Gosse, *Where the Boys Are*, 152–54, 211; Assata Shakur, *Assata: An Autobiography* (New York, 1987), 266–74; Angela Davis, *Angela Davis: An Autobiography* (New York, 1974), 198–216; Kathleen Rout, *Eldridge Cleaver* (Boston, 1991), 95–111; Carmichael, "Solidarity With Latin America," in *Stokely Speaks*, 101–10.

16. *The Autobiography of Malcolm X* (New York, 1964), 334–382; Frantz Fanon, *The Wretched of the Earth* (New York, 1963).

17. Adolph L. Reed, Jr., "Pan-Africanism—Ideology for Liberation?" *The Black Scholar* 3:1(September 1971), 2–13.

18. Carmichael, "The Black American and Palestinian Revolutions," in *Stokely Speaks*, 143.

19. Ibid., 136, 137, 142.

20. Howard N. Meyer, "Understanding Not Panic: One Jew Looks at Black Power," *Negro Digest* 16 (November 1966), 39.

21. Murray Friedman, *What Went Wrong? The Creation and Collapse of the Black-Jewish Alliance* (New York, 1995), 257; James Baldwin, "Negroes Are Anti-Semitic Because They're Anti-White" [1967] reprinted in Paul Berman, ed., *Blacks and Jews: Alliances and Arguments* (New York, 1994), 31–41; Robert G. Weisbord and Arthur Stein, *Bittersweet Encounter: The Afro-American and the Jew* (New York, 1970); Jack Salzman, ed. *Bridges and Boundaries: African Americans and American Jews* (New York, 1992).

22. Julius Lester, *Look Out Whitey! Black Power's Gon' Get Your MaMa* (New York, 1968).

23. Weisbord and Stein, *Bittersweet Encounter*, 85–218; Friedman, *What Went Wrong?*, 195–273; Norman Podhoretz, "My Negro Problem—and Ours" (1963), with Postscript (1993), in Berman, ed., *Blacks and Jews*, 76–96.

24. Clayborne Carson, "The Politics of Relations between African-Americans and Jews," in Berman, ed., *Blacks and Jews*, 135, 134.

25. Carmichael, "The Black American and Palestinian Revolutions."

26. Adam Fairclough, *To Redeem the Soul of America: The Southern Christian Leadership Conference and Martin Luther King, Jr.* (Athens, GA, 1987).

seventeen

AFRICAN AMERICANS AND ISRAEL

GARY E. RUBIN

In 1993, the prominent Jewish writer Cynthia Ozick reviewed the course of African American–Jewish relations in the twenty years since the publication of her essay, "Literary Blacks and Jews." She claimed that "uninformed assaults on Israel by black Americans (who are certainly not alone in this), and a willed misunderstanding of Middle Eastern events since 1967, have done more to destroy Jewish confidence in black goodwill and fairness than any number of homegrown 'Hymietown' quips."[1] Ozick there made a claim found frequently in recent Jewish analyses of Black-Jewish relations since the heyday of the civil rights movement in the mid-1960s. Several writers have argued that hostile African American attitudes toward Israel were a major factor in increasing tensions between Blacks and Jews in the late 1960s and remain a serious impediment to coalition today.

This assertion rests on a simple syllogism: Criticism of Israel is wrong and hostile to Jews. Important Black leaders have criticized Israel. Therefore, important Black leaders are wrong and hostile to Jews.

In attempting to evaluate whether this syllogism holds up to logical and factual analysis, this essay will ask three questions: Which statements by which leaders have caused some Jewish writers to conclude that there exists a "willed misunderstanding of Middle Eastern events" among African Americans? Second, to what degree do the opinions of some Blacks, whose pronouncements on Israel have generated wide public attention, reflect the attitudes of African Americans in general? Third, what objective political and social facts influence Black attitudes toward Israel and how are they likely to change in the near future?

I

The timing and motivation of African American hostility toward Israel, as several recent Jewish analysts have perceived it, is well summed up in a 1995 history of Black-Jewish relations as follows:

The roots of this current can be found, once again, in the late-1960s transformation of the civil rights movement into a race revolution. That shift
spurred a movement by some elements of the black intelligentsia to link
themselves more closely with the struggle of colored peoples throughout
the world against colonial oppression, notably including Palestinian Arabs
living under Israeli occupation in the West Bank and Gaza.... [R]ather
than recognize Zionism as the national liberation movement of the Jewish
people—a movement not unlike those that gave rise to many newly created African countries—these writers portray the Jewish state as an out-
post of Western imperialism and its actions as a counterpart to "Jewish
exploitation" in black ghettos.[2]

The basis for this conclusion is laid out in standard histories of Black-Jewish
relations in this era. Proponents of this viewpoint essentially marshal three types
of evidence for Black hostility toward Israel. First, they argue that in the late
1960s, a group of nationalist-oriented African Americans began to attack Israel as
a colonialist-oppressive state and that their views influenced Black attitudes
toward Israel generally. A typical review of this period cites the following developments as indicative of emerging African American evaluations of Israel:

—In an interview with Black scholar C. Eric Lincoln, Malcolm X "voiced
   resentment at 'the Jews who with the help of Christians in America and
   Europe drove our Muslim brothers (i.e., the Arabs) out of their homeland where they had been settled for centuries and took over the land for
   themselves.'"[3] This is one of several quotes attributable to Malcolm X
   in which he listed Zionism as among the major manifestations of white
   imperialism threatening the flowering of Black nationalism.
—The Chicago publication *Muhammad Speaks* regularly "used loaded
   phrases such as 'Israeli persecutors' and 'Israeli occupation of Palestine.'
   One [article] spoke of 'Nazi-like tactics exercised by the Zionists against
   the defenseless civilian population in the occupied Arab lands.'"[4]
—Black nationalist leader Stokely Carmichael began to attack Israel consistently in the late 1960s, using phrases such as the "trickery of
   Zionism," the "evil of Zionism," and "Zionist aggression."[5]
—At Chicago's New Politics Convention of 1967, which some observers
   saw as a repudiation of the integrationist aims of the civil rights movement,[6] one of the thirteen resolutions demanded by the Black Caucus
   condemned the "imperialist Zionist war," referring to the Six Day War
   which the overwhelming majority of Jews, including many of the organizers of the convention, regarded as defensive and necessary for Israel's
   survival.[7]
—The most controversial attack by emerging African American groups on
   Israel during this period was doubtless the June-July 1967 newsletter of

the Student Non-Violent Coordinating Committee (SNCC) which appeared precisely at a time when American Jews feared for Israel's continued existence during the Six Day War. The letter firmly identified Israel with Western colonialism and oppression of Black and Arab people. It listed some thirty-two "points of information" that combined anti-Zionist rhetoric with classic anti-Semitic themes. Its last point, for example, charged, "That the famous European Jews, the Rothschilds, who have long controlled the wealth of many European nations, were involved with the original conspiracy with the British to create the 'State of Israel' and are still among Israel's chief supporters. That the Rothschilds Also Control Much of Africa's Mineral Wealth."[8]

This analysis argues that hostility toward Israel was so ingrained in parts of the African American community that it surfaced even in disputes about wholly unrelated issues. One of the flashpoints of the bitter New York City schools strike in 1968 was a leaflet left in teachers' mailboxes in the Ocean Hill–Brownsville district claiming that Black schoolchildren could not possibly be taught by "Middle East Murderers of Colored People." Tenants rights groups asserted that they would not be pushed out of their neighborhoods in the way that Arabs were being displaced in the Middle East.[9]

The second type of evidence cited by some historians of Black hostility to Israel focuses not on the nationalistic forces of the late 1960s, but on leaders of established African American organizations. Statements and actions by prominent Blacks were less rhetorically sharp than the attacks of the radicals, but were taken very seriously because they emanated from positions of power in Black America.

A major event in the tendency of many Jews to see Black leadership as problematic for Israel occurred in 1979 when Andrew Young, a former top aide to Martin Luther King in the civil rights struggle, who was then serving as U.S. Ambassador to the United Nations, met in New York with the U.N. representative of the Palestine Liberation Organization. Jewish groups reacted sharply, calling the meeting a violation of U.S. policy to refrain from negotiating with terrorist groups. Though they did not call for him to step down, Young resigned over this controversy, causing African American resentment at what they perceived as Jewish pressure on one of their most prominent public figures, and Jewish anger against what many saw as a hostile act toward Israel by a civil rights leader.[10] A leading historian of the period concluded, "It is impossible to exaggerate the impact of Young's resignation....Young's ouster shattered any possible reconciliation between Jewish and Black leaders."[11]

The Young meeting and resignation were soon followed by a series of meetings led by Southern Christian Leadership Conference head Rev. Joseph Lowery with PLO representatives in New York and with Lybia's leader Muammmar Qaddafi, a bitter opponent of Israel. The group presented Qaddafi with a "Decoration of Martin Luther King."[12]

The most visible lightning rod on Israel, as on several other issues in Black-Jewish relations, has been the Rev. Jesse Jackson. In 1979, Jackson made a high-ly publicized trip to the Middle East, where he embraced Yasir Arafat at a time when most Israelis and American Jews considered Arafat an unacceptable terror-ist. Shortly after his return, Jackson made a heavily reported speech declaring that Zionism was a "poisonous weed" that was choking Judaism. The great majority of American Jews considered Zionism an integral part of their Judaism.[13]

At the same time as these events were occurring, however, several Black lead-ers were publicly embracing Israel. In 1975, a group of prominent African Americans led by veteran civil rights leader Bayard Rustin founded Black Americans in Support of Israel (BASIC). Members of this group included Clarence Mitchell of the NAACP, David Dinkins, who would later become Mayor of New York, and then-Congressman Andrew Young. BASIC condemned the United Nations resolution equating Zionism with racism, opposed terrorism, and encouraged the Black Congressional Caucus to back aid for Israel.[14]

Among Black leaders promoting a positive view of Israel, Jesse Jackson, iron-ically enough, emerged as the most prominent in the late 1980s and 1990s. Reversing his previous stands, Jackson described Zionism as a national liberation movement and conducted an official and positive visit to Israel in 1994.[15]

Despite the evidence of both positive and problematic attitudes toward Israel by Black leadership, it is often the negative statements that figure most promi-nently in histories of the period. The Young, Lowery, and Jackson incidents took place during a time of disenchantment between the two communities and were perceived as contributing to growing tension. The support for Israel by important African American voices seemed lost in a welter of pronouncements on the weak-ening of the historic Black-Jewish coalition.

The third type of evidence cited for African American hostility toward Israel focuses on the writings of Black intellectuals. Dominating this field is the tower-ing figure of Harold Cruse. In his landmark 1967 work, *The Crisis of the Negro Intellectual*, Cruse includes a chapter on "Negroes and Jews—The Two Nationalisms and the Bloc(ked) Plurality." In his analysis of Black and Jewish intellectual and political trends, Cruse writes, "Thus, pro-Zionist influences with-in Negro civil rights organizations are strategically aiding and abetting Negro integration (assimilation), albeit, Zionists, themselves, do not believe in integra-tion (assimilation) for Jews."[16] In this passage, as in the book in general, Cruse focuses on the power and independence of Black political and intellectual leader-ship. But his treatment of Zionism as purely a movement for power rather than a just realization of the aspirations of Jews for their own state after centuries of exile has offended many Jewish readers. To them, Cruse and his followers represent one more instance of the failure of African American leadership to understand the cen-trality of Israel for Jews.

How significant are these pronouncements on Israel by Black nationalists, mainstream leaders, and intellectuals? Do they amount to a full-scale crisis in the relationship between the two communities? In evaluating the influence of Israel on African American–Jewish relations, analysts have basically adopted three positions.

Critic Paul Berman, echoing several Jewish assessments of this period, lists two major reasons for the rise of African American–Jewish tensions in the 1970s: "So there was a lot of bad blood over affirmative action. And when the second great point of disagreement between a large number of blacks and Jews emerged—the argument over Zionism and Palestinians—the bad blood turned worse."[17] In this view, Black attacks on Israel were as damaging to Jewish interests as domestic conflicts over affirmative action, since they identified Israelis as oppressors and Palestinians as fellow victims of Blacks. Thus, African American criticism of Israel emerges as a major factor in the battering of the coalition.

African American analysts of this period tend to place much less emphasis on the position of Blacks on Israel. To them, statements on Israel were not highly significant in themselves, but were rather reflections of deeper problems between Blacks and Jews that stemmed from domestic conflicts. Historian C. Eric Lincoln, for example, wrote, "the suspicions of Arab support and Jewish hostility are very grossly overdrawn, if not altogether figments of fantasy....[T]his is hardly hardcore anti-Semitism. It is more like American students who wear Viet Cong flags and cheer for Ho Chi Minh because they are disenchanted by the common Americans they know so well, but willing to be charmed by the exoticism and the romanticism of people they know little about."[18] Since African American statements on Israel stem not from deep knowledge or involvement with Middle East issues, Lincoln argued, they can not be taken seriously as a major influence on Black-Jewish relations.

Some Jewish analysts of this period tend to agree with Lincoln's conclusions. Robert G. Weisbord and Arthur Stein, for example, argued that, "At the core of their [Black radicals of the 1960s] outlook are grievances against the white West in general and the United States in particular. Unable to make appreciable progress toward economic, political, and social equality in America, their strategy has been to forge ties with the Third World."[19] Thus, the Israel issue is not itself the generator of conflict but rather the product of a more basic confrontation rooted in American causes.

A third approach assesses not so much the degree to which conflicting views over Israel are significant factors in the relationship, but rather how the entire argument reflects mutual African American–Jewish misunderstanding. African American scholar Cornel West has written, "Without a sympathetic understanding of the deep historic sources of Jewish fears and anxieties about group survival, Blacks will not grasp the visceral attachment of most Jews to Israel. Similarly, without a candid acknowledgement of Blacks' status as permanent underdogs in American society, Jews will not comprehend what the symbolic predicament and literal plight of Palestinians in Israel means to Blacks."[20] The debate over Israel and Zionism in this view becomes yet another venue in which each community ignores the needs and values of the other in pursuit of its own interests and world outlook.

In sum, African American nationalists, mainstream leaders, and intellectuals have strongly expressed views on Israel that many Jews regard as both inaccurate and harmful to their interests. Scholars have differed substantially on the seriousness of the attack and its centrality to Black-Jewish relations. The questions remain as to how widespread negative attitudes toward Israel are among African Americans and what their practical consequences might be.

II

When Cynthia Ozick wrote about "uninformed assaults on Israel by black Americans," which "black Americans" did she mean? When Paul Berman spoke of a "great point of disagreement between a large number of blacks and Jews" over Israel and Zionism, what precisely is meant by a "large number"?

The unacknowledged methodology of authors like Ozick and Berman is to quote African Americans who have made what they consider to be problematic pronouncements on Israel and then to assume that these statements have widespread backing among Blacks in general. However, there is no need to speculate about the attitudes of the African American population toward Israel; solid survey data exist that specify their opinions in some detail.

Like any data source, public opinion surveys are hardly perfect in measuring a community's attitudes on any given subject. Still, existing surveys have at least three advantages over Ozick's and Berman's speculations in assessing African Americans' opinions and feelings about Israel. First, these studies, while sponsored by Jewish organizations with a keen interest in gauging support for Israel among the general public, were actually conducted by well-established firms employing standard scientific instruments for measuring public opinion.[21] Second, while Berman, Ozick, and similar writers tend to cite a few choice quotes and to extrapolate their conclusions to African Americans more generally, the surveys base their findings on interviews with large and scientifically selected samples.[22] Third, these surveys, conducted by different firms and organizations over a twenty-five-year period, yield data that are consistent from study to study and therefore reinforce the validity of each survey's findings. Their conclusions are therefore much more solid than the mere supposition that citations attributed to visible individuals speak for larger sections of the community as a whole.

An analysis of thirteen public opinion surveys taken between 1970 and 1977 yielded two major findings typical of studies done on Black Americans' attitudes toward Israel:

—Black respondents' level of support for Israel tended to be lower than that of whites, by an average of 13 percent. This comparison held true at every level of education and for every age group.

—Still, Blacks were a pro-Israel population. Their net response to each question on the surveys was more favorable than unfavorable to Israel, though their pro-Israel differentials were less than those of white respondents.[23]

These findings have been reinforced several times. A study published in 1982 reported, for example, "that Blacks were pro-Israel, but less so than whites." Specifically, it found 35 percent of whites "highly favorable" to Israel, 40 percent "somewhat favorable," and 25 percent "unfavorable." The comparative numbers for Blacks were 20 percent "highly favorable," 45 percent "somewhat favorable," and 35 percent "unfavorable."[24]

Analysis of other surveys adds detail to this general picture. A February 1987 Roper Poll sponsored by the American Jewish Committee included a question on comparative "sympathy with Israel and with the Arab nations." On this item, 51 percent of white respondents indicated greater sympathy with Israel, 8 percent with the Arab nations, 29 percent either equally with both sides or neither, and 12 percent had no answer or said they did not know. Among Black respondents, 24 percent expressed greater sympathy for Israel, 11 percent for the Arab nations, 41 percent for both or neither, while 24 percent said they did not know or had no opinion. Two points stand out in these responses. First, they follow the established pattern of African American support for Israel, but at lower levels than whites. Second, they show a much greater tendency among Blacks to have no opinion or not to answer. For all the assumptions by some writers that there exists among Blacks a virulent hostility toward Israel, the data show that for many this is simply not a very important issue.[25]

The 1987 AJC-Roper Poll also demonstrates that the way in which questions are asked greatly influences responses. As noted, both whites and Blacks show substantially greater sympathy for Israel than for Arab nations. But in response to a question on whether Israel is a reliable ally of the United States, the pro-Israel margin shrinks significantly for both groups, with whites agreeing that Israel is a reliable ally by a margin of 51 percent to 29 percent and Blacks agreeing by a margin of only 40 percent to 36 percent. This finding indicates a significant degree of ambivalence in the pro-Israel stance of respondents.[26]

Moreover, these results are subject to the influence of changing events. An American Jewish Committee–Roper April 1988 survey, taken six months after the outbreak of the Palestinian uprising against Israeli rule in the West Bank and Gaza Strip (the Intifada), showed white respondent patterns converging to the opinions previously expressed by Blacks. Thus, among whites, 38 percent expressed greater sympathy for Israel and 11 percent for the Arab nations, a substantial decline in pro-Israel support from the February 1987 study. Among Black respondents, differential sympathy held fairly steady from the 1987 survey, with 27 percent favoring Israel and 13 percent the Arab nations. African Americans continued to show less interest in this issue, with 25 percent either giving no answer or saying they did not know, compared with 14 percent of whites who gave these answers.[27]

Other findings of the 1988 survey show ambivalence toward Israel by both white and Black respondents. The margin of white respondents agreeing that Israel is a reliable ally of the United States slipped to only 45 percent to 36 percent in this poll, while only 33 percent of Black respondents agreed that Israel is a reliable ally and 40 percent disagreed. On this issue, then, African Americans raise serious questions about Israel's connection to the United States, but do so at a time when other Americans are more prone to ask questions about American-Israel ties as well.

On other items concerning Israel during the difficult time of the Intifada, white and Black respondents gave almost identical answers. Thus, 29 percent of whites and 27 percent of Blacks thought Israel's response to the Palestinian uprising was too harsh, while 12 percent of whites and 10 percent of Blacks rated it as too lenient. Among white respondents, 31 percent thought the media showed bias against Israel, and 38 percent felt that it did not, while 26 percent of Blacks perceived media bias against Israel and 29 percent did not. In sum, some erosion of support for Israel during the Intifada occurred among both Blacks and whites, but this trend took place within a context of remaining majority support for Israel in both populations.[28]

The 1988 AJC-Roper Poll also contained an important question on the salience of this issue to respondents. Asked about their preferred solution to the problem of Palestinians in the Middle East, small numbers of both Blacks and whites backed a variety of solutions ranging from Israeli annexation of the West Bank and Gaza Strip (5 percent of whites and 2 percent of Blacks) to the establishment of a Palestinian state (8 percent of whites; 7 percent of Blacks). The majority of both groups, however, had no firm opinion on this matter, with 58 percent of white and 64 percent of Black respondents replying that they did not know what their preferred solution would be, either because they had not followed the issue closely (34 percent of whites; 43 percent of Blacks) or because they were uncertain (25 percent of whites; 21 percent of Blacks). These findings indicate that Israel is not a relevant enough issue among respondents to generate firm opinions, reinforcing doubts about how seriously pronouncements on Israel by visible African Americans are taken among the larger Black population.[29]

A follow-up American Jewish Committee–Roper survey in May 1990 confirmed many of the findings of the previous studies and added a new dimension as well. This survey examined respondents' comparative sympathies not only between Israel and the Arab states, but between Israel and the Palestinians as well. Among white respondents, 41 percent expressed greater sympathy with Israel, 9 percent with the Arab states, 32 percent equally with both or with neither, and 17 percent said they did not know. Among Blacks, 23 percent indicated greater sympathy for Israel, 7 percent for the Arab states, 31 percent for both or neither, and 39 percent did not know. These proportions shifted significantly on the Israel-Palestinian comparison. Among whites, 35 percent expressed greater sympathy for Israel, 15 percent for the Palestinians, 31 percent for both or neither, and 20 percent did not know. Among Black respondents, 26 percent showed greater sympathy for Israel, 15 percent for the Palestinians, 29 percent for both or neither, and 30 percent said they did not know. In sum, both white and Black respondents showed comparatively greater support for the Palestinians than for the Arab nations in general; Black differentials in Israel over Palestinian sympathies were somewhat lower than those of whites; but both groups still favored Israel over both the Arab nations and Palestinians. These conclusions are reinforced by another question in this survey: 41 percent of white respondents in May 1990 believed that Israel was right to refuse to negotiate with the PLO, 30 percent said Israel was wrong to adopt this stance, and 29 percent did not express an opinion. Among Black respondents, 26 percent thought Israel right to refuse to negotiate with the PLO, 27 percent said Israel was wrong, and 35 percent had no opinion.[30]

The most negative findings reported on African American attitudes toward Israel appeared in a November 1992 survey conducted by the firm of Marttila and Kiley for the Anti-Defamation League. This study took place following a period of tension between Israel and the United States over negotiations with the Arab states and Palestinians and the status of the West Bank and Gaza Strip. Yitzhak Rabin had been elected Prime Minister of Israel in June 1992, but his policies had not yet begun to reverse the stance of the previous Likud government, as they did later.

The survey clearly concluded, "Black Americans have among the least favorable attitudes toward Israel of any demographic group." This evaluation stemmed from several items on which Blacks scored significantly lower on pro-Israel ratings than other respondents. Among what the survey called "the general public," 34 percent had a favorable impression of the current Israeli government, while 36 percent had an unfavorable impression. Among Blacks, 18 percent had a favorable rating and 42 percent an unfavorable one. By a fairly narrow margin of 44 percent to 37 percent, the public at large believed that the United States should continue to give preference to Israel in the Middle East, while only 28 percent of Blacks agreed that this preference should continue and 42 percent disagreed.[31]

In evaluating these results, it is necessary to understand that Blacks were by no means unique in their responses. Indeed, the authors noted that a large part of the "coalition of voters which propelled Democrat Bill Clinton to the White House has neither much interest in the Middle East peace process nor good will toward Israel." Thus, Israel received relatively high unfavorable ratings not only from Blacks (42 percent), but also from liberals (44 percent) and voters under age 40 (42 percent). Liberals (45 percent) and Democrats (43 percent) joined Blacks (42 percent) in feeling that there is no longer reason for the United States to give preference to Israel. Thus, any questioning of support for Israel during this period of strained U.S.-Israel relations was not unique to African Americans, but occurred among several other identifiable groups as well.[32]

Even during this difficult time, the familiar pattern of basic Black support for Israel continued, though at lower levels than that of whites. Respondents to this survey favored Israel over the Arab countries by a margin of 46 percent to 16 percent. Among Blacks, the comparative responses favored Israel by 31 percent to 20 percent. Among both populations, respondents continued to express a more supportive attitude toward Palestinians than toward Arab countries. The general public expressed equal sympathy with Israel and the Palestinians, with each group getting 31 percent, while on this question Blacks favored the Palestinians by a margin of 33 percent to 21 percent.[33] In short, African Americans were one of several groups adopting stances unfavorable to Israel, though they hardly constituted a hard core opposition group.

With the improvement in U.S.-Israel relations that followed the signing of the Israeli-Palestinian Declaration of Principles in 1993, African Americans have moved with the country at large to positions more supportive of Israel. In a March 1995 survey conducted by the Mellman Group for the Israel Policy Forum, 56 percent of respondents agreed that the United States should continue its active efforts to achieve peace agreements between Israel and the Arab countries, while 18 percent disagreed and 27 percent expressed no opinion. Black respondents agreed that the United States should continue its active role by a margin of 54 percent to 12 percent, with 34 percent having no opinion. By a margin of 67 percent to 13 percent, respondents in general held that peace between Israel and the Arabs and stability in the Middle East are in the interest of the United States. Blacks agreed by a margin of 47 percent to 17 percent, with 35 percent expressing no opinion.[34]

Four points stand out in this review of three decades of surveys on African American attitudes toward Israel. First, African Americans show consistent support for Israel over this entire period. Second, that support is at a lower level than that of the public at large. Third, for greater proportions of African Americans than others, this is not a very important issue: Blacks consistently outpace whites in the proportion that express no opinion on Israel-related questions. Fourth, responses of African Americans are subject to the course of events; they are especially prone to express sympathy with the Palestinians as well as with Israel and to strongly back pro-peace positions.

For Jews, there may be cause for concern in lower than average support for Israel, indifference to the issue, and high levels of sympathy for Palestinians. Nevertheless, the sharply critical statements of some African American leaders have clearly not penetrated to the general Black population. At the very least, significant qualifiers are in order in any statement that seeks to identify "black Americans" or "a large number of blacks" as anti-Israel.

III

What practical consequences are African American attitudes toward Israel likely to have? Two areas stand out in which Black positions on Israel may have a substantial impact on general attitudes or on policy.

First, many Jews worry that continued negative statements on Israel by visible Blacks, even if they do not reflect a majority position among African Americans or the stance of established leaders, are damaging to Jewish interests in the United States. However broad or narrow their communal support, the attacks on Israel by Blacks that have drawn wide media attention constitute one of the few readily identifiable locations where positions harmful to central Jewish concerns are being articulated in American society. In the same way, Jews have expressed concern that anti-Semitism in American universities appears in the form of speeches by well-known Blacks such as Kwame Toure and the followers of Louis Farrakhan, often at forums sponsored by African American student associations. Attention-generating statements by individuals, even if they represent only a minority view in the community, can have a telling influence on public discourse and intergroup relations. On two issues American Jews have deemed vital to their interests, Israel and university education, the major opposing forces arise from the Black community, causing significant intercommunal tension.[35]

The second way that African American positions on Israel may have a practical effect is on the issue of U.S. foreign aid to Israel. International assistance must pass through Congress where a substantial Black Congressional Caucus wields some influence.

Even the most pessimistic recent historian of Black-Jewish relations has acknowledged that "the congressional Black caucus has consistently and overwhelmingly favored foreign aid to Israel."[36] Whatever the statements made by some Blacks assaulting Israel or the ambivalence of respondents to surveys, African Americans in Congress have reliably supported substantial U.S. international assistance to Israel.

Congressional Black support for aid to Israel is similar to the supportive stance Caucus members have taken on immigration issues important to Hispanics. Lawrence Fuchs has noted that American Black leadership has historically opposed immigration since they have feared that newcomers would compete with Black labor for scarce jobs. Nevertheless, in the Congressional context, the Black Caucus has supported Hispanic positions on immigration in order to secure the votes of Latino members of Congress on issues of central concern to Blacks.[37] Similarly, Black Caucus members have supported aid to Israel in order to attain Jewish backing for their top priorities.

This explanation for Black Caucus support assumes that aid for Israel is not a fundamental issue to African Americans and can be traded off for coalitional purposes. However, three trends are already occurring that challenge the validity of this assumption and therefore the solidity of continued Black support for assistance to Israel.

First, international affairs, which traditionally ranked low on the public agenda of African Americans, are beginning to rise on the community's list of priorities. A study commissioned by the National Research Council found that Blacks now seek "to influence U.S. policy on Africa in much the same way that Jews have sought to influence policy toward Israel."[38] As concern grows among Black political leadership, particularly on policy toward Africa, actions may be advocated that would compete with Israel for priority attention or resources.

Second, as a result of legal action and rising political consciousness, the number of Blacks in Congress has grown substantially. The Caucus, as a result of its numerical strength and clear agenda, will likely be more assertive in its relations with other communities, demanding, for example, more equal allocation of resources in foreign assistance.[39]

Third, the amount of money available for foreign aid is shrinking. Particularly since the Republican takeover of Congress in the 1994 elections, two trends have threatened foreign assistance: the drive to cut the budget generally and a growing isolationism. Advocates for Israel and Africa may therefore find themselves competing for increasingly scarce resources.

The effect of these three trends on Black Congressional support for Israel cannot be predicted now. It is possible that in an era of shrinking foreign policy resources, African American and Jewish members of Congress will unite to protect international assistance dollars so that their primary areas of interest will continue to draw aid. Conversely, it is conceivable that shrinking dollars will result in tension due to competition for assistance that could go in substantial amounts either to Africa or to the Middle East, but not to both regions. Either outcome could draw on trends now occurring in relations between the two communities. A coalition for foreign aid could grow out of clear majority Black support for Israel evident in opinion surveys, as well as a consistent tradition of pro-Israel voting by the Black Congressional Caucus and support for African assistance by Jewish members of Congress. Competition for resources could stem from relative Black indifference to Israel shown in the same surveys, as well a history of hostility toward Israel and Jewish interests more generally expressed by visible African Americans in the political and academic arenas and a growing interest in promoting the interests of Africa. The next phase of African American opinion and action on Israel is likely to be as complex as their history.

Notes

1. Cynthia Ozick, "Afterword (1993)", in Paul Berman, ed., *Blacks and Jews: Alliances and Arguments* (New York, 1994), p. 72.

2. Murray Friedman, *What Went Wrong? The Creation and Collapse of the Black-Jewish Alliance* (New York, 1995), p. 12.

3. Robert G. Weisbord and Arthur Stein, *Bittersweet Encounter: The Afro-American and the Jew* (New York, 1972), p. 93.

4. Ibid., p. 99.

5. Ibid., p. 101.

6. Friedman, *What Went Wrong?*, pp. 232–33.

7. Weisbord and Stein, *Bittersweet Encounter*, p. 101.

8. Ibid., pp. 102–3.

9. Ibid., p. 106.

10. Friedman, *What Went Wrong?*, pp. 321–22.

11. Leonard Dinnerstein, *Antisemitism in America* (New York, 1994), p. 217.

12. Friedman, p. 328.

13. Ibid., pp. 329–30.

14. Ibid., p. 321.

15. Ibid., p. 348.

16. Harold Cruse, *The Crisis of the Negro Intellectual* (New York, 1984), p. 484.

17. Paul Berman, "Introduction: The Other and the Almost the Same," in Berman, ed., *Blacks and Jews*, p. 18.

18. C. Eric Lincoln, "Foreword," in Weisbord and Stein, *Bittersweet Encounter*, pp. xvi–xvii.

19. Weisbord and Stein, *Bittersweet Encounter*, p. 109.

20. Cornel West, *Race Matters* (Boston, 1993), p. 74.

21. The surveys cited in this section are the American Jewish Committee surveys conducted by the Roper Organization, the Anti-Defamation League survey by Marttila & Kiley, Inc., and the Israel Policy Forum survey by the Mellman Group, Inc.

22. The three Roper Organization/American Jewish Committee surveys cited in this section each interviewed slightly less than 2,000 respondents; the Marttila/ADL survey interviewed a base sample of 800, plus Black and Jewish samples of 400 respondents each; the Mellman Group/Israel Policy Forum survey interviewed 1,005 respondents.

23. Jennifer L. Golub, *What Do We Know About Black Anti-Semitism?* (New York, 1990), p. 16.

24. Ibid., p. 19.

25. David Singer and Renae Cohen, *Probing Public Sentiment on Israel and American Jews: The February 1987 Roper Poll* (New York, 1987), Table 8.

26. Ibid., Table 9.

27. David Singer and Renae Cohen, *In the Wake of the Palestinian Uprising: Findings of the April 1988 Roper Poll* (New York: American Jewish Committee, 1988), Table 9.

28. Ibid., Tables 10, 11, 12.

29. Ibid., Table 13.

30. David Singer and Renae Cohen, *Perceptions of Israel and American Jews: Findings of the May 1990 Roper Poll* (New York, 1990), Tables 9, 10, 14.

31. Marttila and Kiley, *Highlights of Israel/Middle East Results* (New York: Anti-Defamation League, November, 1992), p. 14.

32. Ibid., p. 9.

33. Ibid., pp. 15–16.

34. Data from the files of the Israel Policy Forum, New York.

35. For a fuller discussion, see my essay, "How Should We Think About Black Anti-Semitism?" in Jerome Chanes, ed., *Antisemitism in America Today* (New York, 1995), pp. 150–70.

36. Friedman, *What Went Wrong?*, p. 351.

37. Lawrence Fuchs, "The Reactions of Black Americans to Immigration," in Virginia Yans-McLaughlin, ed., *Immigration Reconsidered* (New York, 1990), pp. 293–314.

38. Gerald David Jaynes and Robin Williams, eds., *A Common Destiny: Blacks and American Society* (Washington, 1989), p. 252.

39. Milton D. Morris and Gary E. Rubin, "The Turbulent Friendship: Black-Jewish Relations in the 1990s," in Peter I. Rose, ed., *Interminority Affairs in the United States: Pluralism at the Crossroads, The Annals*, Vol. 350, November 1993, pp. 53–56.

eighteen

ON IMAGINING FOES, IMAGINING FRIENDSHIP

PATRICIA J. WILLIAMS

n recent years, relations between American Blacks and Jews, as symbolized by the tragic tensions in the Crown Heights section of Brooklyn, New York, have been relentlessly characterized as being in a state of distrust and precipitous decline. It is precisely this sort of broad, simplistic characterization, in the context of infinitely more nuanced encounters, that is itself part of the cause of the breakdown. The term "Black-Jewish alliance" is on the one hand commonly used to invoke a specific history of shared struggles in the United States, from the turn of the century onward. These struggles, from the labor movement to the civil rights movement, were social settings in which the two groups worked shoulder to shoulder in many settings, shoring up and very nearly defining the Left in this nation. As was—and still is—appropriate and efficient in the face of the legalized monolith of U.S. apartheid laws, Blacks and Jews focused frequently on their similarities, on the commonalities of the Holocaust and the Middle Passage, so incomparable in one sense yet so filled with the same unbounded mandate of never forgetting.

On the other hand, after the successes of the civil rights movement, it is clear that the things that divide us demand addressing also. While Blacks and Jews may occupy the same symbolic social space when it comes to the Ku Klux Klan, our divergent histories and daily experiences in the United States make it difficult to presuppose much "sameness" when we deal with each other in other contexts. For example, while both groups share anguishing issues about members who "pass" as either white or gentile, this assimilative force takes on confusing power in regard to one another. "You're white," hurled Blacks in Crown Heights; "Antisemites," Jews hurled back. And of course each side was right in terms of the injurious forays of that verbal war. Members of the Hasidic community used insulting racial epithets and characterizations about Blacks, terms whose history goes back hundreds of years in U.S. history. Black residents of Crown Heights stood on street corners and shouted that Hitler was right. In this context, the use of such shop-worn slogans of hate is a testament to the power of even partial assimilation into the ethic of America's race hatred.

At the same time, I could not help but wonder if this horrible debacle were really about "Black-Jewish relations" in the sense of summoning up the collapse of some historic alliance. The Blacks in Crown Heights were, for the most part, not African American descendants of slavery in the United States, but rather immigrants from various parts of the West Indies and Caribbean. Similarly, I wonder if the fact that the Jews in Crown Heights were mostly members of a fairly self-enclosed Hasidic community introduces a somewhat different tension than that popularly bandied about: they were not "invisible" minorities in the sense that most American Jews are. Their determination not to blend peaceably into the J. Crew mass of suburban manners, morals, and fashionable dress "marks" them in important and dangerous ways—ways that reawaken the sort of unfettered, forcefully unsubtle anti-Semitism that flourished more prevalently only a generation or so ago when most Jews were somewhat more visible by accent, circumcision (in the days before it was widespread), segregation, etc. And Blacks, as participants in this culture, have been no less—nor any more—assimilated into that anti-Semitism than anyone else.

I cannot help wondering if the Crown Heights tension is really about "Blacks versus Jews" at all. That opposition connotes a rather flattened sense of post–civil rights breakdown, as well as a certain neoconservative vision in which Jews have become "zealous Zionists" and Blacks have "lost" their "transcendent moral claim" on national sympathies. Does the construction of the debate in these stereotyped terms contribute anything to the possibility of accord?

Could not the dispute in Crown Heights more fruitfully be recast as one involving Jews who don't feel "white" yet who occupy the identity space of whites, particularly as the beneficiaries of certain public services like that of police protection? At the same time, is it not a dispute involving Blacks who are unaware of themselves as resonantly Christian in this context, yet who, having developed a strong survivalist, even fundamentalist, version of Christianity, are implicated in its history toward Jews indirectly, complexly perhaps, but nevertheless somehow entwined? I daresay it would also help the analysis to take at least some stock of the fact that the steadfastly Messianic Hasidic community in Crown Heights is at odds not just with Blacks but with much of the rest of the Jewish community in this country. Similarly, much of the Black Caribbean community of Crown Heights is not only at odds with the Hasidic community but also at odds with—in some instances quite prejudiced against—Blacks whose ancestors were slaves in the United States. In other words, the issue is, at least in part, whether unassimilated racial, ethnic, and immigrant groups can live in peace not just with one another, but within a culture that resolutely denies their particularity as just too *unpleasant*.

The extent to which any constructive discussion becomes derailed under such circumstances is epitomized by a story one of my students told me: at the height of the Crown Heights tension, one of the local television stations thought it would be a great idea to have a group of Black and Jewish teenagers engaging in conversation that would model tolerance, healing, and general we-are-the-world-ness. The plan encountered immediate problems; among other matters, the Hasidic boys could not have such a conversation in the same room with girls, and the Black youth of Crown Heights seemed a little sullen. So the producers went about remedying this situation by fetching a group of reform Jewish students from Long Island and some pleasant-faced upper-middle class Black kids from private schools—and had them talk about Crown Heights, *in* Crown Heights even, engaging in a "debate" that had less to do with the affected communities than with modeling an imagined melting pot bubbling happily, full of flavor and harmony. But the absurdity of importing people to enact a conversation that the actual neighborhood could never have is directly akin to the Allan Bloom-ian nostalgia for an undifferentiated "American" culture flowing seamlessly from the font of "Western" civilization. Whose anxieties are supposedly redressed by such mythic representations? And is it possible that such representations are not just misleading, but downright oppressive?

The challenge becomes, as years since the civil rights movement have taught us, how we can envision a racially integrated world that will represent not merely the absorption of racial and ethnic minorities into dominant white society, but the fluid mix of race, culture, and much more. Equal opportunity is not only about assuming the circumstances of hypothetically indistinguishable individuals, but also about accommodating the living, shifting fortunes of those who are very differently situated. What happens to a single person may be the repercussive history that repeats itself in the futures of everyone. Nevertheless, in an environment where Blackness and whiteness are the objects of relentless biologized essentialism, it is not surprising that a frequent metaphor for racial harmony, at least since the 1960s, has been embodied in the notion of "grey babies." While I understand that a waved banner of aggressive miscegenation is one kind of logical response to the virulent history of anti-miscegenation in the United States, I do worry that life is not that simple.

When in early 1993 Tina Brown's new *New Yorker* blasted its way into its first national controversy, it did so by meshing—I even want to say mashing—embodied symbols of that violent showdown in Crown Heights. The February 14th issue featured a cover illustration of a Hasidic man kissing a Black woman on the lips. The artist, award-winning cartoonist Art Spiegelman, whose *Maus* books are among the most oddly captivating and moving accounts of the Holocaust ever published, explained his intentions as a Valentine's day wish to New York that life's collisions be as simply resolved as kissing and making up.

But *The New Yorker* cover offended everyone, it seemed; pleased no one; and for all of Tina Brown's protestations that it was *meant* to spark controversy, the controversy that ensued hardly addressed the problems of Crown Heights or racial confrontation in the United States. As lucidly, even childishly resonant, as Spiegelman's wish was on one level, his illustration nevertheless blundered onto a battleground of complicated symbolic meaning. That battleground is fraught with lessons about the kinds of conversations Blacks and Jews need (and need not) to have with one another, and about the pitfalls that even our best efforts at reconciliation seem to encounter. It underscores, moreover, our urgent necessity to press on with the conversation, even when it misfires as dismally as Spiegelman's kiss.

First, it was hard to imagine to whom Spiegelman's fantasy was addressed. Was he trying to speak to the upscale post-ethnic Manhattanites or wanna-be Manhattanites who form so much of *The New Yorker's* readership? Or perhaps to Hasidic Jews, who are not permitted to touch anyone but their own spouses—and certainly not with the closed-eyed, mouth-to-mouth eroticism of Spiegelman's depiction? (Spiegelman was the first to admit that the woman was most likely not "his wife, an Ethiopian Jew.") Or was Spiegelman addressing Blacks, whose experience with artistic representation by whites has always veered to the erotically transgressive? (And imagine *how* transgressive the Jezebel was who could lure a devout Hasidic man from his pursuit of piety.)

This kiss as Spiegelman's chosen metaphor for the kind of complicated political reconciliation that Crown Heights requires strikes me as a sign of how immensely sexualized our culture is—in particular of how sexualized our racial encounters are. And the kiss depicted was a quite sexual one; if there is any doubt about that, consider the same pose with, say, a Hasidic man and Al Sharpton. Perhaps then, in our sexually titillated but homophobic society, the raw sex appeal, even pornography, of the pose would have been all too exaggeratedly visible.) Grey babies have become the optimist's antidote to everything: the pervasive antimiscegenist horror of tainted blood lines that inspires segregation's powerful taboos having been countered time and again by the simplistic antidote of More Miscegenation. (My impatience here parallels my concern with the cheerfully chipper blather so popular these days that hate speech can be countered by the innocent redemption of More Speech. Neither redemptive sex nor whole droning clouds of More Speech will do much if people fail to grapple with—and "grappling with" need not suggest censorship—the complex histories and causes of race hatred and violence.)

But, while political intermarriage may be noble and good, this form of romanticism-as-political solution misses the point. As Calvin Hernton has noted: "One of the most interesting aspects of the race problem was formulated by [Gunnar Myrdal, in *An American Dilemma*,] into a schema which he called 'The Rank Order of Discrimination.' When Myrdal asked white Southerners to list, in the order of importance, the things they thought Negroes wanted most, here is what he got:

1. Intermarriage and sex intercourse with whites
2. Social equality and etiquette

3. Desegregation of public facilities, buses, churches, etc.
4. Political enfranchisement
5. Fair treatment in the law courts
6. Economic opportunities

"The curious thing about this 'Rank Order' was that when Myrdal approached the Negroes, they put down the same items as did the whites, but with one major change—they listed them in reverse order!"[1]

Moreover, if the whole world were grey tomorrow, I think the situation in Crown Heights would still exist, because it can't be cured by convincing everyone that we're all related. Crown Heights is about how—or if—we human creatures can live together while observing very different cultural practices. I do not mean to suggest that racism and anti-Semitism are not key dimensions in the dispute, but rather that resolutions based on innocently assimilative, dehistoricized ideals only blur or aggravate rather than assuage. And that maybe a more respectful—yet perhaps ultimately more difficult—vision would depict a Hasidic Jew and a Caribbean neighbor just nodding and saying "Good morning" to one another as they passed each other on the street they share.

It's a kind of heresy, I know, to suggest that the storybook desire to marry a Capulet and live happily ever after might be oppressive, and again I want to underscore the degree to which, like Spiegelman, I personally believe that the streets of Verona will never be calm until there's a little more love between us. But what concerns me is that the West Side Story solution is a blindly depoliticized one, and obscures the possibility that simple cantankerous coexistence may be more like what we should be aiming for in a democracy based on live and let live.

The Crown Heights situation exemplifies the difficulty of understanding the tensions faced in current race relations: we hear about Black/white, Black/Jewish, Black/brown, Black/Korean confrontations. It is only when it erupts at the level of international figure skating competitions, perhaps, that we are aware of Irish, Italian, or Chinese gangs, to say nothing of White Aryan Resistance gangs, all battling one another dreadfully. The irreducibility of the categories of "Black" and "Jew" in racist and anti-Semitic imagination must be whittled away by persistently detailed descriptions of lived encounters among live neighbors. The genuinely difficult task facing our times is to come up with images that might suggest a model of coexistence that is fluid rather than static, a model of value that does not substitute a facile sociobiology for the actuality of culture.

To illustrate how hard I think the work that faces us will be, let me try to lay out some of my own thoughts about the pitfalls that even our best efforts at reconciling democracy's challenges seem to encounter, as well as my sense of the urgent necessity to continue such conversations, even when they misfire dismally.

In a much-publicized incident at Harvard University a few years ago, a white student hung a Confederate flag from her dormitory window saying that to her it symbolized the warmth and community of her happy southern home. This act produced a strong series of public denunciations from many other students, Blacks in particular, who described the symbolic significance of the Confederacy as a *white* community forged against a backdrop of force, intimidation, and death for Blacks. Eventually one Black student hung a sheet with a swastika painted on it out her window, with the expressed hope that the university would force both her and the white student to remove such displays. The university did not, and eventually the Black student removed her flag voluntarily in view of the fact that it was creating tensions between Black and Jewish students.

While the entire debate surrounding this incident focused predictably on free speech issues, what seemed strange to me was a repeated and unexamined imbalance in how the two students' acts were discussed. On the one hand, there was a ubiquitous assumption that the white student's attribution of meaning to the Confederate flag was "just hers," so no one else had any "business" complaining about it. The flag's meaning became a form of private property that she could control exclusively and despite other assertions of its symbolic power. (Those other assertions are just "their opinion"; all's fair in the competitive marketplace of meaning.)

At the same time, there was an assumption that the swastika's meaning was fixed, transcendent, "universally" understood as evil. The Black student's attempt to infuse it with "her" contextualized meaning (i.e., that of the translated power of what the Confederate flag meant to her) was lost in the face of the larger social consensus of its historical meaning. This larger social consensus is not really fixed, of course, but its monopoly on the well-educated Harvard community's understanding is tribute both to the degree of its overarchingly murderous yet coalescing power in the context of Aryan supremacist movements as well as to our having learned a great deal of specific history about it. The power of that history understandably overshadowed not only that Black student's attempt at a narrower meaning, but also the swastika's meaning in aboriginal American religion or in Celtic runes.

The question remains, however, how some speech is so automatically put beyond comment, consigned to the free market of ideas, while other expressions remain invisibly regulated, even monopolized, by the channels of not merely what we have learned but what we have not learned. I do not want to be misunderstood: I do not question our consensus of the image of genocide embodied in the swastika; I wonder at the immovability of the comfy, down-home aura attending the confederate flag—the sense that as long as it makes some people happy, the rest of us should just butt out. The limits of such reasoning might be clearer if applied to the swastika: without having to conclude anything about whether to censor it, the fact remains that we usually don't cut off discussions of Nazism with the conclusion that it was a way of creating warm and happy communities for the German bourgeoisie.

Let me be clearer still in this thorny territory: I wish neither to compare nor to relativize the horrors of the Holocaust and of the legacy of slavery in the United States. This is not an appropriate subject for competition; it is not a sweepstakes anyone could want to win. What I do worry about is that it is easier to condemn that which exists at a bit of cultural distance from that in which we may ourselves be implicated. And it is easier to be clear about the nature of the evils we have seen in others an ocean away than about those whose existence we deny or whose history we do not know. The easy flip-flopping between "free" and "regulated" signification is a function of knowledge; it underscores the degree to which we could all stand to educate ourselves perhaps most particularly about the unpleas-antries of the past: we should not have to rely upon the "shock" shorthand of cam-pus crises, for example, to bring to our public consciousness the experience of Black history in the good old days of legalized lynching.

I am concerned, furthermore, that the noisy rush to discuss the legalities of censorship and the First Amendment preempts more constructive conversations about how we might reinfuse our civics and our pedagogy with dignity and tol-erance for all. As I have remarked a number of times before, it is as though the First Amendment has become severed from any discussion of the actual limits and effects of political, commercial, defamatory, perjurious or any other of the myriad classifications of speech. It is as though expressions that contain a particularly volatile payload of hate become automatically privileged as political, and more-over, are supported by the First Amendment as a bludgeon of paradox—"I have my First Amendment right to call you a monkey, so you shut up about it." As legal anthropologist Richard Perry observes, hatred thereby gets to cross-dress as Virtue Aggrieved.[2]

II

The ability to negotiate the politics of coexistence on college campuses is direct-ly related to how those leaders of tomorrow, college graduates, will resolve such problems in "the real world." The negotiations in the most banal of everyday encounters are plagued by some of the same symbolic and analytical confusion encountered in the Harvard example. Let me give an example of a Phil Donahue show that I saw some time ago. It was a program that purported to be deeply con-cerned about the rise of anti-Semitism on campuses in general, and the prolifera-tion of Jewish American Princess jokes in particular. "How would *you* feel ...," Donahue kept asking by way of challenge to the studio audience.

The program opened with an extraordinarily long volley of Jewish American Princess jokes, not merely recited, but written in large block letters across the screen—for the hearing impaired presumably, although there was no other part of the program so emphatically emblazoned.

The jokes played on mean-spirited, vulgar stereotypes: they were just plain offensive, even though they were positioned as merely "models" of the subject to be discussed. Although styled as a repudiation, they reenacted the whole problem—over and over and over again—I mean there were a lot of jokes flashed on the screen, and lots of precious TV time was given over to Donahue's long litany, while the audience tittered and giggled its way through this opening volley. It was significant, I think, this tittering: after each joke, the cameras focused intently as a dentist's drill upon the stunned-rabbit faces of the audience, an audience caught in this not-quite-sure-how-to-respond mode that implicated them as they struggled to be good sports while being broadcast live to millions of people. It was a marvelously assimilative moment, like children trying to decide how to be seen at their best. Smile? Frown? Which is the posture of belonging? So they tittered. Nervously.

There is a real risk of destructive impact caught in the power of jokes that make fun of the supposed characteristics of historically oppressed or shunned people. Of course all humor depends on context, but, if it is possible to speak generally, I think that such jokes too frequently are the enactment of a kind of "marking" process, in which communities are described, kinship delimited, the enemy imagined.

The rest of the Phil Donahue show on Jewish American Princesses was a panoply of squirmy ways of dealing with being marked. Donahue's guests included not only a Real Live Jewish Princess, but a Black American Princess, an Italian American Princess, and a WASP Princess as well. While they were all willing to be called *princesses* of a certain flavor, they all denied that they were the *bad* kind of princess. They negotiated this good princess/evil witch divide by at least four different maneuvers:

First, there was the "role model" response: "Yeah well I'm proud to be pushy, and I've made it into a positive attribute, look at how creative I am with the lemons life has handed me. Doesn't bother me a bit" (even though an unfortunate cost of this survival mechanism would seem to be a rather defensive, cynical edge).

Second, there was the "But I really am a princess!" response, along with an attempt to remove the sarcasm from the statement and be taken as literal, real. The Real WASP Princess proclaimed herself as the inheritor of society's privilege and all the other ethnic princesses as mere wanna-be imitations of herself; the Black princess claimed to have been the real princess of a considerably smaller if warmer realm, in having been the apple of her protective family's eye; and the Italian American Princess claimed that her real name *was* "princess," at least that's what daddy always said.

Third, there was the move to concede that, although some women may be like that awful thing at the butt of all those jokes, "all Jewish women are not JAPs." There was, in other words, a concession of the category as validly descriptive, and then the attempt to exclude oneself from it. This is a powerfully defeatist move because it concedes the category as given, and thereby allows the stereotype legitimacy. The response to racist labeling is thus locked into the logic of merely defining oneself within or outside of the label, rather than challenging the prejudice and judgmentalism of the marking process at all. I think that this resort to a "them-us" dichotomy, or an "I'm different" strategy, is perhaps the most prevalent individual response to bigotry, as well as the most destructive.

Fourth, there is the opposite move—and perhaps the most prevalent institutional response to bigotry—the tendency to generalize rather than to exceptionalize, to make shrill self-absorption a general feature of all women, who were portrayed as possessing a variety of generally negative qualities. Women of *all* ethnicities are bitchy, stupid, fluffy, greedy, and sacrificial ran the logic of a narrative that played sexism against anti-Semitism, and played general stereotype against its subcomponents. Thus, "equal opportunity bimbo-ism" was proffered as an odd model of the way in which tolerating intolerance emerges as the new norm for tolerance itself.

The powerfully complicated baggage of this new-age tolerant intolerance was perhaps most painfully visible in the incomprehensibly miscalculated spoof undertaken by actor Ted Danson of his then-girlfriend comedienne Whoopi Goldberg, in which Danson donned blackface, ate watermelon, joked about their sex life and her genitalia, and used the word "nigger" repeatedly. Claiming to be mystified by the storm of public reaction that ensued, much was made of the claim that Whoopi had approved of the material, even helped write it and that therefore it couldn't be racist.

Scarcely two months after that fiasco, Goldberg's recipe for "Jewish American Princess Fried Chicken" was published in a book entitled *Cooking for Litchfield Hills*. The recipe "instructs you to 'Send a chauffeur to your favorite butcher shop for the chicken,' 'Watch your nails' when you shake the chicken in a brown paper bag, and 'Have Cook prepare rest of meal while you touch up your makeup.'"[3] Again there was a big debate about whether it was funny or whether it was anti-Semitic (as though these are necessarily oppositional). Again there was hand-wringing about subject position, although I'm sure that's not what people imagined they were doing. "'This is in worse taste (than the Friar's club debacle) because she could get away with that because she is Black,' said one Litchfield resident."[4]

Let's sidestep for just a moment the complicating detail that Goldberg didn't "get away with" much of anything at all precisely because she employed the body of Danson as the time-honored comedic vehicle of racial minstrelsy—a white man in blackface mouthing stereotypes too familiar to be ironic, albeit supposedly written by a Black woman to parody herself. Rather I would like to examine the comeback shot off by Goldberg's publicist: "Maybe (the critics) are not aware that Whoopi is Jewish, so she is certainly not anti-Semitic."[5] It's a familiar litany: "I heard a Jewish person tell this joke so it's not antisemitic." And of course, a Jewish person wrote this joke for me, so I couldn't possibly be antisemitic just because I'm trying to lighten things up with a little Holocaust humor. In fact, goes the next line of the argument, *you're* intolerant for claiming intolerance. And a bad sport besides. (It is by a reversed, mirror-image logic, perhaps, that two Oakhurst, California, high school youths who dressed up in the white robes and hoods of the Ku Klux Klan and reenacted a lynching of another student for a Halloween party—and who were then rewarded with a prize in the costume competition—sought to justify the event by saying that *no* Blacks were at the party so it was O.K.)[6]

In the political and legal realm, the discussion of race and ethnicity has become increasingly characterized by this sort of casually demeaning stupidity. For me, one of the most powerfully frustrating versions of this dead-end thinking has been the all-out bid to equate affirmative action programs, seeking to include Blacks and dispossessed minorities in American life, with quota programs that have been used to exclude Jews and Asian-Americans. The utter eclipse of the range of affirmative action commitments by the evil specter of quotas demonstrates how any language of reform may be turned inside out by conflating it with historical tropes of negativity, even as its substance is being relentlessly dehistoricized. Whereas segregation and group exclusion were once considered the stigma of inferiority, now, according to the new right consciousness sweeping the land, it is the very identification of Blacks and other racial minorities as groups that is stigmatizing—no matter that the project is inclusion.

In the charged context of affirmative action, programs designed to dismantle systems of favoritism that for centuries "favored" Christian white men and "disfavored" Blacks, Jews, and women have been effectively frozen by a glib and cynically racialized reversal of the vocabulary of preference: so that now presumably it is Blacks who are favored and whites automatically disfavored.[7] The casual ahistoricism of this reversal implies a causal link between the inclusion of Blacks and the oppression of whites—whiteness now generally figured as including Jews and most women.

This backlash taps into myths so powerful that no amount of empirical data seems able to shake their hold. On the one hand the appalling statistics are widely known: about glass ceilings for women, people of color, and certain religious and ethnic groups; about Blacks' dwindling enrollment in colleges and graduate programs; and about underemployment, unemployment, homelessness, and high mortality rates for so many people of color. These statistics are all well-publicized, as are the sentiments of many whites who are quite open about their fear of living in the same neighborhood as Blacks, of attending the same schools, of touching the same food, or even of walking down the same sidewalk. On the other hand, all this evidence and experience of shunning and isolation does not seem to temper even to a small degree the simultaneous perception that Blacks are everywhere better off than whites, taking all the best jobs, having too much fun even when they're in prison, and just generally taking *over* everything (except the banks and the media, still the untrammeled preserve of anti-Semitism's most concentrated virulence).

//

Our kinship on this earth is such an ambiguous affair, a little of this, a little of that, an exercise in how we can invent ourselves to be seen today, survive until tomorrow.

Many years ago, a friend of mine invited me to her home for dinner. As it turned out, her husband was a survivor of Auschwitz. He had been an artist before he had been captured by the Nazis, and while he made his living in an entirely different field since coming to the United States, his wife told me, he still painted as a hobby from time to time. She took me to their garage, and showed me an immense collection of his work. There he had stored paintings that probably numbered in the hundreds: circus-bright landscapes with vivid colors and lush, exquisitely detailed vegetation. Yet in every last one of them, there was a space of completely bare canvas, an empty patch in the shape of a human being. "He never finishes anything," whispered my friend, but I could hardly hear her, for I had never seen such a complete representation of the suppression of personality, the erasure of humanity that the Holocaust exacted.

A few weeks after this, my sister sent me a microfiche copy of a property listing from the National Archives, documenting the existence of our enslaved great-great-grandmother.[8] The night after I received my sister's letter, I dreamed that I was looking at my friend's husband's paintings, all those vivid landscapes with the bare body-shapes, and suddenly my great-great-grandmother appeared in the middle of each and every one of them. Suddenly she filled in all the empty spaces, and I looked into her face with the supernatural stillness of deep recollection. From that moment, I knew exactly who she was—every pore, every hair, every angle of her face. I would know her everywhere.

I retell this story not for its own sake, but to reflect on how difficult it has been to tell at all, mostly because it has almost always affected my relation with those with whom I have shared it in ways that I can never predict: not necessarily in bad ways, but powerfully. Recounting it on an informal basis to a number of my friends, I have been startled by the range of responses to its blended image of historical oppressions. Some have found the story moving, some have been angered by what they perceive as either the flattening or co-opting of the particularity of someone else's story, and for some it is the ultimate proof that I am not cut out for life in the real world. Yet just in the process of telling, I have learned a great deal about my friends—I learned the *why* of their varied responses, the unexpected, invisible connections that they had to "my" story. Once I recovered from being put off by how people were "taking" *my* story, I began to get inklings of the rarely discussed, sometimes painfully suppressed, cultural histories of friends who for the most part identified themselves in the laconic categories of the census—as "white" or "Asian" or "Black" or "all mixed up" or "American" or "nothing in particular." One was the grandchild of a German Lutheran artist killed by the Nazis. Another's mother had fled from North Vietnam to Laos to Cambodia to France.

Someone else was Romany but "passing" because "people don't trust gypsies." I learned a lot about wars in Armenia, potato famines in Ireland, civil war in Ghana, oppression in Latvia, electoral fraud in Palau, independence movements in Scotland, and the literary tradition of magical realism in South America. The whole history of the last three centuries of global displacement of indigenous peoples began to unfold from beneath the serene facade of these very American friends with their Georgia locutions and New York accents and Midwestern vowels and San Fernando Valley inflections—the rich, painful, nuanced, complex, compressed amalgam that is American culture in its most generous sense....

It's complicated, this creation of cultural identity, perhaps a more complicated investment than mere words can capture. As I write, my son, at eighteen months, rolls on the floor of my office, chattering happily to himself. He eyes the floor-to-ceiling bookcases of African literature and Japanese poetry and *Encyclopedia Brittanicas* and Hindu art with satisfaction, turning his body this way and that, examining the literary landscape now sideways, now upside down. He is so extremely comfortable, fascinated, acquisitive. By his gaze, he makes "my" world his. He invests himself, he becomes part of this room. He rolls and sighs and examines and pats his stomach. He is learning where he belongs and that sense of belonging will make a certain property of the familiar.

The familiar is the property of belonging, I guess.

A Ghanaian student, years ago, asked me about the anonymity that I must suffer because of my slave heritage. He could not conceive of such rootlessness, the not knowing that afflicts both whites and Blacks in America, it frightened him. He described the songs by which he could trace his family, his tribe, his ancestors, back for generations. He described it as a system in which there was great respect not just for one's lineage, but for the memorization and oral recitation of that lineage. Words were so special because they bore the remains of one's ancestors and loved ones. It was so important to him that words be handled with care, that they be ordered and precise and caring. He called this the "property" of his life's inheritance. There was no room for carelessness, for that would be to let part of oneself die. I said that I could not conceive of being so thoroughly known. "Our property is much more alienable," I said, almost idly, before I heard its import. He agreed that there was something essentially anti-individualist, even anti-democratic in this memorizing of one's legacy, but he insisted that wisdom has a particular worded shape; to alter it is to result not just in blasphemy but in irretrievable loss.

I do try, from time to time, to imagine this world from which he spoke—a culture in whose mythology words might be that precious, a realm in which words were conceived as vessels for communications from the heart, a society in which words are holy, and where the challenge of life is based upon the quest for gentle words, holy words, gentle truths, holy truths. I try to imagine for myself a world in which the words one gives one's children are the shell into which they shall grow, so one chooses one's words carefully, like precious gifts, like magnificent inheritances, for they convey an excess of what we have imagined, they bear gifts beyond imagination, they reveal and revisit the wealth of history. How carefully, how slowly, and how lovingly we might step into our expectations of each other in such a world.

"I was not hunting for my liberty, but also hunting for my name," said William Wells Brown.

Notes

1. Calvin Hernton. "The Sexualization of Racism," in *Sex and Racism in America*, New York, 1988; see also, Gunnar Myrdal, *An American Dilemma*, 1944, pp. 587–88.

2. Richard W. Perry, unpublished letter of June 1, 1994, on file with author.

3. Jane Furse, "Whoopi cooks up a storm," *The Daily News*, Dec. 1, 1993, p. 3C, col. 1.

4. Ibid.

5. Ibid.

6. Anita Creamer, "Costumes Can't Hide Right and Wrong," *The Sacramento Bee*, Nov. 2, 1993, p. D1.

7. See 110 S. Ct. at 3025–26.

8. Williams, *The Alchemy of Race and Rights* (Cambridge, MA, 1991).

nineteen

BLACKS, JEWS, AND GENDER

The History, Politics, and Cultural Anthropology of a Women's Dialogue Group

LETTY COTTIN POGREBIN

This is the story of a Black/Jewish dialogue group that talked a blue streak for more than a decade and then went silent. I don't mean to suggest that a precipitating crisis contributed to the dissolution of this once vibrant group. More accurately, we just petered out. I think I understand why this happened and how other Black/Jewish dialogues might learn from our mistakes. But I'm getting ahead of my story.

Our group began back in 1984 as a spin-off from the sixty-member Black/Jewish Coalition of New York, which was composed mostly of male business, religious, and community leaders. Organized around the issues of the 1984 Presidential campaign, this larger assemblage had been effective at defusing Jewish anger over Jackson's "Hymietown" slur, and Black anger over a full-page ad headlined "Jews Against Jackson." But after a few months, it was clear to me that most of the participants were unwilling to delve deeper, to accept ambiguity, to expose their vulnerabilities, and to grapple with the emotional component of Black/Jewish relations. The men in particular fell into the habit of proclaiming how much they'd done for race relations and how well-connected they were—a kind of upscale version of "doin' the dozens."

While listening to one of these self-congratulatory speeches, I happened to glance across the room at a Black woman named Harriet Michel and we both rolled our eyes. At the end of that meeting, Harriet and I agreed that we'd had enough of these public masculinity contests. We decided to convene a women's dialogue, a small group of Jewish and African American women who could approach our mutual concerns with honesty, grit, and a feminist perspective.

Getting Started

We modeled ourselves on the consciousness-raising groups of the 1970s which had enabled women of all backgrounds to build on their commonalities and to forge the sisterhood that sustained the early years of the women's movement. However, since we planned to grapple with race, religion, ethnicity, and gender— a full enough plate—we decided not to add class differences into the mix, so we limited the group to our professional peers. Harriet, then director of the New York Urban League, chose two other African American participants—Bernice Powell, president of the New York Coalition of 100 Black Women, and the late Marguerite Ross Barnett, then vice-chancellor of the City University of New York. I chose two other Jewish women—Marilyn Braveman, then director of education and women's issues for the American Jewish Committee, and Jacqueline Levine, past president of the National Jewish Community Relations Council and vice president of the American Jewish Congress. We also decided to include a mediator, a neutral who could guide us through whatever stressful moments might arise. For this role we chose a woman who was neither Black nor Jewish (but could pass for either)—Donna Shalala, a Lebanese Christian, then president of Hunter College and now secretary of Health and Human Services.

Our ground rules were simple: Once a month or so, we met for dinner in each of our homes, alternating between Harlem, the East Side, West Side, and New Jersey. Either we brought pot luck dishes or the host provided the meal and plenty of wine to lubricate the gears of revelation. (My favorite menus, I'll admit, were the ethnically consistent ones—Southern fried chicken and sweet potato pie at a Black member's house; brisket and kugel at the table of a Jewish member.) We scheduled our meetings only when all six of us and our mediator were available, so that no one missed out on the cumulative chemistry of intimacy. From the outset, we agreed to talk straight, no obfuscations, no politesse—and we vowed to work through even the most volatile disputes without ever giving up or slamming out the door. The dialogue thus became a safe space where all confidences were sacrosanct, no thought unspeakable, and no subject off-limits. While our agenda was anything relating to Blacks, Jews, and gender, we agreed on the following givens: The rift between our two communities had widened. We cared enough to want to bridge it. Yet we knew we couldn't go back to the "good old days."

The humorist Calvin Trillin captured the once-upon-a-time trope of Black/Jewish unity when he quoted an apocryphal headline in the old *New York Post*: "COLD SNAP HITS OUR TOWN. JEWS, NEGROES SUFFER MOST." For decades, the common wisdom (especially among Jews) was that our two groups suffered most and suffered together, that we had comparable experiences of dislocation and loss, and maintained a special empathy for one another that was expressed in our politics and our friendships. But we knew we couldn't revisit the years before Ocean Hill–Brownsville, the *Bakke* case, the forced resignation of Andrew

Young—names conjuring bitterness on both sides—years when Blacks and Jews worked together for a goal called "freedom"; when Jews comprised more than half of the volunteers for the Mississippi Summer, and Chaney, Goodman, and Schwerner became our shared martyrs; when our clergy linked arms in massive civil rights marches and everyone sang "We Shall Overcome." Because of these historic connections, some say Jews and Blacks still approach one another with higher expectations than either of us brings to any other group. And our disappointments inflict sharper wounds.

In our women's dialogue, however, we couldn't even assume that there *was* a golden age of cooperation. Our Jewish members subscribed to that version of the past, but some of the African Americans thought the whole thing was a myth born of wishful thinking; they remembered the fifties and sixties as a time of asymmetry and inequality between Jews and Blacks, not an era of collective action and mutual dedication. Such disparate views required that we assume nothing except a willingness to question all assumptions. Which is what we did, meeting after meeting, year after year.

The Dialogue Process

I cannot imagine any group of men sitting around laughing, crying, confessing, letting down their hair and their defenses in quite this way. For the first several months, we talked about how it felt to grow up Black or Jewish in our families and neighborhoods. We described our parents and siblings, told each other how we felt about our looks, our hair, our voices, our bodies. We bonded over the girl stuff, the problems all females share—street hassles, male violence, condescension, sex bias, disproporionate responsibilty for child care and housework, coping with the culture's WASP beauty standards and cruel obsession with youth. Then we moved on to discuss our past interactions with the "other"—the Jews talked about how they experienced the Black people they knew in school or at work, as neighbors or friends; the Blacks did the same about the Jews in their lives. In the process, we learned to accept both our commonalities as women and our differences as Blacks and Jews.

We talked about how, throughout history, our foremothers were routinely subjugated or oppressed as women but when things got really brutal—when they were dehumanized by America's slave masters or slaughtered by Hitler's Nazis—it was not because they were female but because they were Blacks or Jews. This is why, no matter how angry we may be at our husbands, bosses, and boyfriends, we usually stand by our men against a hostile world. Nevertheless, in the privacy of the women's dialogue, we gave ourselves permission to break ranks and expose the gender bias *within* our own communities. We plumbed the deep connections between racism, anti-Semitism, and sexism. We tackled the tough issues and controversial news events of the decade. South Africa and Israel claimed a good chunk of our time, as did the Central Park jogger case and Crown Heights, Jesse

Jackson, the Anti-Defamation League, Ed Koch, Professors Leonard Jeffries and Michael Levin, and Ministers Louis Farrakhan and Khalid Muhammad. We tried to speak the truth and whatever else happened to be on our minds, and several of these exchanges remain vivid in my memory:

A Jewish woman arrived at one of our sessions complaining that a Black cab driver called her a "kike" when he thought her tip inadequate. To which one of the Black woman countered, "That's nothing! I can't get a cab to pick me up at all."

Another time, a Black woman castigated all white women who date Black men, but especially Jewish women who do so.

"If whites are dating Blacks, why make it a *Jewish* issue?" asked one of the Jews.

"Because," said the Black woman, "50 percent of the white partners of Blacks are Jews, and almost all those partners are Jewish *women* dating Black *men*."

"Well then," said the Jewish member, "maybe this proves that Jews, more than other whites, see Black people as human beings worthy of love. Tell me what's so bad about that?"

The sisters told us. White Jewish women siphon off educated, eligible African Americans—the most likely partners for middle-class Black women whose dating options are already severely limited by an ever-dwindling pool of Black males. The facts were sobering: homicide is the leading cause of death among young African American men; Black men die ten times more often than whites of hypertension disease; men in Harlem are less likely to survive to age 40 than men in Bangladesh. Suicide, drug addiction, AIDS, and imprisonment account for another large drain; the male prison population has grown by 80 percent since 1970 and now there are more college age Black men in prison or on parole than in college. More Black men than women drop out of school which explains why at UCLA, for instance, there are twice as many Black female as male students. Add to all this the average rate of homosexuality and one can see why marriageable, healthy, educated Black males are called an endangered species—and why Black women might be indignant when such a man is claimed by a white woman.

The Jewish women understood.

In another discussion, one Jew said she resented Black women's reluctance to join integrated feminist organizations. The African Americans replied that groups like the National Organization for Women and the National Women's Political Caucus are dominated by whites with an elitist agenda. The Jewish women insisted that would cease to be the case only if Black women joined up and altered the agenda from within. After several rounds of this chicken-and-egg argument, the group declared a draw.

In the summer of '84, our meeting fell on the night after Geraldine Ferraro made history at the Democratic Convention. Bubbling with enthusiasm, we toasted Gerry as we chewed over her acceptance speech and reviewed the prospects for the ticket and the pitfalls of a male-female candidacy. When Mondale and Ferraro greet one another, we wondered, should they kiss or shake hands? How would her husband relate to his wife? After a few minutes, I noticed that the Black women were not bubbling quite as effervescently as the Jewish women.

"How come you guys aren't so excited?" I asked. "Is there something wrong with Ferraro?"

"No, but she's white," they answered, almost simultaneously.

"But she's a woman, like you, like us," said I.

"Yeah, but she's white."

"She's also an Italian Catholic but I still feel her achievement as my own," said another Jew. "I think to myself, if an Italian Catholic woman can do it, maybe someday a Jewish woman can be in the White House."

"Maybe so, but it's a big leap from a white Italian to a Black candidate of any kind," said another African American.

"Shirley Chisholm was Black but her 1972 candidacy was only symbolic," replied a Jewish member. "Angela Davis was Black but it made no dent when the Communist Party ran her for president. This time we've got the real thing; it's a tremendous breakthough for women." The Jewish woman gestured toward the Blacks, all of whom were prominent enough to have run for office. "If Gerry Ferraro can be the vice presidential candidate of a major party, *you* could be too."

"Not so!" was the reply. "And that's the point. The woman in me is glad for Gerry but the Black in me has no greater political possibilities today than she did last week. Ferraro's success won't help my people one bit."

Thinking this through, I found it helpful to substitute a Jewish man for the Italian-American woman. If Congressman Ted Weiss had been nominated as Mondale's running mate, would I have been popping my cork? I would have felt proud but I would have seen it as a *man's* triumph, and thus familiar. It would not have greased the track for a Jewish woman or any woman. Suddenly, I understood how Ferraro's moment of glory might not mean the same thing to my Black sisters. It would take Jesse Jackson's strong performance in the 1988 presidential election *added* to Ferraro's breakthrough to make an African American woman's political aspirations plausible.

This discussion raised another critical difference between Black women's marginalization and ours. Because of our white skin privilege, Marilyn, Jackie, and I could identify with the success of a woman trailblazer even though she was not of our ethnic group. In short, Jewish women are allowed to feel like women *first*. We lead with our femaleness or our Jewishness depending on the situation. But racism does not allow Black women a choice of identities. In the eyes of the world, Harriet, Bernice, and Marguerite are Blacks first, and until there was an African American groundbreaker, the earth would stay frozen under their feet. Sexism may be their burden-du-jour at home, but in society at large, racism holds the trump every time.

Listening to one another, we understood how differently our constituencies process events and interpret issues. After the Black teenager Yusef Hawkins was killed in Bensonhurst merely for wandering into a white neighborhood, the Black women insisted that Jews should have expressed more public outrage. The Jews just wanted to stay out of the spotlight; we were glad it wasn't Jewish kids who did it. After the savage attack on the Central Park jogger, the Jewish women asked for more condemnation from the Black community. "It's white society that needs to be condemned," shot back one of the Blacks. "Treat our kids like animals long enough and you can't blame them for acting like animals."

On affirmative action, the Jewish women often had to remind the Blacks that although 70 percent of Americans oppose affirmative action, the majority of American Jews, especially Jewish women, are *for* it. Our dialogue partners were unaware that the great majority of Jewish leaders had spoken out on behalf of affirmative action, though not of quotas, and that two of our largest organizations—the National Council of Jewish Women, and the Union of American Hebrew Congregations—were on record supporting quotas as well. We had to explain that to most Jewish women affirmative action is a *feminist* issue since women of all colors stand to gain from it, and a majority issue since it benefits the whole society. We also had to remind our sisters that most of the Jews who object to quotas do so not because they wish to impede Black advancement but because they remember—and we remembered—when numerical programs were used to exclude Jews from schools, clubs, and workplaces.

If our dialogue group worked harder at debating such issues and decoding our reactions—if we probed deeper into the realm of feeling than other groups I'm familiar with—it may be because we considered ourselves not just representatives of our ethnic communities, but advocates of women.

Finding Commonality

By the time we dug into the hard terrain of racism and anti-Semitism, we knew each other well enough to trust that our truth-telling would not break us apart. We also accepted the fact that we would keep oscillating between that which united us as women and that which divided us as Blacks and Jews.

For instance, early on, we acknowledged that both of our communities have trouble accepting strong women. On the one hand, women were said to be the backbone of our families and the mainstays of our churches or synagogues. On the other hand, strong women draw fire for being "suffocating" (Jewish mothers) or "domineering" (Black mothers). It's our fault that Blacks and Jews are "feminized" peoples. The resulting concern about male weakness is fequently translated into hostility toward women. Supposedly, our feminine wiles and domestic omnipotence put men at a disadvantage. The myth of female sexual and maternal power thus recasts the male in the vulnerable role and justifies his asserting control over "his" women. With those mindsets operating among our own kind, we also get pilloried in the culture at large, where clichés like "Jewish women control Jewish wealth," and "Black women control the Black family" mask the overwhelming concentration of money and power in the hands of white Christian men. In both scenarios, inside and outside our home communities, the woman is the heavy.

Some African American leaders promote the ideal of the docile, submissive woman to compensate Black men who feel belittled by a racist society. But in our dialogue group, the Black women insisted that men must not build their self-esteem at the expense of women. The Black "manhood problem" will not be solved by pulling women down but through massive structural and institutional change—more jobs, better schools, economic development projects, drug treatment, family assistance programs, technical training. Machismo is not the key to human dignity.

The Jewish "manhood problem" seems to originate in the Bible where the weaker or younger son (Isaac, Jacob, Joseph, David, Solomon) typically was the favorite of his mother and of God. Since then, Jewish men around the world have been made into figures of stereotype and scorn. In Europe, they were seen as pale anemic men bent over their books while their wives earned the money, or passive sheep who could not protect their families from the Nazis. In America, they were eggheads, nerds, hen-pecked husbands, peaceniks, or bleeding heart liberals. As an antidote to these wimpish images, some Jews deify the macho Israeli who takes no crap from anyone. Others make themselves masters by domesticating their wives, rendering grown women into dependent children and ornaments of male status.

It is the nature of manhood problems to play themselves out on the backs of women. Often, when a male is the victim of racism or anti-Semitism, his antidote of choice is sexism. The Black man experiences defamation at the hands of whites, and the Jewish man feels the disdain of Christians, not solely as an attack on his race or religion but as a rebuke to his masculine pride. Thus emasculated (i.e., treated like a woman, an inferior), he lords it over *his* perceived inferior, "his" woman, or projects his self-loathing onto all the females of his group and then rejects them in favor of women of the dominant majority. The Black man who wins Mr. Charlie's woman, or the Jew who attracts the WASP debutante, imagines himself more of a man for having taken something that by rights belongs to those in power.

For Jewish men in search of paradigms of male supremacy, the model is the scion of Wall Street or Hollywood, whose manhood is measured not in muscles but in his Mercedes, his corporate Gold Card, and a trophy wife, whom he drapes in furs and jewels to advertise his success. For African Americans, the idol is a Malcolm X, who counseled "stand up and fight like men instead of running around here nonviolently acting like women"; or a Farrakhan, who favors male separatism and Muslim sex role orthodoxies; or an O.J. Simpson, who beat and probably killed his ex-wife yet remains a celebrity athlete.

Accepting Difference

Black/Jewish dialogue takes work but yields its share of revelation. The Black women discovered, for instance, that the Jewish women don't always feel white and are not always treated as white by white Christians but rather as some hybrid, in-between race. The Jews learned that our Black sisters consider us white, *period*. The Jews admitted that we see African Americans as Black before we think of them as Christian or Muslim. Each side bounced back after hearing some of the distorted opinions the other side held about them, and each was relieved to get off its collective chest some of the hostility that none of us would have dared confess elsewhere. Certain facts emerged with great clarity: No longer could Blacks and Jews be drawn together simply because other Americans hate us both. No longer could we reach easy agreement on what constitutes bigotry or insult. No longer could a speech or slogan move us to march together. Now, we often stalked off in opposite directions or faced each other across an abyss, crossing swords over language, power, and resources.

This is not to say that our group automatically divided along lines of color or ethnicity on every issue. On feminism or spirituality, for instance, I usually stood with my Black sisters. But in this dialogue, as in all the Black/Jewish groups in which I've participated, one subject could be counted on to split us down the middle: Louis Farrakhan.

Fighting Over Farrakhan

Our arguments sounded something like this:

Jewish Woman: "I just can't understand the reluctance of mainstream Blacks to repudiate Black anti-Semites instantly and unequivocally. Why is this so hard?"

Black Woman: "Why should each of us have to represent the entire Black race? If I didn't blame you for the behavior of someone like Meir Kahane, why must I answer for the behavior of Farrakhan? Besides, we're powerless, so why do you care what a few of our extremists say about you? And, by the way, how come the only time we hear from Jews these days is when you want us to denounce one of our own?"

J.W.: "Don't denounce him, denounce his behavior."

B.W.: "Since we have so few spokesmen who can engage the attention of the whole community, we have to protect our leaders, not censure them. Even if I disagree with Farrakhan, even if I think Cokely [Steve Cokely, a Chicago political hack who claimed Jewish doctors inject the AIDS virus into Black children] is a fool with no following, I'm not going to attack any Black just to make Jews feel better. And I'm certainly not going after somone like Farrakhan who's been such a good influence on our youth. We're tired of trotting out Martin Luther King,

Jr., and Malcolm X and the same old dead symbols of Black aspiration. We want some *living* heroes for a change."

J.W.: "But the hate message should *invalidate* Farrakhan's hero potential. Would you have ignored that Mussolini dropped poison gas on Ethiopia just because he made the trains run on time? Real leaders send the message to their followers that bigotry is unacceptable. Real leaders aren't afraid of denouncing injustice whoever its targets or perpetrators."

B.W.: "Maybe Jews feel strong enough to go around undermining other Jews, but we have to worry about exacerbating the tensions that already divide the Black community—tensions between the Black middle class [now a quarter of the Black population] and an increasingly entrenched underclass; tensions between moderates like David Dinkins and fringe people like Al Sharpton [a media creation who is known for his flashy gold jewelry, anti-white remarks and crowd-rousing demonstrations]. We were overjoyed when Farrakhan endorsed Jackson's presidential candidacy because until then he had preached separatism and instructed the Nation of Islam not to vote in elections. Now we have this new unity, and you want me to criticize the man who brought thousands more Blacks into the political process?!"

J.W.: "But by not making a statement you *are* making a statement. Or as someone once said, the best way for evil to triumph is for good people to do nothing."

B.W.: "A few of our moderates *have* protested Black anti-Semitism, but others feel they're in a double bind: if they don't speak out, they're unacceptable to Jews whose votes or support they need, but if they do speak out, much of their own rank and file will dismiss them as puppets of the Jews and traitors to Black solidarity."

J.W.: "Jews aren't pulling anyone's strings. We have a proven record of supporting Black leaders. In fact, Los Angeles, Chicago, Philadelphia, and New York wouldn't have elected Black mayors if not for Jewish voters who supported them in far greater proportions than did other whites. And in 1988, after Jackson modulated his rhetoric, he got 9 percent of the total white vote but 10 percent of the Jewish vote, up from 4 percent in 1984. So we're there for Blacks when it counts."

B.W.: "If you really were there for us, you'd stop harping on Farrakhan. Only 1 percent of Blacks are members of the Nation of Islam. There are millions of white anti-Semites. Isn't it hypocritical to keep picking on this one man?"

J.W.: "On the contrary: the fact that we keep raising Farrakhan is a measure of our respect for Black leadership potential. It's precisely because we *do* believe in your empowerment that we cannot ignore Black anti-Semitism. We pay attention to what your extremists say because we believe that these people and their proteges may someday be leaders of the larger community and have power over everyone's lives."

B.W.: "Well, to us Farrakhan's anti-Semitism is nothing but rhetorical excess. It's completely irrelevant to his main message which is a Jewish-style call for economic independence, personal responsibility, and mutual support. What you do for your community is what Farrakhan wants Blacks to do for Blacks. Because of the federal deficit and cuts in social services, self-help is our only hope and Jackson and Farrakhan are its only visible promoters. Farrakhan goes to jails and reclaims our drug addicts and promotes Black entrepreneurs. But whenever he speaks in public, the media reports only what he says about Jews."

J.W.: "Why not point that out to him? Maybe if he edits out the Jew-hating, the press will notice his economic program. No one's going to pay attention to the 'main message' as long as it's surrounded by malice. In fact, how can you be sure his anti-Semitism is only rhetorical? Maybe he consciously *uses* it to gain media attention. Anyway, Jews have learned from experience that no expression of anti-Semitism is 'irrelevant.' Every pogrom begins with a hate campaign. Why not just admit it's wrong?"

B.W.: "Because the Sharptons of the world would destroy us with it. These street agitators gain their power by exploiting the frustrations of the underclass and making them suspicious of traditional Black leaders. Poor Blacks are so disaffected with the system that they're quick to identify with anyone who challenges it. Middle-class, moderate Black leaders like us are running to keep up with them. Our position is too precarious for us to look weak. And if we appear to be kowtowing to the Jews, you know we look weak."

J.W.: "Would it be so hard for a few of you to issue a principled statement like, 'We will not denigrate another people in order to achieve our own self-esteem.' Maybe women like yourselves could say it if the men are too hung up on face-saving."

B.W.: "We can't do it. Look what happened to Laura Blackburn [a prominent lawyer] and Hazel Dukes [president of the New York NAACP]. When they spoke out, they were called Uncle Toms and they lost their credibility altogether."

So it went for hours on end. Even in our intimate group where there was true affection and a will to understand, we spent five or six sessions on Farrakhan and finally declared an impasse. As Leon Weiseltier once wrote, "Not every fight is the result of misunderstanding. There are fights that are the result of understanding." About Farrakhan, we understood but we couldn't stop fighting and neither side moved an inch.

//

At a Black/Jewish retreat in Racine, Wisconsin, Gary Rubin, then an American Jewish Committee expert on race relations, pointed out that culturally and historically, Blacks and Jews learned to respond to insults in opposite ways. Experience has taught the Jewish people to take anti-Semitism very seriously, for what begins with an insult can end in the ovens. Moreover, our Talmudic legacy schooled us to believe that an aggrieved party has a right to demand a retraction and obtain redress. In contrast, experience with slavery and Jim Crow has taught African Americans that insults must be ignored, that in a sense, ignoring an affront *invalidates* it. Black people let today's abuse roll off their backs because they may need to work with their abuser tomorrow. As David Shannon, a minister from Atlanta, put it, "If we'd permitted ourselves to respond to every insult, we'd all have been dead by 1619."

"We don't even criticize our own for what they do to *us*," added Bernice Powell. "When Mayor Wilson Goode dropped a bomb on Black people in Philadelphia, not one Black spoke out."

Bottom line: the Jewish heritage puts the burden on the insulter to retract while the Black heritage puts the burden on the insultee to refuse to respond.

Defining Ourselves and Each Other

In dialogue, the differences between Blacks and Jews are rarely better delineated than when each group speaks about its own "survival," a word both use frequently but with quite dissimilar meanings. For African Americans, survival means factual physical endurance, staying alive in the face of violent crime, drugs, hunger, homelessness, and infant mortality rates that are more than triple that of whites; it means surviving as a viable community when 30 percent of the adults and 75 percent of the young live in poverty, when 44 percent of Black seventeen-year-olds are functionally illiterate, and when the Black unemployment rate is twice the white rate. For Jews, survival means keeping a culture and a religion alive against all odds, discouraging intermarriage, fighting anti-Semitism, and supporting the security of Israel.

In dialogue, it became clear to us that Blacks worry about their actual conditions and fear for the present; Jews worry about their history and fear for the future. Blacks see their survival threatened by poverty; Jews see their survival threatened by affluence, with its temptations of assimilation and moral corruption. To Blacks, racism is a bacteria, potentially curable but presently deadly. To Jews, anti-Semitism is a virus, potentially deadly but presently contained.

Furthermore, fear motivates Jews the way economic and social reality motivates Blacks. Although safe and relatively prosperous at the moment, Jews are a people whose vulnerability is seared indelibly into our collective unconscious. After the Babylonian Exile, four Roman wars, the Christian Crusades, the Spanish and Portuguese Inquisitions, the Czarist pogroms, Stalin, Hitler, and five Arab attacks, we expected our dialogue partners to accept our obsession with anti-Semitism. In turn, our Black sisters expected us to acknowledge the grisly legacy of slavery, the terrors of the Middle Passage, the inhumanity of white Americans, and the continuing scourge of racism.

Competitive suffering. Comparative victimology. In some dialogues, the

Blacks viewed these historical oppressions as a zero sum game: if the Holocaust wins public attention, they thought, slavery loses ground. Many Jews, on the other hand, seemed more intent on staying Number One in the catastrophe ratings than acknowledging the oppression of others. But in our women's group, we connected around gender-linked anguish, the rape of Black slaves and Jewish concentration camp inmates; the unimaginable cruelty of tearing children from their mothers. Surely, there were enough tears to go around, we said, as we made room for each other's suffering, and we listened.

While Black distress was immediate and understandable, it was difficult to explain Jewish paranoia. "In America, though permitted to be rich, Jews are not permitted to be comfortable," wrote political analyst Leonard Fein. We remember how quickly Jews were scapegoated in this country during the gas shortages, the farm crisis, and the Gulf War. We notice that Jews are blamed for the slightest economic reversal no matter how few we are—only 2.5 percent of the U.S. population. (The average American estimates that we're 18 percent!) So, regardless of what Jews may have accomplished or how comfortable we may seem, we continue to fear the swastika and smell the smoke. In fact, the more we flourish, the surer we are that the anti-Semites are out there begrudging our success. As the old joke puts it, paranoids have enemies too.

A friend of mine says he can't relax as long as one swastika appears on a wall in this country or one Jewish cemetery is vandalized. I have a recurrent dream in which my children and I are herded into cattle cars en route to Auschwitz. "One of every three of the world's Jews perished in the Holocaust," I told my Black sisters. "Wouldn't you be afraid if a third of your family had been murdered in your own lifetime?"

"But we had nothing to do with it," answered the Black women. "Why don't you pick on white people for a change?"

They had a point. White anti-Semitism is surely the larger threat, yet it hurts more when Blacks turn against us. Somehow, Black anti-Semitism makes us feel not just threatened but betrayed. So the Jewish women complained about Spike Lee, whose movie *Mo' Better Blues* included the gratuitously stereotyped Shylock characters, Joe and Moe Flatbush; and about the rock group Public Enemy whose best-selling record called Jews "Christ-killers," and whose minister of information, Professor Griff, said, "Jews are responsible for the majority of wickedness that goes on across the globe"; and about Oprah Winfrey who benignly accepted the claim of a guest that Jews murder children for religious ritual; and about Nobel peace laureate Bishop Desmond Tutu, who lectured Jews on "forgiving" the Nazis for the murder of the Six Million.

The Black women listened but what we said didn't always make sense to them. They had grown up in neighborhoods where Jews collected the rent, ran the shops, employed Black domestic workers, checked up on welfare clients, and taught Black children. They worked in New York City where every Jew seems to be thriving. At that moment in time, 30 million American Blacks had only 24 representatives in Congress and no Black senators, while six million American Jews had 31 Jewish members of the House and seven Jewish senators. They also saw that Israel's relatively well-off four-and-a-half million Jews were getting $3 billion in U.S. aid (much of it military) when all of sub-Saharan Africa, with its half billion poor Black people, was getting less than $1 billion. Meanwhile the Third World within our own borders—the South Bronx, Detroit, Watts, the South Side of Chicago—was virtually ignored. Our Black sisters saw Jews favored at home and abroad. They found it incredible that a people so affluent, powerful, and white as we could possibly be quaking at the summit.

To Blacks, America is the nation that enslaved them and continues to deny them equal opportunities. To Jews, it is the promised land that made good on its promises. Blacks worry that their (bad) situation will never improve—therefore their issues are affordable housing, better education, and affirmative action. Jews worry that our (good) situation will never last—therefore our issues are freedom of religion (separation of church and state), freedom of emigration (Soviet Jews, Ethiopian Jews), and a secure Israel. Blacks need relief in the form of economic opportunity and assistance. Jews need relief in the form of reassurance of our continued acceptance. Clearly, these needs are not comparable but they can be experienced with comparable intensity.

Dialogue also revealed how inaccurately each group perceives the power of the other. Blacks are not really in a position to hurt Jews, but because of their superior numbers and a few high profile anti-Semites, Jews fear them. Likewise, although Jews have high political visibility in a few large cities, Jews in general are not really in a position to hurt Blacks, but African Americans believe we are influential enough to suck up all the resources. Blacks are saying, "If we're supposed to be brothers and sisters, how come you're doing so well and we're in the streets?" Jews are saying, "If we're supposed to be friends, why do you keep bad-mouthing me?"

Of course, some of our fabled Black/Jewish togetherness is not a myth. Surveys show our communities to be the most politically like-minded groups in America. The Congressional Black Caucus and the Jewish members of Congress vote together on most issues including those affecting social programs, Israel, and Africa. Although Jews have experienced great economic success, we still vote our consciences not our pocketbooks. Although Blacks have experienced great economic distress, they still vote their consciences not their rage. We share a common vision of justice, a common passion for the liberatory Exodus paradigm. Now we have to build on this compatibility, bring it out of the statistics books and make it work for us—which is precisely the potential of grassroots groups such as our women's dialogue.

Yet, despite its spirited past life, the group began running out of steam sometime in the early 1990s. By 1994, it became harder and harder to schedule meetings; one or another woman was always booked. When we finally found an open date, a member might cancel at the last minute or simply forget to show up. We recognized that the group had lost its primacy in some of the women's lives and, rather than beat it into submission, we let it die a natural death.

Decoding What Went Wrong

Why did this happen? I think one can seek answers without laying blame. Every group has a natural lifespan; maybe ten years was ours. All of us were overworked and spread too thin; maybe it was time to let other priorities claim our time. ("Been there, done that, ready to move on.") Or maybe the group began dissipating when it lost its laser beam focus. In the early years, we were disciplined and tough-minded about keeping our discussions substantive. More recently, we meandered, socialized, gossiped, started being *nice* to one another. Maybe we got too comfortable. Or lazy. Or, dare I say it, bored.

It could be that interest waned when the whole idea of intergroup dialogue lost its cutting edge. The subject of Black/Jewish relations, which was uncharted territory in the eighties, is now overexposed in the media and mainstreamed in community organizations. In the light of this proliferation, our group may have lost the revolutionary fervor and freshness that once animated our discussions. Conversely, it could be that Black/Jewish conflict became so messy and intractable that we despaired of making a difference.

Some answers undoubtedly lie in the group's internal dynamics and the characteristics of its members. Looking back, I'd say the two sides fell out of balance when the Black women began to dominate the discussions by sheer force of their personalities. They were consistently more outspoken and alive, perhaps because they kept adding new blood to their ranks. Marguerite was the first to leave. When she moved to Missouri in 1987, her replacement, Jualynne Dodson, a sociologist and former assistant dean of Union Theological Seminary, kept us all on our toes. Not long afterward, Bernice accepted a job offer in Columbus, Ohio, and we decided to take that opportunity to expand the group to four on each side. We added two new Black women—Pat Reberg, then head of the New York Council of Churches, and Suzan Johnson Cook, pastor of a Manhattan church—and one more Jew, Donna Nevel, a community organizer. (We never did replace Donna Shalala when she left New York. We couldn't think of anyone smart and sensitive enough to fill her shoes.) By the end of the run, Harriet Michel was the only original Black member while all the Jewish founding members were still on board. Perhaps our chemistry had gone a bit stale.

Age and retirement may also have played a role in the energy imbalance. By the latter part of our years together, two of the Jewish women—who are quite a bit older than the rest of us—had cut back on their movement activities or professional lives to such a degree that they sometimes seemed to have entered a downshifting phase of the life cycle.

Another difference was emotional: at first we were all feisty and bold, but as time progressed, the Black women remained willing to express their anger while the Jewish women seemed afraid to let theirs out. I'm not sure if this was because the Blacks had more to be angry about, or if we Jews felt our complaints to be less legitimate. But I do know that when one side believes itself less entitled than the other to take ownership of its feelings, the integrity of the dialogue process is fatally compromised.

Something else tipped the scales: The Jewish women were willing to be critical of Jewish leaders and to condemn any Jew whose position on Black/Jewish issues seemed misguided. (Sometimes we got *too* wrapped up in arcane Jewish community politics, as if these "inside baseball" stories were of interest to everyone.) The Black women, on the other hand, always closed ranks around Black leaders. While they were candid about their community's problems, they all seemed to hold the same lockstep views on incidents that involved Blacks and Jews, and they defended any African American with whom the Jewish world found fault. Or, if they had an ideological dispute among themselves—whether on Tawana Brawley or Crown Heights—they chose not to reveal it to us. After a while, we Jews found this united front hard to believe and somewhat disconcerting.

Most important, I think the group ran out of steam because each side came in with fundamentally different expectations. The Blacks may have been ready to move from dialogue to action that would address the needs of African Americans, while for Jews, dialogue itself *is* the need—it's a short term cure for Jewish insecurity. If Blacks are still talking to us, we tell ourselves, maybe the liberal alliance is not dead, maybe we don't have to fear Black Christians as much as white Christians, maybe they won't all gang up on us.

I think we could have addressed the needs of both groups if we'd found ways to put our skills and experience to use in the community. Together, we could have tackled a single social issue—perhaps working to combat violence against women, a problem that crosses lines of race, ethnicity, and class. We could have helped start other dialogue groups around the city. We could have gone out in pairs and given talks in schools, churches, and synagogues. We might have traveled together to Israel and Africa, or at least to the Holocaust Museum in Washington, D. C., and the Schomberg Center for Research on Black Culture in Harlem. And we should have worked harder to place joint op-ed pieces to counteract the barrage of stories emphasizing Black/Jewish enmity. (Two of us co-authored such a piece in support of David Dinkins' candidacy, but after the *New York Times* turned us down, we never pursued it further.)

At this point, coulda-woulda-shoulda is a futile exercise. Suffice it to say, I miss our group enormously and I'd join another Black/Jewish women's dialogue in a minute regardless of the *Sturm und Drang* that inevitably would repeat itself with a new cast of characters.

Why do Jews and African Americans seem to lock horns more than other minorities? Maybe it's because we take each other seriously. Maybe we still believe that our destinies are interwoven. Or maybe we're inadvertently performing a service for white Christians—functioning as surrogate combatants for the bigots in the dominant culture. Watching us clash with each other in public, other Americans can let off steam vicariously while avoiding the fury that might otherwise be directed at them. But as we satisfy the media's lust for conflict, Blacks and Jews get sucked into the oldest scam in the world: divide and conquer.

It makes no sense for us to pull away from each other. Racist rednecks lump us together; neo-Nazis lump us together; the Klan lumps us together; Posse Comitatus, the Skinheads, the Aryan Nation, and the National Association for the Advancement of White People lump us together. If we were less competitive and more politically savvy we would lump ourselves together, become a lump in America's throat, a pebble in the redneck's shoe, a pea under the mattress of royalty. We would link up and make life uncomfortable for those who hate us.

Together our two groups comprise 15 percent of the population and much of its moral conscience. Both of us are uppity—we demand the right to look and act differently from whites or Gentiles, and yet to be treated similarly—and our uppityness puts us in the same category as feminists of every stripe. You might say women are the Jews of the world, or Blacks are the Jews of America, or vice versa all around. Despite most Jews having white skin, and despite most Blacks being Gentile, both groups remain perennial outsiders, second-class citizens, just as all women are second class in a world that sees men as the norm. This is an important triple parallelism. History has taught us that the fate of each outgroup is inevitably linked to the destiny of the others. An assault on one presages an attack on the other. Working together, we can be each other's early warning system. It should not take a burning Torah or a flaming cross to make us form a bucket brigade.

twenty

BLACKS AND JEWS

A Personal Reflection

MICHAEL WALZER

This is the standard story: once there was a strong political alliance between Blacks and Jews; then came Black power, the 1967 Mideast war, community school boards, affirmative action, the Nation of Islam, and so on; and now there is only trouble and mutual recrimination.

But that's not the way it was...or is. There was never anything like a real alliance, for neither the Black nor the Jewish community is sufficiently united for alliance politics; nor were there ever any negotiations on the terms of an alliance among any group of people that I know about, or any terms informally agreed upon. Individuals and organizations have cooperated in all sorts of ways on all sorts of projects. But what really happened is much more simply described: a lot of Jews went to work in the civil rights movement. Even before the Montgomery bus boycott of 1954 and the student sit-ins of 1960, there were Jews involved in or providing financial support for the NAACP and the National Urban League; and it was mostly the Jews in both the Communist and Socialist parties who took an interest in Black issues in the 1930s. This wasn't anything special, however, for a lot of Jews—many of the same people—also went to work in the labor movement, and in organizations defending civil liberties, and in the New Left, and in the campaign against the Vietnam war, and in the feminist movement. But there was no "Jewish alliance" with Blacks or workers or women or anyone else in any of these political groupings.

I went to North Carolina in 1960 to write about the student sit-ins for *Dissent*, and while I was there, it seemed natural, and it was certainly exciting, to speak at campus meetings and at the Black churches where students and their supporters regularly assembled. I expressed solidarity with the young people sitting in at local lunch counters (I was pretty young myself) and promised to help organize a

Northern support movement. A few months later, I gave similar speeches in Alabama, and was able to describe picket lines at the Boston and Cambridge branches of the stores targeted by Southern Blacks. The co-chairs of Boston's EPIC, the Emergency Public Integration Committee, were both Jewish; so were a high proportion of the picketers we recruited; one of the largest groups came from Brandeis University.

But after a couple of years, I drifted out of civil rights activism, and so did many of my EPIC friends. I don't think that I could now give an accurate account of the process; "drift" is the right word. Did we have some dim sense of being unwelcome? There were no ideological clashes—those were early days. I remember some strained conversations with leaders of the Boston Black community; we didn't invite them to our campuses; they didn't invite us to their churches. (In the North, I spoke only once in a Black church, not in Boston. It was one of the high points of my civil rights years. With the vocal encouragement of the congregation, I imagined myself, briefly, an orator. Why didn't I try to repeat the experience?)

Soon, in any case, my friends and I were caught up in the opposition to America's growing involvement in Vietnam. There were not many Blacks who came with us—though Martin Luther King visited Cambridge in 1967 to help launch Vietnam Summer (the local co-chairs were both Jewish). In fact, I had no more close political associates among Blacks after several years of civil rights work than I had among Vietnamese six or seven years later.

There was, however, something different about Jewish involvement in civil rights—which I missed when I first began thinking about this essay, though it was obvious enough when my *Dissent* co-editor, Mitchell Cohen, pointed it out to me. In all the other movements, I and my friends, or our counterparts, acted as leftists (of one sort or another) who also happened to be Jews. In the civil rights movement, we were emphatically Jewish leftists. Our personal identities, self-knowledge, understanding of our own past, and, most important, our deepest feelings were more engaged in this fight than in any of the others. The community as a whole was also more engaged: many Jewish organizations took public positions and sent their officers to demonstrations. Many rabbis, led by Abraham Joshua Heschel, joined in, their way eased by the religious fervor of the civil rights struggle in the South and by the readiness of Black preachers to invoke the biblical exodus story. Slavery was a cultural memory for the Jews, recent history for the Blacks: it was a powerful unifying theme.

Most of my friends were secular Jews; we didn't need the rabbis, and (I was one of the exceptions here) we didn't listen to the preachers. We had our own memories of Passover seders, and we could quote the prophets and tell stories of Jewish persecution. Southern sheriffs with dogs looked to us like Cossacks...or Nazis. Things that we didn't think about and didn't talk about in the other movements came easily to mind and tongue in this one. We surprised ourselves with the extent of our identifications: of American Blacks as Jews, of ourselves as Blacks. Civil rights, we thought, was our fight.

Black activists obviously (but it wasn't so obvious to us at the time) resented these feelings of moral proprietorship. They knew that civil rights was really their fight, that they, and not we, would have to endure its hardships and live with the consequences of the defeats that were sure to come. A few Jewish kids, some of the rabbis too, made what turned out to be lifelong commitments, and some of their lives, like those of Andrew Goodman and Michael Schwerner, were cut short because of the commitment. These few made the double identification seem more authentic than it was for most of us. We were outriders of the civil rights movement, and after a while, for all our feelings of connection, we rode off—pushed (later on) by Black power militants asserting their own proprietorship, drawn anyway to the Vietnam wars. Most of the Jewish activists of the early and middle '60s continued to support civil rights initiatives—including affirmative action, the most controversial of them—but few of us sought or sustained an internal role in the movement. And over the next several decades, under pressure from an increasingly conservative America, the movement fractured and slowly disintegrated.

II

Black power militancy seemed to me then, and seems to me still, a terrible political mistake. I can understand the need that many Blacks felt to take full charge of their own struggle. Insofar as they did that, they were acting in conformity with the old left maxim: "The liberation of the working class must be the work of the working class." But the workers, after all, were supposed to be the majority of the population when they liberated themselves. American Blacks were and are a minority, with no choice but to engage in coalition politics. That required maintaining links not with "the" Jews but with many Jews and Jewish organizations and also with people in the unions and the white churches and with feminists and even with urban white ethnics inside the Democratic Party. To try to fight alone, without any of these allies, meant to fight with no hope of success. Black power was mostly a politics of gesture—and when it brought no quick victories, the gestures turned nasty.

I want to distinguish carefully between gestures and interests. The two divided Blacks and Jews at roughly the same time, but not in the same way or with the same effects. Crudely put, the divergent interests could have been negotiated and compromised, case by case, were it not for the often threatening symbolism of the gestures.

As the civil rights struggle moved North, Black and Jewish leaders found themselves confronting issues where the professional careers and political ambitions of (some of) their constituents were genuinely at odds. The conflict in Ocean

Hill–Brownsville between a community school board run by Black activists and a largely Jewish teachers' union provides one of the more dramatic examples. I will let this case stand in for many others, for it has all the elements necessary for a general representation. The teachers had a real stake in preventing community boards from purging their schools; the activists really believed (and at the time I thought they were right) that local control was the key to improving their children's educational chances. So the conflict wasn't ideologically constructed, invented, and hyped up by the media—though ideology and hype certainly helped to harden positions on both sides in ways that made certain obvious and fair compromises impossible.

It was insufficiently noticed at the time that much of the drama and the bitterness of this Black-Jewish conflict derived from the fact that it was also a Jewish civil war, with many left intellectuals and even some religious and community leaders supporting the Black activists (the same division among Jews is evident in the 25-year argument about affirmative action). Half of the "replacement" teachers recruited by the local board during the AFT strike were Jewish. I am sure that these people too would have argued that they were defending Jewish interests—not the material and professional interests represented by the union but a larger interest of the Jewish community as a whole in racial equality and Black-Jewish harmony. Some of them worked hard to produce a compromise settlement. But their position was made very difficult when (some) Black activists began circulating anti-Semitic leaflets.

Here is an obvious example of the politics of gesture, for the rhetorical violence of the leaflets, which would have been indefensible even if it served a purpose, was in fact purposeless, merely expressive—as if shouting mattered more to the authors than winning. (Henry Louis Gates argued in a *New York Times* op-ed piece on July 20, 1992, that anti-Semitic rhetoric is best understood as a weapon in a power struggle internal to the Black community. I can only report on how it looked, and still looks, from the outside.) Widely publicized by the union, the leaflets greatly solidified its support, not only among Jews but among New Yorkers generally, and so contributed to the eventual AFT victory. But before that victory, a verbal dance intervened, which has since become familiar: Jewish demands that Black intellectuals and political leaders repudiate the anti-Semitic pronouncements, followed by a reluctant and resentful compliance, followed by Jewish complaints about the reluctance and the resentment, followed…and so on.

There were, of course, Black leaders who acted entirely on their own initiative in condemning Black anti-Semitism. But even they disliked being asked to do this again and again, every time anti-Semitism found expression, as it did with growing frequency, among Black activists in this or that political conflict. They felt, I suppose, that it was humiliating to have to legitimate themselves, to make themselves *kosher*, as it were, over and over. A misunderstanding of major proportions is evident here, for what Jews wanted (and still want), but rarely explicitly asked, of these already legitimate Black leaders was not that they balance gestural anti-Semitism with gestural philo-Semitism, but that they fight and win a political battle in their own community. And this, perhaps, is just what they couldn't do.

It is important to acknowledge that Black anti-Semitism has not produced anything remotely like the underworld of right-wing white fanatics, with their parading militias and arsenals of guns and explosives. These people hate Jews and Blacks with perfect impartiality, and so they might well help to bring the two groups together again. On the other hand, anti-Semitic demagoguery, *when the demagogues are Black*, resonates powerfully in the Black community today. Thousands of urban Blacks (and, most frightening to me, Black college students, whose growing numbers are perhaps the most signal victory of the civil rights movement) will turn out to hear anti-Semitic diatribes. I have to confess that when I read what is said at these meetings, I have a strong impulse to tell my fellow Jews: Whatever the truth about our alliance with Blacks, we had better initiate new alliances now, quickly, with Latino and Asian Americans, in order to protect ourselves. At the same time, of course, we need to look more closely at Black anti-Semitism and to find and mobilize allies in the Black community.

Black anti-Semitism has two aspects. On the one hand, it is very much like the anti-Semitism of Polish peasants: a mix of ancient Christian (or Muslim) prejudice with a more immediate and populist hatred for the local middlemen—shopkeepers, pawnbrokers, landlords, and so on. This sort of thing is powerfully evoked in the autobiographical writings of (for my generation) Richard Wright and James Baldwin. Its old world equivalent produced pogroms in Poland, and it isn't unimaginable that it could do so here (some of the ghetto riots that targeted Jewish shops have been described in this way but only, I think, as a result of a considerable loss of memory about what a Polish pogrom was really like). In fact, in this country, both Polish and Black anti-Semitism has been remarkably inert, politically passive—not all that different, indeed, from the very real and often crudely expressed Jewish prejudice against the Poles and the *Schwartze*, which did not prevent Jews from forming electoral coalitions with these two groups. Similarly, these two groups readily voted with the Jews, even for Jewish candidates, like Herbert Lehman in New York or Howard Metzenbaum in Ohio, say, both elected with strong Catholic working class and Black support. In 1967, Harold Cruse predicted that "Eventually, terroristic tactics will be used in Harlem against white-owned businesses by a nationalist faction, and the Jews will certainly call it anti-Semitism." Almost thirty years later—though there have been a small number of ugly incidents—such tactics have not been seriously urged or used in Harlem (where, in any case, fewer and fewer of the shopkeepers are Jewish …or white): American terrorism has a different location and a different pedigree.

But there is now a second kind of Black anti-Semitism, anticipated perhaps among the Pan-Africanist followers of Marcus Garvey, which is politically active or at least politically ambitious in character and vaguely leftish in tone—an American version of what the German social-democrat August Bebel called "the socialism of fools." Overlapping with the first, it is importantly different too: less local, less immediate, less focused on neighborhood middlemen, far more ideological. It is concerned now with Jews as international figures, secretive and menacing, who supposedly ran the slave trade centuries ago, who control the banks and the mass media today. This is not so different from the creed of the neo-Nazi militias, but with a radical left edge. The Jews are described, collectively, as oppressors of Blacks, Third World peoples, Palestinian Arabs, and anyone else who fits the mythic scheme. The scheme itself is elaborated in pseudoscholarly books and articles (here it differs again from peasant anti-Semitism and resembles that of the Christian Right). It is the work of people who study in libraries, collect weird footnotes, imagine themselves radical intellectuals.

What is most frightening about all this is not its practical effects, for (so far) these have been minor, but its obvious appeal beyond the ghetto, in parts of the new Black middle class, on college campuses, and among the Afrocentric intelligentsia. I don't know what the political future of this second anti-Semitism might be like. That probably depends on the socioeconomic future of the people to whom it now appeals. The more successful they are, the more it will fade away. But if these people come to constitute a kind of lumpen-bourgeoisie, barely holding on to the positions they have, without any hope of upward mobility, they could well form the reserve army of a very unattractive politics. And the American economy seems to be producing groups of this sort, not only at the lowest income level, not only among Blacks.

This is the sort of thing Jews worry about and are right to worry about it (just read, say, Khalid Muhammad's speech at Keane College in New Jersey in 1993). I worry about it too, partly because of its obviously threatening character, partly because it makes any decent left politics so difficult. So it isn't crazy or paranoid or right-wing to insist that Black liberals and leftists take a strong stand against this second anti-Semitism—not only that they respond to this or that outrageous speech but that they launch a political and educational campaign; not only that they repudiate the anti-Semites but that they ostracize them. When Meir Kahane founded the ultra-right Jewish Defense League, ostracism was the almost immediate response of mainstream Jewish organizations. Their leaders didn't try to draw Kahane into a "dialogue." Of course, these leaders were confident that they would be followed by the mass of American Jews. Black leaders today, confronting Louis Farrakhan and his friends, apparently have no such confidence about their own following. And, after the "Million Man March" of October 1995, they have a (possibly exaggerated) sense of Farrakhan's following—which some of them have followed in their turn, in a way that seems to me at once cowardly and reckless. Still, a number of Black politicians and intellectuals have been scathingly critical of Farrakhan. Their commitment to justice and equality is clear, but their political effectiveness, sadly, is less so.

III

Black criticism of Israel is often cited as a central reason for Black-Jewish tensions, but I am inclined to doubt its centrality. Always look—so I was taught long ago—for the local cause, and here the local cause is almost certainly intra-movement relations. Certainly, Jews are sensitive to criticism of Israel; I am sensitive exactly as "Jews" are—especially when the criticism makes no distinction among political forces in Israel or calls into question the legitimacy of the state itself. But my real quarrel in this case is with certain groups on the left, Black and white, where racial difference is submerged in a very curious political agreement: that Black nationalism and Algerian nationalism and Vietnamese nationalism all ought to be supported, while nationalism in general, and Zionism as its supposedly classic exemplar, ought always to be condemned.

My own experience with this curious politics began in 1967, after the Six Day War, when Martin Peretz and I published a piece in *Ramparts* (then struggling to make itself a popular magazine of the New Left), in which we argued that people on the left should both oppose the American war in Vietnam and support Israeli self-defense. For a couple of years after that, I spoke often on campuses around the country, defending that double proposition, often in debates with leftist opponents, all of them white. Black critics of Israel presumably share the ideology of these leftists—and then, perhaps, add to it something more personal, for they tend to identify with Palestinians in a way that none of my debate opponents ever did. I assume that their identification is best explained by the internal politics of the civil rights movement (since they don't seem to identify in the same way with Kurds, say, or the people of the southern Sudan). No doubt, it is also connected to the second kind of Black anti-semitism, with Israel cast in an unlikely role: the leading oppressor of Third World peoples. But, at bottom, this was, and so far as I can tell still is, a left-left fight, not a Black-Jewish fight.

IV

I want to look now at one particularly divisive local issue in order to suggest that a common Black-Jewish politics is still possible. In the late 1960s, Black nationalists like Harold Cruse often accused Jews in the civil rights movement of advocating integration for Blacks but not for themselves. Black supporters of integration were described as tools of the Jews, who had some sinister end in mind: an America in which they alone were distinct and separate. (But what would be the advantage of that?) I recall those arguments today because the same issues arise in the multiculturalism debate. Of course, Jews are as divided as Blacks are about integration and separation; the two divisions are entirely independent of one another. But there is a position in this dispute that is equally useful, so it seems to me, to both groups. I have been defending this position in *Dissent* in recent years and will try, very briefly, to explain it here.

Like other identified and committed minority groups in American society, Blacks and Jews need political and economic integration. They need all the benefits that come from full participation in the political system and in the market, for these are places where recognition is won and resources—power and wealth—are accumulated. Separatism in these spheres is self-defeating and silly. I don't mean to argue against Black shops in Black neighborhoods, only to insist that that can't be the ultimate ambition of Blacks in the economy. Similarly, a handful of representatives from gerrymandered congressional districts can't be the ultimate ambition of Blacks in the political system. Jews have done better in both places, and it was that success that we hoped in the '60s, and still hope, Blacks will repeat.

Affirmative action was and is a program for integration, and it is largely for that reason that it has had so much support from Jews, even though the collective memory of discriminatory quotas predisposes Jews to oppose it (and many Jewish neoconservatives have in fact opposed it, claiming to speak—though they don't speak—for the community as a whole). The aim of affirmative action is to overcome the kinds of political and economic isolation forced on American Blacks by centuries of prejudice—*to bring them in*, as Jews and white ethnic immigrants have come in, to the larger American society. The programs are remedial in nature and, since they carry political and moral costs, they were originally conceived as temporary, founded on the hope that integration can be made a self-sustaining process. If that hope turns out to be unfounded, other or additional egalitarian strategies will have to be tried. In any case, success is measured by integration: the presence of Blacks in significant numbers in political assemblies and government agencies, in entrepreneurial activities, in the professions, and in managerial ranks that are all, given American demography, predominantly white.

But all this says nothing about cultural assimilation. Many (but not all) Jewish activists in the civil rights movement were opposed to assimilation for the Jews—and never supported it for Blacks either. Historically, indeed, multiculturalism is a Jewish idea, first defended, under the name of "cultural pluralism," by the American-Jewish social theorist Horace Kallen in the 'teens and 'twenties of this century. Kallen was arguing against the melting pot theory of American culture, which he identified with European nation-statism, in favor of a new world of ethnic and religious diversity. That is still my position today. Blacks and Jews will have to decide for themselves the extent to which they maintain separate social and cultural institutions. But the success of any form of cultural independence in the United States today requires resources that can only be accumulated through political and economic integration.

Consider the hospitals, day care centers, nursing homes, family services, schools, and cultural societies run by the Jewish community today (and also by Catholics, Lutherans, and so on). These are paid for in part by fees, in part by philanthropic funds raised in the community, and in part by government money in the form of entitlements and matching grants. American Blacks are not at present running institutions of this sort on anything like the same scale, but there is no reason why they can't or shouldn't do so—through their churches or other communal organizations—except for their political and economic weakness. And that is a weakness that will only be overcome by greater integration.

At this concrete level, it is obviously wrong to claim that Jews want these kinds of institutions for themselves, but not for Blacks. An extensive network of hospitals, day care centers, and so on, run by the Black community would make American society stronger overall; no one has any reason to oppose this. We should think of it as "meat and potatoes multiculturalism," because these welfare institutions, and the churches and philanthropies and mutual aid societies that underwrite them, create real space for the everyday enactment of a culture and for the cooperation and camaraderie, the common celebrations and consolations, of its members. By contrast, contemporary Afrocentrism with its anti-white and, often, its anti-Jewish rhetoric, is the gestural version of cultural politics. It doesn't prepare the children, who are its chief audience, for political or economic integration, and so it opens no paths toward a serious cultural independence. Or, rather, it points only to a sectarian separatism, like that, perhaps, of the Hasidim or the Amish—and there is no evidence that most Black Americans, anymore than most Jews or white Protestants, really want anything like that.

Given an inclusive politics and an open and fair economy, the United States can afford a great deal of cultural diversity. We can expect Blacks and Jews to be among the leaders in working out the theory and practice of this multiculturalism. But they won't succeed in their efforts unless they work together at the same time for political inclusiveness and economic fairness. Both groups have a history here that pushes them leftward in roughly similar ways. Despite the writings of Jewish and, more recently, of Black neoconservatives, egalitarian commitments continue to orient and shape the everyday politics of both communities. They still can't, and don't have to, forge a formal alliance; coalitional politics in a democracy is more rough and ready than that. Indeed, the voting record of Blacks and Jews in recent elections suggests that in some rough and ready way, the coalition already (or still) exists. But its full articulation, and the good feeling this would bring, await a serious campaign against gestural militancy and Jew-baiting in the Black community.

The burden falls that way right now, though few people talk about it openly in these terms. If I insist on them here, it isn't in order to deny that political work is necessary in the Jewish community too, to sustain the old commitment to racial equality. I put the fight against Black anti-Semitism first because it is so visible in American politics today and because I believe that there are Black intellectuals and political leaders ready to take on this fight, ready to take the crucial step toward an American left-liberalism that might, by reckoning with its recent past, give itself a future.

twenty-one

WALKING THE TIGHTROPE

Some Personal Reflections on Blacks and Jews

CORNEL WEST

I grew up in a Black world without Jews. Yet my evolving worldview about life and love, faith and struggle was and is deeply shaped by the Jewish world— be it the Bible, Marx, Durkheim, Freud, Kafka, Wittgenstein, or Lukacs. Most of the flesh-and-blood Jews I have encountered are descendants of Eastern European immigrants who arrived in America at the turn of the century. And the vast majority of my Jewish friends tend to be progressive intellectuals and activists. So my personal reflections on Black-Jewish relations preclude any broad generalizations or monolithic formulations.

My first significant and sustained interaction with Jews—especially in college and graduate school—was exciting and exhilarating. I had never been so impressed with such an engaging group of white Americans so deeply concerned about white supremacy and other social evils. In our numerous discussions in study groups, classes, cafes, and political organizations, we informed and inspired one another in regard to our democratic socialist visions, analyses, and strategies for social change. We also reveled in critical evaluations of artists and writers in highbrow and popular culture. And though we never worshiped the New York intellectuals, I always had a good word and strong argument for my favorites—Delmore Swartz, Dwight Macdonald, Harold Rosenberg, Irving Howe, and Michael Harrington (two non-Jews out of five). Yet none of these figures compared to my major intellectual heroes at this young age—Turgenev, Kierkegaard, Marx, Chekhov, Niebuhr, Wittgenstein, Du Bois, Baldwin, Ellison, Schopenhauer, and Nietzsche (two Jews out of eleven).

This period lasted roughly from the late sixties to the mid-seventies. The rise of visible Jewish neoconservative thinkers shattered my parochial perceptions of the Jewish intelligentsia. In stark contrast to the cosmopolitan sensibilities of my Jewish progressive friends, I detected a strong dose of tribalism in the complex, convoluted, and hardly convincing arguments of Jewish neoconservatives.

Ironically, this postwar quest (1967, 1973 wars against Israel) for Jewish identity was influenced by the post–civil rights quest for Black identity—a quest predominant among my Black intellectual friends and comrades. On the domestic front, the astonishing entry of many American Jews into the middle class produced a new cultural situation. Increasing exogamous marriages, diluted Jewish rituals, and dull suburban life raised crucial issues of Jewish continuity and identity. On the Israeli front, the very survival of the country was at stake, and U.S. support—financial and military—was indispensable for its sustenance. The pressing issues of affirmative action (the relative weighing of merit, fairness, and public interest) and Zionism (the relative weighing of Jewish survival, secular democracy, and Palestinian subordination) loomed large—even among my Jewish progressive friends.

This painful and poignant struggle in the Jewish world perplexed me for two reasons. First, I considered affirmative action neither a panacea to vicious racist practices of the past nor a fetish to wipe clean class constraints in American life. Instead, I viewed affirmative action as a weak strategy to break the back of a tight well-to-do white male network that had disproportionate access to power, wealth, status, and influence. So retreat on affirmative action was a sure sign of a progressive or liberal failure of nerve and commitment. Second, I was never a Zionist (like Martin Luther King, Jr., Bayard Rustin, and W. E. B. Du Bois). I strongly believe that Jewish survival depends on statehood for security. But I also believe that in the long run only a secular democratic state—with no special Jewish character— can secure Jewish survival. Hence, I was confused by the intense secular argument for a full-fledged meritocracy in America and the heartfelt Zionist claims for a Jewish state in Israel. As a radical democrat, my dilemma was how to fight the subtle forms of white and male supremacy still operating alongside affirmative action, shatter the silence on class constraints, and put forward a moral critique of Zionism without downplaying the need for Jewish survival or falling into anti-Semitic traps. Needless to say, most of my Jewish leftist friends were progressive Zionists. So we argued intensely and respectfully as comrades.

In parts of the Black world, my position was viewed with great suspicion: Why do you spend so much time with Jewish progressives who will soon betray you on the altar of Jewish interests and networks? Are not Black-Jewish alliances the occasion for Black deference and Jewish paternalism? Why do you engage Jewish Zionists in such a charitable manner when you put forward such harsh criticisms of Black nationalists? Is it possible to forge Black-Jewish coalitions with integrity without attempting to create conditions under which Black progressives, liberals, and nationalists can coalesce?

Since I take seriously the dual strategies of Black operational unity and multiracial democratic alliance, I struggled with these challenging questions. How does one remain true to radical democratic ideals that oppose all forms of xenophobia and target corporate power for downward redistribution of wealth, while always acknowledging the tremendous weight of white supremacy in American society? I have worked with Black nationalists since the late sixties—in Black united fronts, Black political parties, and Black religious formations—precisely because they rightly target the most explosive issue and rawest nerve in American life: white supremacy. Yet I do so as a radical democrat, not as a Black nationalist. Nationalism of any form is for me a species of tribalism that warrants moral rejection. And since all forms of nationalism I know are deeply patriarchal and homophobic, I have great suspicions of them. Just like organized religion. Yet some good can come from them, so I selectively work with them.

My dilemma sharpened in the eighties with the presidential campaigns of Jesse Jackson and the rise of Minister Louis Farrakhan in the eyes of white America. Since then Black-Jewish relations have worsened. Jackson's "Hymietown" remark set off waves of Jewish rage. Farrakhan's response to Jewish threats against Jackson set off even more. And we all became locked into a spiral of accusations and demonizations. In the Jewish world, Jackson could not say enough to warrant forgiveness and Farrakhan was dubbed the new Hitler. In the Black world, Jackson and Farrakhan were viewed as heaven-sent for sustaining forms of Jewish identity and fund-raising predicated on anti-Semitism in America. The double standards for Black and white anti-Semitic rhetoric were appalling. Both worlds grasped only snippets of the truth—namely, that progressive and liberal forces in general were collapsing in America while the two most progressive and liberal groups (Blacks and Jews) were involved in a heartfelt yet cathartic sideshow. The media sensationalized it and projected a polarization more symbolic than real. Yet even symbols shape reality after much media interference.

With the white media discoveries of Leonard Jeffries and Khalid Abdul Muhammad, the obsession in the Jewish world with Black anti-Jewish rhetoric increased. And given the growing influence of Howard Stern and other xenophobic loose-tongued Jewish talk radio hosts, the concern in the Black world with Jewish anti-Black rhetoric increased. In short, the paranoia of two of the most paranoid groups in America was getting out of control—and clashing in ugly ways. Candid dialogue was badly needed.

Michael Lerner and I saw this need in 1988 and acted on it. We worked for five years on our book, *Jews and Blacks: Let the Healing Begin* (1995). We toured the country, lectured in over twenty cities—in Black churches, Jewish synagogues, bookstores, community centers, colleges, high schools. The audiences were all multiracial. The responses were overwhelming. The spirit of honest conversation, collective struggle, and racial healing was inspiring. Yet we received no financial support for our proposed Black-Jewish conference and we were trashed both by visible neoliberal Jewish intellectuals and vociferous progressive Black intellectuals. And with the advent of the O.J. verdict and Million Man March, our efforts for Black-Jewish healing were in shambles. Lerner and I continued to agree to disagree, even as our agreements and disagreements grew deeper, but as a twosome we felt more and more isolated.

The sheer viciousness of the intellectual attacks on my work and life from the

Jewish world caught me a bit by surprise. I've been on the battlefield for over two decades, so I am accustomed to principled criticisms and ad hominem ones. But the recent wave of venom and vitriol directed at me is new. Needless to say, I try to learn what I can from such contemptuous criticisms, keep my stride, and do my work. And with all of us being the cracked vessels that we are, there will always be degrees of mendaciousness and tendentiousness, envy and jealousy, misunderstandings and misinterpretations in our human exchanges. Furthermore, the degraded state of public conversation in American culture leads us to lower our intellectual expectations in regard to a spirit of empathy, charity, or generosity. But the virtual absence of fair-mindedness, the predominance of such intellectual obscenity and personal vulgarity bespeaks a gangsterization of the mind that behooves all of us to resist. Even among tormented and tortured journalists aspiring to serious intellectual work such as Leon Wieseltier we expect more than third-rate hatchet jobs predicated on homework undone in the guise of lowbrow wit and middlebrow wordplay. Similarly, we look for more than paternalistic rankings (Ellen Willis), glib reputation assessments (Sean Wilentz), or weak efforts at mediation in leading liberal and progressive weeklies and quarterlies (Andrew Delbanco). In other works, the degeneration of Black-Jewish relations is suffocating certain pockets of our intellectual life. How sad!

This degeneration can be seen in the responses of some of my old Jewish friends to the attacks. Silence. Avoidance. Evasion. Capitulation. Deference to power. Cowardly careerism. In other words, hardly any serious grappling with my texts or actions—just a shadow game with close colleagues and tribal loyalties. Many of my supportive Jewish friends reach these same conclusions. And most of my Black friends simply say we told you so.

For me, this painful situation raised a number of existential and vocational questions. What were the fundamental reasons I persisted in promoting Black-Jewish coalitions? How would I define the sources of hope for such unpopular efforts? What is the most wise and moral response to such ugly disrespect and degradation? My fundamental commitments are to human decency, mutual respect, and personal integrity. The common thread of these commitments is compassion or empathy. Needless to say, for a Christian, this thread flows from the love ethic of Jesus Christ; for a human being, it serves as the basis of a democratic mode of being in the world. Those great existential democrats—from Walt Whitman, Maurice Maeterlinck, John Dewey, Ida B. Wells-Barnett, Louis Armstrong, Abraham Joshua Heschel, Audre Lorde, and John Coltrane—all promoted forms of human connection mediated with compassion without dissolving diversity and differences. My own investment in Black-Jewish alliances is not simply a political effort to buttress progressive forces in American society. It also is a moral endeavor that exemplifies ways in which the most hated group in European history and the most hated group in U.S. history can coalesce in the name of precious democratic ideals—ideals that serve as the sole countervailing force to hatred, fear, and greed.

This political effort and moral endeavor will always cut against the grain. Jewish racism and Black anti-Semitism are not only as American as cherry pie; they also are human responses to insecurities and anxieties. For a Christian and radical democrat like myself, the go-cart of compassion is dialogue based on a fundamental respect for the "other." This dialogue requires active listening and candid speaking. The aim is neither verbal conquest nor rational coercion; rather it is to provide an occasion for openness so that a spirituality of genuine questioning can take root in one's mind, heart, and soul. Such questioning is the vehicle for intellectual change and existential transformation. The openness that precedes such questioning requires that we be vulnerable enough—hence trusting enough—to be questioned in a transformative mode. This is why no one should be refused to enter such openness. Or to put it another way, no one is so far beyond the pale—so worthy of utter disrespect and contempt—that we give up on them in our dialogical efforts. Why so? Because of human fallibility and unpredictability. Dialogical dogmatism is a form of intellectual exclusion that chooses interlocutors with whom one is comfortable; it rests upon an unacknowledged ignorance of others and an undeniable arrogance toward others. Dialogical dogmatism is ideologically promiscuous—it lies with liberal and conservative, Left and Right, Black and Jewish ideologues. The kind of dialogue I am calling for will always transgress the "respectable" bounds of dialogical dogmatists—yet it is the lifeblood of radical democracy and political breakthroughs. There is never any guarantee for success; yet the sheer existence of such dialogue is already a kind of success—for it means that decency, respect, and integrity are still alive.

So in the midst of disrespect and degradation, I promote the practical wisdom of dialogue—that thin reed in the whirlwind of our times doomed to strong lip-service and weak action that stakes a high moral ground in a cynical age. Like anyone, my rage and anger flows and sometimes overflows—yet my commitment to dialogical action, alongside other forms of democratic action, is profound.

In regard to my defense of sustaining dialogue with Black nationalists or my critical support of the Million Man March, my Jewish critics are eager to put forward loquacious utterances and engaged editorials highlighting my wrongheadedness. Again, I try to listen and learn from their criticisms, but I also recognize the double standards at work. I must denounce, isolate, and make no contact with xenophobic Black nationalists, but certain progressive Jewish intellectuals have no duty to identify and criticize the Negrophobic sentiments of their neoliberal or progressive friends. No serious or substantive Black-Jewish cooperation can emerge on such a one-way street.

Where then do we go from here? Black-Jewish relations—at the symbolic level—are in shambles. Yet there are significant Black-Jewish efforts on the ground: in local communities between churches and synagogues, in the trade-union movement, between the Anti-Defamation League and Black grassroot activists, among electoral coalitions and elected officiates. First, we have to change our ways. We must stop playing games with one another. We must be candid in

Paul Buhle teaches American Civilization at Brown University. His publications include *Marxism in the United States: Remapping the History of the American Left* (1987; rev. ed. 1991) and *The Immigrant Left in the United States* (1996).

Clayborne Carson is Professor of History at Stanford University and Editor and Director of the Martin Luther King, Jr., Papers Project. He also is the author of *In Struggle: SNCC and the Black Awakening of the 1960s* (1981; 2nd ed. 1995).

Jerome A. Chanes is Director of Cultural Services at The National Foundation for Jewish Culture. He is the editor of *Antisemitism in America Today: Outspoken Experts Explode the Myths* (1995).

Thomas Cripps is a historian who lives and works in Baltimore. He has written five books on motion picture history including, most recently, *Making Movies Black* (1993) and *Hollywood's High Noon* (1996).

David Brion Davis is Sterling Professor of History at Yale University. His publications include *From Homicide to Slavery: Studies in American Culture* (1986) and *The Antislavery Debate: Capitalism and Abolitionism as a Problem in Historical Interpretation* (1992).

Hasia R. Diner is Paul S. and Sylvia Steinberg Professor of American Jewish History at New York University. Her publications include *In the Almost Promised Land: American Jews and Blacks, 1915–1935* (1977) and *A Time for Gathering: The Second Migration, 1820–1880* (1992).

David M. Goldenberg is Associate Director of the Center for Judaic Studies and Adjunct Associate Professor in Post-Biblical Literature at the University of Pennsylvania. The editor of *Jewish Quarterly Review*, his own publications have focused on the literature, language, and history of Judaism in the Rabbinic and Roman periods.

Cheryl Greenberg is Associate Professor of History at Trinity College. She is the author of *"Or Does it Explode?": Black Harlem During the Great Depression* (1991).

William Chester Jordan is Professor of History and Director of the Shelby Cullom Davis Center for Historical Studies at Princeton University. His most recent publications include *Women and Credit in Pre-Industrial and Developing Societies* (1993) and *The Great Famine: Northern Europe in the Early Fourteenth Century* (1996).

Jonathan Kaufman, a national reporter for *The Wall Street Journal*, was a co-winner of a Pulitzer Prize for articles on racism and job discrimination that appeared in *The Boston Globe* in 1984. He is the author of *Broken Alliance: The Turbulent Times Between Blacks and Jews in America* (1988).

Robin D. G. Kelley is Professor of History and Africana Studies at New York University. He is the author of *Hammer and Hoe: Alabama Communists During the Great Depression* (1990) and *Race Rebels: Culture Politics and the Black Working Class* (1994).

Earl Lewis is Professor of History and Afroamerican and African Studies at the University of Michigan. He is the author of *In Their Own Interests: Race, Class, and Power in Twentieth Century Norfolk, Virginia* (1991).

Waldo E. Martin, Jr. is Professor of History at the University of California, Berkeley. He is the author of *The Mind of Frederick Douglass* (1985).

Deborah Dash Moore is Professor of Religion at Vassar College. She is the author of *To the Golden Cities: Pursuing the American Dream in Miami and Los Angeles* (1994) and coeditor of the forthcoming *Jewish Women in America: An Historical Encyclopedia*.

Letty Cottin Pogrebin is a founding member of *Ms.* magazine. The author of eight books, her most recent titles include *Deborah, Golda, and Me: Being Female and Jewish in America* (1992) and *Getting Over Getting Older: An Intimate Journey* (1996).

Gary E. Rubin, formerly the Executive Director of Americans for Peace Now, is currently the Director of Public Policy at the New York Association for New Americans. His recent articles include "How Should We Think About Black Antisemitism?" in *Antisemitism in America Today: Outspoken Experts Explode the Myths* (1995) edited by Jerome Chanes.

Jack Salzman, former Director of the Center for American Culture Studies at Columbia University, is Deputy Director for Education, Media, and Public Programs at The Jewish Museum. He is the editor of *Prospects: An Annual of American Cultural Studies,* and, with David Smith and Cornel West, of the five volume *Encyclopedia of African American Culture and History* (1995).

Theodore M. Shaw is the Associate Director–Counsel of the NAACP Legal Defense and Education Fund, Inc. He has litigated civil rights cases throughout the United States on the trial and appellate levels, as well as in the Supreme Court. In addition, he is an Adjunct Professor of Law at Columbia University.

Jason H. Silverman is Professor of History at Winthrop University. His publications include *Unwelcome Guests: Canada West's Response to American Fugitive Slaves, 1880–1865* (1985) and *The Peopling of America: A Synoptic History* (1994).

Michael Walzer, a member of the Institute for Advanced Studies at Princeton University since 1980, is the Editor of *Dissent*. His publications incude *Exodus and Revolution* (1985), *Interpretation and Social Criticism* (1987), and *Pluralism, Justice, and Equality* (1995).

Nancy J. Weiss is Dean of the College, Princeton University. Her books include *Farewell to the Party of Lincoln: Black Politics in the Age of FDR* (1983) and *Whitney M. Young, Jr., and the Struggle for Civil Rights* (1989).

Cornel West is Professor of Afro-American Studies and the Philosophy of Religion at Harvard University. His most recent publications are *Race Matters* (1993) and, with Michael Lerner, *Jews and Blacks: Let the Healing Begin* (1995).

Patricia J. Williams is Professor of Law at Columbia University. Her publications include *The Alchemy of Race and Rights* (1991) and *The Rooster's Egg* (1995).

selected readings

Berman, Paul, ed. *Blacks and Jews: Alliances and Arguments.* New York: Delacorte, 1994.

Bernal, Martin. *Black Athena: The Afroasiatic Roots of Classical Civilization.* 2 vols. New Brunswick, NJ: Rutgers University Press, 1987.

Berson, Lenora E. *The Negroes and the Jews.* New York, Random House, 1971.

Bracey, John and August Meier. "Toward a Research Agenda on Blacks and Jews in United States History," *Journal of American Ethnic History*, 12, 3 (Spring 1993): 60–67.

Branch, Taylor. *Parting the Waters: America in the King Years 1954–63.* New York: Simon and Schuster, 1988.

Carter, Dan T. *Scottsboro: A Tragedy of the American South.* Baton Rouge: Louisiana State University Press, 1969.

Carson, Clayborne. *In Struggle: SNCC and the Black Awakening of the 1960s.* Cambridge: Harvard University Press, 1981.

Chanes, Jerome A., ed. *Antisemitism in America Today: Outspoken Experts Explode the Myth.* New York: Birch Lane Press, 1995.

Cruse, Harold. *The Crisis of the Negro Intellectual.* New York. William Morrow, 1967.

Davis, David Brion. *Slavery and Human Progress.* New York: Oxford University Press, 1984.

Diner, Hasia. *In the Almost Promised Land: American Jews and Blacks 1915–1935.* Westport, CT: Greenwood Press, 1977.

Dinnerstein, Leonard. *AntiSemitism in America.* New York: Oxford University Press, 1994.

Garrow, David. *Bearing the Cross, Martin Luther King, Jr., and the Southern Christian Leadership Conference.* New York: William Morrow, 1986.

Greenberg, Cheryl. *"Or Does It Explode?": Black Harlem in the Great Depression.* New York: Oxford University Press, 1991.

Greenberg, Jack. *Crusaders in the Courts: How a Dedicated Band of Lawyers Fought for the Civil Rights Revolution.* New York: Basic Books, 1994.

Halpern, Ben. *Jews and Blacks: The Classic American Minorities.* New York: Herder and Herder, 1971.

Hentoff, Nat, ed. *Black Anti-Semitism and Jewish Racism.* New York: Richard W. Baron, 1969.

Hertzberg, Steven. *Strangers in the Gate City: The Jews of Atlanta, 1845–1915.* Philadelphia: Jewish Publication Society of America, 1978.

Hill, Herbert and James E. Jones, Jr., eds. *Race in America, The Struggle for Equality.* Madison: University of Wisconsin, 1993.

Kaufman, Jonathan. *Broken Alliances. The Turbulent Times Between Blacks and Jews in America.* New York: Scribner's, 1988.

Lefkowitz, Mary. *Not Out of Africa: How Afrocentrism Became an Excuse to Teach Myth as History.* New York: Basic Books, 1996.

Lerner, Michael. *Black and Jews: Let the Healing Begin.* New York: Putnam, 1995.

Ottley, Roi. *New World A Coming: Inside Black America.* Boston: Houghton Mifflin, 1943.

Peck, Abraham J., ed. *Blacks and Jews, The American Experience.* Cincinnati, OH: The American Jewish Archives, 1988.

Raboteau, Albert J. *A Fire in the Bones: Reflections on African American Religious History.* Boston: Beacon, 1995.

Rogin, Michael. *Blackface, White Noise: Jewish Immigrants in the Hollywood Melting Pot.* Berkeley: University of California, 1996.

Ross, B. Joyce. *Spingarn and the Rise of the NAACP.* New York: Atheneum, 1972.

Salzman, Jack, ed. with Adina Back and Gretchen Sorin. *Bridges and Boundaries: African Americans and American Jews.* New York: George Braziller, 1992.

Washington, James M., ed. *Jews in Black Perspectives: A Dialogue.* Rutherford, N.J.: Fairleigh Dickinson University, 1984.

Weisbord, Robert G. and Arthur Stein. *Bitterswet Encounter: The Afro-American and the American Jew.* Westport, CT. Negro Universities Press, 1970.

Weiss, Nancy J. *The National Urban League, 1910–1940.* New York: Oxford University Press, 1974.

Cornel West, *Race Matters.* Boston: Beacon, 1993.

Malcolm X *(continued)*
  growth of influence, 111, 184–85; idol,
  as, 391; Nation of Islam, beginnings of,
  179; popularity of, 186; separate Black
  economy, 346
Malcolm X (film), 212, 258
Maltz, Albert, 225n.34, 267
Mandeville, John, 29, 44n.31
Marches: Million Man March, 4, 192, 406,
  413, 415; Mississippi, voting rights march,
  1966, 177; Selma to Montgomery voting
  rights march, 1965, 181–82, 191;
  Washington, World War II, 158–59
Marching On (film), 266
Margaret, Saint of Antioch, 57–59
Margold, Nathan, 135
Marine Transport Workers, 203
Marranos Jews, 68–70
Marshall, James, 134
Marshall, Louis, 133–34, 136, 241
Marshall, Thurgood, 183
Martin, Tony, 3, 8, 23–24
Martin, Waldo, 15, 341–55, 418
Marx, Karl, 202
Marx, Rabbi Robert, 117
Marxism, 198
Maslow, Will, 165, 335n.1
Massell, Sam, Jr., 284
Masses and Mainstream, 210
Masses magazine, 204
May family, 143
McCarthyism, 211
McCay, Claude, 204
McCoy, Rhody, 113, 115, 247
McGhee, Sipes v., 161
McKinney, Cynthia, 327, 336n.14
McKinney, E. R., 225n.33
McLean, Albert, 259
Meadows, Ben, 209
Meany, George, 217
Medieval times. *See* Middle Ages
Meier, Golda, 332, 339n.26
Mellman Group for the Israel Policy Reform,
  366
Meritocracy, 326
The Messenger, 126, 144, 204
Metzenbaum, Howard, 405
Meyer, Max, 143
Mfumi, Kwasi, 5
Michaux, Elder Solomon Lightfoot, 267
Micheaux, Oscar, 259
Michel, Harriet, 385–86, 389, 398

Middle Ages, 8; black (color), concept of, 53,
  59–60, 63n.22; hagiographic romances,
  57–58; images of Jews, 53–60; travel
  diaries, 30–31. *See also* Zohar
Middle East. *See* Israel
Midrash: black skin as curse, 38n.3; images
  of Blacks in, 31, 32
Migration: African Americans, to cities, 278;
  African Americans, to north, 9, 154–55,
  231, 246; Jews, Brazil, 70; Jews, to
  American urban centers, 154–55. *See also*
  Immigration
Miller, Alex, 164
Miller, Joseph C., 65
Miller, Kelly, 92, 126
Miller v. Johnson, 327–31, 338nn.21,22,
  339n.26
Milliken v. Bradley, 337n.15
Million Man March, 4, 192, 406, 413, 415
Mississippi: murder of civil rights workers,
  111, 182, 283, 335n.1, 387, 403; voting
  rights march, 1966, 177
Mississippi Freedom Democratic Party, 183
Missouri v. Jenkins, 337n.15
Mitchell, Clarence, 360
Mo' Better Blues (film), 396
Mobile v. Bolden, 309
Moody, Anne, 341–42
Moore, Audley, 206
Moore, Deborah Dash, 13–14, 275–94, 418
Moore, Henry, 161
Moore, Richard B., 204
Moore v. Dempsey, 133
Mordecai, Major Alfred, 80
Mordecai, Samuel, 76
Morgenthau, Rita Wallach, 130
Moses, Isaiah, 77
Moses, Lucy Goldschmidt, 137
Moses, Major Raphael J., 77
Moses (Biblical figure), 36, 325
Moskowitz, Henry, 130, 135
Muhammad, Akbar, 33
Muhammad, Elijah, 3, 346
Muhammad, Khalid Abdul, 3, 406, 413
"Mulatta Rose," 236
Muse, Clarence, 209, 261–62, 265
"My Negro Problem—and Yours" (Podhoretz),
  2, 183–84
Myrdal, Gunnar, 179, 374–75

NAACP. *See* National Association for the
  Advancement of Colored People (NAACP)